W9-BVF-017

The New Century Handbook

FIFTH EDITION

Christine A. Hult
Utah State University

Thomas N. Huckin
University of Utah

Longman

Boston Columbus Indianapolis New York San Francisco Upper Saddle River
Amsterdam Cape Town Dubai London Madrid Milan Munich Paris Montreal Toronto
Delhi Mexico City Sao Paulo Sydney Hong Kong Seoul Singapore Taipei Tokyo

Senior Sponsoring Editor: Virginia L. Blanford
Senior Development Editor: Michael Greer
Director of Development: Mary Ellen Curley
Senior Marketing Manager: Susan Stoudt
Senior Supplements Editor: Donna Campion
Senior Media Producer: Stefanie Liebman
Production Manager: Savoula Amanatidis
Project Coordination, Text Design, and Electronic Page Makeup: Nesbitt Graphics, Inc.
Cover Design Manager: John Callahan
Cover Designer: Kay Petronio
Photo Researcher: Rona Tuccillo
Senior Manufacturing Buyer: Alfred C. Dorsey
Printer and Binder: R. R. Donnelley and Sons Company–Crawfordsville
Cover Printer: Lehigh-Phoenix Color Corporation

For permission to use copyrighted material, grateful acknowledgment is made to the copyright holders on pp. C1–C3, which are hereby made part of this copyright page.

Cataloging-in-Publication Data on file at the Library of Congress

Copyright © 2011, 2008, 2005 by Pearson Education, Inc.

All rights reserved. No part of this publication may be reproduced, stored in a retrieval system, or transmitted, in any form or by any means, electronic mechanical, photocopying, recording, or otherwise, without the prior written permission of the publisher. Printed in the United States.

1 2 3 4 5 6 7 8 9 10—DOC—13 12 11 10

Longman
is an imprint of

www.pearsonhighered.com

ISBN-13: 978-0-205-74412-1
ISBN-10: 0-205-74412-5

Contents

Preface

"Handbooks are all the same." That's the mantra. And to some extent, it's true: Handbooks, which began as pure and simple grammar references, now almost all include content not only on grammar and usage but also on the writing process, research, writing for different purposes, document design—and on and on. So what makes this handbook different?

The main difference is that *The New Century* was the first handbook written from the ground up acknowledging the emerging role of technology in student writing. Other handbooks have appeared since *The New Century's* first edition, and older handbooks have stepped on the electronic bandwagon. But this handbook remains at the forefront. If you want a handbook that understands how students research and write today, this is the one.

What's New in this Edition

Much has changed since the first edition appeared, almost ten years ago. Technology is no longer a set of tools that writers use. Rather, it comprises a complete environment—a context for multimodal communication almost unimaginable before the turn of the twenty-first century, a place for us all to connect through word, image, and sound.

We can identify three stages in the electronic revolution:

- First, **word processing brought computers into the writing classroom** and offered us a remarkable new ability to put words on paper—to cut and paste, to revise, to move text from document to document.
- Second, **the Internet changed the face of research** by opening up library databases, online encyclopedias, and so much more at the click of a button.
- And now, we are plunging headlong into the third electronic revolution: **the advent of community**. Social networking, Web 2.0 platforms (*Twitter, Facebook*), and mobile technologies and smartphones all allow us to share information in a variety of modes (image, text, speech, video) with hundreds, thousands, even millions of readers or viewers or "friends" who

exist in a global cyber community. Suddenly, we are all both *consumers* and *creators,* all part of multiple, overlapping, linked communities.

Research tells us that the students appearing in college writing classrooms today create more "texts" daily than students in any preceding generation. But writing instructors know that quantity does not necessarily equal quality, and that students' prowess with electronic communication devices may not always translate into successful experiences in academic writing. The third revolution—the revolution of community—has brought a particular challenge for writing instructors: Many students use the available technology skillfully, but fail to recognize that as audiences and purposes for their writing differ, so must their writing itself use different conventions and employ different rhetorical choices. More and more, instructors need to find ways to help students understand the differences among writing on a friend's *Facebook* wall, sending out a tweet, posting a comment on a blog site, texting mom—or creating an academic research paper.

Building on its traditional emphasis on rhetorical principles in an electronic context—even more important in an age of global communication—the fifth edition of this handbook has been significantly refocused to reflect the realities of the world that students inhabit.

- **Digital rhetoric and multimodal communication.** A new Chapter 1, "Saying What You Mean to Say in a Digital World," underlines the complex role of *composing* in a digital age by focusing on multimodal communication, acknowledging that successful communication now includes visual and other nonverbal modes.
- **Critical analysis.** Chapter 2, "Critical Reading and Viewing," has been extensively rewritten to acknowledge the increasing importance of critical analysis in a complex world, and the need for all students to be able to understand and evaluate "text" in various forms: images, video, animation, and spoken word, as well as writing.
- **The organic writing process.** Part 1 now more closely aligns with the organic, nonlinear nature of the writing process most instructors present to their students. The chapters on preparing and drafting have been integrated into a single chapter to suggest the fluidity of writing's early stages, and the chapters on writing paragraphs and argument now precede the chapter on revision.
- **The basics in a digital world.** Parts 6 through 12, on grammar, punctuation, and mechanics, have been revised to help students understand that

the most basic components of writing often differ depending on audience and medium, and to show that they must be aware of appropriate conventions for each writing venue.

- **Electronic document design.** Part 4 on document design has been extensively revised to reflect the electronic environment in which students now create a wide variety of documents in a wide variety of media, and to emphasize the rhetorical foundations—an understanding of audience and purpose—of design.
- **Help with—and warnings about—technology.** A wealth of new TechHelp and TechAlert! boxes brings these valuable resources into today's—and tomorrow's—electronic environment.
- **Finding credible sources.** New sections on disciplinary resources (in Part 3) help students identify credible online sources.
- **Current documentation guidelines.** The documentation chapters (Chapters 12 and 13) have been fully updated to reflect new guidelines from both the Modern Language Association (2009) and the American Psychological Association (2010) for citing sources, particularly electronic sources.

Throughout, the handbook has been updated or revised with an emphasis on helping students differentiate among various writing contexts, particularly electronic contexts (public, academic, formal, informal).

The Core of The New Century Handbook

Although technology is central to *The New Century Handbook,* its core remains its focus on rhetorical principles. To produce effective writing, students must be able to understand and analyze context, and we believe that this handbook is second to none in the clarity and accessibility of its coverage of rhetoric. *The New Century Handbook* also includes an abundance of guidance about disciplinary conventions, and its coverage of the nuts and bolts of a handbook (documentation and grammar) is authoritative and extensive.

Part 1: The Composing Process

Even more than in previous editions, the chapters in Part 1 emphasize the need to internalize rhetorical principles—logic, audience, persona—as a basis for successful writing. Part 1 opens with a new chapter on rhetoric in a digital age, and a completely revised Chapter 2 that focuses on multimodal communication—the need to think critically and analytically about not only language but image, animation, and sound. The remaining chapters have been reorganized to reflect a more holistic, organic writing process; the chapters on argument and paragraphing are now followed by the chapter on revision.

Part 2: Research, Documentation—and Avoiding Plagiarism

Fully revised and updated to reflect recent changes in MLA (2009) and APA (2010) styles, these chapters explore the research process from beginning (finding a topic, formulating a thesis) to end (documenting sources in the final paper). Guidelines for evaluating sources—especially online sources—and integrating sources appropriately into academic papers are clear, straightforward, and authoritative. This edition includes extensive information and sample documents showing how to avoid plagiarism—the single biggest concern of instructors today.

Part 3: Writing and Researching in the Disciplines—How the Discourse Differs

What questions are typically asked in biology as opposed to history? What evidence is acceptable in each discipline? Separate chapters on writing in the humanities (with two sample MLA student papers), in the natural sciences, and in the social sciences (with a sample APA paper) provide students with detailed guidance to help them write across the academic curriculum.

Part 4: Designing Documents

These chapters acknowledge that design is an integral part of the writing process; students now create documents in a variety of media. The emphasis is both on the rhetorical focus of design—the need to accommodate audience and purpose—and on the ethical need to use visual materials appropriately. Basic principles of design and composition are introduced in one chapter, and a second discusses specific types of documents (brochures, newsletters, Web pages, and Web sites).

Part 5: Electronic Communication

A thoroughly revised Chapter 21 explores the world of instant messages, text messages, emails, blogs, and more, in which we are all immersed today, and also looks at electronic communication within courses. Other chapters focus on writing in contexts beyond academic papers—business writing, oral presentations, and essay examinations—as well as creating portfolios of written work for evaluation or job searches.

Parts 6–11: The Heart of a Handbook: Grammar, Usage, Mechanics—and the Power of Language

The chapters in these parts not only provide comprehensive, authoritative guidance on the basics of using language, but now also reflect our contemporary communications environment. They are designed to help students understand that what is acceptable as a *Facebook* wall post may not be acceptable in an academic paper. Accessible and compelling chapters offer guidance on how to write effective sentences and choose effective words (including a chapter on language and power that looks at bias, stereotypical language, and the power of language to include and exclude). These sections provide a wealth of examples and streamlined explanations, as well as section titles that reflect the errors themselves rather than the grammatical terms for them—responding to a common complaint from handbook users.

Part 12: Tips for Multilingual Writers

This chapter offers strategies for students whose first language is not English in understanding the conventions and rhetoric of American academic discourse, with a focus on common errors.

Tools for Writing and Researching Electronically

In addition to the comprehensive content outlined above, *The New Century Handbook*, is packed with useful features designed to support writing and research in the twenty-first century.

TECH HELP Although most college students are computer "natives," they aren't necessarily aware of all the tools that a typical software program can provide. Throughout this book—and listed inside the back cover—are boxes that offer guidance in using the wide array of "hidden" resources (based on the most common word processing program, *Microsoft Word*) that can help students compose and format their writing in college and beyond. TechHelp boxes are specific and instructional, including useful strategies for incorporating software functionalities into the writing process.

Combining Documents

Word-processing programs provide multiple ways to accomplish the same task. Here are two ways to combine documents.

1. Insert the two documents into a blank document using the INSERT FROM FILE command. This command is found on the INSERT tab.
   a. Create a new blank document.
   b. INSERT the contents of your prewriting document (INSERT >TEXT>OBJECT>TEXT FROM FILE).
   c. INSERT the contents of your outline document (INSERT >TEXT>OBJECT>TEXT FROM FILE).
   d. Move appropriate information from the prewriting document to the outline document (using COPY and PASTE).
   e. Save the combined document as a first draft with an appropriate new name.
2. Combine the two documents using multiple windows:
   a. Open your prewriting document and your outline document, each in its own window (OFFICE BUTTON > OPEN). Resize the windows so that you can view them both at the same time (VIEW>WINDOWS > ARRANGE ALL).
   b. Moving between the windows by using the SWITCH WINDOWS option, COPY and PASTE appropriate information from the prewriting

TechALERT!

Electronic Language: TM and IM Shorthand

Abbreviations commonly used in text-messaging, instant-messaging, and emailing—such as *pls, tx, u, msg, gr8, w/, b/c, lol, BTW, TIA, FYI*, and *ASAP*—should be avoided in formal writing.

See 21b-4

TECH ALERT! Computers provide tremendous benefits for writers—but they can also overlook obvious errors. TechAlert! boxes throughout this handbook point to potential problems for writers who rely too heavily on electronic resources:

- **Electronic Language Alerts** support the rhetorical focus of this handbook. Students are offered specific guidance about electronic conventions (emoticons, single-letter substitutes for words, and all-lowercase writing, for example) that are not acceptable in academic papers.
- **Grammar Checker Alerts** point out the many shortcomings of grammar and spell checkers and urge students to use these features wisely, not as final arbiters of grammar, style, and spelling.

E-Text Links provide keys to additional resources—audio, video, and Weblinks—available in the *New Century Handbook* interactive e-Text.

Additional Support for Becoming a More Effective Writer

In addition to thorough coverage of the writing process, usage and style, grammar, mechanics, and punctuation, this handbook contains an array of helpful features.

- **Guidelines and Checklists** offer clear, accessible summaries and quick reviews of important information.

Parallelism

Not putting all items in a list in parallel form

FAULTY	The building is 72 feet wide, 130 feet in length, and has a height of five stories.
PARALLEL	The building is 72 feet wide, 130 feet long, and five stories high.

Not using enough parallelism to make the meaning clear

UNCLEAR	Human language is different from other animals' communication systems, just as the elephant's trunk doesn't look like the nostrils of non-elephants.
CLEAR	Human language is as different from other animals' communication systems, as the elephant's trunk is different from other animals' noses.

- **Common Errors lists,** found primarily in Parts 6–12, provide handy snapshots of the most common errors we confront in grammar and usage.
- GO BUTTONS. Go buttons in the margins throughout the book send students to additional content on the topic being discussed.
- **15 sample student papers and other student work**—like Web site evaluations—offer authentic examples of the

writing process and final papers, as well as models of how to integrate sources correctly and incorrectly.

- Exercises provide ample opportunities for students to apply the principles they are learning and review important points.

What Else is Available?

PEARSON mycomplab MyCompLab uniquely integrates a composing space and assessment tools with market-leading instruction, multimedia tutorials, and exercises for writing, grammar, and research. Instructors can use MyCompLab, an eminently flexible application, in ways that best complement individual courses and teaching styles. You can recommend it to students for self-study, set up courses to track student progress, or leverage the power of administrative features to be more effective and save time. The assignment builder and commenting tools developed specifically for writing instruction bring instructors closer to their student writers, make managing assignments and evaluating papers more efficient, and put powerful assessment within reach. Students receive feedback appropriate to their own writing, which encourages critical thinking and revision and helps them to develop skills based on their individual needs. Learn more at www.mycomplab.com.

Interactive Pearson eText. An e-book version of *The New Century Handbook* is also available in MyCompLab. This dynamic, online version of the text includes a wealth of additional resources—videos, audios, Web links, and chapter review materials—and is integrated throughout with MyCompLab to create an enriched, interactive learning experience for writing students.

CourseSmart etextbook. *The New Century Handbook* is also available as a CourseSmart etextbook. This is an exciting new choice for students, who can subscribe to the same content online and search the text, make notes online, print out reading assignments that incorporate lecture notes, and bookmark important passages for later review. For more information, or to subscribe to the CourseSmart etextbook, visit www.coursesmart.com

vango notes VangoNotes. Study on the go with downloadable chapter reviews; listen on any MP3 player. Wherever you are, whatever you're doing, review and practice by purchasing a single chapter or complete text download from Audible.com.

The New Century Handbook Exercise Book provides over 70 additional exercise sets to supplement those found in the book itself. (A separate Answer Key is available to instructors.)

The Instructor's Manual and Multimedia Resource Guide, written by the handbook's authors, includes chapter highlights, teaching suggestions, classroom activities, collaborative activities, usage notes, linguistic notes, computer novice notes, ESL notes, cross-references to related literature in composition, additional exercises, and exercise answers.

Acknowledgments

We wish to thank the many people who have helped us make this edition of *The New Century Handbook* even more responsive to the needs of first-year writing students and instructors. This includes not only reviewers of this text, but also the many researchers and writers in the fields of rhetoric, composition, and linguistics whose work informs our own.

We acknowledge and thank the entire team at Pearson Longman, who supported this handbook from the beginning. Specifically, we thank Joseph Opiela, whose vision for this book both inspired its beginnings and continued to shape it through development. For their expert guidance and constant support throughout the revision of this fifth edition, we thank sponsoring editor Ginny Blanford and development editor Michael Greer. And to the production team—production manager Savoula Amanatidis, managing editor Donna DeBenedictis, senior manufacturing buyer Al Dorsey, and cover design manager John Callahan, all at Longman, our tireless project editor Karen Stocz, our talented designer Jerilyn Bockorick, and a remarkable team of copyeditors and proofreaders at Nesbitt Graphics; we are grateful for the creativity and relentless attention to detail that make this handbook unique.

We have benefited tremendously from the many reviewers who provided suggestions for this new edition. These include Connie S. Adair, Marshalltown Community College; Samantha Blackmon, Purdue University; Andrew DePalma, University of Connecticut; Dawn Elmore-McCrary, San Antonio College; Lori Emerson, Georgia Institute of Technology; Kathleen Furlong, Glendale Community College; Joanne Gates, Jacksonville State University; Michael

Lewis Goldberg, University of Washington, Bothell; John Gooch, University of Texas at Dallas; Jean E. Graham, The College of New Jersey; Charles Hebert, Greensboro College; Marion G. Heyn, Los Angeles Valley College; James W. Kershner, Cape Cod Community College; Robert S. Mann, Des Moines Area Community College Urban Campus; Donald Moore, University of Southern Indiana; Samantha A. Morgan-Curtis, Tennessee State University; Sarah O'Connor, James Madison University; Priscilla Oguine, Seton Hall University; Norman Prinsky, Augusta State University; Bill Reisner, Kapiolani Community College; David Sharpe, Ohio University; John W. Taylor, South Dakota State University; Natasha Whitton, Southeastern Louisiana University; and Heather Wood, University of Texas at Dallas.

Two university librarians, Perry Willett at the University of Michigan and Paul Glassman at Hofstra University, provided invaluable information about how today's students proceed through research projects, and almost 250 students at four universities, including our own, responded to questionnaires about how they research and write. The guidance provided by these librarians and students informed much of the content in our research chapters.

For their technical expertise and innovative ideas for teaching and learning, we thank Kelli Cargile Cook, David Hailey, and Chris Okelberry, all of Utah State University. We were fortunate to have in our classes student writers who were willing to share their work with us, and with the larger readership of this handbook. Student writers whose work appears in these pages include Brandy Blank, Heidi Blankenship, Jennifer Bodine, Ron Christensen, Annie Gabbitas, Janevieve Grabert, Eric Horne, Allan Johnson, Abbey Kennedy, Myndee McNeill, Jeff Meaders, Wensdae Miller, Benjamin Minson, Angela Napper, Chris Nelson, Wyoma Profitt, Heather Radford, Kirsten Reynolds, Sarah Smith, Kaycee Sorensen, Tim Syndergaard, DeLayna Stout, Jon Weber, Bryce Wilcox, and Adam Whitney.

Lastly, we say thanks to our friends and families who supported us in our personal lives so that we could free up the time and the energy to work on this challenging project. Specifically, we wish to thank our respective spouses, Nathan Hult and Christiane Huckin.

Christine A. Hult

Thomas N. Huckin

part

1

Writing in a Digital Age

1 Saying What You Mean to Say in a Digital World

FAQs

- What writing skills are most important in today's digital environment? (1a)
- How can writing well help me in college and beyond? (1b)
- What do we mean by rhetoric and the rhetorical appeals? (1c)
- How has technology changed the way we write? (1d)
- How can this handbook help me become a more effective writer? (1e)

The world of writing has remade itself over the last two decades. *Writing* is no longer limited to the act of putting words on paper. Writing might now be better defined as communicating—using the tools of the vast digital environment in which we function to inform, inspire, and persuade. How have we gotten to this point?

See Fig. 1.1

- Twenty years ago, **word processors** allowed us to revise our writing with a mouse and cursor instead of correction fluid. Suddenly we could move whole paragraphs around in an essay by a simple cut and paste. The processes of rewriting and revising became easier and more fluid.

See Fig. 1.2

- Ten years ago, the **Internet** brought an overwhelming wealth of information to our fingertips. We typed in a word, and we had a thousand sites to visit. No longer did we need to hunt desperately through a library card catalog for sources—but suddenly we found ourselves with too much information, and too little knowledge about how to evaluate what we found.

See Fig. 1.3

- In the last five years, **social networking** and so-called **Web 2.0 applications** (like eBay, Wikipedia, or Twitter) have transformed the nature of our relationships and our community. Suddenly we are all part of a world of "friends," sharing and receiving information non-stop. This huge, accessible array of tools means we can *create* as well as *consume* information.

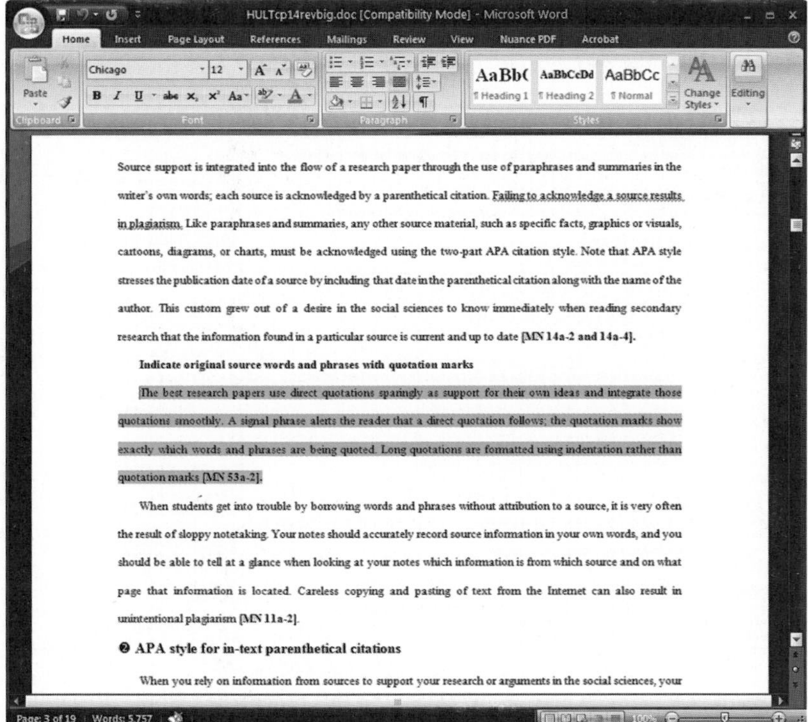

Figure 1.1 The advent of word processing software in the 1980s transformed the writing process by making it vastly easier to revise and edit text.

How will this third revolution in our electronic environment affect the way we write? And what will the *fourth* revolution look like? One thing seems certain: No matter what innovations come next, we will continue to want to share our ideas, our feelings, and our opinions with others, and we will do it through some form of writing.

1a Why do we write?

When we talk about *writing* now, we don't always mean using language. We mean putting elements together—words, images, animations, symbols, abbreviations—in ways that inform, inspire, and persuade. Sometimes we use

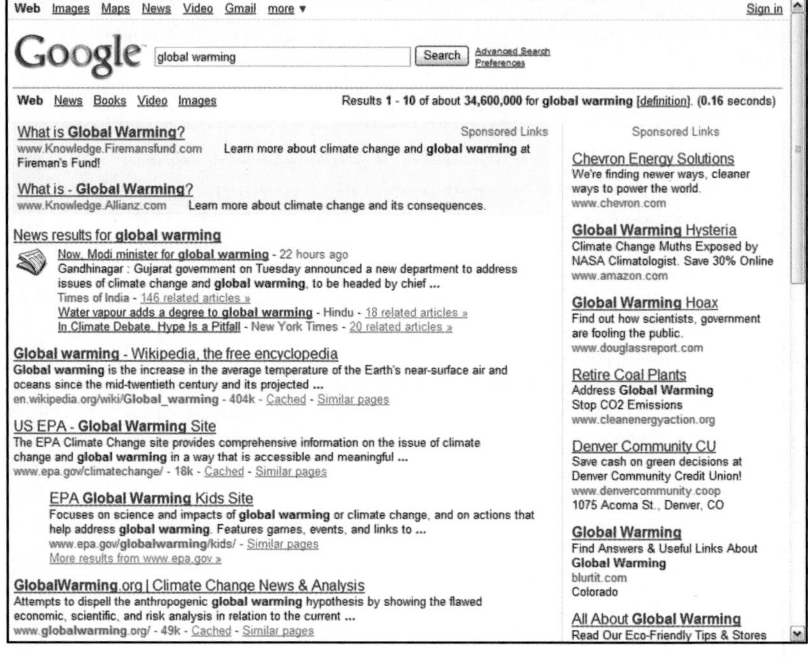

Figure 1.2 ▶ In the 1990s, the rapid growth of the Internet and web-based search engines transformed the research process by making an overwhelming amount of information accessible to anyone with a computer. Today, a Google search for *global warming* returns 34 million entries.

the word *composing* to refer more broadly to this process as a whole. Regardless of the media we are working in, there is one constant: All writing is for an audience. Sometimes the audience for your writing is one person: yourself (a to-do list, your journal). More often the audience is larger: your fellow students, your friends, or the electronic community you find online.

Most writing is motivated by one of four basic goals or purposes.

- **We write to communicate.** Our goal is to share information.
- **We write to learn.** Our goal is to clarify our own thinking.
- **We write to be creative.** Our goal is to express ourselves.
- **We write to persuade.** Our goal is to convince others of something.

❶ Writing to communicate

Think about how we communicate every day.

- We talk on our cell phones.
- We text-message our parents, children, friends, professors.

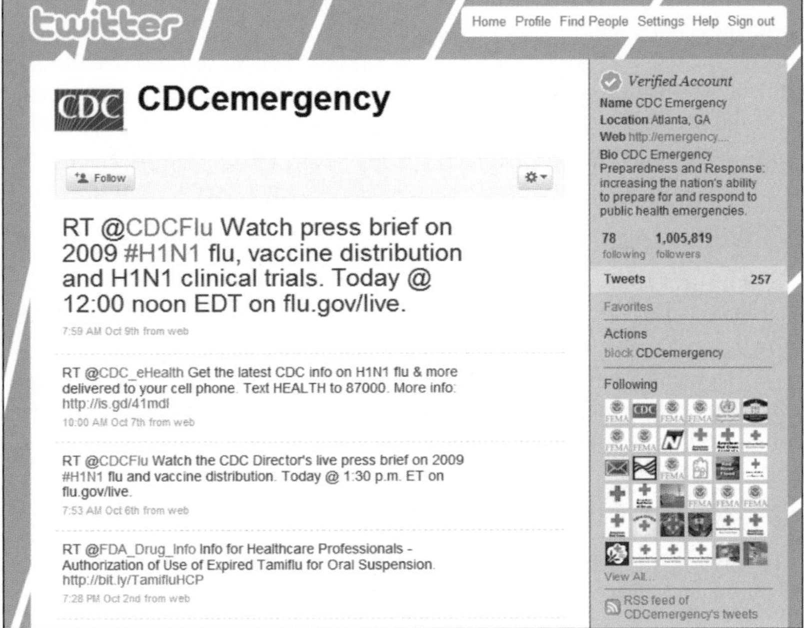

Figure 1.3 The Centers for Disease Control and Prevention began using Twitter in 2009 to provide public health updates, demonstrating the growing importance and public acceptance of social networking as a communication technology.

- We forward a *YouTube* video to a friend—or many friends—with our comments.
- We update our *Facebook* page.
- We leave a note for our roommate, our parents, or our kids about what's in the fridge for dinner.
- We make shopping or to-do lists.
- We even start to draft papers for assignments.

Writing is a way of connecting with others—usually others who share our interests. A group of writers who share common interests and assumptions is called a **discourse community**. You already belong to a number of discourse communities, including your fellow students, your colleagues at work, your family, other members of the organizations to which you belong, your *Facebook* friends, and so on. Every day we share information with these communities through language and images.

EXERCISE 1.1 For one day, keep a copy of every bit of writing you do: text messages, emails, notes to yourself. At the end of the day, make a list of all this writing. How many different kinds of writing did you use to communicate? What media did you use to transmit your writing (cell phone, computer, notebook paper)? What discourse communities are reflected in your writing? (Keep these pieces of writing for use in Exercise 1.2.)

❷ Writing to learn

See Chs. 2-3,
See Part 2

The process of writing helps you clarify your thinking, understand your opinions and beliefs, and grasp the extent of (and gaps in) your knowledge. How often have you started writing without really knowing what you were going to say? How often have you explored your own ideas and discovered what you really thought about the topic as you wrote? Writing has an intimate connection with both reading and research because it encourages you to use both those ways to expand your knowledge.

❸ Writing to create

See Ch. 3

Writing is inherently a creative act. In the act of composing a poem, a video, a blog, or a cartoon, you explore what moves you—what you are passionate about. Your writing inspires emotion: joy, anger, laughter, pain. Writing an essay can be as creative as writing a story or poem, because any piece of writing evolves from your vision of the world. When you create something that conveys your own personal vision or values, you feel emotionally and intellectually satisfied.

❹ Writing to persuade

See Ch. 4

Most of what you write is intended to convince your audience of something. You want to talk a friend into going to a movie with you. You want to trade shifts with a co-worker. You want your professor to accept the argument you're making in your paper. Some people believe that every piece of writing—even a poem—is an argument of some kind, because every piece of writing conveys a point of view and seeks to persuade the audience of that point of view. Because persuasive argument is such a critical purpose in writing and such a common purpose for the kind of writing you will do in college, we devote an entire chapter to it.

1b How important is writing to success in college and beyond?

Your ability to write—to communicate—clearly and effectively is the most important skill you can bring to both college and the workplace. Effective writing will get you good grades in school, and it will get you noticed, and probably promoted, in the workplace.

❶ Writing to succeed in college

In most classes, you will demonstrate how well you understand what's being taught through writing—essays, term papers, research reports, lab reports, and written exams. *Writing* well is the key to *doing* well in college. The challenge is that writing well in one context may not be the same as writing well, or writing effectively, in another. The conventions that you use—style, spelling, abbreviations, grammar—in a text message to a friend are very different from what a college instructor will be looking for in a formal paper. The conventions for writing in a psychology or biology course are also different from those you will want to follow in an English or history course. This handbook will guide you through not only writing a basic essay, but also finding and documenting information from other sources, and writing in the various academic disciplines you may study.

See Parts 1–3

You might think of the last half of this book—the sections that cover grammar, usage, and punctuation and mechanics—as the nuts and bolts, full of rigid rules to remember. But the fact is that the digital world has focused even more attention on your grammatical and stylistic choices because it has introduced a whole host of new writing styles and conventions using a variety of media from cell phones to PDAs. Now more than ever, you need to understand the context in which you are writing—your purpose as a writer and your audience or readers—in order to make the right choices.

See Parts 6–11

❷ Writing to succeed in the workplace

The rise of electronic communication has dramatically altered the workplace. The tools available to us are almost limitless: email, PDF documents, text messages, wikis and other collaborative work groups, blogs, and more. The fact is that we now spend much less time communicating orally—face to face, or on the phone—than we did before computers in the workplace. We all know about colleagues who email each other even when they work in offices next door to one another (or parents who text message children to call them to dinner). Because so much of our workplace communication is now written rather than oral, skilled writers are more valuable than ever.

See Chs. 21–23

All of this writing increases, rather than decreases, the need for clarity, concision, and effectiveness. And the ability to select the right tools for every context has become essential. You must be able to synthesize information, organize your thoughts, and encourage appropriate responses and actions. Just as important, you need to know how to choose appropriate media for your communications, and appropriate communications for your media—that is, you need to understand the conventions of style and usage that are appropriate for each context. Much of this handbook is focused on helping you analyze your audience and your purpose—your **rhetorical situation**—and adapt your style appropriately to that context and discourse community.

1c How do we communicate effectively?

The digital world may change the way we write and offer new media for transmitting writing, but it does not change the basic principles of effective communication—the **principles of rhetoric**.

It is no coincidence that the principles of rhetoric first appeared alongside the earliest democracies, in classical Athens, around the fifth century B.C. Aristotle and other thinkers recognized that, in order to persuade other people and develop a participatory democracy, you need to appeal to

See Fig. 1.4

- **their sense of logic**, or *logos.* You engage people by using reasoning and presenting evidence through the texts that you write, including both words and images.
- **their belief system**, or *pathos.* You engage people through their emotions, appealing to what they know, feel, and think about a subject.
- **their sense of ethics**, or *ethos.* You engage people because you are credible as a speaker or writer who communicates your aims and purposes clearly.

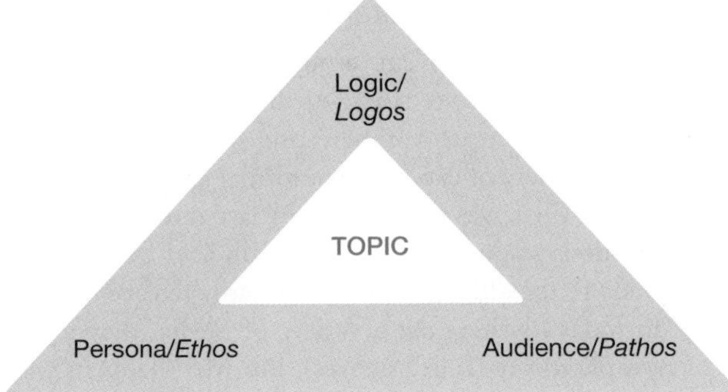

◄ **Figure 1.4** Rhetorical Triangle

See 3b-2

These three **appeals** evolved over time into what we call the **rhetorical triangle**. The three points of the triangle—**logical arguments, audience, persona**—correspond to the appeals defined by the ancient Greeks:

- **Logic** suggests the use of reasoning and evidence to persuade the audience.
- **Audience** suggests the need to understand your reader's belief system in order to create an emotional appeal.
- **Persona**, or *self*, suggests the need to establish your own ethical credibility as a writer with a clear sense of purpose.

Technology has brought some major changes to our writing, perhaps the most overwhelming being the very public nature of most writing today. Rather than sending a note or letter to a single correspondent, we post our innermost thoughts on our *Facebook* pages, we create blogs, we contribute to email threads that may find their way into dozens, hundreds, or even thousands of mailboxes, often without the original author's knowledge. We write academic papers that are reviewed by fellow students in a common process called **peer review**. These processes are almost instantaneous. Where it once took days or even months for a letter to reach its destination, text messages reach their recipients within seconds, and *Facebook* posts are available the instant they are posted to a wide community of friends. We need to remember all of this when we use the wide-ranging media available to us for writing.

1 Using different media for different messages

Although we have seen the advent of numerous media, we haven't entirely discarded the old. Here's a favorite story: At the turn of the 21st century, the *New York Times* decided to create a "time capsule" containing historical information. They asked a variety of experts what format should be used for recording the information—what was most likely to last through the coming centuries. Their unanimous response? Write in ink on acid-free paper. New tools and media are added to the old but do not necessarily replace them.

Not only do today's writers use a variety of media, they also produce a wide range of *types* of writing (called **genres**). But what happens when a traditional genre—a memo, perhaps—is written in a newer medium like email? Do the conventions of that genre (its **discourse conventions**) change or remain the same? Do you need the same kind of salutation in an email letter, for example, as in a hard copy letter?

In a digital world, you need to be able to distinguish—by using rhetoric as your guide—between those occasions when you can use the invented conventions (emoticons, symbols, abbreviations) of online language and those when you need to honor more traditional conventions like traditional spelling, punctuation, and mechanics.

This handbook will help you differentiate among audiences and purposes, so that you can readily use the appropriate conventions for the context in which you are writing. Your writing in almost any genre—and particularly your writing in the workplace or academia—needs to be clear, direct, error-free, logical, and to the point in order to communicate your message effectively.

EXERCISE 1.2 Go back to the copies of your writing you made for Exercise 1.1 and pick one. Using the rhetorical triangle, think about the principles of rhetoric: What logical appeals did you use for writing that particular piece or message? Who was the intended audience? How did you present yourself (as a friend, a mentor, a workplace colleague, a fellow student)? Were your purposes for writing clear? Now think about some alternatives. How might you change this writing to reflect a different logical argument, reader, or persona?

FOR COLLABORATION Working with a group of your peers, discuss your analysis of the rhetorical situation for your writing. Share thoughts on how you might change the rhetorical elements to shape your writing for a different situation.

❷ Using visual language

Graphic novel

We live in a visual world—billboards and advertisements (even interactive ones), computer and television screens, video games, video cell phones. Even traditional print media are becoming more and more visual. Graphic novels are becoming increasingly popular. Contemporary newspapers look very different from old-fashioned ones; they employ a rich array of fonts, headings, and color photographs.

See Fig. 1.5

Visual literacy is the ability to interpret, analyze, and evaluate images critically, just as we do text. When we communicate in a digital world, we have a rich array of tools available for integrating images into our writing. Photographs, cartoons, animations, graphics—all of these are at our fingertips. We are writing and reading not only words but also images, often as part of a coherent text where the elements work together to communicate an argument or inspire an emotion. So learning to write well now means learning how to *design* your communication to achieve the most impact. Effective design is a powerful component in effective writing.

See Part 4

1d How does technology make a difference to our writing?

Much of what you do as a writer in the digital world is very similar to what you did in an analog world. You still need to

- analyze your rhetorical situation,
- determine your topic,
- present evidence to support your position,
- draft, edit, and revise your work,
- and format your work according to the conventions of its medium and context.

What has changed dramatically is the range of tools available for doing this work and the means of transmitting your writing to an audience. These changes have been so exceptional that they have to some extent changed the nature of writing itself.

Logic. These days we write more often to reveal ourselves, rather than to transmit a message or persuade someone to adopt our point of view. Our posts on *MySpace* or *Facebook* often include information that would have been confined to

Figure 1.5 ▶ Newspaper front pages from the Ogden, Utah, *Standard*, from 1890, 2006, and 2009, showing the development of the newspaper from an all-text print medium to a highly visual online environment.

The Standard

INTERNATIONAL RIVALRY

Funds needed for Ogden projects/1B
Mom at Hill AFB honored/2B

Standard-Examiner

Monday, May 1, 2006

Smoking laws on the horizon

New regulations bring mixed feelings

Living soles

Crocodile – 1, chain saw – 0

Remembering Joanne

Layton woman's loved ones recall mother, nurse, sister, friend

Motivation

StandardNET LIVE
WWW.STANDARD.NET

Home Delivery
Digital Edition
Mobile News
RSS Feeds
Local Forums

Traffic Updates
32° Light Snow Nw 8 Mph Humidity: 96%

Main | News | Multimedia | Opinion | Community | Advertising

03-23-09 » Most Views: Shooting Deaths of Four Officers... (729 views) | Most Comments: Earmarking crickets / Special... (10 Comments)

Discover Yourself.
http://ogden.usu.edu
Call 801-626-8141
UtahState UNIVERSITY OGDEN

STANDARD MARKETPLACE
HELP WIDS
CLASSIFIEDS
JOB FINDER
QUALITY CONSIGNMENTS
GO! DINING UTAH
HOME FINDER
RENTAL FINDER
AUTO FINDER
DIRECT REWARDS
UTAH ON SALE

HOT TOPICS

TOP 5 VIEWS AND COMMENTS OF THE LAST 2 WEEKS

MOST VIEWED HEADLINES	VIEWS
Realty agent is charged in scam / Thirty...	7253
Man shoots off finger on first date	4735
HBO, Mormons square off over airing of sacred...	3073
The founders would approve of D.C. seat...	2675
Town dissolution bill gets no hearing	2031

MOST COMMENTED HEADLINES	COMMENTS
Realty agent is charged in scam / Thirty...	201
HBO, Mormons square off over airing of sacred...	108
Don't use Mexico to bring back gun control...	87
Man charged in choking assault	85
The founders would approve of D.C. seat...	28

VIDEO

News Round Up March 23, 2009 04:09

Weber County is planning to

NEWS ROUND UP MARCH 23, 2009
News Round Up for March 23, 2009
04:09

go! TO THE MOVIES NEW! MOVIE REVIEWS SHOWTIMES LET'S GO!

TODAY'S HEADLINES MONDAY, MARCH 23, 2009

SECTIONS: NEWS | SPORTS | BUSINESS | FEATURES | EDITORIALS

Judge says panties will be evidence in Owens trial

FARMINGTON — A judge declined to exclude the blood-stained panties that will serve as key evidence in the murder trial of Edward Lewis Owens, which begins today.

COMMENTS: 0 VIEWS: 229

Woman arrested on burglary charges; suspected of beating man in his home

OGDEN — A woman has been arrested and police are looking for two men in connection with a beating Thursday night.

COMMENTS: 1 VIEWS: 180

Standard Marketplace

Classified ads now on your mobile device.

Click here

a personal and very private diary in previous times—or never written down at all. How have the contexts in which we are currently writing changed the texts themselves? The content and form may be radically different. Because we are using a variety of media, we may use words and images differently, too.

Audience. We are communicating with audiences that may number in the thousands or even millions (if your *YouTube* video goes viral, for example)—or with our professor, one on one. Often our academic writing will be reviewed by our peers as well as our professor. We are writing for multiple, and sometimes unknown, audiences.

Persona. The electronic environment makes us feel anonymous. The anonymity of our personas in the digital world—and the often unknown nature of our audience—brings with it both freedoms and constraints. Your messages may be read by someone you did not originally intend to include—someone from a different culture, a different background, a different set of assumptions. The way you present yourself in your writing needs to acknowledge that possibility.

1 Using technologies in the writing process

Writing is not a neat or orderly process; it is often very messy. If you're like most writers, your writing process proceeds in fits and starts, with repeated cycles of drafting, researching for information, rereading what you have written, revising and editing, and then writing new material and starting over. You may write in "chunks," piecing these chunks together into a final paper by cutting and pasting files. You may multitask while you are writing, moving easily between researching online, texting friends, and downloading songs to your MP3 player.

As comfortable as you are with your computer, you may not be aware of all the tools it offers to help you with the writing process. Many of us still sit down at the computer to write almost as if it were a typewriter. We don't know about creating style sheets and headers; we don't know about the available dictionaries and thesauruses; we aren't aware that software can format our bibliographies or works cited pages automatically. This handbook provides a wealth of information about word-processing functionalities—primarily through the TechHelp boxes throughout the text—that you can use for every phase of your writing: researching, choosing and narrowing a topic, drafting, editing and revising, and designing your final document. And the

TechALERT boxes will alert you to the dangers of relying too much on those tools by pointing out things like the inadequacies of grammar and spell checkers, the need to evaluate online information, and the need to differentiate between formal and informal language conventions in academic and workplace writing.

❷ Using technologies in the research process

Millions upon millions of pages of information are available to all of us online. Much of this information is provided by corporate sponsors and is designed to sell something; much of it is provided by organizations or individuals with particular agendas (not always obvious ones). Very little of the information available online has been through the formal review process that is typically demanded of, for example, articles published in scholarly journals. The burden of evaluating online information falls squarely on you. You need to hone your own critical thinking skills to deal with this cascade of information. You need to be able to

- distinguish quickly and accurately what information is reliable and what information is not;
- identify what types of information can be used in academic research;
- and understand how to incorporate that research appropriately, by documenting and crediting your sources.

See Chs. 7–10

1e How can this handbook help you succeed as a writer?

Through its emphasis on communication in an electronic environment, and especially through its focus on rhetorical analysis and on the process of writing—planning, researching, drafting, and rewriting—*The New Century Handbook* will equip you with the basic skills you need to become a good writer. This handbook will guide you through the continually changing and ever more challenging technology available to you. You will learn to focus on the rhetorical situation, in all genres and all media, and you will learn to make technology your partner in the act of communication.

2 Critical Reading and Viewing

FAQs

- What is critical thinking? (2a)
- How do I read critically? (2b)
- Should I take notes while reading? (2b-1)
- How can I view images critically? (2c)

Are you a critical *consumer* of information, no matter what the context, discipline, or genre? Understanding how to think, read, and view critically will help you understand how to produce information effectively; thinking critically will make you a better writer.

2a Think critically

We are often overwhelmed by incoming information—like fighter pilots having to evade fire or quarterbacks being swarmed by defenders. **Critical thinkers** understand the need to filter and evaluate that incoming information. That may be the primary purpose of your college education—to help you learn to think critically. *Thinking critically* does not mean *criticizing*. Rather, it suggests that you engage, question, and explore ideas actively, without accepting easy answers.

Just as you need to understand the context for your own writing—the logical argument you intend to convey, the audience you intend to reach, the persona you intend to create as a writer—you also need to understand the context of what you read and view.

See Ch. 1

You are being a critical thinker and consumer when you

- identify those parts of a *Wikipedia* entry that appear to be biased;
- recognize which claims for a health food are based on real evidence, and which are simply the manufacturer's sales pitch;
- understand that the image of an attractive woman in a car ad has nothing to do with the quality of the car, and everything to do with enticing buyers.

Critical thinking, or **active thinking**, involves the same processes no matter what medium you are using to communicate—speaking, writing, listening, reading, viewing. In every instance, you need to

- establish your purpose,
- analyze the topic,
- synthesize the information provided,
- make inferences, and
- evaluate.

These steps are not always linear; they may occur simultaneously, or you may come back to one or more of the steps multiple times. But these steps do represent a process that you need to follow to comprehend fully the information you are consuming—and create the most effective messages when you communicate yourself.

1 Establishing your purpose

Whether you are reading, writing, or speaking, ask yourself:

- Why am I interested in this topic? Why do I want to learn about it?
- What is my goal in reading or writing about it?

Knowing *why* you want to know will help you formulate more specific questions about the topic, and these questions will focus your exploration.

Let's say that you need to buy a new computer. If you're a careful buyer, you won't just pull up *computers* on a Web site and click on the first model that appears. You'll think about the tasks you do most often on a computer. Do you use yours primarily for writing? For social networking? For email? Or do you want to be able to send videos to *YouTube* and embed lots of charts and photographs into the papers you produce? Knowing what you want to accomplish on your computer will help you understand what kind you should buy.

❷ Analyzing the topic

Analyzing something means mentally dividing it into its parts. For example, if you're going to be carrying your new computer around with you, you'll want to analyze it according to its weight, its size, its battery life, and maybe even the design of the case. On the other hand, if it's a desktop model you need, these things matter less and instead you will want to analyze competing models according to processor speed, RAM, hard-drive capacity, and audio quality.

The purposes and interests of your sources of information should also be taken into account—particularly in online research. Analysis often depends, to some degree, on information provided by other people who have their own interests, biases, beliefs, and assumptions. As an information consumer and critical thinker, you should always be aware of other people's orientations and try to keep them in mind as you absorb the information. Information from any source can be lacking in objectivity, so it's a good idea to routinely gather your information from multiple, independent sources and compare them.

EXERCISE 2.1 Imagine you're looking for a used car (or, as they say in the trade, a "pre-owned vehicle").

1. How would you analyze potential models?
2. How might a used-car salesperson or other seller analyze (describe) a car?
3. How would an auto mechanic likely analyze that same car?
4. In each of the above cases, explain how a specific set of purposes gives rise to a particular basis of analysis.

❸ Synthesizing the information provided

Synthesizing is the opposite of analyzing. Instead of taking something apart, synthesis puts things together. But this does not mean that synthesizing merely restores something to the way it was before analysis. Rather, synthesis seeks to find *new* ways of assembling things, *new* relationships among the parts, *new* combinations. Like analysis, this process is governed by the critical thinker's purposes.

For example, let's say you've decided to purchase a laptop, rather than a desktop computer, and you want it to be easy to carry—lightweight and small.

Although you'll be using it mainly to write papers and send emails, you'll also want to play games once in a while, so you need some computing power and a decent graphics card. On the other hand, you're on a tight budget and can't afford either a super lightweight model or one with enormous gaming capability. To solve your dilemma, you'll need to analyze the candidate models along these different scales, but then *synthesize* your findings to get the best combination according to your needs and constraints.

4 Making inferences

Another important critical thinking skill is the ability to make inferences, or "read between the lines." People often do not say exactly what's on their minds. Sometimes their lack of candor is just an effort to be tactful; sometimes it's more deceptive than that. When you interpret what people don't say, or don't fully express, you are making inferences. For example, if a used-car salesperson evades your question about a car's heating system and you thereby infer that something is wrong with the heating system, you are exhibiting an important kind of critical thinking. (Note how *purpose* once again plays a key role—in this case, the purpose or intent of the message producer.)

Many of the logical fallacies discussed later, in 4g—such as the *non sequitur*, either/or reasoning, and begging the question—invite the listener or reader to make *faulty* inferences. The ability to detect such fallacies is also a type of critical thinking.

5 Evaluating

Once you've determined your purpose, analyzed your topic, synthesized your ideas, and made appropriate inferences, you are ready to evaluate the results. Evaluation involves examining everything you have done up to this point and determining what it all adds up to. In the case of buying a computer or a used car, you would want to review what you have learned from going through the first four steps; in particular, you would check to see if the information you have gathered consistently points to the same conclusion. If not, you would want to identify the contradictions and try to resolve them. Perhaps your sources of information are not as knowledgeable as you had thought, or perhaps you haven't asked them the right questions. In any case, this activity is itself a form of critical thinking—the willingness to confront and resolve inconsistencies in your reasoning and information gathering.

If at this point there are still troubling inconsistencies in your evaluation of the topic, you may want to "change the playing field"—that is, broaden your inquiry. This can be done in either of two ways:

Critical analysis

- *Use additional sources of information.* Talk to more people, consult other publications, gain some more firsthand experience.
- *Reexamine the initial premises of your investigation.* It could be that these have changed in the course of your inquiry—or were never quite accurate in the first place.

For example, in your search for a new computer, maybe you've relied too much on the advice of a single friend or a single Web site. Or perhaps you really want to do your writing at home on a desktop computer and can do without a more expensive laptop. Sometimes it is only at this evaluation stage that nagging discrepancies and uncertainties are resolved and critical thinking is fully rewarded.

2b Read actively and critically

A good reader reads actively. As you read, your mind must be actively engaged with what your eyes see on the page or on the screen. You need to see the text on multiple levels—the words, the sentences, the paragraphs, the text as a whole—and you need to think about how it relates to things *outside* the text, such as where it was published, what you know about the author, who its target audience might be, other readings, and your own life experience. In short, you need to situate the text and make sense of it in a larger context.

A good reader also reads critically; that is, he or she reads with an open mind and a questioning attitude. To be a critical reader, you need to go beyond understanding what the author is saying; you need to challenge or question the author. You may question the validity of the author's main point or ask whether the text agrees or disagrees with other writings on the same topic and with your own experience.

❶ Reading thoroughly

Reading thoroughly on all levels is crucial to understanding a text well enough to think and write about it knowledgeably and critically. If you structure your reading process according to distinct steps—previewing and predicting; reading for gist; reading for details; reviewing; and taking notes—you will understand what you read more completely.

Previewing and predicting

Begin any reading session by previewing the material as a whole. By looking ahead, you gain a general sense of what is to come. This will help you to predict what to expect from the text as you read and to better understand what you are reading. Jot down in a journal or notebook any questions that occur to you during previewing.

For example, as you approach a textbook for the first time, look closely at the table of contents to preview the book's main topics. Next, preview the assigned chapter. Page through the chapter, reading all headings and subheadings in order to gain a sense of the chapter's organizational structure. Also look at any words that are in boldface or italic print. These words are highlighted because the author considered them to be especially important. Finally, preview any graphs, charts, or illustrations. These visuals are included to reinforce or illustrate key ideas or concepts in the chapter.

You should also preview shorter works, such as magazine or journal articles, prior to reading them. An article may have an abstract or summary of its main points, prominently set off from the main text. It may include subheadings, which provide an idea of the article's structure. Again, look for highlighted words or graphics in the article, since these can provide clues about key ideas. As a final step in previewing an article, read the opening and closing paragraphs to get an idea of the author's thesis and conclusion.

Reading for gist

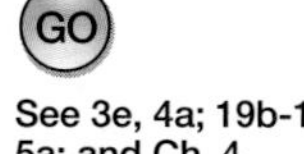

See 3e, 4a; 19b-1; 5a; and Ch. 4

After you preview the text, read it carefully for main points. This step should flow naturally from the previous one, as your previewing should have revealed at least some of the text's main points. Sometimes main points are stated explicitly as thesis statements, headings, topic sentences, or captions to visual aids; at other times you can infer main points from how the author lays out an argument or applies emphasis. In any case, try to get a general sense of what the author is "getting at" in this text.

WEBLINK
Critical reading

Reading for details

Next, read the text again even more closely, this time paying attention to all details. Pace your reading according to the difficulty of the material—the more difficult the material, the more slowly you should read it. You may find that you need to take frequent breaks if the reading is especially dense or contains a lot of new information. You may also find that you need to reread some passages several times in order to understand their meaning. Material assigned for college classes is often packed with information and therefore requires not only slow reading but also rereading.

Reviewing

Once you have completed a thorough reading, go back to the text and review. Pay particular attention to those areas of the text that you previewed. Have the questions you had when previewing been answered? If not, reread the relevant passages. It may also help to review with a classmate or a study group; discuss the text with your peers to be sure that your understanding conforms with theirs. Talking about the text with others will also help communicate your understanding in a meaningful way. If your class has a computer bulletin board or online discussion group, post any questions that you still have about the reading.

Taking notes

Reading invariably stimulates thought. To get the most out of reading, you may find it helpful to record these thoughts in writing. There are a number of ways to do this, including (1) annotating the text while reading, (2) summarizing, (3) keeping a journal, and (4) using a double-column notebook.

Annotating the text while reading. One way to ensure that you are reading actively and critically is to annotate the text as you read. Annotating a text means making summary notes in the margins, as well as underlining or highlighting important words and passages. Typically it is best to preview the material before annotating it. Your annotations should summarize the key ideas in the text. Take care, however, not to overannotate. You need to be selective so that you do not highlight everything in the text. The following excerpt illustrates a student's annotation of a passage from an article on creativity in science and art.

What is the relationship between science and art? There must be a link, as so many scientists are also artists.

What is the kinship between these seemingly dissimilar species, science and art? Obviously there is some—if only because so often the same people are attracted to both. The image of Einstein playing his violin is only too familiar, or Leonardo with his inventions. It is a standing joke in some circles that all it takes to make a string quartet is four mathematicians sitting in the same room. Even Feynman plays the bongo drums. (He finds it curious that while he is almost always identified as the physicist who plays the bongo drums, the few times that he has been asked to play the drums, "the introducer never seems to find it necessary to mention that I also do theoretical physics.")

Art and science cover the same ground—several examples.

One commonality is that art and science often cover the same territory. A tree is fertile ground for both the poet and the botanist. The relationship between mother and child, the symmetry of snowflakes, the effects of light and color, and the structure of the human form are studied equally by painters and psychologists, sculptors, and physicians. The origins of the universe, the nature of life, and the meaning of death are the subjects of physicists, philosophers, and composers.

—K. C. Cole, *The Scientific Aesthetic*

EXERCISE 2.2 One more paragraph from Cole's article is included below. Annotate this paragraph, underlining important ideas and noting key points in the margin.

There are, of course, substantial differences between art and science. Science is written in the universal language of mathematics; it is, far more than art, a shared perception of the world. Scientific insights can be tested by the good old scientific method. And scientists have to try to be dispassionate about the conduct of their work—at least enough so that their passions do not disrupt the outcome of experiments. Of course, sometimes they do: "Great thinkers are never passive before the facts," says Stephen Jay Gould. "They have hopes and hunches, and they try hard to construct the world in their light. Hence, great thinkers also make great errors."

—K. C. Cole, *The Scientific Aesthetic*

Summarizing. A critical thinker is able to abstract or summarize the gist of information read or heard. When you summarize something, you boil it down to its essence, picking out the major points or ideas and restating them in a succinct way. For example, if you had just attended a lecture by a history professor, you might summarize the lecture by writing down the three or four major points made by the speaker. In summarizing, you generally stick to the literal meaning of what you've read or heard.

See 2b-1,
See Ch. 10

Keeping a journal. Many people find it helpful to jot down thoughts while reading and keep them in a journal. Like a diary, a reading journal requires you to put your thoughts into words, an activity that can clarify your thinking about a topic. It allows you to "converse" with yourself, thereby setting up an internal sounding board for your own thoughts. In addition, if you later decide to include these thoughts in an essay or other formal writing, the fact that you have already formulated them will give you a head start. Finally, and most obviously, a reading journal is simply a valuable way to remember things that you might otherwise forget.

Using a double-column notebook. A double-column notebook is a special kind of reading journal that has become increasingly popular in recent years. It combines summarizing and journal keeping. In a notebook, draw a vertical line down the middle of each page (or use the notebook spine itself as the dividing line), thus creating two columns. In the left-hand column, summarize your reading as you go along. In the right-hand column, record your interpretations, evaluations, and other thoughts about the left-hand items. The left-hand column is for literal meaning; the right-hand column is for interpretation and criticism. Here is an example from a reading of "Title IX Lawsuits Are Endangering Men's College Sports," by Glenn Sacks.

SUMMARY	COMMENTS
• Sacks says that between 1992 and 1997, 3.6 men's athletic slots had to be dropped for every women's slot created.	• I wonder what the ratio was before 1992. Should check on this. Might provide a different perspective.
• He seems to assume that football occupies a sacrosanct position in college sports.	• Has anyone thought about making college football semiprofessional? It already seems to be that anyway.
• Sacks says that Title IX demands "rigid proportionality" between the sexes according to overall school enrollment (last paragraph).	• Check on this. It doesn't seem plausible.
• "Over 70% of I-A football programs turn a profit."	• How big a profit? And how many of these programs are there? What about all the others?

TechHelp

Creating a Double-Column Notebook

You can create a double-column notebook by simply setting up a two-column table.

1. Open a new file (FILE > NEW).
2. On your desktop, select TABLE.
3. Click on INSERT > TABLE.
4. For "Number of Columns," insert "2." For "Number of Rows," insert "8" (you can add more rows later, if you need them).
5. Set AUTOFIT to FIXED COLUMN WIDTH.
6. Click OK.
7. At the top of the left-hand column, write "SUMMARY." At the top of the right-hand column, write "COMMENTS." You now have your double-column notebook.
8. Hit SAVE and give your table an appropriate filename.

❷ Understanding what you read

To fully understand a text, you should read it on three different levels: (1) literal meaning, (2) rhetorical meaning, and (3) evaluation/criticism. As you move from one level to the next, you increase your "resistance" to the text, allowing you to question the text's truth value. This three-step process is illustrated with reference to Sacks's essay.

Title IX Lawsuits Are Endangering Men's College Sports

Glenn Sacks

1 In one of UCLA's proudest moments, UCLA-trained swimmers and gymnasts dominated the 1984 Summer Olympics. Half of the gold-medal winning men's gymnastic team were Bruins. Yet, despite producing 22 Olympic swimming competitors and dozens of world-class gymnasts, these UCLA men's teams were eliminated less than a decade later. In fact, over the past five years more than 350 men's collegiate athletic teams have been eliminated nationwide, and the number of men's gymnastics teams has fallen from 200 to just 21. What happened?

High-profile, specific example makes for an attention-getting intro.

2 These athletic programs were not felled by mismanagement, drugs, or rules violations. They were destroyed by Title IX.

3 Title IX of the Education Amendments Act of 1972 barred sex discrimination in any educational program or activity which receives federal funding. In the decades since, women's athletics have burgeoned in high schools and colleges. Title IX was and remains an important and laudable victory for the women's movement.

Basic background info sets the stage nicely.

4 More recently, however, misguided feminist lawsuits and political lobbying have changed Title IX from a vehicle to open up opportunities for women to a scorched earth policy whereby the destruction of men's athletics has become an acceptable substitute for strengthening women's athletics.

Exaggerations like "scorched earth" and "destruction" undermine your objectivity. Implies that feminists are out to "get men."

5 Feminists have used an obscure, hastily prepared bureaucratic action—known now as the 1979 Policy Interpretation—to mandate that the

number of athletes in college athletic programs reflect within a few percentage points the proportion of male and female students on campus. The problem is, as studies have shown, fewer women than men are interested in playing organized sports, even though the opportunity is available.

Even if true (which needs to be shown), this could change.

6 The fact that women now outnumber men in college 57%–43% nationwide makes it even harder for schools to achieve the numerical gender balance demanded by the 1979 Policy—an interpretation never reviewed or approved by Congress. Time and again the Federal Department of Education's Office of Civil Rights (OCR) has investigated schools and allowed them only two options to meet Title IX—create new women's teams for which there often are neither funds nor interested female athletes, or cut men's teams.

A key claim! Needs supporting evidence.

7 Thus women have gained a little but men have lost a lot. According to the National Collegiate Athletic Association (NCAA), for every new women's athletics slot created between 1992 and 1997, 3.6 male athletes were dropped. Kimberly Schuld, director of the Independent Women's Forum's Title IX Play Fair! Project, calls this "clear, government-sanctioned sex discrimination."

Discrimination? Or fairness?

8 Critics of modern Title IX point out that its equity calculations are misleading in part because they count college football's athletes and dollars without considering football's money-making ability. USC, for example, has been hit hard by feminist legal action based on its greater number of male athletes and higher men's athletic budget. What's not considered is that USC's men's teams—largely football—are responsible for over 99% of the near $20 million total revenue of the Athletic Department. In fact, over 70% of Division I-A football programs turn a profit.

Okay, but how typical is this?

How big a profit? And what about the other divisions?

9 Thus schools are caught in a vise. Because schools need football's revenue yet must also equalize gender numbers, they are forced to cut men's non-revenue sports.

Neatly summarizes the gist of his argument.

10 Todd R. Dickey, USC's general counsel, Schuld, and many others argue that football should simply be taken out of the gender equity equation because no other sport earns as much revenue, has such a large number of athletes or staff, and needs as much equipment. "You can't spend as much on women's sports as you can on men's, because there is no women's equivalent for football," Dickey says.

Maybe football is the problem. (Maybe it should be professionalized.)

11 Title IX's modern application has struck hardest at minority men. Lawsuits brought to balance the number of athletic scholarships awarded to men and women have decreased the number and value of men's scholarships, upon which minority men often rely to finance their educations. Black colleges and universities, where female students outnumber males 60%–40% and money is usually tight, have been particularly wounded by feminist lawsuits. And when Title IX forces schools to drop their football programs, as San Francisco State did in 1995, it is black athletes who are hurt disproportionately.

Very effective! Pits one historically disadvantaged group (women) against another (blacks).

12 While modern Title IX has been devastating for male and particularly for minority male athletes, it has also hurt female athletics. By allowing the destruction of men's teams to substitute for increasing the number of women's teams, universities have been stripped of the incentive to build more and better female squads. A school that has six female teams and nine male teams may find it much easier to cut men's teams than to provide the new money and resources to create more women's teams.

The metaphors of violence (struck, hurt, wounded, stripped, destruction) have emotional power but are out of place here.

13 The situation cries out for a flexible athletics policy based on student interest levels instead of rigid proportionality. Title IX states "no person . . . shall, on the basis of sex . . . be subjected to discrimination under any education program or activity receiving federal financial assistance." Misguided women's advocates have used a bureaucratic obscurity to undermine these simple yet high-minded words, and turn Title IX from an instrument used to fight sex discrimination into a policy mandating it.

Assumes there is no flexibility now—which remains to be shown.

Continues to demonize women's advocates and feminists.

Reading for literal meaning

The literal meaning of a text is its explicit meaning as determined by the words on the page and their conventional meanings; it is the "surface" meaning of a text. It comprises all those aspects of a text that are available to anyone who reads that text. Literal meaning does not include hyperbole, metaphor, irony, charged language, tone, or other implicit meanings that must be inferred by the reader.

See 44b

When you start reading a novel, a magazine article, a blog posting, or any other text, you expect to move from sentence to sentence in a smooth flow of literal meaning. Since the deeper meanings of a text (see below) derive from this literal meaning, before you can engage in interpretive or critical reading you must fully understand the literal meaning. Use a good dictionary to help you with any words you don't know. At this stage, you should be a *compliant* reader trying to understand the text on its most basic terms. This is no different from a moviegoer enjoying a sci-fi film as sheer entertainment, rather than analyzing it as a movie critic would.

In "Title IX Lawsuits Are Endangering Men's College Sports," essayist Glenn Sacks makes an explicit argument that Title IX of the federal Education Amendments Act of 1972 is discriminating against male athletes in colleges and high schools. He acknowledges that Title IX has been an enormous boon to women's athletics, but he claims that a 1979 policy interpretation has caused it to be very damaging to men's athletics. Specifically, he accuses feminists of using this 1979 provision to embark on a "scorched earth" campaign against men's athletics, to the point where schools and colleges are being forced to drop hundreds of men's programs in order to comply with federal law and accommodate women's sports. In short, Sacks claims that Title IX has become an instrument of sex discrimination against male athletes in high school and college. This literal meaning of Sacks's essay is plain to see.

Reading for rhetorical meaning

See 1c

Once you have grasped the literal meaning of a text, you should go beyond it to the realm of rhetorical meaning. At this level, you become more conscious of the author's role in constructing the text, giving it a certain "spin," and manipulating the reader. How is he or she using the principles of rhetoric—logical, emotional, or ethical appeals? You also look for clues as to what the author has implied rather than overtly stated, what assumptions the author is making, what audience the author seems to be addressing, and what the author's attitude seems to be as revealed by the tone of his or her writing.

In reading for rhetorical meaning, you should always ask yourself questions such as "In what other way(s) could the author have said this?" or "What *didn't* the author say here that he or she could have?" Often the easiest way to get started in such an analysis is with those words and phrases that draw attention to themselves, for example, because they are loaded terms (as in *fetus* vs. *unborn child*), are emphatic, are deliberately "off-register" or figurative, or are punctuated with "scare" quotation marks.

See 39d, 41f

Sacks's "Title IX Lawsuits Are Endangering Men's College Sports" contains several such examples. In general, Sacks uses a dignified, formal level of diction. However, there are several places in his essay where he uses charged language to add emphasis and establish a more dramatic tone. For example, the word *endangering* in the title is a form of hyperbole, suggesting that men's college sports, like endangered species, are facing extinction. A more accurate term would be *restricting* or *undercutting*. This theme is continued in paragraph 4 with reference to the *destruction* of men's athletics and is now linked to a *scorched earth policy* being pushed by *misguided feminists*. *Scorched earth* is a vivid metaphor, as is the expression *caught in a vise* in paragraph 9; both phrases are likely to catch the reader's attention.

See 39d, 41f

The combined effect of this charged language is to exaggerate and thereby emphasize a polarization of the two sides in this conflict: aggrieved males versus "feminists" and "misguided women's advocates." Although this word choice gives the essay more dramatic power, it also undermines, to some degree, the author's objectivity and credibility.

EXERCISE 2.3

1. In the topic sentences of paragraphs 4 and 5, Sacks prominently uses the word *feminist*. To whom is he referring? What other term could he have used? Why didn't he?
2. Sacks uses the term *sex discrimination* several times in his essay, but to different ends and from different perspectives. Analyze these, and describe how you interpret the term differently according to the context in which it is used.

❸ Evaluating what you read

Finally, you want to read beyond the literal and rhetorical meanings to evaluate the worth of the writing and the validity of the author's ideas or argument. This is the domain of *criticism*. In this mode, you should be even more detached, resistant, and analytical than you were in the interpretive mode. Critical evaluation should be done on two levels, internal and external.

Internal evaluation

See 4c-d, 4f-g

With *internal evaluation*, you restrict your attention, as before, to the text itself. This time, though, you focus on the overall logic of the text. Does it hang together? Does it make sense? If the author is making an argument, does it have enough supporting evidence? Does it consider alternative views? Is it appealing mainly to logic, to authority, or to emotion? Does it have any fallacies?

Look again at "Title IX Lawsuits Are Endangering Men's College Sports." Does Sacks's argument hold up under close scrutiny? Let's start with the overall logic of his argument. According to Sacks, Title IX demands "rigid proportionality" by gender in athletics according to overall college enrollment. Women outnumber men in college enrollment and thus are allowed more places in athletic programs; but men are more interested in playing sports, so men are forced to sacrifice their athletic interests to a far greater degree than women, which is unfair. Is this a sound argument? If his facts are right and if he hasn't left out any relevant information, then yes, his argument would appear to be quite solid. But it rests on at least two claims that are worth examining. First, is it true that Title IX demands strict proportionality? Since 1979 there have been three optional ways, not one, for a school to establish nondiscrimination in college athletic programs: (1) substantial proportionality, (2) evidence of "a history and continuing practice of program expansion for the underrepresented sex," or (3) evidence that a school is "fully and effectively accommodating the interests and abilities of the underrepresented sex." Sacks focuses only on the first of these and misrepresents it as "rigid proportionality," not the *substantial* proportionality called for in the 1979 Policy Interpretation.

Second, are men in fact more interested than women in playing sports? In paragraph 5, Sacks says that "studies have shown" this to be the case, but he fails to cite any. Even if numbers do support his contention, one could point out that interest in women's athletics has "burgeoned," to use his term, from 300,000 at the high school level in 1972 to 3 million today, and from 32,000 at the intercollegiate level to more than 150,000 today. In other words, increased opportunities for women have apparently led to increased interest, a trend that could end up erasing the claimed gender difference altogether.

Sacks's argument appeals to logic and factuality more than to emotion or authority, so it should be evaluated on this basis. In general, he does a good job of supplying factual details (data, names, examples) to support his generalizations. But there are places where one would want even more evidence. For example, is it true that the cutback in men's collegiate athletic teams (paragraph 1) is due solely to Title IX, as implied in paragraph 2? Is it true that the 1979 Policy Interpretation mandates proportionality (paragraphs 5–6)? To what extent do "schools need football's revenue" (paragraph 9)? How is Sacks defining "feminists," and to what extent are they to blame for Title IX's modern application? Such questions could all use concrete evidence or at least reference to appropriate sources.

Are there any fallacies in Sacks's argument? Putting the blame entirely on "misguided women's advocates" appears to be a case of *overgeneralization*, and impugning the character of such women, by accusing them of pursuing a "scorched earth" campaign against men, exemplifies the *ad hominem* fallacy. And the author's simplification of this complex issue to two sides, with schools "caught in a vise," is an example of *either/or reasoning*.

See 4g, 4g-1, 3, 4

EXERCISE 2.4

1. Sacks argues that "the destruction of men's athletics has become an acceptable substitute for strengthening women's athletics" (paragraph 4) and gives an example in paragraph 12, citing "misguided feminists" as the architects of this "destruction." Does his logic hold up? Can you imagine a situation in which a school may opt to cut men's teams yet not find that action fully "acceptable"?
2. Sacks's argument is based on several major assumptions, both stated and unstated, for which he offers no evidence. What are they?

FOR COLLABORATION With one or two classmates, consult the list of logical and emotional fallacies in 4h and see if any of them apply to "Title IX Lawsuits Are Endangering Men's College Sports."

Writing process

External evaluation

In *external evaluation*, you evaluate a text against other texts and against your own experience. These other texts could include writings by the same author or writings on the same topic by other authors. This kind of comparative analysis allows you to see the text in a larger perspective. It also enables you to make an informed guess as to any agenda the author might have or as to anything that might have been *left out* of the text. Most writers who are trying to persuade readers to a particular point of view tend to avoid mentioning facts that might damage their cause. As a critical reader, it is important that you not allow yourself to be manipulated in this way.

Using external evaluation, try to consider this text against other texts and against your own experience. Normally a good starting point for this aspect of critical reading is to note the company it keeps—that is, other texts with which it is grouped. In this case, however, the text was published simply as an opinion piece in the *Los Angeles Times* and then posted separately on the Web. Is this text similar in ideology to the author's other writings? Yes, it would appear so. A quick search of the Web reveals that Glenn Sacks is a staff writer for a conservative political journal called *The American Partisan*, where he is described as "the only regularly published male columnist in the US who writes about gender issues from a perspective unapologetically sympathetic to men" (see http://www.american-partisan.com/about.htm). Other topics he has written on include domestic violence (specifically, battered men), adoption (specifically, notification of the biological father), and child custody (specifically, rights of the natural father). "Title IX Lawsuits Are Endangering Men's College Sports" falls in the same vein. Consistent with conservative ideology, it supports a traditional view (whereby athletics are mainly a male domain) against further encroachment by women. This would explain also his clear animus against feminists and "misguided women's advocates."

To broaden your horizons as a critical reader, it is important that you not restrict yourself to that one author's view but consult a range of opinions. In this case, you could search the Web for writings by other authors, using *Title IX* as your search term. Such a search would turn up some interesting facts not mentioned by Sacks. For example, although more than four hundred men's programs have been cut in the past three decades, even more men's programs have been *added*. Indeed, since 1980, for every two women's sports programs added, 1.5 men's programs have been added. A Web search would also turn up a variety of perspectives on this whole issue. For example, there are those who argue that the OCR does *not* mandate proportionality, that Title IX enforcement already *is* flexible. There are those who claim it is the gargantuan size of football programs that's to blame and that either downsizing or professionalizing college football would take the pressure off other (both men's and women's) programs.

Critical Reading

Internal Evaluation

- ✓ Is the text coherent? Does its logic hang together and make sense?
- ✓ If it constitutes an argument, is it appealing mainly to logic, to authority, or to emotion (7f)?
- ✓ Does it have enough supporting evidence (7c)?
- ✓ Are there any fallacies in the author's reasoning (7g)?
- ✓ Does the author consider alternative views (7d)?

External Evaluation

- ✓ Where was this particular piece of writing published? Does this suggest an ideological slant of any kind?
- ✓ Judging from the author's other writings, what do you think his or her general views or interests are?
- ✓ What purpose or "agenda" might the author have had in writing about this topic?
- ✓ What do other writers have to say about this topic?
- ✓ What might the author have *left out* of the text? Why?
- ✓ How well does the author's representation of the world fit with your own experience?

Sacks hardly acknowledges any of these facts. They are "textual silences" that can be filled in only by a critical reader familiar with different points of view on the topic. Like most editorialists in the public media, Sacks wants to promote his own point of view and is less interested in presenting all sides of the issue. The burden is on you, the reader, to educate yourself on the issue, which can best be done by reading widely and critically and then weighing others' ideas against your own experience.

EXERCISE 2.5

1. Using *Title IX* as your search term, search the Internet for other writings on this subject by other authors. Be sure to look for various points of view, not just authors opposed to Title IX.
2. On the basis of what you found in question 1, what other textual silences do you think there are in Sacks's essay? That is, in arguing for one point of view, what has he left out?

9/11 graphic novel

2c View images actively and critically

In general, the major source of ideas for writing has always been reading. But as visual imagery becomes more and more ubiquitous in our modern world, the viewing of images is becoming increasingly important as a source of input. And like reading, viewing can be done on three different levels: literal meaning, rhetorical meaning, and evaluation/criticism. We will illustrate this three-step process using a photo of a freeway in Virginia and an ad for a sport-utility vehicle, or SUV.

Viewing for literal meaning

See Fig. 2.1

See Fig. 2.2

The literal meaning of an image is its "surface" meaning, the meaning that anyone with a minimal knowledge of the context would attribute to it at first glance. For example, on a literal level, the photo depicts truck and automobile traffic on a highway, passing beneath a sign urging motorists to "report terrorism" via a certain toll-free number. We learn from the caption that the road is the Washington, DC, Beltway and that the photo was taken in April 2003. The literal meaning of the SUV ad is simply that a Saturn VUE

◄ **Figure 2.1** The DC Beltway, April 2003

(*Source:* Used with permission of Seven Stories Press and Michael Williamson)

sport-utility vehicle is parked in an evergreen forest, surrounded by a variety of wildlife.

Viewing for rhetorical meaning

Photo essay

Like written texts, visual images can be manipulated to favor a certain perspective. When viewing for rhetorical meaning, you should try to detect ways in which an image may have been manipulated. Consider, for example, the *composition* of the image:

- How is the image structured? Are some parts connected to others? Are there notable contrasts?
- What parts draw your attention? Why?
- How does this affect your interpretation?

Consider also the *point of view*, or perspective:

- From what angle and distance are we viewing the scene?
- How does this affect your interpretation?
- Would a different point of view make a difference in how you interpret the image, and if so, how?

Figure 2.2 ▶ Saturn VUE Ad

(*Source:* Used with permission of General Motors Corp.)

Finally, consider the *tone* of the image:

- How sharp is the image?
- What colors are used?
- How do these qualities affect your reaction?

Let's consider these points with regard to Figures 2.1 and 2.2. In terms of *composition*, Figure 2.1 is divided into two horizontal parts: the sign and girder above and the cars and trucks below. Our eyes are drawn mainly to (1) the vehicles in the foreground, especially perhaps the dump truck, and (2) the terrorism sign overhead. The vehicles in the foreground catch our attention because of their proximity to us, the sign because of the stark contrast of white lettering on a black background. Most viewers, we think, will shift their gaze back and forth between these two points of focus, creating a linkage between the ordinary (freeway traffic) and the extraordinary (terrorism).

The *point of view* is that of someone standing alongside the highway or parked on the inner shoulder. The angle and close distance make us feel almost as if we were part of the traffic flow, increasing our sense of involvement. If the photo had been taken from a distance or from the side, we would feel more detached from the scene.

The photo consists of a sharp, black-and-white image. This gives it an objective *tone,* typical of photos found in a history book. Indeed, informed by the caption, it conveys the sense of a historic period captured in time—a period when all Americans were traumatized by the specter of post-9/11 terrorism. Even mundane activities like driving on a freeway were haunted by that fear.

In Figure 2.2, the *composition* of the ad is such that it draws our attention mainly to the SUV and certain of the animals, especially the largest of them, the moose. The other animals and birds that compete for our attention include the skunk, puma, red crossbill, goshawk, porcupine, fox, and bear. All of these benefit from having contrasting colors, being of larger size, or being in the foreground. They are all depicted as larger than they would be in real life, making the SUV appear smaller—and therefore less intrusive. The forest itself is pristine—there are no tree stumps or fences, for example. And the vehicle appears to be in some kind of forest clearing; there are no signs of a road. The *point of view* is that of an observer, possibly the driver, standing in the forest and enjoying this Disney-like scene. As for *tone*, the artist has rendered the scene as a painting, thus capturing the kind of tranquility found in paintings by Audubon, Bateman, and other naturalists. The happy tone of the scene is further enhanced by the use of warm, earthy colors. And the keys in the upper-left and lower-left corners are reminiscent of a nature book for children, with the SUV being labeled along with the other animals as if it were just another species of "wildlife."

Viewing critically

Finally, as with reading, you want to go beyond rhetorical meaning and engage in critical evaluation of the image. This stage of viewing requires a consideration of factors both internal and external to the image. Internal evaluation takes into account any aspect of the image itself including any title, caption, or labels. It asks whether the image makes sense—whether its various parts work together in a coherent way. It takes note of any inconsistencies or anomalies that might be considered deceptive. If the image has any title, caption, or labels, internal evaluation assesses how these bits of language fit with the visual image and how they might influence the viewer's perception and interpretation of the image. External evaluation considers factors that are part of

See 2b

the larger context. These include the site where the image is viewed, the "story" it supports, the apparent rhetorical purpose(s) behind use of the image, the apparent rhetorical purpose(s) behind the construction of the image, the veracity of the image in terms of what it purports to represent, and deliberate or unwitting omissions.

As an illustration of this process, consider the photo in Figure 2.1. This photo was taken by a Pulitzer Prize–winning photographer, Michael Williamson. It and about three dozen more of his photos appear in a book (*Homeland*) about 9/11 and its effects on American society. The book's author, Dale Maharidge, writes that the United States today has many parallels to Germany just prior to the Nazi takeover—"the period when working class Germans suffered and the rich were taken care of, leading to the anger that proved so deadly in the 1930s. . . . While the history is not exactly parallel with the German war machine, any superpower with an angry and frightened populace is alarming." He hopes the book "can provide some insight to help us understand the current state of the American mind." Williamson and Maharidge are longtime collaborators who apparently have similar political views; the thirty-eight photos in *Homeland* can easily be interpreted as supporting the book's thesis.

In this photo, the traffic can be seen as representing the American public, a public that is being continually reminded of the threat of terrorism. These reminders, such as the government's color-coded terrorism alerts, come mainly from federal authorities, who are positioned, like the traffic sign in the photo, above the population. We think the photographer deliberately chose this scene because it captured his sense of an impersonal, all-powerful government hovering over, and putting fear into, ordinary working Americans.

There are mainly two sets of words accompanying the image: those in the caption and those on the overhead sign. The caption, "The DC Beltway, April 2003," fits the thesis of the image by invoking the federal government ("DC") and a time when the country had just opened a second front, in Iraq, in the so-called War on Terror. The overhead sign exhorts travelers to "REPORT TERRORISM." Drawing attention with its large upper-case lettering, this message brings to mind similar signs urging motorists to "report littering" or "report bad driving." In this way, it puts terrorism on the same level as these other, more mundane events, implying that terrorism is all around us and can be easily spotted from the road. Such an interpretation is consistent with the book's thesis of an overbearing government keeping the public in a state of fear, perhaps for political gain.

Critical Viewing

- ✓ Where does this image appear?
- ✓ What "story" does it support?
- ✓ What purpose does the image serve in that story?
- ✓ Why did the artist construct the image the way he or she did?
- ✓ How closely do the words accompanying the image, if any, fit with the image itself?
- ✓ How truthful is the image in what it purports to represent?
- ✓ What has been left out of the image that should be there?

How truthful is this image in what it purports to represent? Has anything been left out that should be there? It is difficult to tell from just one photo—and this is a shortcoming of all photos. A single photo represents a single, brief moment in time. For all we know—although this seems unlikely—the "report terrorism" message may have flashed only briefly on the sign, just when the photographer happened to be there. Or the photo could even have been doctored (though Williamson's reputation as a photojournalist makes such a possibility very unlikely).

As for the SUV ad in Figure 2.2, it appeared as a two-page spread in upscale magazines. The ad's designers apparently targeted consumers who might want an SUV but who are sensitive to accusations that SUVs are harmful to the environment. They apparently wanted to counter those accusations by promoting the idea that SUVs can peacefully and harmlessly co-exist with the environment. This theme is reiterated in the slogan at the bottom of the page, "At home in almost any environment." It is not a truthful image; rather, it is a romanticized one. Not only does it portray a scene that could never exist in real life, but it fails to include any of the ways in which SUVs are accused by critics of damaging the environment.

EXERCISE 2.6 Go to *Yahoo! News* at <http://news.yahoo.com/> and click on Photos, then View Slideshows. Select one of the images and use the Checklist for Critical Viewing to critically analyze both the text and the photo.

FOR COLLABORATION Together with one or two classmates, find a current news story featured in one of the major weekly newsmagazines (*Time, Newsweek, US News & World Report*). (You could divide this assignment up so that each person has only one magazine.) Using the Checklist for Critical Viewing, analyze the photos and other visual images (graphs, diagrams, and so on) in these accounts.

3 Planning and Drafting

FAQs

- What should I write about? (3b)
- What if I need to use library sources? (3d)
- What is a thesis, and why do I need one? (3e)
- How do I get over writer's block? (3f)
- How can a computer help me work with my classmates? (3g)

3a An overview of the writing process

Writing involves five stages: planning, drafting, formulating arguments, structuring paragraphs, rewriting (see the Guidelines box). The planning stage encompasses experimenting and exploring, inventing and prewriting, gathering information, and organizing. The drafting stage requires reviewing and then drafting. Formulating arguments involves generating good evidence and building a compelling case. Structuring paragraphs involves making sure that your paragraphs are clearly organized, coherent, and linked in a logical structure. The rewriting stage incorporates revising, editing, and proofreading. These stages are often described as *recursive*, as writers typically move freely among them as they plan, shape, compose, and revise their texts.

Writing process

See Guidelines 3b

3b Experiment and explore

In workplace writing, the topic is often predetermined: an engineer might write a report describing a new piece of computer hardware, a nurse might write a case history of a patient's illness, and so on. One of your major tasks

Guidelines

Stages of the Writing Process

Planning

- **Experiment and explore.** Decide on a topic, and consider your rhetorical stance, genre, and language choice. **3b**
- **Invent and prewrite.** Inventory your knowledge on a topic, prewrite on the topic, and narrow the topic. **3c**
- **Gather information.** Work with peers to brainstorm and discuss your topic. As necessary, find credible sources to support your own ideas. **3d**
- **Plan and organize.** To guide your writing, compose a thesis and construct an organizational plan or outline. **3e**

Drafting

- **Review.** Before you write a first draft, review your prewriting, thesis statement, and outline, and use them as raw material for your paper. **3f**
- **Compose.** Either flesh out your outline by building your text in blocks, or compose from the top down, using your thesis as an advance organizer and writing the piece in a linear sequence. **3f**
- **Collaborate.** Work with your peers as you compose and gather feedback on drafts. **3g**

Formulating Arguments

- **Formulate** an arguable thesis and consider your rhetorical stance. **4a, 4b**
- **Generate** good supporting evidence while incorporating alternative points of view. **4c, 4d**
- **Develop** and test your main points. **4e**
- **Build** a compelling case while avoiding logical and emotional fallacies. **4f, 4g**
- **Structure** the argument. **4h**

Structuring Paragraphs

- **Write** unified paragraphs. **5a**
- **Write** coherent paragraphs with clear organization and sentence-linking techniques. **5b, 5c**
- **Use** sentence structure and vocabulary appropriately. **5d, 5e, 5f, 5g**
- **Write** a compelling introduction and conclusion. **5h**

Rewriting

- **Shift from writer to reader.** Become a skilled reader—think critically and evaluate your own writing. **6a**
- **Revise.** As you revise, add, delete, and rearrange your text, checking for focus, coherence, organization, development, tone, and format. **6b**
- **Edit.** Edit to make your text easier to read. **6c**
- **Proofread.** Proofread to correct errors in punctuation, spelling, and usage. **6d**
- **Collaborate.** Peer review each other's texts. **6e**
- **Rewrite.** Use the peer feedback to make further revisions. **6b**

when given a writing assignment in a college class is to assess what you are being asked to do. Does your instructor want you to analyze or discuss something you have been reading about in class? Does she or he expect you to choose your own topic related to the course and write an argumentative essay? How the assignment is phrased will help you to determine how to approach your own paper.

1 Understanding the assignment

When you first receive an assignment in a course, look carefully at what you are being asked to write. There will often be cue words in the assignment that will give you clues about what your instructor is expecting. Although the cue words in Table 24.1 are in the context of essay exams, the same principles apply to writing assignments. Is the assignment asking you to *analyze, argue, classify* or *describe*? In each case your response will be somewhat different. If you are asked to *analyze*, your paper will divide something into parts and discuss the parts in relationship to the whole. If you are asked to *argue*, you will need to take a position and support it with reasoned arguments and evidence. When *classifying*, you divide some large whole into groups on the basis of shared traits. When *describing*, you systematically explain something's features, sometimes visually or sequentially. To get background information on the subject of the assignment itself, you can explore ideas through the following channels:

See Table 24.1

- Browse through current magazines and newspapers.
- Watch relevant educational programs on television (PBS, Discovery, or The History Channel).

See TechHelp 3b-1

- Converse with friends, family members, or teachers who might have some knowledge or expertise.
- Think about other courses you have taken that are related to the assignment.
- Browse *Wikipedia.*

EXERCISE 3.1 Using one of the search tools available on your Internet browser, explore possible topics of interest to you. Try searching broadly on topics in different categories (for example, "education," "entertainment," or "politics"), just to get some ideas or browse through the newspapers and magazines in the current periodicals section of your library.

FOR COLLABORATION Discuss the list of possible topics with a group of your classmates. Which of the topics do they find interesting or intriguing? What questions about each topic would they be interested in finding an answer to? Keep a list of the most promising topics in your writing journal or in a computer file. Add to this list as more topics occur to you.

TechHelp

Exploring Topics on the Internet

1. For topic ideas, browse *Wikipedia*, the free online encyclopedia written collaboratively by volunteers, at <http://en.wikipedia.org/wiki/Main_Page>. Because almost anyone can edit entries on this site, you'll want to take the actual information with a grain of salt, but it is a good place to brainstorm for topic ideas. You might also want to use *Google* or *Yahoo!* for a similar purpose.
2. Click on a general subject category from *Wikipedia*—for example, Arts, Biography, Geography, History, Mathematics, Science, Society, or Technology.
3. If you click on the Arts portal, you will see a page with a featured article about art, as well as links to many subcategories such as architecture, comics, film, dance, literature, and music.
4. Within each subcategory, search for possible topics that might interest you. For example, if you click on "film," you'll find many topics to explore, such as "special effects," "film awards," "film sequels," and the like.
5. Each time you go one level deeper within the *Wikipedia*, jot down other categories that might provide possible topics for you to write about. Note controversies that appear in the entries. Points of controversy can make for interesting topics.

❷ Considering your rhetorical stance

Once you have selected an area of interest to write about, you can begin to consider the approach that you will take toward your topic, called your **rhetorical stance**. The term *rhetoric* refers to written or spoken communication that seeks to inform or persuade. You can visualize the rhetorical stance in terms of a triangle.

See Fig. 1.4

Logic

Chapters in Part 1 follow the progress of Kirsten Parsons, a college student assigned to write a paper on a computer topic that interests her. The instructor wanted the piece to be written largely from the students' own experiences, from a brief Internet search, and from the class text. After thinking about several possible topics, Kirsten finally settled on the topic of Net theft. She would use logical arguments to persuade her fellow students that petty Net crimes were not much different from other petty crimes, such as shoplifting; they were simply easier to commit.

Constructing Your Rhetorical Stance

Considering Logic

- ✓ Is a problem suggested by my topic?
- ✓ What are my best arguments?
- ✓ What is my intent—persuasive, argumentative, informative?

Considering Persona

- ✓ How do I want to sound to my readers?
- ✓ What kind of language will I use—formal or informal?
- ✓ What role or identity will I assume?

Considering Audience

- ✓ Who are my readers?
- ✓ Are my readers experts or novices on my topic?
- ✓ Are my readers likely to agree with me or not?

Persona

To maintain the interest of her peers, Kirsten decided to take a somewhat lighthearted approach to her topic. She would attempt to play the role of a knowledgeable student, but one with a sense of humor and an understanding of other college students' experiences of the Internet.

Readers or audience

Kirsten decided that her readers would probably be her peers—that is, other college students on her own campus. From talking with other students, she had learned that most seemed to think that it was acceptable to "borrow" material from the Internet. She wanted to alert students that this practice was unethical, if not illegal. She felt that it was important for her fellow students to realize that unattributed use of Internet sources was a form of plagiarism, not unlike stealing.

3 Considering genre and language choice

Genre refers to the kind of writing a piece is, such as novel, essay, poem, song lyrics, or report. Most of the writing you will do in college falls under the broad genre called *academic discourse.* The characteristics of academic discourse include the use of Standard Edited English; that is, academic writers pay close attention to the conventional uses of grammar, spelling, punctuation, and mechanics as described in later sections of this handbook. Other characteristics are a standard format (such as a report or essay format), clear presentation and organization of information, and a formal tone.

The tone of your writing is established through the language choices you make—the words you include in your sentences. A formal tone is conveyed by formal language; for example, you generally would not use contractions or email emoticons in formal writing. Similarly, you typically would not use jargon, abbreviations, or slang in formal academic writing.

4 Considering writing conventions with new media

Writers today use a variety of electronic media to communicate. Cell phones, PDAs (personal digital assistants), smart phones, and netbooks all allow us to stay connected to each other through writing, using electronic tools such as email, text-messaging, instant-messaging, social networking Web sites, and blogs. When we use electronic media, the constraints of the technologies often result in major differences in the writing. Text-messaging on a cell phone is particularly constrained by the medium, which makes long, formal sentences in Standard Edited English difficult to produce. But the kind of writing that is acceptable when produced on your cell phone's keyboard is not necessarily appropriate for an essay in a college course. Skillful communicators know how to shift between types of writing and differing audiences without much difficulty.

You need to learn to pay attention not only to the specific tool with which you are writing, but also to the type of writing that is appropriate for your audience. For example, an email that you write may or may not conform to the traditions of Standard Edited English, depending on the purpose of the email and its audience. If you are writing an email to a prospective employer or a professor, you need to be careful that your correspondence conforms in large measure to the conventions of Standard Edited English. However, if you are sending an email or text message to another student or a family member, you might decide to largely ignore conventions of standard usage, maybe even leaving out capitalization and punctuation altogether. As you prepare to write, think

See Figs. 3.1 and 3.2

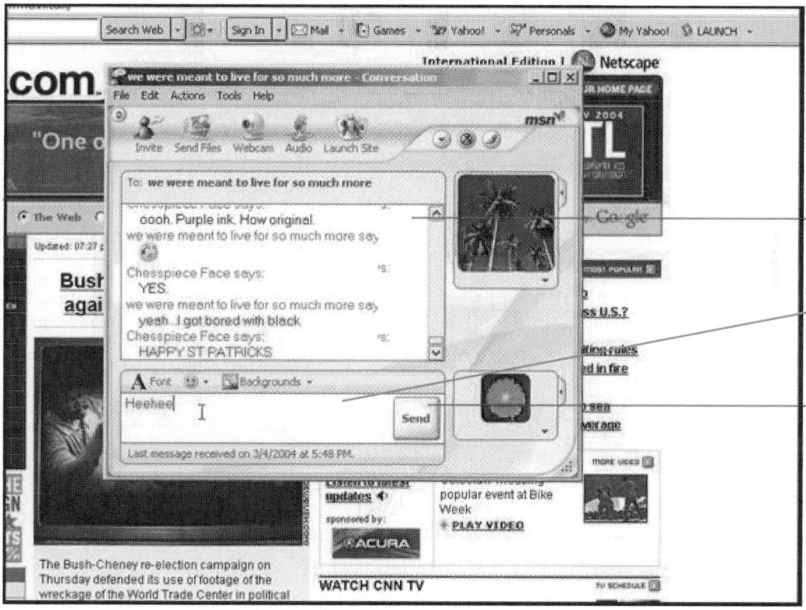

Figure 3.1 Screen showing Instant Messaging discussion

Reading window

Typing window

Send message

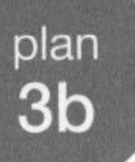

Figure 3.2 ▶
Screen showing student email to professor

Uses formal address

Uses polite tone

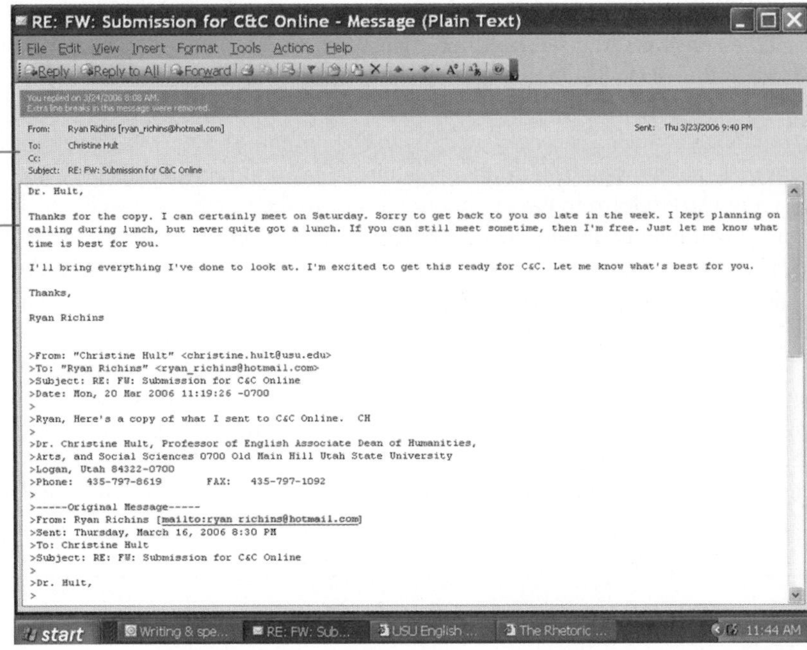

RE: FW: Submission for C&C Online - Message (Plain Text)

File Edit View Insert Format Tools Actions Help

Reply | Reply to All | Forward

You replied on 3/24/2006 8:08 AM.
Extra line breaks in this message were removed.

From: Ryan Richins [ryan_richins@hotmail.com] Sent: Thu 3/23/2006 9:40 PM
To: Christine Hult
Cc:
Subject: RE: FW: Submission for C&C Online

```
Dr. Hult,

Thanks for the copy. I can certainly meet on Saturday. Sorry to get back to you so late in the week. I kept planning on calling during lunch, but never quite got a lunch. If you can still meet sometime, then I'm free. Just let me know what time is best for you.

I'll bring everything I've done to look at. I'm excited to get this ready for C&C. Let me know what's best for you.

Thanks,

Ryan Richins


>From: "Christine Hult" <christine.hult@usu.edu>
>To: "Ryan Richins" <ryan_richins@hotmail.com>
>Subject: RE: FW: Submission for C&C Online
>Date: Mon, 20 Mar 2006 11:19:26 -0700
>
>Ryan, Here's a copy of what I sent to C&C Online.  CH
>
>Dr. Christine Hult, Professor of English Associate Dean of Humanities,
>Arts, and Social Sciences 0700 Old Main Hill Utah State University
>Logan, Utah 84322-0700
>Phone:  435-797-8619        FAX:   435-797-1092
>
>-----Original Message-----
>From: Ryan Richins [mailto:ryan_richins@hotmail.com]
>Sent: Thursday, March 16, 2006 8:30 PM
>To: Christine Hult
>Subject: RE: FW: Submission for C&C Online
>
>Dr. Hult,
>
```


not only about what you want to say but also about how you want to say it and to whom.

EXERCISE 3.2 Using the guidelines given in the Checklist for Constructing Your Rhetorical Stance in 3b-2, outline a rhetorical stance for one of the topics you listed in Exercise 3.1. Describe the rhetorical stance in a brief paragraph.

FOR COLLABORATION Draft a one-paragraph audience profile for an essay you plan to write. Describe your intended audience. After you have written a first draft of the essay itself, exchange papers with another student in your class and write an audience profile for that student's essay. Discuss with your peer how well you each were able to identify the writer's intended audience. Give each other suggestions that might help target the audience better.

3c Invent and prewrite

In the prewriting stage, you invent or discover what you want to say about your subject. As the words *invent* and *discover* imply, during this period you delve into your subject, come up with new ideas, connect these new ideas with prior experiences and knowledge, read about and research your subject, and generally allow your thoughts to take shape. Prewriting also helps you decide what additional information you need to discover (through conversations, reading, and research) in order to write knowledgeably about your subject.

What to write about

TechHelp

Using Computer Journals to Invent and Prewrite

Laptops and netbooks, because they are so portable, allow you to use word processing from the very earliest stages in the writing process. Here are a couple of ways you can invent and prewrite using a computer.

1. **Taking notes in class or in the library.** Some professors allow students to take notes on a laptop while in class. Others prefer not to introduce that distraction, so be sure to check first. If, like many libraries, your library provides a wireless network, you can use your laptop not only to take notes but also to explore topics on the Internet. You can then store ideas and notes in a computer journal on your own laptop. Some libraries even check out laptops for patrons to use while in the library.
2. **Using a computer blog as an online journal.** A **blog** (short for Web log) is a type of online journal, accessible from any machine connected to the Internet, in which you can store your writing ideas or notes. Because you can access a blog from your own laptop, a desktop computer in your dorm room, or a computer located in a campus computer lab, some students find that a blog provides a convenient way to invent and prewrite. However, keep in mind that your blog may be publicly accessible and be careful not to reveal personal or private information in such a public forum.

1 Brainstorming

Brainstorming refers to generating random ideas or fragments of thought about a topic. You may have brainstormed in previous writing classes. It is possible to brainstorm as a group, calling out ideas to the instructor, who writes them on the whiteboard. It is also possible to brainstorm at a computer, either individually or with another classmate. You may also write brainstorming ideas in your writing journal.

KIRSTEN'S BRAINSTORMING

Taking information from the Net. Is it legal? Can we swipe graphics? People copying CDs from each other. Napster? What is Net theft like? Maybe shoplifting? Copyright laws. Hackers and other Net criminals. What is a criminal? If I copied a graphic, was that a crime? Who are hackers? Do I know any? Are they always criminals? Maybe they're just having fun.

EXERCISE 3.3 Following the steps in the TechHelp box below, brainstorm at a computer on the topic you selected in Exercise 3.2. If you do not have a computer available, brainstorm in your writing journal instead.

TechHelp

Brainstorming On-Screen

1. Open a new document in your word-processing program, and make a list of any ideas that occur to you about your topic.
2. Type what you know about your topic, what information you want to cover, and what you still need to find out about.
3. Review your list, and move items into logical groupings.
   a. Convert important items into headings, and group other items under them.
   b. CUT items that do not fit and PASTE them at the end of the list.
   c. DELETE items that seem irrelevant.
   d. Expand ideas by moving your cursor to the appropriate position and inserting new phrases or sentences.
4. Save the brainstorming document on your hard drive or other storage device such as a flashdrive.
5. Update the brainstorming document as you come up with new ideas.

❷ Freewriting

Freewriting is like brainstorming in that it involves writing down thoughts as they come to mind. However, freewriting is typically formulated in connected sentences rather than lists. After freewriting on a particular topic for five or ten minutes without stopping, read over your freewriting. As you read it, you may see relationships between ideas that you had not seen before. You can cut and paste to group related ideas on screen, or circle important ideas and use arrows to show relationships on paper.

KIRSTEN'S FREEWRITING

I think that my topic will be about Net theft. Wondered about the legalities of copying stuff off the Net. A friend asked me the other day if he could copy my CD. Is that the same kind of crime? What about downloading a CD from the Net? Lots of people are worried about giving out their Visa number over the Internet. Is it really secure? Or I wondered, too, about when we use graphics in our other writing. It is so easy now to just go out on the Net, find a graphic, grab it, and paste it into your own paper. Can we do that? I'm concerned about copyright laws. Maybe that graphic is copyrighted, but I don't know that it is. I remember when I was little, I got caught shoplifting. Maybe stealing on the Net is the same kind of petty crime as shoplifting. But it's sure much easier to get caught in a store than on the Net. People can get away with a whole lot more in cyberspace.

MAIN IDEAS FROM KIRSTEN'S FREEWRITING

1. "Borrowing" information from the Internet: CDs, graphics, others? Is this legal? Are there copyright restrictions?
2. Comparisons of Net theft to other petty crimes: shoplifting, copying software, tapes, or CDs. Is it easier to steal on the Net?

EXERCISE 3.4 Using one of the ideas generated by your brainstorming session in Exercise 3.3, freewrite for ten minutes nonstop at the keyboard or in your writing journal. Print out your freewriting session for review, or read over your freewriting from your journal.

FOR COLLABORATION Share your freewriting with a peer or small group of classmates. Identify together the best ideas in each of your freewriting sessions. Pinpoint what seem to be the logical connections among the ideas generated by freewriting.

3 Invisible writing on screen

See TechHelp 3c-3

Invisible writing is a freewriting technique designed to release you from the inhibitions created by seeing your own words on the computer screen. Compulsive revisers find it difficult to ignore the errors they see on the screen and so are unable to write freely at the computer. When you turn off or dim your monitor and write invisibly, your words do not appear on the screen, so you are free to generate ideas without interruption.

EXERCISE 3.5 After dimming or turning the computer monitor off, begin a ten-minute invisible freewriting session, either on the topic you selected in Exercise 3.2 or on another topic.

FOR COLLABORATION Discuss the experience of invisible writing with your peer group.

1. How did it compare with regular freewriting?
2. Did you feel it freed you from editing constraints?
3. Was it more or less frustrating than regular freewriting?

TechHelp

Writing Invisibly on the Computer

You can reduce your anxiety about writing by turning off the computer's monitor.

1. On your computer, open a document in which to store your invisible freewriting.
2. Close any other open windows or applications on your computer. (You do not want to lose valuable data if you should accidentally hit the wrong key.)
3. Turn down the contrast (dim) or turn your monitor off altogether, thus making your writing invisible.
4. When you have finished freewriting, turn the monitor back on and read what you have written.

④ Clustering

See Fig. 3.3

Clustering can help you see relationships among the ideas you have generated in brainstorming or freewriting exercises. Begin a clustering session by putting your topic, in the form of a word or a phrase, in the middle of a sheet of paper. Then, attach to the word or phrase other words or phrases that come to mind, linking and connecting related ideas or subtopics. Through clustering, you can focus on one area of interest to pursue in your paper. Although it is possible to do clustering on a computer, it is easier to do with pencil and paper. The results of Kirsten's clustering session on her topic of Net theft are shown in Figure 3.3.

EXERCISE 3.6 Try clustering your ideas on one of the topics you generated in Exercise 3.1. Make an effort to free associate rather than consciously thinking through the ideas and the relationships among them. This activity should free you for creative thinking.

⑤ Debating

Debating can help you explore a controversial issue from all sides. You might begin by writing down all the generalizations you can think of about the topic. Since Kirsten's Net theft topic has both pro and con arguments, she decided to write contrasting general statements that could then be supported through examples and evidence.

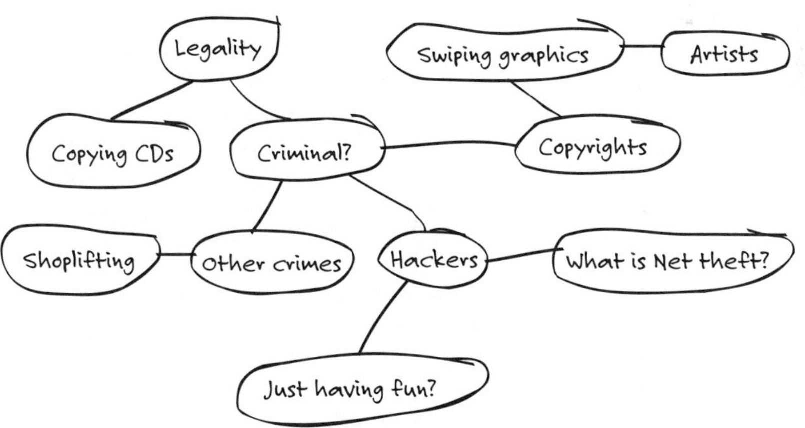

Figure 3.3 Clustering by Kirsten

PRO

1. Using other people's work from the Net is just another form of sharing.
2. The Internet should be "free." To regulate it goes against its very nature.
3. When people put their ideas out on the Internet, they should just assume they're public.

CON

1. Authors and artists who publish on the Internet should not have their work "stolen."
2. "Borrowing" creative ideas, texts, and graphics from the Net is a form of stealing.
3. Net theft is the same thing as shoplifting.

Under each general heading or statement, you then can insert examples or evidence to support the generalization and build your arguments and counterarguments. Once you have constructed a list of generalizations supported by evidence, look over the arguments with an eye toward taking a side and defending it. Begin to think about how your arguments could be arranged to your best advantage and how you could refute arguments on the other side.

EXERCISE 3.7 Pick one of the broad topics you listed in Exercise 3.1, and type into a document all the generalizations you can think of on the topic. Order your generalizations, perhaps by pro and con positions. Then, for each generalization, list two or three specific examples or pieces of evidence. Save and print your prewriting. If you do not have access to a computer, complete this exercise in your writing journal.

FOR COLLABORATION Working with a small group of your classmates, share your prewriting generalizations. Discuss the pro and con positions and/or the specific examples or evidence you have thought of with your group. Are there additional arguments or evidence that you should consider? Have you thought of all the arguments on the other side of your position?

3d Gather information but avoid plagiarism

Particularly if your assignment is to write a research paper, you will need to supplement whatever prewriting techniques you use by gathering information from external sources. The first stage of your research may be informal and *ad hoc*: "googling" the topic, discussing the idea with friends and peers, talking to a professor, reading a few journal articles. The ideas you read about and formulate will lead you into a more systematic and extensive search that is focused on a specific topic. When searching in a focused way, you will likely consult library databases and use a variety of online sources. Formal researching is discussed extensively in Part 2, particularly Chapters 8–10. If your writing task involves significant research, refer to those chapters for guidance.

See Chs. 8–10

❶ Googling or consulting databases

A preliminary *Google* search or a skim through your library database will give you an overview of current discussions about your topic. You can try out several Internet search tools, using a variety of keywords, to see what kinds of information are available on the Internet.

See Ch. 8

❷ Discussing topics in person or online

Informal discussions with classmates, friends, family members, and professors can provide valuable information on your topic. Start with informal discussions before moving to more formal searching. Collaborating with your peers to brainstorm a topic is a good idea. Talking to others about your topic may help you to pose the right questions before beginning a systematic search. Email, instant messages, blogs, and online discussion forums are all good ways to engage in discussions.

❸ Browsing through periodicals

Your library most likely has a section devoted to current periodicals—that is, recently published magazines, newspapers, and journals. You can browse through these to see if your topic is currently being discussed in the media. As you browse, look for articles related to your topic. If you find one, read it for background information. Keep accurate records of everything you read.

TechHelp

Organizing Your Files

1. Using a file management program (such as *Windows Explorer*) or opening the OFFICE menu, create a directory or folder for each course in which you have written assignments (for example, English and history).
2. Within each directory or folder, create subdirectories or additional folders in which to store the work for each assignment.
3. Each time you begin a new writing assignment, save all the work in the appropriate assignment directory or folder.

NOTE: Be sure to keep backup files of important work on a flashdrive or other storage device.

Figure 3.4 ▶ Screen Showing Directory Structure in *Windows Explorer*

Folders for class assignments

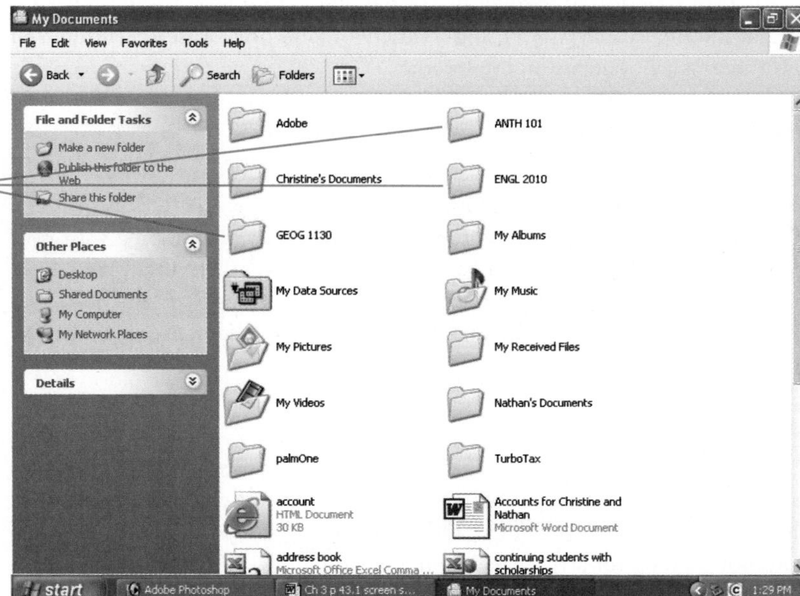

❹ Taking notes

If you are reading, you should read actively and critically and annotate your readings, taking care to use sources responsibly and to avoid plagiarism. If you are listening to a lecture, you should listen attentively and take accurate notes. Be selective. Finally, always identify the source of the lecture notes completely (course, professor, date, and time of the lecture).

See 2b-3; Ch. 10

3e Plan and organize

The structure of your paper will be influenced by all of the items shown in the rhetorical triangle in Figure 1.4. However, no matter how good your information, if your paper is not well organized, your readers will not be able to understand what you are trying to say.

Organizing strategies

See Fig. 1.4

❶ Narrowing your topic

Through prewriting, you develop an awareness of what you do and do not know about a topic. As you look back at your prewriting, think about ways in which you could narrow your topic to a manageable size. Think of any subdivisions there might be within the topic. Try to write down in one sentence what you take to be your specific, narrow topic.

For example, through brainstorming and clustering, Kirsten discovered that her broad topic of Net theft could be subdivided into legal issues, ethical issues, crimes on the Net, computer hackers, and so on. Out of all the possible subtopics, Kirsten decided to narrow the focus of her topic to the practice of "borrowing" information from the Internet.

❷ Formulating a working thesis statement

Once you have written down your narrow topic, try to state in one or two sentences the main point you want to make about that topic. This will be your working **thesis statement**. Your working thesis should ideally have two parts: the first part defines the specific topic to be covered in the essay, and the second part makes a strong point about the topic.

For her working thesis, Kirsten wrote a two-part sentence that defined the specific topic and articulated her main point.

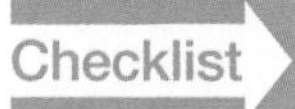

Evaluating a Working Thesis

- ✓ Does the thesis define a specific topic?
- ✓ Does the thesis make a strong point about the topic?
- ✓ Does the thesis provide a blueprint for the paper's development?

Kirsten's Working Thesis: When it comes to "borrowing" information from the Internet, we are gradually becoming a people that can accept lawbreaking as long as we can participate, too.

- ✓ The specific topic is borrowing information from the Internet.
- ✓ The main point is that people accept lawbreaking if they can participate, too.
- ✓ This thesis implies that the paper will explain how we have accepted lawbreaking in the Internet arena. We expect it to explain how easy it is for everyone to "participate" in this kind of lawbreaking.

KIRSTEN'S WORKING THESIS

When it comes to "borrowing" information from the Internet, we are gradually becoming a people that can accept lawbreaking as long as we can participate, too.

An effective thesis statement defines the specific topic and makes a strong point about it. An effective thesis also provides the reader with a blueprint for the direction the paper will take. In other words, the thesis not only states the writer's opinion on the topic but also indicates how the writer intends to support that opinion. Kirsten's thesis implies that her essay will explain how borrowing information from the Internet is a kind of lawbreaking that society has begun to accept.

❸ Evaluating and revising your working thesis

Ask yourself the three questions in the checklist. Is your answer to all three questions "yes"? If not, you will need to revise your thesis. You may need to revise your working thesis several times as you draft your paper. This is why it is called a "working thesis": it can be clarified, modified, or even completely rewritten during the course of the writing process. Allow your thesis to evolve with your understanding of the topic.

EXERCISE 3.8 Draft a few working thesis statements for one of the topics you identified in Exercise 3.1, either typing them into a computer document or writing them in your journal. Evaluate your working thesis statements using the questions in the Checklist for Evaluating a Working Thesis.

FOR COLLABORATION Share your working thesis statements with a peer or a small group. Use the questions in the Checklist for Evaluating a Working Thesis to frame your discussion.

4 Organizing your information

Multimedia storyboarding

Do not hesitate to try a variety of organizational structures and patterns, since word processing makes it very easy to experiment by using the CUT, COPY, PASTE, and OUTLINE features. There is no one right way to organize material. Since we habitually organize experience on the basis of time, space, and logic, these factors often influence the organization of written work.

Time

Organizing by time usually implies imposing a chronological order on information—that is, relating one thing after another in sequence. If you are telling a story in your paper, you will most likely present information in the order in which events occurred. In Kirsten's essay on Net theft, for example, the section in which she tells the story of her own shoplifting experience is organized by time. Similarly, you would probably use a chronological organization when describing how to carry out a process.

See 3h

Space

Organizing by space implies providing a visual orientation for your readers. If you are describing something, you need to orient your readers spatially in order for them to be able to follow your writing. Spatial description will most likely proceed in an orderly fashion from a given vantage point. For example, if you are describing your college dorm room, you might begin at the far corner of the room and work your way across the room to the doorway.

See 5b

Logic

By far the most frequently used principle of organization in college writing is logic. With any logical organizational pattern, you are providing your reader with a familiar way of ordering experience, whether through cause and effect, problem and solution, or some other logical pattern. Reviewing possible patterns at this point in your prewriting will help you construct an organizational plan.

EXERCISE 3.9 Consider what organizational principles might govern a paper on the topic you selected in Exercise 3.8. Type your ideas into a computer document or write them in your journal.

FOR COLLABORATION Work with a peer or a small group to write a possible thesis statement that reflects the organizational principles you have chosen.

❺ Writing an outline

An outline should serve as a guide as you write—not a constraint that confines and limits your thinking. You may need to change your outline several times as you make new discoveries during drafting.

Formal outlines

A formal outline is typically structured in a conventional hierarchy, with numbered and lettered headings and subheadings. A formal outline can be either a topic outline, in which words or phrases are used, or a sentence outline, in which complete sentences are used.

Formal Outline Pattern

Thesis Statement
- I. First main idea
  - A. First subordinate idea
    - 1. First example or illustration
    - 2. Second example or illustration
      - a. First supporting detail
      - b. Second supporting detail
  - B. Second subordinate idea
- II. Second main idea

TechHelp

Outlining with Word Processing

There are two basic outline features available to you: the OUTLINE MULTILEVEL LIST feature and the OUTLINE VIEW feature. We will discuss each in turn.

1. OUTLINE MULTILEVEL LIST is a hierarchical list numbering format that you apply to lines of text to help your readers follow the information. It's really a display aid. To begin MULTILEVEL LIST, choose HOME > PARAGRAPH and MULTILEVEL LIST. Click on the list style that you want in order to select your outline display options. The first list option in the list library is the outline numbering style.
2. OUTLINE VIEW is a working mode that helps you lay out and organize your ideas. Because OUTLINE VIEW uses formatting to convey hierarchy, and not the added visuals of numbers and lettering, it offers a clear, clutter-free way to work. To begin working in OUTLINE VIEW, choose VIEW > OUTLINE.
   a. To organize your ideas from scratch, start with a blank document and switch to OUTLINE VIEW. When you switch your document to OUTLINE VIEW, the OUTLINING toolbar appears. Use the toolbar to manipulate the outline as you work. The various arrows on the toolbar will allow you to change between levels of headings (green arrows) and to highlight and move information up or down levels in the hierarchy (blue arrows).
   b. As you create headings and subheadings, *Word* places plus signs (+) next to the higher-level headings to indicate that there are subheadings beneath them. You can add up to nine levels of headings, as well as regular paragraph text (or body text). You can collapse or expand the subheadings by clicking on the plus sign, and you can move entire blocks of text by clicking on the plus sign and then dragging the text to the new place in the document.
   c. When you are finished outlining your document and moving sections around, select another view from the VIEW menu (DRAFT, PRINT, WEB, or FULL SCREEN READING LAYOUT). Try these different layouts to see which you prefer to use while working on your document.

Informal outlines

Informal outlines are not structured as rigidly as formal outlines. For example, in a formal outline, you are not allowed to have a number one subheading unless there is also a number two subheading. Informal outlines allow you to create any hierarchies you like, without paying close attention to issues of format.

Informal Outline Pattern

Thesis Statement
First main idea
    Subordinate idea
        First example or illustration
        Second example or illustration
Second main idea
    Subordinate idea

In constructing an outline that would guide her through her paper, Kirsten used her thesis statement as a blueprint.

KIRSTEN'S NET THEFT OUTLINE

Thesis: When it comes to "borrowing" information from the Internet, we are gradually becoming a people that can accept lawbreaking as long as we can participate, too.

I. Introduction
    A. Scenario
    B. Definition of Net theft
II. Different medium, same crime
III. Standards of honor
    A. Describe what is legal
    B. Describe what is not legal
IV. Redefining a criminal

EXERCISE 3.10 If you have a word-processing program with OUTLINE VIEW, generate a preliminary outline for a paper based on the working thesis and organizational plan you generated in Exercises 3.8 and 3.9. If you do not have a computer outlining program, outline on paper.

3f Compose a draft

Many writers first compose a skeleton of the finished text and then expand it by adding new arguments, supporting examples and evidence, or illustrative details—the "building blocks" of a text. Some writers like to write their central

Composing process

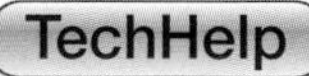

Combining Documents

Word-processing programs provide multiple ways to accomplish the same task. Here are two ways to combine documents.

1. Insert the two documents into a blank document using the INSERT FROM FILE command. This command is found on the INSERT tab.
   a. Create a new blank document.
   b. INSERT the contents of your prewriting document (INSERT >TEXT>OBJECT>TEXT FROM FILE).
   c. INSERT the contents of your outline document (INSERT >TEXT>OBJECT>TEXT FROM FILE).
   d. Move appropriate information from the prewriting document to the outline document (using COPY and PASTE).
   e. Save the combined document as a first draft with an appropriate new name.
2. Combine the two documents using multiple windows:
   a. Open your prewriting document and your outline document, each in its own window (OFFICE BUTTON > OPEN). Resize the windows so that you can view them both at the same time (VIEW>WINDOWS > ARRANGE ALL).
   b. Moving between the windows by using the SWITCH WINDOWS option, COPY and PASTE appropriate information from the prewriting document to the outline document.
   c. Save the combined text as a new document with an appropriate name.
3. If you want to work on more than one document at a time, you can do so by using separate windows. The WINDOW area of the VIEW tab includes several options for viewing windows, including opening a new window, switching windows, arranging and splitting windows.

paragraphs—the middle blocks of a text—first and add the introductory and concluding blocks later.

THE BUILDING BLOCK METHOD. To create blocks, you can use the new document you made from copies of your prewriting and outline documents. Use the headings in your outline to expand and build your text. CUT and PASTE text from your prewriting to place under the headings; then rewrite and amplify the text to create blocks. You can also COPY information from your prewriting window and PASTE it into your document in the other window.

Below is an illustration of how Kirsten built one section of her paper by copying and pasting information from her prewriting file into her outline file; the blocks are in blue.

COMPOSING FROM OUTLINE WITH BUILDING BLOCKS

I. Introduction

A. Scenario

"Look at this new CD I bought!" Jane exclaims to her friend. Interested, Michael eagerly looks at it. "Wow he says!

TechHelp

Saving Document Drafts

1. Each time you begin a new draft, use the SAVE AS feature and name your drafts in sequence: draft1, draft2, and so on. Then, if you decide that your revisions have not been successful, you can always return to an earlier draft.
2. When working on a draft, do not discard work too hastily by using the CUT or DELETE function of your word-processing program.
3. Instead, use the COPY or CUT and PASTE functions. PASTE any information you decide to cut out of your draft at the end of the document or into a new document window so that you can retrieve it later if needed.

TIP. Because you may be revising frequently while you write, be certain that you periodically save your work. You can set an auto recovery feature on your word-processing program that will automatically save at regular intervals. Use OFFICE BUTTON > WORD OPTIONS > SAVE, and click on "save auto recovery info every: ______ minutes."

These guys are my favorite group! Mind if I make a copy of it?"

B. Definition of Net theft

In spite of laws that prohibit the unlicensed copying of music, written materials, and movies, it has become an accepted practice. Graphics, quotes, articles, and many other various things can be copied for personal use, but often no credit is given to the original author.

C. Thesis

When it comes to "borrowing" information from the Internet, we are gradually becoming a people who can accept lawbreaking as long as we can participate, too.

THE TOP-DOWN METHOD. You may prefer to work from the beginning of your paper straight through to the end. You can use your working thesis statement and the corresponding organizational plan to compose in this way.

Overcoming Writer's Block

- **Gain some distance.** Set your writing aside for a few days or hours. Take a coffee or snack break before coming back to your writing task.
- **Keep at it.** When your writing is flowing well, try to avoid interruptions so that you can keep the momentum going.
- **Stop when you know what's next.** This will make it easier to pick up where you left off.
- **Try freewriting.** Often, the act of writing itself will stimulate those creative juices.
- **Use visualization.** Picture yourself writing or picture some aspect of the topic you are writing about. Then describe what you see.
- **Change your point of view.** Try writing from another person's point of view. Or try writing in a different form such as a letter or a memo.
- **Write what you know first.** Rather than beginning with an introductory paragraph, start by writing the portion of your paper that you know the most about.
- **Change your mode of writing.** If you normally type at a computer, try using pencil and paper, or vice versa.

Type or COPY and PASTE your working thesis statement into a new document. With the thesis statement at the top of your screen, begin writing your draft, following the blueprint suggested by your thesis. Save your draft into the appropriate folder on your hard drive so that you can return to it for more work at a later time.

EXERCISE 3.11 Using either the building-block technique or the top-down method, begin drafting in the new document. As you compose, refer back to your prewriting and outline documents. Remember to take advantage of the text-building capabilities of your word-processing program, including the WINDOW and CUT, COPY, and PASTE features.

3g Collaborate

In college classes, as in the workforce, writers often work on projects in writing groups or writing teams. Your teammates can serve as a sounding board for your ideas and arguments. You can compose together at the keyboard, with one team member acting as the scribe. Or you can compose separately and then turn to each other for responses. Your peers can read early drafts and provide you with valuable feedback on your work. Take advantage of the help that can be found in such collaborative writing groups.

See 6e

1 Working with a group

You may or may not be enthusiastic about working with a group, depending on whether your prior experience with group projects was positive or negative. Sometimes one or two students end up feeling that they are doing all the work, or a few students may be bossy or controlling rather than cooperative. However, if you pay attention to group dynamics and role assignments from the start, you should get along fine and together produce an outcome that none of you could have achieved alone.

When you first receive a collaborative assignment, meet with your group to begin brainstorming the possibilities. One person can act as the scribe, typing into the computer all of the ideas generated by the group. Do not cut off creative avenues; brainstorm with the intention of both understanding and opening up the assignment for your group. Once you have a brainstorming list, begin to divide it into component parts, in an effort to outline a plan of action. You might want to "storyboard" your piece—that is, put the components of the overall piece onto 3″ × 5″ note cards and then work together to arrange the pieces to their best advantage.

❷ Writing collaboratively

Once you have come up with an overall plan of action for your writing project, you can assign specific tasks or roles to group members. One writing

TechHelp

Collaborating via Computer

Computers can facilitate collaboration between you and your classmates. You can use computers to write collaboratively, as well as for peer review of each other's work. We will discuss writing collaboratively in this TechHelp box; for information about giving and receiving feedback (peer review), see 6e.

1. **Collaborating in a networked classroom.** If your course is taught in a networked classroom, your teacher may have designated a common drive on the network on which to share work with your peers. Be sure to save work in your class's designated folder on the network drive (e.g., your class may use drive k: as its common drive, with specific folders for work related to each assignment). Clearly label all of your group's files and folders in the common drive for ease of identification.
2. **Collaborating on your class's Web site or blog.** If your class has an online classroom component, you can use the Web tools found on the class Web site to collaborate with your writing group. Common class Web tools include discussion forums, file-sharing spaces, chat rooms, and online journals or blogs.
3. **Collaborating via email or instant messaging.** You can create an email group list or an IM buddy list to facilitate collaboration between you and the members of your writing group. The file attachment option of email is a particularly useful way to share work. Instant-messaging discussions, because they occur in real time, can be especially useful when groups are problem solving together on the assignment.

class was assigned the task of developing a group Web site on a topic related to cyberspace. Together, the students in each group brainstormed the possibilities for their site, first deciding on the nature of the content their Web site would present. Each member agreed to independently write a two- to three-page piece that would be incorporated as a page at the site. Then they assigned each person in the group one of the following roles: *group leader* (organized group meetings, set deadlines, reported progress to the instructor), *group librarian* (recorded relevant Web sites, produced a bibliography, ensured that all links in the site were operational), *group publisher* (took responsibility for the "look" of the site, importing graphics and deciding on appropriate fonts, colors, backgrounds), *group webmaster* (took responsibility for placing all of the group's writing onto the server, making sure that the site was both functional and readable). Because each student in the group knew exactly what his or her contribution would be, group members were able to work together cooperatively. Please remember that if you use any source material for your group project it must be incorporated appropriately to avoid plagiarism

See Ch. 10

FOR COLLABORATION This exercise will provide you with practice in composing collaboratively in a computer classroom. First, exchange keyboards with the person sitting beside you so that your writing appears on the other person's screen. Next, decide who will be writer 1 and who will be writer 2. Writer 1 begins to freewrite on the topic "Why I chose my college major." Writer 2 begins to write when writer 1 types a series of question marks (???). When writer 2 runs out of ideas, she or he types a series of question marks. Continue to exchange ideas for about ten minutes.

❸ Presenting with your group

Once you have completed your collaborative project, in addition to preparing a written version of your group's work, you may be asked to share it publicly through an online document, a poster presentation, or an oral or multimedia presentation. As you think about making your presentation, consider both the content and the logistics of the presentation itself.

The content of the presentation

Make sure that what you are presenting (the content) is interesting and logically sequenced so that your audience can easily follow your train of thought. Visuals must be appropriate to the content. Everything you present needs to be readable by your entire audience no matter where they are in the room. Make sure that if you are using overheads or a *PowerPoint* presentation, all of your slides can be read easily by everyone.

The logistics of the presentation

It will be important that everyone hear all of your group members, so you must make good use of voice as well as making eye contact with your audience. To do this well requires several practice sessions with appropriate group feedback. Consider, too, how you can divide the allotted time appropriately among group members and still stay within the time limits. Work together with your group so that you are all sharing responsibility for the presentation and the burden doesn't fall on one or two group members.

See Ch. 23

EXERCISE 4.4 Write a brief paragraph describing your own writing process, paying particular attention to any composing habits that you have developed over the years. For example, do you have particular tools that you use or a special place where you are comfortable composing? Do you like to have music playing in the background, or is quiet better for you?

FOR COLLABORATION Share your paragraph with a group of your classmates. Discuss the similarities and differences in composing habits among your group.

3h Review a student draft

Following is the first draft of Kirsten Parsons's persuasive paper. You'll remember that the assignment was for students to write an essay on a computer topic of interest, largely from the students' own experiences, from a brief Internet search, and from the class text. Kirsten's topic was Net theft.

Notice the format of this essay. Kirsten has used the standard format as recommended by the Modern Language Association (MLA), according to her teacher's specifications. Her identifying information is in the left-hand corner, 1 inch down from the top margin. Her last name and the page number are listed in a header on the upper right-hand side of each page, spaced 1/2 inch from the top margin. Everything in the essay is double-spaced, including the title and the first line of the text.

There is much that is good about this draft. Kirsten has identified a real problem that many students face—that is, being uncertain of the "rules" when it comes to using the Internet. The topic is compelling, and her comparisons to shoplifting are insightful. But there are things about the paper that can be improved. We have included the instructor's comments (directed at global revisions) on this early draft to highlight some of the areas that need work. Because it is an early draft, the instructor has chosen not to comment on specific grammar, usage, and spelling errors until later in the writing process.

See Ch. 6

Parsons 1

Kirsten Parsons

Professor Hines

English 101–35

15 March 2006

Net Theft Draft

"Look at this new CD I bought!" Jane exclaims to her friend. Interested, Michael eagerly looks at it. "Wow he says! These guys are my favorite group! Mind if I make a copy of it?"

Unfortunately, this is a common request within our society today. In spite of laws that prohibit the unlicensed copying of music, written materials, and movies, it has become an accepted practice to reproduce another's work without paying for it. Similarly, this has spread to the Internet where access to software, phone cards, and other products is convenient and fast. It has become a situation where "legality collides with practicality" (Meyer and Underwood 113). When it comes to "borrowing" information from the Internet, we are gradually becoming a people who accept lawbreaking as long as we can participate, too.

I'm sure all of us once glimpsed a tempting item in a store and after getting no for an answer from Mom or Dad, took matters into our own hands. Sneaking the

I'm not certain what the reference to phone cards and other products is in the above paragraph. There are many kinds of computer theft. It's not really clear what the focus of this paper will be because of all the different examples in this opening paragraph, although your thesis is quite good.

Parsons 2

treasure into a hidden pocket, it probably took only a few moments for your parents to notice something was up. With available technology, Net theft is commonplace. Flowers, phone cards, magazines, books, and software all are vulnerable to cybershoplifting and plagiarism.

Part of the problem is that the physical element involved in actually traveling to a store, and taking something is not necessary for these Net crimes. Imagine walking down the aisle of the local Walmart with the intention of stealing a Hobbes doll, your favorite cartoon character. This scenerio is only possible in a physical world. Because the Net is so unphysical, the risk of being caught, which may deter many thieves in a store, is minimal. Because Net crimes often go ignored, and "everyone" is guilty, more and more people engage in them.

Information about copyright laws, what is legal, and what isn't is available on the Net as well. "Web Issues" at the *Copyright Website* <www.benedict.com> provides information about what can be copied from the Net and how to do it properly. Another page specifically discusses using graphics (*PageWorks* at <http://www.snowcrest.net/kitty/hpages>). Those who decide to break these "laws" run the risk of being ostracized by a group such as Netbusters! This vigilante group seeks to

I really liked this comparison to other petty crimes, like shoplifting. Again, I wasn't sure about your Net comparison, however (flowers, phone cards, magazines, books—how are these vulnerable to Net theft?). Maybe it would be better to just focus on one kind of petty theft—like copying software or "borrowing" materials such as graphics from someone else's Web site.

Parsons 3

prevent what they call "bandwidth robbery" by informing Net users about its devastating results.

If the definition of a criminal is one who has committed a crime, then in the world of the Net, perhaps we all need to serve some time.

I'm not certain of the relevance of the Netbusters example. It needs to be tied in with the rest of the paper. You seem to be going further astray here at the end. You need a strong conclusion that sums things up and returns you to your thesis.

Parsons 4

Works Cited

Meyer, Michael, and Anne Underwood. "Crimes of the 'Net'." *CyberReader.* Ed. Victor Vitanza. 2nd ed. Boston: Allyn, 1999. 111–13. Print.

You will need to cite your Internet sources here as well as your print source. Please check MLA style for the correct format used with Internet sources. We will work on editing for correct grammar and usage on your next draft.

4 Formulating Arguments

FAQs

- How can I get people to understand my point of view?
- How can I get people to respect what I am proposing?
- What is the difference between a convincing argument and a personal opinion?
- What makes a good, arguable thesis? (4a)
- If I'm presenting an argument online, do I need to do anything special? (4j)
- How can I use visuals to support an argument? (4k)

See Ch. 2

When you go on *Facebook* or *MySpace*, you probably have fun sharing ideas with likeminded friends. And you probably avoid disagreements, right? In college, by contrast, disagreement, or argument, is the name of the game: it arises from the critical thinking you're expected to do. Argument in this sense does not mean quarreling; rather, it means taking a position on an issue and supporting it with evidence and good reasoning.

The ability to lay out an argument is essential to success in college, no matter what your major is. It is also indispensable for most professional careers. Doctors, managers, teachers, social workers, lawyers, engineers, salespeople—indeed, all people whose work involves taking a point of view and then persuading others to agree with it—depend on argumentation to accomplish their goals.

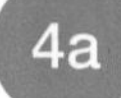

4a Formulate an arguable thesis

See 3e-2

As a first step in developing an argument, you should formulate a good thesis, or claim. A thesis is a statement in which you take a position on an issue—for example, "Voting rights can be extended safely to most of the mentally ill."

In some college assignments, the thesis is given. For example, many standardized tests and final exams have essay questions on a preset thesis. In other cases, your instructor may expect you to formulate a thesis yourself. How do you do that? A good place to start is to follow the suggestions in 3d and 3e:

- gather information from the Internet or a library database;
- discuss topics with classmates or friends either in person or by email, blogs, instant messaging, etc.; and/or
- browse through periodicals.

In general, critical reading, listening, and viewing should raise the kinds of questions that lead to an appropriate thesis. Whether the thesis is assigned or one that you have created yourself, try to shape the thesis and develop the argument so that they become an expression of your own point of view.

See 2b, Chs. 8 and 9

❶ What constitutes an appropriate thesis?

The first requirement for a good thesis is that it be *open to debate.* That is, it should not make a claim that everyone would already agree with. "Smoking is harmful to your health" is not an effective argumentative thesis because almost no educated person would disagree with it. A more interesting, more arguable thesis would be "Smoking should be prohibited in all public places, including bars."

Second, a thesis should be *open to evidence and counterevidence*—you can gather evidence for and against it. For the smoking example, you could search the research literature, Web sites, or newsgroups for scientific evidence about the effects of secondhand smoke; you could look for health statistics on communities that have already enacted such a prohibition; or you could try to locate results of public opinion surveys. If a thesis merely expresses your own opinion about something ("I think smoking is cool"), without citing evidence beyond your own feelings, it offers no claim that can be objectively assessed by others.

Third, a thesis should be *clearly stated.* It should leave no confusion in the mind of the reader as to what you are claiming. Provide definitions or paraphrases of any terms that may be unclear. In the example about smoking in public places, readers would need to know exactly what is meant by the term *public places.* Indeed, the entire argument could hinge on how this term is defined.

Checklist

An Arguable Thesis or Claim

- ✓ Is it debatable—something not everyone will automatically agree with?
- ✓ Can it be supported with evidence available to everyone?
- ✓ Can it be countered with arguments against it?
- ✓ Is it based on more than just personal opinion or subjective feelings?
- ✓ Is it clearly stated, with appropriate definitions of terms?

Here are some examples of appropriate theses:

- Using a cell phone while driving should be against the law.
- Rising gas prices threaten the future of this country.
- The Social Security system should allow people to invest in the stock market.
- American culture is overly obsessed with sports and games.
- The death penalty should be abolished.

2 Using inductive and deductive reasoning

If you have to develop your own thesis, there are two kinds of reasoning that should help you get there. **Inductive reasoning** begins with particular evidence and arrives at some general conclusion. For example, if your mail has been delivered three hours late for the past four days (particular evidence), you might conclude that a substitute carrier is now working your route (generalization). Or let's say the front tire on your bike needs frequent pumping but your rear tire doesn't; you might reasonably infer that your front tire has a small leak. Inductive reasoning is something we use routinely, every day. We use inductive reasoning to try to make sense of things and to come up with new ideas. Because inductive reasoning relies on experience, it is sometimes referred to as "educated guesswork." Inductive reasoning deals with probability, not absolute truth or validity. Thus, the conclusions it arrives at are not necessarily "true"; rather, they are only probable or plausible.

Deductive reasoning goes in the opposite direction, from general to particular. You start with some generalization—a general claim, principle, or belief—and then you apply it to some specific fact and arrive at some specific conclusion or prediction. Deductive reasoning relies on a strict form of logic, conventionally expressed in a **syllogism**. A syllogism contains a major premise (the generalization), one or more minor premises (the facts), and a conclusion.

MAJOR PREMISE	People who work hard are usually successful.
MINOR PREMISE	Kevin works hard.
CONCLUSION	Kevin will probably be successful.

In deductive reasoning there is a difference between *validity* and *truth*. When a deductive argument conforms to the rules of logic, it is said to be *valid*. In the example above, the minor premise fits logically with the condition set up in the major premise ("People who work hard"), and so the conclusion logically follows. A deductive argument can be *true*, however, only if its premises are true—so if any premise is false, the argument itself is false. For example, if it turns out that Kevin does *not* work hard, the above argument, although valid, would be false.

In everyday use, deductive reasoning often leaves its major premise unstated. This is because major premises are often widely accepted assumptions in a particular culture. Thus, the syllogism given above might be expressed in everyday language as "Kevin works hard—I think he'll be successful some day." Such abbreviated syllogisms (or **enthymemes**) are commonplace in daily life because they convey logical reasoning in shortcut fashion. Unfortunately, the convenience of enthymemes makes them easy to misuse for deception. Here is an example from a political campaign: "The Congressman clearly supports family values. He has five children, after all."

MAJOR PREMISE, UNSTATED	Anyone who has five children supports family values.
MINOR PREMISE	The Congressman has five children.
CONCLUSION	The Congressman supports family values.

By leaving the major premise an unstated assumption, the speaker avoided subjecting it to public scrutiny. If he had stated it explicitly, people in the audience might have raised questions about its truth, about the vagueness of the term *family values*, and so on. This example illustrates the fallacy of begging the question.

See 4h-2

Of course, there is no guarantee that induction and deduction by themselves will lead to good, arguable theses. The claim that "Kevin will probably be successful" would not make a good thesis, as it is not open to evidence and counterevidence. The claim that "the Congressman supports family values" works better as a thesis, especially if it is a public issue in the Congressman's district. But it would first need to have the term *family values* defined in a way that allowed for evidence to be marshaled for and against it.

Inductive and deductive reasoning often work together, and the combination has a better chance of producing a good, arguable thesis. For instance, you might use inductive reasoning to formulate a generalization from particulars, and then use that same generalization as your major premise in deductive reasoning. Here is an example.

INDUCTIVE REASONING

PARTICULARS	You keep reading or hearing news reports about mass shootings in southern and western states.
PARTICULARS	You have read in several places that there are more guns per capita in southern and western states than in other states.
GENERALIZATION	More gun ownership leads to more gun-related violence.

DEDUCTIVE REASONING

MAJOR PREMISE	More gun ownership leads to more gun-related violence.
MINOR PREMISE	The new concealed weapon ordinance in our city is causing more people to buy guns.
CONCLUSION	The new concealed weapon ordinance will cause the rate of gun-related violence in our city to increase.

This conclusion would serve as a good thesis for an argument because it is an important public issue, is debatable, can be supported or refuted with evidence, is not just based on personal opinion, and is clearly stated. Note also how the underlying premises themselves satisfy these requirements.

3 Working through a thesis

Not every claim, or thesis, ends up the way it began; most writers develop a thesis somewhat by trial and error, refining their ideas as they gather more information. For an essay in her composition class, Angela Napper decided to write about cybercensorship. She had heard that administrators at her college were considering new rules that would prohibit students from accessing certain Web sites in the school's computer labs. She felt this would be an infringement on academic freedom, so she decided that her thesis would be something like "Censoring Internet usage is inappropriate in a college environment." But this was only her *working thesis.* As she explored the subject and worked through her ideas with a classmate, she realized that the issue of cybercensorship was far broader than just its effect on college students. She also decided that she should make her thesis more specific, more open to evidence—that is, more arguable. After further research and collaborative brainstorming, Angela decided to focus not on the inappropriateness of cybercensorship in college but on the constitutionality of such censorship in the broader public sphere. This resulted in a *revised thesis*: "Citizens need to take a stand to protect their rights to privacy and freedom of information on public computers as these rights are guaranteed to them in the Constitution under the Bill of Rights."

See 3c

Angela's thesis is a good one. First of all, it is not a statement that everyone would automatically agree with. In fact, after the terrorist attacks of September 11, 2001, many people would argue that citizens must sacrifice some of these rights for the sake of greater national security. Second, her thesis can be debated with evidence and counterevidence. Angela could cite the relevant parts of the Constitution and court decisions that either support or undermine her thesis. Third, her thesis is clearly stated.

Although a thesis should be stated early, it should be preceded by any background information the reader needs to make sense of it. Delayed presentation of the thesis is especially appropriate if the audience is either ignorant of the subject or likely to disagree with or be skeptical about the thesis. Delaying the thesis tells the reader that you are not "jumping to conclusions" but instead are thoughtfully and impartially working through the issue. Since readers in college are trained to be skeptical, you should not feel that you have to state your thesis up front (unless, of course, your instructor tells you to).

EXERCISE 4.1 Analyze each of the following claims to decide (a) whether or not it expresses a clear and arguable thesis and (b) what kinds of evidence and counterevidence would be relevant to it. In cases where the claim is not an arguable thesis, reformulate it into one.

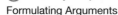

1. Toni Morrison is the best living American author.
2. The National Park System would be better off if it were privatized.
3. Overpopulation is threatening our quality of life.
4. It is a bad idea for governments to attempt to regulate delivery of information via the Internet.
5. Within a decade, soccer will replace baseball as our national pastime.

4b Consider your purpose and audience

See 3b-2

At some point early in the process of developing an argument, you need to carefully consider your purpose and audience. In general, the reason for making an argument is to persuade other people to your point of view. But depending on the situation, you may have any of the following more specific purposes:

- To persuade those who are undecided to agree with you.
- To reinforce the views of those who already agree with you.
- To change the minds of those who disagree with you, or at least deter them from acting against you.
- To test your *own* commitment to this point of view.
- To display (to your instructor) your ability to work through a problem.

See 3b-2

Notice how each of these purposes has a distinctly different audience. It is extremely unlikely that one argument presented one way to all audiences will be successful with each of them. Different people with different backgrounds, beliefs, and so on will often respond differently to the same argument. Thus, you'll have a better chance of succeeding if you shape your argument to address the interests and values of each audience.

A good time to start this process is while working through your thesis. Angela did this when she conducted extra research on her initial topic and found it to be broader in scope than she had realized. In all cases, you should try to develop a thesis that:

See 3e

1. defines a specific topic,
2. makes a strong point about the topic, and
3. provides a blueprint for the paper's development.

As for positioning your thesis, if you have an audience that you think will be either skeptical or uninformed on the issue, you should build up to your thesis by first presenting appropriate background information. Conversely, if you have a knowledgeable, supportive audience, you can proceed more quickly to your thesis.

4c Consider the genre

When you take a class in college, you are doing more than just reading the course materials, taking lecture notes, and doing the required writing assignments and tests. You are also, for the time being, entering a field of study inhabited and nurtured by a community of scholars, and to do well, you need to develop some sense of that larger context. This includes understanding how people in that field typically present arguments. Every field of study has certain standard ways, or *genres*, of laying out arguments. Biology and chemistry, for example, depend heavily on lab reports and research papers. English most often uses the interpretive essay. In history, there is heavy reliance on document analysis. In business, case analyses are common. Each of these genres has its own characteristic features. Knowing the expected genre features can help guide you in the development and presentation of an argument.

For example, in sociology, political science, or environmental science, professors commonly assign various readings and then ask students to write a short paper called a "response paper." A response paper usually consists of an introduction, a descriptive summary of the assigned reading, a personal evaluation, and a concluding generalization. The assigned reading is most often some kind of argument, and your evaluation of it should be an argument as well (whether pro or con). These genre features, coupled with the argumentative nature of the assigned reading and your evaluation of it, should shape your response. In your introduction, you would zero in on the main thesis of the reading. Your summary of the reading would recapitulate the main points of the author's argument, perhaps noting what kind of reasoning it utilizes. Your personal evaluation would critique that argument and then present a counterargument of your own, based partly on your personal experience. And the concluding generalization would incorporate your own thesis. All of this in the space of three or four pages.

In Angela's case, her assignment was to write an essay for her first-year composition class. Her instructor had told the class that he expected the essay to have

- an attention-getting introduction with a thesis statement,
- enough background information to understand the issue,
- a series of paragraphs with supporting evidence for her thesis,
- brief acknowledgment and refutation of any opposing points of view, and
- a good conclusion.

See 4i-1

Angela recognized that these requirements conformed to the parts of the classic five-part method of structuring an argument, and so she set up an outline using this structure as her scaffold.

4d Generate good supporting evidence

Central to the strength of an argument is the evidence cited to support it. There are four main types of evidence: factual data (including statistics), expert opinion, personal experience, and examples.

Factual data include any information presented as representing objective reality. Factual data most often consist of measurable, or quantitative, evidence such as distances, amounts, and ratios. But factual data can include historical events, longstanding assessments, and other widely attested observations about the world. Objectivity makes factual data difficult to refute. Therefore, in most academic disciplines, factual data are considered to be the most powerful form of evidence you can present.

A collection of numerical data, *statistics* are usually compressed in a way that points to a certain interpretation. Because statistics typically represent a large body of data, they can be compelling as evidence. But they can also be manipulated in deceptive ways. If you gather your own statistics, be sure you know how to analyze them correctly. If you take statistics from other sources, try to use only sources that are considered reliable (for example, the US government or prestigious academic journals).

Expert opinion can also be persuasive, because it represents the studied judgment of someone who knows a great deal about the subject at hand. If a famous literary critic said that *Twelfth Night* was one of Shakespeare's finest plays, quoting this expert's statement would strengthen any argument you made along those lines. But expert opinion has its limitations. First, a quotation taken out of context may not convey what the expert really meant. Second, experts sometimes fall prey to the influence of some special interest. Not long ago, experts employed by the tobacco industry testified that tobacco was not addictive. Finally, experts can simply be wrong in their judgments and predictions.

Personal experience is less objective than either factual data or expert opinion, but it can be highly compelling. Personal experience is especially effective when presented in the form of a narrative. The story you tell may represent only your own experience—and thus lack generalizability—but since it is coming directly from you it has a certain vividness that is missing from more detached accounts. Personal experience is not the same as personal opinion: the former is an account of an experience—something you have personally tested against reality—while the latter may be nothing more than a snap judgment. Arguments do not go far on opinion alone.

Examples are effective because, like personal experience, they are concrete, vivid, and therefore easy for readers to relate to. (Just think of how much you appreciate good examples in the textbooks and other instructional materials you read!) Unlike personal experience, examples are supposed to be generalizations about a larger category. That is, they are good only to the extent that they are typical of an entire class of phenomena. If you present an odd case as a "typical example," you could well be criticized for overgeneralizing.

See 4h-1

Angela's essay on cybercensorship is printed on the following pages. Note what kinds of evidence she used to support her thesis.

Napper 1

Angela Napper

Professor Hult

English 101

13 October 2008

Cybercensorship

Introduces the issue in attention-getting terms: "the debate rages . . ."

Presents her thesis

Gives an example as background information

With more and more regulations being formed about what citizens are allowed to view on the Internet, concerns as to the constitutional rights of these citizens are being raised. At public libraries, at colleges and universities, and at businesses the debate rages as to how much privacy users should have and whether censorship of certain materials is needed to protect the public welfare. More and more it is becoming clear that citizens need to take a stand to protect their right to privacy and freedom of speech on public computers as these rights are guaranteed to them in the US Constitution, specifically the First, Fifth, and Fourteenth Amendments.

Recently, the Board of Supervisors in Chesterfield County, Virginia, passed a law to prohibit access to any material deemed by the community to be pornographic or obscene. This includes any information on sex education and any Web sites containing prohibited words. Consequently, a site containing a recipe for chicken breasts would be banned. The new policy seems to be popular with some local residents. They have even started a Liberty Watch group in which citizens make a point of monitoring what those around them are accessing on the Web. Anything they deem illegal by the new standards is reported to the local authorities (Oder and Rogers).

With this type of system in place, citizens' right to access information—as guaranteed in the freedom of speech and freedom of press clauses of the First Amendment and the equal protection clause of the Fourteenth Amendment—is greatly infringed upon. The morals and beliefs of those in power have been forced upon everyone. It is exactly this type of regulation that the Founders were trying to escape when they created the United States, a country where everyone would be free to live their lives as they chose, assuming they were not hurting others. I fail to see how attempting to access a recipe for chicken is hurting anyone. For that matter, gaining information on sex education is not infringing on the well-being of the community. Rather, it is likely improving the overall well-being by preventing unwanted pregnancies and diseases. Educator David Thornburg points out, "Libraries in schools and communities should be the last places to use censorship of any kind. Once the door to censorship is opened, how do we ever get it closed again?"

Presents main supporting evidence for her thesis

Uses quotation from authority to reinforce her point

The debate between freedom of speech and censorship is also raging at a number of universities.

Shifts to another location that has the same issue; should resonate with other students

At Snow College in southern Utah, administrators added software that blocked student access to all information deemed nonacademic. They said the motivation behind their actions had nothing to do with moral censorship. Rather, they claimed that students playing games and viewing pornography were using up too much computing time and power. Students who needed to use campus computers for homework had to wait in long lines and deal with slower computers. With the new policy in effect, the rate of hits on blocked sites (versus approved sites) dropped from thirty-five percent to less than five percent per day. This reduction speeded up the computers for those who used them for academic purposes. Students complained that they were never asked about their opinion beforehand and were not told about the decision after it had gone into effect. When asked what they would do if the student body voted against the new policy, school officials said the policy would be removed (Madsen).

Similarly, Indiana University banned the downloading of MP3s on school computers because it was using up too much of the school's bandwidth. Opposition came from a group called Students Against University Censorship who began circulating a petition around the nation with the goal of gaining popular support as well as legal representation in their fight against these censorship policies. Their aim was to gain public support so as to have more power in a court of law or in negotiations with officials who could strike down censorship at universities nationwide (Ferguson).

However, some universities are in favor of giving students free rein. The University of Nevada, Las Vegas, refuses to put limits on what students can access on school computers or in the dorms. Officials state that they respect the students' rights and they want to make them feel at home when they are living in the dorms, which means allowing them access to all sites. If anyone on campus is offended by what another student is viewing, the offending student is simply asked to relocate to a more private computer. This type of policy respects the rights of all involved. It does not infringe on the freedom of speech rights of the students, while at the same time students who feel uncomfortable by material being viewed around them are accommodated appropriately (Ferguson).

This more reasonable approach provides support for her argument.

More and more the battleground is moving into the workplace. Employers are looking to monitor what their employees access during work hours so as to prevent them from wasting company time on personal entertainment. Currently, over two thousand companies have begun using *Cyber-Patrol,* software that filters out any Web sites the company does not want its employees to access. Microsystems Software, Inc., the company that

This counter-example serves nicely to restrict her thesis; gives her more credibility.

designs this software for corporations, claims it is not censoring anything but only filtering. It allows managers to personally inspect Web sites that have been accessed by company employees. Since every Web site *Cyber-Patrol* blocks has been viewed by a person, there is not blanket censorship based on what words a site may contain. All sites are placed into one of three categories: CyberYes, CyberNo, and Sports/Entertainment. With this system, any company can choose whether it wants its employees to be able to access sports and entertainment sites during work hours. It can also restrict any sites that have been deemed pornographic or violent (Markels).

Highlights the public vs. private dimension of this issue, setting up the next section

This type of restriction seems less in violation of citizens' rights because it is designed to be used only in the workplace. Most would agree employers have the right to monitor what their employees are doing during office hours because the employers own the machines and are paying the employees for their time. Similarly, it might be argued that public libraries and universities also own their computers and consequently should have the right to censor them. It must be kept in mind, however, that those computers were purchased using taxpayers' money, so in reality they belong to the public. *Cyber-Patrol* is also improved in its format in that each Web site is individually viewed. Web sites with recipes for chicken breasts would consequently not be banned.

These same issues of the public's right to privacy have become a point of controversy in the post-9/11 era. Under provisions of the USA-PATRIOT Act, various governmental agencies such as the FBI and the Department of Homeland Security have been monitoring private citizens' Web use and emails. By gaining access to the records of any Internet service provider, government officials can track all people who have hit on any given site, or all of the sites accessed by any given computer. The government claims that such actions are necessary to prevent further terrorist attacks in the United States. Opposition to such government surveillance is led by Jerry Berman, the executive director of the Center for Democracy and Technology in Washington. He and his supporters claim that the government is moving too fast, not stopping to consider the long-term effects that this monitoring could have. The government's response to this claim is that it must use all the tools it can if further attacks are to be prevented. I think this is a scare tactic on the part of the government. Although we may need new laws to stop future attacks by terrorists in the United States, it is also vital to ensure that citizens' rights are not crushed in the process. As one human rights researcher has said, "If allowed to be controlled by a government, instead of a tool for democracy, the Internet may be employed as a

This example adds complexity to the issue, making it even more interesting.

Refutes the counter-example, making her argument stronger

Concludes with a concise summary of the main points and an apt quotation

tool by which more modern dictatorships can monitor and control their citizens" (Hansen).

With the debate raging as to how much privacy Americans are entitled to when it comes to the Internet and what information they should be able to access, it is the citizens' job to take a stand and fight for their rights. It is only by doing so that the ideals of freedom of speech and right to privacy that the Founders so highly valued will be preserved. As Supreme Court Justice William O. Douglas once said, "The right to be let alone is indeed the beginning of all freedom."

Works Cited

Ferguson, Kevin. "Net Censorship Spreading on University Campuses." *Las Vegas Business Press* 28 Feb. 2000: 20. Print.

Hansen, Stephen A. "Policing the Internet: Cybercensorship and Its Potential Impact." Slide presentation and lecture. *AAAS Science and Human Rights Program*. American Association for the Advancement of Science, 1999. Web. 9 Oct. 2009.

Madsen, Grant. "Snow College Officials Defend Net Censorship: Blocking Pornography Was Not for Moral Reasons." *Salt Lake Tribune* 16 Jan. 1999: D3. Print.

Markels, Alex. "Screening the Net; Microsystems Cleans Up Web for Kids, Workers: Screening the Internet for Nudity, Profanity." *Salt Lake Tribune* 5 May 1997: B1. Print.

Oder, Norman, and Michael Rogers. "VA County Public Library to Filter All Access." *Library Journal* 126 (2001): 15. Print.

Puzzanghera, Jim. "Privacy Advocates Argue Anti-Terrorism Plans Harm Free Society." *San Jose Mercury News* 27 Sept. 2001: 17. Print.

Thornburg, David. "Children and Cybercensorship." *PBS TeacherLine*. Public Broadcasting Service, 22 Aug. 2002. Web. 6 Oct. 2009.

What kinds of evidence does Angela use to support her argument? Mainly, she relies on a number of extended *examples* in which citizens' rights to privacy and freedom of speech are being eroded through the use of cybercensorship. By using a broad selection of settings (libraries, colleges, businesses, government surveillance), she conveys a sense of how widespread the danger is. She also cites the *opinions of experts* ranging from Supreme Court Justice Douglas to Jerry Berman, the executive director of the Center for Democracy and Technology. She also gives source information for many of the statements in her paper. Angela uses *factual data* as well, in the form of objective accounts of the different cases and of the applicability of the US Constitution to them.

EXERCISE 4.2 Of the different kinds of evidence that Angela used, which—in your opinion—is most compelling? Why? What other evidence could she have used?

FOR COLLABORATION Together with a classmate, find a written argument that one of you finds persuasive but the other does not. (The opinion page in the campus newspaper or local city newspaper would be one place to look; a political blog might be another.) Then analyze—dispassionately!—why you differ in your reactions. As noted above, people with different backgrounds, beliefs, and values will often respond differently to an argument as well as to the evidence used to support it; this may explain why you and your classmate have the different responses you do.

4e Take note of evidence for alternative views

In gathering evidence, do not go looking just for evidence that supports your case; take note of evidence supporting other positions as well, including evidence that argues directly against your case. On issues that are of any interest or value, the evidence will not be entirely one-sided; there will be evidence supporting alternative views. When you acknowledge the counterevidence, you gain credibility as a careful, conscientious thinker, thereby strengthening your argument rather than weakening it. (This is especially true in academia.) Conversely, readers may interpret your failure to present counterevidence as either a less than full effort to address the issue or an outright attempt to hide negative evidence. Remember, you do not have to make an overwhelmingly lopsided argument in order to prevail; you simply have to show that there is more support *for* your thesis than *against* it. In most college writing, an awareness of the complexity of an issue is considered a sign of intellectual maturity.

Another advantage of gathering counterevidence early on is that it forces you to review your thesis and, if necessary, modify it. In formulating your thesis, you may have overlooked some arguments against it. Maybe you overgeneralized, used either/or reasoning, or committed some other fallacy. If so, this is a good time to reformulate your thesis and make it more defensible. (Getting your fellow students involved in this effort can be helpful; see 6e for more on collaborating.)

See 4h

Angela's essay includes two different kinds of counterevidence against her thesis. First, she notes that some college administrators have been restricting students' Internet access not to censor their access to inappropriate material but to save on computing resources, thus ultimately giving students more access to appropriate uses of the school's computer systems. Second, she says that private companies have a legitimate right to restrict employees' use of company computers because these computers are owned by the company and the employees are paid to do the company's work, not to entertain themselves. She also acknowledges the government's desire to promote greater security against terrorism as a reason for its increased cybersurveillance of American citizens.

EXERCISE 4.3 What other counterevidence could Angela have used? How could she have responded to it?

EXERCISE 4.4 Log on to a newsgroup, chat room, or other Web site where arguments are taking place. (Some interesting newsgroups are *talk.politics, ab.politics, alt.society.resistance, alt.fan.rush-limbaugh*, and *alt. politics. radical-left.*) Print out two conversational threads, each involving several exchanges: one in which the participants make some concessions to each other's point of view and another in which they do not. Do the threads differ in tone, argumentative force, or intellectuality? Write a short paper describing the differences you find.

See 23c

4f Develop and test your main points

Once you have formulated an appropriate thesis and compiled enough information to make a case for it, you need to develop and test the main points you want to make. This is the heart of an argument, where you lay out your reasoning in step-by-step fashion.

1 Deciding what your strongest points are

In any argument, some points are stronger than others: they are

- more central to the issue at hand,
- make more sense in terms of logical reasoning,
- have more evidence supporting them, and
- have less counterevidence opposing them.

In constructing your argument, you need to try to identify those points that seem to be strongest. You might start by simply listing all the points you can think of to support your thesis. Then ask yourself this question: Which of these points are most central to the issue I am addressing? Any controversial topic will give rise to a hierarchy of concerns, which will vary from one person to another. If you ignore a concern that is of overriding importance to a particular reader, you will lose the argument with that reader. For example, in the debate over abortion, the stated overriding concern of most "pro-life" adherents is the sanctity of human life. No amount of arguing in terms of freedom of choice, population control, or women's rights is likely to sway such an audience if the sanctity of human life issue is ignored. These readers will just say that you are missing the point. Thus, an important step at this stage is to analyze your audience and determine how they rank their concerns about the topic under discussion.

What do you do if your strongest points do not coincide with the main concerns of your audience? One strategy is to *redefine* their concerns and your points so that there is a closer fit. For example, if you were writing about abortion from the "pro-choice" side, you could argue that the sanctity of human life encompasses individual freedom, including the freedom of women to decide what happens to their own bodies. Another strategy is to accept the differences between yourself and your audience and prepare to make your argument anyway. Even a losing argument can have value, so long as it is a strong argument. It may gain the respect of your opponents, temper their views, resonate unexpectedly among disinterested parties, "plant a seed," or have other beneficial results. But for these good things to happen, you must at least acknowledge your opponents' point of view. Indeed, in some cases, your strongest points will be refutations of your opponents' strongest points.

❷ Developing and checking your points

Starting with your strongest point, use careful step-by-step reasoning to develop each point. To make sure your points are logically sound, analyze their structure according to a method devised by philosopher Stephen Toulmin. This structure consists of six parts: claim (or point), data (supporting reasons), warrant (general principle connecting data to claim), backing (for the warrant), qualifier (of the claim), and possible rebuttal (or counterargument, with a response). Here is an illustration of how Toulmin logic can be used to check one of Angela Napper's claims—namely, that the Constitution guarantees citizens the right to access information.

POINT OR CLAIM	American citizens have the right to freely access information.
DATA	The Constitution guarantees freedom of speech and freedom of the press.
WARRANT (implied)	Freedom of speech and freedom of the press imply a freedom to *listen* to speech and *read* the press—that is, to access information.
BACKING	The Founders believed that people should be free to live their lives as they choose (provided they do not hurt others) and that a democracy requires a well-informed citizenry.
QUALIFIER	The right to access information does not include the right to impose on other people's privacy or misuse company or university equipment.
REBUTTAL	People should not be allowed to use public computers to view immoral material. (Response: People have a constitutional right to access whatever information they please, and no one else has the right to impose his or her own standards of morality on them.)

Checklist

Sound Reasoning in an Argument

- ✓ Have I arrived at a clearly stated, arguable thesis (4a)? What is it?
- ✓ What is the evidence for my thesis, and how does it function as support for the thesis (4d)?
- ✓ What are the main underlying assumptions—or warrants—that logically connect my claims to my evidence?
- ✓ If these warrants are unstated, will they be obvious to everybody in my audience?

Notice that the validity of Angela's argument depends on an implied warrant. Is this warrant valid? Many people in our culture might think so.

When careful readers judge your arguments, they will be scrutinizing your chain of reasoning. Thus, be aware of the warrant you use for each point you make. Often, the warrant is assumed rather than actually stated. But if critical readers do not share your assumptions, they will say that your claims are *unwarranted*. Any assumptions that might not be shared by your readers should be stated explicitly.

EXERCISE 4.5 Identify a point in Angela's essay other than the one analyzed above. Using the same data-warrant-claim structure, analyze this point.

4g Build a compelling case

See Fig. 1.4

The primary goal of any argument is to make the best case you can. The three basic ways to make a case are by using logical reasoning, asserting your and others' authority, and appealing to the readers' emotions. Though we discuss them separately below, oftentimes the most effective case is one that combines all three.

❶ Appealing to logic

In college, certainly the most important type of support you can give an argument is logical reasoning. Indeed, one of the main purposes of education is to promote the ability to communicate effectively with a broad, skeptical audience (in both professional and public life), and logical reasoning is the primary tool for doing so. In particular, you should avoid logical fallacies. In whatever field of study you undertake—sociology, history, engineering, or biology—your instructors will pay close attention to the logical reasoning you use. They will want to know that you can develop an argument step by step, laying out a chain of reasoning that compels skeptical readers to respect your thinking.

See 4h,
See Chs. 15–18

There are many effective patterns for developing an argument. They include linking cause and effect, making comparisons and contrasts, defining and classifying, narrating a series of events, generalizing from particulars (*induction*), drawing particular inferences from general rules (*deduction*), and providing relevant examples and analogies.

See Ch. 5

❷ Appealing to authority

People are usually greatly influenced by the credibility or reputation of the person trying to persuade them. That is why advertisers like to use highly esteemed celebrities such as Tiger Woods and Christina Aguilera to push their products. The appeal to authority takes advantage of people's natural desire to simplify their lives. If Tiger says that Omega watches are the best, it is easier to take his word for it than to go to the local library and look up the research findings in *Consumer Reports.*

More discerning readers are not so likely to be influenced by celebrity endorsements but may well be influenced by expert judgments. When invoking the authority of true experts, it is important to

- find experts who are addressing an issue within their field of expertise,
- use actual quotations rather than paraphrasing,
- include enough context to make the quotation an accurate reflection of the expert's statement, and
- provide a reference so that skeptical readers can look up the quotation for themselves.

An even more important type of authority is your own. Since you are the person who has gathered the information and assembled the argument, your own credibility (or *ethos*) will be under scrutiny. If readers have any reason to doubt your honesty, fairness, or scholarly integrity, they will treat what you say with a good deal of skepticism. Here are some things you can do to safeguard and enhance your credibility:

- Avoid making exaggerated or distorted assertions.
- Acknowledge opposing points of view and counterevidence.
- If you use other people's ideas or words, give them explicit credit.
- If appropriate, mention your credentials (without bragging).
- Use good reasoning throughout.
- Maintain a respectful, civil tone.
- Pay attention to details of writing such as grammar, style, spelling, and punctuation.

❸ Appealing to emotion

A third powerful way of supporting an argument is by tapping into the readers' emotions. Although this type of persuasion is generally not emphasized in academic and technical writing, it can be highly effective so long as it is used in conjunction with a more logical appeal. In many other kinds of writing (such as political discourse, journalism, and advertising), emotional appeals are used frequently.

Here are some ways to add emotional power to an argument:

See 4k

- Describe the issue in a way that relates it to the readers' values or needs.
- Include examples that readers can identify with, such as stories featuring sympathetic human beings.
- Use a powerful visual aid.

EXERCISE 4.6 In your opinion, what type of support does Angela's essay rely on most heavily? Identify examples in her essay of a logical appeal, an appeal to authority, and an emotional appeal, and evaluate, in writing, the effectiveness of each.

4h Avoid logical and emotional fallacies

A **fallacy** can be either a false statement or a false line of reasoning. As a critical reader and a careful writer, you should always be on guard against both types of fallacies. With regard to false statements, your best defense is good, solid factual knowledge. For example, if someone claims that Mexico is a monarchy, you can expose such a fallacy by noting that Mexico has not been a monarchy since the nineteenth century.

Lines of reasoning pertain more to the formal aspects of argument. Here, you should be on the lookout for any logical or emotional errors. Such errors can all be classified as *non sequiturs*—that is, claims that "do not follow" logically from the premises on which they are based. Some of the most common fallacies are discussed below.

❶ Overgeneralization and oversimplification

When you make a broad statement on the basis of too little evidence, overlooking important differences, you are *overgeneralizing* or *oversimplifying*. Usually the tip-off to this fallacy is the use of absolute qualifiers such as *all*, *every*, *none*, or *never*.

EXAMPLES All Democrats are liberals.

Corporations never look beyond quarterly profits.

Everyone knows about the ozone layer.

Examples are also vulnerable to oversimplification, because an example, by definition, is a claim for generality. If you present something as an example of a broad category, make sure it truly represents that entire category. Otherwise, you will be guilty of overgeneralizing.

EXAMPLE American cars are bigger gas-guzzlers than import cars. For example, the Ford Explorer gets only sixteen miles per gallon while the Toyota Corolla gets thirty-two.

The first sentence may be correct, though it should be qualified by a term such as *on average*. But the example used to support it is misleading. The Explorer is not a typical American car (in terms of gas mileage) and the Corolla is not a typical import car. Furthermore, they are different types of vehicles, so comparing the two is like comparing apples and oranges.

❷ Begging the question

When you make an argument at too superficial a level and leave the underlying issue(s) unaddressed, you are *begging the question*. This is also known as "assuming what needs to be proved," or *circular reasoning*. Often, begging the

See 4f-2

question involves unstated but controversial warrants. In some cases, the unstated warrant is the missing premise of an enthymeme.

EXAMPLE Sex education should be eliminated from the public schools. We shouldn't be encouraging our young people to engage in sex.

This is a fallacious enthymeme.

MAJOR PREMISE, UNSTATED Sex education encourages students to engage in sex.

MINOR PREMISE We do not want to encourage students to engage in sex.

CONCLUSION Sex education should be eliminated.

The unstated warrant in the major premise is unproven and indeed highly controversial. By using it as an unstated assumption, the speaker is guilty of begging the question.

3 Attacking the person instead of the evidence (*ad hominem*)

Also called the *ad hominem* (Latin for "to the man") fallacy, the tactic of attacking the person instead of the evidence is commonly practiced in public discourse. It tries to divert attention from the real issue by discrediting the opponent's character.

EXAMPLE My opponent wants you to believe that she will give you good representation in Congress, but can you really trust someone who admits to having smoked marijuana?

A candidate's personal life, past or present, may have little to do with how she performs as a public servant, yet this is a ploy commonly used in political campaigns and elsewhere to sway people.

4 Using either/or reasoning

The either/or fallacy results from assuming that there are only two ways of looking at a particular issue. Psychologists call it the *black-or-white syndrome*. Also called the *false dilemma*, this fallacy is commonplace in the media (with its predilection for getting "both sides of the story"), in our adversarial system of justice, and in our two-party political system. But reality teaches us that there are typically *many* sides to a story. To be a good thinker, avoid falling into the either/or trap.

EXAMPLE Bill is an avid hunter and gun collector. He is opposed to any gun control legislation, saying, "You're either in favor of the Second Amendment or against it."

Bill's statement constitutes a false dilemma, because it ignores any middle ground where gun ownership could be maintained as a constitutional right, yet regulated in the way that other rights, such as freedom of speech, are regulated.

NOTE Many gun advocates reject any such middle ground, believing that it would result in a chipping away and ultimate loss of their rights. This is known as the *slippery slope fallacy*: "Once you start down that slope, there's no stopping."

❺ Using faulty cause-effect reasoning

Just because two events occur closely in time does not necessarily mean that one caused the other. As statisticians are careful to point out, correlation is not always causation.

EXAMPLE Tax cuts can lead to higher economic growth. From 1990 to 1995, the ten states that raised taxes the most created zero net new jobs, while the ten states that cut taxes the most gained 1.84 million jobs, an increase of 10.8 percent.

It could be that it was the lack of new jobs that caused the first group of states to raise taxes (to pay unemployment compensation, for example), not the other way around.

A special case of faulty cause-effect reasoning is the *post hoc* fallacy (for the Latin *post hoc, ergo propter hoc*, or "after this, therefore because of this"). In this fallacy, an assumption is made that because one event occurred after another, the first event caused the second. It could be, however, that the two events are unrelated.

EXAMPLE Two days ago I signed up with a new Internet service provider, and now my computer is acting up. Maybe I should go back to my old provider.

It is of course *possible* that one action caused the other, but it is by no means certain. Any number of things unrelated to the Internet service could be causing those computer problems.

❻ Using false analogies

False analogies start with true analogies and then try to extend them beyond reason, claiming similarities that do not exist.

EXAMPLE Just as the Founders said that a well-regulated militia was necessary to the security of a free state, modern-day militias like the Montana Freemen are the best guardians of our freedom.

Such a statement may seem reasonable at first reading, but analysis of its logic reveals serious flaws. Contemporary "militias" such as the Montana Freemen are sectarian groups with no official standing; thus, they are very different from the militias of the late eighteenth century, which more closely resembled today's National Guard.

❼ Using the bandwagon appeal (*ad populum*)

The *bandwagon appeal* is a common emotional ploy that tries to pressure you into going along with the crowd. It plays on people's natural urge to belong to a group.

EXAMPLES Everyone agrees that a free-market economy is best.

The general consensus is that Pearl Buck was not as great a writer as Toni Morrison.

See Ch. 2

Since "everyone agrees," if you don't agree too there must be something wrong with you! Remember, though, that the hallmark of a well-educated person is the ability to think critically, which requires an independent mind.

❽ Using a red herring

Anything that draws attention away from the main issue under discussion (in the way that the scent of a fish might distract hunting dogs) is a *red herring*. Politicians are notoriously adept at using this type of evasive tactic, as are advertisers.

EXAMPLE At a press conference, Senator Gladhand is asked about campaign contributions he has received from X Corporation and how they will affect his votes in the Senate. He responds by saying that X Corporation is a "good citizen" and that "American business contributes greatly to America's prosperity."

By shifting attention to American business and away from this particular corporation, the Senator is guilty of using a red herring.

Red herrings can be seen in much modern advertising (especially on TV), where instead of addressing the merits of the product, the ad diverts attention to something else (a beautiful landscape, beautiful people, funny dogs, and so on).

9 Assuming that two wrongs make a right

Another way to deflect attention away from an issue is by using the "two wrongs make a right" fallacy. In this ploy, the arguer defends an accusation of wrongdoing on his or her part by claiming that the other side is guilty of similar or worse wrongdoing. For example, if a local politician defended the city's high crime rate by saying that crime is even worse in other cities, she would be diverting attention away from the real issue, her own city's crime rate.

10 Appealing to bias

Using words with strong positive or negative connotations can exploit the biases of an audience. Like other emotional fallacies, the appeal to bias disregards rational thought but can still be effective in influencing readers or listeners. A bumper sticker saying "Your kids and my taxes go to St. Pedophile's" might be effective with readers who have an anti-Catholic bias. More fair-minded readers, however, would notice its loaded language ("St. Pedophile's") and gross overstatement and quickly dismiss it.

EXERCISE 4.7 The Internet, like other media, is fertile ground for logical and emotional fallacies. Log on to one of the political newsgroups and find two examples of fallacious reasoning. Analyze each according to the principles discussed in this chapter.

See 21c–2

4i Structure the argument

There are numerous ways to structure an argument. After looking at four of the most common ones, we will consider ways to decide which method to select and whether to use an inductive or a deductive arrangement.

❶ Using the classic five-part method

The classic method, which dates back to antiquity, has five parts.

1. Introduce the topic, explain why it is important, and state or imply your thesis.
2. Provide enough background information so that readers will be able to follow your argument.
3. Develop your argument. If you did not state your thesis in step 1, state it here. Support it with appropriate evidence, compelling appeals, and sound reasoning.
4. Acknowledge and refute possible objections and counterarguments, using good evidence and reasoning. Various objections can be dealt with in different parts of the paper. For example, you may want to cite one or more counterarguments early in the paper in order to introduce some of your main points as refutations.
5. Conclude by reemphasizing the importance of the issue and the main points of your argument.

Angela Napper's essay on cybercensorship follows this pattern exactly.

❷ Using the problem and solution method

The problem and solution method involves describing a problem and then proposing one or more solutions to it. This pattern is common in reports, memos, and other forms of business and technical writing. For example, a memo might state, "Some people can't get here in time for our 10:00 a.m. meetings. Do you think we could change the starting time to 10:15?" The key to this method is to clearly identify the problem before stating the solution. The problem and solution method is a good choice when (1) the audience agrees on the nature of the problem and (2) the possible solutions are few in number. In situations where these conditions do not exist, you are likely to have to spend too much time defining the problem and discussing the various solutions. A good example of the problem-solution method can be found in the sample memo in 3h.

❸ Using the Rogerian method

The aim of the Rogerian method is to defuse a hostile audience. The arguer begins by characterizing the opponent's position in terms the opponent can accept and then presents his or her own position in a form that respects both the opponent's and the arguer's views. Once a dialogue has been established, the differences between the two sides can be explored. For example, in her essay on Net theft, Kirsten Parsons begins by noting that unlicensed copying off the Internet "has become an accepted practice," one that "we know we can get away with." By framing the issue in this way (in particular, by using the collective pronoun *we*), she establishes common ground with her readers before going on to argue against Net theft.

See 3f

❹ Using the narrative method

Storytelling is a powerful and persuasive form of presentation, especially if the narrator has a lot of credibility with the audience. But because a skeptical reader may not be willing to generalize from the experience of the narrator, the personal narrative is not effective in college writing unless it is backed up by other kinds of support.

See 3h

In her essay, Kirsten Parsons uses two stories in making her argument. She starts off with a brief narrative illustrating a common instance of unwitting Internet theft. Written in the form of a dialogue, it is likely to engage readers' interest. Then, on page 2, she imagines shoplifting a Hobbes doll from Walmart, using this story to argue that Net theft carries much less risk of detection than physical theft from a store. But she backs it up with references to Web sources that discuss the issue in broader terms.

❺ Selecting a method

Which method works best? The answer depends mainly on how your audience is likely to react to what you have to say. In any argument, your readers will probably agree with you on some issues and disagree on others. The usual strategy is to structure the argument so that the agreed-upon parts come first and the more contentious parts later. This way, you can establish common ground with your readers before going on to more difficult matters.

TechHelp

Keeping Track of an Argument

1. Analyze your audience and topic, and then select an appropriate argument structure.
2. Open the outlining feature of your word-processing software.
3. List your main points from most important to least important, and plug them into the outline according to the argument structure you have selected.
4. Under each point, indicate your supporting evidence and basic line of reasoning.
5. Check the hierarchical structure of your outline. Make sure each point is distinct and independent. If two points say similar things, select one as a main point and make the other a supporting point under it.
6. Draft your paper as you normally would, but shift to your outline occasionally to make sure you are staying on track.

If you know, for example, that your readers are concerned about the same problem you are, the problem and solution method would be a good choice. If your readers know you personally and respect your experience and knowledge, you could start out with a personal narrative. If you and your readers have broadly divergent viewpoints, the Rogerian method is useful because you start out by stating the readers' position—something you know you can agree on. The classic method is popular in college writing because all it presumes about the readers is that they will take the time to read the entire paper carefully; thus, the first few paragraphs can be devoted to introducing the topic and providing whatever background information the readers need.

Although each of these four patterns can be used in its pure form, they can also be combined in different ways. For example, you could tell a personal narrative in the first part of the problem and solution method, or you could take a Rogerian approach in the first part of the classic method to establish common ground with a hostile reader. Indeed, expert writers often combine techniques in interesting ways.

EXERCISE 4.8 Outline Angela's essay, showing how it follows the classic five-part structure.

4j Electronic argument

Traditional forms of argument, as described above, depend on a model of communication in which a writer (or speaker) produces a complete argument that is then read and evaluated by a passive, "captive" reader. With the advent of Internet-based forms of communication, however, argument itself has taken on new forms. Email, newsgroups, listservs, blogs, and instant messaging all use an interactive, dialogic form of communication that promotes an interactive form of argument. In this conversation-like environment, there is great pressure on participants to take turns, with no one dominating the floor. The interaction provides little opportunity for any one person to lay out an extended argument in its entirety; rather, one must be content to offer a quick, abbreviated argument or even, in some cases, just make a single point.

The give-and-take nature of these electronic forms of argument calls for some adaptations.

1. If you want to contribute an argument to an ongoing discussion (for example, in a newsgroup or a blog), make sure you are up to date on how the topic has been discussed up to that point. By reading previous posts, you can avoid simply repeating what has already been said (which might only irritate other participants).
2. Do provide enough context, however, so that the reader knows what you are referring to. One or two sentences should suffice.
3. Limit your response to whatever you can say on a single screen. In most cases, this means making only one or two well-supported points. Most people do not want to scroll through page after page of print.
4. Consider adding links to Web sites containing relevant supporting information.

See 20b-4

5. Make your point concisely and precisely. Take time to edit and proofread.
6. Before hitting the SEND button, read your message over and make sure you're comfortable with its content and tone. Remember that electronic postings are often read by a larger and more diverse audience than the writer anticipates.

Another, albeit less interactive, form of electronic argument can be found on Web sites. Unlike either traditional arguments (laid out in one piece from

TechHelp

Designing an Argument for a Web Site

1. Make the opening screen both visually and textually appealing, so as to capture the interest of your readers. Establish the issue that your argument addresses.
2. Decide on your main pieces of supporting evidence and put clearly labeled links to these items on the opening screen.
3. Cluster your claims and your supporting evidence so that each page of your Web site has unified content.
4. Use graphics only as needed to support your argument, not for decoration.
5. Include a "For Further Reading" link to other Web sites dealing with the same topic as well as some that present alternative views. This material could enrich the reader's experience and, if nothing else, will enhance your credibility.

See 20b-4

See 19c

See 20a-2

See Ch. 20

start to finish) or the interactive types of arguments just described, Web site arguments are dispersed over hypertext links. For example, the main claims may be on a single page, but the supporting evidence may be found on other pages or even at other linked sites. Visitors can navigate the site in any number of ways, and so a creator who wishes to present an argument has to somehow induce visitors to navigate the site in a way that brings out the full force of that argument. Following the general principles of good Web site design should help, as should the more specific guidelines in the TechHelp box above.

See 21d

EXERCISE 4.9

1. If one of your classes has an electronically managed course environment (*Blackboard*, *WebCT*, etc.) with a discussion board, log on to it and make a comment to an ongoing argument, using the above guidelines.
2. If your campus newspaper or local newspaper has a "reader comment" feature, find a story that captures your interest and write a response to it, using the above guidelines. (Your local newspaper may let you use a pseudonym.)

4k Visual argument

Visual images can communicate ideas in powerful ways, and this power extends to argument. Consider, for example, the poster from *Adbusters.com* shown below.

See Fig. 4.1

The image of what appears to be Joe Camel sitting in a hospital bed with his sunglasses off and a downcast look on his face is highly attention-getting. Because it's so different from the standard Joe Camel ads we're used to seeing, we're inclined to look closely at it. This causes us to notice the words *Joe Chemo* and perhaps even read the "Surgeon General's warning" that "smoking is a frequent cause of wasted potential and fatal regret." We quickly understand that this is a parody of the Camel ads: the likable icon of smoking now undergoing chemotherapy (presumably against lung cancer) is meant to persuade viewers to stop smoking.

In this case and in countless others, the visual and the verbal work together; both are indispensable. Together they make what could be considered

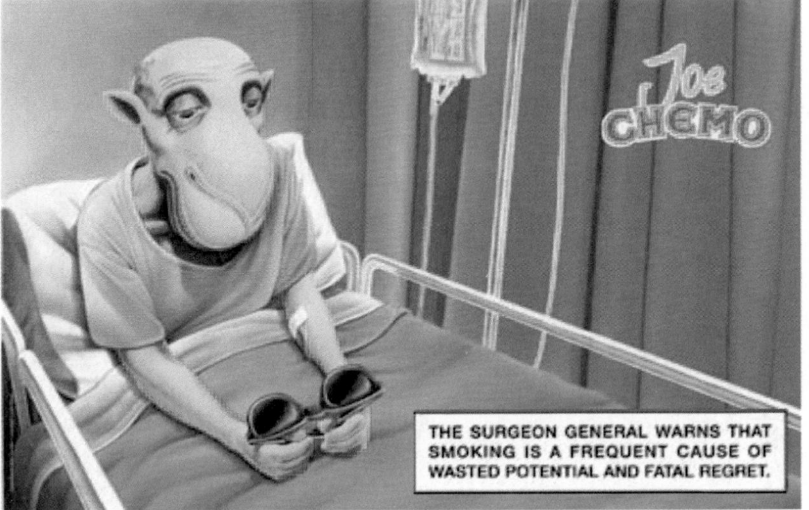
Joe
CHEMO
THE SURGEON GENERAL WARNS THAT SMOKING IS A FREQUENT CAUSE OF WASTED POTENTIAL AND FATAL REGRET.
Source: www.adbusters.com

Figure 4.1 Joe Chemo Ad.

the *beginning* of an argument in that they implicitly express a thesis: the poster implicitly makes a claim about the danger of smoking. Visual images are often powerful in drawing attention to some issue, but visuals alone cannot present a full argument. That is, visuals by themselves cannot make a clearly stated claim (4a), cannot provide sufficient supporting evidence (4d), cannot consider and refute alternative views (4e), cannot build a compelling case (4g), and cannot avoid logical and emotional fallacies (4f); for all these things, you need language. But visual images and language together can form a very powerful combination.

Figure 4.2 ▶ Carbon Dioxide Emissions from Residential Energy Use

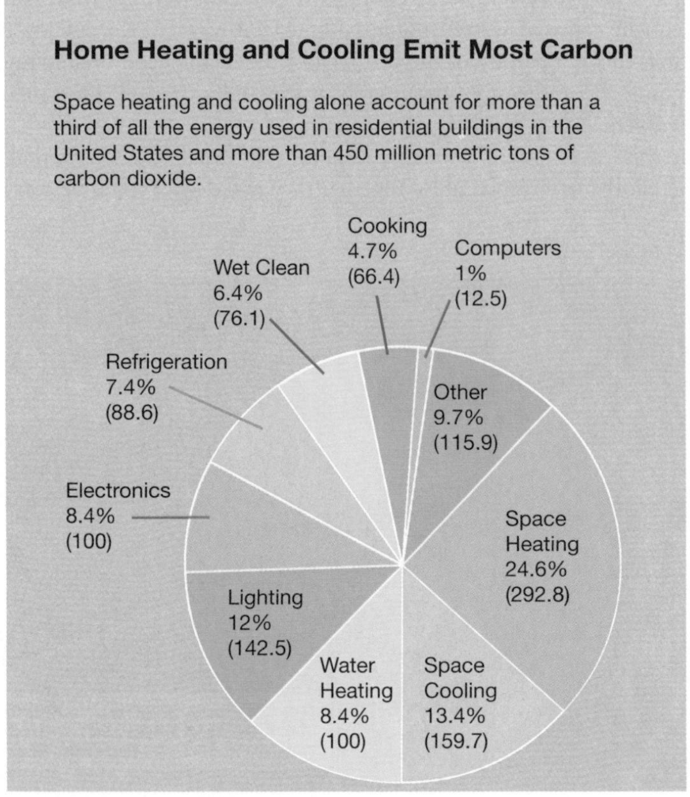

Source: CQ Researcher, December 2008

Although argument is conducted mainly through language, it can be strongly supported by pictures, graphs, or other forms of visual representation. Figure 4.2. is taken from a report that argues for ways to reduce our carbon footprint. Although the pie chart shows that there are many different sources of carbon dioxide emissions from the average residence, the caption focuses on heating and cooling as the main culprits. In this way, the two media work together: the colorful chart draws our attention and emphasizes the large role played by heating and cooling, while the words and numbers give us precise data and a main point.

See Ch. 25

Whenever you are constructing an argument paper or oral presentation, look for ways to enhance your argument with visual support. (For further discussion of the use of graphics, see 19c.)

FOR COLLABORATION Together with one or two classmates, find an argument essay that lacks visual support (some suggestions: the essay by Glenn Sacks in Chapter 2, the essay in this chapter by Angela Napper, or an article in the campus newspaper). Working separately, come up with ideas for adding visual support. Then compare the results and discuss them.

5 Structuring Paragraphs

FAQs

- Why do I need to learn how to structure paragraphs?
- What is a topic sentence, and why is it important to my writing? (5a)
- How long should my paragraphs be? (5f)
- How do I link my paragraphs together? (5g)
- How do I write effective introductory and concluding paragraphs? (5h)

Writing paragraphs

A **paragraph** is a sentence or group of sentences that develops a main idea. Paragraphs serve as the primary building blocks of essays, reports, memos, and other forms of written composition. In Shakespeare's time, a single paragraph could go on for pages, but English paragraphs have evolved into shorter and shorter units. This trend seems likely to continue, as it is now common to find paragraphs of only one or two sentences in news reports, advertisements, memos, and Internet communications.

Well-written paragraphs facilitate quick skimming and help readers stay focused on the main ideas so that they can understand and evaluate the text. To promote this kind of readability, paragraphs should be unified, coherent, and adequately developed, while flowing from one to the next as smoothly as possible.

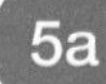

5a Write unified paragraphs

A **unified paragraph** focuses on and develops a single main idea. This idea is typically captured in a single sentence, called a *topic sentence.* The other sentences in the paragraph, the *supporting sentences,* should elaborate on the topic sentence in a logical fashion.

❶ Using a topic sentence

A **topic sentence** gives readers a quick idea of what the paragraph as a whole is about. It is a good idea to place the topic sentence at the beginning of a paragraph, where it provides a preview of the rest of the paragraph. A topic sentence should, if possible, do four things:

- provide a transition from the preceding paragraph,
- introduce the topic of the paragraph,
- make a main point about this topic, and
- suggest how the rest of the paragraph will develop this point.

Here is an example:

> During the past decade or two, children have slipped into poverty faster than any other age group. One of six white U.S. children, two of every five Latino children, and almost one of every two African-American children are poor. These figures translate into incredible numbers—approximately *18 million* children live in poverty: 9 million white children, 4 million Latino children, and 5 million African-American children. [Underscores added.]
>
> —James M. Henslin, *Sociology*

The opening sentence of this paragraph serves as a transition from the preceding paragraph (on child poverty as a new social condition), establishes the topic (child poverty in the United States), makes a main point about it (the percentage of individuals living in poverty is growing more quickly for children than any other age group), and allows the reader to guess that the rest of the paragraph will provide evidence supporting this point.

In a series of paragraphs, the first sentence of each paragraph should serve as a transition from the preceding paragraph. Often, you can make the first sentence both a topic sentence and a linking sentence, as it is in this example (a continuation of the preceding example).

> According to sociologist and U.S. Senator Daniel Moynihan, this high rate of child poverty is due primarily to a general breakdown of the U.S. family. He points his finger at the sharp increase in births outside marriage. In 1960, only 5 percent of U.S. children were born to unmarried mothers. Today that figure is *six times higher*; and single women now account for 30 percent of all U.S. births. The relationship to social class is striking, for births to unmarried mothers are not distributed evenly across

> the social classes. For women above the poverty line, only 6 percent of births are to single mothers, while for women below the poverty line this rate jumps to 44 percent. [Underscores added.]
>
> —James M. Henslin, *Sociology*

The expression "this high rate of child poverty" restates the main topic of the preceding paragraph and thus links the two paragraphs. The topic sentence immediately expresses a new idea ("is due primarily to a general breakdown of the U.S. family"), which represents the main point of this paragraph. The rest of the paragraph supports this point with relevant statistics.

In Web messages, especially email, using short topic sentences and tightly linked paragraphs will help you to avoid the conversational tendency to ramble on with an unfocused message.

2 Placing the topic sentence

The paragraph opening is not always the best location for a topic sentence. Sometimes writers use the first sentence of a paragraph to provide a transition, making the second sentence the topic sentence. In the following example, the writer uses this technique in consecutive paragraphs.

> Of all the places I visited, of all the people I met, one keeps coming back to me again and again: Karma Ura, the Bhutanese scholar and cancer survivor. "There is no such thing as personal happiness," he told me. "Happiness is one hundred percent relational." At the time, I didn't take him literally. I thought he was exaggerating to make his point: that our relationships with other people are more important than we think.
>
> But now I realize Karma meant exactly what he said. Our happiness is completely and utterly intertwined with other people: family and friends and neighbors and the woman you hardly notice who cleans your office. Happiness is not a noun or verb. It's a conjunction. Connective tissue. [Underscores added.]
>
> —Eric Weiner, *The Geography of Bliss*

The topic of the first paragraph ("There is no such thing as personal happiness") is introduced not in the opening sentence but in the second sentence. The first sentence serves a transitional function, connecting this paragraph to the one preceding it. Likewise with the second paragraph: the first sentence serves only as a transition to the second sentence, which contains the paragraph topic.

Occasionally a topic sentence falls at the end of a paragraph, either as a summary or as a restatement of a topic sentence appearing earlier in the paragraph.

> Analytical, creative, and practical thinking often are used together. For example, consider the question of why people become depressed. You would use analytical thinking to evaluate the quality of a theory of why people become depressed. You would use creative thinking to come up with your own theory of why people become depressed. But because you would draw on other people's thoughts, you would necessarily combine analytical and creative thinking. You would use practical thinking to decide how to help someone who is depressed come out of his or her depression. But in order to help the person, you would need to analyze which theory of depression to use and you would have to formulate your own ideas about how to help the person. So, in thinking as a student of psychology and helping someone, you would combine the three kinds of thinking: analytical, creative, and practical. [Underscores added.]
>
> —Robert J. Sternberg, *Pathways to Psychology*

Sometimes no topic sentence is needed. If a paragraph continues the topic covered in the preceding paragraph or simply narrates a series of events or a set of details whose common theme is obvious, you may decide that an explicit topic statement is unnecessary.

EXERCISE 5.1 Open one of your textbooks to the beginning of a section and examine the first five paragraphs. Do they all seem unified? Does each paragraph have a topic sentence? If so, where is it located?

EXERCISE 5.2 Examine the paragraphs in Kirsten Parsons's paper (see 3h). Do they all have topic sentences? Are the topic sentences properly positioned? Are they well worded? Could some of them be improved? If so, how?

5b Write coherent paragraphs with clear patterns of organization

All paragraphs should be *coherent*: each sentence should connect logically with those preceding and following it, enabling readers to move smoothly from one idea to the next. One way to create coherent paragraphs is through the use of organizational patterns.

Among the countless ways to organize paragraphs, certain patterns are especially common: general to specific, cause and effect, comparison or contrast, definition, classification, problem and solution, narrative or process description, exemplification, and physical description. These organizational patterns mirror typical ways people categorize experience. Readers look for familiar patterns, so the more explicitly you signal those patterns, the easier it will be for readers to see the logic connecting your ideas.

1 Organizing by general to specific

The sample paragraphs in 5a-1 both illustrate general-to-specific organization, in which a general statement is followed by specific supporting details. This is one of the most common paragraph patterns, and the general statement serves effectively as a topic sentence. Here is another example of general-to-specific ordering.

Generalization, topic sentence

Specific details

> Every society creates an idealized image of the future—a vision that serves as a beacon to direct the imagination and energy of its people. The ancient Jewish nation prayed for deliverance to a promised land of milk and honey. Later, Christian clerics held out the promise of eternal salvation in the heavenly kingdom. In the modern age, the idea of a future technological utopia has served as the guiding vision of industrial society. For more than a century utopian dreamers and men and women of science and letters have looked to a future world where machines would replace human labor, creating a near-workerless society of abundance and leisure.
>
> —Jeremy Rifkin, *The End of Work*

This paragraph leads off a chapter in Rifkin's book called "Visions of Techno-Paradise." Rifkin uses the general-to-specific pattern to first situate his discussion in universal terms ("every society") and then narrow his focus to the "near-workerless society" that will be the subject of the chapter.

It is possible, though much less common, to organize a paragraph in the reverse order—that is, from specific to general. The specific details grab the reader's attention and are followed by increasingly more general comments culminating in a summarizing statement.

2 Organizing by cause and effect

Many pieces of writing link phenomena through cause-and-effect relationships. The cause-and-effect organizational pattern is especially appropriate for explaining why something happened the way it did or predicting some future sequence of events. Paragraphs organized with this pattern usually include transitional words and phrases such as *therefore, thus, as a result, since, because, consequently, for this reason,* and *thereby.* Two of these are italicized in this example.

> Fetal alcohol syndrome (FAS) occurs when alcohol ingested by the mother passes through the placenta into the infant's bloodstream. *Because* the fetus is so small, its blood alcohol concentration will be much higher than that of its mother. *Thus,* consumption of alcohol during pregnancy can affect the infant far more seriously than it does the mother. Among the symptoms of FAS are mental retardation, small head, tremors, and abnormalities of the face, limbs, heart, and brain. [Italics added.]
>
> —Rebecca J. Donatelle and Lorraine G. Davis, *Access to Health*

Topic sentence

Cause-effect details

❸ Organizing by comparison or contrast

Many writing situations call for comparing or contrasting two or more ideas, issues, items, or events. Comparison focuses on similarities; contrast focuses on differences. In either case, the writer evaluates two or more subjects on the basis of one or more criteria. Transitional words and phrases commonly found in comparison or contrast paragraphs include *however, on the one hand/on the other hand, similarly, in contrast, just as, while, but,* and *like.*

A paragraph based on the comparison or contrast pattern should be structured either (1) by evaluating one subject completely and then turning to the other or (2) by focusing on each criterion, one at a time. For example, in a comparison of the two sociological theories known as structural functionalism and conflict theory, arrangement by *subject* might look like this:

Subject A: Structural functionalism
- *Criterion 1:* How it views society
- *Criterion 2:* What it emphasizes

Subject B: Conflict theory
- *Criterion 1:* How it views society
- *Criterion 2:* What it emphasizes

Arrangement by *criteria,* on the other hand, would look like this:

Criterion 1: How it views society
- *Subject A:* Structural functionalism views society as . . .
- *Subject B:* Conflict theory views society as . . .

Criterion 2: What it emphasizes

Subject A: Structural functionalism emphasizes . . .

Subject B: Conflict theory emphasizes . . .

Which type of structural arrangement is better? It depends on where you want to focus the reader's attention—on the subjects or on the criteria.

The following paragraph is organized according to subject. The liberal view of affirmative action is contrasted to the conservative view, and the criteria used (such as group fairness and individual fairness) are secondary.

Topic sentence

A: Liberal view

B: Conservative view

> The role of affirmative action in our multicultural society lies at the center of a national debate about how to steer a course in race and ethnic relations. In this policy, quotas based on race (and gender) are used in hiring and college admissions. Most liberals, both white and minority, defend affirmative action, saying that it is the most direct way to level the playing field of economic opportunity. If white males are passed over, this is an unfortunate cost we must pay if we are to make up for past and present discrimination. Most conservatives, *in contrast*, both white and minority, agree that opportunity should be open to all, but say that putting race (or sex) ahead of people's ability to perform a job is reverse discrimination. They add that affirmative action stigmatizes the people who benefit from it because it suggests that they hold their jobs because of race (or sex), rather than merit. [Italics added.]
>
> —Adapted from James M. Henslin, *Sociology*

4 Organizing by definition

In academic writing, defining important new terms sometimes requires a complete paragraph. The term is usually introduced in a topic sentence at the beginning of the paragraph and elaborated on in the sentences that follow. Here is a typical example of a paragraph organized by definition, from an introductory biology textbook.

Topic sentence: definition

> *Nucleic acids* are large complex organic molecules composed of carbon, oxygen, hydrogen, nitrogen, and phosphorus atoms. Nucleic acids are polymers of individual monomers known as *nucleotides.* Nucleotides are molecules built up from three basic parts: a special 5-carbon sugar, a phosphate group, and a molecule generally known as a nitrogenous base.

Individual nucleotides can be linked together by covalent bonds to form a polynucleotide. There are two basic kinds of nucleic acids: *ribonucleic acid (RNA)*, which contains the sugar ribose, and *deoxyribonucleic acid (DNA)*, which contains the sugar deoxyribose. Despite their name, nucleic acids are not strongly acidic. [Italics added.]

Details

—Kenneth R. Miller and Joseph Levine, *Biology*

A paragraph organized by definition should include a formal definition—that is, a statement "*X* is a *Y* that ______________," where *X* is the *term* being defined, *Y* is the *class* it belongs to, and ______________ is a set of *distinguishing features*. In the above example, such a definition is found in the first sentence: "Nucleic acids are large complex organic molecules [that are] composed of carbon, oxygen, hydrogen, nitrogen, and phosphorus atoms."

EXERCISE 5.3 Search the Web to find an interesting article of at least 300 words in a newspaper or other source. Download it. Then use the FIND function of your word processor to locate all instances of *however, on the one hand/on the other hand, similarly, in contrast, just as, while, but*, and *like*. In each case, identify the subjects that are being compared.

❺ Organizing by classification

To make sense of the world, people routinely classify things according to their characteristic parts. Classification is an essential part of the analytic work you do in school. Whenever you search the Internet or a library, for example, you focus your quest by using a search system that classifies topics in helpful categories. In academic writing, entire paragraphs are often devoted to classifying some concept. Paragraphs organized by classification normally introduce the topic in the first sentence and the various subtopics in the following sentences. Using these subtopics as the grammatical subjects of their respective sentences, as in this example, creates grammatical parallelism, which makes it easy for readers to see the structure of the paragraph.

See 5e

The United States Army traces its origin to the American Continental Army of 1775. The Army has primary responsibility for military operations on land. Its basic combat units are infantry, armor, and artillery. *The infantry* remains the Army's backbone. Transported to the front lines by helicopter or personnel carrier, foot soldiers engage the enemy in direct

Topic sentence

Three subtopics set off by parallelism

small-arms combat in order to seize and hold ground. *Armor* is the cavalry of the modern army, except that the armored soldiers today move into battle in tanks instead of on horseback. *Artillery* operates the cannons of the battlefield and antiaircraft missile installations. [Italics added.]

—Robert L. Hardgrave, Jr., *American Government*

6 Organizing by problem and solution

In the problem and solution organizational pattern, a particular problem is identified and one or more solutions are proposed. Usually the writer states the problem explicitly, though sometimes it is only implied. Posing the problem in the form of a question is especially attention-getting.

Problem (topic sentence)

Solution

What can be done about drug abuse among students? First, we should distinguish between experimentation and abuse. Many students try something at a party but do not become regular users. The best way to help students who have trouble saying no appears to be through peer programs that teach how to say no assertively. The successful programs also teach general social skills and build self-esteem (Newcomb & Bentler, 1989). Also, the older students are when they experiment with drugs, the more likely they are to make responsible choices, so helping younger students say no is a clear benefit.

—Anita E. Woolfolk, *Educational Psychology*

EXERCISE 5.4 An Internet or library research project is frequently a search for a solution to a problem—finding specific information on an issue that the researcher wants to explore and clarify. Such a search often turns up key words and ideas that suggest an even more interesting issue.

Choose an issue to research. Write it down as the problem, and then list two or three "solutions," or pieces of information you hope or expect to find in your search. This list could be the outline for a descriptive paragraph with a problem and solution pattern.

Conduct the search, and list the information you actually discover in a second column. Do you need to revise your problem statement in light of what you found? Write a coherent problem and solution paragraph using the information.

7 Organizing by narrative or process description

Narratives and process descriptions present events in a time-ordered sequence. A **narrative** tells a story; a **process description** depicts a step-by-step procedure. In either case, the writer recounts events in chronological order, using verb tenses consistently and not jumping from one time frame to another.

When narrating the plot of a literary work, you normally use the present tense, as in this brief description of Ibsen's *Enemy of the People*.

> The play is set in a little town which makes its living from the tourists who come to take its famous baths. Dr. Stockmann discovers that the waters have been contaminated by the local sewage system. He insists that the facts must be revealed, and expects that the city authorities will be grateful for his discovery. To his astonishment he finds that he has become an enemy of the people because he insists that the truth be known and the evil corrected. Doggedly he decides to fight on for truth even though the whole community is against him.
>
> —Vincent F. Hopper and Bernard D. N. Grebanier, *Essentials of European Literature*

Topic sentence

Time-ordered sequence of events

When writing a process description, keep the verb tenses consistent, and use an occasional transitional word such as *first, second, finally, after, then,* or *while.* Notice the transitional words in this process description paragraph.

GO See 28e

> Land reclamation is the careful burying and grading of refuse that is dumped into prepared sites, such as deep trenches, swamps, ponds, or abandoned quarries. *After* the refuse has been dumped, it is sprayed with chemicals to kill larvae and insects. *Then* it is compacted by heavy equipment, covered with a thick layer of clean earth, and graded so that it blends with surrounding land. [Italics added]
>
> —*The New Book of Knowledge*

Topic sentence

Process description

8 Organizing by exemplification

Examples are a powerful way to make difficult concepts understandable. A paragraph organized by **exemplification** often follows a general-to-specific pattern. The concept to be explained is introduced in general terms at the beginning, and then one or more specific examples are offered to make it meaningful, as in this paragraph.

General claim

Supporting examples

The importance of equality is often contrasted with that of liberty. Indeed, someone's position in the alleged conflict between equality and liberty has often been seen as a good indicator of his or her general outlook on political philosophy and political economy. For example, not only are libertarian thinkers (such as Nozick 1974) seen as anti-egalitarian, but they are diagnosed as anti-egalitarian *precisely because* of their overriding concern with liberty. Similarly, those diagnosed as egalitarian thinkers (e.g., Dalton 1920, Tawney 1931, or Meade 1976) may appear to be less concerned with liberty precisely because they are seen as being wedded to the demands of equality.

—Amartya Sen, *Inequality Reexamined*

9 Organizing by physical or spatial description

A descriptive paragraph paints a picture of a person, place, or object by appealing to the reader's senses (sight, sound, touch, taste, or smell). It emphasizes details, which should be carefully selected to give the reader a vivid sense of what is being described. The following example brings to life something that most people can only imagine—the microscopic structure of ordinary soil.

Topic sentence

Physical details

The spaces between the soil grains offer a variety of habitats. The smaller pores and channels are filled with water, the larger ones mostly with air. Clay soils have narrow, threadlike channels that twist and taper downward; in sand, as might be imagined from seeing it on the beach, there are air pockets in the tiny spaces between the grains. Draped upon the skeleton of the soil are the sinews and flesh of a teeming life: each particle, even the finest, has a tight-fitting film of oxides, water, bits of organic matter. This skin is what gives life to the soil underfoot.

—Peter Farb, *Living Earth*

FOR COLLABORATION Textbooks make heavy use of the organizational patterns described on the previous page. Working with a classmate, each of you take a textbook from one of your other courses and open it randomly to any page containing three or more whole paragraphs. Together, analyze and discuss these paragraphs in terms of their organizational patterns.

⑩ Organizing by mixing patterns

Although many paragraphs can be structured using one of the organizational patterns just described, you may sometimes want to express ideas in a way that does not conform to any one pattern. In such cases, do not be afraid to mix two or more organizational patterns. Just make it clear what pattern you are following at any one time. Here is an example of a paragraph that mixes patterns.

> Popular music has never been a stranger to controversy or opposition. Herman Gray has noted three periods of particularly strong opposition: the response to jazz in the early part of the century, the reaction against rock 'n' roll in the 1950s and 1960s, and the most recent wave of controversy associated with heavy metal and rap. No matter what the genre, certain themes such as a fear of the connection between music and sexuality tend to run through all three periods. Such concerns may be expressed either as the fear that sensual rhythms can overcome rationality or that lyrics that push the boundaries of decorum can undermine moral values. Because of these fears, each genre has been linked at various times to drug abuse, lawless behavior, and general moral decline. In turn, all of these problems have been projected to some degree onto race.
>
> —Reebee Garofalo, *Rockin' Out*

Topic sentence

Classification

Details

Cause-effect

This paragraph basically follows the exemplification pattern, with sentences 2–6 exemplifying the generalization stated in the first sentence. But sentence 2, describing "three periods," is a classification statement. And sentences 5–6, marked by "Because . . . ," follow the cause-and-effect pattern. As long as pattern shifts are clearly marked, mixed paragraphs can be comprehensible and coherent.

EXERCISE 5.5

1. What paragraph patterns do you see Kirsten Parsons using in her draft essay?
2. Examine the first four paragraphs in this chapter, and determine what patterns of organization they exemplify. (Remember that a paragraph may use more than one pattern.)

FOR COLLABORATION The topic sentence often suggests the organizational pattern that governs the rest of a paragraph. Try to guess what pattern might follow each of these topic sentences. Then compare and discuss your answers with those of a classmate.

1. *Self-disclosure* is the sharing of personal information with others. ____________
2. Self-disclosure can be a double-edged sword, for there is risk in divulging personal insights and feelings.____________
3. Self-disclosure can affect our dealings within health-care settings. ____________
4. Stores are exploiting your senses and sentimentality in order to make you comfortable, happy, and willing to spend more money.____________
5. In *Ties That Stress: The New Family Imbalance*, David Elkind writes that in today's postmodern family, the needs of hurried children have been sacrificed to the needs of their harried parents.____________

5c Write coherent paragraphs with sentence-linking techniques

Beyond using standard patterns of organization, you can increase the coherence of your paragraphs by creating clear connections between sentences. This can best be done through the use of transitional expressions, repetition of words or phrases, or references to earlier information.

1 Using transitional words and phrases to link sentences

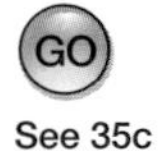

See 35c

Transitional words and phrases such as those listed in the Guidelines box in 5c-1 are useful for linking sentences. These expressions differ somewhat in degree of formality. For example, *furthermore* and *consequently* are more formal than *besides* and *so.* Being aware of these differences will help you strike a consistent tone in your writing.

Notice how effective the transitional expressions are in making this paragraph more readable.

> In many cultures, if not all, touching between adults can indicate sexuality; *however*, the conditions under which it does vary greatly. *For instance*, in the United States, men do not walk around holding each others' hands, unless one is blind or otherwise infirm and the other appears to be helping him get around. *Otherwise* this is seen as a strong indication

Guidelines

Using Common Transitional Words and Phrases

	Use
To show cause and effect	*therefore, thus, consequently, as a result, for this reason, so, so that*
To compare	*similarly, likewise, in like manner, also*
To contrast	*however, on the one hand/on the other hand, in contrast, conversely, but, yet, nevertheless, nonetheless, on the contrary, still*
To show addition	*and, in addition, also, furthermore, moreover, besides*
To indicate time	*before, now, after, afterwards, subsequently, later, earlier, meanwhile, in the meantime, while, as long as, so far*
To give examples	*for example, for instance, specifically, namely, to illustrate, that is*
To conclude or summarize	*in conclusion, to conclude, in summary, to summarize, in short, in other words, therefore, thus, in reality*
To generalize	*in general, for the most part, as a general rule, on the whole, usually, typically*
To emphasize a point	*indeed, in fact, as a matter of fact, even*
To signal concession	*of course, naturally, although it is true that, granted that*

of homosexuality. This is true of female pairs *as well*. *Yet*, in some countries, such as Egypt or at least some of Latin America, same-sex hand-holding or arms around the waist or shoulder indicates solidarity only. In those cultures, *typically*, one wouldn't touch a decent woman in public. [Italics added.]

—Elaine Chaika, *Language: The Social Mirror*

❷ Repeating key words to link sentences

A paragraph almost always has key words. Repetition of these words helps the reader focus on the topic at hand. Exact repetition can become tiresome, however, so good writers sometimes use synonyms or paraphrases. (The THESAURUS feature of your word processor can help you choose synonyms.)

Exact repetition can also be used for special effect. In this example, repetition of the word *growth* acts like a drumbeat, emphasizing the authors' skepticism about the virtues of economic growth.

> Modern economics worships *growth. Growth* will solve poverty, the theory goes. *Growth* will increase our standard of living. *Growth* will reduce unemployment. *Growth* will keep us apace with inflation. *Growth* will relieve the boredom of the rich and the misery of the poor. *Growth* will bolster the GNP, boost the Dow and beat the Japanese. A rising tide lifts all boats. [Italics added]
>
> —Joe Dominguez and Vicki Robin, *Your Money or Your Life*

After introducing the key word *growth* in the first sentence, the writers repeat it six times in the next six sentences. The reiteration of *growth* keeps the reader's focus on the main topic of the paragraph and thus increases its coherence.

Pronouns allow you to refer to the main topic without repetition. If one sentence after another has the same topic, you can often refer to it with a pronoun without confusing the reader. For example, the writers could have substituted *It* for *Growth* at the start of the third sentence. Using pronouns can also help reduce wordiness. Just make sure the pronouns always have clear referents.

See Ch. 36,
See Ch. 33

❸ Using old and new information to link sentences

Another way to link sentences is to refer to "old information," something readers are already familiar with, at the beginning of a new sentence. These references to old information usually consist of repeated words, pronouns, or words marked by *the* or *this*, inserted into the subject position. Here is an example from a textbook on public speaking.

See 26b

> In a classic study, Ralph Nichols asked both good and poor listeners what their listening strategies were. *The poor listeners* indicated that they listened for facts such as names and dates. *The good listeners* reported that they listened for major ideas and principles. *Facts* are useful only when you can connect them to a principle or concept. In speeches, *facts* as well as examples are used primarily to support major ideas. *You* should try to summarize mentally the major idea that the specific *facts* support. [Italics added]
>
> —Steven A. Beebe and Susan J. Beebe, *Public Speaking*

Notice how the grammatical subjects of sentences 2–5 repeat concepts that are mentioned earlier and that two of these repetitions include the article *the*. The concepts "good [listeners] and poor listeners" are first mentioned in the first sentence. Both of these concepts are then referred to as old information in sentences 2 and 3. The concept "facts" is new information in sentence 2 but old information in sentences 4–6. In all cases, the reference to the old information occurs at the beginning of the sentence. Even the pronoun *you* starting off sentence 6 refers to old information; it acknowledges the ongoing existence of the reader and is preceded by the *you* in sentence 4.

Keeping the sentence subject fairly short makes it easier for readers to understand the sentence and see how it fits into the paragraph as a whole. Using repeated words or pronouns to refer back to old information should help you keep sentence subjects short. Notice how short the sentence subjects are in the preceding example paragraph: *The poor listeners, The good listeners, Facts, facts, You, facts.*

EXERCISE 5.6

1. Use the guidelines in section 5c to analyze the coherence of the paragraphs in Kirsten Parsons's draft essay. Make appropriate changes where necessary.
2. Photocopy a page from one of your textbooks. Underline the grammatical subject of each sentence. (The subject is usually that part of the main clause that precedes the verb; see 28b if you need help.) What is the average length of the sentence subjects? How many of them refer to old information?

5d Be consistent with verb tense, person, and number

See 28e

Verb tenses help create a time frame for readers. When you jump from one verb tense to another within a paragraph, you disrupt the paragraph's coherence and risk confusing the reader. Consistent use of pronouns also helps readers. For example, after using the first-person plural (*we, us, our*), do not switch to the singular (*I, me, my*) or to second or third person (*you, they, . . .*) unless there is a good reason to do so.

See Ch. 35

Watching Monday Night Football on ESPN has become a ritualistic practice for countless American sports lovers. Every Monday night during the NFL season, ~~we would~~ millions of fans gather to watch the "old pigskin" being thrown around. This activity can be experienced in the comfort of ~~your~~ one's own home, at parties, or in popular sports bars. ~~A typical viewer will~~ Viewers especially enjoy the opening segment of the program, with all its pyrotechnics and special effects. ~~They~~ The producers really know how to put on a show at ESPN! ~~If you~~ For those who like football, MNF is not to be missed.

5e Use parallelism to make paragraphs coherent

Many paragraphs contain embedded "lists"—that is, sets of sentences that have equivalent values and roles. In such cases, it is important to establish **parallelism** between the sentences by giving them the same grammatical structure. This helps the reader to easily see the relationship between sentences. (Chapter 38 discusses parallelism *within* sentences.) Notice how the two parallel sentences in this paragraph set off the contrast between two living situations.

> [Centuries ago,] divorce was common and easy for most Native American women. *If a woman was living with her husband's family, she simply took her belongings and perhaps the children and went home to her parents. If the couple was living with the wife's parents or if the dwelling was considered hers, she told the man to leave, throwing his clothes and paraphernalia out after him.* Common grounds for divorce were sterility, adultery, laziness, bad temper, and cruelty. [Italics added]
>
> —Carolyn Niethammer, *Daughters of the Earth*

To make it easy for the reader to spot the two situations she is talking about, Niethammer describes them in separate, grammatically parallel sentences (*If a woman was living with . . . If the couple was living with . . .*).

Another good example of parallelism can be found in the sample paragraph about economic growth in 5g.

EXERCISE 5.7

1. Analyze the paragraphs in Kirsten Parsons' essay draft for consistency of verb tense, person, and number. If you spot any errors, suggest appropriate changes.
2. Pick three paragraphs from one of your textbooks, and identify the techniques (such as use of an organizational pattern, sentence links, repetition, or parallelism) that give them coherence.
3. From a Web page, copy three interesting paragraphs that use repetition. Put them into a new document, and use the FIND function to locate all occurrences of key words. If there seems to be too much repetition or not enough, rewrite the paragraphs to better use repetition and other techniques that improve coherence.

5f Decide on appropriate paragraph length

Each paragraph should be long enough to adequately develop its main point. Thus, paragraph length depends mainly on how complicated the topic is. The important thing is to make paragraphs complete and unified. As long as you do this, your paragraphs are not likely to be excessively long or excessively short.

Also, bear in mind that desirable paragraph length can vary from one type of writing to another. In college essays, most paragraphs are likely to be three to six sentences long. In contrast, email messages often have short paragraphs, sometimes with only one or two sentences, like a conversation. Similarly, newspaper reports usually have very short paragraphs (one to two sentences), in part to grab the reader's attention. But newspaper editorials aim for more reflective reading and so have somewhat longer paragraphs (two to three sentences). Paragraphs in the *Encyclopaedia Britannica* may contain twelve or more sentences.

5g Link paragraphs with key words

In any series of paragraphs, a reader should be able to move easily from one paragraph to the next. If a paragraph picks up where the preceding one left off, provide at least one link in the first sentence of the new paragraph.

Determining When to Start a New Paragraph

It is appropriate to start a new paragraph when

- You have adequately covered one topic and are shifting to a new one.
- The current paragraph is getting too long and you want to give the reader some "breathing space."
- You want to emphasize a point by using it as the opening sentence of a new paragraph.
- You want to set off a contrasting point.

Links can be transitional words and phrases or expressions referring to old information and preceded by terms such as *this, these,* or *such.*

> Economic recovery after the war was especially strong in West Germany. Between 1950 and 1958, West Germans doubled their industrial output. The people of West Germany who were facing starvation in 1945 enjoyed one of the highest standards of living by the late 1950s.
>
> "This 'economic miracle'" continues theme of first paragraph
>
> There were several reasons for *this "economic miracle."* The Marshall Plan provided crucial financial aid toward recovery. Under the Marshall Plan, the United States channeled almost $1.4 billion in aid to Germany. Also, since many industrial plants had been destroyed during the war, the Germans rebuilt modern, much more efficient ones. [Italics added]
>
> —Burton F. Beers, *World History*

EXERCISE 5.8

1. Analyze the paragraphs in Kirsten Parsons's essay draft to see if there are connecting links between them. If they don't, how could she change them?
2. Select an essay from a book you have used in one of your courses or an editorial from a daily newspaper, and choose one section of four or five paragraphs. In the first sentence of every paragraph except the first, identify all the words and phrases that help connect that paragraph to the one preceding it.

5h Construct effective introductory and concluding paragraphs

The beginning and the end of a document are the two places where readers are most likely to give full attention to what they are reading. Thus, it is particularly important that you write effective opening and closing paragraphs.

See 6b-7

1 Writing an introductory paragraph that will focus the reader's attention

When readers start to read a piece of writing, they want to know what it will be about and whether it will be interesting—and they want to know quickly. Therefore, you should write an opening paragraph that is informative and interesting. The opening paragraph should always be appropriate to the genre: an academic essay requires a different sort of opening than, say, a letter of complaint. In all genres, however, an introductory paragraph should accomplish four things. It should

1. identify the topic of the piece,
2. stimulate reader interest,
3. establish a tone or style, and
4. enable readers to anticipate what comes next.

See 4a

For an essay, the opening paragraph should also include a thesis statement.

Here is an example of an ineffective introductory paragraph. It comes from a student paper on how the media can affect our behavior.

ORIGINAL

> Some people think that watching TV or seeing movies is only entertainment, that it doesn't affect their behavior. Are you one of them? If so, you will be surprised to learn that media effects are extremely powerful. This paper will talk about those effects. It will describe how the media contributed to the Nazi hate that killed so many Jews and fueled Ted Bundy's killing spree. We should, as a nation, stand up to the tyranny of violent media.

This is a weak introduction for several reasons. First, it's unlikely to stimulate reader interest. Few readers, even if they are media addicts, will let themselves be put in the role laid out in the opening sentences. Second, we don't have a clear sense of what's to come, other than a description of Nazi propaganda and Ted Bundy's killing spree. Finally, there's no clear tone or style to this introduction. It jumps from a direct appeal to the reader to a description of media effects to, finally, an exhortation about media "tyranny."

Consider now the revised version:

REVISED

Identifies the topic and stimulates reader interest

Establishes a tone

States the thesis

Reese's Pieces candies played only a small role in the popular film *ET*, but sales of the candy were boosted by 65 percent after the movie. A similar effect was seen in an episode of *Happy Days*. Fonzie decides to get a library card and mentions that the library is cool: "Anybody can get one of these suckers [library cards] and you can meet chicks there, too." After the show aired, there was a 500 percent increase nationally in library card registration. If the media affect little decisions such as what candy we buy or whether or not we decide to register for a library card, could they affect the big decisions that we make? In this paper I will argue that the media play a leading role in some of the problems we have in society today.

This version is much more compelling. It starts with two vivid examples of the topic under discussion—examples that a college audience can relate to. Thus, it not only identifies the topic but does so in a way almost sure to stimulate reader interest. The next two sentences then nicely raise the stakes, from candy selection to "big decisions" and "problems that we have in society." We can guess what's likely to come next—a discussion of media effects and how they have a strong effect not just on individual decision making but on our society as a whole. All of this is carried off in an engaging style that is likely to encourage the reader to read on.

Here is another example of an effective opening paragraph:

Identifies the topic (happiness)

Stimulates interest with examples readers can relate to

If Daniel Gilbert is right, then you are wrong. That is to say, if Daniel Gilbert is right, then you are wrong to believe that a new car will make you as happy as you imagine. . . . You are wrong to think that you will be more unhappy with a big single setback (a broken wrist, a broken heart) than with a lesser chronic one (a trick knee, a tense marriage). You are wrong to assume that job failure will be crushing. You are wrong to expect that a death in the family will leave you bereft for year upon year, forever and ever. You are even wrong to reckon that a cheeseburger you order in a restaurant—this week, next week, a year from now, it doesn't really matter when—will definitely hit the spot. That's because when it comes to predicting exactly how you will feel in the future, you are most likely wrong.

Implies a thesis: allows reader to anticipate an explanatory discussion

—Jon Gertner, "The Futile Pursuit of Happiness"

See Ch. 24

While some types of writing, such as business letters and memos, have fairly conventional openings, other types of writing give you more latitude in ways to draw reader interest. For example, if you are writing an exploratory essay, you have some freedom in how you construct your opening paragraph. You can adopt a relaxed style, and you can hint at your thesis instead of stating it explicitly. If you are writing an argumentative essay, your readers will expect you to use a more formal style and tighter structure, and they will look for an explicit thesis in the first paragraph.

❷ Writing a concluding paragraph that creates a sense of completeness

The concluding paragraph of an extended piece of writing should not leave the reader hanging but, rather, should neatly tie things up. Except in a very short essay, the concluding paragraph should reiterate your main point, preferably not by simply restating it but by adding something to it. Ideally, it should also stimulate the reader to think beyond what you have already said. See the Guidelines box on Effective Strategies for Concluding Paragraphs; sometimes two or more of these techniques work well together.

Following is an example of a good concluding paragraph. It comes at the end of an essay comparing American and Asian ways of life.

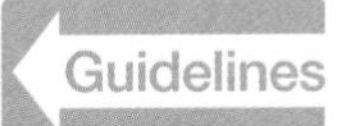

Effective Strategies for Concluding Paragraphs

- Pick up on a theme or idea that was mentioned at the beginning.
- Give an apt quotation.
- Pose a thought-provoking question.
- Reiterate your main point.
- Advocate a course of action.
- Speculate about the future.

Picks up on theme mentioned at beginning

Reiterates main point

Speculates about the future

Advocates a course of action

The Asian approach to the division of labor is not one that Americans want to emulate, or can. Except in emergencies we have believed in satisfying individual desires rather than suppressing them. But, to come back to the central point, we shouldn't fool ourselves about the sheer effectiveness of the system that the Asian societies have devised. Their approach to child-rearing, as to economic development, is worse for many individuals but better for the collective welfare than ours seems to be. The Asian model is not going to collapse of its own weight, unlike the Soviet communist system. So the puzzle for us is to find ways to evoke similar behavior—moderation of individual greed, adequate attention to society's long-term interests, commitment to raising children—within our own values of individualism and free choice.

—James Fallows, "A Few Pointers"

Here are "before" and "after" versions of a concluding paragraph from a student essay titled "The Human Genome Project: Ethical, Social, and Legal Considerations."

ORIGINAL

The genetic revolution brings us breathtaking new technology that calls for extreme caution. The ability of genetic science to determine our birth and predict our future health is increasing at an amazing pace, and the overwhelming amount of new information puts government under increasing pressure to pass legislation.

Although this version reiterates the main theme of the essay, it fails to introduce anything new or stimulate the reader to think beyond what's already been said. The revised version is much more engaging.

REVISED

Gives an apt quotation

Reiterates main point

"Without adequate safeguards, the genetic revolution could mean one step forward for science and two steps backward for civil rights. Misuse of genetic information could create a new underclass: the genetically less fortunate" (Jeffords 1252). A Gallup poll by the Institute for Health Freedom found that 93 percent of adults questioned want their permission to be obtained before their genetic information is used. Under current practice those 93 percent would have their constitutional right to privacy taken away.

> This is a breathtaking new technology we have, and extreme care should be taken. The ability of genetic science to determine our birth and predict our future health is increasing at an amazing pace, and the overwhelming amount of new information should tell our government representatives that it is time to enact new legislation regulating it.

Advocates a course of action

This revised version is far better than the original for several reasons. First, it draws the reader in with a powerful quotation. Second, it presents new information in the form of survey data, underscoring the political explosiveness of this topic. And finally, it concludes with a clear call for action.

EXERCISE 5.9

1. In light of the above discussion, evaluate the introductory paragraph and the concluding paragraph of Kirsten Parsons's essay draft on Net theft (see 3h). For practice, construct an alternative version of each paragraph, using one or more rhetorical devices not used by Kirsten.
2. Apply the same procedure to an essay found in one of your course readings, in a news magazine or newspaper, or on the Internet.

6 Rewriting

FAQs

- Can I be a fair judge of my own writing? (6a)
- How can the computer help me revise my writing? (6b)
- What is the difference between revising and editing? (6b–6c)
- How do I proofread on screen? (6d)
- How do I give feedback to my classmates? (6e)

6a Shift from writer to reader

To be a skillful reviser, you must put yourself in the place of your reader. When you read your own work, however, you may have trouble seeing what you have actually written. Instead, you may see only what you *intended* to write. This section offers some strategies to help you shift roles from writer to reader when you review your writing.

❶ Allowing time to review your draft

If possible, allow at least a day between the time you finish a draft and the time you read it over to revise, edit, and proofread. You will be astonished at how much more clearly you can view your writing if you take a break from working on it. If you are facing a tight deadline, even several hours away from the work can be helpful. Try to schedule more than one session for revising. Writing stored electronically is much easier to revise because you do not need to retype or recopy the entire text after each change.

❷ Reading your own work critically

As you read your work critically, pay attention to different major elements during each subsequent reading. These elements are focus, coherence, organization, development, tone, and format.

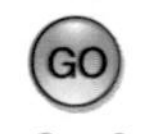
See 6a-2

Focus

Focus refers to how well you adhere to your topic and your thesis throughout a piece of writing. As you reread a draft, check that each paragraph relates in some way to the thesis. Is each of your examples and supporting details needed for your argument? It is more important to maintain focus than to add length. Your readers expect you to fulfill the commitment made by your thesis. If you go off on a tangent, they may lose interest.

See 5a

Coherence

The various components of a piece of writing should "stick together," from sentence to sentence and from paragraph to paragraph. This writing glue is known as **coherence**. Make certain that your sentences and paragraphs are linked through transitional words and phrases. Your goal is to make your writing *cohere*—that is, form a unified whole.

See 5b

Organization

If your piece is well organized, it follows a direction set by the thesis and the opening paragraphs. If you have decided on a particular pattern of **organization**, check to be sure you followed through with that pattern. For example, if you decided to use the cause-and-effect pattern, make certain that you covered both causes and effects. You may find as you reread a draft that some paragraphs would be more effective in a different order or that your closing argument is not your most persuasive and so should not be last.

See 5b

Development

Development refers to the depth of coverage given key ideas. As you reread the text, you may identify points that are underdeveloped. Look particularly for ways in which you have supported your thesis and developed each part of your organizational pattern. For example, if you decided on a problem and solution pattern, have you developed each alternative solution sufficiently, arriving at a best solution? Be certain that each of your main points is backed up within its own paragraph by supporting details, illustrations, or examples.

See 5b-6

TechHelp

Revising Your Document

1. Change the way your text looks in any of these ways:
   a. Change the spacing of your text lines from double to triple.
   b. Change the font size from 12 points to 15 points.
   c. Insert a page break after each paragraph.
   d. Change the margin width from 1 inch to 2 inches.
2. Save the reformatted text under a different name.
3. Print out the reformatted text.
4. Read each paragraph of the printed text carefully, using the Checklist of Critical Reading Questions for Revision
5. Write suggestions for revisions in the margins.
6. Try different views (draft, print, Web, or full screen reading layout), using the VIEW menu.

See 6a-2

Tone

The language you chose to use conveys the **tone**—that is, your attitude toward your topic and your readers. Your tone may be formal or informal, perhaps even humorous. Revisit your rhetorical stance to determine whether the tone you adopted is appropriate to your persona, logical arguments, and readers. If you are writing on a serious topic, you are likely to use a formal tone. Your sentences and paragraphs will be relatively long; your word choices may be abstract; you will use very few personal references and contractions—in general, you will establish a considerable distance between yourself and your readers. If you are writing on a less solemn topic, you may strike an informal tone. Your sentences and paragraphs will be shorter; you will use less abstract language; you may include contractions and perhaps first-person pronouns—your readers will feel a closeness to you, the writer.

GO
See 3b-2

See 3b-3

Format

If your draft is more than a page or two long, consider using the **format** to help the reader navigate the text. By using headings to delineate the major parts, you can help the reader recognize the organizational structure. However, if a piece is relatively short, headings are usually more distracting than helpful.

Critical Reading Questions for Revision

Focus

- ✓ Do I have a clearly stated thesis that controls the content?
- ✓ Do all the major points refer back to and support my thesis?
- ✓ Are all the examples and illustrations relevant to my point?

Coherence

- ✓ Are individual sentences and paragraphs held together by transitions?
- ✓ Are the transitions I have used the best available?
- ✓ Have I avoided overusing any transitions?

Organization

- ✓ Are the major points arranged in the most effective order?
- ✓ Are my strongest arguments placed near the end?
- ✓ Are the supporting points arranged to their best advantage?
- ✓ Have I followed through with the organizational pattern I selected?

Development

- ✓ Is my thesis adequately supported?
- ✓ Are my major points backed up by specific details and examples?
- ✓ Is there at least one paragraph for each major point?
- ✓ Are my paragraphs developed proportionately?

Tone

- ✓ Is my tone appropriate to my rhetorical stance and consistent throughout?
- ✓ Do my language choices reflect my intended tone?
- ✓ Have I eliminated contractions and first-person pronouns if the piece is formal?

Format

- ✓ Does the "look" of my text help convey its meaning?
- ✓ Is the font I have used readable and appropriate to the topic?
- ✓ Are the headings descriptive and helpful in orienting the reader?
- ✓ Have I used graphics and illustrations appropriately?

Note, too, that using headings is more common in some fields than in others. For example, papers written in APA format tend to have headings, while those in MLA format may not. Also, make sure that the font you choose is appropriate to the final product; a font that is suitable for a brochure might not be appropriate for a research paper. Standard fonts for all types of writing include Times New Roman and Courier.

See 19b-7

❸ Preparing a revision outline

One technique that may help you evaluate a piece of writing is preparing a revision outline. When you have a first draft and perhaps some peer or instructor comments on it, you can create a revision outline by updating the original outline for the piece to reflect the weaknesses of the draft. To begin to plan for revising, add comments in brackets to the revision outline concerning items you need to change in your draft.

Kirsten used the revision outline in Figure 6.1 to plan changes to her first draft on Net theft.

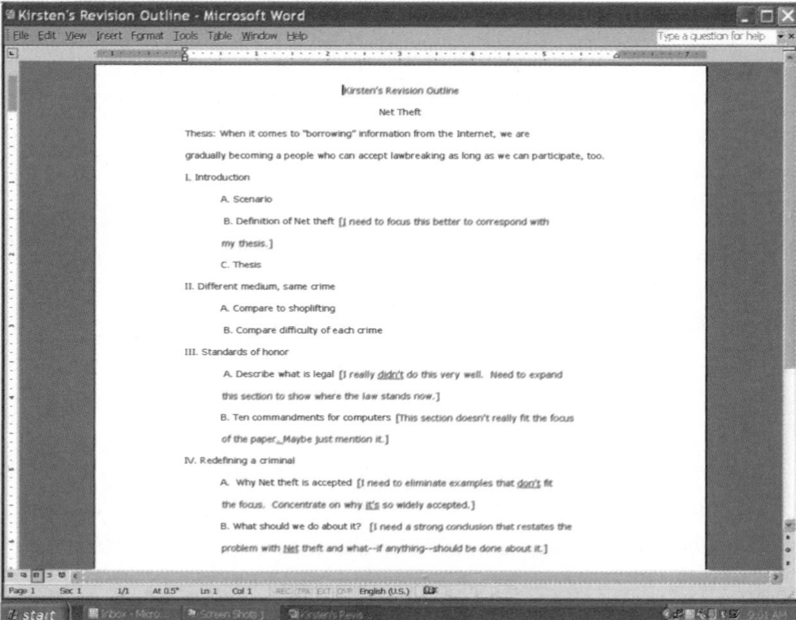

Kirsten's Revision Outline

Net Theft

Thesis: When it comes to "borrowing" information from the Internet, we are gradually becoming a people who can accept lawbreaking as long as we can participate, too.

I. Introduction

A. Scenario

B. Definition of Net theft [*I need to focus this better to correspond with my thesis.*]

C. Thesis

II. Different medium, same crime

A. Compare to shoplifting

B. Compare difficulty of each crime

III. Standards of honor

A. Describe what is legal [*I really didn't do this very well. Need to expand this section to show where the law stands now.*]

B. Ten commandments for computers [*This section doesn't really fit the focus of the paper. Maybe just mention it.*]

IV. Redefining a criminal

A. Why Net theft is accepted [*I need to eliminate examples that don't fit the focus. Concentrate on why it's so widely accepted.*]

B. What should we do about it? [*I need a strong conclusion that restates the problem with Net theft and what--if anything--should be done about it.*]

Figure 6.1 ▶ Kirsten's Revision Outline

EXERCISE 6.1 Reread the rough draft of a paper you are working on. Using the Checklist of Critical Reading Questions for Revision, come up with an overall plan for revising your draft. Prepare a revision outline, and add comments about those items you intend to revise.

See 6a-2

6b Revise

Revising tips

Critical reading can highlight problems of focus, coherence, organization, development, tone, and formatting in your paper. Revising involves adding to the text, deleting from the text, and rearranging information within the text to fix those problems. Using a word-processing program makes these tasks easy. Knowing what to add, delete, and rearrange is the tricky part.

1 Revising for focus

Revisit your working thesis, and revise it to more accurately reflect the overall point of your text. Then revise each paragraph, one by one, to ensure that each is focused on only one idea, which supports the thesis. Try changing the format of your text to help you revise each paragraph. Delete any paragraphs that are not related to the thesis.

See Ch. 5

Kirsten revised her second paragraph to focus more clearly on the idea of "borrowing" from the Internet. Notice how she eliminated references to phone cards and other products and included music, software, written texts, and graphics instead.

> Unfortunately, this is a common request ~~within our society~~ today. In spite of laws that prohibit the unlicensed copying ~~of music, written materials and movies,~~ ^in some circles^ it has become an accepted practice to reproduce another's work without paying for it. Similarly, this ^practice^ has spread to the Internet where access to ^music^ software, ^written texts, graphics,^ ~~phone cards,~~ and other products is convenient and fast. ~~Graphics quotes, articles and many other various things~~ ^These items^ can be copied for personal use with ease, but often no credit is given to the original author.

❷ Revising for coherence

Wherever you notice that sentences do not flow smoothly in your draft, add appropriate transitional words and phrases. Look particularly at the links between paragraphs. Insert transitions to help the reader follow the flow of the text. Words or phrases such as *however, on the one hand/on the other hand, but,* and *in addition* can help the reader see the relationships between ideas. Add these words to your text at appropriate places. If you are using one transitional word too frequently, check the thesaurus in your word-processing program for alternatives.

See 5c-1

❸ Revising for organization

Once you have decided how to improve the organization of your text, use CUT, COPY, and PASTE to move parts of your text. Rearrange the words,

TechHelp

Rewriting Your Document

1. **CUT.** Highlight the text that you want to CUT from your document by using the mouse. When the text is highlighted, click on the scissors (CUT) icon. The cut text will be transferred to the word-processing program's clipboard until you decide to PASTE it somewhere else in the document or in another document or application, such as an email message.
2. **COPY.** Highlight the text to be copied and click on the double page icon (COPY). The text to be copied will still appear in your document, but a copy of it will also be transferred to the clipboard until you decide where to PASTE it. Use COPY when you want to preserve your original document intact.
3. **PASTE.** Move the cursor to the location in the document where you want the cut or copied text to appear. Click on the clipboard icon (PASTE) to paste the text from the clipboard into your document.
4. **MOVE OR DRAG TEXT.** You can also "click and drag" highlighted text to a new location in a document instead of using CUT and PASTE. After highlighting the text, click on the selected text with your mouse and, while still holding down the mouse button, drag the text to the new location. You will see a small square next to the cursor arrow to indicate that text is being dragged. When you release the mouse button, the text will be pasted into the new location.

sentences, and paragraphs into the most effective order. Be sure to check for coherence after rearranging.

4 Revising for development

Your argument is stronger if you include many concrete examples or details. If you are writing an informal piece, do not hesitate to add anecdotes or narratives of personal experiences to give life and personality to your writing. If you are writing a formal paper, you can add information from sources that support your arguments, provided you appropriately document those sources. Additional explanatory details, evidence, examples, or illustrations from your notes can be inserted into your text.

See Chs. 12–14

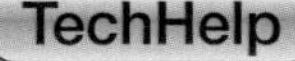

Comparing Document Drafts

1. Regardless of what software you use, the simplest way to compare two drafts is to open both files concurrently in two windows and scan for differences. The advantage of this method is that you are not likely to mix up the documents or inadvertently change something in one instead of the other. The disadvantage is that differences are more difficult to spot.
2. When you begin to revise a document, turn on the TRACK CHANGES feature from the REVIEW menu. Select HIGHLIGHT CHANGES so that your changes will be visually highlighted on your document. You will have the option later of accepting or rejecting the highlighted changes—either individually or for the entire document. You will want to accept or reject changes frequently to prevent your document from becoming illegible.
3. If you forgot to turn on TRACK CHANGES, you can still use the COMPARE DOCUMENTS feature. Open one of the documents and then select COMPARE. The differences between the two documents will be highlighted. Check to see that your revisions were substantive—that is, you did not merely tinker with the text but actually added, deleted, or rearranged material in a significant way.
4. You may also wish to use the SHOW DOCUMENT SOURCE option found on the COMPARE menu.

See Fig. 6.2

While working on her revision outline, Kirsten discovered that she needed to focus and develop her discussion of the legalities of the Internet (item IIIA in her outline). She rewrote the paragraph as follows:

ORIGINAL PARAGRAPH

Information about copyright laws, what is legal and what isn't is available on the Net as well. Web Issues at the Copyright Website (www.benedict.com) provides information about what can be copied from the Net and how to do it properly. ~~Another page specifically discusses using graphics (PageWorks available at http://www.snowcrest.net/kitty/hpages). Those who decide to break these "laws," run the risk of being ostracized by a group such as Netbusters! This vigilante group seeks to prevent what they call "bandwidth robbery" by informing Netusers about its devastating results. The Netbusters homepage has a place to report clandestine computer activities if you know of any perpetrators.~~

REWRITTEN PARAGRAPH

Organizations and individuals have tried to establish standards of conduct for Internet use. For example, the Computer Ethics Institute wrote its Ten Commandments for Computer Ethics, which includes such obvious "rules" as "Thou shalt not use the computer to steal" (Roach). But what is stealing when it comes to materials found on the Internet? The *Copyright Website* asserts that any texts or graphics that you find on the Internet are by their very nature published and thus are "copyrighted" (O'Mahoney). This means that in order to use anything from someone else's Web site, you need their permission. If you put a comic strip such as Calvin and Hobbes onto your homepage, you run the risk of being sued for violation of copyright.

Revising tone and style

❺ Revising for tone

In rereading, you may decide that your tone is either too formal or too informal. To revise your tone to be more formal, expand contractions into their full forms, combine some short sentences to make longer sentences, and

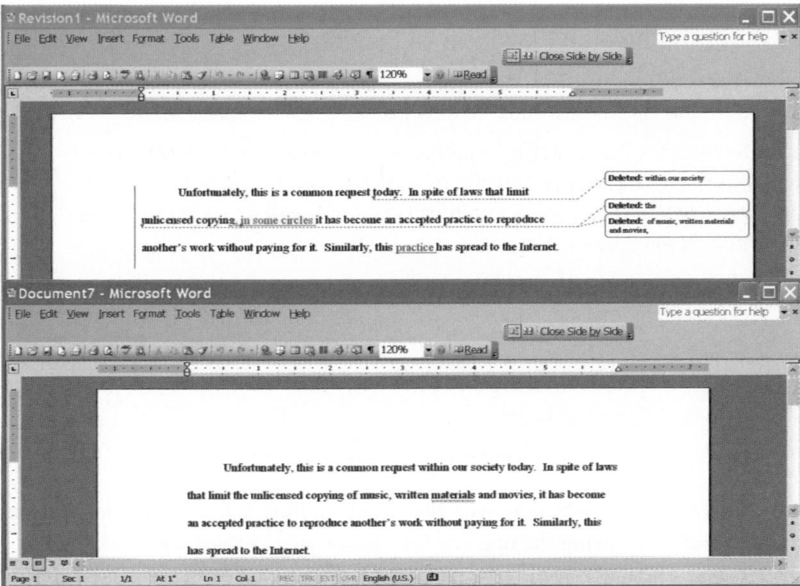

◀ **Figure 6.2** Comparing versions of a document with and without TRACK CHANGES

change informal diction or slang into more formal wording. The TechHelp box on the next page offers guidance in using the FIND AND REPLACE function of your word-processing program as you revise for tone.

6 Revising for format

To convey your information in a more visual way, you may want to add formatting more commonly found in a brochure or a newsletter. You can import and insert graphics to illustrate your text at appropriate points. Try using different fonts by selecting them from the FONT menu. Remember, though, that readability of your text is the most important goal; choose fonts accordingly.

See 20a or 20b

See 19b-7

7 Writing effective openings, closings, and titles

Openings

Writing introductions

Writers have very little time in which to grab the reader's attention—usually only a few seconds. That is why a piece's opening, or lead, is so important. But

TechHelp

Using the SEARCH Function to Revise

1. Activate your word-processing program's FIND AND REPLACE function from the EDIT menu. (Note: It may be called EDIT > REPLACE.)
2. Instruct the computer to search your document for a troublesome word, phrase, or punctuation mark (for example, the apostrophe in contractions). A contraction may be a marker of a less formal tone than is called for in your paper.
3. As the computer moves to each case of the word, phrase, or punctuation mark in succession, you can decide whether to change it or not.
4. Revise any other troublesome words, phrases, or punctuation marks by initiating further searches.

See 5h

do not let concern over how you will begin become a stumbling block. Many writers find that leaving the opening for the last stages of revision works best.

If appropriate for a particular writing assignment, you can be inventive in your opening paragraph. To grab a reader's attention, try starting your lead with an anecdote or story, quotation, dialogue, or descriptive scene. For example, Kirsten decided to begin with dialogue. Note that in her revised opening, Kirsten also corrected the punctuation for dialogue.

> "Look at this new CD I bought!" Jane exclaims to her friend. Interested, Michael eagerly looks at it. "Wow," he says. "These guys are my favorite group! Mind if I make a copy of it?"

Although some academic writing, by tradition, demands it, most experienced writers will not begin a piece with the thesis, or statement of purpose, such as "This paper will explore the pros and cons of drilling an auxiliary well in Smithfield Canyon." The following example illustrates a traditional academic lead.

AN ACADEMIC LEAD

> This essay examines issues of diversity and literacy education primarily in terms of the concept of *difference* via a new term: *non-negotiable difference.* It argues that networked classrooms provide writing instructors

with unique extra-linguistic cues (body language) that can help teachers and students become more responsive to racial difference.

—Todd Taylor, "The Persistence of *Difference* in Networked Classrooms: *Non-Negotiable Difference*"

See 5h-1

Closings or conclusions

Writing conclusions

A conclusion usually takes the form of a summary, which points the reader back to the text itself, or speculation, which points the reader outside of the text.

A SUMMARY CONCLUSION

Few Interneters would disagree that stealing and reselling software or credit cards is wrong. But fewer still would feel guilty about copying the latest game version of Doom, or some such, rather than forking out $39.95. Unfortunately, that often admirable ethos makes it easier for genuine crooks to perpetrate—and justify—their crimes.

—Michael Meyer and Anne Underwood, "Crimes of the 'Net'"

A SPECULATIVE CONCLUSION

Nevertheless, in the litigations and political debates which are certain to follow, we will endeavor to assure that their electronic speech is protected as certainly as any opinions which are printed or, for that matter, screamed. We will make an effort to clarify issues surrounding the distribution of intellectual property. And we will help to create for America a future which is as blessed by the Bill of Rights as its past has been.

—John Perry Barlow, "Crime and Puzzlement"

Do not feel obligated to limit yourself to a summary conclusion. Sometimes a speculative conclusion will work better. This type of conclusion is most appropriate for papers that point the reader in a new direction, that reflect on the implications of some topic, or that suggest the need for further research.

See 5h-2

Titles

Because the title is the first thing a reader sees, it must spark interest in the reader. The title helps the reader anticipate the topic and perhaps the writer's particular point of view. Kirsten's title, "Net Theft," is descriptive and intriguing, if not particularly clever. It is more important that the title be related to the content than that it be cute or funny.

EXERCISE 6.2 Try out several titles and openings for your piece. Be inventive and playful. To catch your reader's attention, write an opening scene, describe a character, tell a story, give a startling fact or statistic, or make an

TechHelp

Using the Grammar Checker Appropriately

Grammar checkers can be useful in pointing out potential trouble spots, but they have serious shortcomings. First, they overlook many potential problems. Second, grammar checkers flag many things that are not actually problematic. Sometimes the computer misreads a sentence; other times it applies a rule too simplistically. Ultimately, it is up to you to identify and correct any problems in your writing.

1. Customize the grammar checker to your needs.
   a. Open the REVIEW menu, and click on SPELLING AND GRAMMAR.
   b. Click the OPTIONS box, and select PROOFING from the left menu. This page allows you to change how Word corrects and formats your text.
   c. Next to "Writing Style," click on the SETTINGS box, and select the required options for commas in a series, punctuation with quotations, and the number of spaces between sentences. Check all of the grammar options to select them. You can always deselect some later if you so desire.
2. Open a piece of writing that you want to check, and run the grammar checker by clicking on SPELLING AND GRAMMAR from the REVIEW menu—both spelling and grammar checks will run simultaneously.
3. For each item the grammar checker flags, consider the recommended alternative. If you do not understand why something was recommended, consult the HELP wizard (open by clicking the F1 key). If you need more detailed information, consult the relevant section of this handbook.
4. Using all of this information, make your own decision about whether to change an item or leave it as is. Remember, a computerized grammar checker may be wrong; it does not consider your rhetorical stance and its suggestions are only suggestions.

See Checklist 6c-4

See 3b-2

outrageous claim. Then try out several possible conclusions for your piece. Write both a summary conclusion and a speculative conclusion.

FOR COLLABORATION Share your titles, openings, and closings with a peer or a small group of classmates. Which titles and openings do they find most effective? Do they prefer the summary conclusion or the speculative conclusion? Write down any suggestions you receive from your peers.

6c Edit

The goal of editing is to make writing easier to read. During revision, you concentrate on making the piece focused, organized, and well developed. During editing, you concentrate on refining words and sentences. Like a car buff putting the final finish on a classic automobile, an editor "finishes" a piece of writing—in general, refining what has been done and making it aesthetically pleasing as well as functional.

As with revising, writers need to distance themselves from their words before editing to become objective readers of their own writing. Listening to the words as the text is read aloud helps you to see where you need to clarify an idea or where you may have used too many words or expressed thoughts awkwardly.

See Checklist 6c-1

1 Checking sentence structure

Sentence-level editing

As you edit your draft, make sure that your sentences are structured according to the conventions of academic writing. Over the years, scholars have developed a standard formal English used for academic writing. Following the conventions of Standard Edited English will mark you as an educated, careful writer.

See Ch. 41

Once you have checked sentence structure, look for sentence variety, making sure that you have not started most or all of your sentences in the same way or used the same sentence pattern over and over. The most effective writing contains sentences that are both clear and varied. Adding an introductory phrase to one sentence or moving a clause in another will help you achieve variety. Notice how Kirsten revised these sentences.

Editing

Sentence Structure

✓ Are all of my sentences complete (Ch. 31)?

✓ Have I avoided both comma splices and run-on sentences (Ch. 32)?

✓ Do paired elements have parallel structures (Ch. 38)?

Wordiness

✓ Have I avoided using unnecessary words, such as *in order to* instead of simply *to* (Ch. 36)?

✓ Have I replaced two-word and three-word phrases, such as *new innovation* and *repeating recurrence*, where one word is sufficient (Ch. 40)?

Repetition

✓ Have I avoided excessive use of a single word (Ch. 40)?

✓ Have I avoided repetition of a single idea that is not the thesis (Ch. 40)?

Verb Usage

✓ Have I primarily used active rather than passive voice (28g)?

✓ Have I replaced overused, general verbs with more vivid, specific verbs where possible (41a)?

Other Errors

✓ Is my end punctuation correct (Ch. 46)?

✓ Is my internal punctuation correct (commas, Ch. 47; semicolons, Ch. 48; colons, Ch. 49)?

✓ Have I used quotation marks appropriately (Ch. 51)?

✓ Have I used other punctuation marks appropriately (Ch. 52)?

✓ Is my spelling correct (Ch. 45)?

✓ Are my mechanics correct (capitals and italics, Ch. 53; abbreviations and numbers, Ch. 54; hyphens, Ch. 55)?

TechHelp

Checking Sentence Structure on the Computer

1. Scroll up from the end of the document, reading it backwards sentence by sentence.
2. Use the FIND and REPLACE function.
   a. Ask the computer to search for each period in the document (begin either at the start or at the end of the document).
   b. Each time you stop at a period, look carefully at the group of words that precedes it to be sure they form a complete sentence.
   c. Use the FIND AND REPLACE function to review the other punctuation by locating first the commas and then the semicolons.

See Ch. 26

See Chs. 46–52

> Blood rushes to your ears and your heart begins to pound, as your body reacts to the rush of adrenaline. Casting a nervous glance around the nearby aisles, *you decide that* the coast is clear. *You extend* ~~Extending~~ your arm, ~~you~~ grab the orange tiger, place it in your backpack*, and* walk nonchalantly towards the exit.

❷ Checking for wordiness

Many writers tend to overwrite their drafts, using a phrase or clause when a word will do. Unnecessary words can obscure the meaning or make the reader work harder than necessary to understand it. These three examples show how Kirsten edited sentences in her draft for wordiness.

See Ch. 36

> Unfortunately, this is a common request ~~within our society~~ today.
>
> [Kirsten omitted three words that convey no additional meaning.]
>
> Not only ~~are these~~ *is this* ~~practices~~ wrong from a moral *standpoint* ~~viewpoint,~~ but legally, ~~they are~~ *it is* forbidden as well. [By using pronouns to refer back to the previous sentence, Kirsten eliminated wordiness.]

Walking into a store and taking something without paying for it is obviously not *legal* ~~encouraged in our society~~. [Again, Kirsten omitted words that convey no additional meaning.]

See 5c-2

See 6c-2

❸ Checking for repetition

Repeating words is not necessarily a bad thing. Using a key term more than once in a text may help you achieve coherence. However, you do not want to use nonessential words repeatedly. Notice that Kirsten deleted the nonessential word *society* twice as she edited her draft sentences.

❹ Checking for verb usage

Weak verbs can lead to ineffective writing. Review your verbs to be certain that they are appropriate and effective. Kirsten edited the verbs in one of her final paragraphs as follows:

The problem, as Meyer and Underwood also point out, is that the "Wild West culture of the Internet promotes an anything goes attitude in Net surfers" (113). Most Internet users *would agree* ~~think~~ that stealing phone card numbers and selling them is wrong. However, many would not *agree* ~~think~~ that sharing a pirated copy of a game was illegal or even wrong. Similarly, many would not *find* ~~think~~ that using a cool graphic *from* ~~found on~~ someone else's page was unethical

TechHelp

Checking Word Choice on the Computer

1. Make a list of words that you suspect you may have overused.
2. Use the FIND and REPLACE function of your word-processing program to find each instance of each word in your document.
3. Use the THESAURUS function to help you think of alternative wording.
4. Be sure you are familiar with any word you decide to use from the thesaurus so that you use it appropriately for the context.

or illegal. The freewheeling world of the Internet ~~finds~~ considers Capitalist rules like "copyright" to be offensive.

Knowing Typical Grammar Checker Rules

Cross-references to sections in this book appear in parentheses.

✓ Make clear comparisons (27f, 36i).
✓ Prefer active voice to passive voice (28g, 36d).
✓ Make subjects and verbs agree in number (29a).
✓ Avoid long noun strings (30b).
✓ Use comparative and superlative forms correctly (30e).
✓ Avoid multiple negatives (36j).
✓ Avoid sentence fragments (31).
✓ Avoid sentences beginning with *and, but*, or *plus* (31a-2).
✓ Use *who, which*, and *that* correctly (33b).
✓ Avoid misplaced modifiers (34).
✓ Avoid excessively long sentences (36a).
✓ Avoid wordiness (36e).
✓ Avoid long strings of prepositional phrases (36f).
✓ Avoid common word confusions (41a).
✓ Avoid informal expressions in formal writing (41c-1).
✓ Avoid jargon (41d).
✓ Avoid overused phrases and clichés (41f-3).
✓ Avoid sexist expressions (42c).
✓ Use homophones correctly (45b).
✓ Avoid common apostrophe errors (50d).
✓ Avoid capitalization errors (53).
✓ Avoid hyphenation errors in compound words (55a-55b).
✓ Make nouns and their quantifiers agree in number (56f).
✓ Do not use more than one modal auxiliary verb at a time (28c, 57h).

❺ Checking for other errors

In addition to editing for *style*, you will want to edit your text for usage, punctuation, spelling, and mechanics. To be acceptable in college courses as well as in most work settings, your writing must conform to the conventions of Standard Edited English. As the writer, you are responsible for making the text comprehensible as well as technically correct.

See Checklist 6c-1

EXERCISE 6.3 Edit your text, using a combination of strategies outlined in this section. Refer to the sections of the handbook referenced in the Checklist for Editing for help. When you have finished editing, run your word-processing program's grammar checker. Consider its advice carefully before making changes to your text.

6d Proofread

Proofreading strategies

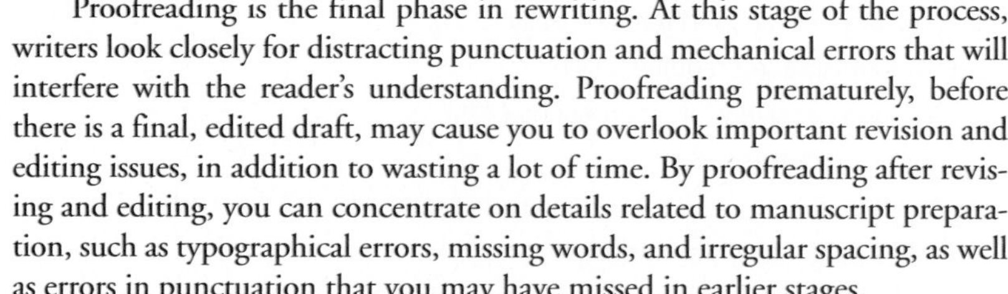

Proofreading is the final phase in rewriting. At this stage of the process, writers look closely for distracting punctuation and mechanical errors that will interfere with the reader's understanding. Proofreading prematurely, before there is a final, edited draft, may cause you to overlook important revision and editing issues, in addition to wasting a lot of time. By proofreading after revising and editing, you can concentrate on details related to manuscript preparation, such as typographical errors, missing words, and irregular spacing, as well as errors in punctuation that you may have missed in earlier stages.

Recent studies have shown that writers who read their texts on screen may not see them as clearly or read them as carefully as do writers who read them in print. Also, proofreading requires reading each word individually, and doing so on a computer screen can be tiring to the eyes. If you choose to proofread on screen, take frequent breaks. Experiment with your own proofreading technique, which may be a combination of on-screen and printout proofreading.

EXERCISE 6.4 Proofread your text, using the suggestions in the Guidelines box on the following page to read it both on screen and in print. Evaluate which method seems to work better for you. Were you able to identify more errors or different errors with either method?

TechHelp

Proofreading On-Screen and in Print

1. When proofreading on screen, use the cursor arrow to scroll down one line at a time, forcing yourself to read each line slowly before reading the next one.
2. Use the VIEW menu to see the text in a variety of layouts: print, full screen reading, Web, outline, or draft layout.
3. View the text two pages at a time, displayed side by side on the monitor. Select the full screen reading layout, and click on the VIEW OPTIONS box in the upper right corner of the screen and then select SHOW TWO PAGES.
4. Move the cursor to the end of the text, and read the sentences in reverse order.
5. Read the text aloud from the screen, slowing down as necessary to attend to the text more closely.
6. If you have a text-reading program, instruct the computer to do the reading aloud, and then listen for errors.

Proofreading Strategies

- **Scroll rapidly through your text** to check for spacing, margins, indents, widows and orphans (single lines and words left alone at the top or bottom of a page), page numbering, and so on.
- **Print the text.** Then wait several hours, or longer if possible, before proofreading it. Whenever possible, proofread a printed copy in addition to proofreading on screen.
- **Use a pointer or ruler** to force yourself to read slowly and deliberately.
- **Proofread the text several times,** using several different layouts from the VIEW menu. Each time, you will pick up additional errors.
- **Change your reading technique** to a proofreading one. Normal reading involves skimming; a typical reader "reads" only two or three words per line. In contrast, proofreading requires that you look carefully at every word and punctuation mark.
- **Ask someone else**—a friend, a relative, or a classmate—**to proofread** the printed text as well.
- **Read your paper aloud**—either to yourself or to a peer, friend, or writing center tutor.

6e Give and receive feedback electronically

When you participate in peer response groups, you are taking part in a writing tradition that is as old as writing itself—writers helping fellow writers. We (the authors of this handbook) often share work with our colleagues, giving and receiving feedback on our professional writing. In fact, we are so much in the habit of gathering feedback on our written work that we feel uncomfortable with the idea of sending anything for publication before it has received a reading from at least one other person, whether that person is a member of our writing group, a coauthor, or an editor. When gathering other opinions, remember that, ultimately, the writing is your own and the feedback you receive should be taken in the spirit of help offered. Comments from readers should not dictate to you the "right" way to write a piece.

1 Using various media for feedback

See 3c-1

In addition to using various media to collaborate with your peers, you can also use various media to give and receive feedback on writing. Types of media include networked classrooms with common drives, class Web sites or blogs, and—perhaps most common—email. Using these various media, it is possible to share with peers anything from a thesis statement to a full draft.

Once you have access to a peer's writing, whether it is located on the class's Web site in file-sharing space or is sent to you as an email attachment, you have various ways in which you can respond. Here are a few suggestions:

See Fig. 6.3

- Read the peer's writing and write your own comments in an email message, clearly pointing out specific lines and paragraphs for which you are suggesting revisions.

See Fig. 6.4

- Open the peer's document and make your own comments in a different colored font or using CAPS or a boldface font. Be sure to save the file with a new name so as to avoid confusion (e.g., CH comments on Blaire draft1.doc).

GO See 6e-3, See Fig. 6.5

- Open the peer's document and make your comments using the DOCUMENT COMMENT feature. Save the file with a new name. You may also wish to use the TRACK CHANGES feature if you are making editing suggestions on the draft.

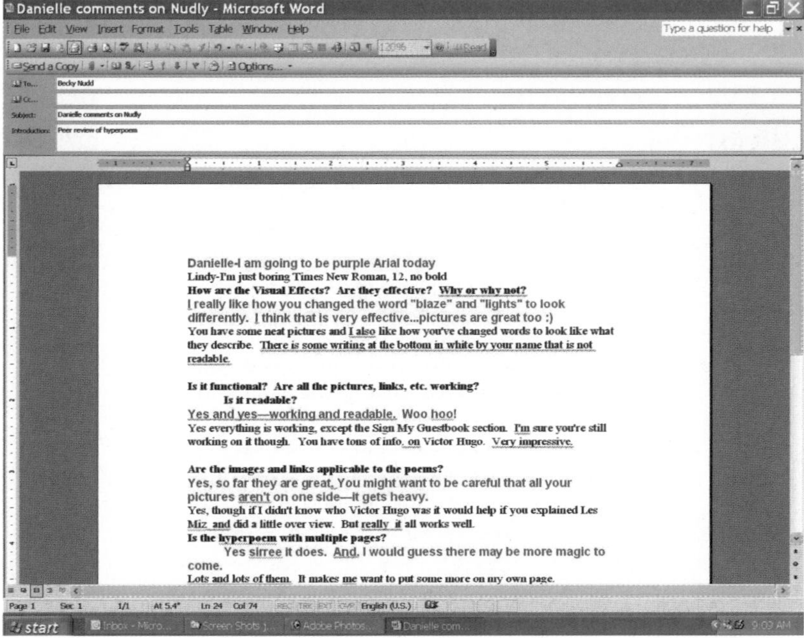

Danielle-I am going to be purple Arial today
Lindy-I'm just boring Times New Roman, 12, no bold
How are the Visual Effects? Are they effective? Why or why not?
I really like how you changed the word "blaze" and "lights" to look differently. I think that is very effective...pictures are great too :)
You have some neat pictures and I also like how you've changed words to look like what they describe. There is some writing at the bottom in white by your name that is not readable.

Is it functional? Are all the pictures, links, etc. working? Is it readable?
Yes and yes—working and readable. Woo hoo!
Yes everything is working, except the Sign My Guestbook section. I'm sure you're still working on it though. You have tons of info. on Victor Hugo. Very impressive.

Are the images and links applicable to the poems?
Yes, so far they are great. You might want to be careful that all your pictures aren't on one side—it gets heavy.
Yes, though if I didn't know who Victor Hugo was it would help if you explained Les Miz and did a little over view. But really it all works well.
Is the hyperpoem with multiple pages?
Yes sirree it does. And, I would guess there may be more magic to come.
Lots and lots of them. It makes me want to put some more on my own page.

Figure 6.3
Email Message with Comments from Peers

- Open the peer's document and make your comments using the FOOTNOTE feature (select INSERT > REFERENCE > FOOTNOTE and follow the instructions for inserting a footnote at the bottom of a page or following the text).

See Fig. 6.6

❷ Giving feedback

Peer review gives students in a writing class a sense of audience. Peer reviewers can tell you whether they understand the purpose, whether the thesis is clear, and whether the supporting evidence is sufficient. But a peer's response is only as helpful as it is sincere. Just telling a peer that the writing is "good" is not particularly useful. As a peer reviewer, you can be most helpful by showing interest in and enthusiasm for the work and by questioning and constructively commenting on the piece.

In order to respond appropriately, you should first read the entire draft, looking for global (general) features of organization and development. In a first

Figure 6.4 ▶ Peer Comments Using CAPS and Colored Font

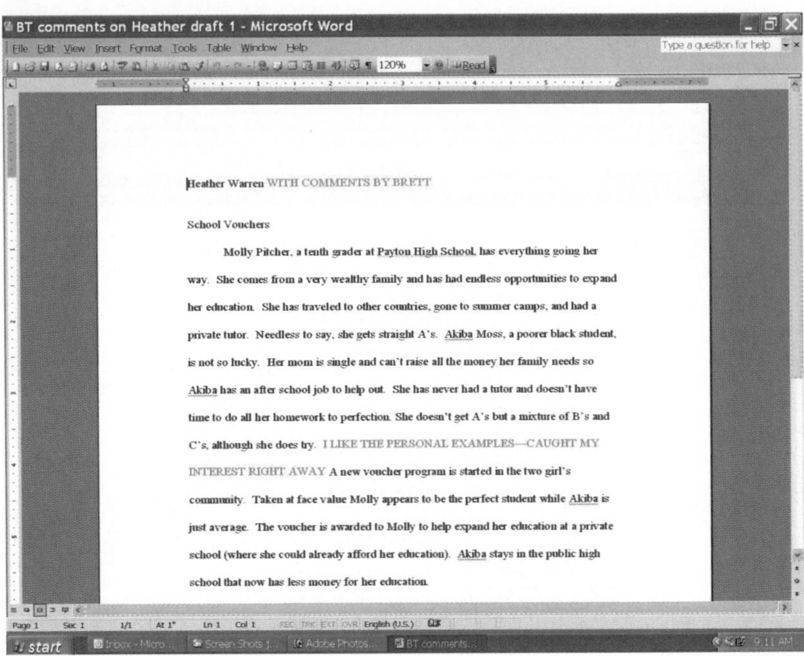

BT comments on Heather draft 1 - Microsoft Word

Heather Warren WITH COMMENTS BY BRETT

School Vouchers

Molly Pitcher, a tenth grader at Payton High School, has everything going her way. She comes from a very wealthy family and has had endless opportunities to expand her education. She has traveled to other countries, gone to summer camps, and had a private tutor. Needless to say, she gets straight A's. Akiba Moss, a poorer black student, is not so lucky. Her mom is single and can't raise all the money her family needs so Akiba has an after school job to help out. She has never had a tutor and doesn't have time to do all her homework to perfection. She doesn't get A's but a mixture of B's and C's, although she does try. I LIKE THE PERSONAL EXAMPLES—CAUGHT MY INTEREST RIGHT AWAY A new voucher program is started in the two girl's community. Taken at face value Molly appears to be the perfect student while Akiba is just average. The voucher is awarded to Molly to help expand her education at a private school (where she could already afford her education). Akiba stays in the public high school that now has less money for her education.

See 3b-2

reading, try to establish what you take to be the writer's rhetorical stance. During a second reading, make specific comments on the finer points (such as style and mechanics). Comments should be phrased as praise, suggestions, and questions, not as barbed criticisms. Learning to be a sensitive peer reviewer will help you to be a better writer; to respond appropriately, you must put yourself in the writer's shoes.

The instructor may provide a list of questions or prompts to use as you read a peer's paper. If so, try to address each item completely and candidly. Here are some ways in which you can respond generally (globally) and specifically (locally) to a peer's writing.

Responding globally

On the first reading, respond to the overall piece of writing, looking for the writer's rhetorical stance and global features of development and organization.

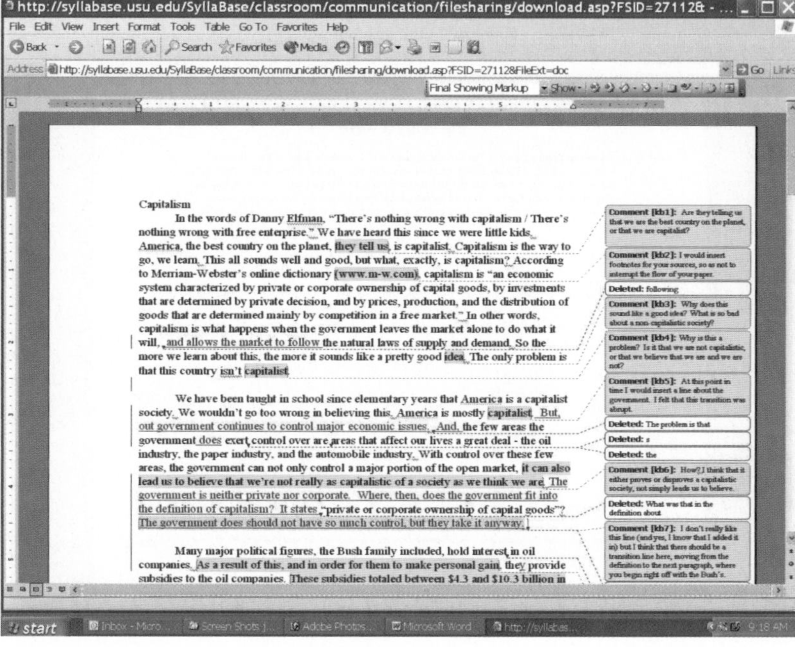

Capitalism

In the words of Danny Elfman, "There's nothing wrong with capitalism / There's nothing wrong with free enterprise." We have heard this since we were little kids. America, the best country on the planet, they tell us, is capitalist. Capitalism is the way to go, we learn. This all sounds well and good, but what, exactly, is capitalism? According to Merriam-Webster's online dictionary (www.m-w.com), capitalism is "an economic system characterized by private or corporate ownership of capital goods, by investments that are determined by private decision, and by prices, production, and the distribution of goods that are determined mainly by competition in a free market." In other words, capitalism is what happens when the government leaves the market alone to do what it will, and allows the market to follow the natural laws of supply and demand. So the more we learn about this, the more it sounds like a pretty good idea. The only problem is that this country isn't capitalist.

We have been taught in school since elementary years that America is a capitalist society. We wouldn't go too wrong in believing this. America is mostly capitalist. But, out government continues to control major economic issues. And, the few areas the government does exert control over are areas that affect our lives a great deal - the oil industry, the paper industry, and the automobile industry. With control over these few areas, the government can not only control a major portion of the open market, it can also lead us to believe that we're not really as capitalistic of a society as we think we are. The government is neither private nor corporate. Where, then, does the government fit into the definition of capitalism? It states "private or corporate ownership of capital goods"? The government does should not have so much control, but they take it anyway.

Many major political figures, the Bush family included, hold interest in oil companies. As a result of this, and in order for them to make personal gain, they provide subsidies to the oil companies. These subsidies totaled between $4.3 and $10.3 billion in

Comment [kb1]: Are they telling us that we are the best country on the planet, or that we are capitalist?

Comment [kb2]: I would insert footnotes for your sources, so as not to interrupt the flow of your paper.

Deleted: following

Comment [kb3]: Why does this sound like a good idea? What is so bad about a non-capitalistic society?

Comment [kb4]: Why is this a problem? Is it that we are not capitalistic, or that we believe that we are and we are not?

Comment [kb5]: At this point in time I would insert a line about the government. I felt that this transition was abrupt.

Deleted: The problem is that

Deleted: s

Deleted: the

Comment [kb6]: How? I think that it either proves or disproves a capitalistic society, not simply leads us to believe.

Deleted: What was that in the definition about

Comment [kb7]: I don't really like this line (and yes, I know that I added it in) but I think that there should be a transition line here, moving from the definition to the next paragraph, where you begin right off with the Bush's.

Figure 6.5 Peer Review Using DOCUMENT COMMENTS and TRACK CHANGES

1. The writer's purpose, persona, and audience seem to be . . .
2. I identify with . . .
3. I like . . .
4. I wonder about . . .
5. I suggest . . .

Responding locally

On the second reading, respond to specific features of the text.

- Are the ideas understandable, and is the logic clear?
- Is the writing style appropriate and the tone consistent?
- Is the sentence structure correct?
- Is the writing concise?
- Are the verbs vigorous and active?
- Are the sentences clear and easy to read?

Figure 6.6 ▶
Peer Comments Using Footnotes

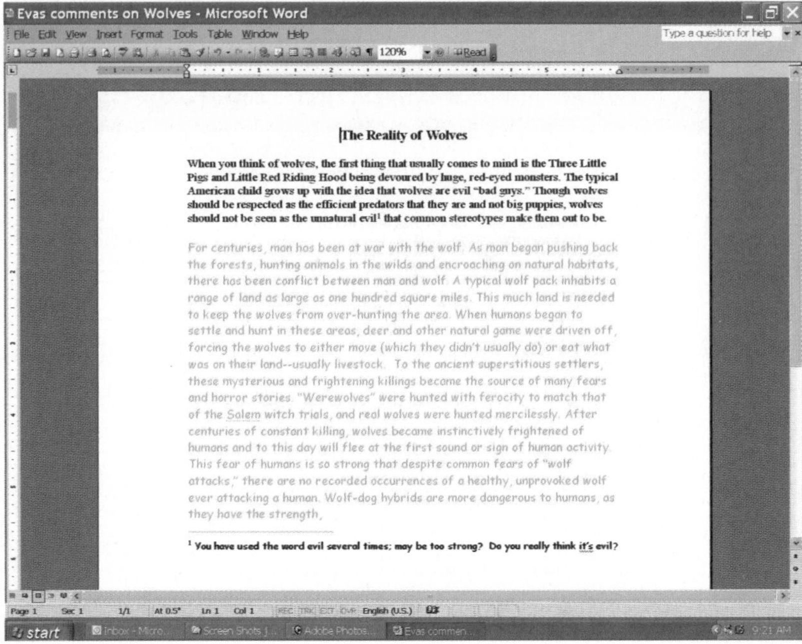

- Is the punctuation correct?
- Is the format appropriate and the font readable?

❸ Receiving feedback

Prior to exchanging drafts, list any specific concerns you have about the draft on which you would like some reader feedback. When comments are returned to you, read them with an open mind. Just as you need to criticize the work of peers with a generous spirit, you also need to receive criticism without becoming defensive. Remember that you can learn a great deal from others who read your work. Try to get enough distance from your own writing so that you do not take comments personally. Your peer is reviewing your *writing,* not you personally. Not all feedback you receive will be useful. Take it with a grain of salt—another's opinion may simply differ from yours. Once you have read and absorbed the peer comments, write down a specific plan for revising your draft.

See 6a-3

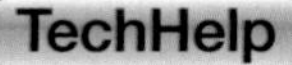

Using Document COMMENT Function

Most word-processing programs will allow you to insert comments into a document that you are reading.

1. To establish your identity, choose WORD OPTIONS from the OFFICE Button. Under the POPULAR OPTIONS tab, fill in your name and initials to personalize your copy of Word. These will show up along with your comments. Make certain that SHOW HIGHLIGHT and SHOW TOOL TIPS are both checked on the DISPLAY tab on the WORD OPTIONS screen.
2. To insert a comment, choose NEW COMMENT from the REVIEW menu. A comment box will appear in the margin of your screen. Type in your comment. The comment box will not interfere with the text itself and can be deleted at any time by using a right mouse click on the box to activate the drop-down menu.
3. To view your document with or without the comments, click on FINAL SHOWING MARKUP, found on the REVIEW menu.

Comment [Ch 1]: My comment.

NOTE: Your commenting options may differ slightly from these, depending on the word-processing software you are using.

FOR COLLABORATION Exchange drafts with a peer, either on paper, by email, or via your class's LAN. Read your peer's work straight through once, with an eye toward global features such as purpose, audience, and tone. Then, read it again carefully before commenting. If you are reading on screen, use the word processor's commenting feature (see the TechHelp box above).

6f Review a model student paper

Consider the revised version of Kirsten's essay on Net theft. Kirsten followed her revision outline as she rewrote this piece. As you compare the first draft with this draft, notice that Kirsten worked to better organize and focus her piece. She worked particularly hard on parts II and IV of her outline, where the paper had begun to fall apart in her earlier draft. She also edited sentences to make them clearer and proofread carefully to catch grammatical and mechanical errors.

See 6a-3

Giving Peer Feedback

- **Read the piece through carefully,** noting first what you take to be the writer's rhetorical stance: his or her intended purpose, persona, and audience.
- **Formulate your comments carefully,** phrasing them as suggestions and questions, not as criticisms. Remember, you are reading a draft, not a finished product.
- **Respond globally and then locally** with both general and specific suggestions for revisions. It is not helpful to the writer if you just say "this is good" without saying why you think so.
- **Give positive feedback** and praise where appropriate. It is important that you be sincere in your comments.
- **Respond completely to any prompts provided by the instructor.** Follow the specified process for commenting: handwriting comments in the margins, typing document comments, or making verbal comments in a read-around group.

It is a truism in the writing field that there are no finished pieces of writing, only deadlines. Any piece can be revised and improved. In what ways do you think this draft is an improvement over Kirsten's first draft? Are there elements Kirsten could still work on to make them more effective?

Receiving Peer Feedback

- **Provide a list of any specific concerns** you have about your draft on which you would like some reader feedback.
- **Read comments with an open mind,** without becoming defensive.
- **Ask for an explanation** if you don't understand a peer's comments. Some comments may be confusing or ambiguous.
- **Accept only those comments that will help you to improve your piece.** Remember that you retain the ownership of your writing.
- **Reject comments** that seem to be leading you off in a direction that you did not intend.
- **Write down a specific plan for revising** your draft and/or write a revision outline.

Parsons 1

Kirsten Parsons

Professor Hines

English 101–35

15 April 2006

Net Theft

"Look at this new CD I bought!" Jane exclaims to her friend. Interested, Michael eagerly looks at it. "Wow," he says. "These guys are my favorite group! Mind if I make a copy of it?"

Unfortunately, this is a common request today. In spite of laws that prohibit unlicensed copying, in some circles it has become an accepted practice to reproduce another's work without paying for it. Similarly, this practice has spread to the Internet, where access to music, software, written texts, and graphics is convenient and fast. These items can be copied for personal use with ease, but often no credit is given to the original author. Not only is this wrong from a moral standpoint, but legally, it is forbidden as well. It has become a situation where "legality collides with practicality" (Meyer and Underwood 113). In other words, breaking the law is more convenient than obeying it, and since we know we can get away with doing it, our conscience gives in. When it comes to "borrowing" information from the Internet, we are gradually

Student and course identification

Opening scenario

Introduction

Print source: authors and page number

Thesis

Parsons 2

becoming a people who accept lawbreaking as long as we can participate, too.

Compare to shoplifting

I'm sure all of us once glimpsed a tempting item in a store and, after getting "no" for an answer from Mom or Dad, took matters into our own hands, sneaking the treasure into a hidden pocket. It probably took only a few moments for your parents to notice something was up. I remember well a discussion about why taking the package was wrong. Then my Dad took me back to the store, where an apology was made and my Strawberry Hubba Bubba Bubblegum was paid for.

Define Net theft

Walking into a store and taking something without paying for it is obviously not legal; ironically, this principle seems to break down where the Net is concerned. With available technology, Net theft is commonplace. Written texts, software, graphics, and music all are vulnerable to cyber-shoplifting. Though it is not encouraged per se, it is not really discouraged either. Isn't this just stealing masked by softer adjectives such as "sharing" or "borrowing"? Granted it is less noticeable, but that doesn't change the fact that you didn't pay for it.

Compare difficulty of each crime

Part of the problem is that the physical element involved in actually traveling to a store and taking something is not necessary for these Net crimes. Imagine

Parsons 3

walking down the aisle of the local Wal-Mart with the intention of stealing a Hobbes doll, your favorite cartoon character. Blood rushes to your ears and your heart begins to pound, as your body reacts to the rush of adrenaline. Casting a nervous glance around the nearby aisles, you decide that the coast is clear. You extend your arm, grab the orange tiger, place it in your backpack, and then walk nonchalantly toward the exit. Then the alarm goes off and you are caught holding the goods!

This scenario is only possible in a physical world. Because the Net is so unphysical, the risk of being caught, which may serve to deter many thieves in a store, is minimal. Net theft is committed within the reach of the refrigerator! Imagine that while Net surfing you find a "Calvin and Hobbes" cartoon on a commercial Web site. You think it would look great on your homepage. With a click of the mouse, you grab the graphic and paste it onto your own page. Who has ever heard of someone being arrested for copying a graphic? Because Net crimes often go ignored, and "everyone" is guilty, more and more people engage in them. The consequences seem to be less punitive, and thus we give in to the influence of the Wild Net.

Net theft is easy to commit

Organizations and individuals have tried to establish standards of conduct for Internet use. For

Standards of conduct

Parsons 4

example, the Computer Ethics Institute wrote its Ten Commandments for Computer Ethics, which includes such obvious "rules" as "Thou shalt not use the computer to steal" (Roach). But what is stealing when it comes to materials found on the Internet? The *Copyright Website* asserts that any texts or graphics that you find on the Internet are by their very nature published and thus are "copyrighted" (O'Mahoney). This means that in order to use anything from someone else's Web site, you need their permission. If you put a comic strip such as "Calvin and Hobbes" onto your homepage, you run the risk of being sued for violation of copyright.

Online source without page number

The problem, as Meyer and Underwood also point out, is that the "Wild West culture of the Internet promotes an anything goes attitude in Net surfers" (113). Most Internet users would agree that stealing phone card numbers and selling them is wrong. However, many would not agree that sharing a pirated copy of a game was illegal or even wrong. Similarly, many would not find that using a cool graphic from someone else's page was unethical or illegal. The freewheeling world of the Internet considers capitalist rules like "copyright" to be offensive.

Summary of the conflict

In the tangled world of the Internet, not all of the new dilemmas that have surfaced will be solved

Conclusion

Parsons 5

immediately. However, if the definition of a criminal is one who has committed a crime, then in the world of the Net, perhaps we all need to serve some time.

Parsons 6

Works Cited

Meyer, Michael, and Anne Underwood. "Crimes of the 'Net.'" *CyberReader*. Ed. Victor Vitanza. 2nd ed. Boston: Allyn, 1999. 111–13. Print.

O'Mahoney, Benedict. *The Copyright Website*. 2005. Web. 1 Apr. 2006.

Roach, Kitty. *PageWorks*. 1996–2004. Web. 1 Apr. 2006.

Print source

Online source: Web site

Online source: Web site

part

2

Research

7 The Research Project

FAQs

- What does it mean to do research? (7a)
- How will I ever get it all done? (7b)
- Can I take notes on my computer? (7c)
- What is a bibliography? (7d)
- What are background sources? (7e)
- How do I focus my search? (7f)

See Ch. 3

See Fig. 7.1

The process of writing a research paper does not differ markedly from the process of writing an essay, described in Part 1. The writing stages outlined in Chapter 3—preparing, composing, and rewriting—still apply. The difference is one of scope. A research paper is longer than most essays and contains more information from external sources, found by doing research. Figure 7.1 shows an overview strategy for writing a research paper. The steps outlined in Figure 7.1 are discussed below.

Research paper advice

7a Become a researcher

Why research? Work in many academic and professional disciplines, including law, medicine, engineering, and psychology, depends heavily on research. In all fields, researchers conduct studies to answer important questions, to solve problems, to prove cases, and to argue positions. In college, your main reason for researching may be to carry out an assignment in a particular course. For example, in a literature course, you may be asked to research an

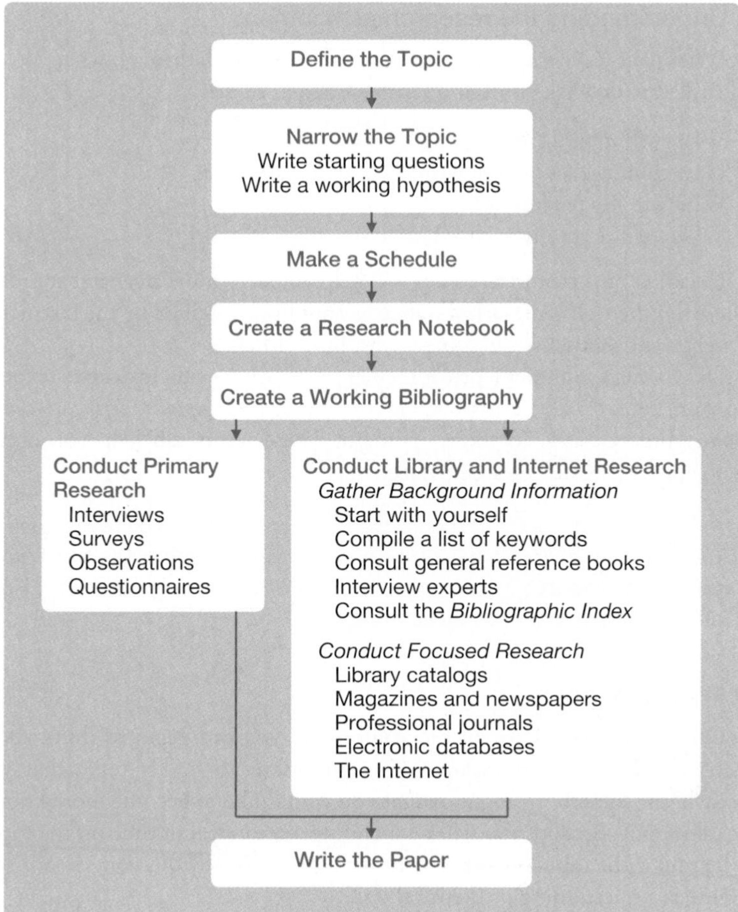

Figure 7.1 A Strategy for Writing a Research Paper

author's life or critiques of literary texts; in a political science course, you may be asked to research a political campaign or a political trend. Whatever your motivation for researching, you need to become seriously engaged in the research process.

❶ Understanding the research assignment

When you receive a research assignment, first think through what you are being asked to do. Ask yourself questions such as these:

- What will my purpose be?
- How should I sound as a writer?
- Who will my readers be?
- Where will I get my authority?

See 3b-2

Deciding on a rhetorical stance will help you determine a general approach to the assignment. If a rhetorical stance has not been specified by the instructor, you may want to discuss the subject with him or her.

See Table 24.1

Does your assignment provide clues as to what your instructor expects from you? Look for key terms, such as *analyze, discuss, explain, define, evaluate, compare*, and *persuade*, in the assignment. These terms can help you decide how to approach your research project.

FOR COLLABORATION Discuss the implications of the key terms *analyze*, *discuss*, *explain*, *define*, *evaluate*, *compare*, and *persuade* with a small group of your peers. How might each word lead to a different research paper? Refer to Table 24.1 as you discuss these terms.

Getting started

❷ Finding a topic

Once you have a sense of the assignment, you can begin to think about possible topics for your research. It is important to find a topic that you already know something about or that you would like to become more knowledgeable about. Because you will be spending a great deal of time on the topic, it is helpful if the topic provokes some kind of response from you, even if that response is a questioning or skeptical one.

Research typically begins with good questions. You need to think about how to use the information you find in your research to answer a question that a particular subject has inspired in you.

- *Look at course textbooks you are currently using.* Is there a debate discussed in a textbook that has not yet been resolved? For example, perhaps in your history textbook you read that there is a difference of opinion among historians concerning the nature of the interactions between Native Americans and the Puritans. Out of this debate might come a question for your research: "What was the relationship between the local indigenous population and the Puritans in the early colony of Plymouth Plantation?"

- **Browse through a specialized encyclopedia**, such as the *Encyclopedia of Psychology* or the *Encyclopedia of Educational Research*, for some ideas.
- **Look for potential research questions on the Internet.**

See TechHelp 7a-4

Once you have some preliminary ideas for a topic, discuss them with a reference librarian, your instructor, and other students in your class. Listen particularly to your instructor's advice on the appropriateness of topics. Although there are no "bad" topics *per se*, there are topics that may prove difficult, given the constraints of the assignment. Your instructor will be able to tell you if topics are overused (for example, capital punishment and abortion), too trendy (for example, rock stars, fads, and fashions), or too trivial or specialized (for example, family interaction in *The Simpsons*). Take your instructor's advice so that you do not find yourself struggling with an unworkable topic.

FOR COLLABORATION Investigate a few possible topics. Discuss the options with peers, classmates, a librarian, and your instructor. Narrow your choices down to one or two workable topics that you can later investigate more thoroughly.

3 Selecting a specific topic

Kaycee Sorensen, the student whose research paper is included in Chapter 11 as a model, was given the assignment of writing a research paper on a technological subject. She was not sure what technological issue she wanted to write about, so she decided to browse the Web as a way of generating some specific topics. After browsing in the *Yahoo*! search directory, Kaycee noticed the topic of Shopping and Services listed under the category Business and Economy. She decided to look into the topic to find out more about how people were using the Internet in new ways to shop for goods and services.

See 8d-1

4 Narrowing and focusing the topic

Search tools are useful not only for getting topic ideas but also for narrowing a general topic area or dividing a subject into several component parts.

TechHelp

Exploring Topics on the Internet

Using an Internet search engine such as *Google* or *Yahoo*!, browse for topic ideas.

1. *Yahoo*! offers a topical list at the following URL: http://dir.yahoo.com. From this site, you can browse through a variety of topics to get ideas of subjects that interest you and how they might be categorized or related. For example, if you click on Society and Culture you find subcategories such as Crime, Environment and Nature, Food and Drink, and so on. These may give you some ideas of what to write about, as well as link you to websites.
2. *Google* also offers a topical directory listing at the following URL: http://www.google.com/dirhp. You can use this directory as a way of exploring subjects. For example, if you click on Home you will find subtopics such as Consumer Information, Apartment Living, Shopping, and so on.

For example, under the broad topic of Business and the Economy found at *Yahoo*!, Kaycee selected the specific topic of cybershopping, passing over other possible technological topics such as intellectual property or ethics and responsibility. She then narrowed the topic of cybershopping to exclude sites devoted to making retail sales since she was interested in the advantages and disadvantages of cybershopping but not in sites that promoted online retail sales.

See 3e-1

Asking research questions

Once you have identified a specific topic, the next step is to focus the topic by asking pertinent research questions that you will attempt to answer—your "starting questions." For example, Kaycee was curious about the prevalence of online shopping in our culture. Posing research questions allowed Kaycee to begin her background reading in search of answers, rather than reading aimlessly in an unfocused way. For the specific topic of cybershopping, Kaycee's starting questions were as follows:

See 3d-1 to 3d-3

Is the number of online shoppers increasing?

Is shopping via the Internet a viable option for consumers?

Is it safe to use a credit card for online shopping?

Developing a hypothesis

As you work through the research process, attempting to answer your starting questions, you should come up with a hypothesis—a tentative statement of what you anticipate the research will reveal. A working hypothesis specifically describes a proposition that research evidence will either support or challenge. As you begin to gather background information on your topic, you should develop a hypothesis that will help you to focus your research. Kaycee moved from her starting questions to a working hypothesis as follows:

TOPIC

Cybershopping

RESEARCH QUESTIONS

Is the number of online shoppers increasing?

Is shopping via the Internet a viable alternative for consumers?

Is it safe to use a credit card for online shopping?

WORKING HYPOTHESIS

The number of online shoppers is increasing, which means that cybershopping is becoming a convenient, affordable, safe option for consumers.

A working hypothesis should be stated in such a way that it can be either supported or challenged by the research. Kaycee's research will either support or challenge her working hypothesis. The hypothesis is called "working" because you may find that you need to change or revise it during the course of the research.

❺ Developing a search strategy

A search strategy is a plan for proceeding systematically with research. Once you have decided on your starting questions and working hypothesis,

TechHelp

Web Searches: Using *Google* and *Google Scholar* Effectively

Google has become the standard in Internet search tools. Another service offered by *Google*, called *Google Scholar*, offers searching tailored for academics. The trick to applying both tools effectively to academic projects is using keyword searches to your best advantage. An effective keyword search presents you with many legitimate sources to choose from while weeding out those that are either irrelevant or unreliable. Note that even if you use targeted keyword searches successfully, you will still need to carefully evaluate any electronic sources culled from a general Web search engine for their credibility.

See 9a

Searching with *Google*

Locate the *Google* homepage by typing *http://google.com.* Take a few minutes to explore its many features and to read the search help information provided. Here are some suggestions:

- Select keywords carefully. They should be both specific and descriptive—for example, *2006 basketball statistics* rather than *basketball* or *Salt Lake City 2002 Olympics* instead of *Olympics*.
- Use a phrase search to find an exact match. Enclose your search query in quotation marks so as to get results for the exact terms you entered in the order you entered them—for example, "*global warming*" rather than *global warming*.

Searching with *Google Scholar*

Locate the *Google Scholar* homepage by typing *http://scholar.google .com* or clicking on the link on the main *Google* page.

- By using *Google Scholar*, you can search broadly for scholarly literature across many disciplines. *Google Scholar* helps you identify the most relevant research across the world of scholarly research. It allows you to search a range of sources in one search. You can also locate the full text of various articles through your own library or on the Web.
- *Google Scholar* sorts articles by "weighing the full text of each article, the author, the publication in which the article appears, and how often the piece has been cited in other scholarly literature." It attempts to provide researchers with the most relevant results first.

you are ready to outline your search strategy. Your first decision will be about the nature of your research. Will you be relying mostly on library and Internet research or on field research?

The two main types of research are primary research and secondary research. **Primary research** entails field research such as generating information or data through interviewing, administering questionnaires, or observation. **Secondary research** involves finding information in secondary, or published, sources found in the library and on the Internet. You need to decide which type or types of research your project demands. Can you find what you need in secondary sources, or will the research be partly or completely primary in nature? What kinds of sources does your instructor expect you to use? Today, secondary sources take a variety of forms: books in the library, articles in journals and magazines, newspapers and government documents, computerized hypertexts found on the Internet.

See 7f-5

See 7f-1 to 7f-4

The goal of a search is to build a working bibliography—a list of possible sources that may or may not eventually be used in the final paper. A working bibliography is typically about twice as long as the final bibliography for a research paper because many of the sources you identify will turn out not to be applicable to your paper or not to be available in time for you to use in your research. By searching for sources in a systematic way, you avoid aimlessly wandering around the library or surfing on the Internet.

See 7d

See TechHelp 7a-5

7b Make a schedule

If you have never done a research project before, you may be overwhelmed at the thought of such a large and complex task. If you break the job down into smaller parts, it will seem much more manageable. Formulating a time frame in which to complete your research project will also help. If your instructor has not given you deadlines, set your own dates for accomplishing specific tasks.

EXERCISE 7.1 Using one of the sample schedules on pages 178-179, draw up a time frame for your own research, with specific target dates for each step in the research process.

Schedules for Writing a Research Paper

Semester-Long Research Project:

Week 1.
- Select a preliminary research topic.
- Articulate starting questions.
- Begin background research.
- Schedule a time frame.
- Begin to focus the topic (see 7e).

Week 2.
- Build a working bibliography by using online library catalogs, databases, and the Internet (see Chapter 8).
- Begin to locate library and Internet sources (see 7f).

Week 3.
- Read, evaluate, and take notes on sources (see 10a).
- Print out information from the Internet.
- Write down complete bibliographical information and make a note of URLs (see 7d-2).

Week 4.
- Conduct any primary research.
- Complete the reading and evaluation of sources.
- Identify gaps in the research and find more sources if necessary (see 7f).

Week 5.
- Begin preliminary writing by summarizing key information.
- Brainstorm on the topic.
- Write a few possible thesis statements (see 11a).

Week 6.
- Write a working thesis statement.
- Sketch an outline of the paper (see 11a-2, 11b).

Week 7.
- Write a rough draft.
- Keep careful track of sources through accurate citations, taking care to distinguish quotes and paraphrases (see Chapter 10).
- Write a References or Works Cited list (see Chapters 12–14).

Week 8.
- Revise and edit the rough draft.
- Spell check and check sentence structure and usage.
- Check documentation of sources.
- Solicit peer responses to the draft (see 6e).
- Revise based on any peer reviews or instructor comments.

Week 9. ► Print and proofread the final copy.
► Have a friend or classmate proofread as well (see 6d, 6e).

Four-Week Research Project:

Week 1. ► Select and narrow topic; schedule time frame; search library databases and Internet.

Week 2. ► Locate sources; read, evaluate, take notes on sources; continue to build bibliography.

Week 3. ► Write thesis statement; sketch outline; begin rough draft; keep careful track of sources.

Week 4. ► Complete draft, solicit peer responses; revise and edit draft; print and proofread final copy.

7c Create a research notebook

See TechHelp 3d-3

See TechHelp 7d-1

If you are using a laptop, you can take advantage of its storage capabilities to develop an electronic research notebook. Create a directory, and label it your research notebook directory. In this directory, you can create files to record your topic and your starting questions, notes from your background research and focused research, and your working bibliography (if you do not have bibliography software such as *NoodleBib*). As you investigate your topic, record not only what others have said on the subject—potentially useful quotations (or paraphrases or summaries of those quotations)—but also your own impressions and comments. You can use research notebook files to develop your thesis statement, to lay out an informal outline or organizational plan for your paper, and to write all preliminary drafts of your paper.

If you do not have a computer, you might set up a ring binder with dividers for all of the files just described:

- Topic and starting questions
- Thesis statement and outline
- Research notes and comments
- Working bibliography
- Drafts 1, 2, 3, as needed

❶ Recording notes in a notebook

See Ch. 9

See Fig. 7.2

See Fig. 7.4

Whether your notebook is paper or electronic, be sure to keep your recorded notes—quotations from material written by other people or paraphrases or summaries of their ideas—separate from your own comments and ideas in order to avoid inadvertent plagiarism. If your notes are handwritten, you might use two columns when recording information: one for notes taken from the source and the other for comments, analyses, and queries. If your notes are electronic, you can use your word-processing program's COMMENTS feature to insert your comments and analyses into the notes taken from sources.

When you are taking notes, it is important to record bibliographical information at the same time so that you have complete citation information for all of your sources. An example of the type of information you might record in your notes, as well as the bibliographical information you need to record for each source, can be found in Figure 7.4 on page 184.

EXERCISE 7.2 Create a directory or folder to serve as your electronic research notebook. Divide it into subfolders to use as you pursue your search (a folder for your working bibliography, another for notes from sources, and so on).

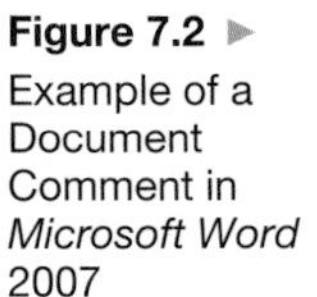

Figure 7.2 ▶ Example of a Document Comment in *Microsoft Word* 2007

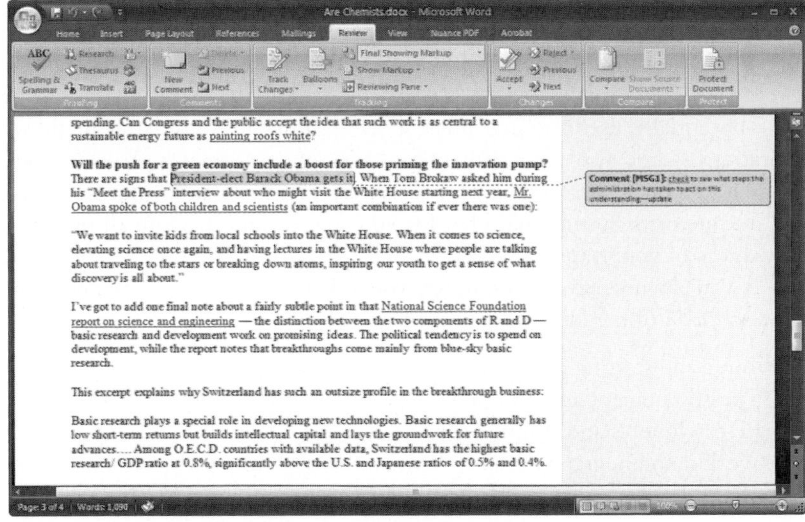

spending. Can Congress and the public accept the idea that such work is as central to a sustainable energy future as painting roofs white?

Will the push for a green economy include a boost for those priming the innovation pump? There are signs that President-elect Barack Obama gets it. When Tom Brokaw asked him during his "Meet the Press" interview about who might visit the White House starting next year, Mr. Obama spoke of both children and scientists (an important combination if ever there was one):

Comment [MSG1]: check to see what steps the administration has taken to act on this understanding—update

"We want to invite kids from local schools into the White House. When it comes to science, elevating science once again, and having lectures in the White House where people are talking about traveling to the stars or breaking down atoms, inspiring our youth to get a sense of what discovery is all about."

I've got to add one final note about a fairly subtle point in that National Science Foundation report on science and engineering — the distinction between the two components of R and D — basic research and development work on promising ideas. The political tendency is to spend on development, while the report notes that breakthroughs come mainly from blue-sky basic research.

This excerpt explains why Switzerland has such an outsize profile in the breakthrough business:

Basic research plays a special role in developing new technologies. Basic research generally has low short-term returns but builds intellectual capital and lays the groundwork for future advances.... Among O.E.C.D. countries with available data, Switzerland has the highest basic research/ GDP ratio at 0.8%, significantly above the U.S. and Japanese ratios of 0.5% and 0.4%.

❷ Taking notes with photocopies, printouts, and downloads

Photocopies and database printouts

Making your own photocopies and printouts of sources has several advantages:

1. You will have the actual wording of the authors at your fingertips, so you will not have to rely on your notes for accuracy when quoting (reducing the chances of inadvertent plagiarism).
2. You can highlight for future reference passages that are important to your research.
3. You can make your own notes on the photocopies or printouts.

See Fig. 7.3

Be sure that you record complete bibliographic information on all photocopies and printouts from books, newspapers, journal articles, or full-text library databases. You will make your life much easier if you can avoid retracing your steps because you neglected to write down a publication date for a source. Refer to Chapters 12–14 for the complete bibliographic information that needs to be listed for each type of source you use in your research.

See Chs. 12–14

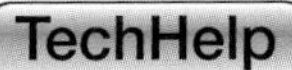

Printing Internet Sources

When you are researching on the Internet, it will be easier for you to print out copies of relevant Web pages than to take notes by hand. If you wish to use a specific section of a Web page as a source, highlight that section using your computer's mouse and then choose PRINT > SELECTION from the PRINT dialog box. In this way, you will print only the parts you need, not the entire Web site. Like photocopies, printouts of sources from the Internet will need to have complete bibliographic information. In addition to the usual information for all sources (the author, title, and publication data), for Internet sources you will need to note the date you accessed the page, and the dates when the site was posted and last updated. It is also a good idea to write the complete URL of the page(s) you are referring to down for future reference.

Figure 7.3 ▶ Example of Annotated Internet Printout

Need to learn more about this organization and its political motives

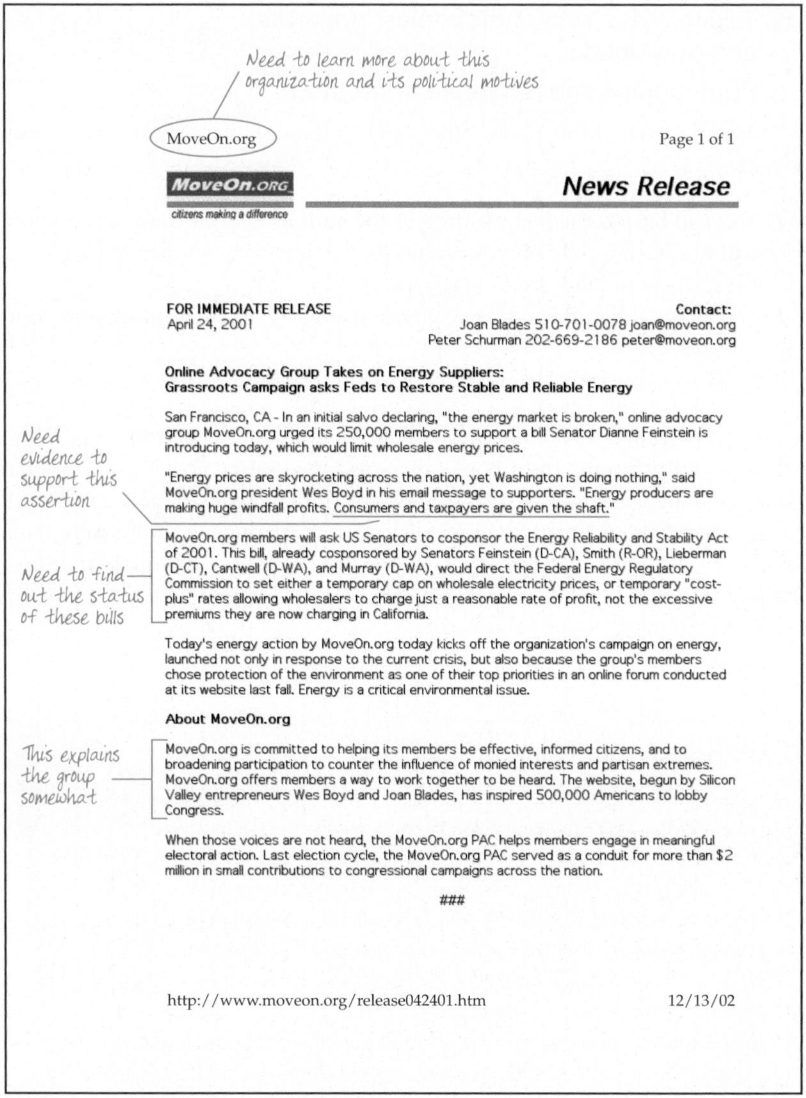

MoveOn.org Page 1 of 1

MoveOn.ORG
citizens making a difference

News Release

FOR IMMEDIATE RELEASE
April 24, 2001

Contact:
Joan Blades 510-701-0078 joan@moveon.org
Peter Schurman 202-669-2186 peter@moveon.org

Online Advocacy Group Takes on Energy Suppliers:
Grassroots Campaign asks Feds to Restore Stable and Reliable Energy

San Francisco, CA - In an initial salvo declaring, "the energy market is broken," online advocacy group MoveOn.org urged its 250,000 members to support a bill Senator Dianne Feinstein is introducing today, which would limit wholesale energy prices.

"Energy prices are skyrocketing across the nation, yet Washington is doing nothing," said MoveOn.org president Wes Boyd in his email message to supporters. "Energy producers are making huge windfall profits. Consumers and taxpayers are given the shaft."

Need evidence to support this assertion

MoveOn.org members will ask US Senators to cosponsor the Energy Reliability and Stability Act of 2001. This bill, already cosponsored by Senators Feinstein (D-CA), Smith (R-OR), Lieberman (D-CT), Cantwell (D-WA), and Murray (D-WA), would direct the Federal Energy Regulatory Commission to set either a temporary cap on wholesale electricity prices, or temporary "cost-plus" rates allowing wholesalers to charge just a reasonable rate of profit, not the excessive premiums they are now charging in California.

Need to find out the status of these bills

Today's energy action by MoveOn.org today kicks off the organization's campaign on energy, launched not only in response to the current crisis, but also because the group's members chose protection of the environment as one of their top priorities in an online forum conducted at its website last fall. Energy is a critical environmental issue.

About MoveOn.org

MoveOn.org is committed to helping its members be effective, informed citizens, and to broadening participation to counter the influence of monied interests and partisan extremes. MoveOn.org offers members a way to work together to be heard. The website, begun by Silicon Valley entrepreneurs Wes Boyd and Joan Blades, has inspired 500,000 Americans to lobby Congress.

This explains the group somewhat

When those voices are not heard, the MoveOn.org PAC helps members engage in meaningful electoral action. Last election cycle, the MoveOn.org PAC served as a conduit for more than $2 million in small contributions to congressional campaigns across the nation.

###

http://www.moveon.org/release042401.htm 12/13/02

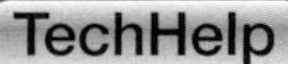

Downloading Internet Sources

Another method of obtaining information is to download or save Internet pages directly into your own computer files (using FILE > SAVE AS). When downloading or copying and pasting files from the Internet, you need to be especially careful not to import information directly into your own work without citing the source appropriately. To keep from inadvertently plagiarizing from the Internet, always include the complete bibliographic information from each source, and put quotation marks around any text that you COPY and PASTE from the Internet. Also, note for yourself the author of the quotation so that you can use that information in a *signal phrase* that introduces the quotation.

See Chs. 12–14; Ch. 10

7d Create a working bibliography

A **bibliography** is any listing of books and articles on a particular subject. As you begin your research, start a **working bibliography**, which will grow as your research progresses. This working bibliography will likely contain some sources that you ultimately will not use in your research paper, so entries need not be in final bibliographic form. However, be careful to accurately record all the information you will need so that you do not have to track down sources twice. Include the author's full name, a complete title including subtitle and edition, the city and state where the work was published, the name of the publisher, and the date of publication. When you write your research paper, you will compile a **final bibliography**. It will include only the sources that you actually used in writing the research paper, and it will be formatted according to a particular documentation style. The final bibliography will be named according to the documentation format you are using: in the Modern Language Association (MLA) style, it is called *Works Cited*; in American Psychological Association (APA) style, it is called *References*; and in the Council of Science Editors (CSE) style, it is called *Cited References.*

See 7d-1

See Chs. 12–14

❶ Recording bibliographic information

See 10a-2

You can prepare a working bibliography manually on index cards or electronically on a computer file. If you use index cards, record bibliographical information (author, title, and publication data) on one set of cards and content notes on a separate set. Figure 7.4 shows both a sample bibliography card and a sample note card with the appropriate information recorded.

See TechHelp 7d-1

Using a computer to record bibliographic information is very efficient because you can easily reformat the information later, when you prepare your final bibliography. Some word processors are equipped with bibliographic software that automatically formats the information.

Figure 7.4 ▶ Bibliography Card and Note Card

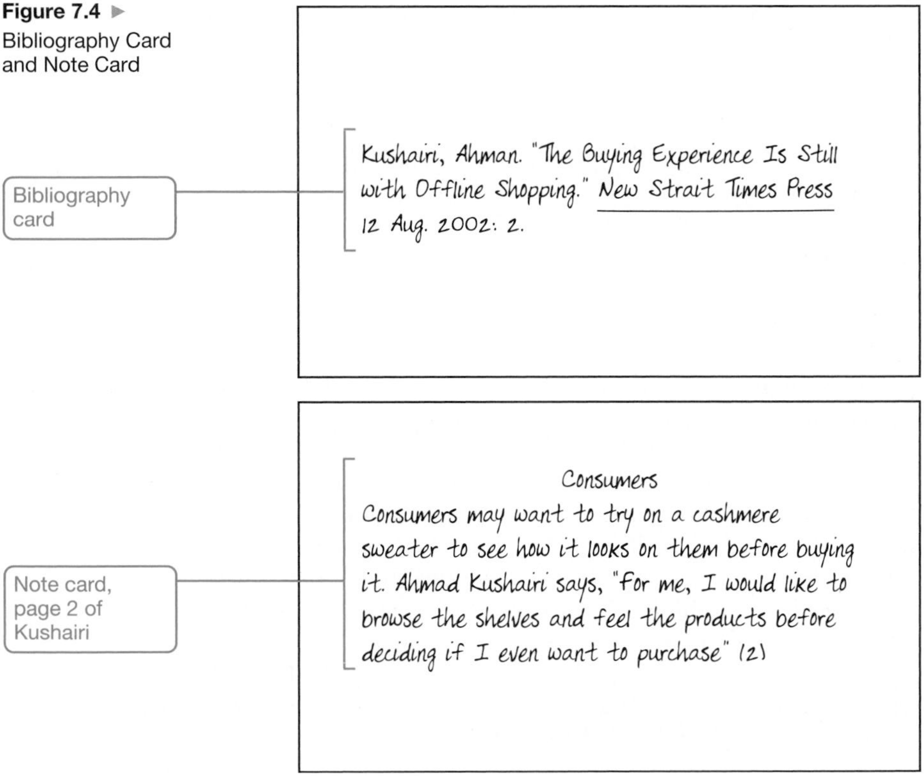

Bibliography card

Kushairi, Ahman. "The Buying Experience Is Still with Offline Shopping." <u>New Strait Times Press</u> 12 Aug. 2002: 2.

Note card, page 2 of Kushairi

Consumers

Consumers may want to try on a cashmere sweater to see how it looks on them before buying it. Ahmad Kushairi says, "For me, I would like to browse the shelves and feel the products before deciding if I even want to purchase" (2)

Using a Computer Bibliography Program

1. Open the bibliography software, such as *NoodleBib* used in *MyCompLab* from Pearson Education or *Citation Machine*, which is a free online service found at <http://citationmachine.net>.
2. Follow the directions for entering data for the particular style (e.g., MLA or APA); usually you will be asked to select the type of source (e.g., print book or Internet journal article) and enter information by category (author, title, publication data).
3. Wait for the bibliography program to generate your bibliography, based on the information you provide. It will format the information appropriately for a particular documentation style you have selected and place it in alphabetical order. Some bibliography programs will convert from one documentation style to another—for example, MLA to APA style.
4. Name and save your bibliography, as well as any Works Cited lists you may have generated from it.

NOTE. You still need to check your bibliography carefully to be certain the program has generated it in the correct format.

See Ch. 12

See Ch. 13

Here is Kaycee's working bibliography, which was generated electronically.

Better Business Bureau Program. 2002. Web. 22 Mar. 2003.

Chan, Christine, et al. "Online Spending to Reach $10 Billion for Holiday Season 2001." *Nielsen/NetRatings* 20 Nov. 2001. Web. 28 July 2002.

Cox, Beth. "E-commerce: Color It Green." *Cyberatlas* 3 Aug. 2002. Web. 12 Apr. 2003.

Frey, Christine. "Online Shopper: Advantages of Plastic." *Los Angeles Times* 18 Oct. 2001: T8. Print.

Greenspan, Robyn. "E-shopping Around the World." *Cyberatlas* 5 Aug. 2002. Web. 23 Mar. 2003.

❷ Writing an annotated bibliography

One type of bibliography that is frequently required by instructors is an *annotated bibliography*, so called because it includes annotations—a brief descriptive paragraph about each source. You might find it useful to compile an annotated bibliography for your own use, because it is an ideal way to keep track of what is contained in each source. Below are a few entries excerpted from an annotated bibliography for a research paper about wolves in the national parks using APA citation style.

Annotated References

Batastini, J., & Buschena, D. (2007, May). Measuring the impacts of wolves on the "market" for elk hunting: Hunter adjustment and game agency response. *American Agricultural Economics Association*. Retrieved from AgEcon Search database.

This paper provides estimates of the effects of wolves on hunter opportunities, where these opportunities are influenced by actions taken by both the game agency and hunters in response to the spread of wolves.

Byron, E. (2008, February). Season set for Montana wolf hunting. The *Helena Independent Record*. Retrieved from http://www.helenair.com/articles/2008/02/21/state/top/55st_080221_ wolves.txt

As reported in the *Helena Independent Record* online newspaper, wolf hunting season was set for the first time ever in Montana, the day before the formal announcement that the predators would be removed from the list of animals protected by the Endangered Species Act was expected.

Dinger, D. (2000). Throwing *Canis Lupus* to the wolves: United States v. McKittrick and the existence of the Yellowstone and Central Idaho experimental wolf populations under a flawed provision of the Endangered Species Act. *Brigham Young University Law Review, 2000*(1), 377. Retrieved from Business Source Premier database.

This BYU Law Review article discusses how the battles over whether wolves should be reintroduced to their historic ranges have reached the courts.

ESA. (1973). *Endangered Species Act* as amended through the 108th Congress. United States Fish and Wildlife Service Website. Retrieved from http://www.fws.gov/endangered/ESA/content.html

This Web site includes a complete description of the Endangered Species Program and is produced by the U.S. Fish & Wildlife Service.

NOAA Fisheries. (2008). *Endangered Species Act*. NOAA Fisheries Website. Retrieved from http://www.nmfs.noaa.gov/pr/laws/esa/

This Web site, produced by the "Office of Protected Resources," of the NOAA, provides an overview of the Endangered Species Act.

Robbins, J. (2004, June). Lessons from the WOLF. *Scientific American, 290*(6), 76–81. Retrieved from Business Source Premier database.

This *Scientific American* article reports that bringing the top predator back to Yellowstone has triggered a cascade of unanticipated changes in the park's ecosystem.

Utah Wolf Management Plan. (2005). Wolves in Utah. Retrieved from http://www.wildlife.utah.gov/wolf/

This is the report produced by the Utah Division of Wildlife Management outlining the future plans for wolf management in the state.

Wellman, J., & Propst, D. (2004). *Wildland recreation policy* (2nd ed.). Malabar, FL: Krieger Publishing Company.
Building on the historic origins of the National Park Service and USDA Forest Service, this book shows how the policy process affects current outdoor recreation management issues.

3 Printing or saving online sources

See 7c-2

If you are using sources from online databases, you may want to print out copies for later review or download them onto your own computer disk using the FILE > SAVE AS command. In either case, be sure that complete bibliographic information appears on the pages or in the files. If it does not, enter the bibliographic information on your working bibliography page. Include the following information:

1. author's name, if available;
2. publication information for print and online versions;
3. the URL;
4. the date of posting or updating;
5. the date you accessed the site.

If you print material from the Web, your browser may automatically include source information, but be sure to check. If you cannot find the complete address, or URL, on your printed copy, record it by hand.

EXERCISE 7.3 Establish a consistent format for entering the bibliographic information on your research, either as bibliography cards, on printouts, or as a computerized working bibliography.

FOR COLLABORATION Meet with a group of three or four classmates to discuss your working bibliographies. Share ideas about sources and databases that you found useful in your search. Suggest possible places to look for information that your classmates might not have thought about. What leads were particularly helpful to you? What dead ends did you encounter? What search challenges are you still facing?

7e Gather additional background information

Now is the time to gather additional background information, using your starting questions and working hypothesis as a guide. This information will help you conduct more focused research later on.

1 Starting with yourself

At the start of a research project, write down everything you already know about your topic. The list may be quite extensive or rather short. The important thing is to inventory your own knowledge first so that you can systematically build on that knowledge base. Also check your biases and assumptions about the topic, asking yourself the following questions.

1. Do I already have a strong opinion about this topic?
2. Have I "rushed to judgment" about it without looking at all the facts?
3. Am I emotionally involved with the topic in some way that might bias my judgment?

If your answer to any of these questions is "yes," think seriously about whether you will be able to keep an open mind as you read about the topic. If not, you might want to choose another topic.

2 Interviewing experts or joining a discussion group

Even if your assignment does not specifically require primary research, it is a good idea to talk to experts in the field, if possible. You may know a professor or a family friend who is familiar with the topic. Make an appointment to talk to that person and get his or her views on the topic. It is not necessary to conduct a formal interview—an informal conversation is generally sufficient. If there are online discussion groups on your topic, join in the conversation or follow others' exchanges to gain a better understanding of your topic.

See Ch. 21

3 Consulting the *Bibliographic Index*

After surveying your own knowledge, reading background sources, and talking to experts, you should be able to narrow the focus of your topic. At this time, you may wish to consult the *Bibliographic Index*, an annual listing of bibliographies, arranged by subject. This index lists all the bibliographies on a particular subject in a given year (a bibliography of bibliographies). Browsing through this index for several recent years will give you a sense of the subject and its subtopics; in addition, you may find some pertinent sources on your topic.

EXERCISE 7.4 Using the suggestions outlined above, investigate background sources on your topic and begin to focus your research. Cast a wide net as you begin your research; you can always revise and refine your focus based on the information you locate. When you have completed your background reading and research, begin to search and read in a more focused way.

7f Conduct focused research

Once background reading has helped you understand your subject, narrow it to a manageable size, and formulate a hypothesis, you are ready to read about your topic in a more focused way. Conducting focused secondary research involves locating—through magazines, newspapers, journals, books, government documents, and the Internet—the specific information you need to write your paper.

See 7f-5

1 Using the library's online catalog

See Fig. 7.5

The digital catalog is one of the most visible computer tools in libraries today. Computerized systems, which have replaced the traditional card catalog, are designed to handle various library functions, such as circulation, cataloging, and location of materials within the library collection. Most computerized catalogs are searchable by author, title, and subject; in addition, computerized catalogs are searchable by keyword or by a combination of subject and keyword.

See Guidelines 7f-1 and Guidelines 8c-2

Many libraries offer instruction in the use of the computerized catalog. If yours does, take advantage of it and spend the time you need to learn how to confidently use your library's computer system. Typically, a library's

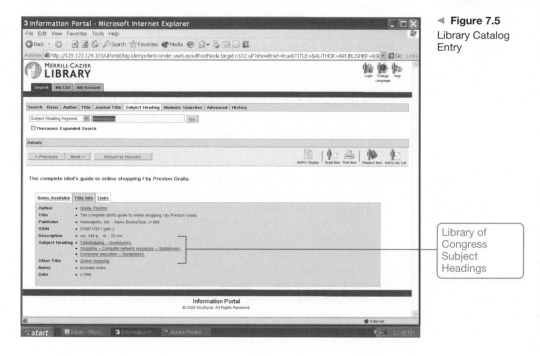

Figure 7.5 Library Catalog Entry

computerized catalog indexes books, government documents, and audiovisual materials.

❷ Using the library's online databases to locate journals and magazines

The most reliable way of conducting a search on any academic subject is through your college library's database services. Your library will provide you with access to numerous indexes that list sources, as well as to full-text sources on academic subjects. The advantage of searching through your library's databases is that you eliminate a lot of the extraneous "noise" that you get from a *Google* search. If you simply type keywords into *Google*, you will get commercial sites, advertising sites, popular press, personal blogs, and so on. A *Google Scholar* search is better than a general *Google* search, but

See TechHelp 7a-5

Keyword Searching

1. **What is a keyword search for?** A keyword search allows you to search for the term or terms that you have identified as being most important for your project.
2. **Where does the computer search for the keywords?** The computer will locate all items in the database, catalog, or index that include the particular keywords anywhere, from the title to the body to the bibliography.
3. **Can the computer supply other related words?** Typically the computer will not be able to supply synonyms for the keywords you have identified. You need to think of as many keywords as possible.
4. **What terms should I use as keywords?** You will have to use your knowledge of the topic, gained through background reading, to come up with keywords. For example, if you are searching the subject of UFOs, you might use *UFO* as a keyword. But you might also want to try *flying saucers* or *paranormal events.*
5. **Can I do a keyword search on the Internet?** The same kind of keyword searching discussed here can be done on the Internet.

GO See Ch. 8

still it may lead you only indirectly to the full-text databases to which your library subscribes. The best place to start is with your own library.

Library databases you should try

Each library organizes its databases differently, so you will need to take the time to become acquainted with the system used on your campus. Your reference librarians and any online help system provided at your library's Web site can get you started. For example, at Utah State University, the library's opening search screen (Electronic Resources and Databases) provides a full range of information that can be found via the library's Web portal—everything from full-text collections to searches by academic subject, specialized database searches, and encyclopedias and dictionaries.

See Fig. 7.6

Keywords will help you locate sources

You will need to first make a list of keywords on your topic. If you are researching global warming, for example, you want to use all the possible

See Guidelines 7f-1

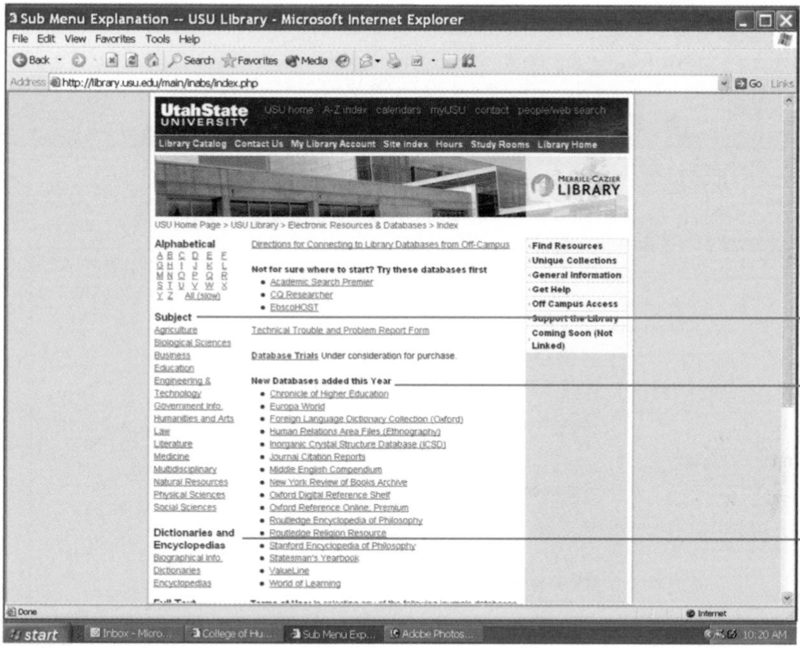

Figure 7.6 Electronic Resources and Databases from Utah State University's Library

Subject databases

Newspaper databases

Dictionaries and encyclopedias

keywords that you can think of, as well as any that turn up in your background reading. Find a good general database at your library's Web page, such as *Academic Search Premier* (from *EBSCOhost*) or *LexisNexis Academic*. Type in your keywords, using AND to narrow the search or OR to expand the search. Check any limiters you might want, such as the last five years or full-text only.

See Fig. 7.7

Keep track of sources and databases

It is very important to keep track of all the sources you locate through a particular database. If you ever need to find the article again, you will need to know where it was located. Notice on Figure 7.8 that there is an ADD menu item to the right of each article as well as a folder icon at the top of the page. As you browse the titles, you can add them to a folder in which you store all the relevant information from this particular search. Once items are in the folder,

Figure 7.7 ▶
Academic Search Premier with Keywords and Limiters

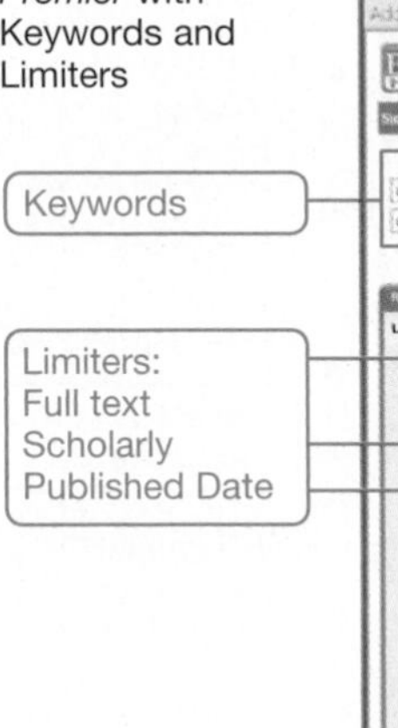

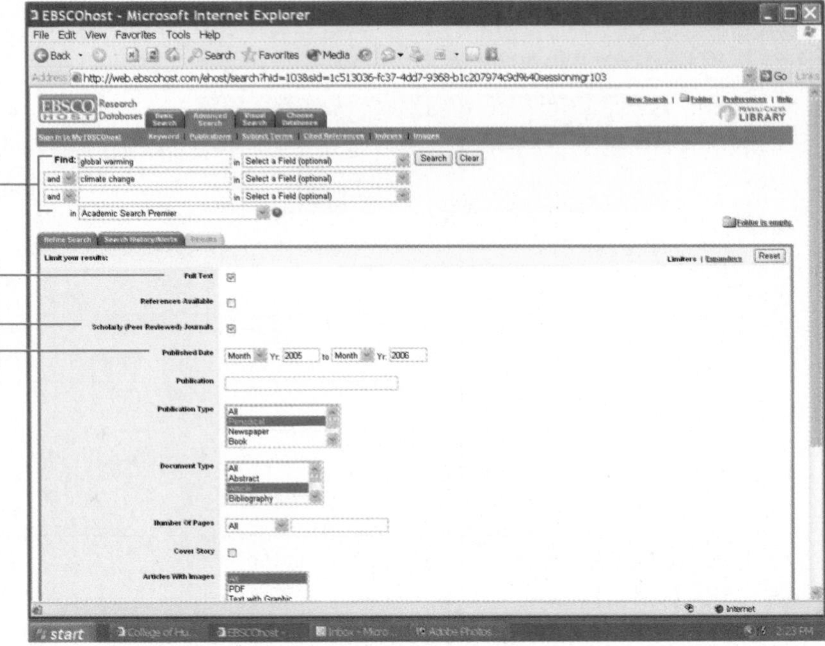

See Fig. 7.8

you can save to a disk, print, email, or archive at *EBSCOhost* those items you wish to retain for future reference.

❸ Use online newspaper databases

Your library will most likely subscribe to full-text newspaper databases as well as other library databases. Check the opening screen of your library's electronic resources page for a link to databases such as *ProQuest Newsstand* or *Utah Digital Newspapers Project*. A search via *ProQuest Newsstand* yielded numerous recent articles on UFOs and paranormal events. It is also possible to search the archives of major newspapers such as the *New York Times*, but such searches often involve a fee for service.

See Fig. 7.9

❹ Use other Internet resources

The Internet is now an important research tool in all fields of study. A biologist observed that he can locate information crucial to his research in

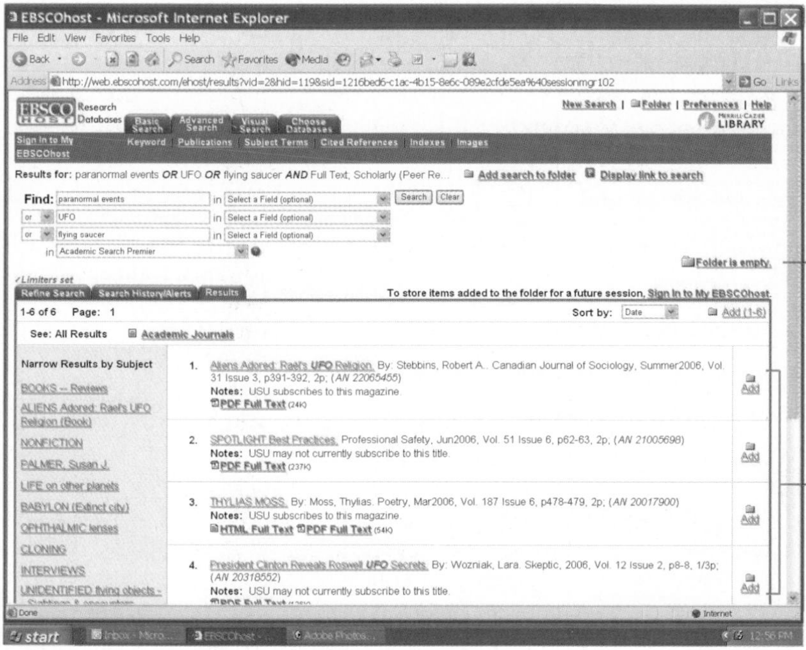

Figure 7.8 Results from Search to Add to a Folder

Folder

Click to add source to folder

minutes via the Internet, when it used to take days or even weeks of searching through print sources. Since the Internet has become so crucial to research, we devote an entire chapter in this handbook to the topic. In Chapter 8 we follow Kaycee Sorensen's use of the Internet to research her topic of cyber-shopping. In addition to finding information via library databases. Kaycee discovered information related to her topic on the Internet. It is often better to begin with the library's databases, to be sure that you are reading from reputable sources.

See Ch. 8

See 7f-2

❺ Doing primary, or field, research

In all disciplines, researchers use primary research methods to gather information and search for solutions to problems. For example, when a chemist performs an experiment in the laboratory, that is primary research; when an

Figure 7.9 ▶
Newspaper Full-Text Database Search

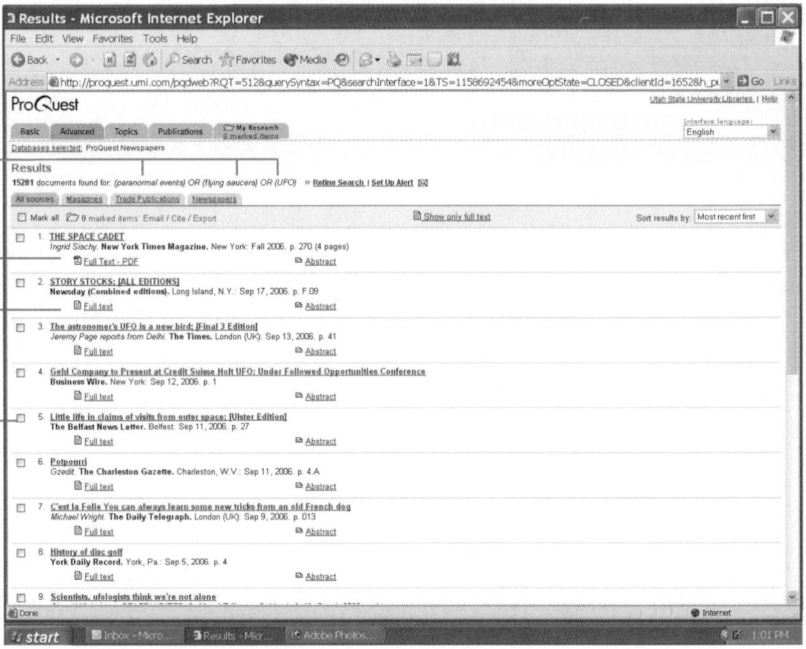

Keywords

Click for Abstract

Click for Full Text

Mark to save in folder

Results - Microsoft Internet Explorer

File Edit View Favorites Tools Help

Address http://proquest.umi.com/pqdweb?RQT=512&querySyntax=PQ&searchInterface=1&TS=1158692454&moreOptState=CLOSED&clientId=1652&h_pu

ProQuest

Utah State University Libraries | Help

Basic Advanced Topics Publications My Research 0 marked items

Interface language: English

Databases selected: ProQuest Newspapers

Results

15281 documents found for: (paranormal events) OR (flying saucers) OR (UFO) » Refine Search | Set Up Alert

All sources Magazines Trade Publications Newspapers

Mark all 0 marked items: Email / Cite / Export Show only full text Sort results by: Most recent first

1. THE SPACE CADET
Ingrid Sischy. New York Times Magazine. New York: Fall 2006. p. 270 (4 pages)
Full Text - PDF Abstract

2. STORY STOCKS; [ALL EDITIONS]
Newsday (Combined editions). Long Island, N.Y.: Sep 17, 2006. p. F.09
Full text Abstract

3. The astronomer's UFO is a new bird; [Final 3 Edition]
Jeremy Page reports from Delhi. The Times. London (UK): Sep 13, 2006. p. 41
Full text Abstract

4. Gehl Company to Present at Credit Suisse Holt UFO: Under Followed Opportunities Conference
Business Wire. New York: Sep 12, 2006. p. 1
Full text Abstract

5. Little life in claims of visits from outer space; [Ulster Edition]
The Belfast News Letter. Belfast: Sep 11, 2006. p. 27
Full text Abstract

6. Potpourri
Gzedit. The Charleston Gazette. Charleston, W.V.: Sep 11, 2006. p. 4.A
Full text Abstract

7. C'est la Folle You can always learn some new tricks from an old French dog
Michael Wright. The Daily Telegraph. London (UK): Sep 9, 2006. p. 013
Full text Abstract

8. History of disc golf
York Daily Record. York, Pa.: Sep 5, 2006. p. 4
Full text Abstract

9. Scientists, ufologists think we're not alone

See 7a-1

archaeologist goes on a dig, that is also primary research. For our purposes, *primary research*, also called *field research*, will refer to the kind of field collection of data that you as a college undergraduate can do. Of course, there is a great deal to learn about the primary, or field, research methods commonly used in various disciplines; we will consider just a few field research techniques that can be adapted for use in a research project—observation, surveys, and interviews.

Observation

Observation is best suited to the collection of nonverbal data. The observer watches people behave in customary ways in a particular environment or setting and takes notes. You might observe where people stand in an elevator, for example, or how they cross a street at an unmarked crosswalk.

Conducting Effective Observations

1. Articulate a general goal for the observation.
2. Gather background information.
3. Plan your observation carefully so as not to unduly influence the behaviors of those you are observing.
4. Take accurate notes during your observation and accumulate them in a research notebook.
5. Analyze your observation notes for trends or patterns.

Through observation, you accumulate *field notes*, which are used to analyze trends and discern customary behaviors. The disadvantages of observation include lack of control over the environment, lack of quantifiable data, and small sample size.

Surveys

Ideally, an entire population would be studied to gain insights into its society. However, polling an entire population is seldom feasible, so surveys are used to sample small segments of the population selected at random. Researchers have refined sampling techniques to be extremely accurate. One common kind of survey is the questionnaire, a form that asks for responses to a set of questions. Designing questions is a science that has been developed over the years. For an example of a paper that uses data from a student-generated questionnaire, see the social science paper in Chapter 18.

See 18-c

Interviews

The advantages of the interview include flexibility (the questioner can interact with the respondent), speed of response (the questioner immediately knows the responses), and nonverbal behavior (the questioner can gather nonverbal as well as verbal responses). However, because interviews take time, fewer responses can be gathered. Another disadvantage is that the character of the interviewer him- or herself can influence the outcome of the interview.

Conducting Effective Interviews

1. Articulate a general goal for the interview, and make an initial contact with the subject.
2. Confirm the appointment the day before.
3. Be prompt, have your questions ready, and stick with the time allotted for the interview.
4. Ask your questions exactly as you wrote them down.
5. Politely probe any unclear or incomplete answers.
6. Review your notes immediately following the interview.
7. Follow up with a thank-you note.

EXERCISE 7.5 Using the suggestions and resources described in this section, conduct focused research on your topic. Include both secondary (print and Internet) sources and primary (field) sources, as appropriate to your topic.

FOR COLLABORATION Interview a classmate using the interview guidance provided above. When you have completed your interview, report to the class what you learned about your subject. Discuss with your classmates what makes an effective or ineffective interview.

8 Using the Internet for Research

FAQs

- How can the Internet help me with my research? (8a)
- What kind of information is available on the Internet? (8b)
- How can I find anything on the Web? (8c)
- What is a search tool? (8c-1)
- What does an Internet search look like? (8d-1)
- What does a search of a library subscription service look like? (8d-2)

Searching the Internet is time-consuming, messy, and often frustrating for students, with numerous dead ends and false starts. Sometimes you will find far too many sources and sometimes none at all. Searching smarter can help. We recommend persistence and also attention to using search tools wisely.

See 8a-c

8a Use Internet sources throughout the research process

When beginning to research on the Internet, you should follow a search strategy, as outlined in 7a-5.

See 7a-5

❶ Finding and exploring topics

You do not need to wait until you are well into your research to turn to the Internet. In fact, because Internet search tools are often organized by topic and subtopic in subject directories, you can use them to explore topic options in the preparing stage of the writing process. For an example of how one student used the Internet to explore a research topic, see 7a-3.

See 8c
See TechHelp 3b-1 and 7a-3

❷ Conducting background and focused research

Once you have decided on a topic, you can use the Internet to find background information and to search in a more focused way. Many of the reference materials used in the library for background information (such as dictionaries, encyclopedias, and handbooks) are also available through the Internet. Internet libraries, online collections, and library subscription databases are discussed in 8c-2.

See 8c-2

❸ Collaborating and exchanging feedback

Email and online discussion forums are ideal for trying out your topic ideas on your instructor and your peers. As you research and write your paper, take advantage of the forums the Internet provides for sharing information—trade ideas, drafts, research sources, and revision feedback.

See Ch. 21
See 3d-2, 3g, 6e

8b Get to know the Internet and the Web

By far the easiest and most popular way of accessing information from the Internet is via the **World Wide Web**, or the Web for short.

❶ Surfing the World Wide Web: Browser tools and homepages

The World Wide Web, a huge spider web-like structure that encompasses computer networks throughout the world, seems to have been woven overnight. No one spider wove this web; anyone and everyone can contribute. This is probably the Web's greatest strength as well as its greatest weakness. It is a strength because no single organization could have compiled the varied and vast amounts of information placed on the Web for anyone to access. It is a weakness because the lack of control creates an information hodgepodge, with the trivial and wildly inaccurate alongside the profound and factual. When looking for information on the Web, you may find everything from vanity homepages to the latest scientific information from a NASA space probe.

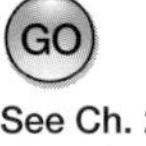
See Ch. 21

Internet browser tools

If you are using a computer in a campus lab, there will probably be icons on the opening screen for the two most popular browsers, *Mozilla Firefox* and *Internet Explorer*. They have comparable features and are free. If you are using a recent version of *Windows*, you will find that *Internet Explorer* has already been installed on your computer. Upgrades for both of these browsers can be found at their respective Web sites and **downloaded** to your own computer.

See Fig. 8.1 and 8.2

Both *Explorer* and *Firefox* include many useful tools that will help you as you conduct your research on the Internet.

Keeping track of your search

Both *Firefox* and *Explorer* help you keep track of important Web sites and retrace the steps of your Internet search. The GO feature keeps a running list of the Web sites you have visited during your current Internet session. It will disappear when you close down your browser.

◀ **Figure 8.1**
Firefox Browser

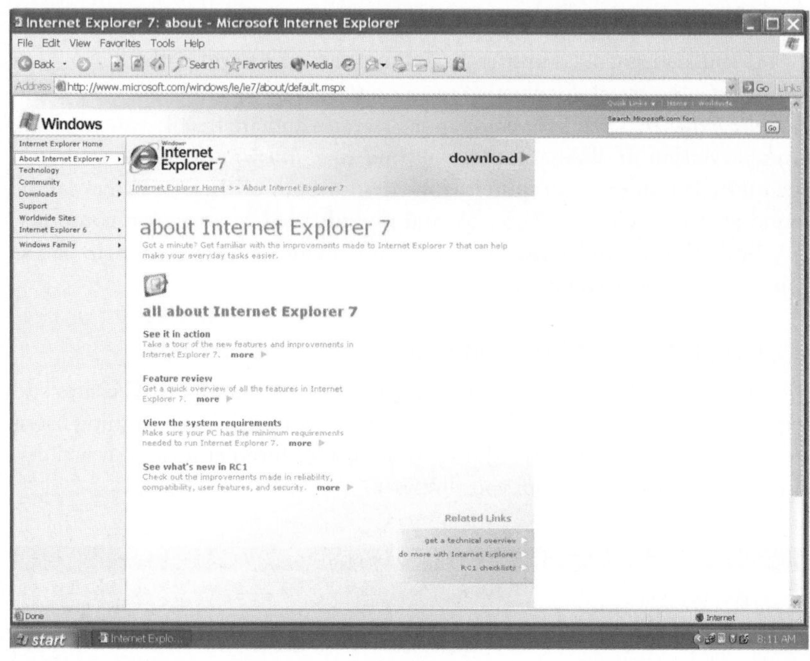

Figure 8.2 ▶ *Internet Explorer* Browser

See TechHelp 8b-1

If you have found a page that you want to visit frequently, you can add this site's address to your list of favorites. You can add a page to your favorites by visiting that page and then choosing ADD TO FAVORITES from the bookmark menu or button. You can also arrange your favorite sites into folders.

To retrace your steps after an Internet search, you can use the HISTORY feature of your browser (found as a button on the toolbar in *Explorer*). You can customize your history to keep track of Web pages visited within a certain length of time. This is useful if you visited a site recently but can no longer recall its address or how you found it.

❷ Respecting copyright and avoiding plagiarism

The amazing growth of the Internet has spawned numerous debates about censorship and freedom of information. At issue is the amount of control that governments and copyright owners should be able to exercise with regard to information found on the Internet. Electronic sharing of information

Using the FAVORITES or BOOKMARK Feature

Marking Internet Sites Using *Internet Explorer*

1. Add sites to your list of favorites by clicking on the ADD TO FAVORITES button on the FAVORITES menu.
2. Click on ORGANIZE FAVORITES to sort them into folders.

Marking Internet Sites Using *Mozilla Firefox*

1. Click on BOOKMARKS > BOOKMARK THIS PAGE to add a page to your list of bookmarks.
2. Click on BOOKMARKS > MANAGE BOOKMARKS to arrange or organize the sites you have bookmarked into folders.

via the Internet is predicated on the copying of files—including files of digitized music, art, graphics, or films—from one computer to another. This ability to copy the work of others has led some people to ask legislators to place restrictions on copying, or "borrowing," information from the Internet.

Current legal interpretation of copyright law indicates that anything (such as text, graphics, or music) placed on the Internet by an individual or group is

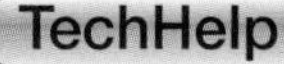

Using the HISTORY Feature of Your Web Browser

Checking Your History in *Internet Explorer*
To check the history of your search, click on the HISTORY button found on the toolbar. *Explorer* will display a search history menu on the left side of your browser window. The HISTORY feature can be customized using the TOOLS menu from the menu bar.

Checking Your History in *Mozilla Firefox*
To find the HISTORY feature, click on the GO menu at the top of the page. *Firefox* will display a search history menu on the left side of your browser window. You may wish to customize your history by using the VIEW menu button, which allows you to sort the history of sites you visited by date, most-visited site, and so forth.

Using Web Materials Ethically

- When writing your own Web pages, download only images or texts that are considered "freeware"—that is, that are offered by the site to users free of charge. If you are not certain, you should email the author or site sponsor for permission to either download the material or link to it from your own page.
- If you wish to use a portion of another's work on your Web page, the general rule is that duplicating ten percent or less of the work constitutes fair use. To use more than this from a source you must secure permission. Be sure to include the statement "Reprinted by permission" when you have secured permission.
- Of course, you should include appropriate citation information on the original source, for both material for which you have obtained permission and material that does not require permission, such as freeware and material used according to fair use copyright standards. (See the *Copyright Website* listed in 8b-2.)

See Ch. 10

presumed to be copyrighted by its authors. However, the ease with which information can be copied and distributed via the Internet makes it nearly impossible to enforce such a rigid interpretation of copyright law. The debate over rights is likely to continue to rage, as commercial authors and publishers seek to receive just compensation for their work and Internet boosters try to preserve the free flow of online information. The *Copyright Website* at <http://www.benedict.com> provides detailed information on recent copyright controversies. Another site with good information is the *Copyright Management Center* at <http://www.copyright.iupui.edu>.

Finding online information

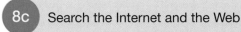

8c Search the Internet and the Web

When you use information from an Internet source, remember that it probably has not been reviewed by anyone other than members of the organization that maintains the site. For example, a review of computers on Gateway

Computer's Web site is likely to be biased in favor of Gateway products, and a discussion of gun control at the National Rifle Association's site will reflect that organization's views.

See Ch. 9

❶ Using search tools to locate information on your topic

How do you go about finding specific information on a particular topic? The most reliable way is to use your library's databases. For a broader Internet Search, you can use a search tool. Some search tools, often called **search engines**, use an automated system to sort pages based primarily on the use and placement of keywords. *Google* and *Yahoo*! are examples of search engines. Search engines automatically find and catalog new sites as they are added to the Web, indexing information by title and keywords.Remember that using these broad search tools will yield many unreliable sources that you will need to sort through and weed out.

See 7f-2,
See Guidelines for Using Search Tools 8c-2

◄ **Figure 8.3** *Google* Directory for Topic Search

Type in Keyword

Directory of topics

TechHelp

WEBLINK
Search tools

Using Social Bookmarking Sites

The Internet is constantly evolving and new tools are developed that help users connect to each other. One such innovation is social bookmarking—designed to help users log and share their bookmarks or favorites on the Web with others interested in the same topic.

Advantages of Social Bookmarking

Social bookmarking sites such as *delicious.com* or *digg.com* allow users to save, categorize, and post their bookmarks on the Web. These bookmarks can either be shared or kept private by each user. If you want to find out what Web sites other users have bookmarked or which sites are the most commonly visited for a particular topic, a search of the bookmarking site can be conducted. Another advantage is that your bookmarks will be available to you on the Web no matter which computer you are using at the time (e.g., your parents' home computer, a public computer in the library, or your personal laptop.)

Searching with keywords

By searching your library's collection you will no doubt already have identified keywords that you can use in a search engine. Enter a **keyword** that identifies your topic and search for **hits** of that keyword—Web pages on which the word appears. Many search tools also permit more sophisticated, customized searches, but the options differ from one search tool to another. Check the search tool's help screen for ways to customize your search, particularly if you are getting hundreds or even thousands of hits for your search term.

See 7f,
See Guidelines for Using Search Tools 8c-2

Using Boolean operators

One of the ways in which search tools allow you to narrow your search is by means of **Boolean operators**—for example, AND and NOT. The same principles used to search by keyword in a library database also apply to searching on the Internet. For example, if you type *childcare in Oregon,* you may get all of the hits for *childcare* in addition to all of the hits for *Oregon,* yielding thousands of sources. But if you combine the terms using the Boolean operator AND, you ask the search engine to find only those sources that include both

See Guidelines for Using Boolean Operators for Internet Searching 8c-2

childcare AND *Oregon* in the same source (the AND limits the search). To limit the search even more, you could add the Boolean operator NOT: *childcare AND Oregon NOT preschool.* Then, any sources mentioning preschool would be eliminated from the list.

Using quotation marks

Another way to focus the search is by using quotation marks, which indicate that the words must appear in a particular order in the text. For example, *"global warming"* would tell the search tool that you are not interested in *global* or *warming* by itself; you want only the two terms in combination, exactly as written inside the quotation marks. In a search on global warming, one student found that *Yahoo!* yielded over 27 million hits for *causes of global warming* without quotation marks and 375,000 hits for *"causes of global warming."*

The only way to see if your search is yielding the results you are after is to browse through the listing of sites found by the search tool. Most search tools provide a brief description of the site, so you can quickly ascertain whether or not the search is finding relevant sources. If it is not, try again with new search terms, subject areas, or limiters (such as Boolean operators). Make use of the search tool's help screen if you are not achieving the results you desire.

2 Using Internet library subscription databases

As discussed in 7f-2, most libraries subscribe to database services so that their patrons can search Internet databases for articles. Full-text databases provide access to the complete text of an article. Find out which of these services your library subscribes to. Some common ones are *LexisNexis* and *EBSCOhost.*

See 7f-2
See 8d-2

Searching virtual libraries

Many libraries make some of the information from their collections available via the Internet. For example, the online collection of the University of California is available at the site listed in the Guidelines for Using Internet Libraries and Collections. You can also use *LibCat,* which provides links to hundreds of libraries with Web access, or *LibWeb,* which provides links to online document and image collections of libraries around the world.

See Guidelines for Using Internet Libraries and Collections 8c-2

Guidelines

Using Search Tools

About.com http://about.com	Information database for "what you need to know about," using human guides who are topic experts
AltaVista http://www.altavista.com	Large, comprehensive database; keyword searching only; supports Boolean searching
Excite http://excite.com	Subject directory and keyword searching available; supports Boolean searching
Google http://google.com	Subject directory and keyword searching available
HotBot http://hotbot.com	Subject directory and keyword searching; includes newsgroups and email; supports Boolean searching
Ixquick http://ixquick.com	One of the world's largest metasearch tools, searching fourteen other tools simultaneously
Lycos http://lycos.com	Subject directory and keyword searching available; supports Boolean searching
Yahoo! http://yahoo.com	Subject directory and keyword searching available; includes news, chat, and email; does not support Boolean searching
Zworks http://zworks.com	Searches multiple search tools simultaneously; ranks the results of searches for relevancy by search tool; also filters to be relatively child-safe

Searching government documents

The federal government maintains numerous sites that you may want to use for research. The *White House* Web site offers an online photographic tour of the White House and provides links to important information about the federal government, including pending legislation, recently produced government documents, and cabinet activities and reports. (See also the *Thomas* Web site for legislation.) At the site produced by NASA, you can find

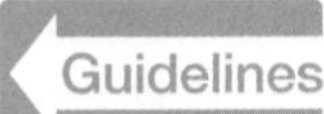

Using Boolean Operators for Internet Searching

Online databases use Boolean operators to combine two or more terms in ways that the computer recognizes. The Boolean operators most commonly used are AND, OR, and NOT.

1. Be sure to use the appropriate Boolean operator.
   a. AND (&) limits the search, because both keywords must be found in the search. For example, if you wanted to find information only on cats as pets, you could limit your search with the AND operator, typing in *pets AND cats.* The search would then be limited to those sources that included both words.
   b. OR (|) expands the search, because any text with either keyword will be included in the search results. For example, if you wanted to expand your search to include both dogs and cats, you would use the OR operator, typing in *dogs OR cats.* Both groups would then be included in your search.
   c. NOT (!) limits the search by excluding any text containing the keyword after the operator. For example, if you wanted to exclude dogs from your search of pets, you could do so with the NOT operator, typing in *pets NOT dogs.*
2. Enter Boolean operators in UPPERCASE letters (unless you use the symbols).
3. Leave a space before and after each Boolean operator.
4. If your phrase is complex, involving several Boolean operators, use parentheses: *(pets AND cats) AND (NOT dogs).* The same search can be indicated using symbols: *(pets & cats) & (! dogs).*

information on space flights, space research, and aeronautics. By using a search tool, you can locate specific information on hundreds of other government Web sites, including city and state sites.

Searching online periodicals

Newspapers and magazines that are published on the Web can be a good source for a research paper, particularly for background information. Several publishers offer online versions of their publications to consumers. Often you can access the full texts of articles that appear in the print version. For example, the *New York Times* is available online, as is *Time* magazine. If you know the name of the publication, you can search for it using one of the search tools

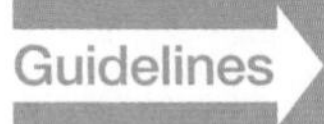

Using Internet Libraries and Collections

Academic Info http://academicinfo.net	Gateway to quality educational resources categorized by discipline
Educators' Reference Desk http://www.eduref.org	Includes the ERIC database with over one million abstracts on education topics
Internet Public Library http://www.ipl.org	Reference site built by the University of Michigan
LibCat http://www.librarysites.info	Links to hundreds of online libraries and library Web sites
Librarians' Internet Index http://lii.org	About eleven thousand links compiled by public librarians; highest-quality sites included with annotations
OAIster http://oaister.umdl.umich.edu/o/oaister	Links to free, academically oriented digital resources
University of California–Berkeley LibWeb http://sunsite.berkeley.edu	Links to online documents and image collections around the world
University of California–Riverside Infomine http://infomine.ucr.edu	Lists over 115,000 online sources by academic subject; reliable annotations

described in 8c-1. In addition, some Web sites will link you to major newspapers and magazines. For example, News Directory's twenty-four-hour *Newsstand* provides links to thousands of magazines and newspapers from around the world, cataloged by region and organized by topic (business, health, religion, sports, travel, social issues, and so on). Finally, you can use a search tool such as *Google* or *Yahoo*! to search for news in magazines and newspapers by selecting "Latest Headlines" or "Today's News" from the subject index.

See 8c-1,
See TechHelp 7a-4

Note that URLs change often. If the URL we have listed does not work, try shortening the address or searching by title. Also, go to <http://www.ablongman.com/hult> and click on the Web site for this handbook to get updates on URLs and additional sites to search.

Guidelines

Finding Documents from Government Sites

Bureau of the Census http://www.census.gov	Social, demographic, and economic information; index a–z; searchable by place, location, and word
Bureau of Justice Statistics http://www.ojp.usdoj.gov/bjs	Statistics on all criminal justice topics—law enforcement, drugs, crime, and so on
Bureau of Labor Statistics http://stats.bls.gov	Statistics by region, searchable by keyword; economy at a glance
Congressional Quarterly http://www.cq.com	World-class information and insight on government and politics
Department of Education http://www.ed.gov	Educational initiatives, news, publications, programs
Fish & Wildlife Service http://www.fws.gov	Information related to fish and wildlife
Library of Congress http://lcweb.loc.gov	Centralized guide to information services provided by the Library of Congress
National Institutes of Health http://www.nih.gov	Health information, grants, health news; database searchable by keyword
National Library of Medicine http://www.nlm.nih.gov	Free *Medline* searches; other medical databases
NASA http://www.nasa.gov	Tracking of current space flights and missions, including space shuttle missions
Statistical Abstract of the U.S. http://www.census.gov/statab/www	Collection of statistics on social, economic, and international subjects
Thomas (congressional legislation) http://thomas.loc.gov	Full text of current bills under consideration by US House and Senate
White House http://www.whitehouse.gov	Information on federal government initiatives, tours, etc.

Finding Online Periodicals

CNN Interactive http://www.cnn.com	CNN news from around the world; includes audio and video clips
Excite NewsTracker http://news.excite.com	News headlines from *Excite* (includes Reuters and UPI)
Google NewsTracker http://news.google.com	News headlines by topic
London Times http://www.timesonline.co.uk/global	Daily contents from the *London Times*
Lycos News http://news.lycos.com	News headlines from *Lycos* news service (includes CNN, ABC, Reuters, and others)
New York Times http://nytimes.com	Daily contents of the *New York Times*
Yahoo! Today's News http://dailynews.yahoo.com	News headlines from *Yahoo!* news service (includes CNN, ABC, Reuters, and others)

EXERCISE 8.1 Open your Internet browser and explore several of the search tools described above, including library links, government links, and newspaper links. Take an online tour of the White House, try searching the *New York Times* database, or find an online version of a local or regional newspaper. (Search for the newspaper by title, using any available search tool.)

8d Model searches of the Internet and library databases

1 Follow a student Internet search

To show you how a search might work, in this section we follow the Internet search of Kaycee Sorenson.

1. The first step in her search strategy was to look for a topic on the Internet, using the *Yahoo*! subject directory as a launching point. When Kaycee opened the *Yahoo*! guide, she saw several potentially interesting subject categories. Kaycee noticed the topic of "Shopping and Services" listed under the category "Business and Economy."

See TechHelp 7a-3

Since she had an interest in online shopping, she decided to look for relevant sources listed in that category.

Her starting questions were these:

- Is the number of online shoppers increasing?
- Is shopping via the Internet a viable solution for consumers?
- Is it safe to use a credit card for online shopping?

2. She typed the words *online shopping* into the search screen and asked *Yahoo*! to search just "Shopping and Services."

See Fig. 8.4

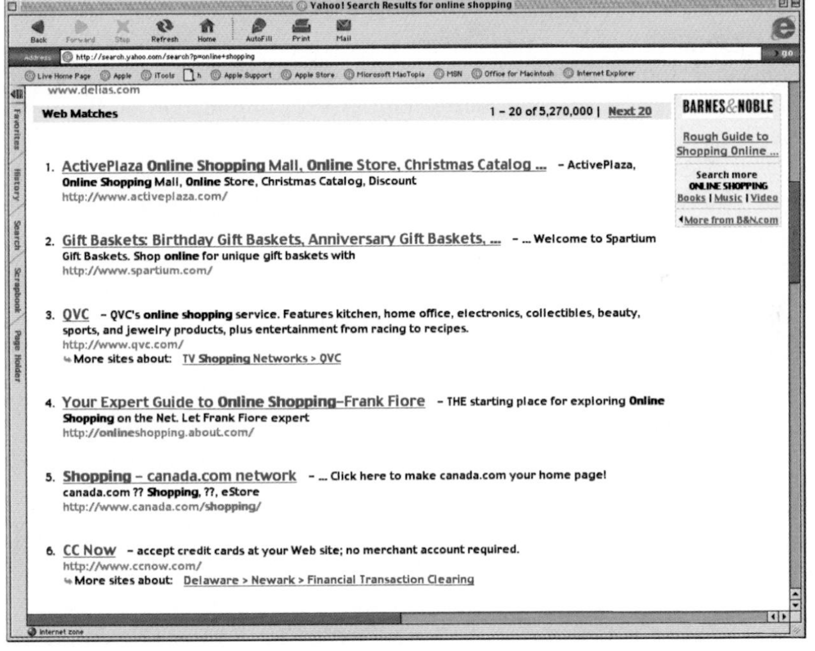

Figure 8.4 Searching the "Shopping and Services" Topic on *Yahoo*!

That search yielded more than five million hits for Web sources that contained either the word *online* or the word *shopping*. Kaycee also noticed that many of the sites were commercial businesses that offered consumers online shopping opportunities. Kaycee realized that her search terms were much too broad, so she needed to narrow her search further, especially since many of the links were irrelevant to her research topic. She first put the search terms in quotation marks so that *Yahoo*! would look for the keywords together in sequence. When she typed *"online shopping"* in quotation marks and clicked SEARCH JUST THIS CATEGORY, the search was still too broad. Kaycee then tried the combination *ecommerce + security* to further focus her search. She used the + sign to indicate that all results must have both the term *ecommerce* and the term *security* in them. The result of this search was closer to what she was after—with a range of articles and Web sites that were both commercial and noncommercial.

3. After browsing through the sources, following the links, and reading some of them to evaluate the sites for their relevance to her research questions, Kaycee printed out a few for later use, including the *Cyberatlas* and the shopping guide from *Hypermart.net.* Kaycee then went to her library to find books, magazines, newspapers, and journal articles with information on her topic. She located several magazines and newspapers that were useful, including *Money* magazine and *Capital Times.* Her use of the library's database service to search for journal articles is described in the next section. Remember that you should always seek a combination of different types of sources rather than relying exclusively on Web sites.

❷ Follow a student search of a library subscription database service

One of the best ways to search for journal articles that are academic in nature is through your library's subscription database services. You will need to check your library's Web site to find out which services it subscribes to. These databases will put journal articles on your topic at your fingertips. Often they include the full text of the article itself. That is, you can actually read the article online rather than having to locate it within the paper-bound volumes in your library.

See 7f-2

1. Kaycee used the library subscription databases extensively during her search for information on cybershopping. She first went to her library's

homepage to find out which databases (listing articles by topic) were available. She found a long list of databases by discipline. Notice that the databases are listed by subject in the left-hand margin and alphabetically in the main window. A check mark indicates a database that is suitable for general research; a page icon represents a database that includes full-text articles. Kaycee's librarian recommended *EBSCOhost* as a comprehensive database to use for academic research.

See Fig. 8.5

2. When she clicked on *EBSCOhost*, it took her to a list of databases from which to choose. By checking a box in the margin, she could search several databases simultaneously. She decided to try the *Academic Search Elite* to see what kinds of articles would be listed there.

See Fig. 8.6

This link brought her to a search page where she could enter her keywords and other relevant information to limit her search results. Kaycee's librarian had recommended that she use the advanced search because it would allow her to combine terms such as *Internet* and *shopping*. Kaycee refined her search by asking the database to find *Internet AND shopping* but *NOT retail*.

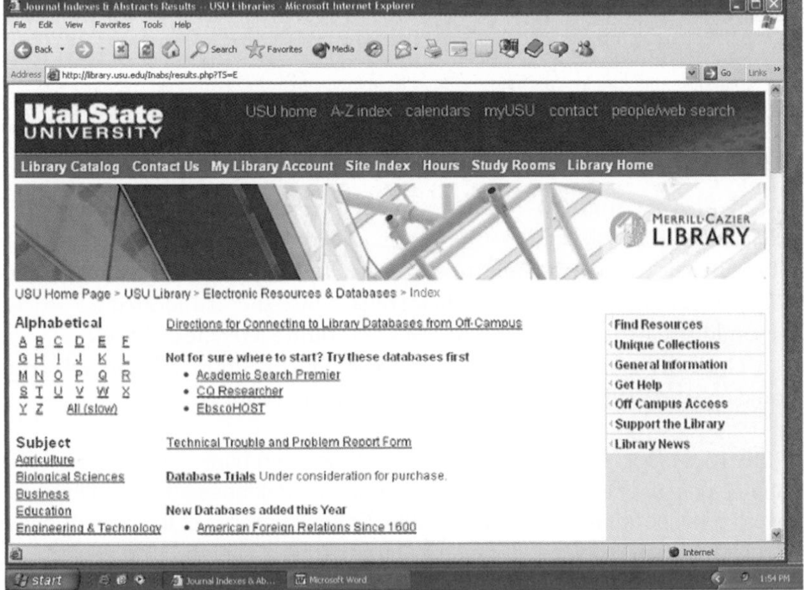

◄ **Figure 8.5**
Library Subscription Databases

Figure 8.6 ▶ EBSCOhost Academic Search Elite database Search results page

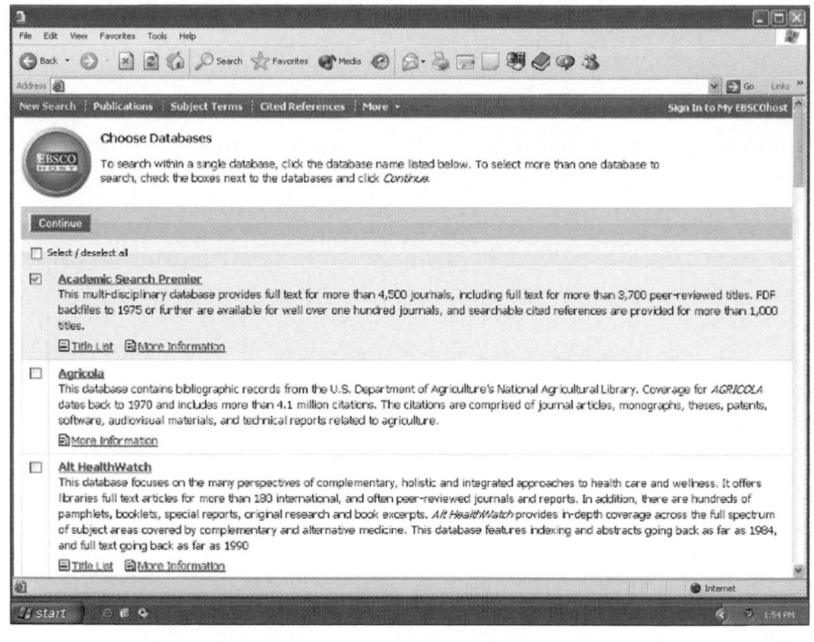

See Fig. 8.7

She did this to avoid sites that promoted retail shopping, such as Old Navy's online catalog. She also limited her results by asking for full-text journals that were peer reviewed and published within the last three years.

3. She got fourteen results from these terms. A few of them looked promising, so she clicked the ADD button to add those to her personal citation folder. By clicking on the links to either the PDF or the HTML full-text version, she could read the articles themselves. Once she had located an article, she could also download, print, or save it for future reference.

See 7f-2

This brief tour through the *EBSCOhost* illustrates how valuable subscription databases through your library's Web site can be for your research.

See Fig. 8.3

EXERCISE 8.2 Pick a topic that interests you and begin a search. First use the *Google* directory to work your way down the database; then type in a keyword and see what results you achieve. Check out some of the links. Are you finding relevant sources? If not, try narrowing your search using AND or NOT; you can also combine terms in quotation marks.

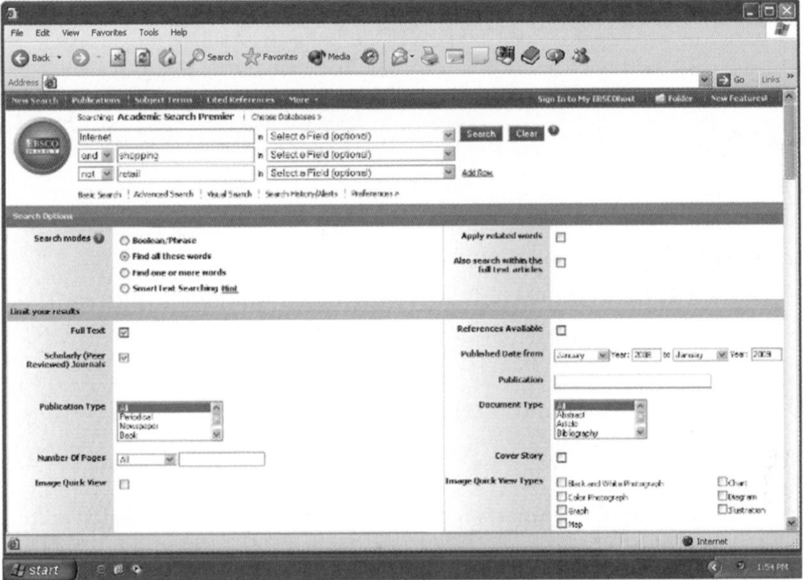

◀ **Figure 8.7** Advanced Search results page

FOR COLLABORATION Write a brief paragraph about your understanding of copyright as it applies to information (texts, graphics, photos) you find on the Internet. Share your paragraph with a small group of your classmates. Do you all agree on what is ethical and fair use of Internet materials? Share your collective understanding with the rest of the class in order to generate your own class standards of fair use.

EXERCISE 8.3 Search a full-text database to which your library subscribes. Follow the steps above in 8d-3 for Kaycee's search. Use the keywords you have listed thus far in your research. Print out or save to a disk or flash drive any relevant articles you locate.

See 8d-3

9 Evaluating Print and Electronic Sources

FAQs

- What makes a print source reliable? (9a-1)
- How important is the date something was published? (9a-1 and 9a-2)
- How can I evaluate an author's credibility when researching online? (9a-2)
- What makes an Internet source reliable? (9a-2)

One of your most important tasks as a researcher in today's digital culture is to evaluate what you read. The tendency to believe everything you read, either in print or online, is a dangerous one.

Some—though certainly not all—print sources undergo a process of peer review and evaluation before they are published. (*Peer review* is the practice of sending material to experts in the field for evaluation before it is published.) Peer-reviewed sources can generally be trusted to present information accurately. In contrast, the screening process for Internet materials is unpredictable. Many people who create Web sites or blogs have a sense of personal integrity, but others are less than forthright in the ways they use the medium to promote themselves or their viewpoints. Reading with a critical eye is always important, but it is particularly vital in dealing with Internet information.

See 2b, Fig. 9.1

9a Choose legitimate sources

Because you will be relying on your sources to provide evidence and authority to support your hypothesis, you need to choose legitimate, credible sources. Your credibility or *ethos* as a researcher may be at stake. Whether you are evaluating print or online material, choosing legitimate sources is a two-step process:

See 3b-2

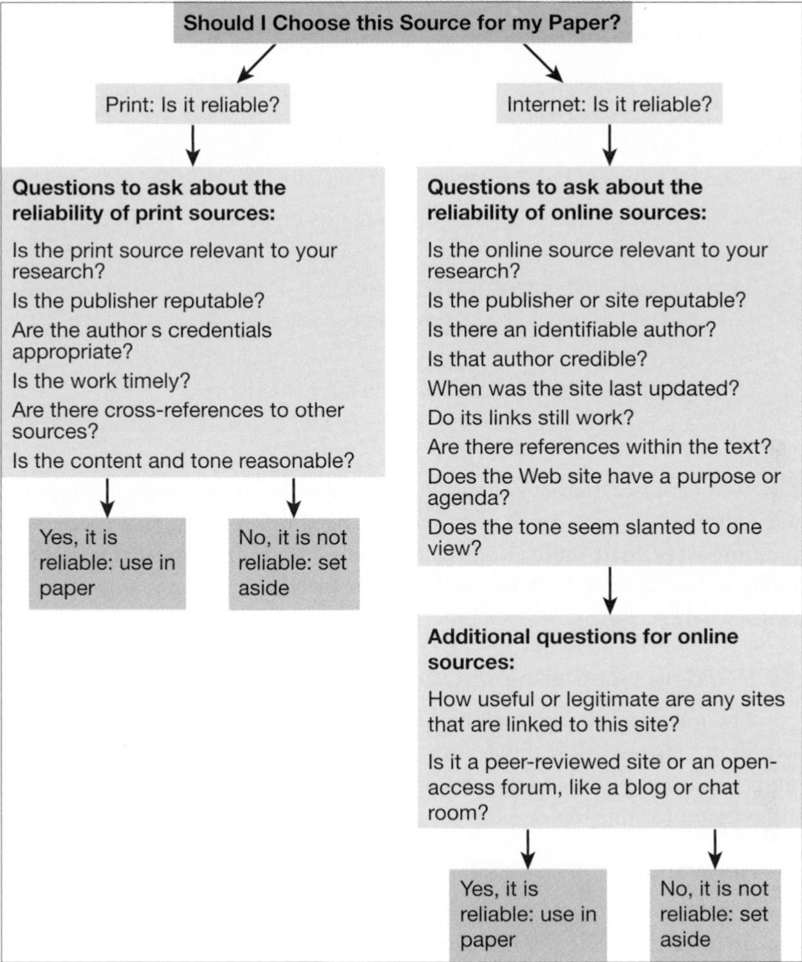

Figure 9.1
A Strategy for Evaluating Sources

1. Decide whether or not the source is relevant and reliable enough to be worth reading.
2. Decide whether or not the source is worth using in your research paper.

For both print and online sources, you apply the same basic criteria for determining the source's legitimacy and applicability to your research project.

TechHelp

Finding a Site's Homepage

A well-designed Web site will include a link to the homepage on every page of the site. If a site does not have such a link, however, you can "travel up" the URL directory to locate the site's homepage.

1. Open your browser and locate the site that interests you.
2. Look at the URL that appears in the LOCATION or ADDRESS line of your browser.
3. Back your way up the URL path by deleting the section of the address that follows the last slash (/) in the address. Hit ENTER to retrieve the new page.
4. Keep doing this until you have reached the homepage.

See 9b

See 9a-2

However, because Internet content is not regulated—anyone with a computer and online access can contribute—you will need to ask additional specialized questions to evaluate online research materials. For this reason, advice on evaluating online sources, with its own medium-specific guidelines, appears in its own separate section.

Evaluating sources

❶ Deciding whether a print source is reliable

The mere fact that something has been published does not guarantee its veracity or accuracy. For this reason, it is essential to be able to peruse print sources efficiently with an eye toward deciding whether they are legitimate and relevant to your topic.

Relevance

Is the source relevant to your research? Does the source address the topic you are researching? Sometimes a title will mislead you; checking subheadings in articles and tables of contents in books can help you see whether a source is actually on another topic entirely or on a narrow aspect of your topic. If a source is not relevant, move on.

Publisher or sponsor

Who is the sponsoring organization or publisher? Is the article in a popular magazine like *Vanity Fair* or a professional journal like the *Journal of Behavioral*

School Library Journal Mobile

School Library Journal

The world's largest reviewer of books, multimedia, and technology for children and teens.

Because geogra... can be flat-out am...

Home | Print Issue | Reviews | Articles | Technology | Supplements | Newslett...

SLJ | Library News | Web | Reviews

SEARCH

ALA ANNUAL COUPONS

FREE informative and exciting webcast events that keep you up-to-date on best practi...

Share | RSS | Subscriptions | Reprints/License | Print | Email

Searching for the Perfect Summer Reading List?

The Coretta Scott King Committee offers some terrific choices

-- *School Library Journal, 6/19/2009 9:47:00 AM*

This summer, help celebrate the 40th anniversary of the Coretta Scott King Book Awards by encouraging kids to explore and learn with outstanding books by African American authors and illustrators. Based on Coretta Scott King awardees, this summer reading list has something for every reader and interest, everything from Mother Goose rhymes to music to sports and much more-all told from the African-American perspective. These books provide satisfying reading experiences for all children, while promoting understanding and appreciation of the culture of all peoples. Enjoy.—*Coretta Scott King Committee*

Preschool

Publication

Author

Timeliness

◄ **Figure 9.2** Screen Shot of a print Journal Article with Annotations

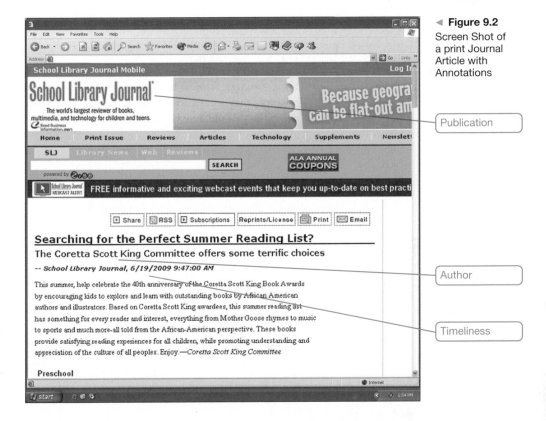

Sciences? For many college papers, the popular press—and particularly major newspapers like the *New York Times* or news magazines like *Time* or *Newsweek*—can certainly be useful, particularly as background information. Generally you can rely on the information found in publications produced by academic entities. But no information, regardless of its publisher or sponsoring agency, should be accepted at face value without critical evaluation.

See 2a

Author

Who is the actual author of the material? Books and journals may include an "About the Author" section, or the author's affiliation may appear on the title page. If no biographical data are provided, you may want to seek additional information to confirm an author's credentials—either at the library, within the sponsoring publication, in a biographical reference text, or via an Internet search. The sponsoring organization or publisher may provide the author with some degree of credibility; we assume, for example, that writers for *Newsweek* or the *Chicago Tribune* have appropriate credentials. This does not mean, however, that information found in magazines and newspapers—and even journals—should not be read critically, particularly for biases.

See Fig. 9.2

Timeliness

When was the article or book published? In many fields, the timeliness of information is as important as the information itself. For example, if you are researching a medical topic, you want to be certain that your sources are completely current. With print sources, you need to be especially careful about when a piece was written. Months or even years may go by between when something is discovered and when it finally appears in print. In rapidly changing fields, access to current information is crucial.

TechHelp

Web Searches: Using the Internet to Assess Author Credibility

For both print and online sources, you can use an Internet search to help you evaluate an author's credibility.

1. Open a search tool such as *Google*.
2. Type the author's name in the SEARCH box.
3. Choose PHRASE SEARCHING if it is available. If not, put the author's name in quotation marks to try to ensure that results will include only the individual you want.

When we typed the name *Nicholas Negroponte* into a *Google* search, we found hundreds of columns in *Wired* magazine written by Negroponte. In addition, we found biographies, book reviews, speeches, interviews, and photographs. We learned that Negroponte is founder and director of MIT's MediaLab. Overall, we felt confident that Negroponte was an expert in the field.

Cross-references

Is the source you are looking at cited in other works on the subject? Is the author cited in other works? You can sometimes make decisions about a work's credibility by considering how—and how often—the work is cited by other sources. You may find that one author's name comes up repeatedly in references and discussions. That author is probably an expert on the topic; it would be worth your while to find material written by that person. Likewise, once you have identified a source as reliable, you can use the references it includes to other sources to locate additional research material.

See TechHelp 9a-1

Rhetorical stance: audience, writer's persona and purpose, logical arguments

What is the intended audience for the piece? What discourse community is being addressed? What is the author's purpose and how does his or her persona come across? What logical arguments does the author draw on? The title of an article may help you establish which readers are being targeted. Journals and magazines typically are geared to particular target audiences, whom they assume share certain biases and opinions. If you are aware of these biases before you read a piece, you will be able to keep the information in context. What are the author and publisher trying to accomplish? Are they trying to sell a product or market an idea? Are they trying to persuade you to accept a particular point of view? Read the editorial policy of a magazine or newspaper to get an idea of the publication's purpose or agenda. Skim the piece quickly to get a sense of the arguments being marshaled by the author.

Content: tone and bias

Does the rhetoric used in the article or book suggest moderation and reason? Are the data included well-documented? Is the tone strident or preachy, or does it seem moderate and reasonable? Is the argument logically developed, or do there seem to be gaps in the evidence or obvious fallacies in the reasoning? How does the content match or contradict what others have said on the subject?

See Ch. 4

❷ Deciding whether an Internet source is reliable

The same general criteria are used to evaluate both Web sites and print sources. An additional challenge in evaluating electronic material is that some of the questions you will need to ask—about who an author or sponsoring

Assessing the Appropriateness of Print Sources

- **Title and subtitle.** Check both the title and the subtitle for relevance to your topic. For example, you could not be sure that a book titled *Wishes, Lies, and Dreams* was appropriate without reading the subtitle: *Teaching Children to Write Poetry.*
- **Copyright page.** Check this page, just after the title page, to find out who published the book, where it was published, and when.
- **Table of contents.** Check the titles of parts, chapters, and sections. The outline of a book can show you the topics covered and the detail of that coverage.
- **Abstract.** Read the abstract, if included. It will provide you with a concise summary.
- **Preface.** Read the preface. This is where the authors generally set out their purpose.
- **Chapter headings and subheadings.** Check the headings and subheadings to find out what specific subtopics will be discussed.
- **Conclusion.** Read any conclusion or afterword. It may give you another sense of the authors' stance.
- **Author note.** To evaluate credibility, read anything provided about the authors.
- **Index.** If available, check the Index for a listing of topics included in the book.
- **Bibliography.** Look at the list of references at the end of the article or book. It can tell you how carefully authors researched and can lead you to other related information.

organization is and when the site was published or last updated—may be difficult to answer because the information is hard to find, intentionally hidden or vague, or, in the most extreme cases, just not there.

Relevance

Do the title and subtitle of the online source suggest that it addresses your research topic and questions? Although titles and subtitles are a good initial indicator, remember that titles of online sources, like those of print sources, can be misnomers. An "About This Site" or "About This Organization" link is especially worth reading because it functions as a mission statement for the Web site's

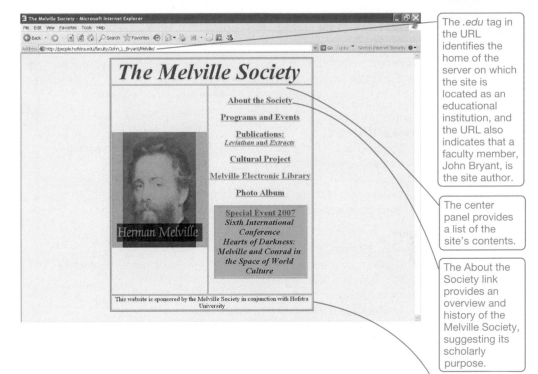

The *.edu* tag in the URL identifies the home of the server on which the site is located as an educational institution, and the URL also indicates that a faculty member, John Bryant, is the site author.

The center panel provides a list of the site's contents.

The About the Society link provides an overview and history of the Melville Society, suggesting its scholarly purpose.

The line at the bottom indicates who sponsors the site.

▲ **Figure 9.3** Home page of the Melville Society, an organization devoted to study of the works of American author Herman Melville. The site is housed at Hofstra University and offers information about publications and events sponsored by the Melville Society, as well as links to other sites that contain information about Herman Melville's life and work.

sponsoring organization, and it can also serve as a map for the site's contents. (The Melville Society site in Figure 9.3 has an About the Society section, as well as links to other independent sites containing Melville scholarship.)

See Fig. 9.3

Publisher or sponsor

Who is the site's publisher or sponsor? How credible is that person or group? What is their agenda or purpose? Well-known academic organizations and trustworthy commercial sources (such as publishers of reputable online journals, magazines, or newspapers) are generally considered reliable. However,

TechHelp

Web Searches: Using Domains and URLs to Assess Internet Sources

Although no organization regulates Internet content for its reliability or accuracy, the domain type offers hints about the source of a site. Those hints, in turn, will help you assess the site's content for legitimacy.

.edu

Typical Sponsor

Educational institution such as a college or university; often contains reliable, scholarly information.

Sample Sites

University of Michigan http://www/umich.edu

Purdue University Libraries http://www.lib.purdue.edu

.gov

Typical Sponsor

Department or agency of the federal government; presents information regarding research or policy issues

Sample Sites

U.S. Census Bureau http://www.census.gov

Mammalian Gene Collection, an initiative sponsored by the National Institute of Health http://mgc.nci.nih.gov

.fl.us, .il.us, etc.

Typical Sponsor

State or local government office. (URLs will vary, but tend to include the state abbreviation, followed by *.us*.)

Sample Sites

Florida Department of State http://www.dos.state.fl.us

Illinois Criminal Justice Information Authority http://www.icjia.state.il.us/public

.org

Typical Sponsor

Nonprofit organization or, in some cases, an individual; may contain biases favoring that organization's point of view

Sample Sites

American Red Cross http://www.redcross.org

United Nations Children's Fund http://www.unicef.org
Natural Resources Defense Council http://www.nrdc.org

.com

Typical Sponsor

Commercial business or other for-profit organization; need to be evaluated carefully for potential bias

Sample Sites

Amazon http://amazon.com
Project Bartleby http://www.bartleby.com

.net

Typical Sponsor

A network traditionally, but can be anything from an individual to a corporate Internet provider; need to be evaluated carefully for potential bias.

Sample Sites

Earthlink http://www.earthlink.net
Anthro.Net Research Engine: Anthropology and Archaeology http://www.anthro.net
American Music Resource http://www.amrhome.net

.mil

Typical Sponsor

The US military; limited usefulness unless your topic has a military focus

Sample Sites

Official U.S. Air Force Site http://www.af.mil
Official U.S. Marine Corps Site http://www.usmc.mil

.ca, .uk, etc.

Typical Sponsor

Country outside the United States (URLs will vary, but tend to include the country abbreviation (e.g, *.uk* for United Kingdom); sites will vary considerably so be sure to review with care

Sample Sites

The British Museum http://www.thebritishmuseum.ac.uk
Government of Canada Website http://www.canada.gc.ca

the viability as an academic research source of any sponsor that falls outside of this relatively finite group is questionable, and you will have to do additional work to confirm who the sponsor is and where the site comes from. Certainly any site for which you cannot identify a sponsor should be discarded as a source for a research project. Even when you can confirm the existence of the sponsoring organization of a Web site, sometimes, it can be hard to tell much about what the group is. One clue to the nature of the sponsoring organization is the URL itself. Internet conventions have been established to assign a standardized tag to Web addresses, called a *domain type.* Domain types tell you something about the nature of the sponsoring organization. Looking at the domain type of a Web site will help you to understand the purpose behind the page—whether educational or commercial, for example. These distinctions between domains are important because they can give you indications about a Web site's reliability as a source.

See 9b-2

See TechHelp 9a-2

Author

Is there an identifiable author, and is he or she credible as an expert on your topic? Many Web sites include either a biographical blurb about an author or an "About the Author" page. The sponsoring organization itself may also provide some level of author credibility. Keep in mind, however, that for Internet sources you may need to do additional research to clarify your evaluation of an author. If you have any doubt about an author's authority, trustworthiness, or possible biases on a given issue, you can and should use his or her name and whatever limited biographical information you obtain from the original source to investigate further—either via the library or using an online search engine like *Google.*

Timeliness

When was the site last updated? Do its links to embedded pages still work? The same general rules about currency and timeliness apply to both Internet sources and print sources. Although the instant access of the Internet compares favorably with the lag time often associated with print sources, determining what Internet information is reliable and how current it is may be more difficult. You will need to check the "small print" of the Web sites you peruse to see how recently they were updated; such information often appears at the very bottom of the main page or is buried under a site map, company or site sponsor name, or copyright link. You should also check to see whether the site's links are still

TechHelp

Web Searches: Identifying Sites as Personal Homepages

Personal homepages, maintained by individuals, will vary the most in terms of reliability. They may contain anything from legitimate scholarship by a professor with expertise in his or her field to the unsubstantiated opinions of an amateur to a personal Weblog diary with photos. Consequently, flagging such sites for more meticulous evaluation of their legitimacy is essential. You can usually determine whether a page is a personal site by asking the following questions:

- Does the site URL include a tilde symbol (~) followed by a name?
- Does the URL seem complicated or unconnected to the subject matter?
- Does the word *user* or *personal* show up either in the URL or somewhere on the page?
- Is it hosted on a popular commercial site, such as *AOL* or *MSN*?

working; "dead" links tend to indicate that the site has not been updated frequently and its contents should be treated with some skepticism.

Cross-references

Is there a Works Cited section or some other kind of reference list? Are there footnotes or endnotes? Are there any hyperlinks within the text? Check out any sources referenced to confirm the site's credibility. On many commercial Web sites, hyperlinked phrases are embedded in the main text. Evaluating these references can reveal the level of scholarship and support the author has for his or her position, as well as the site or author's stances or biases; ideally, it can guide you to other related, useful online information on your topic. (The US Census Bureau site in Figure 9.4 has a "Related Sites" link in the sidebar.)

See Fig. 9.4

Rhetorical stance: target audience, site's ethos, site's use of logical arguments

Does the Web site have an agenda? Does it seem to be targeted to a particular audience? Is it designed to persuade rather than inform? Does it seem to have a logical organizational structure? If the site includes an "About Our Site," "About Our Organization," or "About Our Company" page, read it carefully. This

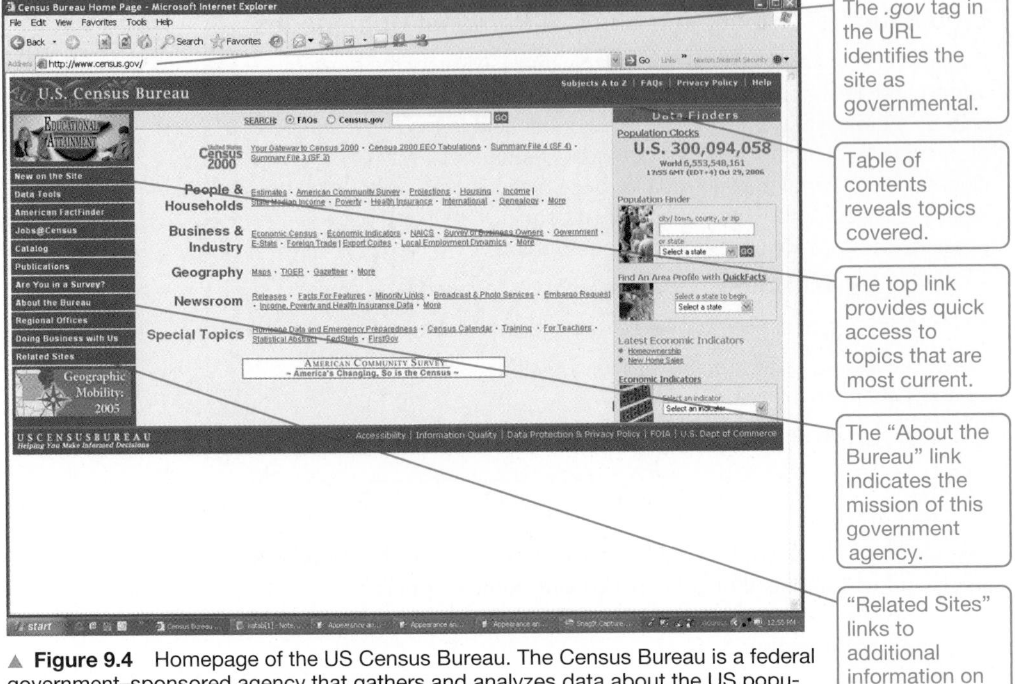

▲ **Figure 9.4** Homepage of the US Census Bureau. The Census Bureau is a federal government–sponsored agency that gathers and analyzes data about the US population and economy. The site presents and archives many of the agency's studies.

should describe its agenda. Regardless of the source, you will need to exercise caution as an information consumer.

Content and Tone

Does the content seem slanted toward a particular viewpoint? If so, is supporting evidence used to back up the claims? As with print sources, careful evaluation of the general tone of a Web site is necessary.

❸ Using special criteria for Web sites and other electronic sources

The following criteria can be used specifically for identifying credible online sources.

Web Searches: Assessing the Appropriateness of Web Sources

- **Title and subtitle.** Check the Web page title—found on the top line of your screen, above the browser window—and the title on the actual page for relevance to your topic. Check the domain type in the URL.
- **Copyright information.** Be sure to see what group sponsors the site; this information should be at the bottom of the homepage. Knowing the sponsor will help you assess a site's reliability.
- **Links to secondary pages.** Does the site include embedded links that elaborate on useful subtopics?
- **Abstract.** If an abstract is included, reading it will provide you with a brief summary.
- **Introduction.** Reading any introductory material should reveal the site's agenda; such material usually appears on the splash page or homepage.
- **Headings and subheadings.** Looking closely at the major divisions on the homepage may tell you how detailed or extensive the site is.
- **Conclusion.** Read any concluding material on the final page of the site. It may give you another view of the site author's stance.
- **Author page.** To establish a site's credibility, you must read any information about the author or site developer(s), which should appear at the bottom of the piece, under an "About the Author" link, or under an "About Our Site" link. Then confirm or expand the picture this gives you by conducting a search on the author's name, using an Internet search tool.
- **Glossary.** Looking at any glossary of terms included on the site may give you a deeper understanding of the topics covered.
- **Links to references.** Checking out the sources referenced (and evaluating their legitimacy) can tell you about the thoroughness, currency, and accuracy of the site's research.
- **Links to related sites.** Evaluating related sites recommended by the site you are considering can reveal the site or author's stances or biases, and it can also lead you quickly to other related, useful information.

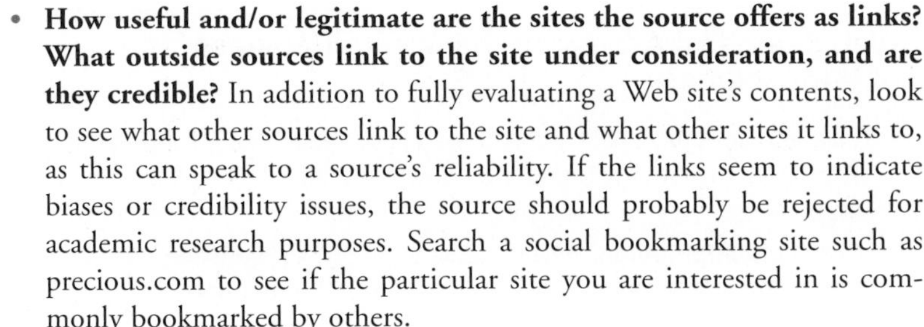

- **How useful and/or legitimate are the sites the source offers as links? What outside sources link to the site under consideration, and are they credible?** In addition to fully evaluating a Web site's contents, look to see what other sources link to the site and what other sites it links to, as this can speak to a source's reliability. If the links seem to indicate biases or credibility issues, the source should probably be rejected for academic research purposes. Search a social bookmarking site such as precious.com to see if the particular site you are interested in is commonly bookmarked by others.

GO See TechHelp 8c-1

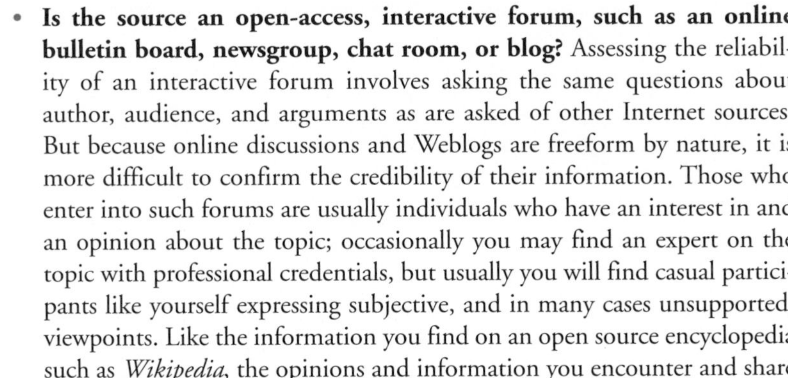

- **Is the source an open-access, interactive forum, such as an online bulletin board, newsgroup, chat room, or blog?** Assessing the reliability of an interactive forum involves asking the same questions about author, audience, and arguments as are asked of other Internet sources. But because online discussions and Weblogs are freeform by nature, it is more difficult to confirm the credibility of their information. Those who enter into such forums are usually individuals who have an interest in and an opinion about the topic; occasionally you may find an expert on the topic with professional credentials, but usually you will find casual participants like yourself expressing subjective, and in many cases unsupported, viewpoints. Like the information you find on an open source encyclopedia such as *Wikipedia*, the opinions and information you encounter and share

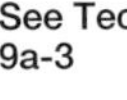

GO See TechHelp 9a-3

TechHelp

Web Searches: Using *Wikipedia* Appropriately

The free online encyclopedia *Wikipedia*, at <http://en.wikipedia.org/wiki/Main_Page>, will often be one of the first hits on a *Google* keyword search. However, you should use information found in *Wikipedia* with caution. Because the entries at *Wikipedia* can be written and edited by any visitor to the Web site, they vary in accuracy and reliability. Use *Wikipedia* as a starting point for exploring a topic, issue, or question. The entries may be useful for generating topic ideas and for locating points of controversy about a particular topic, but in general this is not a good source to cite in an academic research paper. Another potential use for online dictionaries and encyclopedias is to build your keywords and search terms that can lead you out to other more reliable scholarly sources found through a library database search.

GO See TechHelp 3b-1

Evaluating Source Information

The Sponsoring Organization

✓ Where does the information appear—in the popular press, in a scholarly journal or report, on a corporate Web site, on a blog?

✓ Who is the sponsor of the source—an academic association, a publisher, an organization?

✓ For a Web site, what is the domain of the URL—educational, commercial, governmental—and what can that help you determine about the site's content?

The Author

✓ Who is the author? Have you heard of this person? Does the author's name appear in other sources?

✓ What are the author's credentials?

✓ What kind of language does the author use?

✓ What kind of tone has the author adopted?

The Audience

✓ Who is the intended audience for the publication?

✓ Does the publication target obvious biases in its audience?

✓ What are the characteristics of the audience members?

The Agenda

✓ What are the author and sponsoring organization trying to accomplish?

✓ Is an idea or product being marketed?

✓ Are you being urged to adopt a particular point of view?

The Timeliness

✓ When was the piece published?

✓ When was the Web site posted and/or updated?

✓ How important is it that your information be current?

See TechALERT 9a-3

in these forums can be helpful for generating ideas and discovering interesting areas for further research, but they will not be much help as sources for a research paper. As a general rule, verify any information you find in such sources with at least one or two other reliable information sources.

EXERCISE 9.1 Select for evaluation four Web sites. For each site, make a note of the sponsoring organization, the author (if known), the target audience, the site's purpose or agenda, any apparent bias, the tone, and the timeliness of the information. Rank the sites in order of trustworthiness, based on your evaluation, from most trustworthy to least.

9b Follow a student's evaluation of Web links

See Fig. 9.5

To give you a sense of how you might go about evaluating information you find via an Internet search, let's follow a student searching for background information and ideas related to smoking. Mark Robb has been reading about the debate on smoking and addiction. He wants to find out more about both sides of the debate in an effort to begin to answer the question "Is smoking addictive?" Mark knows that the tobacco industry has argued that smoking is not addictive but merely habit-forming, so he begins his search for *"smoking is not addictive"* on *Google.*

1. The first site listed by *Google* is titled "Key Issues: Addiction or Habit?" The site's URL with its *.org* tag suggests an organizational site. When Mark clicks on the site, he finds a homepage called "FOREST." He clicks on the "About FOREST" link to find out about the site's sponsor, and he learns that FOREST stands for Freedom Organisation for the Right to Enjoy Tobacco. Who sponsors the organization? Reading further, he learns that most of its funding is provided by tobacco companies. Despite the assurances of independence on the Web site, Mark believes that any information found in this publication would have to be read with the organization's obvious bias in favor of tobacco and smoking in mind.

2. The second site listed in the *Google* search is titled "Consumer Misperceptions About Tobacco Still Abound. . . ." Mark notes that the URL address includes *nih.gov* (National Institutes of Health). Because the information is located on a reputable government site, he decides to read it. The article "smoking is not addictive" - Google Search - Microsoft Internet Explorer

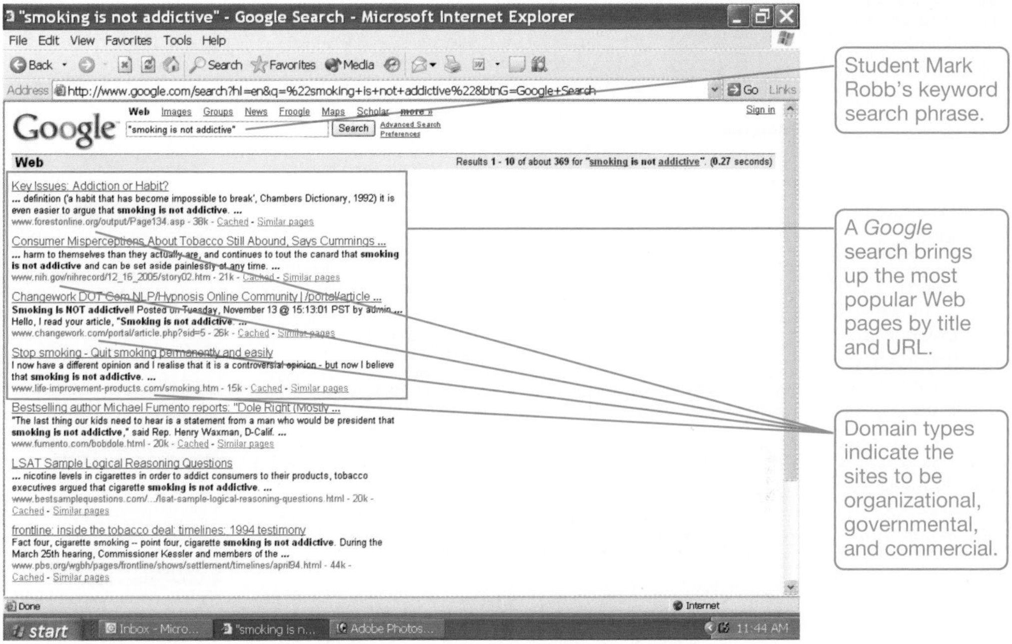

File Edit View Favorites Tools Help

Back Search Favorites Media

Address http://www.google.com/search?hl=en&q=%22smoking+is+not+addictive%22&btnG=Google+Search Go Links

Google Web Images Groups News Froogle Maps Scholar more »

"smoking is not addictive" Search Advanced Search Preferences

Sign in

Web Results 1 - 10 of about 369 for "smoking is not addictive". (0.27 seconds)

Key Issues: Addiction or Habit?
... definition ('a habit that has become impossible to break', Chambers Dictionary, 1992) it is even easier to argue that **smoking is not addictive**. ...
www.forestonline.org/output/Page134.asp - 38k - Cached - Similar pages

Consumer Misperceptions About Tobacco Still Abound, Says Cummings ...
... harm to themselves than they actually are, and continues to tout the canard that **smoking is not addictive** and can be set aside painlessly at any time. ...
www.nih.gov/nihrecord/12_16_2005/story02.htm - 21k - Cached - Similar pages

Changework DOT Com NLP/Hypnosis Online Community | /portal/article ...
Smoking is NOT addictive! Posted on Tuesday, November 13 @ 15:13:01 PST by admin ...
Hello, I read your article, "**Smoking is not addictive**. ...
www.changework.com/portal/article.php?sid=5 - 26k - Cached - Similar pages

Stop smoking - Quit smoking permanently and easily
I now have a different opinion and I realise that it is a controversial opinion - but now I believe that **smoking is not addictive**. ...
www.life-improvement-products.com/smoking.htm - 15k - Cached - Similar pages

Bestselling author Michael Fumento reports: "Dole Right (Mostly ...
"The last thing our kids need to hear is a statement from a man who would be president that **smoking is not addictive**," said Rep. Henry Waxman, D-Calif. ...
www.fumento.com/bobdole.html - 20k - Cached - Similar pages

LSAT Sample Logical Reasoning Questions
... nicotine levels in cigarettes in order to addict consumers to their products, tobacco executives argued that cigarette **smoking is not addictive**. ...
www.bestsamplequestions.com/.../lsat-sample-logical-reasoning-questions.html - 20k - Cached - Similar pages

frontline: inside the tobacco deal: timelines: 1994 testimony
Fact four, cigarette smoking -- point four, cigarette **smoking is not addictive**. During the March 25th hearing, Commissioner Kessler and members of the ...
www.pbs.org/wgbh/pages/frontline/shows/settlement/timelines/april94.html - 44k - Cached - Similar pages

Done Internet

start Inbox - Micro... "smoking is n... Adobe Photos... 11:44 AM

Student Mark Robb's keyword search phrase.

A *Google* search brings up the most popular Web pages by title and URL.

Domain types indicate the sites to be organizational, governmental, and commercial.

▲ **Figure 9.5** Student *Google* Search Results for "*smoking is not addictive*".

outlines a lecture to NIH by a reputable scientist, who uses humor to deliver a scathing indictment of tobacco companies and their campaign to provide smokers with crutches that keep them addicted: one of the crutches he cites is "the canard that smoking is not addictive."

Many other sites from the *Google* search follow the debate between the tobacco industry, which attempts to argue that tobacco is habit-forming but not addictive, and various health organizations, which dispute the tobacco industry's claims. Mark is learning a lot about the background of the smoking debate.

3. The third and fourth sites in the *Google* search are both commercial sites. One presents a 1996 article titled "Personal Health: Cigar Smoking" by science writer Jane Brody, published in the *New York Times*. To be on the safe side, Mark also conducts a *Google* search, using *"Jane Brody" + science* as

See Fig. 9.6

The sponsoring organization reveals itself to be a reliable source.

The publication date suggests the data may be outdated.

A keyword search of the author's name reveals Brody's credentials as a reputable science writer.

The contents heads preview article content.

Links lead to related information on other websites.

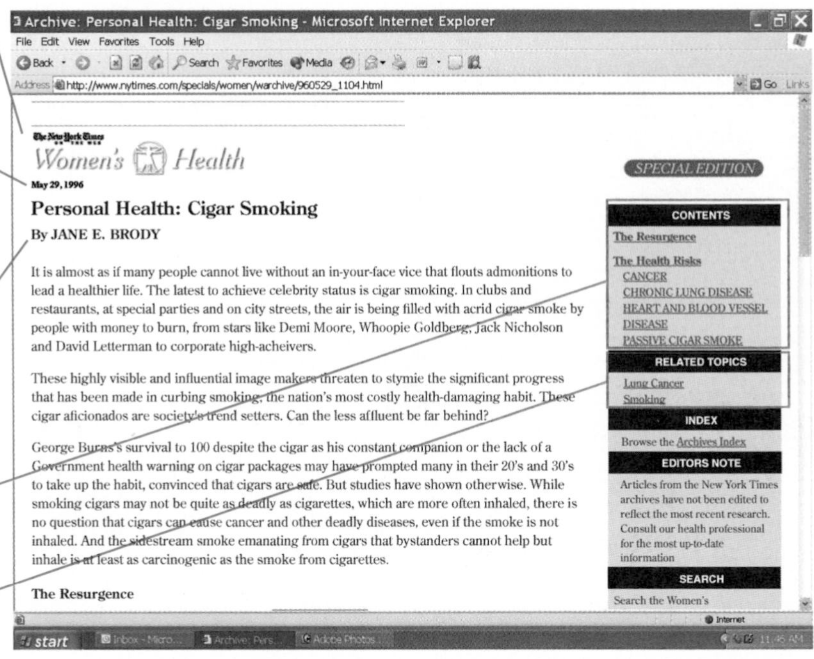

Archive: Personal Health: Cigar Smoking - Microsoft Internet Explorer

File Edit View Favorites Tools Help

Back Search Favorites Media

Address http://www.nytimes.com/specials/women/warchive/960529_1104.html

The New York Times

Women's Health

SPECIAL EDITION

May 29, 1996

Personal Health: Cigar Smoking

By JANE E. BRODY

It is almost as if many people cannot live without an in-your-face vice that flouts admonitions to lead a healthier life. The latest to achieve celebrity status is cigar smoking. In clubs and restaurants, at special parties and on city streets, the air is being filled with acrid cigar smoke by people with money to burn, from stars like Demi Moore, Whoopie Goldberg, Jack Nicholson and David Letterman to corporate high-acheivers.

These highly visible and influential image makers threaten to stymie the significant progress that has been made in curbing smoking, the nation's most costly health-damaging habit. These cigar aficionados are society's trend setters. Can the less affluent be far behind?

George Burns's survival to 100 despite the cigar as his constant companion or the lack of a Government health warning on cigar packages may have prompted many in their 20's and 30's to take up the habit, convinced that cigars are safe. But studies have shown otherwise. While smoking cigars may not be quite as deadly as cigarettes, which are more often inhaled, there is no question that cigars can cause cancer and other deadly diseases, even if the smoke is not inhaled. And the sidestream smoke emanating from cigars that bystanders cannot help but inhale is at least as carcinogenic as the smoke from cigarettes.

The Resurgence

CONTENTS

The Resurgence

The Health Risks

CANCER

CHRONIC LUNG DISEASE

HEART AND BLOOD VESSEL DISEASE

PASSIVE CIGAR SMOKE

RELATED TOPICS

Lung Cancer

Smoking

INDEX

Browse the Archives Index

EDITORS NOTE

Articles from the New York Times archives have not been edited to reflect the most recent research. Consult our health professional for the most up-to-date information

SEARCH

Search the Women's

Internet

start Inbox - Micro... Archive: Pers... Adobe Photos...

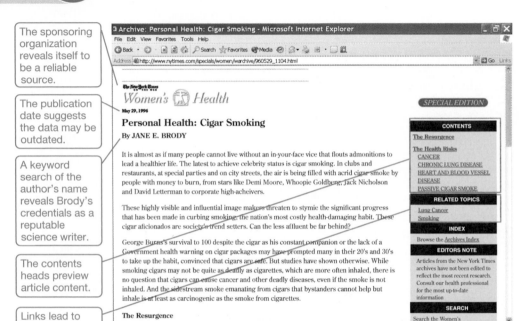

▲ **Figure 9.6** Science writer Jane Brody's May 29, 1996 *New York Times* article, found via student Mark Robb's *Google* search. (See Figure 10.3.)

search terms. Via several different sites, he discovers a list of impressive professional credentials spanning decades—from her degrees in biochemistry and science writing to her extensive publications as a book author and a renowned journalist—which confirm that she is a legitimate authority on his topic. Although the article focuses specifically on cigar smoking, both the author and the source are credible enough that Mark decides to read it. His main questions are about its timeliness and currency, because the article is almost a decade old. Ultimately, he decides to keep the article on hand as a possible reference, noting in his electronic journal that several links to related *Times* articles on the same subject appeared along with the article and might be worth evaluating as well.

The other commercial site is titled "Stop smoking—Quit smoking permanently and easily." Although Mark is skeptical about its usefulness as a source based on its promotional tone, he checks out the site. The link, http//:www.life-improvement-products.com/smoking.htm, seems to present some factual information. But when Mark clicks on the site's homepage link, he discovers that the site author is a person named Derek Brownhill, a British hypnotherapist whose credentials could not be verified by the rather vague biographical information under the "About Derek Brownhill" link. Further investigation reveals that Mr. Brownhill is using the site to promote hypnosis (and his own professional services as a hypnotist) as a viable way to quit smoking. Those pieces of information show the site's clear lack of relevance to Mark's approach to the topic, as well as the site author's biases on the issue, and they make it easy for Mark to eliminate the site as a possible source.

Mark now has access to a great deal of background information on the smoking and addiction issue. He proceeds to read the relevant sources carefully, taking notes in his electronic notebook file. In addition to making notes about content, Mark writes down evaluative information about each source's sponsor, author, agenda, and so on, to remind himself of the source's credibility. Now that he has explored some background ideas about his topic, Mark is ready to move on to a more focused search of the library databases in order to locate scholarly journal articles on his topic. For an example of a model search of a library subscription database service, see 8d-2.

See 8d-2

Mark's brief research tour through the Internet illustrates the importance of evaluating everything you read. In thinking critically about the sites he encounters in his search, Mark poses all of the questions on the Checklist for Evaluating Source Information. He considers the sponsoring organization, the author, the rhetorical stance of the site, and the site's timeliness. By using all these evaluative questions, Mark is able to assess the reliability of the information he finds.

See 9a-3

EXERCISE 9.2 Make a chart or table in which you compare the sites you labeled most trustworthy and least trustworthy in Exercise 9.1. Use the questions in the Checklist for Evaluating Source Information to help you construct your chart. Bring a copy of the chart to class for discussion.

FOR COLLABORATION Share your chart with a small group of your peers. What makes each site trustworthy or not trustworthy? What were some clues to obvious biases? Do your classmates agree with your evaluations? Discuss why or why not.

10 Using Sources and Avoiding Plagiarism

FAQs

- What should I put in my notes? (10a)
- What is plagiarism, and how do I avoid it? (10b)
- What is the difference between paraphrasing and summarizing? (10c and 10e)
- How many quotations do I need, and how do I integrate them into my paper? (10f)

Integrating source information into your own writing is a skill that takes practice. Being careless about your sources can lead to a serious academic offense called plagiarism—with serious consequences such as a failing grade for the course or even expulsion from school.

See Ch.12

Plagiarism is defined as the unauthorized or misleading use of the language and text of another author. Whenever you use exact words or paraphrase or summarize ideas from a source, you need to give proper attribution to that source. Readers must be able to tell exactly what information came from which source and what information is your own contribution to the paper.

See Guidelines 10a

10a Use sources responsibly

When writing a research paper, you must acknowledge any original information, ideas, and illustrations that you find in another author's work, whether it is in print or on the Internet. Acknowledging the work of other authors is called documenting sources. By incorporating source information appropriately, you will avoid plagiarism.

See 10b

Guidelines

Top Ten Ways to Avoid Plagiarizing

1. Take accurate, usable notes.
2. Record complete citation (bibliographic) information along with your notes.
3. Determine when acknowledgment is needed.
4. Avoid copying and pasting information (text or graphics) from the Internet into your paper.
5. Never submit the same paper for two different classes.
6. Never "buy" or "borrow" a paper from the Internet or another student.
7. Paraphrase accurately using synonyms.
8. Summarize information into your own words.
9. Copy quotations carefully and punctuate them correctly.
10. Provide proper documentation for all paraphrases, summaries, and quotations.

❶ Reading critically

If you rely on only one source throughout your paper, you immediately lose credibility with your readers. Readers will question the depth of your research and the level of your knowledge; your competence as a researcher will be called into question. On the other hand, if you use a number of authors to provide supporting evidence, you gain credibility with your readers. So, it is important to read and evaluate several sources.

GO
See Ch. 2
See Checklist 9a-3

Chapter 2 describes the process of reading critically, which involves previewing, reading, and then reviewing. When you read sources for your research paper, pay special attention to reading with a critical eye.

Previewing

Preview the source first. As you preview, pay attention to key words or phrases and try to get a general idea of the work's purpose and structure.

Reading

When you are reading your own books or photocopied articles, use a highlighter or a pencil to underline key ideas. Stop frequently to take notes in

See 7c
See 7a-4

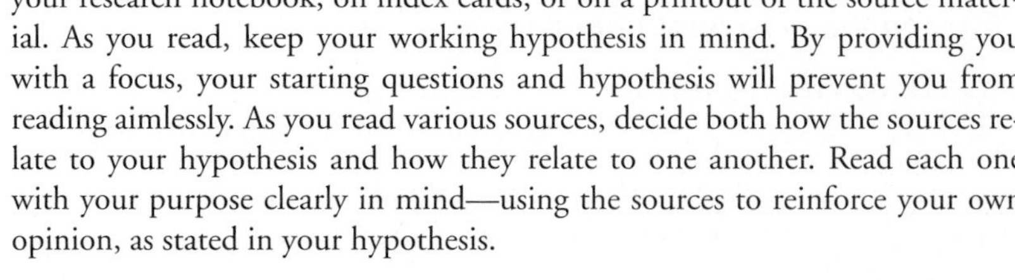
your research notebook, on index cards, or on a printout of the source material. As you read, keep your working hypothesis in mind. By providing you with a focus, your starting questions and hypothesis will prevent you from reading aimlessly. As you read various sources, decide both how the sources relate to your hypothesis and how they relate to one another. Read each one with your purpose clearly in mind—using the sources to reinforce your own opinion, as stated in your hypothesis.

Reviewing

See Ch. 9

As part of your review, assess and evaluate each source, including those you find as you search the Internet. Assessment is a two-step process of deciding whether or not the source is worth reading and whether or not the source is worth using in your paper. Evaluating involves thinking carefully about key elements in the work.

Synthesizing

What kinds of "conversations" are happening between the authors that you are reading? Does one source contradict another, or does it reinforce what you've read in other places? Does a particular source serve as an example of something explained in a more general source? Or perhaps one source gives an excellent definition of the topic you are researching while another describes something in more detail. In your research notebook, be sure that you not only summarize the individual sources but also look for relationships between the ideas in one source and those in another.

❷ Taking accurate, usable notes

See Fig. 10.1

It is important to take accurate, usable notes when you first encounter a source. If you do not, you may have to retrace your steps to relocate a particular source. In the worst-case scenario, the source you need to reference will have been checked out by another library patron or the Internet site will be gone.

Taking content notes and recording bibliographical information

See 7d

Content notes include source information; bibliographical information provides documentation. Be sure to take notes in a research notebook and

Notes from Suzuki - Microsoft Word

Notes from Suzuki, Sept 6, 2006. I think that music in a young child's life should be more than just an occasional break from the ordinary. Interaction with music can develop a child's social, mental and physical skills, and should provide a base for all of the other activities they may participate in. Here's how Suzuki put it: "Musical activities provide children with important experiences that can help them develop physical coordination, timing, memory, visual, aural and language skills. When they work to increase their command of music and exercise musical skills in the company of others, they gain important experience with self-paced learning, mental concentration and a heightened personal and social awareness" (Suzuki, par. 40).

Interaction with music produces increased developments in many areas because it requires the use of many parts of the brain, rather than just an isolated section. In a study by Dr. Lawrence Parsons of the University of Texas-San Antonio, he and his colleagues "Found that there is an area in the right half of the brain that interprets written musical notes and passages of notes, that is known to interpret written letters, and words. Moreover, they report an overall,

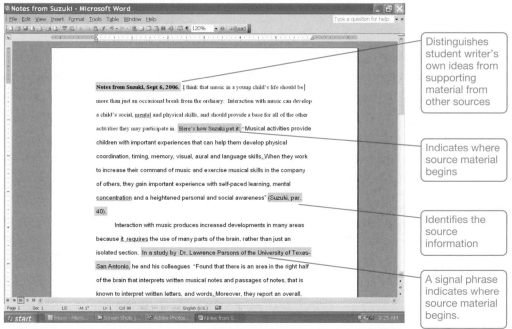

Distinguishes student writer's own ideas from supporting material from other sources

Indicates where source material begins

Identifies the source information

A signal phrase indicates where source material begins.

▲ **Figure 10.1** Notes in a computer file, including quotations and commentary.

See 7d-1, 7c-2, and Fig. 7.3

record sources in a working bibliography. For an example of a working bibliography, see 7d-1. For an example of a printout with notes, see Figure 7.3.

Recording substantive and interpretive information

The most successful research papers incorporate information from several sources into the flow of the paper. The least successful papers tend to make one of the following major mistakes:

- They rely too heavily on just one source for support of the argument.
- They cobble together the opinions of three or four authors, one right after the other, without interpreting their meaning or relationship, often called "patch writing."

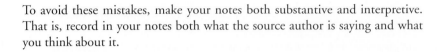

See 7c

To avoid these mistakes, make your notes both substantive and interpretive. That is, record in your notes both what the source author is saying and what you think about it.

Deciding whether to quote, paraphrase, or summarize

See 10c

See 10e

See 10f

When you record content notes from a source, you typically either paraphrase or summarize what you have read. If the information seems especially significant to your research topic or if it provides new insights or ideas that you have not encountered before in your research, you will probably want to paraphrase it. Paraphrasing is an almost line-by-line rewording of the source information. If the information seems less crucial to your topic or if you need little detail to make your point, you may wish to summarize instead. A summary, in contrast to a paraphrase, condenses information. Record information in the form of a direct quotation if it is impossible to put the information into your own words—for example, if the author expressed a thought so memorably that you could not possibly say it otherwise.

10b Avoid plagiarism when you use sources

By following the guidelines in this chapter when you paraphrase, summarize, and quote, you can avoid plagiarism.

1 Determining when no acknowledgment is required: Common knowledge

You need not document "common knowledge." This term refers to information that is generally known or accepted by educated people. Information that you can find readily in general reference works such as encyclopedias or in the popular media is probably common knowledge and need not be documented, though it must be stated in your own words. Be certain that several sources provide the same information before assuming that it is common knowledge. As a general rule, it is better to overdocument than to underdocument and be accused of plagiarizing. When in doubt, document.

Guidelines

Acknowledging Sources

- **Direct quotations, paraphrases, and summaries of outside source material, including Web sites.** Any word, phrase, or sentence that you copied directly from a source must be placed in quotation marks, and complete bibliographic information must be given, including the page reference for the quotation. Similarly, you must acknowledge paraphrases and summary restatements of ideas taken from a source, even though you have cast them in your own words.

  When you summarize, paraphrase, or quote from a Web site, you must give proper acknowledgment to the source. It is not acceptable to cut and paste text or graphics from the Internet without acknowledging the source.
- **Abstracts of articles.** Many online databases provide abstracts rather than complete works. For example, when searching the *ERIC* database, you will find abstracts that tell what an article or document is about, in addition to showing its location and source. What if you use information from the abstract but do not actually read the original? You need to acknowledge the abstract when paraphrasing, summarizing, or quoting information it contains. Note in your bibliography that you are quoting the abstract rather than the source itself.
- **Images, graphics, visuals, charts, or other statistical materials from either print or Internet sources.** Any images, diagrams, charts, or other statistical materials that come from outside sources—be they print sources or Internet sources—need to be credited. This credit is still necessary even if you use data from a source in order to create your own chart or table.

See Chs. 12–14

❷ Determining when acknowledgment is required

Quote, paraphrase, summarize

Essentially, any material that comes from an independent, outside source—whether in print, Internet, audio, or video format—needs to be acknowledged.

One student writing a political science paper on the effects of immigration laws on the makeup of the US population over the past half-century went to the Web site for the United States Citizenship and Immigration Service to

See Figs. 10.2 and 10.3

do some research. Searching the annual statistical yearbooks produced by this government agency, she found relevant data on US immigration, broken down by region and country of last residence, that supported the argument in her essay.

Once the student had written her first draft and was re-evaluating her essay and supporting evidence, however, she realized that citing the large population numbers from the original table was unwieldy and potentially confusing; she decided that percentages would illustrate her point much better and more

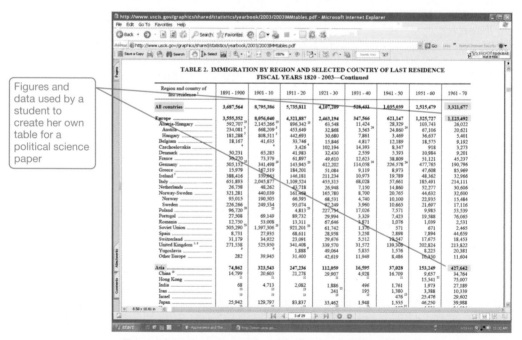

Figures and data used by a student to create her own table for a political science paper

http://www.uscis.gov/graphics/shared/statistics/yearbook/2003/2003IMMtables.pdf - Microsoft Internet Explorer

TABLE 2. IMMIGRATION BY REGION AND SELECTED COUNTRY OF LAST RESIDENCE
FISCAL YEARS 1820 - 2003—Continued

Region and country of last residence[1]	1891 - 1900	1901 - 10	1911 - 20	1921 - 30	1931 - 40	1941 - 50	1951 - 60	1961 - 70
All countries	**3,687,564**	**8,795,386**	**5,735,811**	**4,107,209**	**528,431**	**1,035,039**	**2,515,479**	**3,321,677**
Europe	**3,555,352**	**8,056,040**	**4,321,887**	**2,463,194**	**347,566**	**621,147**	**1,325,727**	**1,123,492**
Austria-Hungary	592,707[23]	2,145,266[23]	896,342[23]	63,548	11,424	28,329	103,743	26,022
Austria	234,081[3]	668,209[3]	453,649	32,868	3,563[24]	24,860[24]	67,106	20,621
Hungary	181,288[3]	808,511[3]	442,693	30,680	7,861	3,469	36,637	5,401
Belgium	18,167	41,635	33,746	15,846	4,817	12,189	18,575	9,192
Czechoslovakia	[4]	[4]	3,426[4]	102,194	14,393	8,347	918	3,273
Denmark	50,231	65,285	41,983	32,430	2,559	5,393	10,984	9,201
France	30,770	73,379	61,897	49,610	12,623	38,809	51,121	45,237
Germany	505,152[23]	341,498[23]	143,945[23]	412,202	114,058[24]	226,578[24]	477,765	190,796
Greece	15,979	167,519	184,201	51,084	9,119	8,973	47,608	85,969
Ireland[5]	388,416	339,065	146,181	211,234	10,973	19,789	48,362	32,966
Italy	651,893	2,045,877	1,109,524	455,315	68,028	57,661	185,491	214,111
Netherlands	26,758	48,262	43,718	26,948	7,150	14,860	52,277	30,606
Norway-Sweden	321,281	440,039	161,469	165,780	8,700	20,765	44,632	32,600
Norway	95,015	190,505	66,395	68,531	4,740	10,100	22,935	15,484
Sweden	226,266	249,534	95,074	97,249	3,960	10,665	21,697	17,116
Poland	96,720[23]	[23]	4,813[23]	227,734	17,026	7,571	9,985	53,539
Portugal	27,508	69,149	89,732	29,994	3,329	7,423	19,588	76,065
Romania	12,750	53,008	13,311	67,646	3,871	1,076	1,039	2,531
Soviet Union	505,290[25]	1,597,306[23]	921,201[23]	61,742	1,370	571	671	2,465
Spain	8,731	27,935	68,611	28,958	3,258	2,898	7,894	44,659
Switzerland	31,179	34,922	23,091	29,676	5,512	10,547	17,675	18,453
United Kingdom[5,8]	271,538	525,950	341,408	339,570	31,572	139,306	202,824	213,822
Yugoslavia	[9]	[9]	1,888[9]	49,064	5,835	1,576	8,225	20,381
Other Europe	282	39,945	31,400	42,619	11,949	8,486	16,350	11,604
Asia	**74,862**	**323,543**	**247,236**	**112,059**	**16,595**	**37,028**	**153,249**	**427,642**
China[10]	14,799	20,605	21,278	29,907	4,928	16,709	9,657	34,764
Hong Kong	[11]	[11]	[11]	[11]	[11]	[11]	15,541[11]	75,007
India	68	4,713	2,082	1,886	496	1,761	1,973	27,189
Iran	[13]	[13]	[13]	241[12]	195	1,380	3,388	10,339
Israel	[13]	[13]	[13]	[13]	[13]	476[13]	25,476	29,602
Japan	25,942	129,797	83,837	33,462	1,948	1,555	46,250	39,988

3 of 29

▲ **Figure 10.2** Page 3 of Table on Immigration by Region and Selected Country of Last Residence, Fiscal Years 1820–2003. The data for 1961–70 in this table, along with data in Figure 10.3, were used by a student to create her own table for a political science essay.

Source: United States Citizenship and Immigration Service, Department of Homeland Security, *2003 Statistical Yearbook of the Immigration and Naturalization Service*, table 2, 2003. Web. 20 May 2006.

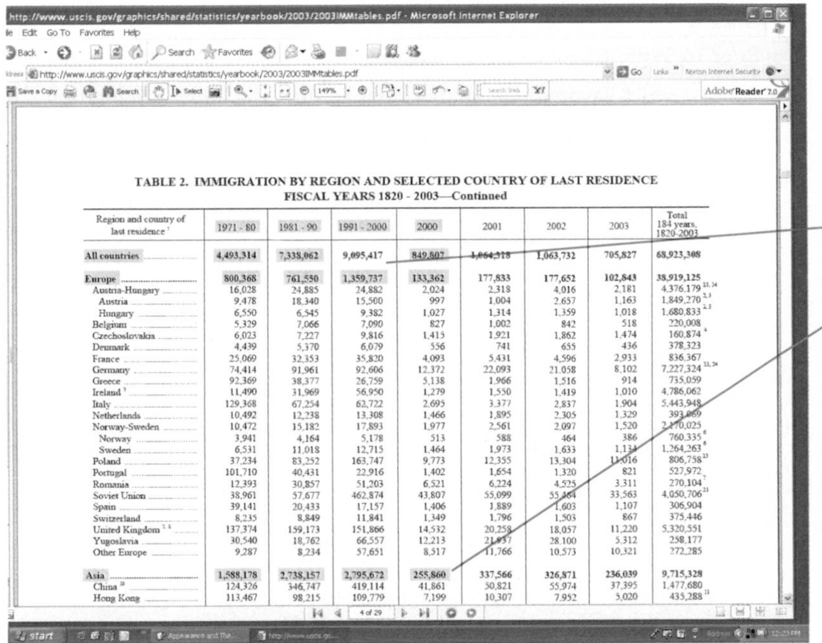

TABLE 2. IMMIGRATION BY REGION AND SELECTED COUNTRY OF LAST RESIDENCE
FISCAL YEARS 1820 - 2003—Continued

Region and country of last residence[1]	1971 - 80	1981 - 90	1991 - 2000	2000	2001	2002	2003	Total 184 years, 1820-2003
All countries	**4,493,314**	**7,338,062**	**9,095,417**	**849,807**	**1,064,318**	**1,063,732**	**705,827**	**68,923,308**
Europe	**800,368**	**761,550**	**1,359,737**	**133,362**	**177,833**	**177,652**	**102,843**	**38,919,125**
Austria-Hungary	16,028	24,885	24,882	2,024	2,318	4,016	2,181	4,376,179 [13,34]
Austria	9,478	18,340	15,500	997	1,004	2,657	1,163	1,849,270 [2,3]
Hungary	6,550	6,545	9,382	1,027	1,314	1,359	1,018	1,680,833 [2,3]
Belgium	5,329	7,066	7,090	827	1,002	842	518	220,008
Czechoslovakia	6,023	7,227	9,816	1,415	1,921	1,862	1,474	160,874 [4]
Denmark	4,439	5,370	6,079	556	741	655	436	378,323
France	25,069	32,353	35,820	4,093	5,431	4,596	2,933	836,367
Germany	74,414	91,961	92,606	12,372	22,093	21,058	8,102	7,227,324 [13,34]
Greece	92,369	38,377	26,759	5,138	1,966	1,516	914	735,059
Ireland [3]	11,490	31,969	56,950	1,279	1,550	1,419	1,010	4,786,062
Italy	129,368	67,254	62,722	2,695	3,377	2,837	1,904	5,443,948
Netherlands	10,492	12,238	13,308	1,466	1,895	2,305	1,329	393,069
Norway-Sweden	10,472	15,182	17,893	1,977	2,561	2,097	1,520	2,170,025
Norway	3,941	4,164	5,178	513	588	464	386	760,335 [6]
Sweden	6,531	11,018	12,715	1,464	1,973	1,633	1,134	1,264,263 [6]
Poland	37,234	83,252	163,747	9,773	12,355	13,304	11,016	806,758 [23]
Portugal	101,710	40,431	22,916	1,402	1,654	1,320	821	527,972 [7]
Romania	12,393	30,857	51,203	6,521	6,224	4,525	3,311	270,104
Soviet Union	38,961	57,677	462,874	43,807	55,099	55,464	33,563	4,050,706 [23]
Spain	39,141	20,433	17,157	1,406	1,889	1,603	1,107	306,904
Switzerland	8,235	8,849	11,841	1,349	1,796	1,503	867	375,446
United Kingdom [5,8]	137,374	159,173	151,866	14,532	20,258	18,057	11,220	5,320,551
Yugoslavia	30,540	18,762	66,557	12,213	21,937	28,100	5,312	258,177
Other Europe	9,287	8,234	57,651	8,517	11,766	10,573	10,321	272,285
Asia	**1,588,178**	**2,738,157**	**2,795,672**	**255,860**	**337,566**	**326,871**	**236,039**	**9,715,328**
China [10]	124,326	346,747	419,114	41,861	50,821	55,974	37,395	1,477,680
Hong Kong	113,467	98,215	109,779	7,199	10,307	7,952	5,020	435,288 [11]

4 of 29

▲ **Figure 10.3** Page 4 of Table on Immigration by Region and Selected Country of Last Residence, Fiscal Years 1820–2003.

The data for 1971–80, 1981–90, and 1991–2000 in this table was used by a student to create her own table for a political science essay.

Source: United States Citizenship and Immigration Service, Department of Homeland Security, *2003 Statistical Yearbook of the Immigration and Naturalization Service*, table 2, 2003. Web. 20 May 2006.

clearly. She used the data from the United States Citizenship and Immigration Service tables in Figures 10.2 and 10.3, dividing the total number of immigrants from all countries by the numbers from Europe and Asia specifically, to calculate the percentages of European and Asian immigrants to the United States for each relevant decade. Using those results, she created her own chart. Below is an excerpt from her final paper, accompanied by the chart she made. Because she neglected to include source documentation within the text or after the table, she committed plagiarism in her research paper.

PLAGIARISM USING STATISTICAL DATA

Absence of in-text source citation and/or citation for the table itself constitutes plagiarism.

Prior to 1965, US immigration had been limited through rigid national quotas, which favored immigrants from Europe. The 1965 Immigration and Nationality Services Act eliminated the old country-of-origin quotas, giving priority to educated and skilled workers and to uniting families. As the percentage shifts in Table 1 indicate, dramatic changes were wrought over a fifty-year period; the result has been increasing numbers of non-European residents, particularly from Asia.

Table 1 Percentages of US Immigrants from Europe and Asia, 1961–2000

Region of Origin	1961–1970	1971–1980	1981–1990	1991–2000
Europe	33.8	17.8%	10.4%	14.9%
Asia	12.9	35.3%	37.3%	30.7%

The use of data without acknowledgment in this paper constitutes plagiarism. In order to document the source properly, the student should have included a parenthetical citation within the text and in the caption of the table, as well as the full source information in her Works Cited list. Below is the same paper excerpt, this time revised to include the necessary documentation to correct the plagiarism.

CITATIONS OF STATISTICAL DATA ADDED TO CORRECT PLAGIARISM

Revised paper includes parenthetical in-text citation.

Prior to 1965, US immigration had been limited through rigid national quotas, which favored immigrants from Europe. The 1965 Immigration and Nationality Services Act eliminated the old country-of-origin quotas, giving priority to educated and skilled workers and to uniting families. As the percentage shifts in Table 1 indicate, dramatic changes were wrought over a fifty-year period; the result has been increasing numbers of non-European residents, particularly from Asia (United States Citizenship and Immigration Service).

Table 1 Percentages of US Immigrants from Europe and Asia, 1961–2000

Region of Origin	1961–1970	1971–1980	1981–1990	1991–2000
Europe	33.8	17.8%	10.4%	14.9%
Asia	12.9	35.3%	37.3%	30.7%

Source: Data based on United States Citizenship and Immigration Service, Department of Homeland Security, *2003 Statistical Yearbook of the Immigration and Naturalization Service,* table 2.

Finally, the entry in the Works Cited list, including the complete citation, should have appeared as follows:

United States Citizenship and Immigration Service, Department of Homeland Security. *2003 Statistical Yearbook of the Immigration and Naturalization Service,* table 2. 2003. Web. 20 May 2006.

3 Unintentional plagiarism

Your notes should accurately record source information in your own words, when possible. You should be able to tell at a glance from your notes when information is from a source and when it is your own commentary or thoughts on a source.

Students taking notes from a source sometimes commit *unintentional* plagiarism by carelessly copying words and phrases from a source into their notes and then using these words and phrases without acknowledgment in a paper. If you follow the reading and notetaking procedures outlined in this chapter, paraphrasing and summarizing in your own words what you have read, you are unlikely to use the author's exact wording inappropriately in a research paper. Unintentional plagiarism can occur even if you have kept a good record of your sources because of poor paraphrases or summaries of source information.

See 10c–10e

Unintentional plagiarism has become more frequent with the increased reliance on electronic sources, which can be easily copied and pasted into an electronic research notebook. For example, Figure 10.4 shows a page

See Fig. 10.4

Quotation marks and in-text citation added to correct plagiarism of text from a source.

Text and figures plagiarized from an original source.

Source citation added to correct plagiarism of a figure.

Rockets - Microsoft Internet Explorer

http://www.english.usu.edu/faculty/chuk/Spring2003/English2010H/argument/katab/katab.htm

Rockets

Introduction
Solid
Liquid
Hybrid
Safety
Economic Issues
Conclusion
Vocabulary
bibilio

" A solid propellant rocket engine is the simplest type of rocket engine. As the name suggests, the entire propellant in this type of engine is solid. The oxidizer and the fuel are combined into one material. Forming this material into one solid hollow tube (casting) provides propellant which easily fits into an airframe. The propellant tube must have a hole running its length to allow for internal combustion of the fuel. The amount of thrust caused by a solid engine is directly proportional to the amount of propellant burning at any instant. This thrust can thus be controlled by varying the shape of the void in the fuel. Some of the more common shapes are shown below, next to a graph of how the thrust varies with time when they are used for an engine. " (Schmidt)

Fig.1. Rockets and thrust. Source: Schmidt.

Shapes that have a large initial burning surface area begin with a large amount of thrust that quickly decreases as burn time continues. The shape chosen for each application is very specific to the needs of the engine at that time. A spark must be provided before the fuel begins to burn. Because the fuel and oxidizer have previously been mixed, there is no need for a complicated ignition system or mixing chamber.

There are disadvantages to the solid propellant system. First, the thrust cannot be controlled once the propellant has ignited. Also, once ignited, a solid propellant system cannot be shutoff. This is dangerous because the rocket will continue to burn until all of the fuel is gone, sometimes with catastrophic results. Also, because the propellant burns the entire length of the rocket, it can get very hot very quickly.

There are a few advantages to the solid engine system. The first is that solid propellants provide for the simplest engines, as there are no ignition devices required. Solid propellants are easier to store. This is because there are no freezing or evaporation temperatures to worry about, as the solid propellants are all stable at reasonable temperatures. Hence, solid propellants are safer to storage. Also, because a solid engine requires ignition to start the combustion, the materials involved are generally much less corrosive.

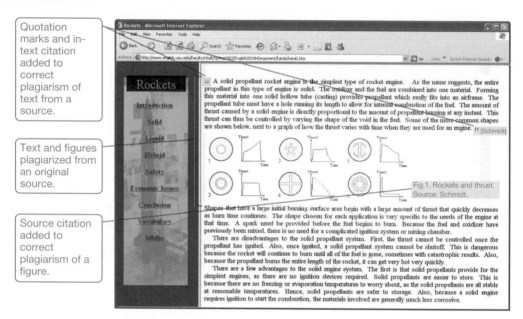

▲ **Figure 10.4** Exhibiting Unintentional Plagiarism

A Page from a Student Web Site Essay in which exact wording and figures are used without including a citation to the source of the information in the body of the essay. (See also Figure 10.5.)

from a student's Web essay, which was submitted electronically in an online classroom. The student dropped the figures and the preceding explanations for those figures into the body of her paper without saying where the figures and accompanying information came from. As seen in Figure 10.5, the original source of the information, Professor Eckart W. Schmidt's online piece *Rocket Propellants*, was listed on the bibliography page of the paper, but was not referenced within the body of the Web text itself—hence, *unintentional* plagiarism. In order to avoid plagiarism and cite the source correctly, according to MLA citation style, the student should have used quotation marks, included a parenthetical reference to Schmidt's work, and also labeled the figure as coming from Schmidt's Web site at the University of Washington.

See Fig. 10.5

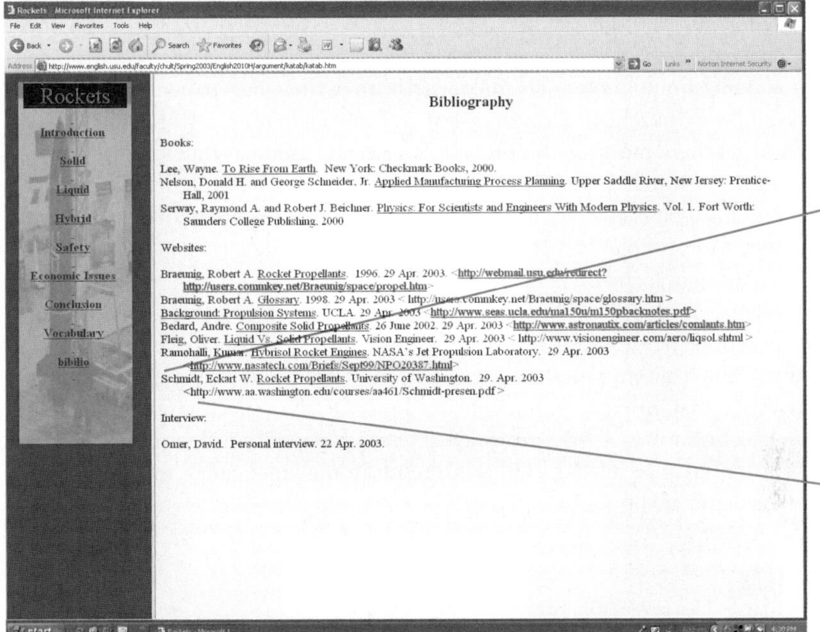

Rockets

Introduction
Solid
Liquid
Hybrid
Safety
Economic Issues
Conclusion
Vocabulary
bibilio

Bibliography

Books:

Lee, Wayne. To Rise From Earth. New York: Checkmark Books, 2000.
Nelson, Donald H. and George Schneider, Jr. Applied Manufacturing Process Planning. Upper Saddle River, New Jersey: Prentice-Hall, 2001
Serway, Raymond A. and Robert J. Beichner. Physics: For Scientists and Engineers With Modern Physics. Vol. 1. Fort Worth: Saunders College Publishing, 2000

Websites:

Braeunig, Robert A. Rocket Propellants. 1996. 29 Apr. 2003. <http://webmail.usu.edu/redirect?http://users.commkey.net/Braeunig/space/propel.htm>
Braeunig, Robert A. Glossary. 1998. 29 Apr. 2003 < http://users.commkey.net/Braeunig/space/glossary.htm >
Background: Propulsion Systems. UCLA. 29 Apr. 2003 <http://www.seas.ucla.edu/ma150u/m150pbacknotes.pdf>
Bedard, Andre. Composite Solid Propellants. 26 June 2002. 29 Apr. 2003 <http://www.astronautix.com/articles/comlants.htm>
Fleig, Oliver. Liquid Vs. Solid Propellants. Vision Engineer. 29 Apr. 2003 < http://www.visionengineer.com/aero/liqsol.shtml >
Ramohalli, Kumar. Hybrisol Rocket Engines. NASA's Jet Propulsion Laboratory. 29 Apr. 2003 <http://www.nasatech.com/Briefs/Sept99/NPO20387.html>
Schmidt, Eckart W. Rocket Propellants. University of Washington. 29. Apr. 2003 <http://www.aa.washington.edu/courses/aa461/Schmidt-presen.pdf >

Interview:

Omer, David. Personal interview. 22 Apr. 2003.

Original source for text and figure on rocket propellants in Figure 10.4
Bibliographic entry for source material used in Figure 10.4 indicates that the plagiarism was unintentional.

▲ **Figure 10.5** Indication That the Plagiarism Was Unintentional
The source of the plagiarized material in Figure 10.4 was correctly cited in the student's bibliography, above. However, to avoid this instance of unintentional plagiarism, the student should have cited the source by author Eckart W. Schmidt parenthetically within the body of the paper after the quoted material and figures. (See annotations to Figure 10.4 for these corrections.)

④ Intentional plagiarism

Sometimes plagiarism is *intentional*; that is, a writer knowingly copies the work of another without proper acknowledgment of the source. Whenever you use words from a source, this must be indicated clearly through the use of quotation marks and documentation at the point in the text where the source information is used. It is not enough to list the author in the footnotes or bibliography. Readers must be able to tell as they are reading your paper exactly what information came from which source and what information is your contribution to the paper.

❺ Other forms of plagiarism

Academic standards specify that students do their own work. This means that you should not ask someone else to write your papers for you, nor should you purchase a research paper from an online research paper mill. Most teachers monitor the process of research itself, so they can tell when a student's research paper is not his or her own work. Of course, it is perfectly acceptable to receive advice on your work—from peers and writing center tutors, for example.

Another form of plagiarism, called *self-plagiarism*, sometimes confuses students. Students assume that if the work is their own, they can submit a paper multiple times for several different courses. This practice is not acceptable. When an instructor assigns an essay or a research paper, he or she assumes that original work will be done for that specific assignment and course. Submitting the same essay or research paper to different instructors is a form of plagiarism that is likely to result in the same penalties as other types of academic dishonesty.

10c Paraphrase sources accurately

See 10b

The objective of paraphrasing is to present an author's ideas clearly, using your own words and phrases. This important skill not only deepens your understanding of the author's ideas but also helps you avoid plagiarism. Here are some suggestions to help you paraphrase.

1. *Place the information in a new order.* In the following example, from an article titled "Finding Medical Help Online" that appeared in *Consumer Reports,* the good paraphrase inverts the sentence structure of the original, whereas the poor paraphrase copies both words and sentence structure from the source and hence leads the student to commit unintentional plagiarism. The source is identified by the author's last name and the page number on which the material appears. (Plagiarized text is underlined.)

ORIGINAL QUOTATION FROM "FINDING MEDICAL HELP ONLINE," SCHWARTZ, P. 28

If you're coping with an illness or want to exchange views about a medical topic, you'll want to find your way to a newsgroup. Despite the name, these are not collections of news items. They are, in effect, virtual bulletin boards open to anyone who cares to participate. The messages generally consist of plain text.

GOOD PARAPHRASE [WITH INVERTED SENTENCE STRUCTURE AND DIFFERENT WORDS]

YES In a recent *Consumer Reports* article, the author suggests finding a relevant newsgroup if you have a particular medical problem or if you want to talk with others about a medical subject. Newsgroups are online bulletin boards that are available to anyone; in spite of their name, they are not news reports. Anyone who wishes to may join in a newsgroup discussion (Schwartz 28).

POOR PARAPHRASE [COPIES WORDS AND SENTENCE STRUCTURE DIRECTLY FROM SOURCE RESULTING IN PLAGIARISM]

NO If you're faced with an illness or want to exchange views about a medical topic, you'll want to find your way to a newsgroup. Despite the name, these are not news items. They are virtual bulletin boards open to anyone. The messages generally consist of ordinary text (Schwartz 28).

2. *Break the complex ideas into small units.* If the author has expressed himself or herself in a rather complicated way, paraphrasing gives you the opportunity to state the complex ideas of the source more simply. Here is another passage from the same article.

ORIGINAL, P. 29

The "perfect" search engine would guide users to every relevant location, ranked in order of usefulness, without leaving anything out and without including anything irrelevant. That engine doesn't yet exist.

GOOD PARAPHRASE [WITH SIMPLIFIED SENTENCE STRUCTURE]

YES Schwartz states that no Internet search tool is yet "perfect." If it were, it would lead you to all the appropriate locations on your topic. It would rank all the Web sites by how useful they were. It would never leave something out that was relevant. It would never include anything that was irrelevant (29).

3. *Use concrete, simple vocabulary in place of technical jargon.* If the author has used technical vocabulary, you can replace some of the technical jargon with more simple, familiar words as you paraphrase. Here are some examples of jargon from these examples that might be changed in a paraphrase.

newsgroup = online bulletin board
search engine = Internet search tool
users = those who are using the Internet
location = Web site found at a unique Internet address

4. *Use synonyms for words in the source.* Just as you can replace jargon with more familiar terms, you can use synonyms (words that mean roughly the same thing) in place of words from the source. Here are some of the synonyms used in the paraphrases above.

illness = medical problem
exchange views = talk with others
medical topic = medical subject
available to = open to
despite = in spite of
news items = news reports

5. *For each important fact or idea in your notes, write down the source page number.* With paraphrases, as with quotations, you must indicate exactly on what page in the source you found the information. Ideally, anyone else reading your work should be able to locate the exact wording from which your paraphrase was taken. If the source has no pages, as is true of many Internet documents, provide the author's last name only.

See Chs. 12–14

See Fig. 10.6

❶ Recording paraphrases in your notes

The following example shows a passage from an Internet newsletter and a student's paraphrased notes. In her paraphrase, notice how the words have been changed or reordered and the sentence patterns altered from the original in order to avoid plagiarism. Notice also that the information is fairly complete, with most of the ideas from the original source retained in the paraphrased version.

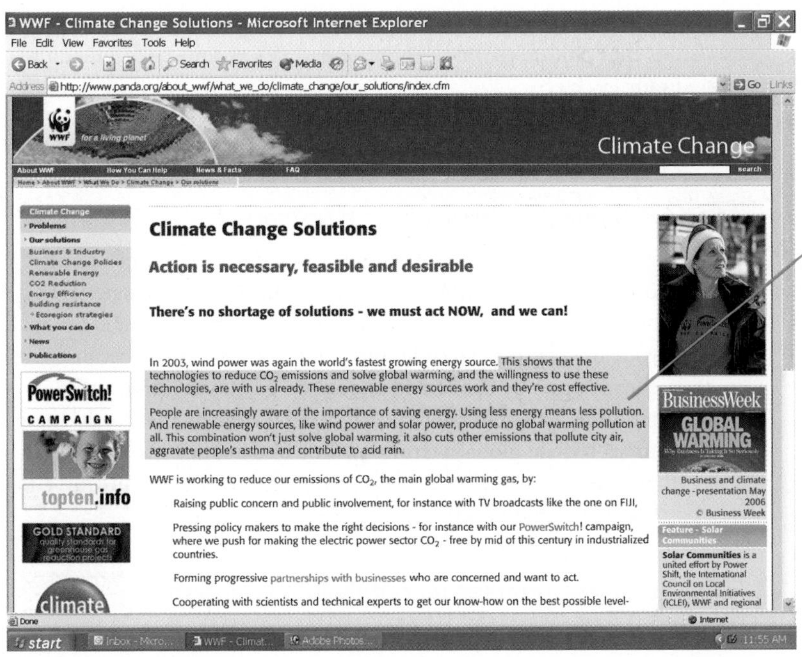

Original quotation being paraphrased by a student

▲ **Figure 10.6** Highlighted Passage from the WWF's *Climate Change* Web Site
The student copied the material verbatim in her electronic notebook and later paraphrased it with proper acknowledgment of the original source.

ORIGINAL (SEE FIGURE 10.6)

There's no shortage of solutions—we must act NOW, and we can!

In 2003, wind power was again the world's fastest growing energy source. This shows that the technologies to reduce CO_2 emissions and solve global warming, and the willingness to use these technologies, are with us already. These renewable energy sources work and they're cost effective.

People are increasingly aware of the importance of saving energy. Using less energy means less pollution. And renewable energy sources, like wind power and solar power, produce no global warming pollution at all.

This combination won't just solve global warming, it also cuts other emissions that pollute city air, aggravate people's asthma and contribute to acid rain.

From World Wildlife Fund (WWF). *Climate Change.* 2003. 1 Nov. 2006 <http://www.panda.org/about_wwf/what_we_do/climate_change/our_solutions/index.cfm>

GOOD PARAPHRASE [FROM STUDENT'S NOTEBOOK]

YES As a source for the world's energy, wind power is increasing the most rapidly, which indicates that the current technologies to solve global climate change already exist. Furthermore, people are willing to use these renewable and affordable resources because they are learning to be concerned about energy conservation and the reduction of CO_2 emissions. At the same time as these new energy sources reduce global warming, they also reduce other pollutants that negatively impact health and cause "acid rain" in our cities (World Wildlife Fund).

❷ Integrating paraphrases smoothly into your paper

Paraphrases from notes should be integrated into a paper in much the same way as direct quotations. You should introduce them with signal phrases and place them in context for the readers, perhaps using the author or title in the introduction. You need to provide documentation indicating the source of the information.

See Chs. 12–14

GOOD PARAPHRASE [INTEGRATED INTO A PAPER WITH A SIGNAL PHRASE AND DOCUMENTATION FOR A WEB SITE]

YES According to an article published at the World Wildlife Fund Web site, we already possess effective and inexpensive technologies to solve the global warming crisis. When consumers use less power, there is a corresponding reduction in air pollution. Furthermore, alternative, renewable power, such as wind and solar, does not result in any emissions that contribute to global warming. Changing energy policies will not only help with the global warming problem but will at the same time reduce pollution in the air we breathe that contributes to poor health and to the problem of "acid rain" (World Wildlife Fund).

Guidelines

Effective Paraphrasing

1. Place the information in a new order.
2. Break the complex ideas into small units.
3. Use concrete, direct vocabulary in place of technical jargon.
4. Use synonyms for words in the source.
5. Accompany each important fact or idea in your notes with the source author and page number.
6. Incorporate the paraphrase smoothly into the grammar and style of your own writing.

EXERCISE 10.1 Select a short article on a topic of interest to you and print or photocopy it. Select a short paragraph from the article. Following the guidelines in this section, paraphrase that paragraph. Provide appropriate documentation for the source, as if you were using the paraphrase in a research paper.

FOR COLLABORATION Bring to class a passage that you have paraphrased as well as the paraphrase itself. Exchange passages and paraphrases with a classmate. Use the Guidelines for Effective Paraphrasing to evaluate the classmate's work, looking specifically at how effectively your peer has captured the original passage in his or her paraphrase without using the language or wording of the original source.

See Guidelines 10c-2

10d Avoid plagiarism when using Internet sources

Students sometimes succumb to temptation and plagiarize information they find on the Internet by copying and pasting it into their own papers and submitting it as though it were their own work. This is a very serious academic offense. No matter how tempting, do not succumb to the lure of copying and pasting Internet information into your own paper. Ignorance of the rules at your school is no defense when you are caught plagiarizing. Following the guidelines in this chapter will ensure that you do not commit this academic offense.

See Figs. 10.7 and 10.8

See Chs. 12–14

Figures 10.7 and 10.8 illustrate where one student, Brian Fowler, went wrong. He was failed for the entire course when his professor discovered the plagiarism on his final examination. Could he have used information from *SparkNotes.com* appropriately in a course paper? Certainly. To do so, he would have included in quotation marks any information quoted from the Web site, placed a footnote or a parenthetical citation at each point in the paper where source information was either paraphrased or quoted, and provided a reference list at the end of the paper that detailed the source information so that the reader could find and read the Web site.

10e Summarize sources briefly

Like paraphrasing, summarizing involves restating the author's ideas or information in your own words, but summaries are typically much briefer than the original information. The goal of a summary is to record the gist of the piece—its primary line of argument—without examples and other departures from the main ideas. As with paraphrasing, you need to be sure that the summary is stated in your own words to avoid plagiarism.

1 Recording summaries in your notes

A student summarized the original wording from the World Wildlife Fund Web site as follows:

GOOD STUDENT SUMMARY IN RESEARCH NOTEBOOK

YES The World Wildlife Fund Web site outlines easy-to-implement solutions to the global warming problem. They suggest changes in both individual energy use and global energy policies as ways to tackle the problem. Changing energy policies will also reduce health problems related to pollution and acid rain (World Wildlife Fund).

Here are some additional suggestions to help you summarize effectively.

1. *Identify key points.* A summary must reflect the main ideas of the source accurately, so you need to read carefully before you write a summary. As you read your own books or photocopied articles, underline or highlight

Brian S. Fowler

Dr. Peter Corcoran

English 4320

Final Exam

Monks and Prioresses
and Friars, Oh My!

Upon reading *The Canterbury Tales* from cover to cover for the very first time, although I had already read several of the tales, a reoccurring theme seemed to jump up and slap me in the face with the telling of each tale, that theme was corruption among church officials. After contemplating what I would ask dear old Geoffrey Chaucer if I had a moment to sit and chat with him for a spell, I would definitely ask him how he really felt about the church and why he chose to portray these church officials in such a dysfunctional manner.

The religious figures Chaucer represents in *The Canterbury Tales* all deviate in one way or another from what was traditionally expected of them. Generally, their conduct corresponds to common medieval stereotypes, but it is difficult to make any overall statement about Chaucer's position because his narrator is so clearly biased toward some characters—the Monk, for example—and so clearly biased against others, such as the Pardoner.

Plagiarized text

Figure 10.7
Brian Fowler's Paper
The highlighted information was copied directly from *SparkNotes.com*. (See Figure 10.8.)

The paper continues with numerous passages copied directly from SparkNotes.com without documentation.

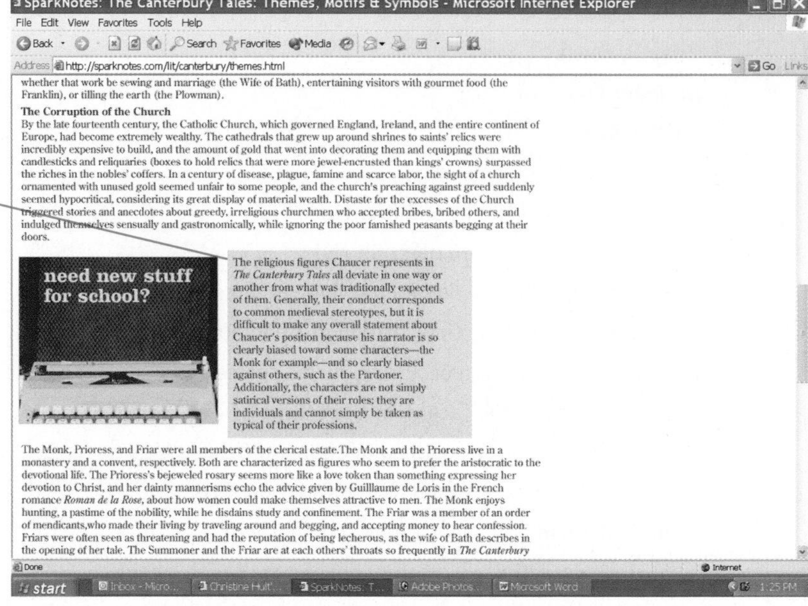

SparkNotes: The Canterbury Tales: Themes, Motifs & Symbols - Microsoft Internet Explorer

File Edit View Favorites Tools Help

Address http://sparknotes.com/lit/canterbury/themes.html

whether that work be sewing and marriage (the Wife of Bath), entertaining visitors with gourmet food (the Franklin), or tilling the earth (the Plowman).

The Corruption of the Church

By the late fourteenth century, the Catholic Church, which governed England, Ireland, and the entire continent of Europe, had become extremely wealthy. The cathedrals that grew up around shrines to saints' relics were incredibly expensive to build, and the amount of gold that went into decorating them and equipping them with candlesticks and reliquaries (boxes to hold relics that were more jewel-encrusted than kings' crowns) surpassed the riches in the nobles' coffers. In a century of disease, plague, famine and scarce labor, the sight of a church ornamented with unused gold seemed unfair to some people, and the church's preaching against greed suddenly seemed hypocritical, considering its great display of material wealth. Distaste for the excesses of the Church triggered stories and anecdotes about greedy, irreligious churchmen who accepted bribes, bribed others, and indulged themselves sensually and gastronomically, while ignoring the poor famished peasants begging at their doors.

need new stuff for school?

The religious figures Chaucer represents in *The Canterbury Tales* all deviate in one way or another from what was traditionally expected of them. Generally, their conduct corresponds to common medieval stereotypes, but it is difficult to make any overall statement about Chaucer's position because his narrator is so clearly biased toward some characters—the Monk for example—and so clearly biased against others, such as the Pardoner. Additionally, the characters are not simply satirical versions of their roles; they are individuals and cannot simply be taken as typical of their professions.

The Monk, Prioress, and Friar were all members of the clerical estate.The Monk and the Prioress live in a monastery and a convent, respectively. Both are characterized as figures who seem to prefer the aristocratic to the devotional life. The Prioress's bejeweled rosary seems more like a love token than something expressing her devotion to Christ, and her dainty mannerisms echo the advice given by Guillaume de Loris in the French romance *Roman de la Rose*, about how women could make themselves attractive to men. The Monk enjoys hunting, a pastime of the nobility, while he disdains study and confinement. The Friar was a member of an order of mendicants,who made their living by traveling around and begging, and accepting money to hear confession. Friars were often seen as threatening and had the reputation of being lecherous, as the wife of Bath describes in the opening of her tale. The Summoner and the Friar are at each others' throats so frequently in *The Canterbury*

Done — Internet

start — Inbox - Micro... — Christine Hult'... — SparkNotes: T... — Adobe Photos... — Microsoft Word — 1:25 PM

Information copied and pasted into student paper.

▲ **Figure 10.8** Text from *SparkNotes.com* The highlighted text was copied and pasted exactly into Brian Fowler's paper without documentation. (See Figure 10.7.)

key ideas, words, or phrases. Ask yourself, "What is the central idea of this passage?" Try to articulate that idea in your own words, using just a sentence or two.

See 7c-1

2. *Record information.* As you record the key ideas, be certain that you separate your own interpretive comments from the source information. You can do this by using a two-column notebook or document comments.

3. *Create lists and tables.* When you are condensing ideas, sometimes it helps to write them down in the form of a list or a table. In this way, you can capture the most important ideas in the simplest form possible and present them to readers as a listing of key ideas. In the following example, the student has summarized an entire article in the form of a table of key ideas. Notice that the article headings, taken directly from the source, are placed in quotation marks to indicate a direct quotation.

GOOD STUDENT SUMMARY OF THE ARTICLE "FINDING MEDICAL HELP ONLINE"

YES In a recent *Consumer Reports* article titled "Finding Medical Help Online," Schwartz explains how to find the "good stuff" (27). The major parts of the article are summarized in the table below.

Summary of Schwartz Article

"Basic Information about the Internet" (27–28)	Discusses terminology, equipment, hardware, and software issues.
"Newsgroups" (28)	Explains how newsgroups work and how they can provide forums for likeminded individuals to discuss issues.
"Search Engines" (29)	Describes some general search engines and explains how they work.
"Health Web Sites" (29)	Outlines general and specific medical sites that might be useful.
"Strategies for Searching" (30–31)	Walks through a model search, explaining what one is likely to find and how useful it is likely to be.

Source: *Consumer Reports* (Feb. 1997): 27–31.

4. *Check for accuracy.* Just as you did when quoting or paraphrasing from a source, you need to check your summaries to ensure their accuracy. Make sure that the words and phrases are your own. Place any of the author's unique words or phrases in quotation marks and include a page reference. Check to be sure that you have not been interpretive or judgmental about anything the author has said. When summarizing, you should restate the author's main ideas objectively in your own words, without interpretation. Record any interpretive judgments as document comments or clearly distinguish them in a two-column notebook. It is a good idea to reread the source after you have summarized it, just to be certain that you have not inadvertently altered the author's meaning (see Figure 10.9).

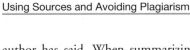

See Fig. 10.9

❷ Integrating summaries into your paper

Introduce a summary with a signal phrase and place it in context for the readers, perhaps using the author's name or article title in the introduction. As with quoting and paraphrasing, you need to provide documentation indicating the source of the summarized information.

See Chs. 12–14

Document comments keep a student's ideas and interpretations separate from an original outside source.

Signal phrase identifies where source material begins.

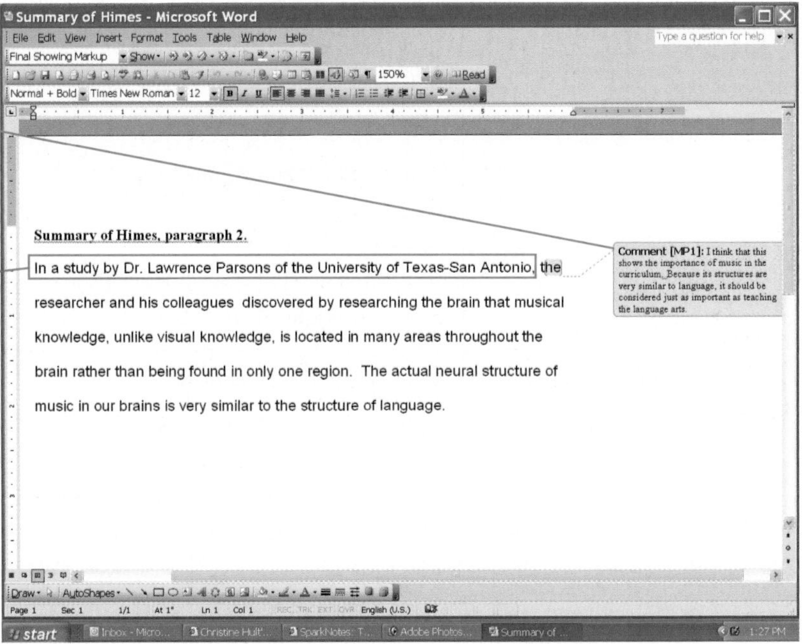

▲ **Figure 10.9** A Summary of Source Material, with an Interpretation by the Student Writer in a Document Comment

Using COMMENTS allows you to keep your own ideas separate from original source material.

10f Avoid plagiarism when you summarize

Using your own words and providing documentation for the source will produce a summary that avoids plagiarism. In the following examples, the unacceptable summary makes the mistake of using the same wording and sentence structure as the original source (underlined words are plagiarized) as well as failing to provide documentation. The acceptable summary recasts the main idea in the student's own words and provides proper attribution to the source itself, an article from *New York Times* online titled "With Cable TV at M.I.T., Who Needs Napster?".

See Fig. 10.10

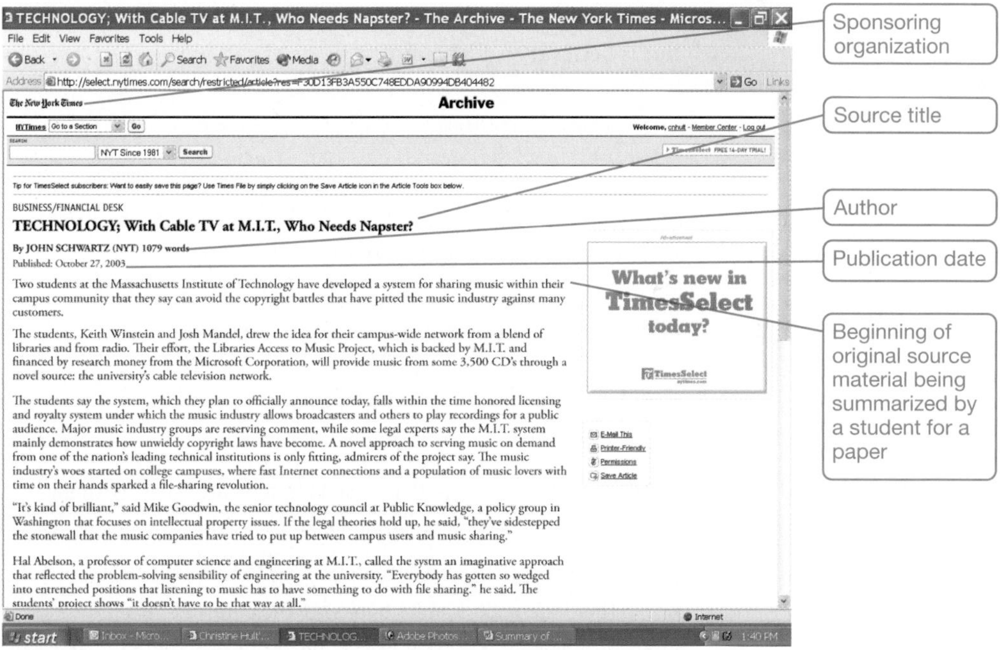

TECHNOLOGY; With Cable TV at M.I.T., Who Needs Napster? - The Archive - The New York Times - Micros...

File Edit View Favorites Tools Help

Address http://select.nytimes.com/search/restricted/article?res=F30D13FB3A550C748EDDA90994DB404482

The New York Times — Archive

NYTimes Go to a Section Go — Welcome, cnhult - Member Center - Log out

NYT Since 1981 Search — FREE 14-DAY TRIAL!

Tip for TimesSelect subscribers: Want to easily save this page? Use Times File by simply clicking on the Save Article icon in the Article Tools box below.

BUSINESS/FINANCIAL DESK

TECHNOLOGY; With Cable TV at M.I.T., Who Needs Napster?

By JOHN SCHWARTZ (NYT) 1079 words

Published: October 27, 2003

Two students at the Massachusetts Institute of Technology have developed a system for sharing music within their campus community that they say can avoid the copyright battles that have pitted the music industry against many customers.

The students, Keith Winstein and Josh Mandel, drew the idea for their campus-wide network from a blend of libraries and from radio. Their effort, the Libraries Access to Music Project, which is backed by M.I.T. and financed by research money from the Microsoft Corporation, will provide music from some 3,500 CD's through a novel source: the university's cable television network.

The students say the system, which they plan to officially announce today, falls within the time honored licensing and royalty system under which the music industry allows broadcasters and others to play recordings for a public audience. Major music industry groups are reserving comment, while some legal experts say the M.I.T. system mainly demonstrates how unwieldy copyright laws have become. A novel approach to serving music on demand from one of the nation's leading technical institutions is only fitting, admirers of the project say. The music industry's woes started on college campuses, where fast Internet connections and a population of music lovers with time on their hands sparked a file-sharing revolution.

"It's kind of brilliant," said Mike Goodwin, the senior technology council at Public Knowledge, a policy group in Washington that focuses on intellectual property issues. If the legal theories hold up, he said, "they've sidestepped the stonewall that the music companies have tried to put up between campus users and music sharing."

Hal Abelson, a professor of computer science and engineering at M.I.T., called the systm an imaginative approach that reflected the problem-solving sensibility of engineering at the university. "Everybody has gotten so wedged into entrenched positions that listening to music has to have something to do with file sharing." he said. The students' project shows "it doesn't have to be that way at all."

What's new in TimesSelect today?
TimesSelect

E-Mail This
Printer-Friendly
Permissions
Save Article

Done — Internet

start — Inbox - Micro... — Christine Hult'... — TECHNOLOG... — Adobe Photos... — Summary of ... — 1:40 PM

Sponsoring organization

Source title

Author

Publication date

Beginning of original source material being summarized by a student for a paper

▲ **Figure 10.10** *New York Times* Article: The original source for the student summaries.

ORIGINAL

Two students at the Massachusetts Institute of Technology have developed a system for sharing music within their campus community that they say can avoid the copyright battles that have pitted the music industry against many customers. . . . The M.I.T. system, using the analog campus cable system, simply bypasses the Internet and digital distribution, and takes advantage of the relatively less-restrictive licensing that the industry makes available to radio stations and others for the analog transmission. The university, like many educational institutions, already has blanket licenses for the seemingly old-fashioned analog transmission of music from the organizations that represent the performance rights. . . . Although the M.I.T. music could still be recorded by students and shared on the Internet, Professor Abelson said that the situation would be no different from recording songs from conventional FM broadcasts. The system provides music quality that listeners say is not quite as good as a CD on a home stereo but is better than FM radio.

POOR SUMMARY [COPIES WORDS AND SENTENCE STRUCTURE DIRECTLY FROM SOURCE AND LEAVES OFF DOCUMENTATION]

NO Two M.I.T. students have developed a system for sharing music within their campus community to avoid copyright battles. Their system provides music quality that listeners say is not quite as good as a CD but better than FM radio.

GOOD SUMMARY [RECASTS THE MAIN IDEA INTO STUDENT'S OWN WORDS AND PROVIDES SOURCE DOCUMENTATION]

YES To allow students on the M.I.T. campus to share music with each other without violating copyright laws, two students have developed a system of sharing music by using the campus cable TV network. This ingenious system bypasses the Internet altogether and provides music via cable TV that is better in quality than what can be heard on the radio (Schwartz).

Guidelines

Effective Summarizing

1. Identify the main points as you read the source.
2. Put those main points into your own words.
3. Condense the original, keeping the summary short.
4. Use a table or a list, when appropriate, to summarize the information.
5. Be objective rather than interpreting or judging source ideas.
6. Integrate the summarized ideas into the flow of your prose.
7. Provide proper documentation for the source you are summarizing.

EXERCISE 10.2 Using the same article as in Exercise 10.1, choose one brief section or page to summarize. Remember that a summary is a condensed version of the original source. Write up your summary and turn it in to your instructor. Be sure to include a printout or photocopy of the original source, with the relevant sections marked to indicate the key ideas.

10g Quote sources sparingly

See Chs. 12–14

See Ch. 51

Quotations are exact wordings taken from sources. When you use a direct quotation, you must integrate it smoothly into the flow of your ideas. You need to use signal phrases to alert your reader that a quotation is coming. You also need to document the source appropriately and punctuate it correctly.

❶ Deciding when to use direct quotations

See 10c–10e

It is usually preferable for you to paraphrase or summarize source material so that the information is in your own words and in your own writing style. Too many direct quotations lead to a very choppy paper because the reader encounters so many writing styles. A short quotation of a sentence or two or a block quotation can be used if the author's wording is so memorable that you simply are unable to paraphrase it. Such quotations set the author's wording apart from your text, drawing attention to what is quoted.

If you decide to use a long quotation of more than four lines in your paper, you are obliged to explain your choice to your readers. In other words, you should introduce the quotation and tell the reader something about it, explaining how it relates to the argument that precedes and follows it. (We discuss this in more depth below.) Particularly in literary analysis papers where your argument is supported by the text you are analyzing and by other literary critics, you may find yourself using several short quotations throughout your paper. For an example of how such quotations are effectively integrated into the flow of your own argument, see Heidi Blankley's analysis of the novel *Regeneration.*

See 16c

❷ Integrating quotations into the grammatical flow

The quotation should flow smoothly with the grammatical structure of your own sentence.

NOTE The citation style in the examples below is MLA. The climate change example is a quotation from an Internet source and therefore has no page number.

NO Carnegie Mellon researchers study climate "Scientists disagree about whether climate change will be a serious problem in the next 50 to 100 years" (Morgan and Smutz). [Grammar problem—fused sentence]

YES Researchers at Carnegie Mellon University claim, "Scientists disagree about whether climate change will be a serious problem in the next 50 to 100 years" (Morgan and Smutz). [Quotation integrated grammatically]

❸ Using signal phrases

In a signal phrase, you include the author or source organization's name (*researchers at Carnegie Mellon University*) as well as a verb or a form of a verb that tells something about the author's position (*claim*). Some verbs that are commonly used in signal phrases are listed in the Guidelines for Verbs to Use in Signal Phrases for Quotations in 10g-3. You can use a variety of signal phrases to show your own interpretation of the author's point and to provide for stylistic variety. Signal phrases can precede the quotation, interrupt it, or follow it, as in the examples below (the signal phrases are underlined). Signal phrases can also be helpful in showing the reader where source information begins and ends.

See 10g-3

SIGNAL PHRASE PRECEDES QUOTATION

Rivers provides an insightful revelation about gender roles: "He distrusts the implication that nurturing, even when done by a man, remains female" (Barker 107).

SIGNAL PHRASE INTERRUPTS QUOTATION

"Stable introverts," another study found, "are the highest academic performers" (Furnham and Medhurst 197).

SIGNAL PHRASE FOLLOWS QUOTATION

"Extroverts prefer locations where socializing opportunities abound," report Campbell and Hawley (141).

If you provide the author's name in the signal phrase, you need only put the page number in parentheses.

NO "During the years with The Nature Conservancy and IUCN, I did some science, some conservation, and a little writing. What I always came back to was the writing—the more heart-filled, the better. In the end, I think I always knew the words would win out" (Pyle 59). [No signal phrase]

YES As Robert Michael Pyle *explains,* "During the years with The Nature Conservancy and IUCN, I did some science, some conservation, and a little writing. What I always came back to was the writing—the more heart-filled, the better. In the end, I think I always knew the words would win out" (59). [Signal phrase with the verb *explains*]

❹ Providing interpretations or explanations

Too often, inexperienced writers simply "dump" quotations into their papers without providing interpretations, which is invariably ineffective. You cannot assume that a quotation can stand on its own merits. Rather, you are obliged to explain to your readers why you are using a particular quotation. Compare the following examples, with and without introductory explanations.

NO "Everyone in the group contributes to the overall level of emotional intelligence, but the leader holds special sway in this regard.

Verbs to Use in Signal Phrases for Quotations

acknowledges	confirms	objects
advises	contends	observes
advocates	criticizes	offers
affirms	declares	opposes
agrees	denies	recommends
alleges	describes	remarks
allows	disagrees	replies
answers	discusses	reports
asserts	disputes	responds
avows	emphasizes	reveals
believes	explains	says
charges	expresses	states
claims	finds	suggests
concludes	interprets	thinks
concurs	lists	writes

Emotions are contagious, and it's natural for people to pay extra attention to the leader's feelings and behavior" (Goleman, Boyatzis, and McKee 174). [No introductory explanation]

YES Goleman et al. confirm that it is only when groups exhibit the qualities of emotional intelligence that they can be perceived as smarter than individuals. The authors assert, "Everyone in the group contributes to the overall level of emotional intelligence, but the leader holds special sway in this regard. Emotions are contagious, and it's natural for people to pay extra attention to the leader's feelings and behavior" (174). [Includes introductory explanation with signal verbs *confirm* and *assert*]

❺ Using ellipses and brackets to indicate omissions and changes

In order to better integrate a quotation into the flow of your own prose, you may sometimes wish to alter the quotation by omitting a portion of it, adding a clarifying word or phrase, or altering a verb, a pronoun, capitalization, or punctuation.

See Ch. 52

A set of three spaced periods, called an *ellipsis*, is used to indicate any information that has been left out of the original quotation. Brackets are used to show any words or phrases within the original that you have changed to conform to the grammar of your own sentence. The example below illustrates both ellipses and brackets.

> YES Researchers at Carnegie Mellon University claim, "Scientists disagree about whether climate change will be a serious problem . . . [since] nobody knows for sure whether climate changes caused by human actions will be large enough and fast enough to cause serious damage" (Morgan and Smutz). [Shows omissions and changes]

Sometimes it is necessary to change the tense or form of a verb to conform to the grammar of your own prose.

> "One of the worst things," Dr. Minor said, "was the way in which insurance companies insinuate[d] themselves into my dealings with patients" (33). [The original verb in the present tense changed to past tense.]

Effective Quoting

1. Use direct quotations sparingly as support for your own ideas.
2. Use primarily short quotations (one or two sentences).
3. Be extremely careful to be accurate when copying a quotation.
4. Attribute quotations to their sources and punctuate them correctly.
5. Integrate quotations smoothly into the stylistic flow of the paper.
6. Incorporate quotations in a way that is grammatically correct.
7. Provide an explanation to place the quotation in context.
8. Use the author's name or the work's title to introduce the quotation.
9. Use ellipses and brackets when words or phrases are omitted from the quotation.
10. Provide proper documentation for all quotations.

See 51a

See 51e

See 52g, 52k

For clarity's sake, often a pronoun in the original will be replaced by the noun referent.

> "When [Dr. Minor's] sons said they wanted to be doctors, he insisted that they work a while as hospital orderlies to see his world from a different perspective" reports a recent *Newsweek* article (32). [The possessive pronoun *his* is changed to *Dr. Minor's* to make the referent clear.]

You may need to change a lowercase letter to a capital letter to make the quotation fit grammatically into the flow of your own prose.

> "[D]octors and hospitals," observes a recent *Newsweek* article, "remain prime targets in the battle to reduce medical spending" (32). [In the original, *Doctors* is not capitalized.]

❻ Using indentation to set off a block quotation

In MLA style, quotations longer than four lines should be set off from the regular text by indenting every line of the quotation ten spaces from the left margin and double-spacing lines throughout. Because the format sets apart the quotation, it is not necessary to use quotation marks. The line spacing and right-hand margin remain the same as for the regular text. A long quotation should always be introduced by a signal phrase. Notice the punctuation at the end of the following block quotation: the period comes before the page number in parentheses rather than at the end (as it does for quotations run into the text). The last sentence exemplifies a quotation with run-in text.

> Aronson describes the isolation that is commonly felt by those caring for patients suffering from Alzheimer's disease:
>
> > As the chronic illness develops and the physical and behavior signs of the patient become more pronounced, the caregiver senses his or her isolation even more intensely. Friends and relatives may socialize less frequently. Telephone calls and visits may become few and far between,

> and the physical and emotional burdens of caring for the patient increase. (167)

The author goes on to describe "the other experiences common to caregivers, including frustration, resentment, and trouble with letting go" (167–68).

10h Avoid plagiarism when you quote

Every time you copy information from a source, indicate through quotation marks on your note card or in your research notebook that you have taken the exact wording from the original. Figures 10.11 and 10.12 show a note card and an electronic research notebook with information that a student intended to quote because she felt that the author expressed a key idea in forceful language. This particular quotation came from an article found on the Internet. Note that since Internet sources typically do not provide page numbers, the student could not indicate a specific page in the notes. She also created a corresponding bibliography entry for this source.

See 7d-1

Quotation on Climate Change

According to researchers at Carnegie Mellon University, "Scientists disagree about whether climate change will be a serious problem in the next 50 to 100 years. The main reason for this disagreement is that nobody knows for sure whether climate changes caused by human actions will be large enough and fast enough to cause serious damage." (Granger Morgan and Tom Smuts, Global Warming and Climate Change, part 2, U.S. Global Change Research Information Office, 1994, 28 July 2006 <http://earthscape.org/p1/mog01/part2.html>

Figure 10.11 Note Card with Direct Quotation

Figure 10.12 ▶ Computer Notebook with Direct Quotation Using quotation marks around direct quotes in your research notes will clarify when you are quoting and when you are paraphrasing.

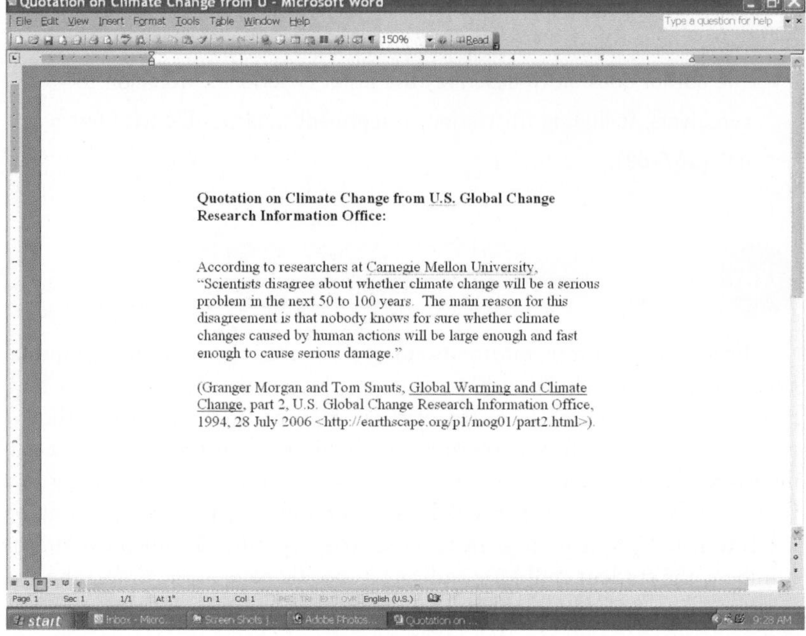

Quotation on Climate Change from U - Microsoft Word

Quotation on Climate Change from U.S. Global Change Research Information Office:

According to researchers at Carnegie Mellon University, "Scientists disagree about whether climate change will be a serious problem in the next 50 to 100 years. The main reason for this disagreement is that nobody knows for sure whether climate changes caused by human actions will be large enough and fast enough to cause serious damage."

(Granger Morgan and Tom Smuts, Global Warming and Climate Change, part 2, U.S. Global Change Research Information Office, 1994, 28 July 2006 <http://earthscape.org/p1/mog01/part2.html>).

EXERCISE 10.3 From the article you printed or photocopied in Exercise 10.1, choose a sentence or two in which the author states an important idea in memorable words. Imagine that you will be using the quotation in a research paper. Introduce the quotation by providing a context, and then write the quotation, using correct grammar and punctuation.

See 10g-5

FOR COLLABORATION Exchange rough drafts of your paper with a peer. Use the Guidelines for Effective Quoting (10g-5) to evaluate your peer's rough draft, looking specifically at how effectively he or she has integrated direct quotations into the flow of the paper.

11 Writing the Research Paper

FAQs

- Is it okay to use "I" in my paper? (11a-3)
- How do I arrange all the information? (11b)
- How do I write a draft? (11c)
- How do I revise? (11d)
- Should I use footnotes? (11e-1)
- Is it okay to add a photo or graphic? (11e-3)

A major difference between a research paper and most essays is that you will be using information from sources, in addition to your own ideas, as support for your thesis. The guidelines in this chapter will help you write a successful research paper.

Research paper advice

11a Review your rhetorical stance and thesis

The most effective way to decide which sources will work in your research paper and how to present them is to review your rhetorical stance by reassessing your topic, persona, audience, and argument.

1 Reassessing your persona, and audience

See 3b-2, 7a

How do you want to come across as a writer and what, ultimately, is your purpose for writing the piece? Ask yourself, "Who is my audience?" You may not be able to determine for certain whom your readers will be, but you can assume that they will be intelligent people with an interest in your topic. Since it is unlikely that they will be experts in the field, you should define terms carefully and avoid using jargon or technical vocabulary.

❷ Refining your argument

Has your working hypothesis helped you to arrive at a position you wish to argue in your paper? If not, revise it. Remember that in a research paper you will usually take a side on a debatable issue. You will use logical arguments to support the side you are taking in the debate.

Testing your hypothesis

See 7a

Kaycee Sorensen's starting questions about online shopping had to do with its growth, its convenience, and its safety. As she looked over the material gathered in her research, Kaycee was convinced that online shopping was an excellent option for consumers. In other words, she confirmed that her research had supported her working hypothesis.

> The number of online shoppers is increasing, which means cybershopping is becoming a convenient, affordable, safe alternative for consumers. [Yes, Kaycee determined that this hypothesis was supported by the research.]

Writing a thesis statement

See 3e-2 and 3e-3

A thesis statement for a research paper is similar to a thesis statement for an essay. That is, it states for readers the central idea that the paper will argue. Many times, the working thesis statement is revised during the actual writing process. Kaycee decided to write a thesis that stated her conclusions about online shopping.

> Working thesis: Cybershopping is a safe alternative for consumers.

Revising the thesis

See 5a

Your instructor may require that your thesis (and thus your research paper) have an argumentative edge. If so, make sure that you have taken a stand that can be supported through arguments in the paper. If your research paper is informational rather than argumentative, your thesis should reflect the fact that you are reporting data rather than taking a stand on an issue. Your thesis statement should clearly tell readers what direction your paper will take. Readers should not be surprised at the end by a position that was not acknowledged in the paper's introduction.

AN ARGUMENTATIVE THESIS

Whatever the causes, males and females have different perspectives on computers and their uses.

AN INFORMATIONAL THESIS

This paper will trace the evolution of computers from the first room-sized mainframes to the current hand-held notebooks.

After Kaycee had written a first draft of her paper, she revisited her working thesis statement. Although it stated in brief form her central idea for the paper, it was not specific enough to provide an accurate blueprint of what she had argued in the paper itself. She revised her thesis to be more specific and to reflect her argumentative stance. The revised thesis now states both the central idea and her opinion about it.

Revised thesis: Consumers should shop online because, despite fears of safety and identity theft, its simplicity, the convenience of comparison shopping, and access to a variety of merchandise make online shopping the logical and best choice for consumers.

3 Deciding on a voice and tone

Academic papers should be informative and serious, but they need not be dull or dry. You still can and should put your own personality into a piece. However, check with your instructor before using the informal first-person "I" in your research paper. Try to strike a balance in your tone, making it pleasing to readers.

See 3b-3

Before you begin to draft your research paper, answer the following questions about voice:

- Do I want to sound forceful and authoritative?
- Do I want to sound reasonable and moderate?
- Or, do I want to sound passionate and concerned?

Notice the voice in the following passage, taken from Kirsten's paper on Net theft.

See Ch. 3

> I'm sure all of us once glimpsed a tempting item in a store and, after getting "no" for an answer from Mom or Dad, took matters into our own hands, sneaking the treasure into a hidden pocket. It probably took only a few moments for your parents to notice something was up. I remember well a discussion about why taking the package was wrong. Then my Dad took me back to the store where an apology was made and my Strawberry Hubba Bubba Bubblegum was paid for.

The voice in this passage is light and friendly. Kirsten seems to be speaking directly to her readers. Contrast that voice with Kaycee's.

> Transaction security is the first thing to be aware of when shopping on the Internet, and data encryption provides the most secure way to send information from site to site without having anyone in between being able to read it. When an Internet user sends information, the data is encrypted, or put into code. Anyone who tries to read the information while it is en route to the site will find it impossible. Secure Sockets Layer (SSL), the standard for sending secure data, protects against snooping and possible tampering and then verifies that the site to which the data is sent is authentic.

In this passage, Kaycee sounds authoritative and knowledgeable. The much more serious voice is appropriate for a research paper.

11b Plan a structure

Some writers like to work from an organizational plan or outline, fleshing out the skeleton by incorporating additional information under each of the major points and subpoints. Others prefer to begin writing and have the structure evolve more organically. An outline or plan should be a guide as you write, not a constraint that limits your thinking. Whatever structure you select must include a format for incorporating opposing viewpoints.

❶ Developing an organizational plan or outline

GO
See 3e-5

As you write your outline, remember that you are trying to make the information or argument accessible to readers as well as clear and comprehensive. If you used note cards, sort them by heading and subheading into related ideas and information. If you used a computer research notebook, sort your materials by using the CUT, COPY, and PASTE features of your word-processing program.

After Kaycee decided on the stand she would take in her paper, as articulated in her thesis, she outlined an organizational structure in which she systematically answered each of her starting questions so that her argument would be easy for a reader to follow and understand. In order to explain cybershopping to her readers, Kaycee decided on the following plan.

> Introduction: Personal anecdote about online shopping
>
> The growing interest in online shopping
>
> The reasons for this growth: convenience, good deals, improved access to new technology, it's quick and easy
>
> Counterarguments to thesis: those who resist, their concerns—security, seeing items before purchase
>
> Ensuring transaction security, privacy, and avoiding credit card fraud
>
> Conclusion: Ease and convenience outweigh the potential risks.

She entered these headings into her electronic notebook, stored in a computer file in her hard drive.

See 3e

❷ Including opposing viewpoints

In an argumentative research paper, it is crucial to present the counterarguments—that is, the arguments that oppose your position. In her paper, it was important for Kaycee to acknowledge that some consumers are reluctant to do their shopping online. In her revised thesis, she acknowledges those concerns ("despite fears of safety and identity theft"). Then she refutes these concerns on pages 6 and 7 of the research paper by showing that security can be ensured if consumers take reasonable precautions.

11c Write a draft

When writing your first draft, use concrete and simple language to explain your research conclusions in your own words. Ideally, you should type your draft on a computer to make revision easier. Be certain to back up your computer documents and save to a disk frequently so as not to lose any of your work.

❶ Choosing a drafting strategy

For writing a first draft, you will need to establish a strategy that fits your writing style. Here are a few different ways in which writers of research projects proceed:

See 3f, 6a-3, 7c

- Write a draft systematically from a plan, using the building-block technique.
- Write a draft from piles of notes arranged according to a blueprint from the thesis.
- Write a sketchy first draft without looking at the notes—just writing down everything you remember from the research; follow up by fleshing out the partial draft with more complete information while referring to your notes.
- Write a rough first draft and then write a revision outline that suggests ways in which the draft needs to be changed.
- Write a draft by cutting and pasting information from an electronic research notebook.
- Write a draft while looking at annotated photocopies, printouts, and downloads.

❷ Applying the drafting strategy to blend material

In writing a first draft, it is best to put down your own understanding of the topic first, rather than relying too heavily on your sources. After you have written your draft, you can go back and add specific sources to support your arguments. Readers want to know what *you* think about the subject. They do not want to read a string of quotations loosely joined by transitions. Once you have drafted your paper, important data, facts, illustrations, and supporting evidence gleaned from your sources can be added to your arguments to give them authority and force.

See 10c-2, 10e-2, 10f

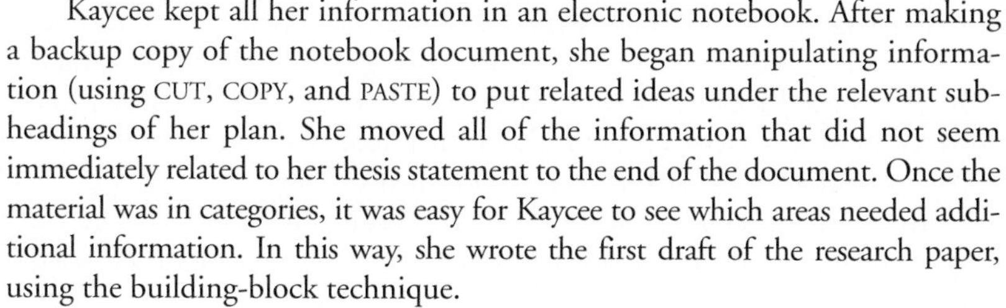

Kaycee kept all her information in an electronic notebook. After making a backup copy of the notebook document, she began manipulating information (using CUT, COPY, and PASTE) to put related ideas under the relevant subheadings of her plan. She moved all of the information that did not seem immediately related to her thesis statement to the end of the document. Once the material was in categories, it was easy for Kaycee to see which areas needed additional information. In this way, she wrote the first draft of the research paper, using the building-block technique.

See 3f

❸ Writing a working title

Writing a title can help you succinctly state the topic your research paper will cover. Try out a few titles before deciding on one. It should be brief yet descriptive.

See 6b-7

❹ Writing an introduction and a conclusion

Because a research paper typically covers more information than an essay, it may take a couple of paragraphs to introduce the topic effectively. Kaycee used two opening paragraphs for her research paper. The first paragraph provides an interesting opening anecdote that leads the reader into the topic of the paper. The second, leading up to her thesis, explains to readers how prevalent online shopping is becoming. Kaycee's conclusion sums up the major points in her argument and restates her stance on the subject.

EXERCISE 11.1 Write an introductory paragraph for a research paper. First, write a straightforward academic paragraph with a serious tone. Then write a second version of the opening paragraph that is light in tone and perhaps even humorous. You might tell a story or describe a scene.

FOR COLLABORATION Discuss these two opening paragraphs with your classmates. Which do you like better? Which seems more appropriate for your research paper?

11d Review and revise the draft

See 6e

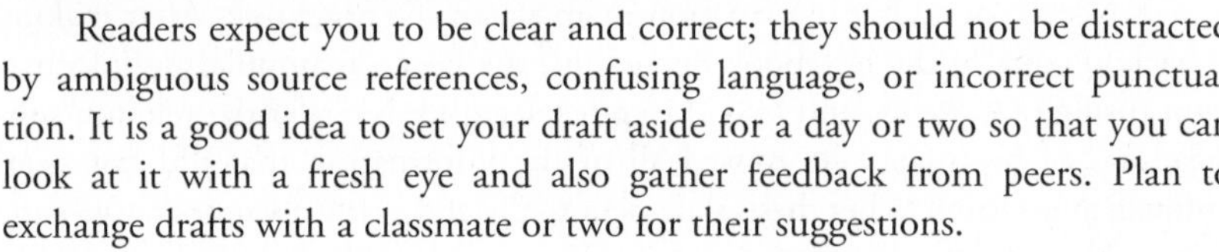

Readers expect you to be clear and correct; they should not be distracted by ambiguous source references, confusing language, or incorrect punctuation. It is a good idea to set your draft aside for a day or two so that you can look at it with a fresh eye and also gather feedback from peers. Plan to exchange drafts with a classmate or two for their suggestions.

See 11e

You need to reread your rough draft several times, both on the computer screen and in hard copy. Each time you read it, pay attention to a different aspect of the paper:

See 6b–6d,10b–10d

1. Think about the overall structure and style of the paper.
2. Check grammar and punctuation.
3. Make sure source materials are incorporated smoothly and accurately into the text.
4. Consider formal details such as conventions of documentation and format.

See Ch. 6

After your paper has been typed and spell checked, proofread it several times to catch and correct all typographical and mechanical errors.

TechHelp

Using INSERT to Number Pages

1. To insert page numbers into your document, use the INSERT menu and click on PAGE NUMBERS. The dialogue box will give you choices as to the location (top or bottom of the page) and alignment (left, right, or center) of the page numbers. Selecting FORMAT PAGE NUMBERS will give you the opportunity to make other decisions about numbering format (e.g., roman numerals, where to start numbering, etc.).
2. If you want to format a running header (top of the page) or footer (bottom of the page) that appears on every page, choose the HEADER OR FOOTER dialogue box. You can select from among a number of formats to use in a header or footer while in these dialogue boxes.

11e Follow formatting conventions

See 3h

The research paper format recommended by the Modern Language Association (MLA) is the same as that outlined for essays. MLA recommends placing your identifying information in the upper left-hand corner, 1 inch down from the top margin, rather than using a title page. However, check with your instructor about his or her preference for a title page with a research paper. MLA also calls for putting your last name and the page number in the upper right-hand corner of each page, 1/2 inch from the top margin. Everything in your research paper is double-spaced, including the title and the first line of the text. Notice that Kaycee uses a personal anecdote as a catchy opener, followed by her introduction and thesis statement. She then develops her argument in the body paragraphs, and she ends with a strong conclusion. The final pages of the research paper detail her works cited, using the MLA documentation system.

See Chs. 12–14

The documentation conventions common to different disciplines are described in detail in Chapters 12–14. The main systems are the Modern Language Association (MLA) system, typically used in the humanities and fine arts; the American Psychological Association (APA) system, used in the social sciences; the *Chicago Manual of Style* (CMS) system, used in business; and the Council of Science Editors (CSE) system, most often used in the sciences. Ask your instructor if there is a particular format you should use. If not, select the format from the discipline most closely related to your research topic.

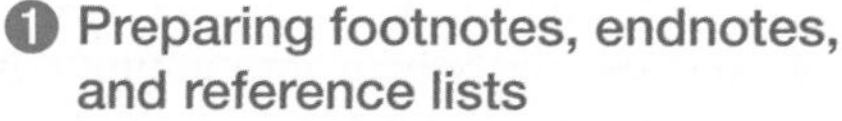

1 Preparing footnotes, endnotes, and reference lists

Depending on the conventions of the particular discipline, your paper may or may not have footnotes or endnotes. All research papers must include a listing of the sources used in the paper. Again, the way this listing is titled and formatted will depend on the particular discipline.

Footnotes and endnotes

Footnotes or endnotes are used most often in the humanities, where CMS style is common. In research papers in the sciences, citations generally appear

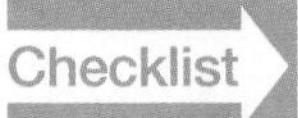

Revising a Research Paper

- ✓ Does the paper fulfill the promise made by the thesis?
- ✓ Do the arguments flow smoothly and logically?
- ✓ Is sufficient attention paid to counterarguments?
- ✓ Does the introduction lead effectively into the paper?
- ✓ Does the conclusion either summarize or describe implications?
- ✓ Is the paper focused, adequately developed, and coherent?
- ✓ Are the sources integrated smoothly into the flow of the paper?
- ✓ Is information in quotes, paraphrases, and summaries accurately related and clearly acknowledged?
- ✓ Are the parenthetical citations clear and accurately tied to the works-cited entries?
- ✓ Are the works-cited entries properly formatted?
- ✓ Is the format of the piece appropriate for a research paper?
- ✓ Has the paper been edited and proofread to eliminate errors?

GO See 3e-3, 5h, 6b-7, 6c–d, 10b-d, 11b, 11e, Chs. 12–14

See 12a-3

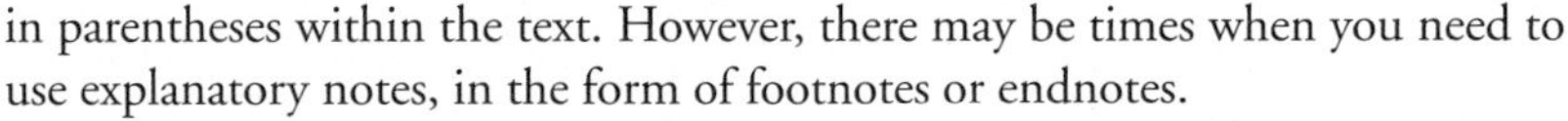

in parentheses within the text. However, there may be times when you need to use explanatory notes, in the form of footnotes or endnotes.

Works Cited or References lists

See 7d

See Chs. 12–14, 7d-1, and TechHelp 11e-1

A Works Cited list or a References list is an alphabetical listing of sources at the end of a paper. Your word-processing program may have a feature that will help you to manage sources, place them into appropriate citation styles, and alphabetize references automatically. Check your word-processing program's HELP menu to ascertain whether this feature is available and to learn how to use it.

❷ Understanding formatting conventions

Word processing can help you create a text that is professional in appearance. If you are to communicate effectively with readers, in the end you must attend to both form and content. However, be sure to make attention

TechHelp

Using a Computer FOOTNOTE Program

1. To insert a footnote or endnote into your paper, place the cursor at the point in the text where you want the superscript number to appear.[1] On the REFERENCES tab, in the FOOTNOTE group, click INSERT FOOTNOTE or INSERT ENDNOTE. The note number will be inserted as a superscript number and the corresponding number will appear either at the bottom of the page as a footnote or at the end of the paper as an endnote; type in your note. If you double-click on the footnote or endnote number, it will return you to the reference number in the document. You can apply the consecutive numbering of notes to the whole document or to only a specific section of the document. This feature is especially useful for documents with multiple chapters.
2. The computer will automatically generate the footnote or endnote and place it at the bottom of the appropriate page (footnote) or in a consecutive list at the end of the paper (endnote). It will renumber the notes if some are added or subtracted from the document. For an example of a footnote, see the bottom of this box.

[1] Type in the information for the footnote at the bottom of the page.

to format your last consideration. Too often, writers using word processors spend an excessive amount of time playing with the appearance of the text—varying the fonts, for example—rather than concentrating on content.

Most word-processing programs offer formatting features such as underlining, boldface, and italics, with which you can vary the appearance of the text and highlight important information. However, you should check with your instructor about his or her preferences before you spend a lot of time adjusting the format of your paper. Your goal should be to make the paper look professional. It is best to be conservative and justify the text on the left side of the page only.

See 19b

See Chs. 12–14

3 Incorporating visuals into your research paper

It has become acceptable for students to incorporate visuals (photos and graphics) into their research papers. However, it would be a good idea for you

TechHelp

Using PAGE SETUP and FORMAT

1. To format your page, use the PAGE LAYOUT tab. You will find options to set the margins, the paper orientation (portrait or landscape), the size of the paper (letter or legal), the layout (columns, backgrounds, watermarks), borders, line numbers, and so on. Choose margins that are consistent with the formatting style you are using in the paper (MLA, APA, CMS, or CSE).
2. Use the PARAGRAPH menu on the PAGE LAYOUT tab to make formatting changes to individual paragraphs, such as double or single spacing or indenting. Again, use the formatting specified by the documentation style you are using.
3. Use other features on the PAGE LAYOUT menu to adjust fonts, arrange the positions of texts and pictures, choose backgrounds, colors and themes, and so on.
4. Use the INSERT tab to insert graphics, pictures, text boxes, diagrams, charts, tables, links, or objects such as images or symbols.

See Chs. 12–14

Incorporating Visuals into Your Research Paper

1. **Integrate the visuals into your text carefully**. Visuals complement text but do not substitute for it. Readers will only be irritated if it seems visuals have been inserted as mere decoration.
2. **Explain the visual's significance in words**. If you are using graphs or charts, you need to explain their significance in your text and refer specifically to each one (e.g., "see Table 1").
3. **Use clip art selectively**. Clip art is free artwork that is available in image archives in your word processor and on the Web. Don't include clip art unless you have some specific reason for doing so. It is frequently overused.
4. **Don't mix clip art and photographs**. For visual consistency, it's best to use only one type of graphic medium in a single paper. Also be consistent with any text boxes, lines, and other graphics.

5. **Insert tables and photos**. You can create tables and photos in other programs (such as *PowerPoint* or *Photoshop*) and insert them into your paper at the appropriate location.
6. **Wrap text around the graphic**. For ease of reading, it's often a good idea to place your visual so that the text wraps around it. Your word-processing program will allow you to edit the placement of the graphic in relationship to the text.
7. **Respect copyright protections**. Be sure to secure permission to use any visuals that you have not developed yourself.

to check with your instructor before doing so. Listed in the Guidelines for Incorporating Visuals into Your Research Paper box are some issues to consider to make your visuals as effective as possible.

See Ch. 19

11f Review an annotated student research paper

The following research paper, written by Kaycee Sorensen, is formatted following the MLA system of documentation. Annotations are included to explain the various conventions.

See Ch. 12

Although MLA style does not call for a title page, here is a format you could use if your instructor prefers one.

Title, centered

Online Shopping:

Risky (but Better) Business

Student identification, centered

By

Kaycee Sorensen

Course identification and date

Professor Hult

English 2010 H, Section 01

3 May 2003

Sorensen 1

Kaycee Sorensen

Professor Hult

English 2010 H, Section 01

3 May 2003

Online Shopping:

Risky (but Better) Business

Recently, I shopped at the Logan Old Navy to find a new pair of jeans, but since I wear an uncommon size, I could not find exactly what I wanted. The attendant in the fitting rooms suggested that I visit *OldNavy.com* to find what I was looking for. She gave me all the information I would need to find the jeans and purchase them online, and when I visited *OldNavy.com,* I found the jeans, and they were cheaper than in the store. Needless to say, I bought more than just the jeans because of the wonderful prices. This was not my first experience, but because of the price, the convenience, and access to more items, I became excited to seek out new online shopping venues. 1

I am not alone in my growing interest in online shopping. According to *Nielson/NetRatings*, 498 million people worldwide now have access to the Internet from home, and just as these people are using the Internet for quick access to information and electronic communication, millions of them are also turning to the Internet for shopping purposes (Hupprich and Bumatay). 2

Student's last name and page number in upper right-hand corner

Title, centered; subtitle helps to create interest

Personal narrative used as attention-grabbing introduction

Paragraph 2 describes the current controversy; appeals to authority

Internet source without a page number

Sorensen 2

Thesis—main point

Consumers should shop online because, despite fears of safety and identity theft, its simplicity, the convenience of comparison shopping, and access to a variety of merchandise make online shopping the logical and best choice for consumers.

Topic sentence (see 5a)

Personal experience used as extended example in support of thesis

The convenience of online shopping became clear 3
to me not only as a consumer but also as a retailer. During the holidays, I work for Sears in Frisco, Texas. Our store is new and we still only serve the urban areas, so many people travel from rural areas to shop. While working over Christmas I helped one such woman who needed to shop for items for the baby she was expecting. She could not purchase everything she needed in this one trip and did not want to have to make the drive numerous times, so I suggested she go online to see what *Sears.com* had to offer. After visiting the site she decided to order all of her baby furniture from the comfort of her own home. She informed me that though she was able to buy most of the items she needed online, she would come back to the store to shop for baby clothes, which were not available online.

No citation needed for common knowledge

Rural customers are not the only consumers who 4
benefit from online shopping. More and more shoppers use the Internet to comparison-shop before purchasing items online or in a store, so they save money. There are

Sorensen 3

price-comparison tools on the Internet, and some, such as *PriceGrabber.com,* find the best price for a particular item and then calculate the tax and shipping costs. This site and others can be used to get price quotes for items varying from airline tickets to cashmere sweaters.

Many customers may want to try on a cashmere 5
sweater to see how it looks on them before buying it, even if they have to pay more to do so. For example, Ahmad Kushairi says, “For me, I would like to browse the shelves and feel the products before deciding if I even want to purchase.” Online retailers are aware of this and try to target these consumers by providing new technologies. For example, My Virtual Model Inc. has created a tool that allows customers to “try clothes on” before purchasing them. This technology has “increased online sales” by leading to 26 percent more purchases than average and increasing the average order size by 13 percent. Virtual models are being used by numerous online retailers, such as Lands’ End, Limited Too, Lane Bryant, and Nutri/System (“Virtual Model”).

Retailers also target consumers by offering deals 6
through special online promotions such as credit card companies offering deals to their cardholders. For example, American Express, Visa, MasterCard, and Discover have promotions that include free shipping and discounts

Transitional sentence used to link paragraphs

Direct quotation from a print source that is one page only

Paraphrase of a print source

No page number when source is only one page long

Summary of a one page print source, restating and condensing

Transitional sentence, followed by topic development describing other benefits to consumers

Paraphrase of an author quoted in another source on teen behavior

Paraphrase of an Internet source quoted in another source to explain a study about the complexities of online shopping behavior

ranging from 5 to 25 percent. To receive these deals, however, customers must first visit the credit card site, and they will usually have to use promotion codes or visit the retailers' sites from a link on the credit card company's site. The discounts change frequently and vary among the various credit card companies. Credit card companies can also offer promotions for local businesses and attractions, so consumers can register their e-mail address to learn of the offers before they are posted on the site (Frey).

7 In addition to good deals and access to new technology, online shopping offers a place for consumers to shop quickly and easily online, as well as quickly and easily offline. One segment of the population that has benefited the most is teenagers. Jared Blank, an analyst for Juniper Matrix, points out that teens today "use the Internet as a shopping mall—a place to meet friends, play games, and shop—even without the intent to purchase. Teens spend almost as much time on Amazon.com as adults, even though few of those teens can make purchases on the site" (qtd. in "Nearly One-Third").

8 Teens are not the only segment of the consumer population who browse for goods online and then choose to shop in brick-and-mortar stores. According to the NPD Group, Inc., 92 percent of online consumers use the Internet to shop and/or purchase online (qtd. in Pastore).

Sorensen 5

Cyberjournalist Michael Pastore points out that NPD's data shows that even those consumers not making purchases online are still influenced by what they see on retailers' Web sites. Eighty-four percent of occasional buyers, who made at most one online purchase in the past six months, describe their usual use of the Internet for shopping online and then going offline to purchase. Pamela Smith, vice president of NPD Online Research, explains:

> Measuring online sales alone cannot capture the full benefit of a retailer having an Internet presence. We know that even consumers who don't typically purchase online are using retailers' web sites to browse and decide what to buy. . . . Although it may not result in a purchase at that time, it could translate directly into an offline sale. (qtd. in Pastore)

Indented quotation in MLA style (see 12a, 19b-3, 51a-2)

Ellipsis used to show that part of the quotation was left out (see 52k)

Figure 1, which outlines how online shoppers describe how they typically use the Internet for shopping, illustrates Smith's point.

9 Since the NPD study was completed, our nation has experienced an economic downturn, but online spending has increased. A study titled "The State of Retailing Online 5.0" reports that "fully 56 percent of holiday retailers reported online profits in 2001, compared to only 43 percent in 2000" (qtd. in Cox).

More statistical support to bolster the argument

Statistical information used to support the argument regarding online shopping behavior

Sorensen 6

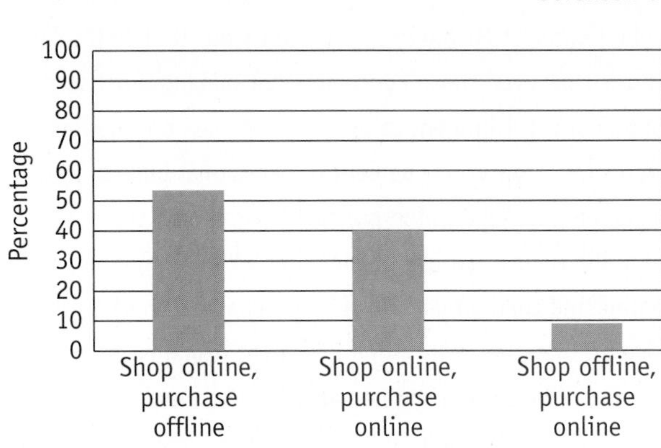

Fig. 1. How shoppers typically use the Internet
Source: Pastore.

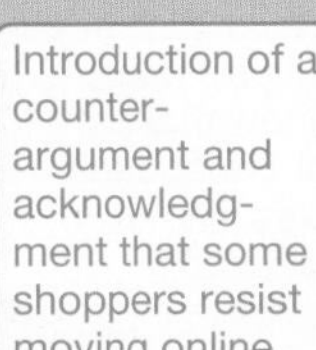

Introduction of a counter-argument and acknowledg-ment that some shoppers resist moving online

Although online shopping trends and spending are 10
growing, there are still consumers who resist purchasing products over the Internet. One reason many people may choose to browse for goods online and then purchase them offline is their concern about identity theft. In fact, a report by Taylor Nelson Sofres points out, “Almost one-third (30 percent) of Internet users who have not shopped online stated that they didn’t want to give credit card details (up by 5 percent from 2001) and 28 percent cited general security concerns” (qtd. in Greenspan). In order to confidently shop online, consumers must be sure that the retail site

Sorensen 7

is safe and secure and that no one can steal personal information from the site. According to *The Shopping Guide*, which is an online shopping directory sponsored by Microsoft Internet, consumers can protect themselves by considering three things: transaction security, privacy, and credit card fraud ("Online Shopping Safety").

Refutation of the counter-argument to allay fears

Transaction security is the first thing to be aware 11
of when shopping on the Internet, and data encryption provides the most secure way to send information from site to site without having anyone in between being able to read it. When an Internet user sends information, the data is encrypted, or put into code. Anyone who tries to read the information while it is en route to the site will find it impossible. Secure Sockets Layer (SSL), the standard for sending secure data, protects against snooping and possible tampering and then verifies that the site to which the data is sent is authentic. *Netscape Security Center*, which is an informational site published on the Internet browser's homepage, explains that shoppers, when sending or receiving confidential information, should make sure that their data is always being checked by SSL (see Fig. 2). SSL works with certain versions of browsers, such as *Netscape*, *Internet Explorer*, and *AOL*, and can also be

Topic sentence for paragraph 11

Development of the topic using a paraphrase of an online source

Sorensen 8

Citation of a source without an author

verified by simply calling the vendor. Oftentimes, a padlock will appear in the bottom left corner to tell you if the site is secure ("How Encryption Works").

Transitional sentence, followed by further development of the topic of consumer protection

Transaction security can also be ensured by 12
checking the credibility of a source. One way to do this is to look for the Better Business Bureau Online Reliability Seal, which guarantees that a retailer has been in business for at least one year, has become a member of a local Better Business Bureau (BBB), and has agreed to arbitration in case of a dispute over sale. The BBB says that online advertisements with excessive

Visual: screen shot of *Netscape Security Center* on availability of security information

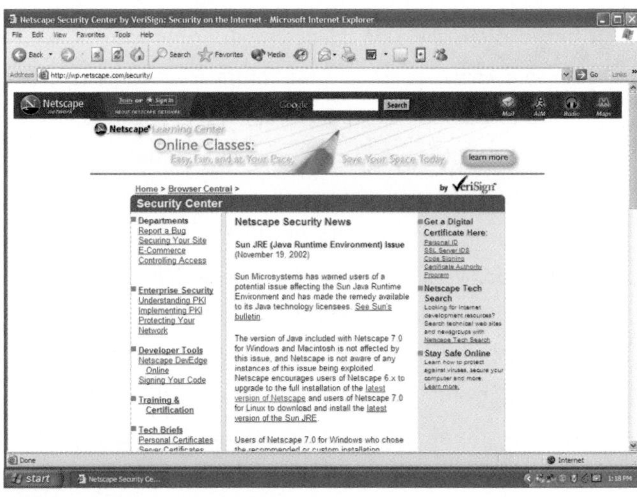

Fig. 2. *Netscape Security* Homepage.
Source: "How Encryption Works."

Sorensen 9

capital letters, dollar signs ($$$$$) and exclamation points (!!!!) at every turn, misspellings, and grammatical errors may indicate a sleazy operation (*Better Business*).

Privacy is another important consideration for 13
online shopping, and consumers may worry that once their data gets to the receiver safely, a hacker may come in and steal uncoded information. Most retailers move data off their Internet server after receiving it so it will be inaccessible to hackers. Each company has a different policy, so it is best to check with customer support or the help section for specifics.

Further development of the topic of consumer protection

The Online Shopping Guide also advises that shoppers 14
need to check the policy on credit card fraud and to be aware of any guarantees that online retailers make about identity theft ("Online Shopping Safety"). Ellen Stark reminds us that despite what policies individual companies have, the Fair Credit Billing Act ensures that a bank cannot hold a customer liable for more than $50 in fraudulent charges. So, no matter what concerns consumers have about a hacker stealing their identity and charging products to stolen credit card numbers, the federal government has provided consumers with protection.

Appeal to logic regarding identity theft

In-text citation of one-page source, with author's name in signal phrase

Despite concerns about safety and identity theft, 15
more and more people are turning to the Internet to meet their consumer needs. Retailers are aware of this

Summary and conclusion (see 5h)

Sorensen 10

trend and are anxious to attract new customers to their sites, and they are therefore willing to improve site safety and user-friendly technology to entice shoppers. While some people choose to shop online because they find shopping in brick-and-mortar stores annoying and time-consuming, others just enjoy the fact that not only can they shop without leaving their homes but they can shop without even getting dressed. Others would rather simply click on a button to order goods than stand in checkout lines or battle for parking spaces in a crowded mall lot. Whatever the reason for initially shopping online, many consumers, like myself, not only enjoy the benefits of ease and convenience of e-commerce but also believe that it will only get better.

Action to be taken, plus useful links for consumers

Now that you know about online shopping, you are 16
probably wondering where to shop online. These are just a few links to some of my favorite online shopping sites. Just remember, just because you shop online does not mean you buy online. You can shop around and then visit the store as you normally would; this will save you a few hours—or days!

amazon.com	landsend.com	shop.com
bn.com	oldnavy.com	target.com
fossil.com	sears.com	wal-mart.com

Sorensen 11

Works Cited

Better Business Bureau Program. 2002. Web. 22 Mar. 2003.

Cox, Beth. "E-commerce: Color It Green." *Cyberatlas* 3 Aug. 2002. Web. 12 Apr. 2003.

Frey, Christine. "Online Shopper: Advantages of Plastic." *Los Angeles Times* 18 Oct. 2001: T8. Print.

Greenspan, Robyn. "E-shopping around the World." *Cyberatlas* 5 Aug. 2002. Web. 23 Mar. 2003.

"How Encryption Works." *Netscape Security Center*. Web. 5 Apr. 2003.

Hupprich, Laura, and Maria Bumatay. "Nielsen/NetRatings Reports a Record Half-Billion People Worldwide Now Have Home Internet Access." *Nielsen/NetRatings* 3 June 2002. Web. 3 Apr. 2003.

Kushairi, Ahmad. "The Buying Experience Is Still with Offline Shopping." *New Strait Times Press* 12 Aug. 2002: 2. Print.

Alphabetical listing of all sources used (see Chapter 12)

Internet: Professional site, with date of publication followed by date of access.

Name of professional site

Date of publication

Date of access

Print: newspaper

Internet: online newsletter

Article titles are enclosed in quotation marks; each important word starts with a capital letter

Print: newspaper

Article found via a library reference database

Name of the database

Internet: article from an online publication

Print: magazine

Print: newspaper

Sorensen 12

"Nearly One-Third of Teens Make Offline Purchases after Window Shopping Online." *PR Newswire Association, Inc.* 18 July 2001: Financial News Section. *Academic Search Elite*. Web. 20 Mar. 2003.

"Online Shopping Safety and Security." *The Shopping Guide* 8 Aug. 2002. Web. 12 Apr. 2003.

Pastore, Michael. "Web Influences Offline Purchases, Especially among Teens." *Cyberatlas* 3 Aug. 2002. Web. 18 Mar. 2003.

Stark, Ellen. "There's Help on the Way If You Face a Credit Card Dispute." *Money* May 1996: 41. Print.

"Virtual Model Tech Hikes Lands' End Sales." *Capital Times* 27 Sept. 2001: 6E. Print.

12 MLA Documentation Style

FAQs

- What is the purpose of documentation?
- How can I integrate my sources responsibly? (12a-1)
- How do I document MLA sources within the text of my paper? (12a-2)
- How do I create a Works Cited list in MLA style? (12a-4)
- How do I cite electronic sources in MLA style? (12b)

For complete student papers using MLA style, see Chapter 11, Writing the Research Paper, pages 284–296 and Chapter 16, Writing in the Humanities, pages 401–403 and 405–412.

Providing a documentation trail that leads back to the original sources is a feature that distinguishes scholarly writing from writing found in the popular press. Scholars and researchers in all disciplines base their own work on the work that others have done in the past. The thread of knowledge can be traced from one scholar to another. In scholarly writing, providing readers with evidence of that thread of knowledge is essential, not only so that readers can trace the thread if they so desire but also to let them know that the information is from reliable sources.

12a Document using MLA style

MLA Web site

The Modern Language Association (MLA) documentation style has been adopted by many scholars in the fields of language and literature (Joseph Gibaldi, *MLA Handbook for Writers of Research Papers*, 7th ed., New York: MLA, 2009). The MLA style consists of two parts:

- In-text citations (found in parentheses), which include the author's last name and the page number of the source information, and
- A list of works cited, arranged alphabetically by authors' last names, found at the end of the paper.

❶ Integrating sources and avoiding plagiarism in MLA style

In Chapter 10, Using Sources and Avoiding Plagiarism, we talked in general about the importance of using sources accurately and responsibly in your research papers. To help you do so, the MLA citation style provides for a two-part system of source identification: (1) in-text citations within the body of the paper and (2) a Works Cited list at the end of the paper. By using the MLA documentation style, you can integrate your source information appropriately and ethically without inadvertently committing plagiarism.

GO See Ch. 10

GO See 12a-2 and 12a-4

Plagiarism, a serious academic offense, is often committed by students inadvertently in the following two ways.

1. Failing to acknowledge a summary or paraphrase of a source in the body of the paper through a signal phrase and in-text citation
2. Using the original author's words without putting the borrowed words or phrases in quotation marks or including a parenthetical citation

Guidelines

See 10g and Guidelines 10g-3

Using the MLA Citation Style

1. **Introduce your source** using a signal phrase that names its author or include the author's last name with page number in parentheses at the end of the citation: *According to Jones*, . . . (332) or (Jones 332).
2. **Paraphrase or summarize** the information from your source. It's best to use direct quotations sparingly. Preferably, recast the source information into your own words. If you do use any words or phrases from the author, be sure to include them in quotation marks.
3. At the conclusion of your paraphrase, summary, or quotation, **insert in parentheses the page number on which the information was found**, followed by a period: (*332*). or (*Jones 332*).
4. At the end of your paper, **list the source with complete bibliographic information on your Works Cited page**.

See 12a-2

See 12a-4

❷ MLA style for in-text citations

When you rely on information from sources to support your arguments in the humanities, your readers will want to know who wrote each source and where it can be located. MLA documentation therefore requires that you provide that information—the author's last name and the page number where your source information can be found—in the body of your paper in the form of an in-text citation, also called parenthetical references, which is linked to the Works Cited page. Following are some guidelines for incorporating parenthetical references in the text of your research paper.

1. Author Named in a Signal Phrase

If you introduce a paraphrase or direct quotation with the name of the author, simply indicate the page number of the source in parentheses at the end of the cited material.

> Attempting to define ethnic stereotyping, Gordon Allport states that "much prejudice is a matter of blind conformity with prevailing folkways" (12).

No page number is necessary when an entire work is cited or for unnumbered Web pages. (Note that titles of independently published works are italicized.)

> Conrad's book *Lord Jim* tells the story of an idealistic young Englishman.
>
> The World Wildlife Federation's Web site has links to many helpful sites about the environment.

2. Author Named in Parentheses

If the author's name is not used to introduce the paraphrased or quoted material, place the author's last name along with the specific page number in parentheses at the end of the cited material, before the end punctuation. Do not separate author and page number with a comma.

> When Mitford and Peter Rodd were first engaged, "they even bought black shirts and went to some Fascist meetings" (Guinness 304).

A Directory to MLA Style

In-Text Citations

Works Cited Entries

Books

Periodicals (Journals and Magazines)

3. Multiple Sentences Paraphrased

Indicate every instance of paraphrased or summarized material. If an entire paragraph is taken from a single source, mention the author's name at the beginning of the paragraph and cite the page numbers where appropriate.

> As Endelman shows, the turbulence of the interwar years—"political agitation, social discrimination, street hooliganism" (191)—culminated in the formation of the British Union of Fascists. He states that anti-Semitism "was common enough that few Jews could have avoided it altogether or been unaware of its existence" (194).

4. Work by Two or Three Authors

Include the last names of all the authors (the last two connected by *and*) either in the text or in the parenthetical reference. Because the following references are to entire works, no page numbers are necessary.

> Goodsell, Maher, and Tinto write about how the theory of collaborative learning may be applied to the administration of a college or university.

> We need to think daily about the implications of our future liberation (Eastman and Hayford).

5. Work by Four or More Authors

In citing a work by four or more authors, either provide the names of all the authors or provide the name of the first author followed by the abbreviation *et al.* ("and others").

> In *The Development of Writing Abilities*, the authors call writing that is close to the self "expressive," writing that gets things done "transactional," and writing that calls attention to itself "poetic" (Britton, Burgess, Martin, McLeod, and Rosen).

or

> In *The Development of Writing Abilities*, the authors present a theory of writing based upon whether a writer assumes a participant or a spectator role (Britton et al.).

6. Work by a Corporate Author

When the author is an organization or corporation, treat the group's name the same way as the name of an individual author. If the name is long, try to incorporate it into the text rather than including it in a parenthetical note.

> The book *Discovering Microsoft Office,* by the Microsoft Corporation, "describes the many multilingual features available in *Outlook*" (143).

7. Work in More Than One Volume

If the work consists of more than one volume, provide the volume number, followed by a colon, just before the page number. When referring to an entire volume of a multivolume work, add a comma after the author's name, followed by *vol.* and the volume number.

> In Ward's introduction to the collected works of Sir John Vanbrugh, he states that "the Vanbrugh family seems to have been both ancient and honorable" (1: x).

> The collected plays of Vanbrugh show the range of his talent (Ward, vol. 2).

8. Different Works by the Same Author

When the Works Cited list refers to two works by the same author, include in the parenthetical reference the title (which may be abbreviated), as well as the author and the page number of the source. If the author's name is included in the text, cite only the title and page number in parentheses.

> Her first volume of memoirs, published in 1975, tells the story of her brother's friend, whom her mother would not allow her to choose for games at parties (Mitchison, *All Change Here* 85). In her prewar novel, Mitchison, who was the housebound wife of an Oxford don, derives a strange solution to England's economic problems (*We Have Been Warned* 441).

9. Works by Two or More Authors with the Same Last Name

Include both authors' first and last names in the signal phrase or in parentheses to distinguish two authors who have the same last name.

> Luci Shaw reveals deep spirituality in her poem titled "Made Flesh" (31). Martin Shaw's poem "Respite" is more philosophical (45).

10. Work Cited Indirectly

If possible, take information directly from the original source. However, sometimes it is necessary to cite someone indirectly, taking material from a quotation in another source—particularly in the case of a published account of someone's spoken words. To indicate an indirect quotation, use the abbreviation *qtd. in* (for "quoted in") before listing the source.

> High school teacher Ruth Gerrard finds that "certain Shakespearean characters have definite potential as student role models" (qtd. in Davis and Salomone 24).

11. Two or More Sources Within the Same Citation

When referring to two or more sources within the same parenthetical reference, use semicolons to separate the citations. For the sake of readability, however, take care not to list too many sources in a single citation.

> The works of several authors in the post-war years tend to focus on racial themes (Mitchison 440; Mosley 198).
>
> If students are allowed to freely exchange ideas about a work of literature, they will come to examine their own sense of the work in light of the opinions of others (Bleich 45; Rosenblatt, *Literature as Exploration* 110).

12. Anonymous Work

Sources such as magazine articles, Web sites, and reports by commissions may not list an author. Such works are listed by their title on the Works Cited page. For the in-text citation of an anonymous work listed by title, use an abbreviated version of the title, in parentheses, plus the page number when available.

The article points out the miscommunications that can occur between men and women because of differences in communication styles ("It Started" 110).

In many Native American cultures, the feather often symbolizes a prayer ("Feather").

13. Work of Literature

Since classic works of literature are often available in different editions, including location information, such as chapter number, section number, act number, and scene number, in the parenthetical citation will help your reader locate the reference in any edition of the work. Include this location information after a page reference, where appropriate. When citing classic poetry or plays, use line numbers instead of page numbers. Generally, use arabic numbers rather than roman numerals.

In the novel *Lord Jim,* Conrad describes the village of Patusan and its inhabitants (242; ch. 24).

In *Paradise Lost,* Satan's descent to earth is described in graphic detail (Milton 4.9-31).

As Laertes leaves for France, Polonius gives the young man trite and unhelpful advice such as "Beware/Of entrance to a quarrel, but being in,/Bear't that th' opposed may beware of thee" (*Hamlet* 1.3.65–67).

14. Work in an Anthology

If you are citing a work found in an anthology (collection), use the name of the author of the particular work you are citing, not the editor(s) of the anthology. List the page numbers as they are found in the anthology.

The American Dream crosses many ethnic boundaries, as illustrated by Papaleo (88).

15. Sacred Text

When quoting from the Bible, the Qur'an, or another sacred text, give the title of the version you are using (e.g., *The Revised Standard Version*), the book, and the chapter and verse or their equivalent, separated by a period. If using a signal phrase, spell out the book being quoted. In parentheses, abbreviate the book if its name is five or more letters (e.g., *Phil.* for *Philippians*).

In his letter to the Philippians, the apostle Paul says, "There must be no room for rivalry and personal vanity among you, but you must humbly reckon others better than yourselves. Look to each other's interest and not merely to your own" (*The New English Bible*, Phil. 2.3–4).

16. Entire Work or One-Page Article

When citing an entire work or a work that is only one page long, refer to the author and the title, without any page numbers.

In his book *Losing My Mind: An Intimate Look at Life with Alzheimer's*, Thomas DeBaggio chronicles his battle with Alzheimer's disease.

See item 16

17. Work with No Page Numbers

A work without page numbers is cited like a one-page work. If a work uses paragraph numbers instead of page numbers, use the abbreviation *par.* or *pars.*

The reporter from a recent Family Law Conference sponsored by the American Bar Association, Sarah H. Ramsey, stated, "High-conflict custody cases are marked by a lack of trust between the parents, a high level of anger and a willingness to engage in repetitive litigation" (par. 24).

18. Different Page Numbers in the Same Work

When it is apparent that two citations refer to the same work, there is no need to repeat the author's name. Identifying the appropriate page number will suffice.

In *We Have Been Warned*, Mitchison's prewar novel, she states that "these commercial ideas have crept into all our morality, art and science" (441). She continues in this vein when she asks, "How could he with that racial inheritance and that education—even if he saw through the education very young?" (444).

19. Long or Block Quotation

When a quotation is lengthy (takes up more than four lines), indent it ten spaces from the left-hand margin (or 1 inch). Lines remain double-spaced throughout the indented quotation. Note that the end punctuation is different for indented quotations than for internal citations that are run into the text—the period comes before the parenthetical citation for indented quotations. Also note that no quotation marks are used and that a colon generally introduces the quotation.

> McMurtry's novel chronicles the growing-up years of a young man in rural Texas. In this passage, we see the alienation that Lonnie feels as his family falls apart around him:
>
> > The next day was the last of the rodeo, and I didn't much care. The whole crazy circle of things got so it tired me out. When I woke up that morning I could see Jesse down in the lots, moving around, and I got up to go talk to him. I had looked for him the night before, after the dance, but he wasn't around. . . . There was nobody to cook my breakfast, and I didn't feel like cooking it myself. (112)

20. Electronic or Online Source

When information is from an electronic medium, usually the entire work is referenced. In such cases, incorporate the reference to the work within the sentence by naming the author of the source (or the title, if no author is listed) just as it is listed on the Works Cited page. No parentheses are needed when an entire work is cited.

> One of the features of *The Encyclopedia Mythica* Web site is its archive of cultural myths, such as those prevalent in Native American society.
>
> Andy Packer's homepage lists a number of links to *Star Wars* Web sites.

21. Secondary Web Page Source

When citing a Web site with secondary pages, list separately each secondary page used in the research paper.

According to *Britannica Online*, in Native American mythology, a feather often symbolizes a prayer ("Feather").

Britannica Online shows that mythology has developed in all societies ("Mythology").

22. Quote or Paraphrase from an Electronic Source

See item 21

When quoting or paraphrasing directly from an electronic source, either give the section title in quotation marks or cite the paragraph number (with the abbreviation *par.*), if provided, so that a reader will be able to find the section used in the paper. If no numbering is provided, list the source author or title only. Or, you may wish to incorporate the work's author or title into the sentence containing the information.

The writer discusses his reasons for calling Xerox's online site "a great place to visit" (Gomes, par. 5).

The average global air temperature has risen between 0.3 and 0.6 degree Celsius (Hileman).

3 MLA format for bibliographic footnotes and endnotes

Generally, footnotes and endnotes are not used in MLA style. However, notes may be included to refer the reader to sources that contain information different from that given in the paper. In the text, indicate a note with a superscript number typed immediately after the source that is referred to. Number notes consecutively throughout the text.

- Use a note to cite sources that have additional information on topics covered in the paper.

1. For further information on this point, see Barbera 168, McBrien 56, and Kristeva 29.

2. For an additional study of Smith's fictional characters, see Barbera's *Me Again*.

- Use a note to cite sources that contain information related to that included in the paper.

  3. Although outside the scope of this paper, major themes in the novel are discussed by Kristeva and Barbera.

- Use a note to cite sources containing information that a reader might want to compare with that in the paper.

  4. On this point, see also Rosenblatt's *Literature as Exploration*, in which she discusses reader response theory.

④ MLA style for the Works Cited page

You need to provide your readers with a complete and accurate alphabetical list of all the sources used in your paper so that they can readily find these

Guidelines

Formatting MLA Endnotes and Footnotes

With the endnote style, all your notes appear together at the end of the paper:

- Start a new page following the end of the text, before the Works Cited list.
- Type the title *Notes*, centered horizontally 1 inch from the top of the page.
- Double-space to the first note.
- Indent the first line five spaces (or 1/2 inch) from the left margin and type the note number and a period. The second line will return to the margin.
- Leave one space following the number, then begin the text of the note.
- Double-space between and within all notes.

With the footnote style, each note is at the base of the referenced page:

- Position the text of the note at the bottom of the page on which the reference occurs.
- Begin the footnote four lines below the text.
- Use a note number and a period, followed by a space, then the note itself.
- Single-space within a footnote, but double-space between footnotes if more than one note appears on a page.

On the Works Cited page, include all the sources mentioned in either endnotes or footnotes.

Formatting an MLA Works Cited Page

- **List sources alphabetically** by the last name of the author, using letter-by-letter alphabetization. When no author is given, alphabetize by the first word of the title, excluding *A, An,* and *The.*
- **Type the first word** of each entry at the left margin of the page. Indent all subsequent lines of the same entry five spaces, or 1/2 inch. (This is called a *hanging indent.*)
- **Double-space** the entire list, both between and within entries.

sources if they wish to do so. This list, usually called Works Cited, should appear at the very end of your paper. (If you include works that were useful to you in your research but not directly cited in your paper, the list should be called Bibliography. A bibliography that includes brief summaries of the works is called an Annotated Bibliography.)

Books in MLA style

A citation for a book has four basic parts. Author's Name. *Book Title.* Publication Information. Medium.

- *Author's name.* For books, monographs, and other complete works, include the author's full name as given on the title page—start with the last name first, followed by a comma; then put the first name and middle name or initial, followed by a period.
- *Book title.* After the author's name, give the complete title of the book as it appears on the title page (italicized), followed by a period. Important words in the title should be capitalized. Include the subtitle, if there is one, separated from the title by a colon.
- *Publication information.* Indicate the place of publication, followed by a colon (if several cities are listed, include only the first one); the publisher's name as it appears on the title page, followed by a comma; and the date of publication from the copyright page, followed by a period.
- *Medium.* Indicate the medium of publication, such as *Print* or *Web.* Adding the medium of publication to all citations represents a change in MLA style.

In MLA style, the publication information is abbreviated as much as possible in the bibliographic entry. The city where the book was published is given without a state abbreviation. A country abbreviation may be needed for clarity for some foreign publications (for example, *Ulster, Ire.; Bergen, Norw.*). But if a foreign city is well known (such as London or Paris), a country abbreviation is unnecessary. Abbreviate the publisher's name to one word wherever possible (for example, McGraw-Hill, Inc., to *McGraw*; Houghton Mifflin Co. to *Houghton*). Similarly, abbreviate the names of university and government presses: *Columbia UP* for Columbia University Press; the letters *GPO* for Government Printing Office.

A basic entry for a book in a Works Cited list looks like this:

Author | Book Title

Diamond, Jared. *Collapse: How Societies Choose to Fail or Succeed.*

Publication information | Medium

New York: Penguin, 2005. Print.

To see where this information may be located on the title page and copyright page of a book, see Figure 12.1.

See Fig. 12.1

For guidelines on citing electronic books, see items 52 and 53 below.

1. Book by One Author

Author | Book Title | Publication information | Medium

Bryant, John. *The Fluid Text.* Ann Arbor: U of Michigan P, 2002. Print.

See items 52 and 53

Haire-Sargeant, Lin. *H.* New York: Pocket, 1992. Print.

Manguel, Alberto. *A History of Reading.* New York: Viking, 1996. Print.

2. Book by Two or Three Authors

Write multiple authors' names in the order in which they are given on the book's title page. Note that this order may not be alphabetical. Reverse the name of the first author only, putting the last name first; separate the authors' names with commas.

Fiorina, Morris P., Samuel J. Abrams, and Jeremy C. Pope. *Culture War? The Myth of a Polarized America.* New York: Longman, 2005. Print.

Figure 12.1 ▶ Locating Source Information in a Book

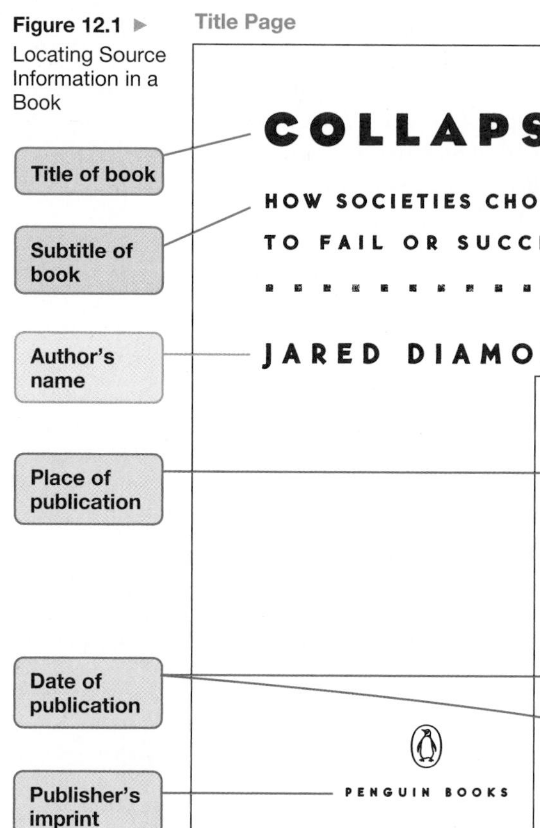

Copyright Page

PENGUIN BOOKS
Published by the Penguin Group
Penguin Group (USA) Inc., 375 Hudson Street, New York, New York 10014, U.S.A.
Penguin Group (Canada), 90 Eglinton Avenue East, Suite 700, Toronto, Ontario, Canada M4P 2Y3 (a division of Pearson Penguin Canada Inc.)
Penguin Books Ltd, 80 Strand, London WC2R 0RL, England
Penguin Ireland, 25 St Stephen's Green, Dublin 2, Ireland (a division of Penguin Books Ltd)
Penguin Group (Australia), 250 Camberwell Road, Camberwell, Victoria 3124, Australia (a division of Pearson Australia Group Pty Ltd)
Penguin Books India Pvt Ltd, 11 Community Centre, Panchsheel Park, New Delhi – 110 017, India
Penguin Group (NZ), cnr Airborne and Rosedale Roads, Albany, Auckland 1310, New Zealand (a division of Pearson New Zealand Ltd)
Penguin Books (South Africa) (Pty) Ltd, 24 Sturdee Avenue, Rosebank, Johannesburg 2196, South Africa

Penguin Books Ltd, Registered Offices:
80 Strand, London WC2R 0RL, England

First published in the United States of America by Viking Penguin, a member of Penguin Group (USA) Inc. 2005
Published in Penguin Books 2006

3 5 7 9 10 8 6 4 2

Copyright © Jared Diamond, 2005
All rights reserved

Maps by Jeffrey L. Ward

THE LIBRARY OF CONGRESS HAS CATALOGED THE HARDCOVER EDITION AS FOLLOWS:
Diamond, Jared M.
Collapse: how societies choose to fail or succeed/Jared Diamond.
p. cm.
Includes index.
ISBN 0-670-03337-5 (hc.)
ISBN 0 14 30.3655 6 (pbk.)
1. Social history—Case studies. 2. Social change—Case studies. 3. Environmental policy—Case studies. I. Title.
HN13.D5 2005
304.2'8—dc22 2004057152

Printed in the United States of America
Set in Minion
Designed by Francesca Belanger

Except in the United States of America, this book is sold subject to the condition that it shall not, by way of trade or otherwise, be lent, resold, hired out, or otherwise circulated without the publisher's prior consent in any form of binding or cover other than that in which it is published and without a similar condition including this condition being imposed on the subsequent purchaser.

The scanning, uploading and distribution of this book via the Internet or via any other means without the permission of the publisher is illegal and punishable by law. Please purchase only authorized electronic editions, and do not participate in or encourage electronic piracy of copyrighted materials. Your support of the author's rights is appreciated.

Author's or Editor's Name

- List the author's last name, first name.
- For multiple authors, list authors in the order they are listed on the title page. (See 12a-4 item 2.)
- For an editor, use the abbreviation *ed.* after the name. (See 12a-4 item 7.)

Book Title

- Use the exact title as it is listed on the title page, not the cover.
- Italicize the title. Follow the conventions of capitalization and punctuation as found in the models for books on the preceding and following pages.

Diamond, Jared. *Collapse: How Societies Choose to Fail or Succeed.* New York: Penguin, 2005. Print.

Medium

- Conclude with the medium of publication, such as *Print.* Adding the medium of publication to all citations represents a change in MLA style.

Publication information

- Begin with the place of publication, followed by the publisher and the date. Punctuate the same as in the models that follow. Use as few words as possible, eliminating such words as Press, Publisher, Inc.
- Give the year as it appears on the copyright page; do not use the date of the latest printing.

TechHelp

Italicizing, Not Underlining

The 2009 MLA style has changed from underlining to italicizing. Show the title of a complete work or a journal in italicized form. See also MLA Web site: http://www.mla.org/style_faq2.

Guinness, Jonathan, and Catherine Guinness. *The House of Mitford*. New York: Viking, 1985. Print.

3. Book by More Than Three Authors

For a book with more than three authors, either write out the names of all the authors listed on the book's title page or write only the first author's name, followed by a comma and the Latin phrase *et al.* (for "and others").

Britton, James, Tony Burgess, Nancy Martin, Alex McLeod, and Harold Rosen. *The Development of Writing Abilities*. London: Macmillan, 1975. Print.

or

Britton, James, et al. *The Development of Writing Abilities*. London: Macmillan, 1975. Print.

4. Organization as Author

When an organization rather than an individual is the author, give the name of the organization as listed on the title page instead of the author, even if the same group also published the book.

Alzheimer's Disease and Related Disorders Association. *Understanding Alzheimer's Disease*. New York: Scribner's, 1988. Print.

5. Book by a Corporate Author

A book by a corporate author is any book whose title page lists a group as the author, rather than individuals. Start with the name of the corporate author, even if it is also the publisher.

Conference on College Composition and Communication. *The National Language Policy*. Urbana: NCTE, 1992. Print.

New York Times Company. *The Downsizing of America*. New York: Random, 1996. Print.

6. Unknown Author

If no author is listed, begin the entry with the title. List the work alphabetically by the first major word in the title.

The American Heritage Dictionary. 4th ed. Boston: Houghton, 2002. Print.

7. Book with an Editor

For books with editors rather than authors, start with the editor or editors, followed by a comma and the abbreviation *ed.* (for "editor") or *eds.* (for "editors").

Barbera, Jack, and William McBrien, eds. *Me Again: The Uncollected Writings of Stevie Smith*. New York: Farrar, 1982. Print.

Cooper, Jane Roberta, ed. *Reading Adrienne Rich: Reviews and Revisions, 1951-1981*. Ann Arbor: U of Michigan P, 1984. Print.

Damrosch, David, Kevin J. H. Dettmar, and Jennifer Wicke, eds. *The Longman Anthology of British Literature: The Twentieth Century*. 3rd ed. New York: Longman, 2006. Print.

8. Chapter or Selection from an Edited Work

An entry for a particular selection begins with the author's name and the title of the chapter or selection. The title is italicized if the work is a book or a play; it is enclosed in quotation marks if the work is a poem, short story, chapter, or essay. Note that the name of the editor or editors follows the book title and is preceded by the abbreviation *Ed.* (for "Edited by"). The inclusive page numbers of the selection follow the publication information. The publication medium is last, e.g., *Print.*

Rushdie, Salman. "Chekov and Zulu." *The Longman Anthology of British Literature: The Twentieth Century*. Ed. David Damrosch, Kevin J. H. Dettmar, and Jennifer Wicke. 3rd ed. New York: Longman, 2006. 2989-98. Print.

Spivak, Gayatri. "Feminism and Deconstruction, Again: Negotiating with Unacknowledged Masculinism." *Between Feminism and*

Psychoanalysis. Ed. Teresa Brennan. London: Routledge, 1989. 206-23. Print.

9. Book with Author and Editor

When citing the book itself, begin with the author's name. The editor's name, introduced by *Ed.* (for "Edited by"), follows the title.

L'Engle, Madeleine. *O Sapientia*. Ed. Luci Shaw. Wheaton: Shaw, 1984. Print.

When citing the editor's contribution to the work, begin with the editor's name, followed by a comma and *ed.* Then list the author's name, introduced by *By*, following the title.

Shaw, Luci, ed. *O Sapientia*. By Madeleine L'Engle. Wheaton: Shaw, 1984. Print.

10. Two or More Items from an Anthology

When citing more than one work from an anthology, list the anthology itself as well as the individual works.

Madison, Soyini D., ed. *The Woman That I Am: The Literature and Culture of Contemporary Women of Color*. New York: St. Martin's, 1994. Print.

11. Two or More Books by the Same Author

Alphabetize entries by the first word in the title. Include the author's name in the first entry only. In subsequent entries, type three hyphens in place of the author's name, followed by a period.

Rose, Mike. *Lives on the Boundary: A Moving Account of the Struggles and Achievements of America's Educationally Underprepared*. New York: Penguin, 1989. Print.

---. *Possible Lives: The Promise of Education in America*. Boston: Houghton, 1995. Print.

12. Article in a Reference Book

An entry for an article in a reference book follows the same pattern as an entry for a work in an anthology. Note, however, that the editor's name and full publication information need not be provided; it is sufficient to provide the edition (if known) and the year of publication. If the article is signed, provide the author's name. (Often the author's name is given in abbreviated form at the end of the article and provided in full form elsewhere.)

Robins, Robert Henry. "Language." *Encyclopedia Britannica*. 2007 ed. Print.

If the article is unsigned, start with the title of the article.

"Lochinvar." *Merriam-Webster's Encyclopedia of Literature*. 1995 ed. Print.

13. Introduction, Preface, Foreword, or Afterword

Start with the name of the author of the specific part being cited, followed by the name of the part, capitalized but not underlined or enclosed in quotation marks. If the writer of the specific part is the same as the author of the book, give the author's last name, preceded by the word *By*. If the writer of the specific part is different from the author of the book, give the book author's complete name after *By*. Provide complete publication information for the books, followed by the inclusive page numbers (even if they are given as roman numerals) of the part being cited.

Tompkins, Jane. Preface. *A Life in School: What the Teacher Learned*. By Tompkins. Reading: Addison, 1996. xi-xix. Print.

14. Book in Translation

Begin the entry with the author's name and the title of the book. After the book's title, insert the abbreviation *Trans.* (for "Translated by") and give the translator's name. If the book also has an editor, give the names of the editor and the translator in the order in which they are listed on the title page.

Kristeva, Julia. *Powers of Horror: An Essay on Abjection*. Trans. Leon S. Roudiez. New York: Columbia UP, 1982. Print.

15. Second or Subsequent Edition of a Book

If a book is not a first edition, identify the edition in the way that it is identified on the book's title page: by year (*1993 ed.*), by name (*Rev. ed.* for "Revised edition"), or by number (*2nd ed., 3rd ed.*).

Strunk, William, Jr., E. B. White, and Roger Angell. *The Elements of Style*. 4th ed. New York: Longman, 2000. Print.

16. Work in More Than One Volume

When citing more than one volume of a multivolume work, insert the total number of volumes in the work before the publication material.

Doyle, Arthur Conan. *The Complete Sherlock Holmes*. 2 vols. Garden City: Doubleday, 1930. Print.

17. One Volume of a Multivolume Work

When citing one volume of a multivolume work, include only the particular volume number before the publication information. At the end of the citation, following the date, MLA recommends providing the number of volumes in the complete work.

Poe, Edgar Allan. *The Complete Poems and Stories of Edgar Allan Poe*. Vol. 1. New York: Knopf, 1982. 2 vols. Print.

18. Book in a Series

If the title page indicates that the book is part of a series, insert the series name (do not italicize it or enclose it in quotation marks) and the series number, if any, before the publication information.

Ball, Arnetha F., and Ted Lardner. *African American Literacies Unleashed: Vernacular English and the Composition Classroom*. Studies in Writing and Rhetoric. Urbana: NCTE, 2005. Print.

Jameson, Frederic. Foreword. *The Postmodern Condition: A Report on Knowledge*. By Jean-François Lyotard. Trans. Geoff Bennington and Brian Massumi. Theory and History of Lit. 10. Minneapolis: U of Minnesota P, 1989. vii-xxi. Print.

19. Republished Book

Insert the original publication date, followed by a period, before the publication information for the work being cited.

Dewey, John. *Experience and Education*. 1938. New York: Collier, 1963. Print.

20. Government Document

If the author of a government document is unknown, start with the name of the government, followed by the name of the agency that issued the document, abbreviated. The title of the publication, italicized, follows, and the usual publication information and medium completes the entry.

United States. FBI. *Uniform Crime Reports for the United States: 1995.* Washington: GPO, 1995. Print.

(*GPO* stands for Government Printing Office.)

21. Published Proceedings of a Conference

Write an entry for proceedings in the same way as for a book. Provide information about the conference after the title of the proceedings.

Chambers, Jack A., ed. *College Teaching and Learning*. Selected Papers from the 13th Intl. Conf. on Coll. Teaching and Learning, Apr. 2002. Jacksonville: Florida Community Coll. at Jacksonville, 2002. Print.

22. Pamphlet or Newsletter

Cite a pamphlet the same way as a book.

Five Wishes. Aging with Dignity Pamphlet. Princeton: Robert Wood Johnson Foundation, 2008. Print.

23. Title Within Another Title

If there is a title of another book within the title of the book you are citing, do not italicize the title within the title.

Steinbeck, John. *Journal of a Novel: The* East of Eden *Letters*. New York: Viking, 1969. Print.

24. Sacred Text

When citing an individual published edition of a sacred text, begin the entry with the title, including the specific version, if any.

The Torah: The Five Books of Moses. Philadelphia: Jewish Society of America, 1962. Print.

Periodicals (journals and magazines) in MLA style

A citation for an article in a periodical follows a format similar to that for a book:

Author's Name. "Article Title." Publication Information. Medium.

- *Author's name.* As with a book, include the author's complete name as listed either in the journal's table of contents or at the beginning of the article itself. For multiple authors, use the order of names shown in the journal.
- *Article title.* Use the complete title of the article as listed in the journal's table of contents. Enclose the title in quotation marks.
- *Publication information.* Complete publication information for a source from a periodical includes several elements.
  - For an article in a journal, the entry should include the name of the journal itself (italicized), the volume and issue numbers, often the date of publication, the inclusive numbers of the pages on which the specific article appears, and the medium of publication.
  - For an article in a newspaper or a magazine, the entry should include the name of the periodical (italicized), the date (formatted as day month year: *22 June 2006*), and page numbers for the entire article. (If the article is not on consecutive pages, provide only the first page number followed by a plus sign, +.)
  - Omit opening *The, A,* or *An* from the name of the periodical.
- *Medium.* The publication medium comes last. Adding the publication medium to all citations represents a change in MLA style.

In Works Cited entries for sources from periodicals, use of accurate punctuation and formatting is critical. Punctuation helps readers identify the kind of information being provided. The journal title should be italicized; the date should be enclosed in parentheses; a colon should follow the date and precede the page numbers.

A basic citation for a journal article in a Works Cited list looks like this:

Author — Article title — Publication information

Cooper, Marilyn M. "Bringing Forth Worlds." *Computers and Composition*

22.1 (2005): 31-38. Print.

Medium

See Fig. 12.2

To see how this information can be located in a journal, see Figure 12.2.

For information about how to cite online periodical articles, see items 55–58 below.

See items 55–58

25. Article in a Journal Paginated by Volume

For all scholarly journals, include both the volume and issue number. This represents a change from prior MLA style. The issue is indicated by placing a period after the volume number, followed by the issue number—for example, *57.4* signifies volume 57, issue 4, regardless of pagination.

Author | Article title

Coogan, David. "Service Learning and Social Change: The Case for Materialist Rhetoric." *College Composition and Communication* 57.4 (2006): 127–35. Print.

Journal title

Volume number | Issue number | Year of publication | Consecutive pages | Medium

Holbrook, Sue Ellen. "Women's Work: The Feminizing of Composition." *Rhetoric Review* 9.2 (1991): 201–19. Print.

When there are two or more authors, write the authors' names in the order in which they are given on the first page of the article. Note that this order may not be alphabetical. Reverse the name of the first author only (putting the last name first); write the other names in normal order. Write the rest of the entry in the same way that you would an entry for a journal article with one author.

Kidda, Michael, Joseph Turner, and Frank E. Parker. "There is an Alternative to Remedial Education." *Metropolitan Universities* 3.3 (1993): 16–25. Print.

Shamoon, Linda K., and Deborah H. Burns. "A Critique of Pure Tutoring." *Writing Center Journal* 15.2 (1995): 134–51. Print.

26. Article in a Journal Paginated by Issue

Include both volume and issue numbers regardless of pagination by volume or issue. Put a period after the volume number, and write the issue number after the period—for example, *5.1* signifies volume 5, issue 1.

Figure 12.2 ▶ Locating Source Information in a Journal

Journal Cover

Volume 22, Number 1, 2005 ISSN 8755-4615

ELSEVIER

Computers and Composition

An international journal.

Special Issue on the Influence of Gunther Kress' Work

Editors
Gail E. Hawisher
University of Illinois Urbana-Champaign
Cynthia L. Selfe
Michigan Technological University

Name of Journal

Table of Contents Page

Computers and Composition
AN INTERNATIONAL JOURNAL

CONTENTS

Volume 22, Number 1, 2005

Special Issue on the Influence of Gunther Kress' Work

Publication information

Publication date

Title of article

Author of article

Page numbers

Author's Name

- Begin with the author's name. If there is no author, as for a magazine article, begin with the title.

Cooper, Marilyn M. "Bringing Forth Worlds." *Computers and Composition* 22.1 (2005):
31-38. Print.

Medium

- Conclude with the medium of publication, such as *Print*. Adding the medium of publication represents a change in MLA style.

Article Title

- Enclose the complete title of the article in quotation marks.

Publication Information

- The journal name (excluding *A, An, The*) is italicized, followed by the volume and issue number, date and inclusive pages. If publication information does not appear on the title page, check the copyright page (often the inside front cover on journals). See models for journals and magazines for correct MLA punctuation.
- For all scholarly journals, include both the volume and issue number. This represents a change in MLA style.

Kogen, Myra. "The Conventions of Expository Writing." *Journal of Basic Writing* 5.1 (1986): 24–37. Print.

Mohanty, S. P. "Us and Them: On the Philosophical Bases of Political Criticism." *Yale Journal of Criticism* 2.2 (1989): 1–31. Print.

27. Magazine Article

A basic citation for a magazine or newspaper article in a Works Cited list looks like this:

Author — Article Title

Carreyrou, John. "How a Hospital Stumbled Across An Rx for Medicaid." *Wall Street Journal* 22 June 2006: A1+. Print.

Publication information — Medium

GO
See Fig. 12.3

To see how this information can be located in a newspaper, see Figure 12.3.

If the article is unsigned, begin with the title. For a weekly or biweekly magazine, provide the day, the month (abbreviated, except for May, June, and July), and the year, followed by a colon and the inclusive page numbers.

"It Started in a Garden." *Time* 22 Sept. 1952: 110–11. Print.

For a monthly or quarterly magazine, give only the month or quarter and the year before the inclusive page numbers. (If the article is not printed on consecutive pages, give the first page number followed by a plus sign.)

MacDonald, Heather. "Downward Mobility: The Failure of Open Admissions at City University." *City Journal* Summer 1994: 10–20. Print.

28. Newspaper Article

Provide the name of the newspaper in italics, but do not use the article (*The, An, A*) that precedes it (*Boston Globe*, not *The Boston Globe*). If it is not included in the newspaper's title, add the city of publication in brackets following the title. Nationally published newspapers, such as *USA Today*, do not need a city of publication in the reference. Next, provide the day, month (abbreviated, except for May, June, and July), and year. (Do not list volume or issue numbers; however, if the edition is given on the newspaper's masthead, do include it, followed by a colon.) Conclude the entry by providing the page

For Emmylou Harris, Harmonic Convergence

An Americana queen on the road with Dire Straits' Mark Knopfler

LEISURE & ARTS | D7

Indiana U-Turn: All Out for Honda

A town once hostile to foreign cars is now battling to build them

MARKETPLACE | B1

The Digital Route Up the Family Tree

Genealogy projects are moving more ancestral data online

PERSONAL JOURNAL | D1

THE WALL STREET JOURNAL.

© 2006 Dow Jones & Company. All Rights Reserved

DOW JONES WSJ.com THURSDAY, JUNE 22, 2006 - VOL. CCXLVII NO. 145 - ★★ $1.00

Living Expenses

How a Hospital Stumbled Across An Rx for Medicaid

Mt. Sinai Helps Patients Avoid The ER, Paring State Costs And Aiding Its Bottom Line

Dr. Chassin Goes After Salt

By John Carreyrou

After being diagnosed with congestive heart failure three years ago, Norma Soto became a regular at the emergency room of New York's Mount Sinai hospital. Each visit was lucrative for Mount Sinai because Medicaid covered Ms. Soto's expensive treatment.

"I'd end up spending hours there," recalls the unemployed 54-year-old, who lives alone in public housing in

An Acute Problem

What's News—

Business and Finance

SOME CARDIAC CENTERS are cutting back on the use of drug-coated stents and substituting uncoated devices due to rising concerns over blood clots. The safety debate could signal turmoil in a field dominated by Boston Scientific and Johnson & Johnson.

■ Big drug buyers are extracting steep discounts from pharmaceutical firms on some medicines.

■ Merck is selling Zocor to some managed-care firms at below the expected generic price.

■ FedEx posted a 27% jump in fourth-quarter profit and said it sees no signs of an economic slowdown. Shares climbed 5.1%.

■ Morgan Stanley said earnings more than doubled, results analysts credited to CEO John Mack.

■ Morgan Stanley will try to convince a Florida court next week to overturn the Perelman verdict.

World-Wide

■ THE U.S. PRESSED insurgent attacks as disorder in Iraq flared anew.

■ The Senate fell short of moving to an up-or-down vote on a minimum-wage raise.

■ House Republicans put off renewal of the Voting Rights Act in dispute on bilingual ballots and whether the tighter scrutiny of the South is unfair.

Migration Is Making Old-Style Politics Difficult in Mexico

Voters Dwindle, Absentees Don't Register, Patronage Loses Its Traditional Hold

By Joel Millman

TECOMATLÁN, Mexico—So many voters from this parched mountain section of Puebla state have moved to New York that it's become known as "Puebla York." That's put political candidates in a quandary: How do you campaign for votes when the voters are missing?

Burning Oil

Behind Rise of Iran's President: A Populist Economic Agenda

Ahmadinejad Wins Power Promising Lavish Outlays; Inflation Is a Major Worry

Crunch Time at Biscuit Factory

By Bill Spindle

TEHRAN—Iran's new president, Mahmoud Ahmadinejad, has grabbed the world's attention with his bombast over Tehran's nuclear program and saber rattling against Israel. At home, however, the president's popularity is soaring thanks to another reason: his enthusiastic embrace of economic populism.

Fuel Economy

◄ **Figure 12.3** Locating Source Information in a Newspaper

Author's Name

► List author's name first, if an author is provided. If not, begin with the title of the newspaper article itself. (See item 28.)

```
Carreyrou, John. "How a Hospital Stumbled Across An Rx for Medicaid." Wall Street
    Journal 22 June 2006: A1+. Print.
```

Article Title

► Use the exact title and enclose it in quotation marks.

► Follow the conventions of capitalization and punctuation as found in item 28.

Publication Information

► Begin with name of the newspaper followed by the date of publication (day, month, year). Punctuate as in item 28.

► List the newspaper section number and page number. If the article continues beyond the initial page, include a plus sign to indicate additional pages.

Medium

► Conclude with the publication medium, e.g., *Print.*

numbers, preceded by the section number or letter if each section is separately paginated, with the publication medium last, e.g., *Print.*

Rose, Marla Matzer. "JetBlue Bound for Port Columbus." *Columbus Dispatch* 13 July 2006: B1. Print.

Titze, Maria. "Warning: Trust in Courts Needed." *Deseret News* [Salt Lake City] 16 Jan. 2001: A1. Print.

"Twenty Percent Biased against Jews." *New York Times* 22 Nov. 1992: A1. Print.

29. Editorial

Provide the name of the editorial writer (last name first), if known, and then the title of the editorial (in quotation marks). Next, write the word *Editorial*, but do not italicize it or enclose it in quotation marks. End the entry with the name of the newspaper, magazine, or journal and the standard publication information including medium of publication.

"Six Who Serve Their Council Districts." Editorial. *Boston Globe* 31 Oct. 1997: A22. Print.

Warner, Judith. "What Girls Ought to Learn from Boys in Crisis." Editorial. *New York Times* 12 July 2006: A22. Print.

30. Letter to the Editor

Include the designation *Letter* after the name of the letter writer, but do not italicize it or enclose it in quotation marks. End the entry with the name of the newspaper, magazine, or journal and the standard publication information and publication medium.

Lopez, Francesca. Letter. *New York Times*. 12 July 2006: A21. Print.

31. Review

Start with the name of the reviewer and the title of the review. Then insert *Rev. of* (for "Review of"), but do not italicize it or enclose it in quotation marks. Next, provide the title of the piece reviewed, followed by a comma, the word *by*, and the name of the author of the piece being reviewed, if applicable. If the name of the reviewer is not given, start with the title of the review; if no title is given either, start with *Rev. of.* End the entry with the name of the newspaper, magazine, or journal and the standard publication information including publication medium.

Denby, David. "Dressed to Kill." Rev. of *The Devil Wears Prada*. *New Yorker* 10 July 2006: 119–20. Print.

32. Abstract from an Abstracts Journal

Begin by providing publication information on the original work. Then provide material on the journal in which you found the abstract: the title (italicized), the volume number, and the year (in parentheses), followed by a colon and the page or item number. The publication medium is last.

Johnson, Nancy Kay. "Cultural and Psychosocial Determinants of Health and Illness." Diss. U of Washington, 1980. *DAI* 40 (1980): 425B. Print.

(*Diss.* means "Dissertation," and *DAI* is the abbreviation for *Dissertation Abstracts International.*)

Juliebo, Moira, et al. "Metacognition of Young Readers in an Early Intervention Reading Programme." *Journal of Research in Reading* 21.1 (1998): 24–35. *Psychological Abstracts* 85.7 (1998): item 22380. Print.

33. Unsigned Article

If an article has no known author, begin with its title, alphabetizing the citation by the first major word of the title on your references list.

"What You Don't Know about Desktops Can Cost You." *Consumer Reports* Sept. 2002: 20–22. Print.

Other sources

34. Film or Video Recording

Begin with the film's title (italicized), followed by the director, distributor, year of release, and publication medium, e.g., *Film.* You can include other pertinent information, such as the names of the performers, writers, and producers, before the name of the distributor.

The Devil Wears Prada. Dir. David Frankel. Perf. Meryl Streep and Anne Hathaway. Twentieth Century Fox, 2006. Film.

Indiana Jones and the Temple of Doom. Dir. Steven Spielberg. Paramount, 1984. Film.

If citing an individual's work on the film, begin the entry with that person's name and title.

Spielberg, Steven, dir. *Indiana Jones and the Temple of Doom*. Paramount, 1984. Film.

35. Television or Radio Program

Provide the title of the episode (enclosed in quotation marks), if known; the title of the program (italicized); the title of the series (not italicized or enclosed in quotation marks), if any; the network; the call numbers and local city, if any; the date of broadcast and the medium, e.g., *Radio* or *Television.*

"Bingo to You, Sir." *All Things Considered*. Natl. Public Radio. WBUR, Boston. 29 Aug. 2006. Radio.

"Ultimate Bear." *National Geographic World Premier*. National Geographic Channel. 30 Aug. 2006. Television.

36. Sound Recording

For a sound recording that is available commercially, provide the name of the artist, the title of the recording (italicized, unless the piece is identified only by form, number, and key), the manufacturer, and the year of issue. Indicate the medium last.

Ashanti. "Still on It." *Collectables by Ashanti*. Def Jam, 2005. CD.

Ball, Marcia. *Blue House*. Rounder, 1994. CD.

Ormandy, Eugene, cond. Symphony no. 3 in C minor, op. 78. By Camille Saint-Saëns. Perf. E. Power Biggs, organ. Philadelphia Orch. Sony, 1991. CD.

37. Performance

An entry for a play, concert, opera, or dance begins with the title (italicized), includes information similar to that given for a film, and ends with the performance site (for example, the theater and city) and the date of the performance and the medium.

Blues for an Alabama Sky. By Pearl Cleage. Dir. Kenny Leon. Perf. Phylicia Rashad, Tyrone Mitchell Henderson, Sean C. Squire, Deidre N. Henry, and John Henry Redwood. Huntington Theatre, Boston. 5 Feb. 1997. Performance.

38. Work of Art

Provide the name of the artist, the title of the work (italicized), the name of the site that houses the work, and the city. If it is available, include the date the work was created immediately after the title. If the work is part of a private collection, provide the collector's name. When the source is the original work of art, include the medium of composition after the date of composition. When the source is a reproduction, include the medium at the end (e.g., *Web*), followed by the date of access.

Cassatt, Mary. *Breakfast in Bed*. 1886. Oil on canvas. Private collection of Dr. and Mrs. John J. McDonough, Youngstown, OH.

—. *Five O'clock Tea*. Museum of Fine Arts, Boston. Web. June 2008.

39. Published Interview

Provide the name of the person being interviewed; the title of the interview (enclosed in quotation marks), if any; the title of the source in which the interview is published; and any other pertinent bibliographic material, including the publication medium.

Faulkner, William. "The Meaning of 'A Rose for Emily.'" Interview. 1959. The Story and Its Writer: An Introduction to Short Fiction. Ed. Ann Charters. Compact 4th ed. Boston: Bedford-St. Martin's, 1995. 772–73. Print.

40. Unpublished Interview

Provide the name of the person being interviewed, the designation *Personal interview* (not italicized or in quotation marks), and the date.

Jensen, Steven. Personal interview. 12 Apr. 1997.

41. Personal Letter to the Author

Gore, Al. Letter to the author. 12 Dec. 2005.

42. Dissertation—Published

Cite a published dissertation as a book, but add dissertation information before the publication data. Italicize the title of the dissertation, followed by the abbreviation *Diss.* (for "Dissertation"), the name of the degree-granting institution, the date, and the publication information including medium.

Deatherage, Cynthia. *A Way of Seeing: The Anglo-Saxons and the Primal World View*. Diss. Purdue U, 1997. Ann Arbor: UMI, 1997. 9821728. Print.

See item 32

UMI stands for University Microfilms International.

43. Dissertation—Unpublished

Cite an unpublished dissertation as follows:

Balkema, Sandra. "The Composing Activities of Computer Literate Writers." Diss. U of Michigan, 1984.

44. Speech or Lecture

Provide the name of the speaker; the title of the presentation (in quotation marks), if known; the meeting and sponsoring organization, if applicable; the place where the speech or lecture was given; the date and publication medium.

Wiesel, Elie. "Night." Opening Banquet. NCTE Convention. Gaylord Opryland Hotel and Conference Center, Nashville. 16 Nov. 2006. Speech.

45. Map or Chart

Cite a map or a chart the same way you would cite a book with an unknown author, but add the label *Map* or *Chart* to distinguish it.

Wyoming. Map. Chicago: Rand, 1990. Print.

46. Cartoon or Comic Strip

Schultz, Charles. "Peanuts." Cartoon. *Herald Journal* [Logan] 15 Aug. 2002: C6. Print.

47. Advertisement

First name the item being advertised; then add the word *Advertisement* and identify the source where the ad appeared, with the date and page number.

Benadryl Severe Allergy and Sinus Headache. Advertisement. *Prevention* Sept. 2002: 55. Print.

12b Electronic media in MLA style

Coverage of electronic references in MLA style is given in the *MLA Handbook for Writers of Research Papers*, 7th ed. (New York: MLA, 2009), by Joseph Gibaldi. The *MLA Handbook* has simplified the style for electronic citations to provide only the information needed. A URL is typically not required unless your reader will be unable to locate the source without it. If needed, place the URL in angle brackets after the date of access. End the citation with a period after the angle bracket, as in item 83. A citation for an electronic source may have the following five parts:

See item 83

1. Author's or site creator's name
2. Title of the document
3. Information about a corresponding print publication
4. Information about electronic publication
5. Publication medium and access date

Because electronic information can be changed quickly, easily, and often, an access date may be important. The version of a Web site available to your readers may be different from the one you accessed during your research. It is a good idea to print out or save to a disk the electronic source on the day you access it so that you have an accurate record. Below are tips on citing some of the most commonly used electronic sources. In its guidelines for electronic style, the MLA acknowledges that not all of the information recommended for a citation may be available. Cite whatever information is available. You may want to consult your instructor before finalizing your Works Cited list to ensure that you are conforming to his or her requirements for electronic sources.

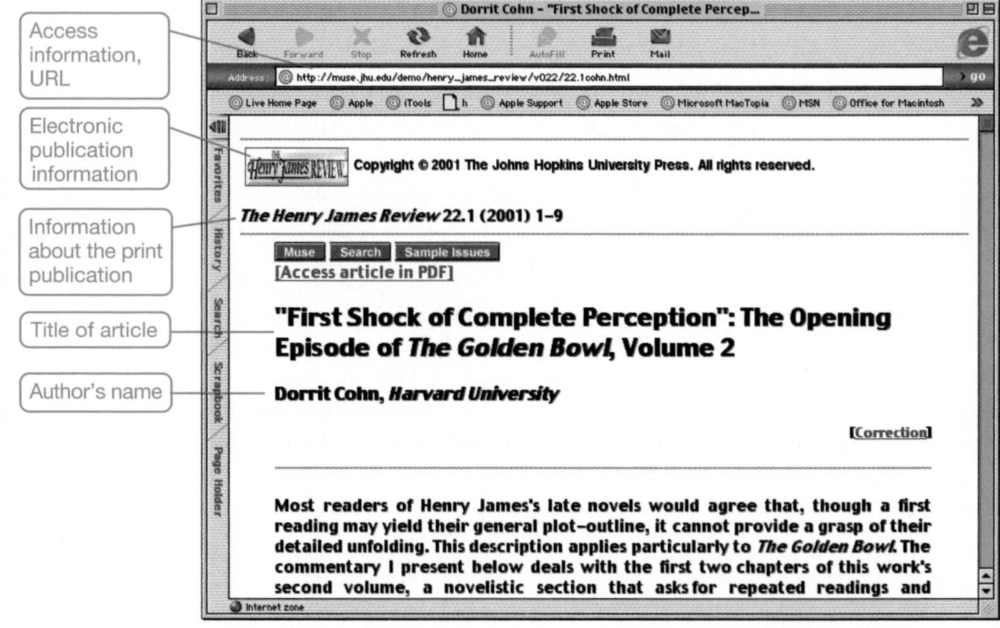

▲ **Figure 12.4** Online Journal Article with a Corresponding Print Version

- *Author's or site creator's name.* Begin your citation of an electronic source with the name of an author, listed last name first, comma, first name, period.

  Cohn, Dorritt.

- *Title of the document.* List next the full title of the document, enclosed in quotation marks. Exceptions include citations of entire Internet sites or online books. If no author's name is given, begin the entry with the document's title.

See items 48 and 52

  Cohn, Dorrit. "'First Shock of Complete Perception': The Opening Episode of *The Golden Bowl*, Volume 2."

- *Information about the print publication.* If the document was simultaneously printed as well as posted to the Internet, list the print information next, following the guidelines for print publications.

See Fig. 12.4

  Cohn, Dorrit. "'First Shock of Complete Perception': The Opening Episode of *The Golden Bowl*, Volume 2." *Henry James Review* 22.1 (2001): 1–9.

- *Information about electronic publication.* Next comes information about the electronic publication, including the title of the site (italicized), the date of electronic publication or the last date the site was updated, and the name of any sponsoring organization. If an editor's name or a version number is provided, include that information as well, following the title. Since it is possible for print and electronic versions to vary, it is necessary to include both types of publication information in your citation. If there is no print version, provide the electronic publication information only.

  Cohn, Dorrit. "'First Shock of Complete Perception': The Opening Episode of *The Golden Bowl*, Volume 2." *Henry James Review* 22.1 (2001): 1–9. *Project Muse Journals*. 2003. Johns Hopkins UP.

- *Medium and Access information.* Finally, provide your readers with information that will tell them the type of electronic medium and the date you accessed the work.

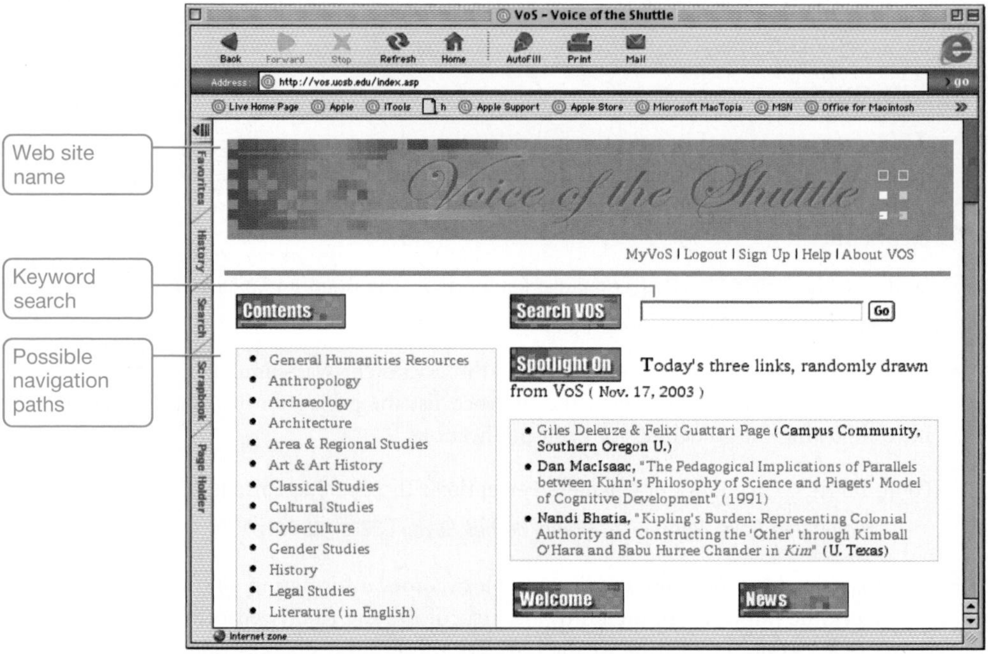

Web site name

Keyword search

Possible navigation paths

▲ **Figure 12.5** An Internet Site with Navigation Paths or Search Option

See Fig. 12.5

Cohn, Dorrit. "'First Shock of Complete Perception': The Opening Episode of *The Golden Bowl,* Volume 2." *Henry James Review* 22.1 (2001): 1–9. *Project Muse Journals*. 2003. Johns Hopkins UP. Web. 24 Apr. 2003.

48. Entire Internet Site

Often it is appropriate to reference an entire Internet Web site, such as a scholarly project or an information database. Include the information available at the site, in the following sequence.

1. The title of the site or project (italicized)
2. The creator or editor of the site (if given and relevant)
3. The electronic publication information: version number (if relevant), date of electronic publication or latest update, the name of the sponsoring organization or institution (if provided)

4. The medium and date of access

Institute for Advanced Technology in the Humanities. 2006. Web. 7 July 2006.

MSN.com. 2006. Microsoft Network. Web. 28 Feb. 2006.

Pew Center on Global Climate Change: Working Together. 2006. Pew Center on Global Climate Change. Web. 15 June 2006.

Rabe, Barry G. "Rave to the Top: The Expanding Role of U.S. State Renewable Portfolio Standards." Pew Center on Global Climate Change. 2006. Web. 15 June 2006.

See Figs. 12.6 and 12.7

Access information, URL

Web site name

Organization's homepage

Site table of contents

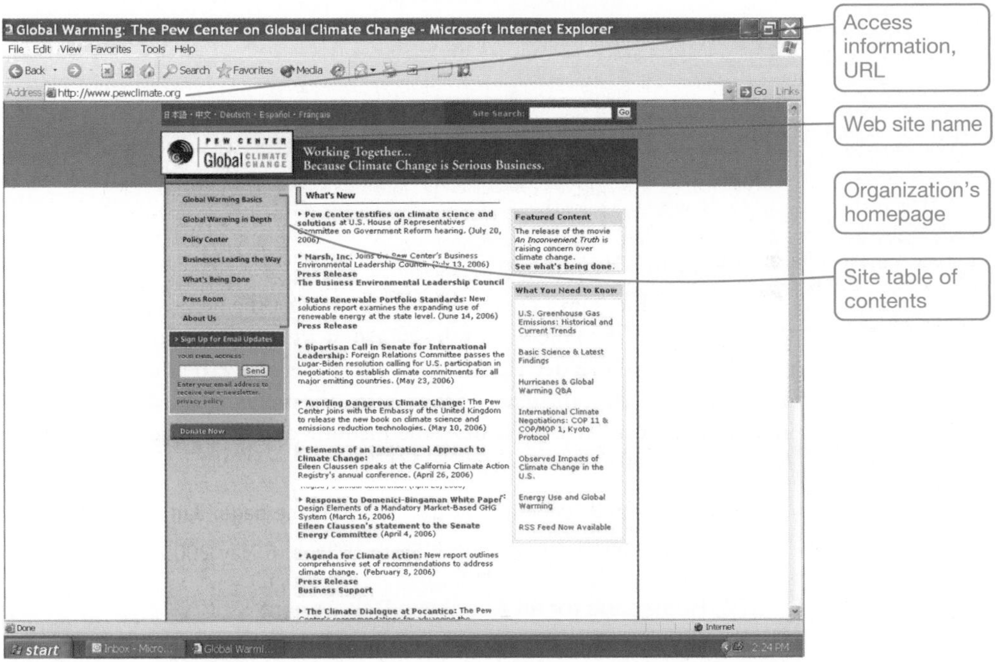

▲ **Figure 12.6** An Entire Internet Site

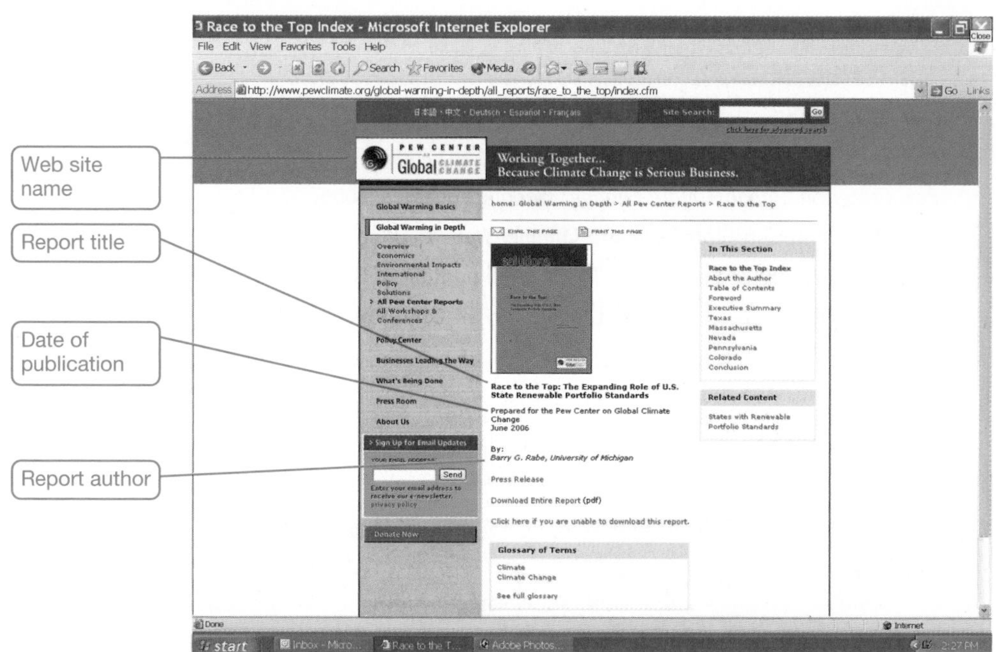

▲ **Figure 12.7** A Report Found at the PEW Center's Web Site

49. Course Homepage

If you wish to cite a course homepage, list first the name of the instructor (last name first), then the title of the course (neither italicized nor in quotation marks). Next comes a description, like *Course home page* (neither italicized nor in quotation marks), the dates of the course, the names of the department and institution that offered the course, the medium and date of access. Note that *home page* is spelled as two words in MLA style.

Edwards, Farrell. General Physics. Course home page. Jan. 2003-May 2003. Physics Dept., Utah State U. Web. 6 May 2003.

50. Homepage for an Academic Department

Begin a citation for a department homepage with the department's name, then a description such as *Dept. home page* (neither italicized nor in quotation marks), the institution's name, the date the page was last updated (if provided), the date of access, and the URL.

See item 49

Department of English. Dept. home page. Utah State U. Web.
16 June 2006.

51. Personal Homepage

When citing someone's homepage, begin with that person's name, followed by the title of the site or, if none is provided, the description *Home page* (neither italicized nor in quotation marks). Next provide the date the site was last updated (if provided), the medium and the date of access.

See item 49

Avila, Alejandro Perez. Home page. 17 Feb. 2003. Web. 1 May 2003.

52. Online Book

The complete texts of many books are available online as well as in print. Provide the following information when citing such works.

1. The name of the author (if only an editor, compiler, or translator is mentioned, give that person's name first, followed by *ed.*, *comp.*, or *trans.*)
2. The title of the work, italicized
3. The name of any editor, compiler, or translator (if not given earlier)
4. Publication information from the printed work, if the work has been printed
5. Electronic publication information, such as the title of the Internet site, editor of the site, version number, date of electronic publication, and name of any sponsoring organization
6. The medium and access date

Woolf, Virginia. *The Voyage Out*. London: Faber, 1914. *EServer*. Ed.
Geoffrey Sauer. 2003. U of Washington. Web. 1 June 2003.

53. Part of an Online Book

Sometimes you will be referring to a part of an online book. In such a case, list the title of the part after the author's name. If the part is a work like a poem or an essay, use quotation marks. If the part is a customary section like an introduction or a preface, do not include quotation marks.

Pope, Alexander. "Epistle I." *Essay on Man*. *EServer*. Ed. Geoffrey Sauer.
2003. U of Washington. Web. 1 June 2003.

54. Online Government Document

When citing government documents, start first with the information from the printed version and conclude with the electronic citation information.

United States. Dept. of Commerce. US Census Bureau. *How the Census Bureau Measures Poverty*. 26 Aug. 2004. Web. 5 May 2006.

55. Article in an Online Periodical

Many magazines, newspapers, and scholarly publications are available in online formats. Generally, citations for online periodicals follow the same sequence as citations for print periodicals. They should include the following information.

1. The author's name (if provided)
2. The title of the work, in quotation marks
3. The name of the journal, magazine, or newspaper, italicized
4. The volume and issue number (or other identifying number, if provided)
5. The date of publication
6. The range or total number of pages, paragraphs, or sections, if they are numbered
7. The medium and date of access

If you cannot find some of this information, cite what is available.

Sheikh, Nabeela. "True Romance." *Jouvert: A Journal of Postcolonial Studies* 7.1 (2002): n. pag. North Carolina State U, Coll. of Humanities and Social Sciences. Web. 23 Mar. 2003.

This journal is published solely online and has no page or paragraph numbers, hence the abbreviation *n. pag.* If page or paragraph numbers were provided, they would be listed after the publication date, for example, *(2002): 21–25.*

56. Article in an Online Scholarly Journal via a Journal Database

See item 55

See Fig. 12.8

In addition to scholarly journals that are published online independently, others can be accessed via an online journal database. If the journal is included in a database, provide the name of the database (italicized) following the print information for the article; end with the date of access and the relevant URL within the database.

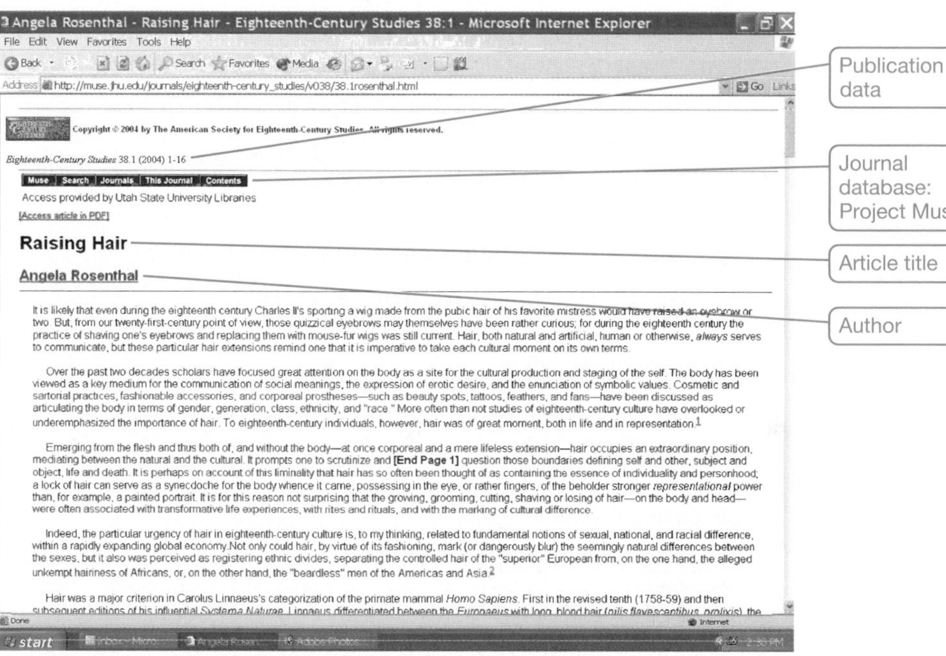

▲ **Figure 12.8** Article in an Online Scholarly Journal Accessed via a Journal Database

Rosenthal, Angela. "Raising Hair." *Eighteenth-Century Studies* 38.1 (2004): 1-16. *Project Muse*. Web. 14 May 2006.

57. Article in an Online Newspaper or on a Newswire

Stout, David. "Bush Asserts Shield Could've Blocked Missile." *New York Times*. New York Times, 7 July 2006. Web. 20 July 2006.

58. Article in an Online Magazine

Citron, Roger. "Process Makes Perfect: John Roberts' Marked, and Positive, Influence on the Supreme Court." *Slate*. Slate, 7 July 2006. Web. 20 July 2006.

59. Online Review

Bast, Joseph L. Rev. of *Our Stolen Future*, by Theo Colborn et al. *Heartland Institute*, 18 Apr. 1996: 27 pars. Web. 25 June 2003.

60. Online Abstract

Reid, Joy. "Responding to ESL Students' Texts." *TESOL Quarterly* 28.2 (1994): 273-92. Abstract. Web. 12 July 2002.

61. Anonymous Article

"London Marks 1-Year Anniversary of Carnage." *MSNBC*. MSNBC, 7 July 2006. Web. 12 July 2006.

62. Online Editorial

"A Nuclear Threat from India." Editorial. *New York Times*. New York Times, 13 May 1998. Web. 14 May 2005.

63. Online Letter to the Editor

Lowry, Heath. Letter. *Deseret News Online* [Salt Lake City]. Deseret News, 23 Mar. 1998. Web. 25 Mar. 2003.

64. Information Database or Scholarly Project

CNN Interactive. Cable News Network,12 July 2000. Web. 12 July 2000.

The Electronic Text Center. Ed. David Seaman. 2002. Web. 1 Jan. 2003.

65. Document from an Information Database

To cite a poem, a short story, an article, or another work within a database, begin with the author's name, if given, followed by the title of the work in quotation marks. If no author's name is given, begin with the title.

Continue with relevant information on the project, including the medium and access date.

Angelou, Maya. "On the Pulse of the Morning." *Electronic Text Center*. Ed. David Seaman. 2002. Web. 1 Jan. 2003.

66. Document or Full-Text Article Found via a Personal Subscription Service

If you are using a personal subscription service, such as AOL, that allows you to locate documents by using keywords, provide the name of the online service (italicized) and the date of access, followed by the keyword.

"Demand for Organic Food Outstrips Supply." *AOL News*. America Online, 7 July 2006. Web. 7 July 2006. Keyword: Health.

67. Document or Full-Text Article Found via a Library Subscription Service

To cite online documents or articles that you derive from a document hosting service that your library subscribes to (e.g., *LexisNexis, ProQuest,* or *EBSCOhost*), follow the citation for the source itself with the name of the database (italicized), the medium, and the date of access. If the library service provides only a starting page for the article's original printed version rather than numbering the pages, provide the number followed by a hyphen, a space, and a period: *115-*.

See Fig. 12.9

Bozell, Brent L., III. "Fox Hits Bottom–Or Does It?" *Human Events* 57.4 (2001): 15-. *Academic Search Premier*. Web. 15 Oct. 2002.

King, Marsha. "Companies Here Ponder Scout Ruling." *Seattle Times* 6 July 2000: A1. *LexisNexis*. Web. 15 Aug. 2000.

68. Nonperiodical Publication on CD-ROM or Disk

Often, works on electronic media are published in a single edition, much as books are. To cite such publications, use a format similar to that used to cite print books, with the addition of the publication medium.

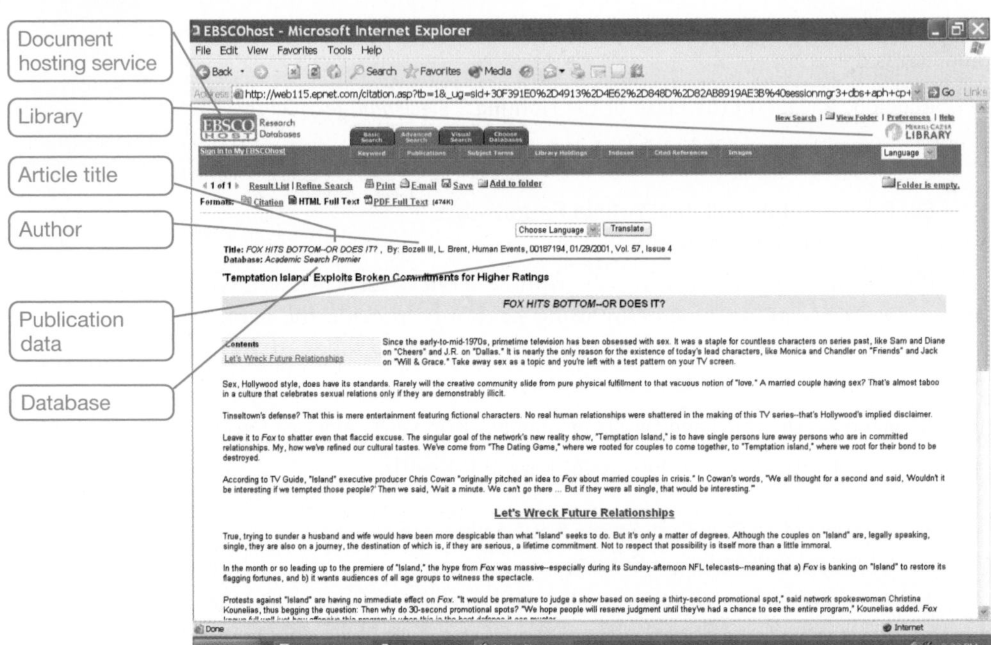

▲ **Figure 12.9** Full-Text Article Found via *EBSCOhost,* a Document Hosting Service

National Geographic Maps. Washington: National Geographic Society, 2006. CD.

69. Database Periodically Published on CD-ROM

When citing periodically published reference works, include the information on the printed source, as well as the publication medium, the name of the vendor (if relevant), and the electronic publication date.

Arms, Valerie M. "A Dyslexic Can Compose on a Computer." *Educational Technology* 24.1 (1984): 39-41. *ERIC*. Sept. 1990. CD.

70. Multidisk Publication

To cite a CD-ROM publication on multiple disks, list the number of disks or the specific number of the disk you used.

Great Literature Plus. 4 disks. Parsippany: Bureau of Electronic Publishing, 1993. CD.

71. Work in More Than One Medium

When a work is published in more than one medium (for example, both as a book and as a CD), you may specify all the media or only the medium you used.

Hult, Christine A., and Thomas N. Huckin. *The New Century Handbook*. 4th ed. New York: Longman, 2008. Print, CD.

72. Work in an Indeterminate Electronic Medium

If you cannot tell what medium the source is in (perhaps you accessed the work from a library's Web site and are unsure whether it is on CD-ROM or stored on the library's Internet server), use the designation *Electronic* for the medium.

Delk, Cheryl L. *Discovering American Culture*. Ann Arbor: U of Michigan P, 1997. Berkeley Public Lib. 20 June 2006. Electronic.

73. Electronic Television or Radio Program

Tarabay, Jamie. "Thousands of Police Hit Baghdad's Streets." *All Things Considered*. 14 June 2006. Natl. Public Radio. Web. 7 July 2006.

74. Electronic Sound Recording or Sound Clip

Beethoven, Ludwig van. "Symphony no. 5 in C, op. 67." June 1998. New City Media Audio Programs. Web. 20 July 2006.

75. Electronic Film or Film Clip

Anderson, Paul Thomas, dir. *Boogie Nights*. 1997. Trailer. New Line Cinema. Web. 13 May 2006.

76. Online Work of Art

Van Gogh, Vincent. *The Starry Night*. 1889. Museum of Modern Art, New York. Web. 20 Mar. 2006.

77. Online Interview

Gregson-Wagner, Natasha. Interview. *Hollywood Online*. May 1998. Web. 15 May 2006.

78. Online Map

"Mellow Mountain: Park City, Utah." Map. *MapQuest*. Web. 17 Feb. 2007.

79. Online Cartoon

Trudeau, Garry. "Doonesbury." Cartoon. *New York Times*. New York Times, 13 May 1998. Web. 3 Dec. 2006.

80. Online Advertisement

3D RealAudio. Advertisement. Web. 20 Aug. 1998.

81. Online Manuscript or Working Paper

Hendrickson, Heather. "Art: Impractical but Essential." Working paper, n.d. Web. 28 Aug. 2006.

(The abbreviation *n.d.* stands for "no date.")

82. Email Communication

For email messages that you wish to cite, provide the writer's name (or alias or screen name); the subject or title of the communication, if any (in quotation marks); the designation *E-mail to*; the name of the person to whom the email is addressed; and the date of the message. Note that *e-mail* is spelled with a hyphen in MLA style.

Gardner, Susan. "Help with Citations." Message to the author. 20 Mar. 2002. E-mail.

83. Online Posting

For a message posted to an email discussion list, include, in addition to the information provided for an email citation, the description *Online posting* and the date of the posting. Provide the name of the discussion list, if known. Then give the medium and date of access. If needed to locate the post, include the URL.

Surendranath, Lindsey. "Secondary Writing Center." Online posting. 30 June 2006. WPA Discussion List. Web. 7 July 2006. <http://wpacouncil.org>.

Citation of a posting to a World Wide Web discussion forum follows the style of an online posting.

84. Downloaded Computer Software

Fusion. Vers. 2.1. 30 June 2002. Digital file.

For student papers using MLA style, see Chapter 11, pages 284–296 and Chapter 16, Writing in the Humanities, pages 401–403 and 405–412.

See Chs. 11 and 16

13 APA Documentation Style

FAQs

- What is the APA style of documentation? (13a)
- How do I avoid plagiarizing? (13a-1)
- How do I let a reader know that I'm using a source within my paper? (13a-2)
- What does a reference list look like in APA style? (13a-4)
- How do I document electronic sources when using APA? (13b)

For a complete student paper using APA style see Chapter 18, pages 439–448.

APA Web site

13a Document using APA style

The documentation style commonly employed in the social sciences was developed by the American Psychological Association (APA). Detailed documentation guidelines for APA style are included in the *Publication Manual of the American Psychological Association*, 6th ed. (Washington, DC: APA, 2010). Since currency of information is critical in the social sciences, an in-text citation identifies each source by the author's name and the date of publication. The date of publication is also emphasized in the References list, which appears at the end of the paper.

1 Integrating sources and avoiding plagiarism in APA style

See 13a-2

APA citation style provides for a two-part system of source identification: (1) in-text parenthetical citations within the body of the paper and (2) a References list at the end of the paper. By using APA style, you can integrate your source information appropriately and ethically without inadvertently committing plagiarism.

See 13a-4

Plagiarism, a serious academic offense, is often committed by students inadvertently in the following two ways.

1. Failing to acknowledge a summary or paraphrase of a source in the body of the paper through a signal phrase and in-text parenthetical citation
2. Using the original authors' words without putting the borrowed words or phrases in quotation marks or including a parenthetical citation

Acknowledge all sources

Failing to acknowledge a source results in plagiarism. Like paraphrases and summaries, any other source material, such as specific facts, graphics or visuals, cartoons, diagrams, or charts, must be acknowledged using the two-part APA citation style. Note that APA style stresses the publication date of a source by

Using the APA Citation Style

1. **Introduce your source** using a signal phrase that names its author, immediately followed by the date of publication in parentheses or include the name and date in parentheses at the end: *Jones (1995) states that . . .* or (*Jones, 1995*).

See 10g-3; Guidelines 10g-3

2. **Paraphrase or summarize** the information from your source. It's best to use direct quotations sparingly. Preferably, recast the source information into your own words. If you do use any words or phrases from the author, be sure to include them in quotation marks and to provide the page number(s), preceded by *p.* or *pp.*, in parentheses.

See 10g

3. If you did not name the author in a signal phrase, at the conclusion of your summary **insert in parentheses the author's last name, a comma, and the date of publication**: (*Jones, 1995*). For a direct quotation or close paraphrase, also provide the page number(s), preceded by *p.* or *pp.*: (*Jones, 1995, p. 75*).

See 13a-2

4. At the end of your paper, **list the source with complete bibliographic information on your References page**.

See 13a-4

See 13a-2 and 13a-4

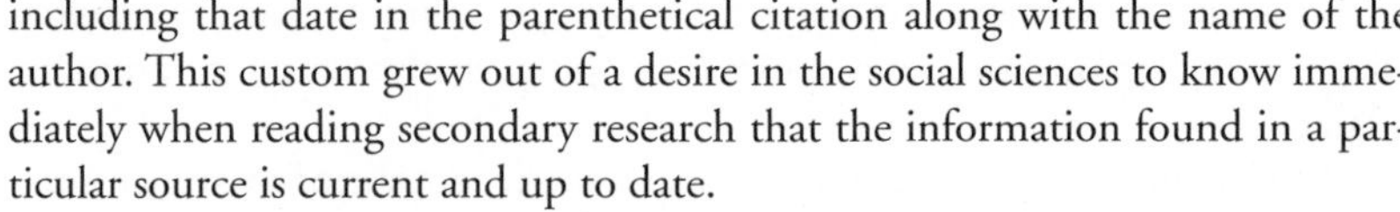

including that date in the parenthetical citation along with the name of the author. This custom grew out of a desire in the social sciences to know immediately when reading secondary research that the information found in a particular source is current and up to date.

Indicate original source words and phrases with quotation marks

The best research papers use direct quotations sparingly as support for their own ideas and integrate those quotations smoothly. A signal phrase alerts the reader that a direct quotation follows; the quotation marks show exactly which words and phrases are being quoted. Long quotations are formatted using indentation rather than quotation marks.

See 61a-2

When students get into trouble by borrowing words and phrases without attribution to a source, it is very often the result of sloppy notetaking. Careless copying and pasting of text from the Internet can also result in unintentional plagiarism.

See 10a-2

❷ APA style for in-text parenthetical citations

When you rely on information from sources to support your research or arguments in the social sciences, your readers will want to know who wrote each source and when. APA style therefore requires that you provide that information—the author's last name and the date of publication—in the body of your paper in the form of an in-text parenthetical citation, which is linked to the References list.

1. Author Named in a Signal Phrase

If the author's name is used to introduce the source in a signal phrase, provide the year of publication in parentheses just after the name.

> Hacking (1995) covers much that is on public record about multiple personality disorder.

2. Author Named in Parentheses

If the author's name is not used to introduce the source, provide the author's last name and the year of publication in parentheses at an appropriate place. Include a comma between the author's name and the date of publication.

A Directory to APA Style

In-Text Citations

References List Entries

Books

Periodicals (Journals and Magazines)

Other Sources

Electronic Media

In antiquity and through the middle ages, memory was a valued skill (Hacking, 1995).

3. Specific Page or Paragraph Quoted

When quoting or directly paraphrasing the author's words, provide a page number (or a paragraph number if the electronic source includes one). Precede the page reference with the abbreviation *p.* (to cite one page) or *pp.* (to cite more than one page).

There may be a causal explanation for multiple personality disorder, because "multiplicity is strongly associated with early and repeated child abuse, especially sexual abuse" (Hacking, 1995, p. 73).

If the quotation is from an electronic source that does not have numbered pages, provide the author and year only.

Vault Reports makes the following request on its Web site: "If you work (or have worked) for a company we write about, or you have recently gone through a job interview, please fill out our Survey and tell us about your experience" (1998).

4. Work by Two Authors

In citing a work by two authors, provide the last names of both authors. Use the word *and* to separate their names in the signal phrase, but use an ampersand (&) to separate their names in an in-text parenthetical citation.

As Sullivan and Qualley (1994) point out, many recent publications take the politics of writing instruction as their central concern.

The explanation for recent turmoil in the academy may be found in politics (Sullivan & Qualley, 1994).

5. Work by More Than Two Authors

In the first reference to a work by three, four, or five authors, provide the last names for all authors. In subsequent citations, use the first author's last name and the Latin phrase *et al.* (for "and others"). When a work has six or more authors, include only the name of the first author, followed by *et al.*, in the first and in all following citations.

> Writing becomes less egocentric as the child matures (Britton, Burgess, Martin, McLeod, & Rosen, 1975).

> According to Britton et al. (1975), mature writers consider their readers more than themselves.

6. Anonymous Work

If no author's name is provided, use either the title or an abbreviated form of the title (usually the first few words) for the in-text citation. Italicize the title of a book, periodical, brochure, or report; use quotation marks around the title of an article or chapter.

> Public schools have become overly dependent on the IQ test as an indication of academic potential (*Human Abilities in Cultural Contexts*, 1988).

> An individual's success in life depends in large measure on the cultural context in which he or she was raised ("Beyond IQ in Preschool Programs," 1994).

7. Work by a Corporate Author

Generally, provide the full name of a corporate author in in-text parenthetical citations.

> Recently published statistics show the gap between the rich and poor to be widening (New York Times Company, 2005).

If the name of the corporate author is long (such as United Cerebral Palsy Association) or if its abbreviation is easily recognized (such as APA), use the abbreviation after including both the complete name and the abbreviation in the first text reference.

FIRST TEXT REFERENCE

> There is a Web site that explains citing information from the Internet (American Psychological Association [APA], 2001).

SECOND AND SUBSEQUENT TEXT REFERENCES

The documentation system commonly employed in the social sciences is presented in great detail (APA, 2001).

8. Different Works by the Same Author

To distinguish citations of two or more works by the same author published in the same year, add a lowercase letter after the date of publication in the parenthetical reference: *(1995a), (1995b).* Assign the lowercase letter after alphabetizing the entries in the References list.

The Art of Wondering: A Revisionist Return to the History of Rhetoric focuses on historical rhetoric in general (Covino, 1988a), while "Defining Advanced Composition: Contributions from the History of Rhetoric" concentrates on advanced composition (Covino, 1988b).

9. Works by Two or More Authors with the Same Last Name

When the References list includes two or more primary authors with the same last name, provide those authors' initials in all citations, even if the publication dates are different.

G. A. Fraser (2001) writes about abuse as the cause of multiple personality disorder.

S. Fraser (1997) has written a memoir about incest and its effect on multiplicity.

10. Two or More Sources

To cite several different sources within the same parenthetical citation, list the sources in alphabetical order by the authors' names and use a semicolon to separate the entries.

Several studies (Prinsky & Rosenbaum, 1987; Record labeling, 1985; Thigpen, 1993) show concern about songs with themes of drugs and violence.

11. Personal Communication

Personal correspondence, such as letters, telephone conversations, lecture notes, and email, should be cited only in the text itself. Do not list the communications in the References list because readers cannot access them. Provide the initials and the last name of the correspondent, the designation *personal communication*, and the date.

J. Tompkins suggests that fear and authority prevent true learning in elementary, secondary, college, and university classrooms (personal communication, August 7, 2004).

The misinterpretation of Herrnstein's study is widespread (H. J. Miller, personal communication, April, 2006).

12. Email Communication

Email communication from individuals should be cited as personal communication within the text and not included on the References list. The in-text citation is formatted as follows:

See item 11

L. L. Meeks provided researchers with the pertinent information regarding teacher training (personal communication, May 2, 2005).

13. Web Sites

When referring to an entire Web site (as opposed to a specific document or page on the site), it is sufficient in APA style to give the address of the Web site within the text itself. Such a reference is not included on the References page.

Patricia Jarvis's Web site includes a great deal of information about recent archaeological digs in the Great Basin (http://www.asu.edu/~ students).

❸ APA style for content notes

The APA discourages use of content notes (footnotes or endnotes)—they can distract readers from the flow of the text. Content notes should be included only if they enhance or strengthen the discussion.

- Make only a single point in each note.
- Number notes consecutively throughout the text, using a superscript number.
- List the notes on a separate Notes page at the end of the text.

4 APA style for the References list

You need to provide your readers with an alphabetical listing of all the works you used as sources. This References list should appear at the end of your paper. The purpose of the References list is to help readers find the materials you used in writing the paper, so the information in it must be complete and accurate.

Books in APA style

A citation for a book has four basic parts:
Author's Name. (Publication Date). *Book title.* Publication Information.

- *Author's name.* Begin a book citation with the author's last name, followed by a comma and the first and middle initials, when known.
- *Publication date.* Next give the year of publication, enclosed in parentheses.
- *Title.* Provide the book's complete title and subtitle, if any, in italics. Capitalize the first word of the title, the first word of the subtitle, and any proper nouns; use lowercase for all other words in the title and subtitle.

See item 32

Guidelines

Formatting an APA References List

- List sources alphabetically by the last name of the author, using letter-by-letter alphabetization. When no author is given, alphabetize by the first word of the title, excluding *A, An,* or *The.*
- Type the first word of each entry at the left margin. Indent all subsequent lines of the same entry five spaces, or 1/2 inch. (This is called a *hanging indent.*)
- Double-space the entire list, both between and within entries.

- *Publication information.* Follow the title with publication information: the city of publication and the publisher, separated by a colon. If more than one location is listed for the publisher, give the site that is listed first on the title page or the site of the publisher's home office, if known. If the city is not a familiar one or if it could be confused with another city of the same name, include a state or country abbreviation. Omit the word *Publisher* and abbreviations such as *Inc.* or *Co.* from publishers' names. Include the complete names of university presses and associations.

For guidelines on citing electronic books, see items 33 and 34 below.

1. Book by One Author

Bolick, C. (1998). *Changing course. Civil rights at the crossroads.* New Brunswick, NJ: Transaction Books.

Hacking, I. (1995). *Rewriting the soul: Multiple personality and the sciences of memory*. Princeton, NJ: Princeton University Press.

2. Book by Two or More Authors

When a book has two to six authors, provide all the authors' names (last name first, followed by initials) in the order in which they appear on the title page. Note that this order may not be alphabetical. Connect the final two names with an ampersand (&). Abbreviate the seventh and subsequent authors as *et al.*

Britton, J., Burgess, T., Martin, N., McLeod, A., & Rosen, H. (1975). *The development of writing abilities*. London: Macmillan.

Hindelang, M. J., Hirschi, T., & Weis, J. G. (1981). *Measuring delinquency*. Beverly Hills, CA: Sage.

3. Book by a Corporate Author

Begin the entry with the full name of the group; alphabetize the entry by the first important word in the name. Should the same group be listed as author and publisher, include the word *Author* at the end of the entry in place of the publisher's name.

American Psychological Association. (2001). *Publication manual of the American Psychological Association* (5th ed.). Washington, DC: Author.

National Commission on Excellence in Education. (1984). *A nation at risk: The full account*. Cambridge, MA: USA Research.

4. Book with an Editor

For an edited book, provide the editor's name in place of an author's name. Include the abbreviation *Ed.* (for "Editor") or *Eds.* (for "Editors") in parentheses immediately following the editor's name.

Peterson's (Eds.) (2004). *Peterson's four-year colleges* (35th ed.). Lawrenceville, NJ: Thomson Peterson's.

5. Chapter or Selection from an Edited Book

To cite a particular chapter or selection in an edited work, start with the author's name, the year of publication, and the title of the selection. Do not italicize the title or enclose it in quotation marks. Next, provide the names of the editors in normal order as they appear on the title page, preceded by the word *In* and followed by the abbreviation *Ed.* or *Eds.* (in parentheses) and a comma. End the entry with the book's title (italicized), the inclusive page numbers for the selection (in parentheses), and the publication information.

Kadushin, A. (1988). Neglect in families. In E. W. Nunnally, C. S. Chilman, & F. M. Cox (Eds.), *Mental illness, delinquency, addiction, and neglect* (pp. 147–166). Newbury Park, CA: Sage.

6. Two or More Books by the Same Author

When two or more entries have the same author, arrange the entries by the date of publication, with the earliest first. If you have two or more works by the same author published in the same year, alphabetize by title and distinguish the entries by adding a lowercase letter immediately after the year: *(1991a), (1991b).*

Flynn, J. R. (1980). *Race, IQ, and Jensen*. London: Routledge.

Flynn, J. R. (1991). *Asian Americans: Achievement beyond IQ*. Hillsdale, NJ: Erlbaum.

7. Article in a Reference Book

If an encyclopedia entry is signed, start with the author's name; if it is unsigned, start with the title of the article. In either case, follow with the publication date. Provide the volume number and page numbers of the article (in parentheses) after the title of the reference book.

Davidoff, L. (1984). Childhood psychosis. In *The encyclopedia of psychology* (Vol. 10, pp. 156–157). New York: Wiley.

Schizophrenia. (1983). In *The encyclopedic dictionary of psychology* (Vol. 8, pp. 501–502). Cambridge, MA: MIT Press.

8. Book in Translation

Indicate the name of the translator in parentheses after the book's title, and follow the name with the abbreviation *Trans.*

Freire, P. (1993). *Pedagogy of the oppressed* (New rev. 20th anniv. ed., M. B. Ramos, Trans.). New York: Continuum.

9. Subsequent Edition of a Book

If a book is not a first edition, indicate the relevant edition in parentheses immediately following the title of the book. Use abbreviations to specify the type of edition: for example, *2nd ed.* stands for "Second edition" and *Rev. ed.* stands for "Revised edition."

See item 8

Lindeman, E. (2005). *A rhetoric for writing teachers* (4th ed.). New York: Oxford University Press.

10. Republished Book

Provide the original date of publication in parentheses at the end of the entry, with the words *Original work published.*

Dewey, J. (1963). *Experience and education*. New York: Collier. (Original work published 1938.)

11. Government Document

Unless an author's name is given, begin an entry for a government document with the name of the agency that issued the publication.

National Center for Educational Statistics. (2006). *The condition of education 2006*. Washington, DC: U.S. Department of Education, Office of Educational Research and Improvement.

12. Published Proceedings from a Conference

Van Belle, J. G. (2002). Online interaction: Learning communities in the virtual classroom. In J. Chambers (Ed.), *Selected papers from the 13th International Conference on College Teaching and Learning* (pp. 187–200). Jacksonville, FL: Community College at Jacksonville Press.

13. One Volume of a Multivolume Work

Doyle, A. C. (1930). *The complete Sherlock Holmes* (Vol. 2). Garden City: Doubleday.

Periodicals (journals and magazines) in APA style

A citation of an article in a periodical or a journal follows a format similar to that for a book:

Author's Name. (Publication Date). Article title. Publication Information.

- *Author's name.* As with a book, include the author's last name, followed by first and middle initials.
- *Publication date.* Include the year and, in some cases, the month of publication, enclosed in parentheses.
- *Title of the article.* Provide the complete title and subtitle of the article, with only the first letters of the title and subtitle and proper nouns capitalized. Do not italicize titles or enclose them in quotation marks.
- *Publication information.* Publication information for an article must include several elements.

- Begin with the full name of the journal or periodical, as it appears on the publication's title page, italicized, with all major words capitalized.
- Follow this immediately with the volume number, also in italics. Do not use the word *Volume* or the abbreviation *Vol.*
- Next, provide the issue number, if available, in parentheses and not italicized whether or not the journal pages by volume or issue.
- Finally, provide the inclusive page numbers for the article. Use the abbreviation *p.* or *pp.* with articles from newspapers, but not with articles from magazines or journals.

See items 35 and 36

14. Article in a Journal Paginated by Volume

Author | Publication date | Article title | Article subtitle

Popenoe, D. (1993). American family decline, 1960-1990: A review and appraisal. *Journal of Marriage and Family, 55*(3), 527-555.

Publication information

Strong, T. (2002). Dialogue in therapy's "borderzone." *Journal of Constructivist Psychology, 15*(2), 245–262.

15. Article in a Journal Paginated by Issue

Provide the issue number (in parentheses and not italicized) immediately following the volume number.

Alma, C. (1994). A strategy for the acquisition of problem-solving expertise in humans: The category-as-analogy approach. *Inquiry, 14*(2), 17–28.

16. Article in a Monthly Magazine

Include the month, not abbreviated, in the publication date.

Dobson, L. (2006, July/August). What's your humor style? *Psychology Today*, 48.

17. Article in a Weekly Magazine

Provide the year, month, and day of publication.

Ratliff, E. (2006, July 2). Déjà vu, again and again. *The New York Times Magazine,* 38.

18. Newspaper Article

Provide the complete name of the newspaper (including any introductory articles) after the title of the article. List all discontinuous page numbers, preceded by *p.* or *pp.*

Pollack, A. (2006, July 13). Paralyzed man uses thoughts to move a cursor. *The New York Times,* pp. A1, A21.

19. Editorial

Add the word *Editorial,* in brackets, after the title of the editorial.

Madigan, C. (2006, July 11). Is the Web changing journalism? [Editorial]. *The Chicago Tribune,* p. A23.

Six who serve their council districts [Editorial]. (1997, October 31). *The Boston Globe*, p. A22.

20. Letter to the Editor

Add the designation *Letter to the editor,* in brackets, after the title of the letter or after the date if there is no title.

Fischer, S. (2006, July 13). [Letter to the editor]. *The New York Times,* p. A22.

21. Review

Provide the name of the reviewer, the date of publication (in parentheses), and the title of the review, if given. Then, in brackets, write the designation *Review of* and the title of the piece that was reviewed.

Ribadeneira, D. (1997, October 31). The secret lives of seminarians [Review of the book *The new men: Inside the Vatican's elite school for American priests*]. *The Boston Globe*, p. C6.

22. Unsigned Article

If the article has no known author, start the entry with the title of the article, and alphabetize by the first important word in the title (usually the word that follows the introductory article).

The blood business. (1972, September 7). *Time,* 47–48.

In the References list, this entry would appear in the B's.

23. More Than One Work by the Same Author in the Same Year

List the works alphabetically by title and use the lowercase letters *a, b, c,* and so on after the dates to distinguish the works.

Hayles, N. K. (1996a). Inside the teaching machine: Actual feminism and (virtual) pedagogy. *The Electronic Journal for Computer Writing, Rhetoric and Literature, 2*. Retrieved from http://www.cwrl.utexas .edu/cwrl

Hayles, N. K. (1996b). Self/subject. In P. Vandenberg & P. Heilker (Eds.), *Keywords in composition* (pp. 217–220). Portsmouth, NH: Heinemann/Boynton-Cook.

Other sources in APA style

24. Film or Video Recording

Begin with the names of those responsible for the film and, in parentheses, their titles, such as *Producer* and *Director.* Give the title (italicized), and then designate the medium in brackets. Provide the country of origin and the name of the studio.

Ossana, D. (Producer), & Lee, A. (Director). (2005). *Brokeback mountain* [Motion picture]. United States: Focus Features.

25. Television or Radio Program

Identify those who created the program, and give their titles—for example, *Producer, Director,* and *Anchor.* Give the date the program was broadcast. Provide the program's title (italicized), as well as the city and the station where the program aired.

Michaels, L. (Executive Producer). (2005, October 1). *Saturday night live*. New York: NBC-TV.

26. Technical Report

Write an entry for a technical report in a format similar to that for a book. If an individual author is named, provide that information; place any other identifying information (such as a report number) after the title of the report.

Vaughn Hansen Associates, in association with CH2M Hill and Water Research Laboratory, Utah State University. (1995). *Identification and assessment of certain water management options for the Wasatch Front: Prepared for Utah State Division of Water Resources*. Salt Lake City: Author.

27. Published Interview

For a published interview, start with the name of the interviewer and the date. In brackets, give the name (and title, if necessary) of the person interviewed. End with the publication information, including the page number(s), in parentheses, after the title of the work in which the interview is published.

Davidson, P. (1992). [Interview with Donald Hall]. In P. Davidson, *The fading smile* (p. 25). New York: Knopf.

28. Unpublished Interview

Follow the format for a published interview.

Hult, C. A. (1997, March). [Interview with Dr. Stanford Cazier, past President, Utah State University].

29. Unpublished Dissertation

Provide the author's name, the date, and then the title of the dissertation, italicized and followed by a period. Add the phrase *Unpublished doctoral dissertation*, a comma, and the name of the degree-granting institution.

Johnson, N. K. (1980). *Cultural and psychological determinants of health and illness*. Unpublished doctoral dissertation, University of Washington.

30. Speech or Lecture

For an oral presentation, provide the name of the presenter, the year and month of the presentation, and the title of the presentation (italicized). Then give any useful location information.

Meeks, L. L. (1997, March). *Feminism and the WPA.* Speech given at the Conference on College Composition and Communication, Phoenix, AZ.

31. Paper Presented at a Conference

Provide information about the location of the meeting, as well as the month in which the meeting was held.

Klaus, C. (1996, March). *Teachers and writers.* Paper presented at the meeting of the Conference on College Composition and Communication, Milwaukee, WI.

13b Electronic media in APA style

The electronic documentation formats found in the *Publication Manual of the American Psychological Association*, 6th ed., were updated in 2010 with new formats for electronic documentation, as shown in the following examples. When citing electronic media, use the standard APA style to identify authorship, date of origin (if known), and title, much as for print material; the Web information is then placed in a retrieval statement at the end of the reference. If you are referencing an electronic version that duplicates exactly a print source, simply use the basic journal reference style for print sources.

32. Online Professional or Personal Site

To comply with APA style, present information in the following general sequence when citing documents found on a Web site:

1. The author's or editor's last name and initial(s)
2. The creation date of the work, in parentheses. Use *n.d.* (no date) if the electronic publication date is not available.

3. The title of the complete work, italicized
4. The relevant subpage or program (if the document is contained within a large, complex site)
5. The designation *Retrieved,* followed by the word *from* and the site title
6. The access protocol or path or URL (Note: Break URL lines only before a slash or before a period; do not follow the URL with a period.)
7. When a Digital Object Identifier (DOI) is available, use the DOI instead of the URL in the reference.

See item 41

Andrews, M. (2006). *Queen Victoria's underwear*. Retrieved from the Victorian Era Online Web site: http://www.victoriana .com

Jarvis, P. (n.d.). *My homepage*. Retrieved from http://www.mtu.edu/ ~students

NOTE No retrieval date is necessary when content is not likely to change, as for a published article or book.

33. Online Book

Provide any data on the print publication before giving details on where the electronic version can be located.

Aristotle. (1954). *Rhetoric* (W. R. Roberts, Trans.). Retrieved from *The English Server* at Carnegie Mellon University: http://www.rpi.edu/~ honeyl/Rhetoric/index.html

34. Article in an Online Work

Generally, citations for articles in online works follow the same sequence as citations for their print counterparts, followed by the retrieval statement.

Kennedy, B. (2004). Plants and people share molecular signaling system. *Science Journal*. Retrieved from http://www.science.psu.edu/ journal/Summer2004/plantsandPeopleSum04.htm

Women in American history. (2007). In *Encyclopaedia Britannica*. Retrieved from http://www.women.eb.com

35. Article in an Online Newspaper or on a Newswire

Green, T. (2006, July 10). The Air and Space Museum is falling. *The Los Angeles Times*. Retrieved from http://latimes.com

36. Article in an Online Magazine

Fantino, J. (2004, March). Crime prevention: Are we missing the mark? *The Police Chief Magazine*. Retrieved from http://policechiefmagazine.org

37. Online Review

Donnelly, P. (2005). Women and patients [Review of the book *Female solution*]. *OBGYN.net*. Retrieved from http://www.obgyn.net/women/women.asp

38. Online Abstract

Gould, M. (2006). Seven ways to improve student satisfaction in online classes. *Distance Education Report, 10*(12), 7. Abstract retrieved from Academic Search Premier database.

39. Online Editorial

Rao, L. (2006, August). Do you know your vitamins and minerals? [Editorial]. *Prevention*. Retrieved from http://www.prevention.com

40. Online Letter to the Editor

Masek, T. (2006, July 10). Dirty tricks and fraud [Letter to the editor]. *The Salt Lake Tribune*. Retrieved from http://www.sltrib.com

41. Article in an Online Scholarly Journal (with Digital Object Identifier)

Brumfiel, G. (2006). Planet hunters seek cheap missions. *Nature. 442* (7098), 6. doi: 10.1038/442006a

42. Document or Full-Text Article Found via a Reference Database

To cite a full-text article you derive from a service that your library subscribes to (e.g., *LexisNexis, EBSCOhost,* or *ProQuest*), follow the same format as for its print counterpart. In general it is not necessary to add database information.

King, M. (2000, July 6). Companies here ponder scout ruling. *Seattle Times*, A1.

43. Nonperiodical Publication on CD-ROM or Disk

To cite works distributed on CD or disk, give the authors, publication date, title, and publication information in standard APA format. After the title, identify the type of electronic medium in brackets—for example, [CD-ROM].

ClearVue, Inc. (2007). *The history of European literature* [CD-ROM]. Chicago: Author.

44. Online Work of Art

Seurat, G. (1884). *A Sunday on La Grande Jatte*. Art Institute of Chicago. Retrieved from http://www.artic.edu/aic/collections

45. Online Interview

Buckley, T. (2006, July 11). Jazz ready for Fisher [Interview with Jerry Sloan]. *Deseret News*. Retrieved from http://desnews.com

46. Online Posting

Although unretrievable communication such as email is not included in an APA References list, more public or retrievable Internet postings from newsgroups or listservs may be included.

Walker, J. (2006, April 17). 2006 graduate research network and travel awards. Message posted to Appalachian Alliance for Computers and Writing Discussion List. Retrieved from http://www.kcte.org/hypermail/aacw-l/archive.200604/0000.html

For a student paper using APA style, see Chapter 18, Writing in the Social Sciences, pages 439–448.

14 CMS and CSE Documentation Styles

FAQs

- What are the CMS and CSE styles of documentation? (14a, 14b)
- How do I avoid plagiarizing? (14a-1, 14b-1)
- How do I let a reader know that I'm using a source within my paper? (14a-2, 14b-2)
- How do I use footnotes in CMS style? (14a-3)
- What does a reference list look like in CMS or CSE style? (14a-4, 14b-3)
- How do I document electronic sources when using CMS or CSE style? (pages 14a-3, 14b-3)

All of the disciplines have in common a need to provide readers with a documentation trail that they can use to retrace the research path. Even though the details of documentation format vary somewhat by discipline, the guiding principles are the same:

1. Show the reader within the text itself, by using in-text citations or footnote numbers, that you are using source information.
2. Provide your readers with complete bibliographical information so that they can find the source should they wish to do so.

Chicago Manual Web site

14a Document using the Chicago Manual of Style (CMS)

The documentation system used most commonly in business, communications, economics, and the humanities and fine arts (other than languages and literature) is outlined in *The Chicago Manual of Style*, 15th ed.

(Chicago: The University of Chicago Press, 2003). This two-part system uses footnotes or endnotes and a bibliography to provide publication information about sources quoted, paraphrased, summarized, or otherwise referred to in the text of a paper. Footnotes appear at the bottom of the page; endnotes appear on a separate page at the end of the paper. The Bibliography, like the Works Cited list in the MLA documentation style, is an alphabetical list of all works cited in the paper.

1 Integrating sources and avoiding plagiarism in the CMS system

See Ch. 10

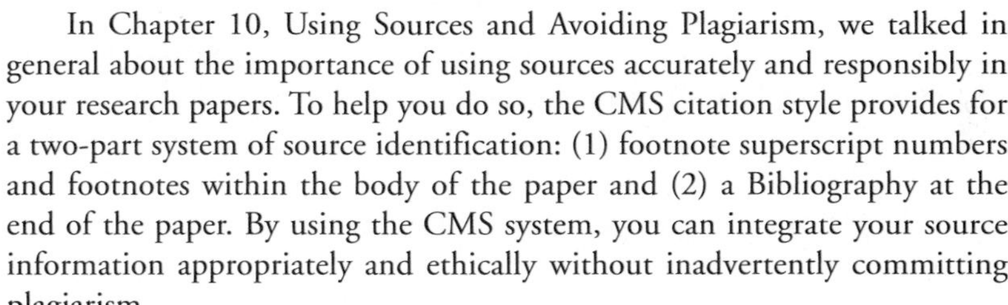

In Chapter 10, Using Sources and Avoiding Plagiarism, we talked in general about the importance of using sources accurately and responsibly in your research papers. To help you do so, the CMS citation style provides for a two-part system of source identification: (1) footnote superscript numbers and footnotes within the body of the paper and (2) a Bibliography at the end of the paper. By using the CMS system, you can integrate your source information appropriately and ethically without inadvertently committing plagiarism.

See 14a-2, 14a-3, 14a-4

Plagiarism, a serious academic offense, is often committed by students inadvertently in the following two ways:

1. Failing to acknowledge a summary or paraphrase of a source in the body of the paper through a signal phrase and footnote number
2. Using the original author's words without putting the borrowed words or phrases in quotation marks or including a footnote number

Acknowledge all sources

A successful research paper uses the writer's own words and expresses the writer's understanding of the answers to specific research questions. In such a paper, sources are used as evidence to support the writer's own argument. Source support is integrated into the flow of the writer's research paper through the use of paraphrases and summaries in the writer's own words; each source is acknowledged by a footnote. Failing to acknowledge a source results in plagiarism. Like paraphrases and summaries, any other source material, such as specific facts, graphics or visuals, cartoons, diagrams, or charts, must also be acknowledged using the CMS footnote citation system.

See 10b-2

Guidelines

Using the CMS Citation System

1. **Introduce your source** using a signal phrase that names its author, with a superscript footnote number following the source information: Jones states that. . . .[1]
2. **Paraphrase or summarize** the information from your source. It's best to use direct quotations sparingly. Preferably, recast the source information into your own words. If you do use any words or phrases from the author, be sure to put them in quotation marks.
3. **Format your footnotes** (listed on the page on which the source was cited) or endnotes (typed in a consecutive list at the end of the paper before the bibliography) according to the CMS format.
4. At the end of your paper, **list the source with complete bibliographic information on your Bibliography page**.

See 10g-3, Guidelines box 10g-3, 14a-2 to 14a-4

Indicate original source words and phrases with quotation marks

The best research papers use direct quotations sparingly as support for their own ideas and integrate those quotations smoothly. A signal phrase alerts the reader that a direct quotation follows; the quotation marks show exactly which words and phrases are being quoted. Long quotations are formatted using indentation rather than quotation marks. When students get into trouble by borrowing words and phrases without attribution to a source, it is very often the result of sloppy notetaking. Your notes should accurately record source information in your own words, and you should be able to tell at a glance when looking at your notes which information is from which source and on what page that information is located. Careless copying and pasting of text from the Internet can also result in unintentional plagiarism.

See 51a-2

See 10b-3

❷ CMS format for in-text citations

In the text, indicate a note with a superscript number typed immediately after the information that is being referenced. Number notes consecutively throughout the text.

In *A History of Reading*, Alberto Manguel asserts that "we, today's readers, have yet to learn what reading is."[1] As a result, one of his conclusions is that while readers have incredible powers, not all of them are enlightening.[2]

❸ CMS format for notes

See TechHelp 11e-1

If you are using footnotes, put each note at the bottom of the page on which the reference occurs.

Guidelines

Using the CMS Citation Style

If you are using footnotes:

- Space down four lines from the last line of text, and position the footnote at the bottom of the page.
- Single-space within each note, but double-space between notes if more than one note appears on a page.

If you are using endnotes, put the notes in a consecutive list:

- Begin a new page at the end of the paper.
- Type the title *Notes* at the top of the page, centered; do not use quotation marks.
- List the notes in consecutive order, as they appear in the text, and numbered correspondingly.
- Double-space all notes, both within and between entries.

The other details of formatting are the same for both footnotes and endnotes:

- Indent the first line of each note, using the paragraph indent.
- Use a number that is the same size as and is aligned in the same way as the note text. Do not use a superscript. Follow the number with a period and a space.
- Begin with the author's name, first name first, followed by a comma. Then provide the title of the book (italicized) or article (in quotation marks). Finally, provide the publication information.
  - For books, include (in parentheses) the place of publication, followed by a colon; the name of the publisher, followed by a comma; and the date of publication. Follow the closing parenthesis with a comma and the number of the page you are citing.
  - For articles, include the title of the periodical (italicized), followed immediately by the volume number; the issue number, preceded by a comma and the abbreviation *no.*; the date of publication (in parentheses), followed by a colon; and the page number.

A Directory to the CMS System

Notes

1. Alberto Manguel, *A History of Reading* (New York: Viking, 1996), 23.

2. Steven Brachlow, "John Robinson and the Lure of Separatism in Pre-Revolutionary England," *Church History* 50 (1983): 288–301.

In subsequent references to the same source, *Chicago Manual* recommends using a short form including the author's last name, a shortened title, and a page number.

SHORT FORM

3. Manguel, *History of Reading*, 289.

The abbreviation *ibid.* (in the same place) is used to refer to a single work referenced in the immediately preceding note. If the page numbers are different, include the page number as well.

4. Ibid., 291.

5. Ibid.

Books in CMS style

1. Book by One Author

6. Iris Murdoch, *The Sovereignty of Good* (New York: Schocken Books, 1971), 32–33.

SHORT FORM

6. Murdoch, *Sovereignty,* 33.

2. Book by Two or Three Authors

List the authors' names in the same order as on the title page of the book.

7. John Sabini and Maury Silver, *Moralities of Everyday Life* (New York: Oxford University Press, 1982), 91.

8. Anne S. Goodsell, Michelle R. Maher, and Vincent Tinto, *Collaborative Learning: A Sourcebook for Higher Education* (University Park, PA: National Center on Postsecondary Teaching, Learning, and Assessment, 1992), 78.

3. Book by More Than Three Authors

In the long form, list all authors; in the short form, use the abbreviation *et al.* (and others) after the first author's name; list all authors in the accompanying bibliography.

9. James Britton, Tony Burgess, Nancy Martin, Alex McLeod, and Harold Rosen. *The Development of Writing Abilities* (London: Macmillan, 1975), 43.

SHORT FORM

9. Britton et al., *Development*, 43.

4. Book by a Corporate Author

10. American Association of Colleges and Universities, *American Pluralism and the College Curriculum: Higher Education in a Diverse Democracy* (Washington, DC: American Association of Higher Education, 1995), 27.

5. Book with an Editor

11. Jane Roberta Cooper, ed., *Reading Adrienne Rich: Review and Re-visions, 1951–1981* (Ann Arbor: University of Michigan Press, 1984), 51.

12. Robert F. Goodman and Aaron Ben-Ze'ev, eds., *Good Gossip* (Lawrence: Kansas University Press, 1994), 13.

6. Book with an Editor and an Author

13. Albert Schweitzer, *Albert Schweitzer: An Anthology,* ed. Charles R. Joy (New York: Harper & Row, 1947), 107.

7. Chapter or Selection from an Edited Work

14. Gabriele Taylor, "Gossip as Moral Talk," in *Good Gossip,* ed. Robert F. Goodman and Aaron Ben-Ze'ev (Lawrence: Kansas University Press, 1994), 35–37.

15. Langston Hughes, "Harlem," in *The Norton Anthology of African American Literature,* ed. Henry Louis Gates, Jr., and Nellie Y. McKay (New York: Norton, 1997), 1267.

8. Article in a Reference Book

The publication information (city of publication, publisher, publication year) is usually omitted from citations of well-known reference books. Include the abbreviation *s.v.* (*sub verbo*, or "under the word") before the article title, rather than page numbers.

16. Frank E. Reynolds, *World Book Encyclopedia,* 1983 ed., s.v. "Buddhism."

17. *Encyclopedia Americana,* 1976 ed., s.v. "Buddhism."

9. Introduction, Preface, Foreword, or Afterword

18. Jane Tompkins, preface to *A Life in School: What the Teacher Learned* (Reading, MA: Addison-Wesley, 1996), xix.

10. Work in More Than One Volume

19. Arthur Conan Doyle, *The Complete Sherlock Holmes,* vol. 2 (Garden City, NY: Doubleday, 1930), 728.

11. Government Document

20. United States Federal Bureau of Investigation, *Uniform Crime Reports for the United States: 1995* (Washington, DC: GPO, 1995), 48.

Periodicals (journals and magazines) in CMS Style

12. Article in a Journal Paginated by Volume

21. Mike Rose, "The Language of Exclusion: Writing Instruction at the University," *College English* 47 (1985): 343.

13. Article in a Journal Paginated by Issue

22. Joy S. Ritchie, "Confronting the 'Essential' Problem: Reconnecting Feminist Theory and Pedagogy," *Journal of Advanced Composition* 10, no. 2 (1989): 160.

14. Article in a Monthly Magazine

23. Douglas H. Lamb and Glen D. Reeder, "Reliving Golden Days," *Psychology Today,* June 1986, 22.

15. Article in a Weekly Magazine

24. Steven Levy, "Blaming the Web," *Newsweek,* April 7, 1997, 46–47.

16. Newspaper Article

25. P. Ray Baker, "The Diagonal Walk," *Ann Arbor News,* June 16, 1928, sec. A.

17. Abstract from an Abstracts Journal

26. Nancy K. Johnson, "Cultural and Psychological Determinants of Health and Illness" (PhD diss., Univ. of Washington, 1980), abstract in *Dissertation Abstracts International* 40 (1980): 425B.

Other sources in CMS (Chicago) style

18. Speech or Lecture

27. Wayne Booth, "Ethics and the Teaching of Literature" (paper presented to the College Forum at the 87th Annual Convention of the National Council of Teachers of English, Detroit, MI, November 21, 1997).

19. Personal Letter to the Author

28. George H.W. Bush, letter to author, September 8, 1995.

Electronic media in CMS (Chicago) style

The *Chicago Manual of Style* (15th edition, 2003) covers formats for electronic media thoroughly, integrating its coverage of electronic documentation formats with coverage of print citations. In general, electronic sources are cited much as print sources are cited. The URL is listed at the end of the citation and is not placed in angle brackets. CMS points out that dates of access are of limited usefulness because of the changeable nature of electronic sources and suggests using the date of access only in fields in which the information is particularly time-sensitive, such as medicine or law. If an access date is needed, place it in parentheses following the URL, as in this example from an online law journal.

29. Ruthe Catolico Ashley, "Creating the Ideal Lawyer," *New Lawyer*, April 3, 2003, http://www.abanet.org/genpractice/newlawyer/april03/ideal.html (accessed July 20, 2003).

20. Online Professional or Personal Site

30. Academic Info, "Humanities," 1998–2000, http://www.academicinfo.net/index.html.

21. Online Posting

Archived source addresses are given separately from any other addresses in citing listserv messages. The date of posting is the only date given.

31. Janice Walker, email to Alliance for Computers and Writing mailing list, April 16, 2006, http://www.ttu.edu/lists/acw-l/2006.

22. Computer Software

To cite computer software, start with the title and then include the edition or version, if any. Next, give the name and location of the organization or person with rights to the software.

32. A.D.A.M.: Animated Dissection of Anatomy for Medicine, Version 2.0, Benjamin Cummings/Addison-Wesley and A.D.A.M. Software, Inc., Reading, MA.

23. Online Book

33. Vernon Lee, *Gospels of Anarchy and Other Contemporary Studies* (London: T. Fisher Unwin, 1908), http://www.indiana.edu/~letrs/vwwp/lee/gospels.html.

24. Article in an Online Professional Journal

34. Peter Appelros, "Heart Failure and Stroke," *Stroke* 37 (2006): 1637, http://stroke.aha.journals.org/current.shtml.

25. Article in an Online Magazine

35. David Glenn, "Sherry B. Ortner Shifts Her Attention from the Sherpas of Nepal to Her Newark Classmates," *The Chronicle of Higher Education*, August 8, 2003, http://chronicle.com.

26. Article in an Online Newspaper

36. Heather May and Christopher Smart, "Plaza Legal Battle Revived," *The Salt Lake Tribune*, August 7, 2003, http://www.sltrib.com/2003/Aug/t08072003.asp.

27. DVDs and Videocassettes

37. "Let's Get Together," *The Parent Trap*, DVD, directed by David Swift, II (1961; Burbank, CA: Walt Disney Home Video, 2002).

4 CMS Format for Bibliography entries

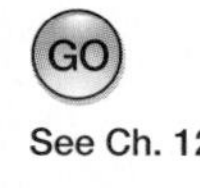
See Ch. 12

For a short paper, it is not essential to provide a bibliography since your footnotes already contain the complete bibliographic information. However, if your teacher requires a bibliography, check to see if using the MLA style for a works cited page as outlined in Chapter 12 will be acceptable. For CMS bibliographic style, you will need to refer to Chapter 17 of the *Chicago Manual.*

CSE Web site

14b Document using CSE style

Although source citations in scientific papers are generally similar to those recommended by the APA—since scientists also are concerned about how current source material is—there is no uniform system of citation. Various disciplines follow their own styles (e.g., styles developed by the American Chemical Society and the American Medical Society). But many scientists use the guide created by the Council of Science Editors (formerly the Council of Biology Editors). The information presented here is from the seventh edition of this guide: Council of Science Editors, *Scientific Style and Format: The*

CSE Manual for Authors, Editors, and Publishers, 7th ed. (Reston, VA: Council of Science Editors in cooperation with The Rockefeller University Press, 2006).

❶ Integrating sources and avoiding plagiarism in CSE style

In Chapter 10, Using Sources and Avoiding Plagiarism, we talked in general about the importance of using sources accurately and responsibly in your research papers. The CSE citation style provides for a two-part system of source identification: (1) parenthetical citations or citation numbers within the body of the paper and (2) a References list that is either alphabetical or numerical at the end of the paper. By using CSE style, you can integrate your source information appropriately and ethically without inadvertently committing plagiarism. Since the CSE citation style closely resembles the APA style, for more on integrating sources and avoiding plagiarism, see 13a-1.

See Ch. 10, 13a-1, 14b-2, 14b-3

❷ CSE style for in-text citations

The CSE style of documentation offers three alternative formats for in-text citations, each of which is linked to an end-of-paper reference list:

- *The citation-sequence (number) style*, in which numbers within the text (assigned based on when the sources are first cited) are used to refer to end references
- *The name-year style*, in which in-text references consist of the last name of the author(s) and the year of publication
- *The citation-name style*, in which an alphabetical reference list is created and numbered, and the number for each source is used within the text as a superscript, no matter where the in-text reference appears. This is the style used by the CSE manual. The models below use the citation-name style for in-text citation.

Temperature plays a major role in the rate of gastric juice secretion[3].

Recent studies[3,5,8-10] show that antibodies may also bind to microbes and prevent their attachment to epithelial surfaces.

A student paper in the CSE citation-name style can be found in Chapter 17, Writing in the Natural Sciences, on pages 420–431.

See Ch. 17

A Directory to CSE Style

References Page Entries: Citation-Name Style

❸ CSE style (Citation-Name) for the References list

As in all documentation systems, the CSE's References list must contain all the sources cited in the paper. The title of this page may be References or Cited References. Since the purpose of this list is to help readers find the materials used in writing the paper, information must be complete and accurate.

The following list reflects the CSE citation-name style, since that is the format most commonly used in CSE-style research papers. List authors with last names first, followed by initials. Capitalize only the first word of a title and any proper nouns. Do not enclose titles of articles in quotation marks, and do not underline or italicize titles of books. Abbreviate journal names of more than one word. Include the year of publication. Cite volume and page numbers when appropriate.

Formatting a CSE References List

In any CSE References list, double-space both within and between entries.

Citation-Name Style

- Order the list alphabetically by author or editor. Once the alphabetical list has been created, number the list.
- Type citation numbers, beginning with 1, flush with the left margin. Leave two spaces and then begin the entry. Align any following lines on the first letter of the entry itself.
- Order the information within entries as follows: Author or editor name. Title of book or article. Publication information (location: publisher; date).

Books in CSE style

1. Book by One Author

1. Kruuk H. The spotted hyena: a study of predation and social behavior. Chicago: Univ Chicago Pr; 1972.
2. Abercrombie MLJ. The anatomy of judgment. Harmondsworth (Eng.): Penguin; 1969.

2. Book by Two or More Authors

3. Hersch RH, Paolitto DP, Reimer J. Promoting moral growth. New York: Longman; 1979.

3. Book by a Corporate Author

4. Carnegie Council on Policy Studies in Higher Education. Fair practices in higher education: rights and responsibilities of students and their colleges in a period of intensified competition for enrollment. San Francisco: Jossey-Bass; 1979.

4. Book with Two or More Editors

5. Buchanan RE, Gibbons NE, editors. Bergey's manual of determinative bacteriology. 8th ed. Baltimore: Williams & Wilkins; 1974.

5. Chapter or Selection from an Edited Work

6. Kleiman DG, Brady CA. Coyote behavior in the context of recent canid research: problems and perspectives. In: Bekoff M, editor. Coyotes: biology, behavior, and management. New York: Academic Pr; 1978. p. 163–188.

6. Government Document

7. Mech D. The wolves of Isle Royale. National Parks fauna series. Available from: United States GPO, Washington; 1966.

Periodicals (journals and magazines) in CSE style

7. Journal Article by One Author

8. Schenkel R. Expression studies of wolves. Behavior. 1947;1: 81-129.

8. Journal Article by Two or More Authors

9. Sargeant AB, Allen SH. Observed interactions between coyotes and red foxes. J Mamm. 1989;70:631-633.

9. Article with No Identified Author

10. Frustrated hamsters run on their wheels. Nat Sci. 1981;91:407.

10. Newspaper Article

11. Blackman J. Aldermen grill Peoples officials on heating costs. Chicago Tribune. 2001 Jan 16; Sect. 1A:2(col. 3).

11. Magazine Article

12. Aveni AF. Emissaries to the stars: the astronomers of ancient Maya. Mercury. 1995 May:15-18.

Other sources in CSE style

12. Unpublished Interview

13. Quarnberg T. [Interview with Dr. Andy Anderson, Professor of Biology, Utah State University, 1988 Apr 15].

13. Dissertation

14. Gese EM. Foraging ecology of coyotes in Yellowstone National Park [dissertation]. Madison (WI): University of Wisconsin; 1995. 124 p.

14. Unpublished Manuscript

15. Pegg J, Russo C, Valent J. College cheating survey at Drexel University. [Unpublished manuscript, 1986].

15. Personal Letter

16. Fife A. [Letter to President Calvin Coolidge, 1930]. Located at: Archives and Special Collections, Utah State University, Logan, UT.

Electronic media in CSE style

16. Online Professional or Personal Site

17. Gelt J. Home use of greywater: rainwater conserves water—and money [Internet]. 1993 [cited 2003 Nov 8]. Available from: http://www.ag.arizona.edu/AZWATER/arroyo/071.rain.html

17. Online Book

18. Bunyan J. The pilgrim's progress from this world to that which is to come [Internet]. London: Kent; 1678 [cited 2005 Jan 16]. Available from: http://www.bibliomania.com/0/0/frameset.html

18. Article in an Online Journal

19. Lechner DE, Bradbury SF, Bradley LA. Detecting sincerity of effort: a summary of methods and approaches. Phys Ther J [Internet]. 1998 Aug [cited 2004 Sep 15]. Available from: http://www.apta.org/pt_journal/Aug98/Toc.htm

19. Article in an Online Newspaper

20. Roan S. Folic acid may mask vitamin deficiency. Salt Lake Tribune [Internet]. 2003 Aug 7 [cited 2006 Aug 8]. Available from: http://www.sltrib.com/2003/aug/08072003/thursday/81868.asp

20. Electronic Posting to a Listserv

21. Kasianowicz J. Careers in biochem. In: MEDLINE-L [Internet]. Washington: Bureau of Weights and Measures; 2003 Mar 2. Accessed 2005 Apr 23.

For a student paper using CSE style, see Chapter 17, pages 420–431.

part 3

Writing in the Disciplines

15 Writing in the Disciplines

FAQs

- Do disciplines ask different questions? (15a-1)
- How do I provide evidence in different disciplines? (15a-2)
- Is there a difference in writing formats and styles by discipline? (15b-1 to 15b-2)
- How do I learn all the new words in my major? (15b-4)

As a college student, regardless of your major, you are probably taking courses in the sciences, such as geology or chemistry; the social sciences, such as sociology or political science; and the humanities, such as philosophy or English literature. You may also be taking "applied" courses in home economics, agriculture, engineering, or business. Each of these disciplines seeks understanding and knowledge in traditional ways; each shares basic research processes. Exploring the relationships among disciplines will help you interpret and use the methods and processes employed by researchers.

See 15a

Writing that is clear and logically developed is key to communicating information regardless of the discipline. The basic principles of researching and writing are vitally important in all disciplines. However, the types of questions asked and evidence used, the customary ways in which the information is reported, the language and writing style preferred, and the genre conventions—the **disciplinary discourse**—varies by the field of study. This chapter provides a broad overview of disciplinary research and writing. Chapters 16–18 contain more specific information about researching and writing in the humanities, natural sciences, and social sciences.

See Chs. 16–18

15a Disciplinary research

WAC Clearinghouse

What is research in the disciplines? Broadly defined, all research is systematic inquiry designed to further our knowledge and understanding of a subject. By this definition, nearly everything you do in college is research. You seek to discover information about people, objects, and nature; to revise your findings in light of new information that comes to your attention; and to interpret your experience and communicate that interpretation to others.

1 Questions asked in the disciplines

People are interpretive animals. In our interaction with the world, we seek to represent internally to ourselves what we have experienced externally. We generally assume that the universe is an orderly, reasonable, meaningful place, and that if we but look, we will be able to discern that order. When we are confronted with a problem, we seek a reasonable explanation for it; that is, we "research" the subject to discover its meaning.

See Fig. 15.1

Figure 15.1 shows a person confronted with a problem. As he relaxes under a tree, he is rudely awakened from his reverie. In searching his internal representation of the world, the character finds an explanation for what happened. The humor of the cartoon is the result of its parody of Archimedes, who shouted "Eureka!" when he discovered a new principle of physics, and Newton, who deduced the principle of gravity from a falling apple. Because we are familiar with the orderly procedures people use to solve problems—procedures that this character has not used—we understand that his response is silly.

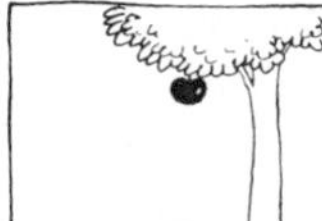

Figure 15.1 Reprinted by permission of Johnny Hart and Creators Syndicate, Inc.

This same issue concerning the falling apple could be researched by a physicist who might ask the following questions: Why does the apple fall? How fast does it fall? How long will it take to reach the ground? Such questions involve broad issues about the nature of the physical universe and the "laws" that govern it. The physicist observes natural phenomena and then develops a systematic body of principles to account for or predict other similar events in the universe.

An economist researching the same issue might focus on the need for a reliable food source in a society, asking such questions as these: How do people meet their basic need for food? What laws of supply and demand operate on the production and distribution of food? An economist also seeks to define the broad issues of how people in society structure their economic relationships. The economist develops a systematic body of ideas to be used in accounting for other similar economic systems or events.

A historian researching this issue would attempt to explain and explore the human experience of the character in the cartoon by asking other questions: What is the significance of the event to this character and to others of his historical period? How does this event relate to other similar events? The historian would account for, reconstruct, and narrate all the events related to this character's so-called discovery that apples cure hunger, relating the discovery to other more general cultural events.

It is clear that researchers in different disciplines ask different questions about the same subject. What distinguishes them is the perspective that the researcher in each field takes.

2 Evidence used in the disciplines

Researchers in the disciplines also have customary ways in which they "test" their hypotheses or provide reasons for their point of view. For example, evidence to a historian may be a diary or a memoir written during a specific historical period; evidence to a psychologist may be a case study of an individual suffering from a particular mental illness. Anyone who is learning about a specific discipline will also be learning how to argue a case and present evidence in that discipline. Evidence can vary from quantitative (using statistical and numerical data) to qualitative (using observations and interviews). Data can be presented in the form of visuals such as tables, graphics, and charts, or it can be described in narratives (stories). Information can be gathered either through primary sources (firsthand data collection) or through secondary sources (reading and reporting on the work of others). Chapters 16–18 discuss these different uses of evidence in the disciplines in more detail.

See Chs. 16–18

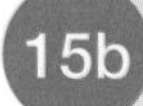

15b Disciplinary discourse

In addition to variations in questions and evidence, disciplines can vary in the ways they present information, sometimes called disciplinary **genres**. Genres are the typical forms that writing and speech can take in various contexts. Your task as an apprentice in a particular discipline is to discover the discipline's genres and practice them in your own writing.

❶ Format

A discipline's genres will incorporate specific formats in which to organize its writing. The *lab report*, for example, is a genre of scientific writing. A typical lab report will contain the same conventional features and formats for many scientific disciplines. Another genre of both natural and social science writing is the informal research report. For examples, see 17c and 18c. Notice the use of headings and subheadings in both of these genres.

See 17c and 18c

The use of visuals is especially important in fields within the sciences and social sciences. Often data are presented in the form of visuals—tables, graphs, and charts. Such visuals can be very effective, particularly in presenting a great deal of data in a compact form.

See 20c,
See Fig. 15.2

Because of the ease with which documents can now be desktop published, writers in all disciplines have access to many more visuals than ever before—clip art, photographs, cartoons, drawings, maps, and so on. These visuals should be used strategically so that your reader is not overwhelmed by competing graphics.

See Fig. 15.2 and 20c

Readers of disciplinary genres expect to find certain organizational patterns, certain types of connections between ideas, and a logical sequence. It is your job as an apprentice in a discipline to find out what genre conventions to follow. Don't hesitate to ask your instructors for suitable models of excellent disciplinary writing.

❷ Style

Another distinguishing feature of disciplinary writing is style—that is, the customary sentence patterns chosen by writers in that discipline. Features of

Figure 15.2 ▶ Table from a Biology Lab Report

Table 1

Test Conditions for Specificity of Enzymes

Treatment	Sugar or Control (4 ml)	Enzyme or Control (2 ml)	Yeast (10 ml)
HYPOTHESIS			
1	Lactose	β-galactosidase	Yeast
2	Melibiose	β-galactosidase	Yeast
3	Lactose	α-galactosidase	Yeast
4	Melibiose	α-galactosidase	Yeast
ASSUMPTIONS			
5	H_2O	α-galactosidase	Yeast
6	Melibiose	H_2O	Yeast
7	Lactose	H_2O	Yeast
8	H_2O	H_2O	Yeast
9	Glucose	H_2O	Yeast

style that can differ by disciplines include *tone* (How objective is the writing? How formal is the tone?), *rhetorical stance* (Do the writers try to achieve distance from their audience? Or do they try to identify with their audience?), and *sentence style* (How long are the sentences and paragraphs in this discipline? Are the verbs active or passive? Are headings and subheadings used?).

③ Documentation

Even though the general principles of documentation are the same—providing your reader with an indication of what sources you used and how to find them—formatting conventions differ by discipline. Documentation in the humanities emphasizes being able to locate a particular quotation on the page on which it was found; hence, internal citations in MLA style use the author's last name and a page number. In contrast, documentation formats in the natural and social sciences emphasize a source's currency and timeliness; hence, internal citations in APA style use the date of publication as well as the author's last name and the page number.

See Chs. 12–14

④ Vocabulary

One of your primary jobs as you study a discipline will be to learn its specialized vocabulary, sometimes called *jargon.* Not only will you need to recognize specialized and technical words when you read, but you will also need to employ them appropriately in your writing. It may be helpful to keep your own dictionary of specialized terms as you study a particular field. The Cross-Curricular Resources Atlas at the back of this book provides a brief introduction to essential vocabulary in a range of disciplines. However, be sure you use the specialized vocabulary or jargon of the discipline only when communicating with other insiders.

GO See 41d

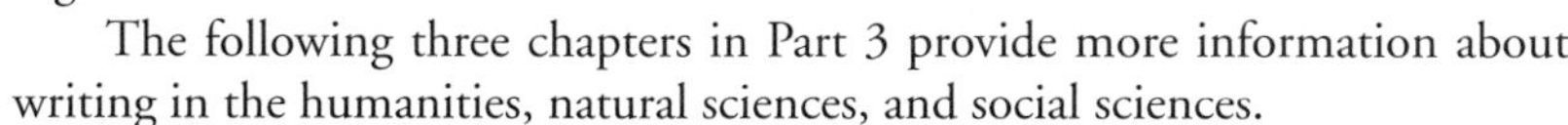

The following three chapters in Part 3 provide more information about writing in the humanities, natural sciences, and social sciences.

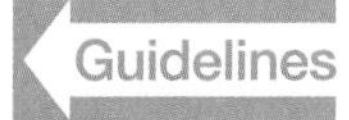

Learning New Vocabularies

- **Begin a learning log or journal.** In either a handwritten journal or a computer file, list new vocabulary words from class and your reading. Be sure to record an example of each word as it is used in a sentence.
- **Take notes.** In lectures, take careful notes, including any new vocabulary used by your instructor. Review your notes after class and highlight or underline the new words. Look them up in the dictionary and write down their definitions in your learning log.
- **Use flash cards.** Create your own vocabulary flash cards, using 3 × 5 index cards. Practice defining the words on the cards with a classmate.
- **Join online discussions.** Online listservs and discussion forums provide a way to "lurk" in your discipline. Read some of the prior posts and note the vocabulary being used. Are there words that recur? Are there new terms? Again, record any new words in your learning log.
- **Keep at it.** Be persistent about noting and practicing your new vocabulary. You will not be able to learn it all at once.

See 23c-1

EXERCISE 15.1 Browse through some journals that are used frequently in your field of study. Do you notice any common elements in format, style, or language? Do some journals follow a style that differs from others in the field? What common elements define the writing genre for your discipline?

FOR COLLABORATION Bring a journal article from your field to class to share with a small group of your peers. Discuss with them how the article exhibits what you see as the genre. Compare articles to determine whether the fields represented have different discourse conventions regarding format, style, and language.

16 Writing in the Humanities

FAQs

- What are the types of writing used in the humanities? (16a)
- I have to write a paper about a poem we read in class. Where should I start? (16b)
- How is a literary analysis paper formatted? (16c)
- Where can I find information for a humanities research paper? (16d)

Disciplines in the humanities include classical and modern languages and literature, history, and philosophy. Humanists deal in significance, insight, imagination, and the meaning of human experience. They write to express their understanding of some aspect of the world. In general, humanists inquire into consciousness, values, ideas, and ideals as they seek to describe how experience shapes understanding of the human condition.

16a Know the different types of writing in the humanities

Written texts in the humanities fall into three broad categories: (1) creative writing, such as fiction, poetry, and drama; (2) interpretive and analytical writing, such as literary and art criticism; and (3) theoretical writing, such as historical, philosophical, and social theories of literature and art.

1 Creative writing

Human beings have always been storytellers. The impulse to create works of literature, whether in the form of oral folk narratives or formal written sonnets, is as old as humankind. Creative writing, or literature, provides readers with an aesthetic experience. Readers expect a literary work to mean something to them—to show them new ways of looking at themselves and the world—in addition to entertaining them.

The major **literary genres,** or types of literature, are poetry, fiction, creative nonfiction, and drama. Biography and autobiography are also sometimes considered literary genres.

2 Interpretive and analytical writing

Readers of literary works ask interpretive or analytical questions: What sort of work is it? Does it have a message? How powerful or meaningful is the message? Critical writing in the humanities is usually either interpretive, analytical, or some combination of the two. **Interpretive writing** discusses the author's intended meaning or the impact of the work on an audience. A book report that summarizes the plot and discusses the significance of a work is an example of interpretive writing. **Analytical writing** takes interpretation one step further, examining the whole of the work in relationship to its component parts. For example, an analytical writer might try to understand how the plot of a play is reinforced by its setting or how a ballet's musical score contributes to its theme. A critical essay that argues for a particular position with respect to a literary work is an example of analytical writing.

3 Theoretical writing

The third type of humanistic writing is **theoretical writing**. Theorists look beyond individual works of literature and art to see how they exemplify broader social and historical trends. For example, a theorist might use the characters in a Dickens novel to speculate about shifts in class structure in nineteenth-century England. Theorists provide links among art, literature, and other disciplines such as history, sociology, and psychology. Their writing involves interpretation and analysis, but their goal is to *synthesize*—to present interpretations in a larger context. Many of the articles published in professional humanities journals exemplify theoretical writing.

Literary analysis

16b Write interpretively or analytically about literature

Much of the writing you will do in college literature courses is interpretive or analytical. Instructors generally expect you to make a claim about a literary work and then support that claim through reasoned arguments and evidence from the work itself. Your goal in writing interpretively or analytically is to shed light on an aspect of the work that the reader might not otherwise see.

See Ch. 5

1 Reading literature critically

See 2b

Begin by reading the work critically. Using the following critical reading process when you read a piece of literature will start you on the way to writing an interpretive or analytical essay.

First, read the work straight through, with an eye toward understanding the text and noting its impressions on you. Does the work make you feel happy or angry? Is there a character, event, or scene that is particularly moving or striking? Does anything in the text confuse or puzzle you? Keep a journal (either on a computer or in a notebook) in which you jot down impressions as you read.

Once you have finished reading the work, skim it in its entirety to highlight important passages, such as pivotal scenes, revealing character descriptions, and vivid descriptive passages. Then try writing a brief plot outline to be sure that you have a clear sense of the chronology. You might also list key characters and their relationships to each other.

Finally, review your marginal notes, outline, and lists to determine what aspects of the work interested you most. Try freewriting at your computer or in your journal, recalling your overall impressions and any important points you may have overlooked earlier.

See 3c-2

2 Determining audience, persona, and arguments

Once you have completed your critical reading, establish a rhetorical stance for your paper. In determining this stance, you will make decisions about your intended persona and the purpose for writing, as well as your intended audience and the best arguments to use to persuade them. If you are writing to complete an assignment, begin by carefully studying the assignment itself.

See 3b-2

As you begin to analyze the assignment, look for key terms such as *analyze* or *discuss*, terms that imply an interpretive or analytical purpose for writing. Your instructor may have specified some aspect of the work that you should write about, or he or she may have left the topic open-ended. In most cases, your instructor will expect you to write an argumentative piece that makes a point about the work and supports that point with examples and illustrations from the text. Examples of some typical assignments follow.

See 24a-3

Typical Assignments

Writing Assignments Calling for Interpretation or Analysis

- Discuss the key ideas or themes that the author of the poem "One Art" is trying to convey. Connect the poem to your own experiences of loss.
- Explain how the setting and location of *Regeneration* affect its major themes.
- Analyze the ways in which the set design for the play *West Side Story* reinforces the plot.

WEBLINK

Writing about literature

Writing Assignments Calling for Character Analysis

- Analyze the relationship between Cathy and Adam Trask in *East of Eden.*
- Explore the character of Lady Macbeth in the play *Macbeth.*

General Assignments That Allow the Writer to Decide the Rhetorical Stance

- Discuss in depth some aspect of one of the novels we read this term.
- Explain how one of the authors we read this term uses imagery.

Think about your persona for the paper. How do you wish to come across as a writer? Will you be objective and fair or heated and passionate? Is your purpose to persuade, to inform, or something else? Your persona is revealed in the paper through the words and sentence structures you choose.

Finally, ask yourself who the audience for the paper will be and what arguments will be persuasive to that audience. Most often the audience, in addition to your instructor, will be intelligent readers who are interested in literature but who may not be acquainted with the particular text you are writing about. Your paper should provide readers with background information about the text so that they will be able to follow your argument.

❸ Developing a claim and writing a thesis

How you interpret or analyze a work of literature will depend on what you have read, your interests, your prior knowledge, the information presented in class, and your general understanding of the text. If you have a choice, always write about something in the work that interests you. You will need to come up with your own critical interpretation or analysis of the work and then write a thesis statement that articulates your claim.

See 3e-1 to 3e-3

Literary works are typically analyzed with respect to some major aspect such as characters or plot. In Guidelines box 16c can be found examples of questions you can use in arriving at a thesis related to one of the major aspects of literary works.

❹ Using the appropriate person and tense

In writing interpretively about literature, it is generally appropriate to use the first person (*I, we, our*) to express your own point of view: "*I* was greatly moved by the character's predicament." However, in academic papers, the third person (*he, she, it, they*) is typically used to discuss information found in sources.

Also, in writing about a work of literature, the commonly accepted practice is to use the present tense (sometimes called the *literary present*) when describing events that happened in the work: "Adam Trask *learns* about his wife's true character slowly." Similarly, use the present tense when discussing what an author has done in a specific literary work: "Steinbeck *uses* Cathy and Adam Trask to illustrate his point about the pure evil that *exists* in human nature."

See 30d-1

❺ Writing your literature paper

Once you have articulated a thesis, you can proceed to write your paper, following the advice in Part 1 of this handbook. In particular, you may wish to review the stages of the writing process. If your assignment specifies that you support your thesis through research, follow the advice in Part 2 on researching your topic. In particular, review Chapter 7 on the research project.

See 3a

See Ch. 7

16c Review some model student papers

Let us now look at how two students approached the task of writing about literature, one to produce a literary interpretation and the other to produce a literary analysis.

Guidelines

Using questions to develop a thesis about a literary work

Characters (major actors)

- How convincing are the characters?
- Is a particular character's behavior consistent throughout the work?
- Does the author reveal the narrator's thoughts?

Plot (what happens)

- How effective is the plot?
- Does it hold your interest and build to an effective climax?
- Does the plot line seem well connected, or is it disjointed and hard to follow? How might this affect an interpretation of the work?

Theme (major idea or main message)

- What is the overall theme or point that the work is trying to make?
- Is the point one that you agree with?
- Does the author convince you that the point is well taken?
- Is the theme used consistently throughout the work, or are there contradictions?

Structure (organization)

- What is the structure, or overall design, of the text itself?
- Does it skip around chronologically or geographically?
- Does one chapter lead logically to the next?
- What is the author trying to accomplish with the particular structure he or she chose?

Setting (where and when the events take place)

- How has the author used setting?
- Are descriptions of people and places particularly vivid?
- How well did the author re-create a sense of place?

Point of View (perspective of whoever presents the ideas)

- What is the point of view adopted by the writer?
- Who is the narrator?
- Did the narrator influence the way you reacted to the work?
- Does the point of view remain consistent?

Rhythm (meter or beat) and Rhyme (correspondence in the sounds of words)

- Are there striking rhythmic patterns or rhyme schemes?
- What is the impact of the work's language?

Imagery (visual impressions created) and Figures of Speech (metaphors and similes)

- Did the author use imagery and figures of speech effectively?
- Is a particular image repeated throughout the work?

Symbolism (use of familiar ideas to represent something else) and Archetypes (traditional models after which others are patterned)

- How have symbols and archetypes been used in the work?
- Does the author repeat a certain key symbol? To what purpose?
- Is there a mythical archetype at work? How effective is it?

Style (writer's choice of words or sentence structures)

- Does the writer characteristically choose certain words or sentence structures?
- Is the language simple and direct, or ornate and formal?

Tone and Voice (persona of the author as reflected through word choice and style)

- What tone or voice has the writer adopted?
- Is the tone appropriate to the theme? To the characters?
- How does the writer's tone affect you as a reader?

1 An example of literary interpretation

In a first-year course on understanding literature, students were asked to interpret Elizabeth Bishop's poem "One Art" and discuss the impact of its major theme—loss. Wayne Proffitt began his task by rereading the poem, circling and annotating words relating to its major theme. He then listed those items he had highlighted in outline form. For his rhetorical stance, he decided on an interpretive purpose, an objective persona, and a novice audience. Next, Wayne wrote his working thesis, which articulated the claim he would make in his paper: "Bishop's poem helps the reader

See Fig. 16.1

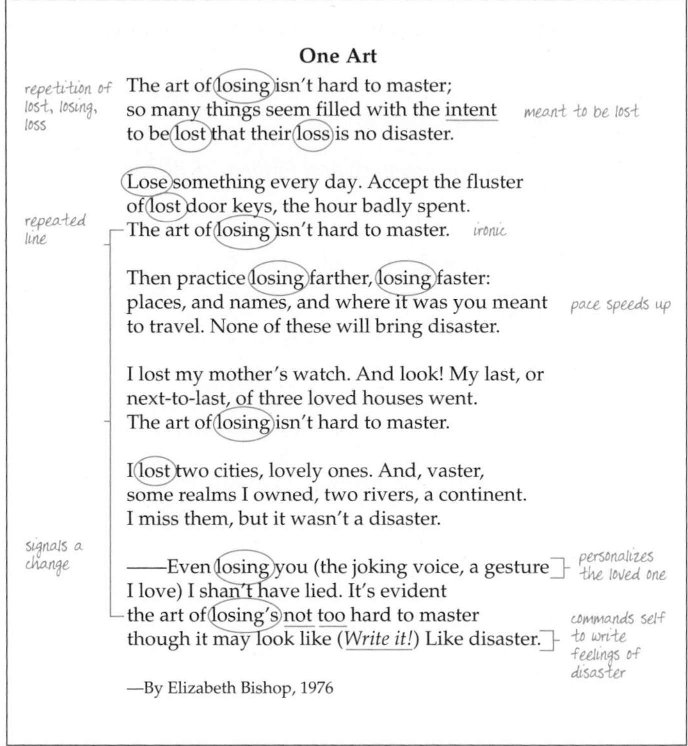

One Art

The art of losing isn't hard to master;
so many things seem filled with the intent
to be lost that their loss is no disaster.

Lose something every day. Accept the fluster
of lost door keys, the hour badly spent.
The art of losing isn't hard to master.

Then practice losing farther, losing faster:
places, and names, and where it was you meant
to travel. None of these will bring disaster.

I lost my mother's watch. And look! My last, or
next-to-last, of three loved houses went.
The art of losing isn't hard to master.

I lost two cities, lovely ones. And, vaster,
some realms I owned, two rivers, a continent.
I miss them, but it wasn't a disaster.

——Even losing you (the joking voice, a gesture
I love) I shan't have lied. It's evident
the art of losing's not too hard to master
though it may look like (*Write it!*) Like disaster.

—By Elizabeth Bishop, 1976

Figure 16.1 ▶ Elizabeth Bishop's Poem with Wayne's Interpretive Annotations

understand the meaning of loss and how loss might eventually be accepted." This thesis makes an interpretive claim about the meaning of the poem. Wayne then went on to write the paper, using the poem itself as his source as he explained and justified his claim.

Proffitt 1

Wayne Proffitt

Professor McKay

English 1116-03

15 May 2006

Emotional Distance and Loss in a Poem by Elizabeth Bishop

Elizabeth Bishop (1911–1979) has only recently been recognized as one of the greatest poets of the twentieth century (Burt). She offers her knowledge of loss with humor and a casual air in "One Art." Bishop's poem helps the reader understand the meaning of loss and how loss might eventually be accepted. It seems that this poem may be autobiographical, as it describes not only things that people in general tend to lose but also specific items that the poet herself has lost during her lifetime. The reader is led through a list of lost objects that the speaker claims were meant to be lost. "So many things seem filled with the intent" that when they finally do get lost it "is no disaster." The reader is advised—in a casual way—to get used to losing things and to practice getting better at letting go. The ironic encouragement of "the art of losing isn't hard to master" helps make clear the speaker's real emotions and attitudes toward losing.

The humorous and casual voice of the speaker becomes quite forced toward the end of the poem,

Last name and page number in upper right-hand corner

No title page. For a model with a title page, see Chapter 11.

Student and course information

Double spaced

Internet source

Interpretive thesis

Words of the author in quotation marks

Interpretation of the change in voice

Proffitt 2

however, and readers suspect that the loss of her loved one was not really one that could be shrugged off. It is almost as if the speaker is trying to gear herself up for the final loss by convincing herself that there is nothing she cannot handle losing. With this armor in place, she attempts to deal with the grief of losing one well loved, but finds that in the end she cannot hold her nonchalance and indifference steadily enough. At this point, perhaps both the speaker and the reader suddenly feel the art of losing for what it really is—an inevitable task—and that it can truly be "disaster" for the one who has lost. The remembered "joking voice, a gesture I love" bring a real beloved person into the poem and emphasize the enormity of the loss. The speaker has difficulty completing the closing sentence and must goad herself to "write it" and be done.

Interpretation of the meaning of loss in the poem

The ability to create such distance between the speaker and the object being discussed increases the impact of the submerged emotion when it is finally allowed to surface. The very distance of this poem's opening stanzas is one of the reasons that the emotional loss at the end of the poem contains so much power. Personal suffering and loss is not openly exposed in this poem, and because of this, careful reading is necessary to see past the distance crafted into the poem. The

Emotional impact of the poem

Proffitt 3

effort of seeing more than is directly stated contributes to the reader's eventual understanding and even sharing of the sense of loss.

Proffitt 4

Works Cited

Bishop, Elizabeth. "One Art." *The Complete Poems 1927-1979 by Elizabeth Bishop*. New York: Farrar, 1983. 215. Print.

Burt, Steve. "Elizabeth Bishop's 'One Art': A Review." *Harvard Advocate* 1998. Web. 20 Apr. 2006.

Print source

Internet source

❷ An example of literary analysis in MLA style

For a sophomore-level course on the British novel, students were asked to analyze a significant theme in one of the novels they read for the course. Heidi Blankley decided to write about the novel *Regeneration.* She was fascinated by the theme of gender stereotypes, which had been discussed in class and also in a conversation she had with her professor during office hours. Her essay illustrates literary analysis—an analytical argument about a work of literature.

In her first two sentences, Heidi articulates her critical stance. Notice how she begins with a quotation stating the general topic of the book (the treatment of shell-shock victims after World War I), followed by her own claim that the book is even more profoundly about the theme of gender stereotypes. This claim, or thesis, provides the reader with a clear understanding of the analysis Heidi plans to make in her paper. As the writer, she must prove to her readers, using examples from the text, that the novel *does* explore the theme of gender stereotyping.

See Ch. 12

The paper exemplifies the MLA documentation and formatting conventions. The list of works cited shows that Heidi read secondary sources about the novel and used information from her class, from a journal article, from a book, and from the Internet as support for her essay.

Blankley 1

Heidi Blankley
Professor Kristine Miller
British Novel
2 April 2005

Ending the Violence

Pat Barker, a contemporary British author and winner of the prestigious Booker Prize, writes novels about England during the war years (Middlemiss). In *Regeneration*, Pat Barker "examines the treatment of shell-shock victims at Edinburgh's Craiglockhart hospital during World War I" (Perry 44). Although Barker's novel is mainly about the acculturation of shell-shock victims from World War I, it is more concerned with the larger issue that lurks behind the battle scenes: gender stereotypes. Barker suggests that the violence created by adhering to the masculine stereotype—that men are brave warriors and not nurturers—is not merely a social problem, but a mythical, psychological obstacle, the effects of which are seeping into all facets of life. If humans are ever to recover from the violence, Barker thinks we must analyze the root of the violence and come to terms with our destructive behavior toward the environment, other species, and one another.

In chapter 4, a relatively bizarre scene occurs which forces the patient, David Burns, to realize he can exert influence on the violence surrounding him. Burns

Writer's last name and page number appear on every page

Student, professor, and course identification

Internet source

In MLA style, source citations typically include the author and the page number, with no comma

Analytical thesis

First example of coming to terms with violence

Blankley 2

boards a bus that takes him away from the hospital at Craiglockhart into the countryside. There he comes into contact with a tree that reeks of death, "The tree he stood under was laden with animals. Bore them like fruit" (Barker 38). Burns's first impulse is to give in to fear and run from the grotesque tree, but Barker has a different plan in mind for Burns. Instead, Burns faces his fear head-on and unties the animals:

Long quotation from the novel is indented 10 spaces

> When all the corpses were on the ground, he arranged them in a circle round the tree and sat down within it, his back against the trunk. He felt the roughness of the bark against his knobby spine. He pressed his hands between his knees and looked around the circle of his companions. Now they could dissolve into the earth as they were meant to do. (Barker 39)

Punctuation precedes the citation for indented quotations only

This scene is so strange and so grotesque that it forces the reader to question Barker's motives for including it. The scene Burns stumbled upon becomes a reflection of the war; the animals represent the hundreds of decaying soldiers. The inhumane hanging of the animals suggests that the soldiers are dying for an inhumane and unnatural purpose. Just as this scene is unnatural in its placement of the animals, so are the massive murders involved with the war (Miller).

Information summarized from class notes

Blankley 3

Furthermore, the circle Burns makes with the decaying animals resembles the cyclical pattern of history; humanity has spawned war after war, apparently without learning anything from its own violence. As the creator of the circle and also the one who sits within it, Burns recognizes that he is both a physical perpetrator of violence and a psychological victim of it. He copes with this paradoxical situation simply by revising gender stereotypes. As he steps into the circle and returns the animals to the earth, he takes on the qualities of a nurturer, a role contradictory to the masculine stereotype. However, although Burns might wish to remove himself from the situation, from his contributions to the war and violence in general, he is still a part of it, the "white root" of it (Barker 39).

The example is related to the theme of gender stereotypes

What Barker is trying to accomplish with this scene is to show that no matter what gender, we are a part of the recurring historical pattern of violence, whether it is toward humans or other creatures. The only way to get out of the circle, as Burns does later in his dream about the scene he had witnessed, is to see ourselves inside the circle: "He folded his arms across his face and . . . began drifting off to sleep. He was back in the wood, outside the circle now, but able to see himself inside it" (Barker 40).

Critical analysis of the scene described

Second example of coming to terms with violence

Brackets show letters changed from the original to fit the sentence

The second example is related to the theme of gender stereotypes

Blankley 4

Another character, Rivers, also displays his sensitivity to the destruction around him. Rivers, modeled after a real-life doctor, is shown by Barker to be a humane and sensitive man (Perry 44). In chapter 13, a bumblebee is trapped inside a room where Craiglockhart officials are holding a meeting. Rivers is unable to concentrate on the meeting and keeps scanning the windows, trying to find the bee because "the noise was unreasonably disturbing" (Barker 132). When he finally finds the insect, he "fetch[es] a file from the desk and, using it as a barrier, guide[s] the insect into the open air" (Barker 132). When he turns back into the room, he finds "everybody, Burns included, staring at him in some surprise" (Barker 132-33); judging from this reaction, we can assume that Rivers's response to the bee is an abnormal one. Perhaps the others in the room were unaware of the bee's presence, or if they were aware, maybe they would have acted like "bloodthirsty little horrors" (Barker 172), smacking the bee with the file instead of rescuing it.

Through his action, Rivers transcends the masculine stereotype, which is why his action is met by surprise from the other men. The release of the bee might simply be symbolic of Rivers's escape from Craiglockhart—for at the end of this chapter, he takes some time off for sick

Blankley 5

leave. But this connection seems too obvious. Barker is once more forcing the reader to question gender stereotypes. By releasing the bee instead of smashing it, Rivers becomes Barker's ideal human. He is a man with the capacity to nurture not only other men but nature as well. In this instance, he represents the balance, a human being acting on natural instinct to save another creature, without questioning his own motives.

Throughout her novel, Barker plays with the myth of regeneration. Typically (in American mythology), the myth of regeneration involves a male character who seeks to escape the bonds of his old life. To do so, he retires from civilization into the purity of wilderness and, after a while, is reborn a newer, wiser man who is more in tune with himself and his surroundings. Although the wilderness in *Regeneration* is civilized, Burns and Rivers try to use the wilderness in the same way. Burns returns to his native home in Suffolk hoping to recuperate from the psychological trauma he experienced in the war. Burns invites Rivers to join him there, hoping Suffolk will have the same invigorating effect on Rivers.

The myth of regeneration is related to the theme of violence

Barker's idea of regeneration appears to apply to violence in general, to the war, and to gender roles.

The theme of violence is analyzed

Ellipses indicate omissions

The two themes of violence and gender stereotypes are connected

The use of metaphor is analyzed

Blankley 6

Early in the novel, Rivers has an insightful revelation about gender roles:

> He distrusted the implication that nurturing, even when done by a man, remains female, as if the ability were in some way borrowed, or even stolen from women—. . . . If that were true, then there was really very little hope. (Barker 107)

If women are the only ones who can be considered nurturers, if men are permanently locked into the role of brave warriors, and if neither females nor males have the capacity to extend the boundaries of these roles, then there is little hope that the psychological trauma of war can be overcome. There is also little hope that the cycle of violence will ever cease, because the masculine gender stereotype depends on war and violence for the man to prove himself as a brave warrior, while the female stereotype depends on wounded soldiers to nurture. The result of clinging to these stereotypes is a perpetual cycle of violence that extends past the war and into the physical qualities of the environment. If the stereotypes are left unquestioned, the cycle of violence will continue, and neither men nor women will be able to recover from the violence.

However, in chapter 15, Barker illustrates a remedy for the destructive cycle of violence with a brilliant metaphor:

Blankley 7

> Rivers knew only too well how often the early stages of change or cure may mimic deterioration. Cut a chrysalis open, and you will find a rotting caterpillar. What you will never find is that mythical creature, half caterpillar, half butterfly, a fit emblem of the human soul, . . . No, the process of transformation consists almost entirely of decay. (Barker 184)

Barker reveals that the only way to abolish war and all the violent behavior equivalent to war is to internalize those traits which are perceived as inherently masculine and inherently feminine—to view the soul as a combination of butterfly and caterpillar, enclosed in the delicate chrysalis of the earth. War is a transition period, a devastating event which can lead to the positive transformation of social roles, if we let it.

In her article on women's fiction, Pykett suggests that "Pat Barker, like a number of other recent women writers, does not interrogate or deconstruct history . . . but rather she seeks to recover and reclaim the past on behalf of those who have been silenced and marginalized by history" (75). In this novel, the shell-shock victims are those who have historically been silenced. Barker gives them a voice in *Regeneration*. Through them, she

Introduces the quotation with the author's name in a signal phrase

Conclusion returns to thesis idea

Blankley 8

suggests that it is possible to heal society if we cease adhering to the stereotypical male and female gender roles. What we need in order to solve the trauma of war and to prevent future violence are not heroes or warriors, but a reconsideration of gender, a restructuring of the rules so that men may reveal their "feminine" sensitivity without being typecast as effeminate, homosexual, or motherly.

MLA citation style

Novel

Internet source

Class notes and interview

Nonfiction book

Book title is italicized

Second line is indented

Journal

Initial capitals are used in article titles, which are also put in quotation marks

Journal name is italicized

Blankley 9

Works Cited

Barker, Pat. *Regeneration*. New York: Plume, 1993. Print.

Middlemiss, Perry. Homepage. 1 Jan. 1997. Web. 15 Mar. 2005.

Miller, Kristine. Class notes and personal interview. 10 Mar. 2005.

Perry, Donna. *Backtalk: Women Writers Speak Out*. New Brunswick, NJ: Rutgers UP, 1993. Print.

Pykett, Lyn. "The Century's Daughters: Recent Women's Fiction and History." *Critical Quarterly* 29.3 (1987): 71–77. Print.

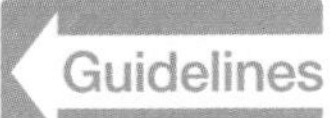

Useful Web Sites for Research in the Humanities

Art and Architecture

The American Institute of Architects <http://www.aia.org>
American Federation of Arts <http://www.afaweb.org>
National Association for the Visual Arts <http://www.visualarts.net.au/home/default.asp>
The Center for Creative Photography <http://dizzy.library.arizona.edu/branches/ccp>
Architecture Encyclopedia <http://www.archpedia.com/>
World Wide Arts Resources <http://www.world-arts-resources.com>

English Literature and Language

National Council of Teachers of English <http://www.ncte.org>
Modern Language Association <http://www.mla.org>
English Server–Iowa State University <http://www.eserver.org>
Project Bartleby <http://www.bartleby.com>
Project Gutenberg <http://www.gutenberg.org>
Voice of the Shuttle: English Literature <http://vos.ucsb.edu>

History and Classics

American Philological Association <http://www.apaclassics.org>
American Association for State and Local History <http://www.aaslh.org>
World History Association <http://www.thewha.org>
Perseus Project <http://www.perseus.tufts.edu>

Music

International Society for Music Education <http://www.isme.org>
MENC: The National Association for Music Education <http://www.menc.org>
Music Teachers National Association <http://www.mtna.org/>

Philosophy

The American Philosophical Association <http://www.apa.udel.edu/apa/index.html>

Religion

Comparative Religion <http://www.academicinfo.net/religindex.html>
American Academy of Religion <http://www.aarweb.org>

16d Research in the humanities

See Ch. 8

See Ch. 21

Scholars in the humanities now rely on technology in their research and their writing. Students of the humanities, too, should familiarize themselves with available resources, particularly those in library databases. Take a look at the useful humanities Web sites in the preceding Guidelines box. Numerous humanities discussion groups, bulletin boards, and newsgroups can also be found via an Internet search.

See 21c-2

EXERCISE 16.1 Investigate the Web sites available for one of the disciplines within the humanities. Search by topic for a newsgroup or a bulletin board.

FOR COLLABORATION Bring to class a printout of a Web site that you found in your disciplinary Internet search. Share the information with a small group of your peers. What kinds of resources are available for the disciplines within the humanities?

17 Writing in the Natural Sciences

FAQs

- What kinds of writing assignments can I expect in science courses? (17a)
- What makes scientific writing different from other kinds of writing? (17b)
- Should I use headings in a scientific report? (17c)
- How can I find information for a science research paper? (17d)

Scientists formulate and test theories about the natural and physical world, and their findings are used to solve problems in medicine, industry, and agriculture. Typically, the natural sciences are classified into two categories: pure and applied. The pure sciences include life sciences (such as biology and botany), physical sciences (such as mathematics, physics, and chemistry), and earth sciences (such as geology and geography). The applied sciences include medical sciences (such as forensics, pathology, surgery, and ophthalmology), engineering (mechanical, environmental, aerospace, civil, and electrical), and computer science.

National Academy of Sciences

17a Know the different types of writing in the natural sciences

To solve problems in a systematic way, scientists use the scientific method. Writing plays a critical role in each of the six steps of the scientific method. Whether you are writing up your own work in a research report or summarizing and evaluating other people's work in a review of literature, you need to be familiar with the scientific method.

The Scientific Method

1. Express the problem in writing, clearly and objectively, in the form of a statement, usually called a *problem statement*.
2. Gather all relevant information needed to solve the problem, including information found on the Internet and in library sources such as books and journals.
3. Analyze that information and formulate a *hypothesis*, a statement that predicts what the scientist expects to find by conducting controlled experiments related to the problem under investigation.
4. Design and conduct controlled experiments to test the hypothesis, keeping a detailed record of each experiment and its outcome.
5. Analyze these records to determine how well they support the hypothesis or predicted results.
6. Restate the hypothesis as a conclusion that explains how the experimental data supported, refuted, or modified the initial hypothesis.

1 Research report

Most scientific writing takes the form of research reports, which are based on primary research conducted by scientists. The motivation for much primary research in the natural sciences is an event or experience that challenges existing ideas and promotes inquiry. In general, the aim is to improve the congruency between theories and concepts about the world and actual experiences or experimental results.

Great breakthroughs in the advancement of knowledge occur through primary research, and these developments are announced to the scientific community through research reports. Famous examples of primary research include the studies conducted by the English biologist Sir Alexander Fleming. When he noticed that one of his cultures of *Staphylococcus* bacteria had been contaminated by a microorganism from the air outside, Fleming examined the contaminated plate in detail and observed a surprising phenomenon: where the colonies of bacteria had been attacked by microscopic fungi, a large region had become transparent. Fleming hypothesized that the effect could be due to an antibacterial substance secreted by the foreign microorganism and then spread into the culture. This secretion turned out to be a variety of the fungus *Penicillium*, from which the antibiotic penicillin is now made.

Guidelines

Format for a Scientific Report

- *Abstract*, which summarizes the report in one compact paragraph
- *Introduction*, which states the problem, background information, and the hypothesis
- *Literature review*, which summarizes related research
- *Research methods*, which outlines the processes used in the experiments
- *Research results*, which describes the findings of the experiments
- *Discussion and conclusion*, which relates the research back to the problem and hypothesis and speculates on its implications
- *Endmatter*, which may include notes, references, and appendixes

Whether a research report announces the discovery of penicillin or the results of a student lab experiment, the basic outline is the same, as it parallels the steps in the scientific method. Individual scientists use many variations on this standard format, depending on their audience. Less formal reports may not include an abstract or a literature review, for example. An abbreviated version of the research report may serve as a laboratory report or a progress report.

2 Review of literature

The second major category of scientific writing is the review of literature. A literature review may be a brief summary of the literature on a specific topic; it may be a lengthy critical review of a single work or an extended critical review of several works on the same topic. A literature review may even take the form of annotations—critical or explanatory notes added to another text.

17b Write objectively about science

Science and engineering writing

As a student, when you are writing about the natural sciences, generally you are responding to an assignment. The assignment may specify whether you are to write a research report or a review of literature. If it does not, you are probably better off reviewing the literature on a particular topic, unless

See 17a-1

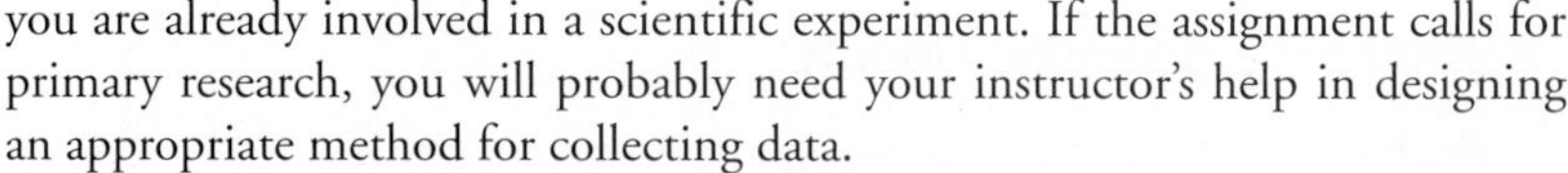

you are already involved in a scientific experiment. If the assignment calls for primary research, you will probably need your instructor's help in designing an appropriate method for collecting data.

If your instructor has not assigned a particular topic, you can turn to the media—television, radio, magazines, and the Internet—for ideas. Look for controversies or new discoveries in the natural sciences and begin to ask questions about them. For example, a television documentary on some of the newest findings from scientific experiments conducted by the international space station might lead you to wonder about the future of the space station and its missions.

See 3b-2

❶ Determining audience, persona, and arguments

Once you have a topic, you can establish a rhetorical stance. Usually you can assume that you are writing for intelligent readers who are interested in the subject but may not know many details about the topic. You should provide enough background information so that such readers will be able to follow your argument. Knowing who your readers are will help you to determine which arguments will be the most persuasive. Because of the focus on objectivity in scientific writing, your persona will typically need to be straightforward and you will most likely adopt a formal tone. Look in the assignment for key terms such as *analyze* or *discuss*, which imply interpretation or critique, as you decide your purpose. Your instructor will no doubt expect you to write a piece that makes a point, supported by your secondary sources. Your instructor can also help you decide if your report should have an argumentative edge or if it should be a more informational piece.

❷ Writing a thesis

To write a thesis, you need to refine your topic. For example, if you decided to write about the space station, you could use print sources and the Internet to find out more about the international space station and then write an informative thesis describing what you found out. If your instructor wanted your report to have an argumentative edge, your thesis could argue for or against the claim that the US government should continue to support the space station.

See 3e-1 to 3e-3

❸ Completing the research and writing your paper

Regardless of the discipline for which you are writing, you should follow the writing process described in Part 1 of this handbook. Refer to Chapters 3 and 6 for advice on prewriting, drafting, revising, and editing. If your paper consists of or includes a literature review, refer to Part 2 for information on library and Internet research. See the list of reference materials commonly used in the sciences, including Internet resources.

See Part 2 and 17d

4 Using visuals

In the natural sciences, visuals such as graphs, charts, and diagrams are often used to convey information and statistical data in a compact format. As an apprentice science writer, you will need to learn the customary ways in which statistical data are presented in your field. Notice how the table included by the engineering students in their report on domestic water supply (page 428) manages to capture in a succinct and readable fashion the weighted selection criteria for water supply alternatives. Refer to 19c for more information about using graphics and visuals in your writing.

See 19c

17c An example of a research report in CSE style

In a sophomore-level engineering course, the students worked with their peers on a primary research project. Following is a report produced by one group of four students. Notice how the students' report begins with a cover memorandum, which includes an executive summary outlining the study and its recommendations. Then, in the body of the report, the students describe their own research, which was designed to determine the method that would best solve the water shortages anticipated in a neighboring community.

The report illustrates an adapted scientific report format. It begins with a cover memo to introduce the problem and proposed solutions. The cover memo also serves as an abstract. Next comes a title page. The sections have headings that parallel the research itself. However, not all of the sections typically found in a research report are included. The students did not include a formal literature review, choosing instead to integrate references within the body of the report. They followed the CSE citation style, using the citation-name system. Notice that the report sections are numbered, a practice common to scientific and engineering reports, as it helps readers find relevant information quickly and easily.

See 14b

Cover memo

TO: Brent Adams, CEE Professor
FROM: Group 4: David Hunter, Carl Jones, Lee Duong, Rhonda Peterson
SUBJECT: RECOMMENDATION FOR CHOOSING AN ALTERNATIVE WATER SOURCE/SYSTEM
REF.: Your letter of request, September 10, 2003
DATE: January 5, 2004
DIST.: Sonia Manuel-Dupont, Project Supervisor

Smithfield City will not have an adequate supply of culinary water in the future. Their current supply is adequate for only another 5 years[5]. We were asked by you to research and derive a solution for this problem. After discussing as a group the various alternatives that could be implemented, we decided on four alternatives that would be the most effective. Each of us in the group researched articles and conducted personal interviews to determine the most appropriate solution. From our findings we have gathered that the most effective alternative is installing a new well that will have enough supply to meet future demand.

Executive summary used in place of abstract

Executive Summary

The population of Smithfield City is growing rapidly. The current water supply for Smithfield is not adequate to meet the needs of the city over the next 25 years. We need to find a source to provide an additional 70 million gallons of water per month to Smithfield City in order to have an adequate water supply for the next 25 years. We have researched the problem in scientific journals and books and have spoken with the Smithfield City Engineer and also others who deal directly with water supply.

Our purpose of communication is to inform you of our 4 researched alternatives: (1) development of a new well, (2) no action, (3) installation of a dual system, and (4) water reuse. Only the development of a new well will supply enough water for Smithfield City over the next 25 years. Development of a new well was ranked best on cost, feasibility, and adequacy, and average on maintenance and impact on the environment. Therefore, we recommend the development of a new well to provide the necessary water for Smithfield City.

Title page

Recommendation for Installing
a Well for Smithfield City

To:
Brent Adams
CEE 361
Professor

From:
Group 4

Dist:
Dr. Sonia Manuel-Dupont
Project Supervisor

January 5, 2004

1.0 Introduction and Problem Statement

The City of Smithfield currently receives most of its culinary water from springs in Smithfield Canyon. There are 8 springs near the top of the canyon and 3 springs located further down the canyon. These springs produce an estimated flow rate that varies seasonally from 1800 gallons per minute in the spring to 1100 gallons per minute in the winter[5]. In addition to the springs, Smithfield has a secondary water supply provided by a 12-inch-diameter, 40-foot-deep well located at Forrester Acres, west of the city. Water is pumped from this well during 3 or 4 months out of the year, only as a secondary water source to provide for residential summer irrigation. This well was modified to be able to supply up to 1500 gallons per minute but rarely runs at such capacity[4]. With full use of the springs and supplementation from the well, a minimum of 77 million gallons of water per month can be supplied to Smithfield at all times.

The current water supply is enough to sustain the residents of Smithfield. However, the population of Smithfield City is growing rapidly; therefore, additional water must be found to supply the future residents of Smithfield. The population, as of now, is about 6800 people[5]. The average water use per service is

Sections numbered per CSE multiple-numeration style

Introduction

Problem statement

Page number centered at the bottom of each page

36,862 gallons per month. Our predictions show that 14,346 people will be living in Smithfield City by the year 2030 and the amount of water they use will average approximately 144.52 million gallons per month, assuming the amount of water use per service remains constant. Appendix B contains the equation used to predict the population growth and a yearly prediction of population for the next 25 years. Appendix C contains information on the current and projected water use.

The difference between the minimum current water supply for Smithfield (77 million gallons per month) and the predicted water use in 25 years (144.52 million gallons per month) is 67.52 million gallons per month. We used 70 million gallons per month as the amount of water that Smithfield needs to meet the water demand in the year 2030.

First-level heads centered

2.0 Four Proposed Alternative Solutions

Literature review included in discussion of proposed solutions

Given the problem of finding an additional water supply, we researched Smithfield's current population and water supply to make predictions for the next 30 years. We also researched 4 different alternatives to find out what would be the best option to meet the expected demand. The alternatives considered were (1) drill a new well, (2) take no action, (3) implement a dual water irrigation system, and (4) recycle graywater.

2.1 Drill a New Well

Second-level heads flush left and underlined

The 1st alternative is to drill a new well for culinary water. This new well will be located on the north end of the Smithfield City golf course. There is a large protected aquifer in that area[5]. The well will be about 400 feet deep, and it will use a 16-inch-diameter pipe. After the water leaves the well, it will pass through a chlorine gas chlorinator. The chlorine mixes with the water to disinfect it. Time is required for the chlorine to treat the water, so the water will enter an 18-inch pipe to slow down the velocity of the water. The water will then travel 2500 feet to connect with the existing water lines[5]. The system will be run automatically. Monitors in the storage tank and water lines will inform a computer when the storage supply is low. The computer will then activate the well to supplement the water demand. When the storage water is sufficiently recharged, the computer will shut down the well, thus conserving energy and the water in the aquifer.

Source cited by superscript number.

2.2 Take No Action

The 2nd alternative is that of no action. This means that Smithfield's water system would remain the same and run at present capacity.

2.3 Implement a Dual Water Irrigation System

The 3rd alternative that was considered is the implementation of a dual water irrigation system. A dual

3

water system consists of 2 parts: (1) a culinary distribution system to provide potable water for residential use and (2) a distribution system to provide untreated, "raw" water for irrigation purposes[11]. Approximately 65 percent of the households in Smithfield are currently using some type of dual water irrigation system. Almost all of those using the current dual system are supplied water by Smithfield Irrigation Company[5]. Implementation of a dual system would consist of routing canals and irrigation lines to those residences that are not using dual water and also to any new homes in the city. Under this alternative, irrigation would be provided separately for everyone, and the strain on the culinary supply would be reduced.

2.4 Recycle Graywater

The 4th alternative that was considered is recycling graywater. Recycling graywater is a relatively inexpensive and effective way to reuse waste water. Graywater is defined as "untreated household wastewater which has not come into contact with toilet waste. Graywater includes used water from bathtubs, showers, bathroom wash basins, and water from clothes washing machines and laundry tubs. It shall not include wastewater from kitchen sinks or dishwashers"[8].
A schematic of graywater reuse for a typical

residential home is listed in Appendix D, Figure D-1. After clear water has been used in a home, it becomes graywater. The water then goes through a settling and filtration process; it then can be reused in some areas of the home. Graywater is most suitably reused for subsurface irrigation such as that of nonedible landscape plants. This cuts down on the amount of culinary water used for lawn irrigation. All of the information (including values) given under this alternative is given under the assumption that, as with the dual system, only 35 percent of the present homes in Smithfield City would be affected by a graywater system. A graywater system will be useless to the people who receive irrigation water separately from their culinary supply. We assumed that the number of connections that currently use water from the canal irrigation system will remain relatively constant through the next 25 years.

3.0 Research Methods

3.1 Five Evaluative Criteria

Each of the alternatives we have described has been examined with respect to 5 criteria. The criteria we have selected, in order of significance, are (1) cost of implementation, (2) feasibility, (3) adequacy of supply, (4) maintenance required, and (5) impact on the environment.

5

Table 1 shows the alternatives and the criteria. The alternatives are ranked on a scale from 0 to 2, 0 being the least favorable and 2 being the most favorable. The rankings are multiplied by a weighting factor of 1, 2, or 3, depending on the importance of the criterion involved. A description of our criteria is as follows:

1. Cost—The complete cost of installation and implementation of the alternative
2. Feasibility—The ease of implementation and whether it is allowable
3. Adequacy—Whether or not it will supply a sufficient amount of water
4. Maintenance—The person-hours and cost for upkeep

Table used to report data

Table 1 Weighted Selection Criteria for Water Supply Alternatives

		Alternatives			
Multiplier	Criterion	Well	No Action	Dual Water	Reuse
3	Cost	2	2	1	0
2	Feasibility	2	2	1	0
2	Adequacy	2	0	0	0
2	Maintenance	1	1	2	1
1	Environment	1	2	1	2
	TOTALS	17	14	10	4

5. Impact on the Environment—How the alternative affects land usage and habitat

Based on our findings and the rankings provided by Table 1, our recommendation to Smithfield City is to construct a new well to provide water for its domestic supply.

In sections 3.2–3.5, students analyze the four alternatives in detail, in light of their criteria.

4.0 Results and Discussion

With the increasing population, Smithfield City has concerns over water demand. Our research shows that with the increasing population, Smithfield will need to provide more water for its citizens. We developed alternatives to help Smithfield meet demands.

Given the 4 alternatives—groundwater well, no action, dual water system, and water reuse—we believe constructing a groundwater well is the best choice for the City of Smithfield. For a reasonable price, an efficient well can be built to meet the predicted needs of Smithfield with low maintenance and minimal impact to the environment. The well could carry Smithfield for many years to come.

Statement of suggested solution to the problem

7

CSE citation-name citation style

Appendix A

References

Personal communication

1. Burgess M, Distributor, Fairbanks Morse Pump Corp. 2003 Dec 3. [Personal communication].

Journal article

2. Carter R. 1994. Trickle-down economy. Sierra. 79: 18-19.

Page nos. Title Journal Volume

3. [DWR] Division of Water Resources. 1992. State water plan—Bear River Basin executive summary [Internet]. Available from: www.nr.state.ut.us/WTRRESC/WTRRESC.htm. Accessed 2003 Nov 8.

4. [Forsgren] Forsgren Association, Inc. 1995. Computer simulation and master plan for domestic water system: prepared for the Smithfield City Corporation. Salt Lake City: Forsgren Assoc., Inc.

5. Gass J, Smithfield City Engineer. 2003 Nov 8. [Personal communication].

Internet source

6. Gelt J. 1993. Home use of greywater: rainwater conserves water—and may save money [Internet]. Available from: www.ag.arizona.edu/AZWATER/arroyo/071.rain.html. Accessed 2003 Nov 8.

Technical report

7. [IAPMO] International Association of Plumbing and Mechanical Officials. 1996. Uniform plumbing code. Los Angeles: Plumbing Assoc.

8. Pope T. 1995. Greywater, a recyclable resource [Internet]. Available from: www.waterstore.com/article1.html. Accessed 2003 Nov 8.

9. [Roscoe] Roscoe Moss Co. 1995. The engineers' manual for water well design. Los Angeles: Roscoe Moss Co.

10. Rowland P. Assistant City Engineer. 2003 Nov 17. [Personal communication].

11. [Vaughn] Vaughn Hansen Associates, in association with CH2M Hill and Water Research Laboratory, State University. 1995. Identification and assessment of certain water management options for the Wasatch Front: prepared for the State Division of Water Resources.

12. Wilding D, Water Department Head. 2003 Dec 2. [Personal communication].

In addition to Appendix A (References), students included the following appendixes:
Appendix B: Population Projections
Appendix C: Projection of Water Flow Rates
Appendix D: Schematic of Graywater Reuse System
Appendix E: Individual Cost of Water Well Construction
Appendix F: Discussion of Cost of Implementation of a Dual System
Appendix G: Calculations for Percentage of Water Use

Research in the Natural Sciences

See Ch. 8

See Ch. 21

Scientists were quick to see that technology could help with research and writing. As a student of the natural sciences, you too should familiarize yourself with the available resources, particularly those in library databases and on the Internet. (See Chapter 8 on types of library databases and Internet resources and how to use them.) An extended listing of useful Internet sites for the natural sciences follows. Numerous natural sciences discussion groups, bulletin boards, and newsgroups can also be found via an Internet search. (See Chapter 21 for information on using computer networks.)

Useful Web Sites for Research in the Natural Sciences

Biology and Animal Science

National Science Foundation <http://www.nsf.org>
American Institute of Biological Sciences <http://www.aibs.org/core/index.html>
Biozone <http://www.biozone.co.nz/links.html>
American Society of Animal Science <http://www.asas.org>

Science writing and ESL

Botany and Plant Genetics

Genetics <http://www.biology.arizona.edu/mendelian_genetics/mendelian_genetics.html>
Bio Online <http://bio.com>

Chemistry

American Chemical Society <http://acswebcontent.acs.org/home.html>
The Learning Matters of Chemistry <http://www.knowledgebydesign.com>

Computers

Electronic Frontier Foundation <http://www.eff.org>
Internet Society <http://www.isoc.org>

Engineering
American Society for Engineering Education <http://www.asee.org>
Cornell's Engineering Library <http://www.englib.cornell.edu>

Environment and Ecology
The Environmental Defense Fund <http://www.environmentaldefense.org/home.cfm>
International Institute for Sustainable Development <http://www.iisd.org>
National Wildlife Federation <http://www.nwf.org>

Geology
Geological Society of America <http://www.geosociety.org>
American Geological Institute <http://www.agiweb.org>
Geological Surveys and Natural Resources <http://www.lib.berkeley.edu/EART/surveys.html>

Health Sciences
National Institutes of Health <http://www.nih.gov>
World Health Organization <http://www.who.int/en>

Mathematics and Statistics
American Mathematical Society <http://www.ams.org>
Math Archives <http://archives.math.utk.edu>
National Council of Teachers of Mathematics <http://www.nctm.org>

Physics and Astronomy
American Institute of Physics <http://www.aip.org>
American Physical Society <http://www.aps.org>

Wildlife and Fisheries
National Audubon Society <http://www.audubon.org>
National Fish and Wildlife Foundation <http://www.nfwf.org>
U.S. Fish and Wildlife Service <http://www.fws.gov>

See 21c-2

EXERCISE 17.1 Investigate the Web sites available for one of the disciplines within the natural sciences. Search by topic for a newsgroup or a bulletin board.

FOR COLLABORATION Bring to class a printout of a Web site that you found in your disciplinary Internet search. Share the information with a small group of your peers. What kinds of resources are available for the disciplines within the natural sciences?

18 Writing in the Social Sciences

FAQs

- What makes writing in the social sciences different from writing in other sciences? (18a)
- What kinds of writing assignments can I expect in social science courses? (18a)
- How should I use the scientific method in a social science report? (18a-1)
- What discipline-specific techniques can I use to write persuasively about the social sciences? (18b)
- How can I find information for a social science research paper? (18d)

The social sciences—psychology, anthropology, political science, sociology, and education—focus on the systematic study of human behavior and human societies. They are comparatively young disciplines; most came into their own in the early twentieth century. In part to establish their academic credibility, they adopted methods used in the natural sciences. Today, many social scientists use the scientific method to study people: they develop hypotheses and then design and conduct controlled experiments to test those hypotheses.

See 17a

18a Know the different types of writing in the social sciences

Social science links

The goal of any science is the systematic, objective study of phenomena. Social scientists cannot observe human emotions and consciousness directly, so they study the only objectively observable aspect of people: behavior. They then write to convey research findings discovered through those observations. Writing often begins with the careful recording of field or observation notes.

From these notes, the social scientist formulates a hypothesis, and then he or she seeks to test that hypothesis through further systematic experiments or observations. Notes from these experiments are then analyzed and compared to the hypothesis. Finally, the social scientist writes a conclusion explaining how the experimental and observational data supported, refuted, or modified the initial hypothesis. The entire process is typically recounted in a research report. Then that research report and others are typically summarized and evaluated by other social scientists in a review of literature.

1 Research or case study report

Most social science writing, like natural science writing, takes the form of research reports and case study reports. Research reports are based on primary research conducted by social scientists using interviews, surveys, questionnaires, and the like.

Because much of what social scientists study has not been examined before, they often collect and analyze their own data, announcing their results in research reports. One well-known example is Stanley Milgram's book-length research report *Obedience to Authority: An Experimental View* (New York: Harper, 1974). Milgram, a Yale psychologist, sought to determine to what extent ordinary individuals would obey the orders of an authority figure. Through his experiment, he hoped to probe the psychological processes that allowed the Germans to carry out mass human extermination during World War II. The research process Milgram used closely followed that of other scientific researchers. He began with a question: How could Hitler have succeeded in marshaling so much support from those who were called on to carry out his inhuman orders? After much preparation, Milgram designed and conducted an experiment to test his hypothesis. Using simulated shock experiments, which he admitted were controversial, Milgram showed that an alarming proportion of adults (65 percent of those tested) were willing to inflict severe and, as far as they knew, permanent damage on strangers simply because they were instructed to do so by an authority figure—in this case the experimenter. From the results of these tests, Milgram concluded that, indeed, many people will follow immoral orders, particularly when acting out of a sense of duty and obligation to someone in command.

Whether it summarizes years of laboratory experiments on human motivation or presents the results of a survey conducted in class, a research report in the social sciences typically follows the same pattern as a research report in the natural sciences. (The structure of a typical research report is detailed in 17a-1.) Many research reports begin with a brief review of the literature, to set the current study in context.

See 17a-1

❷ Review of literature

Researchers need to know what other researchers have found so that they can replicate the experiments, either to confirm or to disprove the hypotheses. Students and scholars should be aware of current controversies in their fields so that they can present balanced reports and make observations and contributions of their own. Scholars in a field often publish reviews of literature, in which they analyze, critique, and discuss journal articles. These literature reviews, or summaries, can take a variety of forms—the same forms found in the natural sciences.

See 17a-2

18b Write persuasively about social science

Most writing in the social sciences is argumentative. You need to take a stand or make a claim about an issue and then argue for that position, supporting your argument with primary research and/or secondary sources.

As a student, when you write about the social sciences generally you are responding to an assignment. If the assignment calls for primary research, you will probably need your instructor's help in designing an appropriate method for collecting data. (For information on how to report primary research, see 17a-1.)

See 17a-1

If your instructor has not assigned a particular topic, you can turn to the media—television, radio, magazines, and the Internet—for ideas. Look for controversies about human behavior and begin to ask questions about them. For example, a magazine article on the influence parents have on their children's use of alcohol or drugs might lead you to wonder if there really is a connection between parenting and drug use. If so, who researched the connection and what exactly did they discover?

❶ Determining audience, persona, and arguments

See 3b-2

Once you have a topic, you can establish a rhetorical stance. First, ask yourself who your audience will be. Usually you can assume that you are writing for intelligent readers who are interested in the subject but may not know much about the topic. You should provide enough background information so that such readers will be able to follow your argument. Knowing who your readers are will help you to determine which arguments will be the most persuasive. Your persona will most likely be straightforward and you will adopt a relatively formal tone. Look in the assignment for key terms such as *analyze* or *discuss*, which imply interpretation or critique, as you decide your purpose. Your instructor will no doubt expect you to write a piece that makes a point, supported by your secondary sources.

❷ Writing a thesis

See 3e-1 to 3e-2

The thesis of a social science paper will generally relate to a claim about a particular kind of observed behavior. With regard to children and drugs, for example, you might claim (based on a literature review and/or observational or survey data) that, indeed, parents are the most important determining factor in whether their children ever experiment with alcohol and drugs.

❸ Completing the research and writing your paper

See Chs. 3 and 6

See Ch. 3, Part 2, and 18d

Refer to Chapters 3 and 6 for advice on prewriting, drafting, revising, and editing. The writing habits that you have developed in English courses will serve you well in the social sciences; try keeping a journal on your reading, exploring through brainstorming or clustering, or working collaboratively with peers. If your paper consists of or includes a literature review, refer to Part 2 for information on library research. See the list of reference materials commonly used in the social sciences.

18c Review a sample research report in APA style

See Ch. 13

In a first-year liberal arts and sciences course, students worked with partners on a primary research project that included a brief review of the literature. Notice how the student authors begin with an overview of the current research on the study habits of introverts and extroverts. Then, they report the results of their own research, which tested the findings in the literature review against the experiences of their fellow students. Brandy and Sarah used a typical research report format for their paper, following the conventions of the American Psychological Association (APA).

INTROVERTS AND EXTROVERTS 1

An Investigation of the Study Habits of
Introverts and Extroverts

Group: True Colors
Brandy Black
Sarah Summers
Liberal Arts and Sciences 124
Professor Long

October 30, 2006

Title page

If the paper is being submitted for publication, include the shortened title to be used as a header on every page of the printed version

Title

Student and course identification; if submitting for publication, use author names and academic affiliation instead

Include the date when submitting for a course assignment

An abstract is a brief (no more than 120 words) summary of the paper, often included in social science papers

Abstract

This research report reviews the literature on student study habits and presents information from our research about ways in which students on our campus study. We reviewed several articles on study habits in journals such as *Psychological Reports, Personality and Individual Differences,* and *The Journal of Research in Personality*. We also investigated the study habits of two student personality types on our campus: introverts and extroverts. Our research included a four-page survey about academic success and study habits (which we asked 15 students to answer) and a six-day study log to chart the length of study time, duration of breaks, and type of studying. This report shows that our own research, for the most part, replicated the findings of many of the national studies.

INTROVERTS AND EXTROVERTS 3

An Investigation of the Study Habits of Introverts and Extroverts

Research about personality types and their study habits has become increasingly important. In particular, psychologists have studied how to recognize personality types of students and how to teach different kinds of students. Because of this national interest, we decided to investigate the study habits of two personality types, introverts and extroverts. We began this study with two general assumptions. First, we thought that introverts would be less socially active in their study habits, spend more time studying, and have a higher degree of academic success. Second, we thought that extroverts would study in groups, study less, and have slightly lower grades. In order to investigate our assumptions, we read several articles in journals such as *Psychological Reports, Personality and Individual Differences,* and *The Journal of Research in Personality.*

We constructed a four-page survey about academic success and study habits which we asked 15 students to answer. In addition, we also created a six-day study log to chart the length of study time, duration of breaks, and type of studying done by the students. The purpose of this research report is to review the literature and to present information from our own research. This report shows that

Title

Double-spaced text

Hypothesis

Background information

Thesis

First-level heading is centered and bold

Others' research is reviewed and summarized

Next level heading is set flush on left margin and bold

In APA style, source citations include last name and date, with a comma

Brackets show wording change

our own research, for the most part, replicated the findings of many of the national studies. Information in this paper will be presented in two sections. First, findings from the larger, national studies will be summarized. Then, findings from our study will follow.

Literature Review

According to national studies, there are three major trends used in tracing the academic life of extroverts and introverts. The first trend is the academic success of the student, classified into self-rated academic success and actual degree of success. The second trend is preferred study locations and situations. The third trend is the number of study breaks taken by extroverts and introverts, measured by frequency and duration.

Academic Success

Several studies chart the success of extroverted and introverted students. These have divided academic success into two categories: self-rated academic success (Irfani, 1978) and the actual degree of success (Furnham & Medhurst, 1995; Olympia et al., 1994). One study showed that more extroverts than introverts rated themselves as academically successful (Irfani, 1978). So, according to this study, "the possibility [that] a student will rate himself academically successful is likely to be

INTROVERTS AND EXTROVERTS 5

greater when the student is extroverted rather than introverted" (Irfani, 1978, p. 505).

In contrast, another national study found that "stable introverts [are] the highest academic performers" (Furnham & Medhurst, 1995, p. 197). This study charted the actual degree of academic success and concluded that "introverts predominate among outstanding students" (p. 207). It was also noted that although introverts are frequently among the top students, the GPA of introverts and extroverts differs only slightly.

Preferred Study Locations and Situations

Several studies addressed preferred study locations and discussed whether students favored working in groups or alone. One report concluded that introverts choose to study where the number of people and amount of stimulation is minimized (Campbell & Hawley, 1982, p. 141). Group study is usually minimal because introverts study better when they are not being distracted. Introverts tend to select study environments that have few or no people, such as their bedroom. When they study in libraries, they prefer locations that allow them to be alone.

When we look at preferred study environments and study groups for extroverts, the results are nearly the opposite. Campbell and Hawley (1982) found that "extroverts . . . prefer locations where socializing

Running heads should be set UPPER CASE and flush left on every page

Direct quotations require a page number in the citation

The relevant literature under each topic is reviewed

opportunities abound and the level of external stimulation is high" (p. 141). Extroverts typically spend more time studying in groups and choose "busier" locations to study in, such as student centers and dining halls. Campbell and Hawley stated that "the typical extrovert is sociable, . . . needs to have people to talk to, and does not like reading or studying by himself" (p. 139). If extroverts do study at the library, they "occupy library study locations which maximize external stimulation" (Campbell, 1983, p. 308). These reports suggest that introverts and extroverts differ in regard to study location and studying in groups.

Number of Study Breaks

Campbell and Hawley (1982) discovered that there were differences in the frequency of breaks and the reason for taking these breaks between introverts and extroverts. Introverts prefer study locations without a lot of external stimuli so they are not distracted or influenced to take breaks. Consequently, they study for longer periods of time before they take a break. On the other hand, because extroverts are sociable and prefer to study in areas where there is a great deal of external stimulation, they are more easily distracted, leading to a higher frequency of breaks.

The hypothesis to be tested is stated

According to the national research reports, we expected to find differences in the study habits of introverts and extroverts in our own research, as follows: extroverts should rate themselves higher than introverts for academic success; the average GPA should be fairly similar between the two groups; introverts should prefer to study alone in quiet places while extroverts should prefer groups in busier places; and introverts should take fewer study breaks.

Methods: The State University Study

The primary research study is described and the results discussed

To determine how state university students would compare to reports found in our literature review, we administered a four-page questionnaire to 15 students. We also asked the students to keep a six-day study log. The methodology used to create this questionnaire follows.

Developing the Research Questions

We designed a questionnaire to learn about the academic life of introverts and extroverts. The main areas we wanted this questionnaire to address were

1. How do students view themselves? As introverts or extroverts? As successful academically?
2. Do introverts or extroverts do better in school?
3. Do introverts and extroverts study differently?

After writing these research questions, we were able to design the actual questionnaire. We randomly selected 15 students in the library who agreed to answer the questionnaire. The students were given a brief personality survey to determine whether they were introverted or extroverted. The subjects were divided into two groups: 8 introverts and 7 extroverts. Thirteen of the students also agreed to keep a six-day study log.

Students analyzed other demographics as well—years in school, gender, marital status, number of roommates, and number of children. Then they analyzed the academic success, time management skills, study habits, and preferred study situations and locations of their subjects by using the questionnaire and study log data.

Results and Discussion

Demographic Information

The following demographic information was obtained in order to categorize our subjects. Students were asked to check off their age from a range of ages 18 through 26. From Table 1 it can be seen that the majority of the students that we surveyed fell in the 18-20 range.

Table is used to report data

Table 1

Age of Subjects

Age	<18	18–20	21–23	24–26
Introvert	0	63%	25%	12%
Extrovert	0	71%	29%	0%

Results of the study are compared to the hypothesis

Conclusions

In comparing the national studies with our state university study, we made several observations about the three major trends we had intended to address. Our first trend dealt with academic success. Both studies agreed that the GPA is only slightly different between introverts

INTROVERTS AND EXTROVERTS 9

and extroverts. In the national studies, more extroverts rated themselves as academically successful. In contrast, our study showed more introverts rated themselves as academically successful.

The second trend dealt with the preferred study locations and situations of introverts and extroverts. The national studies concluded that introverts liked quiet environments; however, our study showed that the majority of introverts preferred to listen to music while studying. Both the national studies and our study concluded that introverts like to be alone while studying and that extroverts prefer group study. Our final trend dealt with the frequency of study breaks. Our study showed that introverts took fewer study breaks than extroverts, which agreed with the national studies.

In two areas, results run counter to hypothesis

APA citation style

Initials

Date

Page numbers

Only first word and proper nouns are capitalized in article or book title

No quotation marks around title

Volume number is italicized; issue number is in parentheses and not italicized

Journal name, in capital and lowercase letters, is italicized

Article in online journal with retrieval statement

Following the References was Appendix A, which included Tables 2–7.

INTROVERTS AND EXTROVERTS 10

References

Campbell, J. B. (1983). Differential relationships of extraversion, impulsivity, and sociability to study habits. *Journal of Research in Personality, 17*(3), 308-313.

Campbell, J. B., & Hawley, C. W. (1982). Study habits and Eysenck's theory of extroversion-introversion. *Journal of Research in Personality, 16*(2), 139-146.

Furnham, A., & Medhurst, S. (1995). Personality correlates of academic seminar behavior: A study of four instruments. *Personality and Individual Differences, 19*(2), 197-208.

Irfani, S. (1978). Extroversion-introversion and self-rated academic success. *Psychological Reports, 43*(2), 508-510.

Olympia, D. E., Sheridan, S. M., Jenson, W. R., & Andrews, D. (1994). Using student-managed interventions to increase homework completion and accuracy. *Journal of Applied Behavior Analysis, 2*(1)7, 85-99. Retrieved from http://www.envmed.rochester.edu/

 18d Research in the social sciences

Social scientists were among the first to realize that technology could help with research and writing. As a student of the social sciences, you too should familiarize yourself with the available resources, particularly those in library databases and on the Internet. (See Chapter 8 on types of library and Internet resources and how to use them.) An extended listing of useful Internet sites for the social sciences follows. Numerous social sciences discussion groups, bulletin boards, and newsgroups can also be found via an Internet search.

See Chs. 8 and 21

Useful Web Sites for Research in the Social Sciences

National Council for the Social Studies <http://www.ncss.org>

Anthropology

American Anthropology Association <http://www.aaa.net.org>
Society for Applied Anthropology <http://www.sfaa.net>

Business and Economics

American Management Association <http://www.amanet.org/index.htm>
American Economic Association <http://www.vanderbilt.edu/AEA>
Library of Congress Business Resource References <http://www.loc.gov/rr/business/>

Ethnic Studies

National Association for Ethnic Studies <http://www.ethnicstudies.org>
University of Texas Internet Resources for African American Studies <http://www.utexas.edu/cola/centers/caaas/resources>
University of Georgia Institute for African American Studies <http://www.uga.edu/~iaas>
Asian Studies Resources <http://www.ibiblio.org/ucis/Asian.html>
University of Texas Asian Studies Network Information Center <http://asnic.utexas.edu/asnic/index.html>

Education

American Educational Research Association <http://aera.net>
Educator's Reference Desk <http://www.eduref.org>
Department of Education <http://www.ed.gov>

(continued)

(continued)

Journalism and Communication
CNN <http://www.cnn.com>
The New York Times on the Web <http://www.nytimes.com>
USA Today <http://www.usatoday.com>
Wall Street Journal <http://www.wsj.com>

Political Science
Political Science Resources on the Web <http://www.lib.umich.edu/govdocs/polisci.html>
International Society of Political Psychology <http://ispp.org>

Psychology
A Guide to Psychology Resources <http://www.guidetopsychology.com>
American Psychological Association <http://www.apa.org>

Sociology and Social Work
American Sociological Association <http://asanet.org>
Bureau of Justice Statistics <http://www.ojp.usdoj.gov/bjs>
Bureau of Labor Statistics <http://stats.bls.gov>
Statistical Abstract of the United States <http://www.census.gov/statab/www>

See 23c-2

EXERCISE 18.1 Investigate the Web sites available for one of the disciplines within the social sciences. Search by topic for a newsgroup or a bulletin board.

FOR COLLABORATION Bring to class a printout of a Web site that you found in your disciplinary Internet search. Share the information with a small group of your peers. What kinds of resources are available for the disciplines within the social sciences?

part

4

Document Design

19 The Basics of Good Design

FAQs

- How can I use principles of basic design to be a more effective writer? (19a)
- What is the standard format for academic papers? (19b-1)
- What tools do I have to organize and highlight information? (19b-2 to 19b-7)
- When is one type of graphic better than another? (19c)
- Is there anything I need to know about downloading graphics and images off the Web? (19d)

The key to designing effective documents—just as with *writing* effective documents—is understanding your audience and purpose. In making design choices, you should always consider who will be reading your document, why you are writing it, and why they will read it. Knowing your rhetorical stance will help you select the appropriate tools to use for your document.

There are three parts of designing an effective document:

Rules of document design

- *basic principles of good design*, which are consistent from one paper to the next;
- *formatting tools*, which allow you to organize and highlight information; and
- *graphic elements*, which allow you to illustrate information more effectively.

Keep in mind that all of these tools represent a *means to an end*—the accomplishment of your rhetorical purpose—and not an end in themselves. Good design enhances your rhetorical purposes—it doesn't simply decorate a page.

19a Follow the three basic design principles: clustering, contrasting, and connecting

Your writing will be more effective if you help your readers along by using basic principles of good design. Each of these—**clustering, contrasting**, and **connecting**—can support your message and encourage your reader to understand the purpose of your paper.

❶ Clustering: grouping closely related items

See Fig. 19.1

Look at the original title page from a student paper. All the information is there, but what you see is five separate pieces of information, each unrelated to the others. What are the logical groupings that the writer (Devon Johnson) could use? We can quickly identify three.

1. The title and subtitle
2. The title of the course and name of the instructor
3. The writer's name—and possibly a date

When Devon revises his title page into clusters, the information is clearer, and the important information stands out.

Most research suggests that we all learn more efficiently when information appears in clusters, or modules, and most textbooks cluster information in a variety of ways. One example is the FAQs box at the beginning of this chapter, where important points about what you'll find in the chapter are clustered together. These questions have a similar origin and purpose, so it makes sense to present them together. Clustering related elements together encourages readers to identify and understand those relationships.

❷ Contrasting: highlighting differences

When you flip through a textbook, which elements stand out? If you respond like most readers, you will say that the headings, which are set in a different (and usually larger and heavier) typeface, stand out from the rest of the text. Setting headings in larger, bolder type contrasts them with other parts of the text and makes it easy for readers to see them—and to understand that they represent important information.

Devon Johnson also uses contrasting typefaces in his title page, where the main title appears in larger, bolder type. The main title, which is the most

Figure 19.1 ▶ Grouping Related Items to Improve Layout

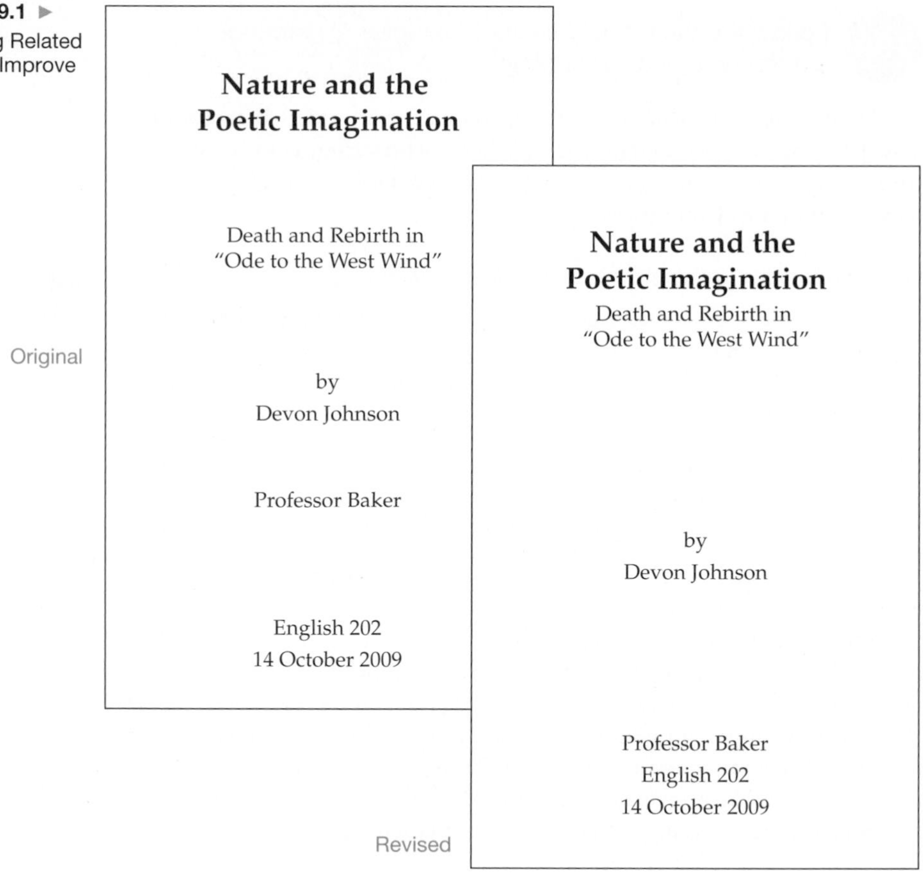

Original

Nature and the Poetic Imagination

Death and Rebirth in
"Ode to the West Wind"

by
Devon Johnson

Professor Baker

English 202
14 October 2009

Revised

Nature and the Poetic Imagination
Death and Rebirth in
"Ode to the West Wind"

by
Devon Johnson

Professor Baker
English 202
14 October 2009

important piece of information on the page, is *foregrounded*—that is, given more visual prominence. The other items on the page, being relatively less important, are given less visual prominence, or *backgrounded.*

❸ Connecting: relating every part to some other part

Information becomes more coherent when important graphic or typographic elements are repeated—that is, when different parts of a document are visually connected so that no single element is left stranded. These connections should not be haphazard, however. The connections you make through design should underscore connections in meaning, value, or purpose. For example, in this handbook, the headings and subheadings are set in different colors and sizes:

- All the chapter titles are one size and one color.

19 The Basics of Good Design

- The most important (or A-level) heads are another.

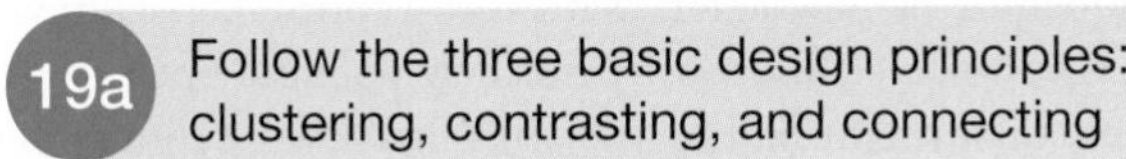

19a
Follow the three basic design principles: clustering, contrasting, and connecting

- The next important (B-level) are a third.

❸ Connecting: relating every part to some other part

Creating these connections among heads makes it easier for readers to skim through the chapters and see how sections are related.

EXERCISE 19.1 Design your own business card or greeting card, adhering to the principles in this section. Try using the document design program on your computer, if it has one.

FOR COLLABORATION Bring examples of advertisements from the Internet, newspapers, or magazines, and discuss with your group the effectiveness of each example. Try to bring both good and bad examples from each genre.

19b Use formatting tools

Thirty years ago, students using typewriters had very limited tools available for formatting papers. They could set margins, and they could use ALL CAPITALS for titles or heads, or indent heads differently. But that was about it. By contrast, you now have an almost bewildering array of tools available—hundreds of fonts that come in not just boldface and italic but in unlimited colors and sizes; imported graphics and images; the ability to turn text into tables or graphs, to wrap text around images, to box text; and on and on. How do you make decisions? As with all effective communication, it depends on who your readers are and what you want to accomplish.

See 19e

If you are writing an academic paper for a college course, the choices you make will be confined by the conventions of the discipline in which you are writing. A business instructor, for example, may want more headings and graphics than an English instructor. You can probably be more creative if you are designing a brochure or newsletter. With many course papers now transmitted electronically, however, your instructor may be more open to your use of formatting tools than might be the case with hard copy submissions. The general guideline in designing and formatting your papers is to check with your instructor about his or her preferences.

1 Using standard academic formatting

Most academic papers follow similar rules for basic formatting like setting margins and spacing text. Following these guidelines will mean that, for most college courses, you are formatting your paper appropriately.

See Ch. 55

Margins. The standard margin for academic papers is 1 inch all around, to give the instructor space in which to write comments. This is also the default margin for most word-processing programs, so there's no need to reset margins. Similarly, most word processors are set to **left justify** your text—that is, start all lines at the left margin and leave the right margin ragged, thus avoiding the need to hyphenate at the end of a line.

If you prefer the more formal look of a commercial publication (like this textbook), you can set your text to **block justify**, starting lines at the left and ending them evenly at the right by clicking the appropriate icon in the toolbar.

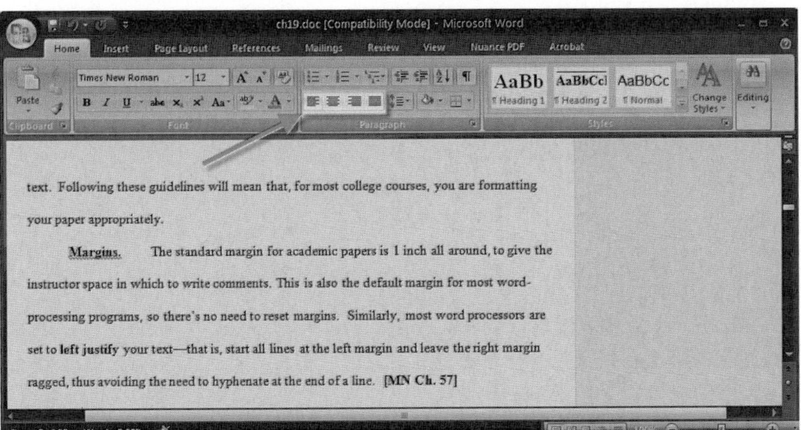

Figure 19.2 The toolbar icons to set left, center, right, or full (block) justified text in Microsoft Word 2007.

Block justification can look more elegant (especially in documents with columns, such as newspapers or brochures), but it can also leave unsightly gaps in lines unless you use appropriate hyphenation. A word processor can resolve this problem by automatically hyphenating lines, but the result may be another problem—too many hyphens. Use your best judgment in such cases. Either make manual adjustments in hyphenation, or revert to a ragged right margin.

Indentations. Academic papers typically use standard (and consistent) indenting: five spaces, or $^1/_2$ inch, at the beginning of each new paragraph. Software word-processing programs allow you to set these margins and this indentation automatically, using the PAGE SETUP command on the FILE menu, and the PARAGRAPH feature on the FORMAT menu.

Quotations that are longer than four lines of prose or three lines of poetry should be set off as a block, with each line indented ten spaces. This is simple to do electronically, either by using the ruler or by highlighting the entire quote and then using the ⇒ icon on the toolbar. In bibliographies, résumés, bulleted lists, and certain other types of writing, you may want to use **hanging indents**, where the first line begins at the left margin and the following lines are indented. Hanging indents can usually be set on the PARAGRAPH menu.

See Ch. 51

TechHelp

Numbering Pages

Page numbers make long papers easier to read and reference. To insert page numbers in Word, click on INSERT > PAGE NUMBERS, and then specify where you want the page numbers to be located. (Most academic papers are numbered in the upper right-hand corner.) Most instructors prefer that the first page not be numbered. Just uncheck the appropriate box on the PAGE NUMBERS menu to disable first-page numbering.

If you want to include additional information (your name, the course number or instructor's name, the date) use the VIEW > HEADER AND FOOTER menu.

See Student Papers: 6f, 11f, 16c, 17c, 18c

Spacing. Most instructors will want you to use double spacing throughout your paper (except perhaps in footnotes). Use FORMAT ⇒ PARAGRAPH to set line spacing in most word-processing programs. You should leave one space after all end punctuation (periods, question marks, and exclamation points), and after commas, semicolons, colons, and each dot in ellipses.

❷ Using headings to organize your message

Headings represent the basic building blocks of any paper—they reflect the underlying structure of the paper and lead readers through the information you are presenting. Headings allow readers to skim a text and identify its basic argument (such readers are common in business and the professions), and they provide signposts for close readers, leading them from one major concept to the next. College instructors may have particular requirements about the use of headings, particularly in short papers, so always check with your instructor about whether she or he wants headings included in your paper.

Headings inform. Headings should always be informative; that is, they should give the reader an idea of what the paper, section, or illustration is about. If this chapter had simply been called Chapter 19, you wouldn't have any idea what it was going to cover. The heads within this chapter tell you where sections begin and end. But long, descriptive labels can be confusing or distracting. *Try for informative headings that are no longer than four or five words.*

Headings reflect structure. Headings can also help you as you write to keep track of your overall plan. If you write an outline before you begin

Creating Headings

Guidelines

- Use grammatically parallel form for same-level headings.
  - **RIGHT:** Using headings effectively
    Formatting headings effectively
  - **WRONG:** Using headings effectively
    How to format heads effectively
- If headings are numbered or lettered, make sure the numbers or letters are accurate, sequential, and consistent.
- Use headings to show a hierarchical relationship. Headings should always reflect the connections between sections and let readers see quickly which sections are more important or larger in scope.

composing, you can often convert the main points of the outline into headings and subheadings for your paper. If you don't start with an outline, good headings should form one when you're done writing—you should be able to pull the headings out and clearly see the underlying organization of the text. Your headings should reflect connections.

See 19a-3

How many headings? Writers generally use from one to four levels of headings, depending on how complex the document is. In this chapter, for example, we use three levels in addition to the chapter title:

1. Level 1, or section headings

Use formatting tools

2. Level 2, or subsection headings

❶ Using headings to organize your message

3. Level 3 headings

Headings inform.

Each of these headings is designed with its own typeface, size, color, and indentation, so the headings are easily differentiated and clearly reflect their relationship to one another. Someone outlining this chapter could easily identify the key concepts and understand what content fits within each concept.

3 Using lists to organize information

Lists are a powerful form of visual clustering, showing how several things form a closely related set. There are two main types of list formats:

- A **numbered** (or **lettered**) list suggests that the items in the list are either ranked (more important to less important, for example) or sequential (steps to be followed in a process, for example). The TechHelp list below, for example, shows an order of steps to be followed.
- A **bulleted list** uses symbols—bullets (•) or checkmarks (✓), for example—to suggest that the items in the list are of equal importance and have no particular order. This list, for example, suggests that both numbered lists and bulleted lists are equally important.

Itemized lists break up the text on a page and can provide visual interest, but they attract a lot of attention from the reader, so be careful not to overuse them. If you use too many lists too close together, their effectiveness will start to blur. A good rule of thumb is to have no more than one itemized list per manuscript page or computer screen.

TechHelp

Creating an Itemized List

1. Introduce the list with a title or brief sentence describing the topic covered.
2. Click on the Numbering or Bullets icon in the toolbar or on the FORMAT menu to initiate the list, and the software will automatically format your list for you.
3. Edit to make sure that all items on the list are in the same grammatical form.

See Ch. 38

❹ Using typography to convey information effectively

It's hard to imagine a time when writers had only one size and typeface or **font** (Courier) available to them, and when type was always black—and yet that was true only thirty years ago, when almost all papers were composed on typewriters. Printing presses have always accommodated a wide range of fonts, or typefaces, but until the advent of computers, these were not available to everyday writers. The apparently endless array of typefaces, sizes, and colors available to us now may make it tempting to "decorate" your paper—just because you can. It's a temptation you should resist. In fact, you may want to check with your instructor about whether she prefers one font, or one size type, over another. Even if your instructor allows varied typography and color, these elements should always be employed rhetorically—that is, you should use fonts and color to reach your audience and achieve your purpose.

Typography refers to all the features associated with individual letters, numbers, and other symbols: font type, font style, font size, color, and case.

Font type refers to the actual design of the typeface. There are two basic categories of typefaces: **serif** and **sans serif**. Serif typefaces—like Courier, Times New Roman, and Garamond—include little decorative touches like tiny tails on the y, or little balls at the top of the f, called *serifs*. Serif typefaces are considered generally friendlier to the eye and easier to read. Sans serif typefaces—Helvetica and Arial for example—have no decorative flourishes and can offer a more modern, high-tech, stripped down look. Sans serif typefaces are typically used in advertisements, signs, and instructions. Whether you choose a serif or a sans serif font, confine yourself to standard typefaces. Very few instructors want to read a paper printed in *Rage Italic*, COPPERPLATE GOTHIC, or Bradley Hand.

Font style refers to the different variants of a single typeface: regular, *italic*, **bold**, or ***bold italic***. Italic, bold, and bold italic type can all be used for emphasis, but they have other uses as well. Standard document style guidelines use italic for titles of books, for example, and bold is often used to introduce new terms, particularly those that are in a glossary or are defined nearby (as in the eBook that is available with this book). Be consistent about using these variants—and be careful about over-using them. A page full of boldface terms risks confusing the reader, who can no longer tell what's important from what's not.

Font sizes, which determine the size of the type on the page, are measured in **points**. You can choose a type as small as 4 points or as large as 144, but for most academic papers, you will want to use 10 or 12 point type, with section headings and titles set larger. More specialized assignments—brochures, or newsletters, or bulletins—may use a wider range of type sizes and styles to distinguish sections and subsections.

5 Using boxes and borders to highlight information

A **box** is a rectangular container within which you can include text, graphics, or a combination of the two (see, for example, the TechHelp boxes throughout this book).

Boxes are especially useful for summarizing main points or procedural steps, because they simultaneously cluster these points or steps and set them off, through contrast, from the rest of the text. Boxes are commonly found in textbooks, handbooks, user manuals, and other instructional documents, but they are rarely used in academic writing. Check with your instructor about whether boxes are acceptable in his or her course. If they are, use them with caution—they can be tricky to position within your text. (To insert a text box, see INSERT menu.)

6 Using color to highlight information

Computers allow us to use color systematically in our writing for clarity, emphasis, and aesthetic appeal. You can use color to provide visual clustering for related items, to show connections among elements, or to create contrast between items—in other words, to support the basic principles of design. Here again, however, you need to think rhetorically—by using color here, am I helping my audience understand my message? Am I making my message more appealing—and therefore more likely to be read? Am I adding an emotional attraction to this document?

If you introduce color into your writing, make sure you use it consistently and systematically.

- Establish a color theme that promotes connections within the document. (The headings in this book use color systematically. Does the use of color help you understand the relationships among the headings?)
- To draw attention to one element, or contrast it with another, put one color against a very different background color.
- Take advantage of established meanings—like red for *warning*, or green for *safety*.

CULTURE/ LANGUAGE NOTE Bear in mind that color associations may vary from one culture to another. Black is associated with death in many cultures—but in others, white is.

Color may play a big role in informal writing in an electronic environment, but in academic papers, you will want to use it sparingly. Especially if your final product is hard copy, remember that only color printers and color copiers will be able to produce or reproduce the colors you have chosen.

The brochures in Figures 19.3 and 19.4 are examples of a poorly designed and well-designed document, respectively. The first doesn't follow basic design principles—it doesn't connect key information, it doesn't cluster information appropriately, and it uses contrasting color and typefaces inconsistently.

7 Using columns to cluster or contrast information

Documents like brochures, newsletters, résumés, and Web pages often use columns to connect or contrast related information or simply to break up a wide page of text. There are basically two kinds of columns:

See Ch. 20 (Sample Brochure), Ch. 22 (Sample Résumé)

- In **newspaper columns**, the text is continuous: It starts on the left, flows down the first column, and then continues at the top of the next column to the right. You can create newspaper columns with the COLUMNS feature on the PAGE LAYOUT menu, or by clicking on the columns icon on the toolbar.
- In **tabular columns**, two independent texts run side by side. Tabular columns are useful if you want to have text in one column and numerical data in another, as in a table, or to show different kinds of corresponding entries, as in a résumé. Tabular columns are created by using the TABLE feature on your toolbar or FORMAT menu.

Uses graphic inappropriately.

Doesn't visually connect key terms. [*Peer Court* and *volunteers*]

Evokes wrong color associations. [*students, offenders*]

Emphasizes wrong words. [courthouse address, *offenders*]

De-emphasizes important words. [*volunteers*]

Uses parentheses and @ sign inappropriately.

Puts related information into footnote.

Uses inconsistent typography.

Lacks visual balance.

SALT LAKE PEER COURT*

Is seeking volunteers (for the 2006/07 school year).

Work directly with **students** as they adjudicate, mediate, and mentor youth **offenders**.

Volunteers are needed (for Thurs. evenings from 6-8 PM) at the ***MATHESON COURTHOUSE, 450 SOUTH STATE STREET***.

Please contact: **Iris Salazar** in the Bennion Center @581-4811
e-mail Little Rainbo@yahoo.com
Kathleen Zeitlin or Lenna Penisi 322-1815

*(An alternative to juvenile court for youth offenders)

▲ **Figure 19.3** A Poorly Designed Flyer

SALT LAKE PEER COURT

An Alternative to Juvenile Court for Youth Offenders

Is Seeking

VOLUNTEERS

(for the 2006/07 school year)

Work directly with students as they adjudicate, mediate, and mentor youth offenders.

Volunteers are needed for Thursday evenings from 6-8 PM at the Matheson Courthouse, 450 South State Street.

PLEASE CONTACT:

Iris Salazar in the Bennion Center 581-4811

(e-mail **LittleRainbo@yahoo.com**)

Kathleen Zeitlin or Lenna Penisi 322-1815

Makes visual connections through color and typeface. [*Salt Lake Peer Court, Volunteers*]

Uses color contrasts for emphasis.

Emphasizes important words. [*volunteers*]

Uses graphic appropriately.

Uses consistent typography.

Uses color functionally.

Uses balanced layout.

Clusters appropriate information. [all contact info at bottom]

▲ **Figure 19.4** A Well-Designed Flyer

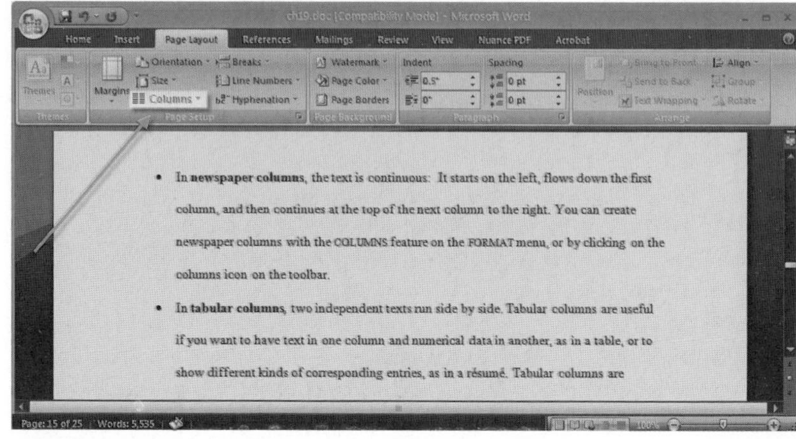

▲ **Figure 19.5** Use the columns icon to access settings for the number and size of columns in Microsoft Word 2007.

The power of illustrations

19c Use graphics appropriately

Graphics, which include tables, line graphs, bar graphs, pie charts, clip art, photographs, cartoons, drawings, maps, and other forms of visual art, can add interest and excitement to any document. They can help you engage your audience and support your message. Each type of graphic has

Guidelines

Using Graphics

1. Place the graphic near the text to which it relates.
2. Introduce each graphic with a text reference. For example, precede the graphic with a sentence ending in a colon or a brief parenthetical comment like "(see Figure 2)."
3. Use a caption that makes the graphic self-explanatory.
4. Keep the graphic as simple and uncluttered as possible.

◄ **Table 19.1** Effects of the Bush Tax Cuts, 2004–2010*

INCOME LEVEL	2004	2006	2008	2010
Lowest 20%	1.7	1.4	1.4	1.2
Second 20%	7.7	6.8	7.0	6.2
Third 20%	11.5	10.0	10.3	9.6
Fourth 20%	18.1	16.3	15.6	13.2
Highest 20%	61.0	65.4	65.7	69.8

*Projected percentage reduction in federal income taxes.
Source: Children's Defense Fund and Citizens for Tax Justice http://www.ctj.org./html/gwb0602.htm.

its own special uses and features. Graphics can add a lot of power to a document, but as with all enhancements, graphics should be used judiciously to emphasize or clarify an important point. Using too many graphics dilutes their effectiveness.

EXERCISE 19.1 Use information from Table 19.1 to create (a) a line graph, (b) a bar graph, and (c) a pie chart. In each case, write a caption that describes what the graph illustrates.

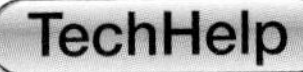

Editing Photographs Digitally

Many effective and easy-to-use photo editors are available, either in your campus computer lab or, as free shareware, on your home computer. All photo editors offer the same basic capabilities—they allow you to rotate, crop, resize, touch up, and apply special effects to pictures. Each program has its own way of doing these things, however, so the best way to learn a particular program is to experiment, explore menu options, and simply spend time getting to know how it works.

TYPE OF GRAPHIC | **USE THIS GRAPHIC TO** | **EXAMPLE**

Tables

Create tables by clicking on TABLE in the toolbar menu.

- Present lots of data in compressed form (as, for example, this table is doing).
- Organize numerical data conveniently.
- Draw readers' attention to data.

	1990	1999	2010	2020
Industrialized Countries	2,849	3,129	3,692	4,169
Eastern Europe, Former Soviet Union	1,337	810	978	1,139
Developing Countries	1,641	2,158	3,241	4,542
Asia	1,053	1,361	2,139	3,017
Middle East	231	330	439	566
Africa	179	218	287	365
Central and South America	178	249	377	595
Total World	5,827	6,097	7,910	9,850

Sources: 1990 and 1999: Energy Information Administration (EIA), *International Energy Annual 1999*, DOE/EIA-0219 (99). Washington: GPO, Feb. 2001. Projections: EIA, *World Energy Projection System*. Washington: GPO, 2002.

Line Graphs

Create line graphs by clicking on the INSERT > CHART icon, then choose a line graph from the available chart types.

- Make data more understandable.
- Show changes over time—especially continuous variation (as opposed to discrete points in time).
- Track several variables at once.
- Allow reader to see differences between data entries more clearly than in a table.

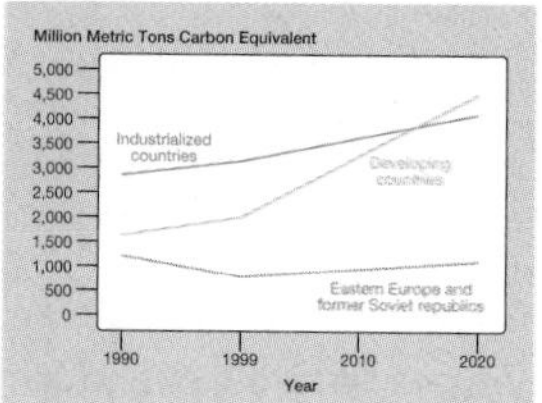

Bar Graphs

- Emphasize discrete points—end points rather than continuous variables.
- Show changes over time.
- Allow reader to see differences between data entries more clearly than in a table.

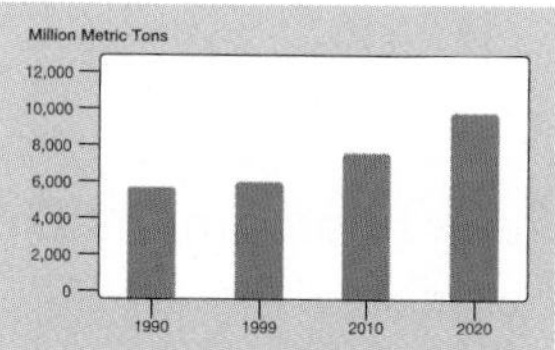

Pie Charts

- Show how a fixed quantity is divided into parts.
- Depict ratios rather than absolute quantities.

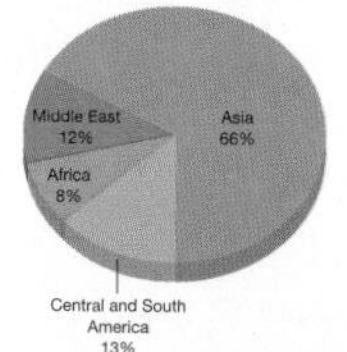

<table>
<tr><th>TYPE OF GRAPHIC</th><th>USE THIS GRAPHIC TO</th><th>EXAMPLE</th></tr>
<tr><td>Clip Art
Most word-processing programs offer small selections of free, downloadable clip art, and more is available by exploring the Web.</td><td>• Include a logo or icon in a brochure or advertisement.
• Add a decorative touch to a document.
Caution: Most instructors do not want academic papers "decorated" with clip art.</td><td></td></tr>
<tr><td>Diagrams
Diagrams, like other illustrations and photographs, cannot be republished (on a Web site, for example) without express permission of the copyright holder.</td><td>• Illustrate scientific, technical, or business documents.
• Provide step-by-step instruction.</td><td>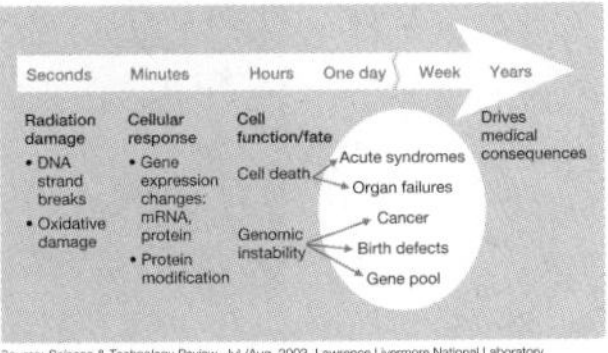

Source: Science & Technology Review, Jul./Aug. 2003, Lawrence Livermore National Laboratory.</td></tr>
<tr><td>Maps</td><td>• Illustrate historical or political documents.</td><td></td></tr>
<tr><td>Cartoons</td><td>• Illustrate persuasive documents.</td><td></td></tr>
<tr><td>Photographs
Digital photo-editors like Adobe Photoshop and Microsoft Picture It! are readily available.</td><td>• Add realism to a piece of writing, offering a "here and now" feeling.
• Illustrate historical conditions.
• Move readers emotionally.</td><td>
Phototake/NYC</td></tr>
</table>

The original and edited photos shown here illustrate how dramatic editing changes can be. The original is off-center, out of focus, and too dark. By cropping, resizing, and sharpening, and then increasing the dark-bright contrast, the photographer created a significantly more dynamic image.

	1990	1999	2010	2020
Industrialized Countries	**2,849**	**3,129**	**3,692**	**4,169**
Eastern Europe, Former Soviet Union	**1,337**	**810**	**978**	**1,139**
Developing Countries	**1,641**	**2,158**	**3,241**	**4,542**
Asia	1,053	1,361	2,139	3,017
Middle East	231	330	439	566
Africa	179	218	287	365
Central and South America	178	249	377	595
Total World	**5,827**	**6,097**	**7,910**	**9,850**

Sources: 1990 and 1999: Energy Information Administration (EIA), *International Energy Annual 1999*, DOE/EIA-0219 (99). Washington: GPO, Feb. 2001. Projections: EIA, *World Energy Projection System*. Washington: GPO, 2002.

◀ **Table 19.2**
Annual World Carbon Dioxide Emissions (million metric tons carbon equivalent)

Use a self-explanatory caption.

Place near related text.

Use an appropriate introductory phrase.

Use a simple, uncluttered design.

EXERCISE 19.2 Find an old photo that needs editing. Scan it into your computer. Then use a photo editor to make it better.

FOR COLLABORATION In a small group, share and discuss the photo you edited in Exercise 19.2. Do the changes create a more dynamic and emotionally arresting image?

TechHelp

Aligning Graphics with Text

1. Position your cursor where you want to insert the image.
2. Click INSERT > PICTURE.
3. Right-click on the image.
4. Click on FORMAT PICTURE > LAYOUT.
5. Select the desired option: to wrap text around the image or put it in front of or behind the image.

Lines highlighted with color.

Lines distinguished by color, dotted, etc.

Three or fewer lines avoid confusion.

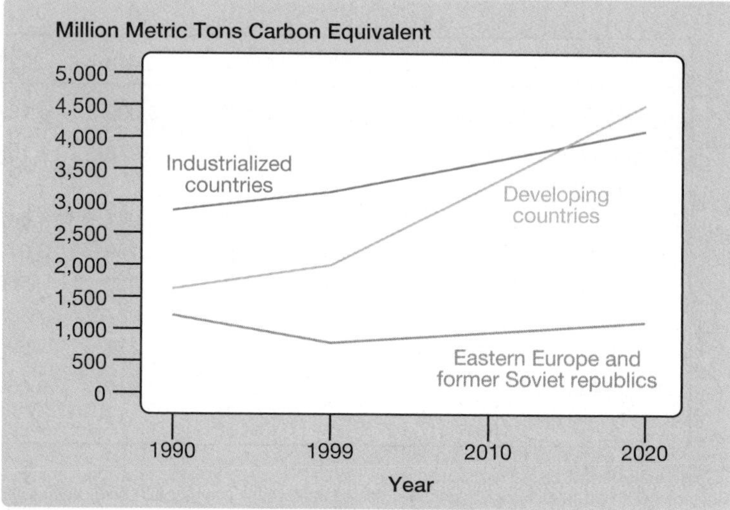

▲ **Figure 19.6 Model Line Graph: World CO_2 Emissions by Region, 1990–2020.** This figure converts the data from lines 1-3 of Table 19.2. Notice how much simpler it is to understand the relationships among the data.

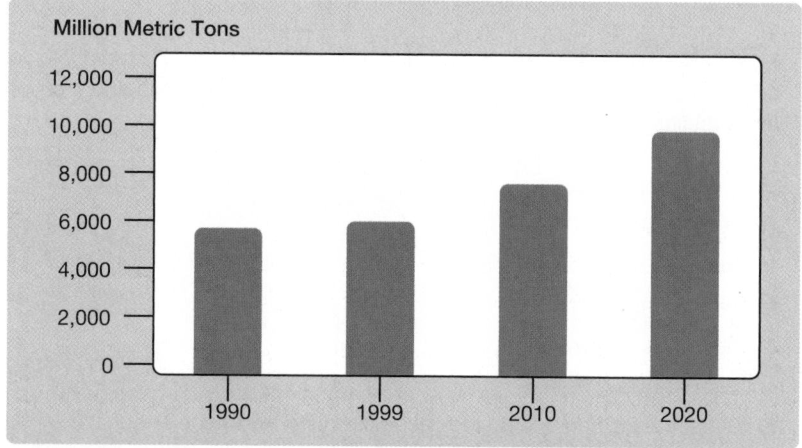

▲ **Figure 19.7 Model Bar Graph: Global CO_2 Emissions, 1990–2020.** The sheer weight of the bars emphasizes, more than the line graph, the increase in global CO_2 emissions that we will likely experience by 2020.

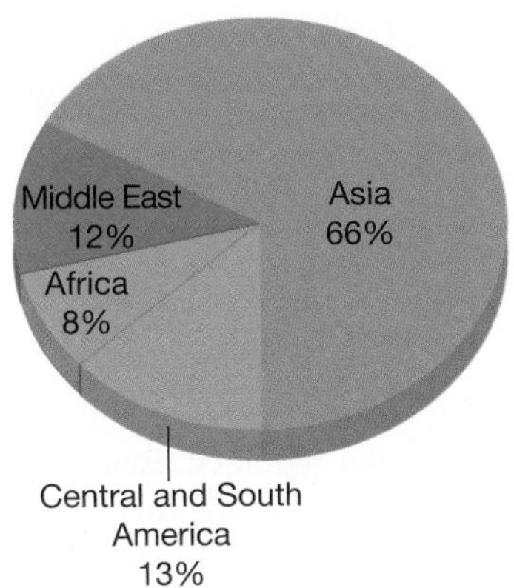

▲ **Figure 19.8 Model Pie Chart: Projected CO_2 Emissions in Developing Countries, 2020.** This pie chart reconfigures the information found in the Developing Countries section of the table in Figure 19.4. The projected accountability region by region for emissions is clearly apparent.

▲ **Figure 19.9 Sample Clip Art.** Scanners and downloading can make the process of integrating clip art into an electronic document very simple.

source: http://office.microsoft.com/en-us/clipart/results.aspx?CategoryID=CM790019351033

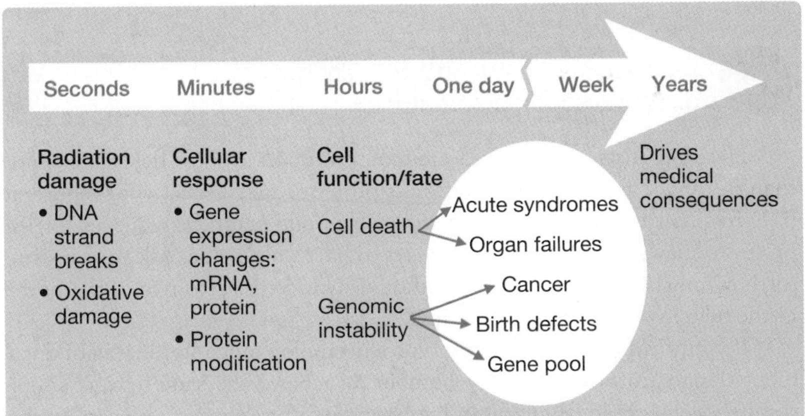

▲ **Figure 19.10 Sample Diagram: Response of an Organism to Heavy Doses of Ionizing Radiation.** This diagram, which shows the short- and long-term effects of the kind of radiation we get from medical procedures and electronic consumer products, captures a large amount of interrelated information in visual form—making it easier to comprehend than a straight text explanation.

Source: *Science & Technology Review*, Jul./Aug. 2003, Lawrence Livermore National Laboratory.

19d Use graphics ethically

Many wonderful images can be found on the Web. However, you need to be aware that all graphics, by virtue of their publication on the Web, are automatically copyrighted by the author. To use another person's graphics from a Web site, you must secure that person's permission. If an email address is included at a site, you can email the person and ask his or her permission to replicate the graphic. Or, you may find a statement on the page permitting certain limited, noncommercial uses of the graphics. **Remember: Using someone else's graphic without prior permission is a form of plagiarism.**

GO See 10a

Many sites on the Web were created specifically to make images available for use by others. A search engine will help you locate these images. For example, the *Google* and *AltaVista* search tools include image directories. Or, you can search by name for the image you are looking for. For example, if you are looking for a picture of a tiger, you can instruct the search engine to search for "tiger image."

19e Respect the norms and conventions of your discourse community

Headings, lists, and graphics are more common in some fields and genres than in others. For example, a business professor may expect your reports to have frequent headings and subheadings, lists, and graphics, while an English professor may expect your literary essays to have only a title. Ask your instructor how much "design" your paper should include. Be sensitive to the norms of the field in which you are working.

If your field of study does not typically employ much in the way of document design features, you may be able to achieve the same effects simply through well-crafted language. In literary essays, for example, you can emphasize main points by putting well-crafted topic sentences at the beginnings of paragraphs and by using parallelism, contrast, and other techniques.

See Ch. 39

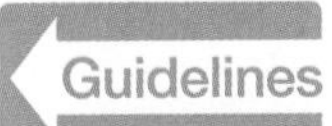

Reviewing a Document Onscreen

Check for and correct any of the following problems.

- **"Widowed" or "orphaned" lines.** Are any single lines stranded at the top or bottom of a page? Do any headings appear at the bottom of a page, with no text beneath them? You can avoid most widows and orphans in Word by clicking on FORMAT ⇒ PARAGRAPH ⇒ **LINE AND PAGE BREAKS**, and then checking the box for Widow and Orphan Control. Other programs have similar capabilities.
- **Interrupted lists.** Do any lists start on one page and end on the next—especially short lists? Readers will have trouble making connections in these cases. Most word-processing programs cannot control for this, so you will have to check all short lists visually.
- **Misplaced graphics or boxes.** Do all graphics and boxes appear on the same page as—or no more than one page away from—the text that refers to them? Are they centered, or appropriately placed on the page? To center a graphic in Word, position it to the left of the correct page, highlight it, and then click on the CENTER button in the toolbar. You can also position the graphic manually using the ruler, or use the PAGE SETUP menu to input the numbers for the placement desired.
- **Errors in page or section numbering.** Are your pages numbered correctly? If you have used numbered heads to identify sections, do these follow sequentially? Errors in numbering are likely to confuse and annoy readers. Your word-processing program can number the pages for you, and using outlining functions consistently through the development of your paper can help prevent problems with section numbering. Still, you should visually survey your paper to make sure all sections are properly numbered.
- **White space.** Are specific elements getting the appropriate emphasis? White space can make different elements (graphics, lists, and titles) stand out. By surveying your document in the PAGE LAYOUT or PRINT PREVIEW mode, you can decide whether your graphic and design elements are appropriately contrasted with the space around them. White space also offers your readers "breathing room" as they leaf through your document. Densely packed documents can seem overwhelming.

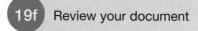

19f Review your document

See TechHelp box 11e-1

Before you print out a document, look at it carefully on screen. Make sure that the page numbers and headers or footers are set up as you want them to be. Reviewing the document is particularly important if you change from one printer to another, as you may need to adjust the formatting of the document to accommodate the fonts, spacing, and different graphics of the new printer.

The best way to review a document on a computer is by selecting either VIEW ⇒ PAGE LAYOUT or FILE ⇒ PRINT PREVIEW and then scrolling through to simulate a reader leafing through the document. A two-page view is especially useful with newsletters and brochures.

EXERCISE 19.3 Find a poorly formatted page from a user manual, junk mail, or the Internet. Referring to the principles discussed in this section, write a critique of the page; then reformat the document.

FOR COLLABORATION Share your critiques and reformatted documents with your group. Choose one document to reformat together, using the group's best suggestions for redesign.

20 Designing Specific Documents

FAQs

- How can using a brochure or newsletter template help me? (20a-1)
- How can I use white space and color effectively? (20a-2, 20b-2)
- What tools are available to help me plan a Web site? (20d)
- What is a storyboard? (20d-3)
- How can I help readers navigate through my Web site? (20d-4)
- How do I actually write for a Web site? (20e)

The basics of good design apply to any type of document you may need to design. Whether your document will ultimately be printed or posted to a Web site, the same general strategies and processes will help you develop and design a more effective document.

See Ch. 19

20a Produce a simple brochure

Desktop publishing

A brochure is designed to inform or persuade an uncommitted audience through use of text and/or graphics. Space is typically limited to a single folded sheet, and layout is designed for emphasis and readability.

❶ Making decisions about content

The content decisions you make when you produce a brochure should be based on a rhetorical analysis. Notice that the description of brochure characteristics addresses not only topic but also purpose, persona, and audience. A brochure is focused on a specific topic, and its purpose is clearly persuasive.

See 3b-2

In this section, we will follow a student as she produces a simple brochure. Felicia Alvarez set out to help advertise the school in which she worked part-time. The topic of the brochure was the school and its philosophy; the purpose was to inform the parents of prospective students about the school; the persona was that of an informed insider who knew much about the school and its philosophy; the readers were parents of prospective students.

Since Felicia was new to brochure writing, she turned to her word-processing program for help. She discovered that she could access, through the OFFICE button, a brochure template that provided a preset format she could adapt to her own needs.

Desktop publishing resources

❷ Making decisions about layout and design

Chapter 19 discusses three basic design principles, called the three C's: clustering, contrasting, and connecting. When you design a brochure, you

TechHelp

Using Document Templates

1. Templates in Word 2007 can be found by clicking the OFFICE button > NEW > INSTALLED TEMPLATES.
2. Select the desired template (for example, brochure, newsletter, memo, or report).
3. Follow the instructions within the template to begin designing your document and its content. For example, the "school brochure" template suggests that you use the body of the brochure to keep parents informed of school events.
4. Insert your own text and graphics into the template, using the model as a guideline for format and content.
5. Revise your document, observing the design principles described in this chapter and in Chapter 19.
6. In most programs, the template may be altered to fit your needs and saved for future use.

NOTE: These steps apply to *Word for Windows* and *WordPerfect*. For other word-processing programs, check your documentation.

See Ch. 19

must attend to all of these principles, paying particular attention to the following considerations.

- *An enticing cover.* To entice readers, use a combination of lively copy and strategically placed graphical images. Felicia decided to use a photograph of children from the school on the cover panel.
- *A cohesive story.* Once you have enticed readers to open the brochure, lead them through the text in a logical way. The text should tell a story; each panel should relate to the previous one and to those that follow. The template helped Felicia construct a logical story line for her brochure.
- *Coherent graphics.* In a brochure, graphics often play as important a role as copy in telling the story. Like the copy, the graphics should be logical and consistent. Several design features were incorporated into the brochure template Felicia used, including font styles and sizes, shaded boxes, icons, and line breaks. Such features help provide visual coherence throughout a brochure. Felicia added a photograph to draw readers in and color to provide additional coherence throughout the brochure.
- *Adequate white space.* Because the space available in a brochure is extremely limited, you should include only essential information. You can always provide readers with a method for obtaining more information, as Felicia did by including a phone number. Small chunks of text broken up by white space and informative headings, plus simple and direct language, help make a brochure readable. Aim for a 3:2 ratio between text and white space—that is, three parts of text for every two parts of white space.

❸ Refining the brochure

Once you have prepared the first draft of your brochure, print it out and evaluate it, keeping in mind the three C's of design. When Felicia printed her draft, she discovered that it did not make good use of the clustering principle—everything was too spread out and the photograph was too small. She revised by clustering related text together and by enlarging the photograph. She liked the contrast provided by the color in the headings and decided to repeat that design element in the shaded boxes.

Then Felicia looked for coherence or connectedness in her brochure. Did all of the elements connect to each other? After experimenting with various combinations of justifications (right, left, block), she decided that left justification would best show how each of the panels was connected to the others.

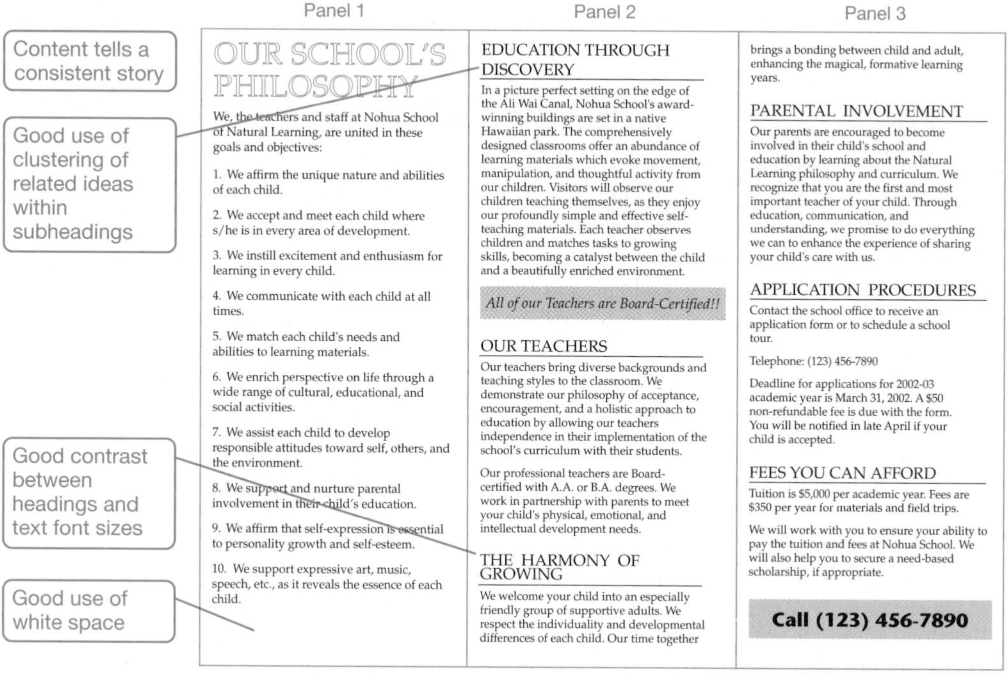

Content tells a consistent story

Good use of clustering of related ideas within subheadings

Good contrast between headings and text font sizes

Good use of white space

Panel 1

OUR SCHOOL'S PHILOSOPHY

We, the teachers and staff at Nohua School of Natural Learning, are united in these goals and objectives:

1. We affirm the unique nature and abilities of each child.

2. We accept and meet each child where s/he is in every area of development.

3. We instill excitement and enthusiasm for learning in every child.

4. We communicate with each child at all times.

5. We match each child's needs and abilities to learning materials.

6. We enrich perspective on life through a wide range of cultural, educational, and social activities.

7. We assist each child to develop responsible attitudes toward self, others, and the environment.

8. We support and nurture parental involvement in their child's education.

9. We affirm that self-expression is essential to personality growth and self-esteem.

10. We support expressive art, music, speech, etc., as it reveals the essence of each child.

Panel 2

EDUCATION THROUGH DISCOVERY

In a picture perfect setting on the edge of the Ali Wai Canal, Nohua School's award-winning buildings are set in a native Hawaiian park. The comprehensively designed classrooms offer an abundance of learning materials which evoke movement, manipulation, and thoughtful activity from our children. Visitors will observe our children teaching themselves, as they enjoy our profoundly simple and effective self-teaching materials. Each teacher observes children and matches tasks to growing skills, becoming a catalyst between the child and a beautifully enriched environment.

All of our Teachers are Board-Certified!!

OUR TEACHERS

Our teachers bring diverse backgrounds and teaching styles to the classroom. We demonstrate our philosophy of acceptance, encouragement, and a holistic approach to education by allowing our teachers independence in their implementation of the school's curriculum with their students.

Our professional teachers are Board-certified with A.A. or B.A. degrees. We work in partnership with parents to meet your child's physical, emotional, and intellectual development needs.

THE HARMONY OF GROWING

We welcome your child into an especially friendly group of supportive adults. We respect the individuality and developmental differences of each child. Our time together

Panel 3

brings a bonding between child and adult, enhancing the magical, formative learning years.

PARENTAL INVOLVEMENT

Our parents are encouraged to become involved in their child's school and education by learning about the Natural Learning philosophy and curriculum. We recognize that you are the first and most important teacher of your child. Through education, communication, and understanding, we promise to do everything we can to enhance the experience of sharing your child's care with us.

APPLICATION PROCEDURES

Contact the school office to receive an application form or to schedule a school tour.

Telephone: (123) 456-7890

Deadline for applications for 2002-03 academic year is March 31, 2002. A $50 non-refundable fee is due with the form. You will be notified in late April if your child is accepted.

FEES YOU CAN AFFORD

Tuition is $5,000 per academic year. Fees are $350 per year for materials and field trips.

We will work with you to ensure your ability to pay the tuition and fees at Nohua School. We will also help you to secure a need-based scholarship, if appropriate.

Call (123) 456-7890

▲ **Figure 20.1** Felicia's Brochure

So she changed the justification on the title, which the word-processing program had centered. She checked to make sure that all the text fonts were compatible, with the exception of titles (for contrast). She added a caption to the picture. Finally, she opened the brochure in the two-page VIEW window to verify that the alignment was consistent throughout. The finished brochure appears in Figure 20.1.

GO See TechHelp box 20a-1, Fig. 20.1

EXERCISE 20.1 Write a brochure to announce a party or to advertise a business or an event. First, decide who your readers will be and what information you will want to include. Then select a brochure template from your word-processing program. Enter text for the cover and for the other panels. Revise the brochure using the 3Cs of document design.

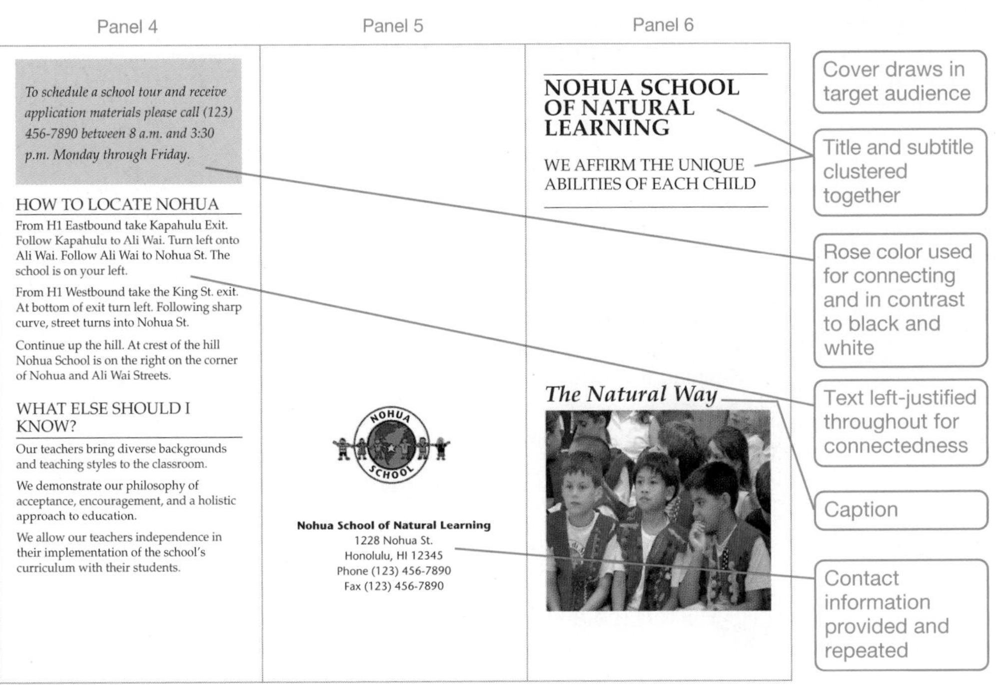

▲ **Figure 20.1** (cont.)

FOR COLLABORATION When you have completed the brochure, print it out, and ask a few friends or classmates to respond to these questions:

1. What clues does the cover provide about the brochure's contents, and what emotional effects does it create?
2. What story does the brochure tell?
3. How well do the graphics help to convey the story?
4. Is the brochure easy to read? Why or why not?

Revise your brochure based on the feedback you gather.

EXERCISE 20.2 Find a brochure on your campus—in a library or student activities office. Write a one-page critique of the brochure, commenting on how well it meets the brochure writing criteria as outlined in this section.

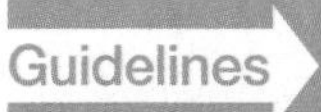

Guidelines

Writing Brochures

- **Deciding on the content and writing the text**
  - **a.** Conduct a rhetorical analysis.
  - **b.** Choose a template.
  - **c.** Write and insert the text.
- **Deciding on the layout and design**
  - **a.** Design an enticing cover.
  - **b.** Tell a cohesive story.
  - **c.** Add coherent graphics.
  - **d.** Include adequate white space.
- **Refining the brochure**
  - **a.** Check for clustering.
  - **b.** Check for contrast.
  - **c.** Check for connectedness.

20b Produce a simple newsletter

Newsletters are extremely versatile print publications that deliver timely information to a target audience with similar interests, such as business customers or employees of an organization, and are generally informative rather than persuasive. Many newsletters are printed front and back on 11″ × 17″ paper and folded, to create an 8½″ × 11″ page size. They sometimes include an additional one-page, two-sided insert, for a total of six pages. The design and production decisions you must make for a newsletter are similar to those for a brochure. However, in a newsletter you have more space to work with.

1 Making decisions about content

See 3b-2

As always, you first need to consider your rhetorical stance, looking at the topic in terms of purpose, persona, and audience. Since readers already have some stake in the organization, business, product, or service that sponsors the newsletter, you can assume they will be interested in the subject matter. But you still want to make your writing lively and engaging.

❷ Making decisions about layout, design, and mode of delivery

Be sensitive to the needs of busy, selective newsletter readers by including a table of contents on the first page and providing headings, subheadings, lists, and graphics to help readers find information quickly and easily. Observing the three C's—clustering, contrasting, and connecting—is particularly important in newsletter design. Available design elements include different type fonts, pull-out quotations that are set off from the regular text and printed in larger type, special initials, rules (lines), boxes, color, and graphics.

Newsletters are typically printed in columns, with a masthead, or banner, at the top of the first page, followed by text arranged in either two or three columns per page. Use white space as an element of contrast—to draw attention to something else and provide a place for readers to pause. Do not "trap" white space in the fold area of a two-page spread. Instead, use white space creatively to draw the reader's eye toward important information.

Use graphic elements such as color, pictures, and text art for emphasis. Generally, the banner is the first graphic a reader sees in a newsletter, so other graphics should coordinate with the banner, in accordance with the design principle of connectedness. Pick up and repeat colors or visual elements from the banner, for example, elsewhere in the newsletter. Graphics can occupy one, two, or three columns in a newsletter. Of course, the larger the graphic, the stronger the emphasis. You might consider using a small graphic in the lower right-hand corner of the first page, to balance the banner at the top of the page.

See 19c

Newsletters today are often delivered electronically rather than printed and mailed. If you decide to produce and distribute an e-newsletter, your decisions about layout and design may be affected by the space or format constraints of email servers. You'll need to convert your newsletter into HTML by using the SAVE AS WEB PAGE option in the OFFICE button > SAVE AS menu.

See 20e

❸ Refining the newsletter

Most word processors have newsletter templates. Cecelia Chung decided to publish her research paper in newsletter format. In the OFFICE button > NEW menu on her word-processing program, she found a newsletter template.

The template left space for a table of contents, which would be generated automatically as Cecelia supplied the copy for headings and subheadings. Once she had the various elements in place, Cecelia inserted her research paper file

Guidelines

Writing Newsletters

- **Deciding on the content and writing the text**
  - **a.** Conduct a rhetorical analysis.
  - **b.** Choose a template.
  - **c.** Write and insert the text.
- **Deciding on the layout and design**
  - **a.** Choose a banner.
  - **b.** Select a color scheme.
  - **c.** Include white space.
  - **d.** Place graphics.
  - **e.** Select fonts for the text, and add headings and a table of contents.
- **Refining the newsletter**
  - **a.** Check for clustering.
  - **b.** Check for contrast.
  - **c.** Check for connectedness.

into the template. The template arranged the text automatically into columns. Cecelia then began the job of formatting the newsletter to make it reader-friendly and visually appealing.

See Fig. 20.2

Part of the finished newsletter appears in Figure 20.2. Note that unlike many newsletters, this example does not contain independent "stories" but rather is a published research paper. Most newsletters will include several stories rather than one continuous argument.

EXERCISE 20.3 Analyze the design of Cecelia's newsletter with respect to the three C's. Write your evaluation of Cecelia's application of each design principle. Or, evaluate a newsletter that you have seen on your campus or at work.

EXERCISE 20.4 Design your own newsletter, using a template found on your word-processing program. Or, design a class newsletter as a collaborative project.

FOR COLLABORATION Once you have written a draft of your newsletter, exchange it with a classmate for peer review.

Figure 20.2 Cecelia's Newsletter

Banner

Global Climate Change

Cecelia Chung November 14, 2006

Global Warming: What, How, Why Care?

Larger bold font for heading

Global Warming: Is It Really Happening?

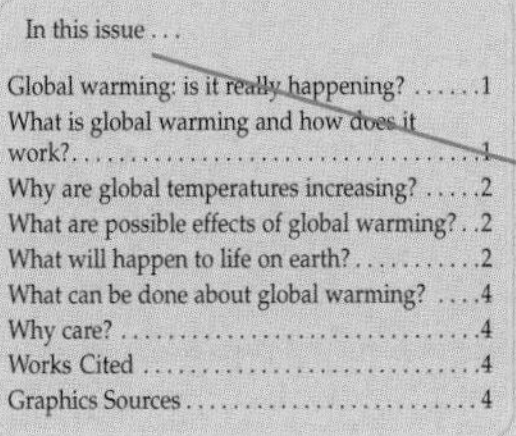
In this issue . . .

Table of Contents

Global warming, at least as measured by climate experts, *is* really happening. Over the last 100 years, it has been estimated that the average global air temperature has risen between 0.3 and 0.6 degree Celsius (Hileman). Though there is debate over other aspects of global warming, scientists generally agree that global temperatures have risen.

However, a big source of disagreement is whether this is a normal or an abnormal warming. Too little is known about long-term global temperature cycles, some say, to determine if this is abnormal. Reliable weather data, it is true, have only been kept for the last century or so (Montague 1). As a result, some question whether there is significant cause for alarm about global warming as a real problem. While I agree that some caution is warranted when predicting the final outcome of this warming trend, I feel that to disregard the problem altogether is extremely short-sighted, because the effects of even a temporary, normal warming trend are potentially devastating for earth and its inhabitants. Most people would agree. It is in our best interests to know as much as possible about global warming, its causes and potential effects. Before we discuss the true nature of the controversy, let's look at how global warming works.

What Is Global Warming and How Does It Work?

Global warming is an increase in average air temperature on earth's surface, as measured from many points across the globe. Global warming, in its simplest form, is a product of two factors: so-called greenhouse gases and radiation from our local star, the Sun. The idea is that sunlight enters earth's atmosphere, hits molecules of atmospheric gas on earth's surface, and is converted to other forms of energy such as heat. Sometimes this energy is prevented from escaping back into space by a "blanket" of gases such as carbon dioxide, and a net gain of heat occurs (Britt). Without

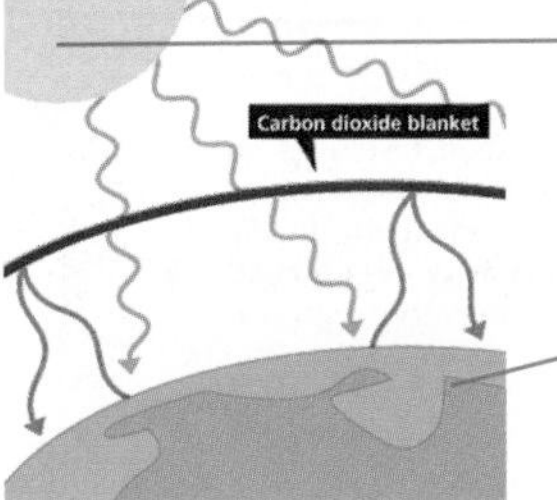

Colors coordinated with banner

Graphic in lower right for balance

Figure 20.2 (cont.)

Running head

Two-column format

White space

2 Global Climate Change November 14, 2006

these gases, our planet would be about 60 degrees Fahrenheit colder than it is today (Montague 1), too cold for many terrestrial life forms that now thrive here. But there is concern that too much heat buildup caused by unnatural levels of so-called greenhouse gases will be dangerous for our planet.

Why Are Global Temperatures Increasing?

Now that scientists have established that global warming is taking place, the next ques-

changes, increased rates of glacial melting, subsequent sea-level increases, and air and sea-surface temperature increases, sometimes with resulting shifts in plant and animal species.

Models predict that, if current theories hold true, temperatures will rise between 1 and 3.5 degrees Celsius by 2100 (Hileman). Temperature increases are expected to be highest over land, changing climates and affecting habitat suitability for terrestrial species, which may be forced to migrate or go extinct. These temperature increases are also ex-

Matching colors

White space around graphic draws eye outward to the text

3 Global Climate Change November 14, 2006

southern California, conducted by John McGowan and Dean Roemmich of the Scripps Institute of Oceanography, has shown a 2–3 degrees Fahrenheit temperature increase in the sea-surface temperature in the last fifty years (Svitil 36). This has led to density changes in the surface waters, which have had broad implications for the suitability of the habitat for the species living there.

Changes in habitat naturally lead to changes in energy resources as species unable to cope with change die out or disperse to other areas. As one population shrinks, other dependent species populations are stressed for food resources, in turn stressing the populations dependent upon them. In the study previously mentioned, changes in density stratification of the water altered the amount of chemical nutrients carried up from the bacterial beds in the depths of the ocean. As nutrient levels declined near the surface, plants dependent upon these nutrients suffered declines in population, which in turn reduced populations of plant-dependent phytoplankton. The population-

However, some predictions state that temperatures will rise exponentially as compounding factors come into play. According to Krebs, as temperatures rise, rates of successful migration will be affected by individual mobility (locomotion), energy resource mobility, reproductive rate, habitat dispersal, and geography. Since a population can only migrate as quickly as its slowest-moving resource, and only to places with suitable habitat unblocked by barriers beyond their capacity to overcome (such as deserts, mountains, oceans), many species will be unable to migrate quickly enough to keep up with rates of climate change (115).

For example, historical models have shown that the geographic range of American beech has moved just 0.2 km per year since the last Ice Age. However, to keep pace with current predictions of climate change, beech will have to move 7–9 km per year to the north (Krebs 113). Thus, the beech is destined to extinction unless we intervene. I predict that many species, both plant and animal, will be unable to move quickly enough to keep up

Figure 20.2 (cont.)

4 Global Climate Change November 14, 2006

ing in abundances and will affect conditions in many economies. It is impossible for humanity to escape entirely unaffected by even a minor warming trend.

What Can Be Done about Global Warming?

Already, many groups and individuals are concerned and taking action about global warming and the problems it may bring. The cooperative effort of local, national, and international entities is necessary, because the potential effects of global warming are so huge. Global warming will affect not only individuals but businesses and governments as well.

Businesses dependent upon world conditions are especially concerned about global warming, for economical if not environmental reasons. Two of these are the global insurance and banking industries. These industries are working with the United Nations to reduce environmentally damaging activities. This is largely because, says UN Environment Program director Hans Alder, "They know that a few major disasters caused by extreme climate events . . . could literally bankrupt the industry in the next decade" (Hertsgaard C1).

Why Care?

Global warming is, after all, a global problem. The effects of global warming, destructive and severe, will be felt increasingly by everyone. Scientists agree that it is happening, so we should all support efforts to research and combat its causes. The changes global warming will eventually cause are unknown in their severity and scope but already we can feel some of them. Let's take action to prevent further escalation of global warming.

Works Cited

Britt, Robert. "The Heat Is On: Scientists Agree on Human Contribution to Global Warming." *Ion Science* 1995. Web. 13 Nov. 2006.

Hertsgaard, Mark. "Who's Afraid of Global Warming?" *Washington Post* 21 Jan. 1996: C1. Web. 13 Nov. 2006.

Hileman, Bette. "Climate Observations Substantiate Global Warming Models." *Chemical and Engineering News* 27 Nov. 1995. Web. 13 Nov. 2006.

Krebs, Charles J. *Ecology: The Experimental Analysis of Distribution and Abundance.* 4th ed. New York: Harper, 1994. Print.

Montague, Peter. "Global Warming—Part 1: How Global Warming Is Sneaking Up on Us." *Rachel's Hazardous Waste News* 26 Aug. 1992: 1. Web. 22 Nov. 2006.

Svitil, Kathy A. "Collapse of a Food Chain." *Discover* July 1995: 36–37. Print.

Graphics Sources

Carbon dioxide blanket. 13 Nov. 2006 <http://www.injersey.com/Media/IonSci/features/gwarm/gwarm.html>.

Friendly sun. 13 Nov. 2006 <cuisun9.unige.ch/eao/www/gif/New_Sun.color.gif>.

Web design

20c Generate a basic design for the Web

Web documents differ from print documents in two important ways:

1. They tend to be more visual (that is, they include more graphics and photographs).
2. They are hypertextual and weblike in structure (that is, they have electronic links).

You may not associate design with writing. Perhaps you think of design in terms of designing graphics or designing page layouts. But designing is something that happens during any writing process. We will use the term *design* to refer broadly to the ongoing planning involved in developing and writing for a complicated project such as a Web site. When a Web page is well designed, the author's message is successfully conveyed to readers, and the look and content of the page match the author's purposes.

1 Using visuals effectively

See Fig. 20.3

When Web authors consider document design, formatting, and graphics, they make decisions similar to those made by writers of print documents. The role of visual features in conveying meaning is greater in Web documents: Web authors typically use images instead of words to show readers how to find information and to help them understand concepts. They employ visual tools such as color, background images, typographical distinctions, spacing, graphics and icons, lists, and tables and frames. Increasingly, Web sites use **multimedia,** incorporating sound and even movement (or **hypermedia**) to convey their messages. Web designers need to pay close attention to the size of multimedia and graphics files, however, since large files can take a long time to download.

2 Using hypertext effectively

One of the greatest challenges in writing hypertext is to make it easy for readers to navigate through the links. Careful design is the key to constructing a successful Web site.

See TechHelp 8b

EXERCISE 20.5 Find two Web sites that you think are visually appealing. Describe what makes them interesting. How has each site's author used color, graphics, and other media? Bookmark the sites.

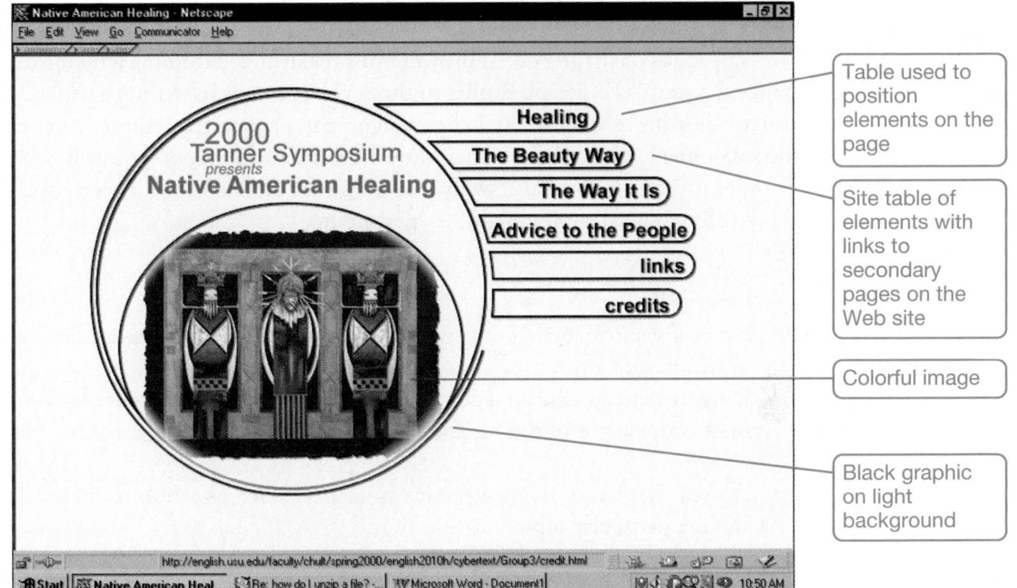

▲ **Figure 20.3** A Student Web Page Illustrating Design Features

FOR COLLABORATION Print copies of the homepages for your classmates, or post them to your class's common directory. Discuss the sites, and your evaluation of them, with your classmates.

20d Plan your Web document

As you think about how you want your Web site to look, keep in mind the basic strengths and limitations of this medium. Although the Web allows you to be extremely creative in using graphics, photos, colors, and even video and sound, the Web authoring language **HTML** (HyperText Markup Language) is not as versatile as many desktop publishing programs. For example, constructing columns for a Web page is more complex than producing a newsletter in columns using a word-processing program. In addition, the number of fonts available may be limited.

❶ Deciding on a rhetorical stance

See 3b-2

See 7a

The kinds of writing decisions you must make in determining a rhetorical stance for your Web site are similar to those you confront in writing a paper. If you are creating a Web site as a class assignment, analyze the requirements of the assignment. Think about what knowledge and information you will need in order to write a successful Web site. If you are to choose your own topic, think through what topics might be appropriate.

Purpose

- Do you want to share your own creative work—such as poetry, fiction, music, or art—with others?
- Do you want to educate your audience about a topic that concerns you, such as the plight of the African elephant or the health dangers of nuclear waste?
- Do you want to provide a service to readers, such as a link to materials about a particular topic?

Persona

- What kind of background would be most suitable for the site?
- What colors would be appropriate?
- Which images would enhance the site?
- What text would reflect best on you as an author?

Audience

See 20d-4

- Is the text so dense that it is difficult to read on screen?
- Will the text be interesting to readers?
- Are there too many graphics?
- Does the site allow readers to skim and read selectively?
- Are there enough navigational tools?
- Will the page hold readers' attention?

❷ Learning about design technology

You do not compose a Web site directly on the World Wide Web. Instead, you create the text and graphics as files on your computer's hard drive or on disk, using a software program designed for this purpose. When the files are complete and stored in appropriate folders and directories, you transfer them from your computer or the lab's server to your college's Internet server or to an Internet service provider **(ISP)**.

Naming and storing your Web files

Naming Conventions. Servers may be picky about what file names they will accept, so you need to decide on a simple yet understandable system for naming the files that will make up your Web project. For example, use only lowercase letters in Web file names, and do not use any spaces or characters such as periods since those can cause problems for servers. Web file names should be kept short and must end in either *.htm* or *.html.* (At one time, these extensions distinguished Mac from PC Web files, but they have since become interchangeable.) Graphics files will typically end in either *.gif* or *.jpg* since these are the image formats recognized by Web browsers.

Creating a directory for your project. It is a good idea to create a project directory or folder on your hard drive or disk in which to store all documents and graphics related to a particular Web project. As you construct your Web site, you will probably create a number of separate documents and graphics files that will later be connected to each other with hypertext links. If you keep them all in the same location on your disk or hard drive, you will find it easier to organize your Web site. Furthermore, you will be able to transfer all of the related files to your Internet server at once if they all reside in the same folder. Be certain to make backup copies of everything you are using for your Web site, and remember to save frequently as you work on the project.

Understanding how Web files are stored. Before you begin your Web project, it is important to understand how Web files are stored on your college's or service provider's computer system. If your college provides Internet access for students and faculty, it will have dedicated storage space on a large computer that is used as the campus Internet server. To use your college server, you will need to secure an account, which will include a user name and password unique to you.

Basic design elements

As you think about your Web site, you will need to consider whether or not to use some basic design elements such as tables, frames, and style sheets to structure the Web pages. Depending on your site's purpose and the needs of

TechHelp

Publishing Your Web Pages

With FTP (file transfer protocol) software like *WindowsFTP:*

1. Open the software and supply the information requested about destination server and location. (Ask your instructor or lab supervisor for this information if you are using a campus server.)
2. Use the buttons that appear on the screen to transfer files.

See Fig. 20.4

Or, use your browser to transfer FTP files:

1. Type *ftp://* followed by your server address in the address line, rather than *http://*.
2. Use COPY and PASTE to transfer files from your computer to the destination server.

With an ISP (Internet service provider):

1. Identify the ISP you will use. These include *Yahoo!, Google* and *MSN*, as well as free sites like *GeoCities* (<http://geocities.com>) or *AngelFire* (<http://angelfire.com>). Keep in mind that free sites may automatically include advertising banners along with your Web pages.
2. Follow the instructions at the ISP site to upload your Web files.

your audience, you can select among these design options. We will provide a brief explanation below, but you will need to research them further if you wish to try them yourself.

Using tables and frames. Web page authors use tables and frames to control page layout and organize text and graphics.

Tables allow you to select the number of columns and rows that will be used on each page and what data will "fill" cells formed by the intersection of those columns and rows. If you select zero width for the table border, the table itself will not appear on the page. Instead, the table will provide you with "cells" in which you can insert appropriate data.

See Fig. 20.5

Frames differ from tables in their ability to display multiple files in different portions of the frame shown in the browser window. The frame itself consistently appears on the page, but different Web pages may be displayed within the frame windows.

See Fig. 20.6

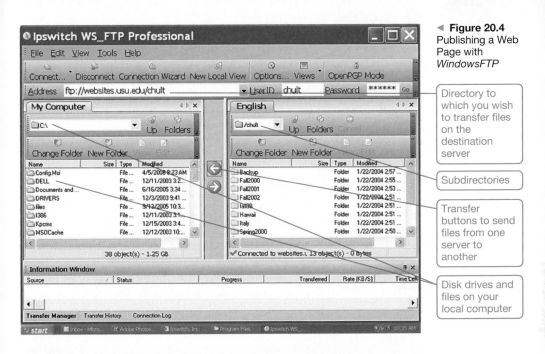

Figure 20.4 Publishing a Web Page with *WindowsFTP*

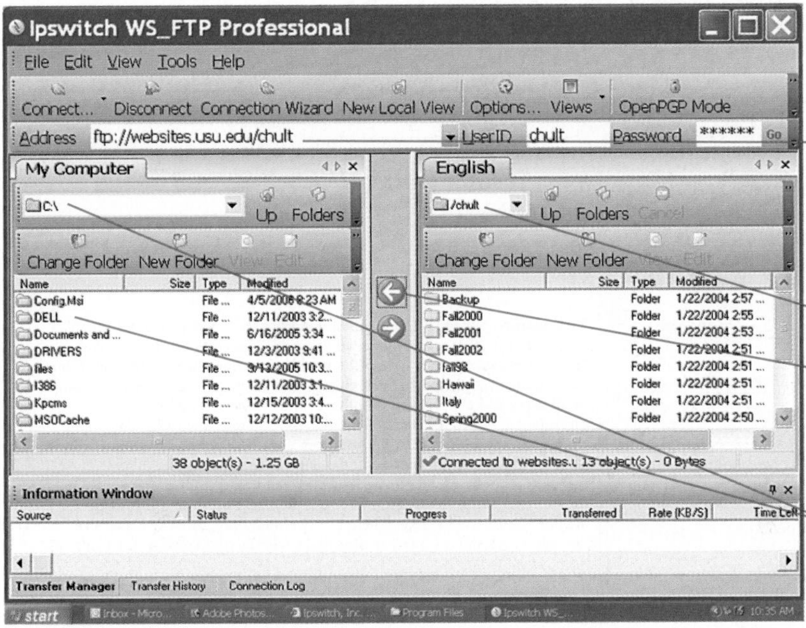

Directory to which you wish to transfer files on the destination server

Subdirectories

Transfer buttons to send files from one server to another

Disk drives and files on your local computer

Figure 20.5 Using Tables to Organize Content on a Student's Web Page

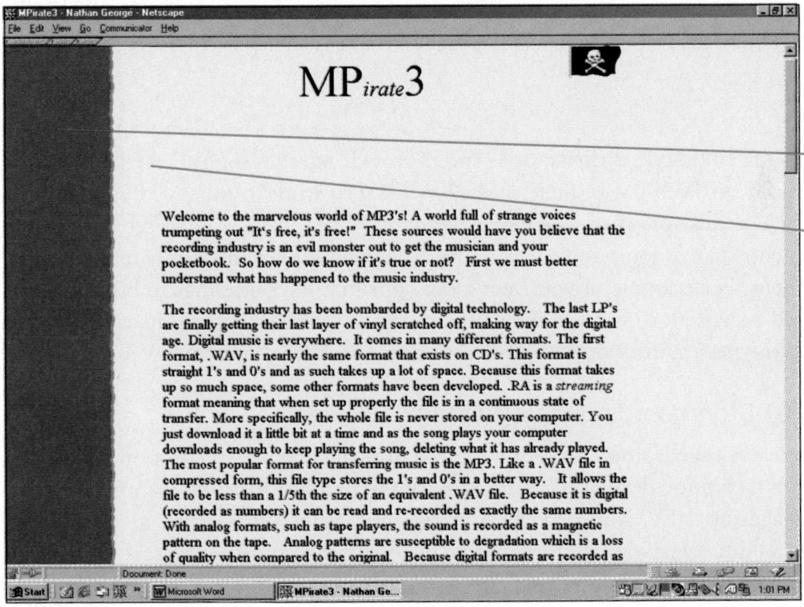

Column 1 of table

Column 2 of table

MP*irate*3

Welcome to the marvelous world of MP3's! A world full of strange voices trumpeting out "It's free, it's free!" These sources would have you believe that the recording industry is an evil monster out to get the musician and your pocketbook. So how do we know if it's true or not? First we must better understand what has happened to the music industry.

The recording industry has been bombarded by digital technology. The last LP's are finally getting their last layer of vinyl scratched off, making way for the digital age. Digital music is everywhere. It comes in many different formats. The first format, .WAV, is nearly the same format that exists on CD's. This format is straight 1's and 0's and as such takes up a lot of space. Because this format takes up so much space, some other formats have been developed. .RA is a *streaming* format meaning that when set up properly the file is in a continuous state of transfer. More specifically, the whole file is never stored on your computer. You just download it a little bit at a time and as the song plays your computer downloads enough to keep playing the song, deleting what it has already played. The most popular format for transferring music is the MP3. Like a .WAV file in compressed form, this file type stores the 1's and 0's in a better way. It allows the file to be less than a 1/5th the size of an equivalent .WAV file. Because it is digital (recorded as numbers) it can be read and re-recorded as exactly the same numbers. With analog formats, such as tape players, the sound is recorded as a magnetic pattern on the tape. Analog patterns are susceptible to degradation which is a loss of quality when compared to the original. Because digital formats are recorded as

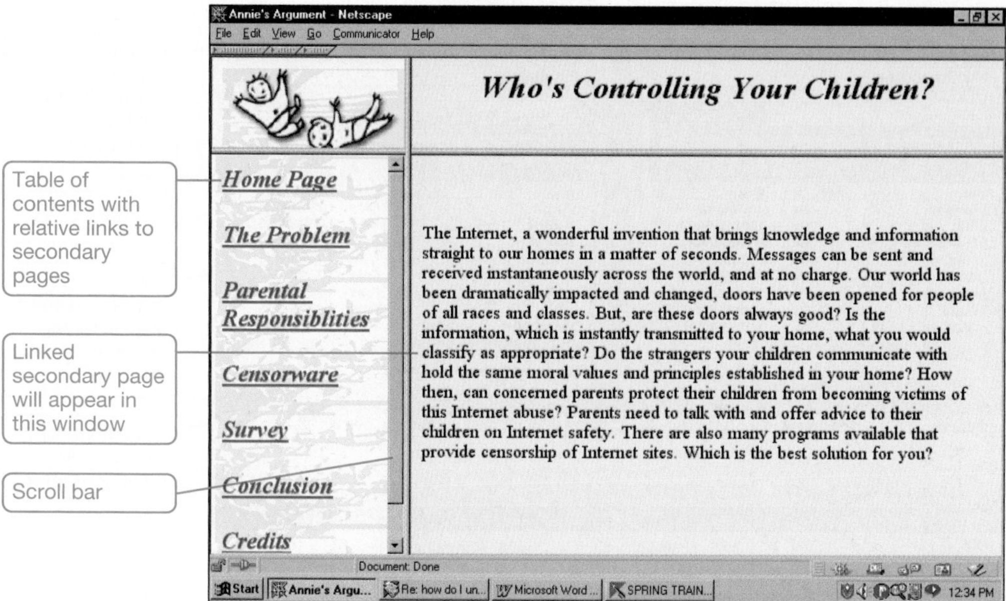

▲ **Figure 20.6** Using Frames to Organize Content on a Student's Web Page

Using style sheets. Style sheets provide another sophisticated way to format your Web pages. Style sheets for the Web work in much the same way as style sheets for word-processing programs. They allow you to set default elements such as fonts and colors that will then be applied uniformly to your document. For example, if you want all of your first-level headings to be black on a red background, you can define the header 1 style to associate the colors, fonts, and typestyle that you'd like them to appear in throughout your Web document.

❸ Storyboarding your Web presentation

Storyboarding—that is, making a drawing of a work's component parts—is a technique developed by journalists and graphic artists to plan newspapers, magazines, TV commercials, movies, and other media that mix text with graphics. One way to storyboard a Web site is to outline the text and sketch the graphics for each page on 3″ × 5″ index cards. Pin the cards to a bulletin board, and then move them around until you have a unified story. You can show the links between the cards by stretching a piece of string from one card to another. You can also storyboard by doing small, "thumbnail" page plans on a sheet of paper. Figure 20.7 illustrates two types of organizational structures used for Web sites: linear and hierarchical. In a simple Web site with a straightforward story, the pages can be linked in a linear sequence, with one leading to the next in a straight line. The pages of a more complicated Web site should be linked in a hierarchical structure or with multiple linkages that provide readers with numerous options. You need to provide enough information about yourself on each Web page that readers can contact you with questions or comments: your name, email address, and the date you last updated the page.

See Fig. 20.7

④ Planning navigation

See Fig. 20.3

As Figure 20.3 shows, a Web site begins with a homepage (the first page), which also serves as an introduction to the site. It often includes several secondary pages (**relative links**), which are accessed from the homepage. Each page (designated by a different file name) should be no more than two or three screens long. For high-impact pages, try limiting the length to what will fit on one screen so that readers can see the entire page at a glance without scrolling. You can also include on your pages **remote links** to other Web sites located elsewhere on the Internet.

Links are highlighted words and phrases within a document that allow readers to get from one page to another. **Navigational buttons** are graphical icons, such as arrows, symbols, buttons, or pictures, that will take readers in a particular direction or to a particular location. You may need to include text in addition to the graphic, as on the "Contents" and "Works Cited" buttons in Figure 20.8, if the purpose of the graphic is not readily apparent. Navigational buttons may be included at the top, bottom, or one side of each page within a multipage Web site.

See Fig. 20.8

⑤ Applying the basic design principles to a Web site

Web design and production

Given the vast quantity of information on the World Wide Web, accommodating the busy, selective reader is imperative. The homepage is the first page readers will see when they access your site, so it should introduce your site concisely, providing an overview of the content and organization of the site. Do not waste readers' time with decorative design elements; rather, include elements that will enhance readers' understanding of your message. Observing the basic

LINEAR ORGANIZATION
Mary Parker's Homepage
Picture
Personal Interests
Photography
Hiking
Mountain Biking
Favorite Music
Classical
Rock
Folk
Résumé
HIERARCHICAL ORGANIZATION
Picture Mary Parker's Awesome Homepage
Link to WSU
Personal
Music Résumé
WSU's Homepage
Personal: Photography
Link to some of my best photos in Web album (home)
Music: Classical
List of my favorite Bach pieces and remote links to two Bach-related Web sites (home)
Résumé
(home)
Personal: Hiking
Link to photos of hiking in Zion (personal)
Music: Rock
List of my favorite Sting songs and remote links to two Sting-related Web sites (home)
Personal: Mountain Biking
Link to photos of bike trip to Canada (personal)
Personal: Folk
List of my favorite Kathy Kallick songs and remote links to two Kallick-related Web sites (music)

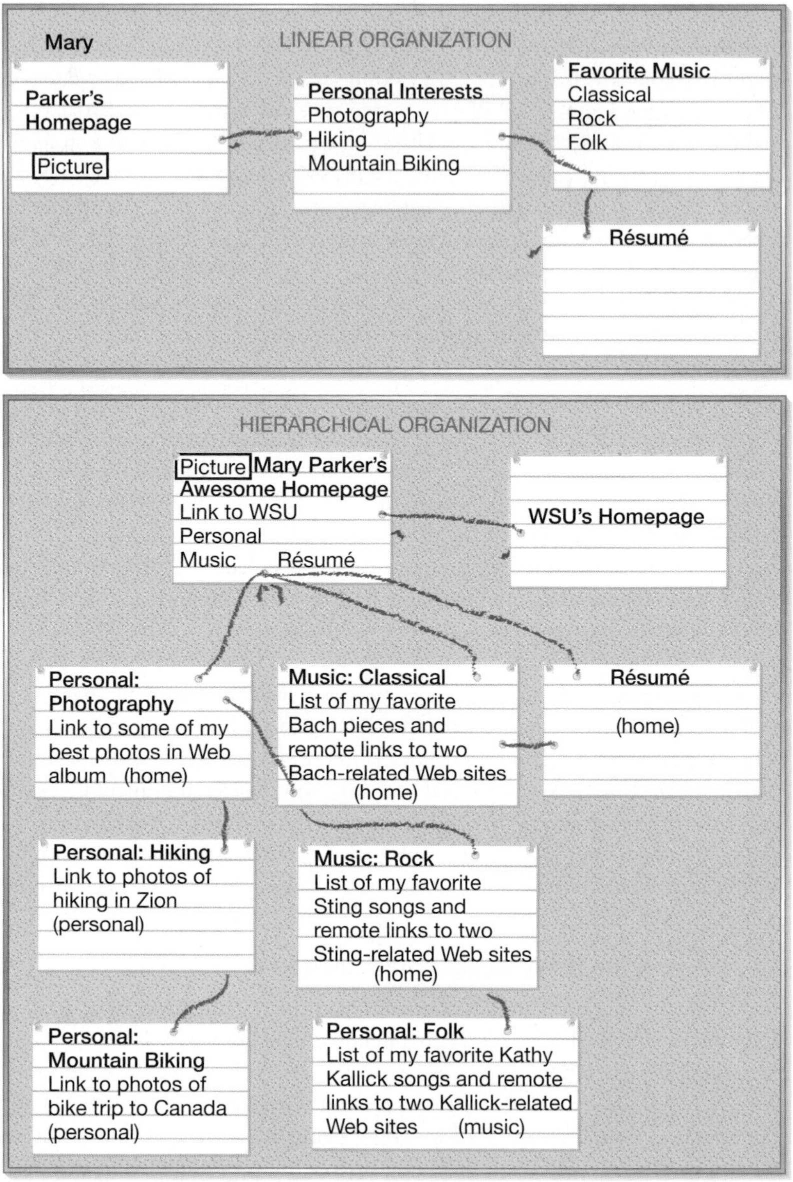

Figure 20.7 ▶ Two Types of Storyboards for a Web Site

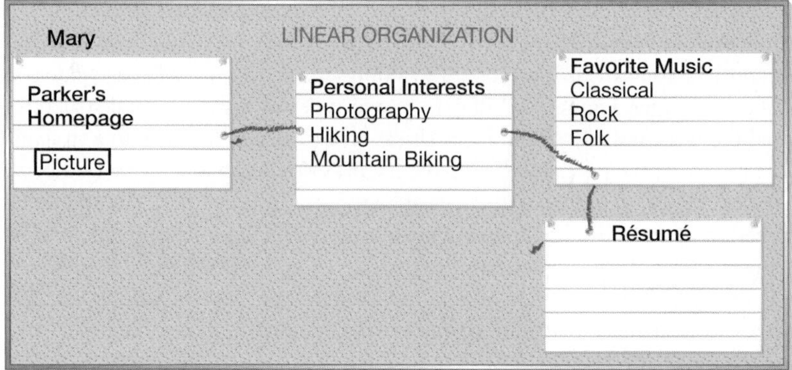

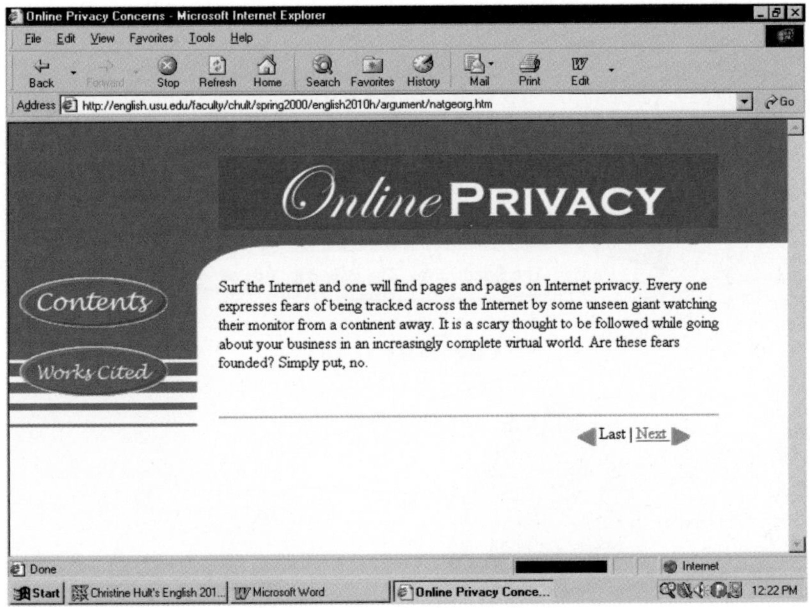

◀ **Figure 20.8**
One Page of a Student Collaborative Web Site with Navigational Buttons

design principles exemplified by the three C's—clustering, contrasting, and connecting—may be even more critical to Web design than to print design.

See Ch. 19 and Fig. 20.9.

Clustering: grouping closely related items

When designing Web pages, position chunks of information that are related in meaning close to one another. Emphasize clusters of information by placing white space around them. Group important elements at the top left and lower right of the screen, as readers of the English language are trained to move their eyes from left to right. Use numbered and bulleted lists to show relationships among items in a group.

Contrasting: highlighting differences

Use contrasting fonts or font sizes to highlight basic elements. For example, you might use the largest HTML headings (H1) for titles and smaller HTML headings (H3) for any subtitles. Use colors or patterns to contrast other elements on the page.

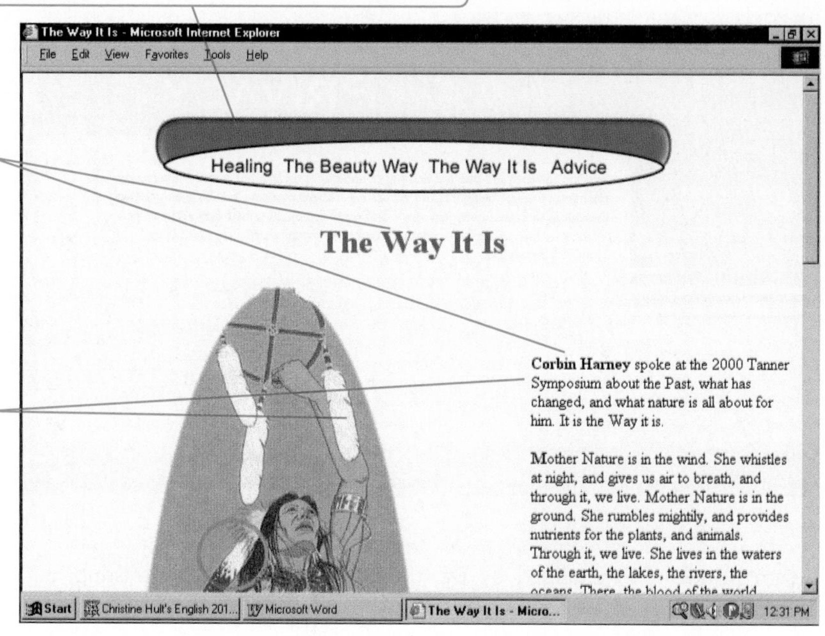

▲ **Figure 20.9** The 3 C's of Design as Used by a Group of First-Year Students

Connecting: relating every part to some other part

See 20a, 20b-3

See Fig. 20.10

Adhering to the principle of connectedness is especially important for Web authors. Since readers can access the pages within a site in any sequence, use a design template and a consistent graphic, title, or logo to foster visual connectedness. Furthermore, because readers can easily become lost when reading hypertext, it is important to include navigational aids to connect all pieces of the Web site. One way to do so is to provide a "home" link on every secondary page that takes readers back to the homepage. You might also supply a site map, showing how all of the pieces are connected. It is a good idea to provide readers with alternative routes through the site's pages so that they are not forced along a single path. Busy, selective readers will appreciate the optional routes.

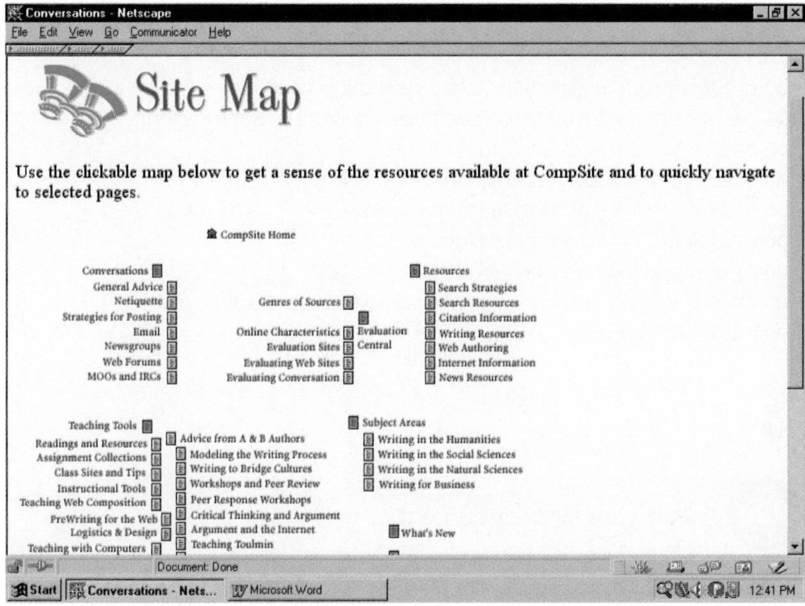

Figure 20.10
A Site Map

EXERCISE 20.6 Begin planning and designing a Web site. Set goals, and then create a storyboard with 3″ × 5″ cards or sketches in a notebook. Pay careful attention to planning the navigation through various linked pages. What pages need to be linked to each other? Draw arrows on your storyboard to indicate links. To ensure that readers are not left stranded on a page, plan to provide icons or buttons that lead them home or forward.

FOR COLLABORATION Exchange drafts of your Web sites with a classmate for peer review. Comment specifically on the features of the Web site that are visual or that use hypertext.

EXERCISE 20.7 Visit the *Voice of the Shuttle* "Laws of Cool" page (<http://vos.ucsb.edu/shuttle/cool.html>). Find a site that you think illustrates effective Web design. List the reasons you find the design compelling, referring to criteria outlined in this chapter. Share your sites and your evaluation with the class.

Some Dos and Don'ts of Web Design

DO organize your information before designing your site.
DO aim for pages that are no more than two or three screens long.
DO accommodate text-only browsers.
DO use a template and repeat visual elements.
DO use other Web pages to learn new code.
DON'T include unnecessary design elements.
DON'T use graphics files of over 30 K (kilobytes).
DON'T use copyrighted text or graphics without permission and acknowledgment.

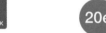

HTML tutorial

20e Write your Web document

Once you have an overall plan for your Web site, you can begin to compose the actual pages. The text of a Web site is as important as how it looks—Web pages communicate through *both* text and graphics. There are several methods for composing Web pages; you may select one or use a combination of methods.

❶ Using an HTML editor

See 8c

HTML editor or composer software is designed to help you write Web pages. The most commonly used commercial HTML editor is *Dreamweaver*. Free HTML editors can be downloaded from the Internet; to find free software, type "HTML editor" as a search term in *Google*. To learn how to use the software you download, refer to its written and online documentation or Help manual.

❷ Using a text-editing or word-processing program

If you use a word-processing program, you need to enter the HTML coding by hand. When authors first began writing for the Web, this difficult and time-consuming method was the one they used—they typed in all the HTML codes that the browser would need to interpret and display Web pages. Despite the availability of sophisticated editors and composers, it is sometimes still necessary to insert codes manually to achieve the result you desire. It is important to understand enough HTML coding to be able to revise and rewrite the code that underlies any of your Web pages. We suggest using a tutorial such as NCSA's *Beginner's Guide to HTML* to learn the basics of coding.

❸ Using a translator program

Translator programs change word-processing or database files into Web files. *Microsoft Word, WordPerfect, Excel,* and *PowerPoint* all include a SAVE AS WEB PAGE option. This is a useful option if you have already written extensive

TechHelp

Creating and Previewing Your Web Page with *Word*

- First, make sure that the *Word* Web templates have been loaded onto your computer. To find the templates, go to the OFFICE button and click on NEW. One of the types of templates available to you should be WEB PAGE.
- Click on WEB PAGE. *Word* will construct a Web page that includes the basic underlying codes necessary to begin any Web document. (*Word* uses the WYSIWYG principle—What you see is what you get.) You will not see the underlying HTML codes unless you go to the VIEW menu and view the HTML source.
- Create your page, following the principles outlined in Chapter 19 and in this chapter for good content and design, and save it by selecting SAVE AS > WEB PAGE.
- Select WEB PAGE PREVIEW from the FILE menu, or click on the WEB PAGE PREVIEW icon on your Web toolbar. (You can preview your page and then return to working on it in *Word*, as long as you save it before each preview.)
- Any Web page that you have saved as a file can be opened directly in a Web browser by choosing OPEN PAGE from the FILE menu of either *Explorer* or *Firefox*. A window will open that allows you to browse your disk drives and select the HTML file that you want to open.

text or presentation material that you wish to convert quickly into a Web file. Translating allows you to take full advantage of all the features of your word-processing program (spell checker, grammar checker, thesaurus, etc.), which may not be available to you in an HTML editor or composer.

EXERCISE 20.8 If you have access to *Microsoft Word*, open the VIEW WEB LAYOUT button to see how your text would look as a Web page. Save your file on your hard drive or on a disk, using SAVE AS WEB PAGE from the OFFICE button menu. Try using the Web toolbar to make changes to your Web page.

part

5

Writing for Different Purposes

21 Electronic Communication

FAQs

- How do I know the appropriate etool to use for each kind of communication? (21a)
- Can I email my instructor? What are the rules? (21b)
- How do I use online networks effectively? (21c)
- How do I set up or become a member of an electronic mailing list? (21c-1)

While you are in college you are learning how to learn, and one of the main skills you should want to develop is the ability to adapt to changing technologies. Given the current technological environment, we have written this chapter with the following three goals in mind:

1. To walk you through the major forms of electronic communication currently available to you, with an emphasis on the most user-friendly and popular etools.
2. To provide you with basic guidelines on how, when, and why to use particular tools in the academic setting.
3. To give you guidance on how to make your online communications appropriate, effective, and persuasive, depending on the particular etool you are using.

21a The rhetoric of etools

See 3b-2

In this world of multiple electronic communication options, you need to pay close attention to your rhetorical stance. As we discussed in Chapter 3, *rhetoric* refers to written or oral communication that seeks to persuade a particular audience about a particular topic. In every act of communication, the rhetorical triangle is in operation, as your audience, your persona, and your chosen arguments interact with your topic. Depending on the aim of your writing, some electronic tools may be better than others. For example, it is probably not appropriate to text-message your professor because of the informality of the medium, whereas it may be perfectly acceptable to send an email message, provided you use an appropriate tone—that is, don't start out your email "Yo, Prof." Just as it is not appropriate to talk to your teachers, supervisors, or bosses the same way you talk to your friends or family, it is not appropriate to *write* to them the same way. Below are some suggestions to help you navigate the rocky shoals of rhetoric when using etools. The etools most appropriate for particular types of communication are summarized in the TechHelp box in 21a-1.

See 21a-1

TechHelp

Determining Which Etool to Use

Type of Communication	Via PC	Via PDA	Via Cell Phone	**Instant message**	**Listserv**	**Newsgroup**	**Web-log**
Collaborative project for school or work	☑	☐	☐	☑	☐	☐	☐
Peer review of a draft	☑	☐	☐	☐	☐	☐	☐
Informal or personal discussion; hobby	☑	☑	☑	☑	☑	☑	☑
Formal discussion, school or work	☑	☐	☐	☐	☑	☑	☐
Quick question or request	☑	☑	☑	☑	☑	☐	☐
Long dialogue or extended conversation	☑	☐	☐	☐	☑	☑	☐
Journal entry or travelogue	☑	☐	☐	☐	☐	☐	☑

❶ Tone and formality in electronic communications

Levels of formality vary widely among electronic communications. For example, instant messages and text messages are very informal and chatty in tone. On the other hand, email can be formal or informal, depending on the rhetorical stance you wish to adopt. Remember, the stance is based on your audience, as well as your persona (how you wish to come across). If you are writing to your professor to clarify an assignment, you will want to address him or her formally, make the request politely, and come across as an engaged and diligent student. Don't ask a professor "what you missed" when you weren't in class! That is the number one complaint professors have about student emails.

❷ Public versus private conversations

Electronic communication often blurs the line between what is a private and what is a public conversation. Sometimes we act as though everything we say online is private, between ourselves and our immediate correspondent. However, you should remember that email, text messages, and chat-room conversations are in a sense "public," since they can be archived on someone's computer or cell phone, forwarded to others, and even subpoenaed in a court of law. Take particular care not to write anything from a school's computer that you don't want made public—because it just might end up that way.

Of even more concern are postings to personal Web pages, blogs, *Facebook*, and so on, where students often put a great deal of personal information, sometimes to their own detriment. Again, use good judgment about what you put out on the Internet, because unscrupulous individuals can distort the information and use it for their own purposes. Do not forget that what may at first glance seem like a private communication may in fact become extremely public.

❸ Multi-tasking

Although the ability to multi-task is a good skill to develop, it can get us into trouble. Sometimes we try to do too much at once, and our communications become sloppy as a result. For example, even though it might seem efficient, it may not be a good idea to email a professor with a question while taking notes in another class, text-messaging with a friend, or surfing the Internet. When your mind is on more than one task, you are likely to do none of them very well. When in doubt, focus on one thing at a time—particularly if the person you are communicating with is important to you or the communication situation is a formal one. If you inadvertently make a mistake in etiquette or hit the SEND button too soon, the written record of your error in judgment may come back to haunt you.

21b Use email effectively

In the academic world, email is now the standard for communicating information between and among professors and students. However, professors may have particular preferences with respect to email use in their class. It is a good idea to ask a professor whether he or she has any specific preferences, such as no email on evenings or weekends. A few professors will not give their email address out to students at all, but most find it a convenient way to communicate information to the entire class and to field questions that may arise outside of class time.

Using Email Appropriately

Guidelines

Professor to Student

- Clarifications of syllabus
- Changes in deadlines
- Need for professor to miss class because of illness
- Additional information about assignments
- Reminders of due dates
- Comments on working drafts

Student to Professor

- Request for clarification of an assignment
- Request for clarification of lecture information
- Need for student to miss class because of illness
- Question about writing topic or research assignment
- Request for help locating additional information
- Request for comments on working draft

1 Writing and sending email messages

By the time you enter college, you probably have been using email for many years. This section provides a general description of how email programs work, although details may differ from program to program. You should find out what program is the standard on your campus and learn more about it on your own.

Using specific subject headings

On the subject line, type a very specific subject that alerts your recipient to the message's topic. Rather than sending a message that is long and complex and covers several topics, it may be better to send a second message with a different subject line to keep your ideas focused.

Copying other recipients

On the "CC" or "BCC" line, include addresses of additional recipients who may be interested in the content of your message. Use your email client's BCC (Blind Carbon Copy) feature to preserve the privacy of recipients. Put one recipient in the To field (and that can be your own email address to keep other addresses *really* private) and put all other addresses in a BCC field. That way everyone gets the message but no one can see the other recipients' addresses. Think carefully about whom you want to copy; many people receive hundreds of emails daily and would prefer not to be copied on messages unless they have expressed a specific interest or need to know.

Using attachments to share your work

See 21b-6

Most email programs will allow you to attach a document, picture, or other file to your email message. Be sure that the document you attach is in a format that can be opened by your recipient. When in doubt, attach documents saved in **rich text format** (*.rtf), which can be read by most word-processing programs. Also be sure not to attach any extremely large files that may overwhelm the recipient's mailbox.

Adapting style and tone to audience

As discussed earlier in this chapter, you need to be sure that the level of formality of your message suits the occasion and the recipients. Although informal email is acceptable among friends and classmates, it is generally best to adopt a more formal tone and use Standard Edited English for other situations, such as emails to professors, large groups of recipients, and prospective employers.

Signing your message

Always sign your message so that recipients know how to respond. Most email programs allow you to create and store a signature file that you can insert at the end of emails, and many automatically insert this file if instructed to do so.

Formatting an email message

Your email program will probably offer multiple options for text format, including font style and size, HTML coding, and so on. When selecting your format, think primarily in terms of readability. Using a dark background, for example, or very small type can make messages difficult to read.

❷ Responding to email messages

Your email program will allow you to reply to the sender or to everyone on the recipient list.

Double-checking the recipient list

When responding to an email, you can use the REPLY TO or REPLY TO ALL option, depending on whether you want to reply only to the sender or to everyone who received the original email. Make sure you consciously decide which to use, rather than always clicking on REPLY TO ALL. One of the major annoyances cited by those who use email frequently is being included in mindless replies to groups of recipients rather than to individuals.

Double-checking subject headings

Check to be certain that the subject line reflects the content of your reply. If you have changed the subject of your message midstream, be sure to change the subject line as well. And if your message is in response to a long trail of emails, you may want to revise the subject heading to more clearly reflect the actual content of your message. You will also want to clean up the content of the message to include only relevant information.

Including material from the original message

If you include the original message, you may wish to incorporate your response directly into the text of the previous message, but be careful to delineate your text from the original text in some fashion. You can set your text apart using a colored font, CAPS, italics, or bold, depending on the capability of your email program. Be careful to delete any information in the previous stream that is irrelevant or sensitive.

Forwarding a message

See 23b-1

You may wish to forward messages to additional recipients. If you decide to forward a message, check carefully to see whether personal messages within the current message need to be deleted first. Be particularly careful about forwarding long email trails without reading every message. If you have any doubt about forwarding a message, secure the original sender's permission before doing so. Be conscious of exposing all the recipients' email addresses to others. Use the BCC to hide email addresses and clean up the body of the message to make sure everyone's emails are not included. If you are going to pass along something you think is worthwhile, you should take the time to clean up both the TO/BCC list *and* the body of the email. Of course, there are situations where it is best to not forward a message, for example, any chain letter, that list of top ten jokes, the political satire you pulled off the Web, and the link to the latest *YouTube* video. Hard as it may be to hear, most people who receive these things are too polite to tell you to cut it out.

Sending multiple emails to the same recipient

Be judicious about sending numerous messages to the same recipient. Emails should be brief, but most recipients would prefer a slightly longer coherent message to a series of quick thoughts. Try to gather your thoughts first and craft one email that covers the topic thoroughly, rather than sending a number of short emails as ideas occur to you.

3 Gathering and maintaining email contacts

Email is a great way to maintain contact with classmates in a work or study group. Collect your classmates' email addresses just as you would their phone numbers, and store these addresses in the address book on your email program so that you do not have to retype them each time you want to send a message. Most email programs allow you to store multiple addresses in a distribution group under one heading, such as "study group." If you routinely send messages to the same group of people—your coworkers or classmates, for example—consider creating a group for those addresses and then send to the group rather than individuals.

If you do not know the address of a student on your campus, check your college Web site's homepage. Typically, there will be an email directory for students and faculty at your school. Note, however, that not all schools allow outside access to their student directories.

Here are some other Internet sites that offer help in locating email addresses; note that some may charge fees to find addresses for you.

Bigfoot	<http://www.bigfoot.com>
Internet Address Finder	<http://www.iaf.net>
World Email Directory	<http://www.worldemail.com>

If you cannot locate someone's address through one of these sources, try typing the person's name into a *Google* search—or simply call and ask!

EXERCISE 21.1 Look in several email directories for the email address of a friend or acquaintance in another state. Discuss your results with classmates. How successful were you? What problems, if any, did you have? Brainstorm about other similar searches you might want to conduct. Describe what you learned that might be useful in the future.

FOR COLLABORATION Using your email program, set up a study group with a group address list that includes all the members. Mail a few test messages to one another, and use the REPLY TO ALL function to respond. Discuss ways in which this email study group might help you with your classwork.

❹ Practicing good email etiquette

Netiquette rules

Internet users have developed a set of conventions to help keep the medium friendly and courteous. These conventions have been nicknamed **netiquette**. In addition to the Guidelines box on netiquette, keep the following cautions in mind:

- **Flaming**—using angry or abusive language in an electronic setting—is considered harassment and is completely inappropriate in email messages.

If you are flamed, do not reply in kind. Either ignore the message or respond calmly. **Spamming**—sending numerous messages, such as chain letters or advertisements, randomly to a large number of recipients—is both irritating and bothersome because it needlessly clutters up everyone's electronic mailbox.

- It is not appropriate to use class email addresses to ask someone for a date. Nor is it appropriate to write personal emails to classmates whom you do not know outside of class. Class email addresses should be used only for activities related to class work.

The rhetoric of email

See 21a

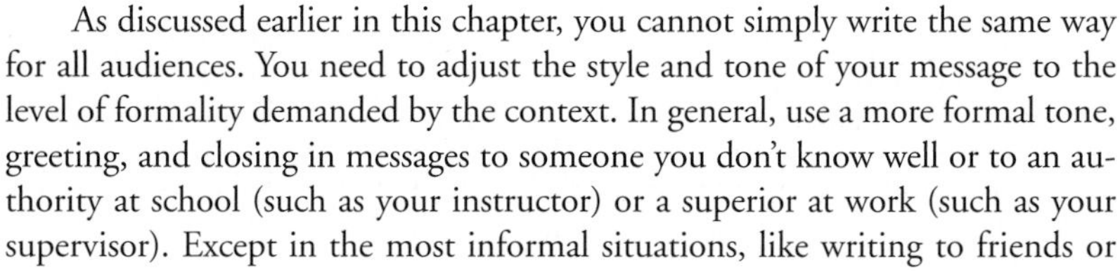

As discussed earlier in this chapter, you cannot simply write the same way for all audiences. You need to adjust the style and tone of your message to the level of formality demanded by the context. In general, use a more formal tone, greeting, and closing in messages to someone you don't know well or to an authority at school (such as your instructor) or a superior at work (such as your supervisor). Except in the most informal situations, like writing to friends or

Guidelines

Netiquette

- **Always type a subject heading** for your email that describes the message's content accurately and specifically.
- **Use an appropriate salutation.** For informal messages, you can use just a name; for business or academic messages, use a standard salutation (Dear Ms. Smith, Dear Dr. Kennedy).
- **Keep messages brief and to the point.**
- **End messages with your name and email address** so that the recipient is clear about who is sending the message and can respond to it.
- **Forward messages only if you have a compelling reason to do so.** People who send you emails are communicating with *you,* not some undetermined audience.
- **Do not quote from an email message** unless the writer has given you explicit permission to do so.
- **Avoid using all capital letters.** This is the electronic equivalent of shouting.
- **Reread your message before sending it.** If there is any chance that the message could be misinterpreted, take time to revise it.

family, you should always use the conventions of Standard Edited English as described in this handbook. Take care to proofread carefully so that your writing is clear and error-free before you send it off. Taking care at this stage can help you avoid embarrassment later.

❺ Using email shorthand

Because email is conversational, users have evolved a kind of shorthand based on email diacritics; asterisks, emoticons, and other characters or punctuation used to add emphasis or other flavoring to email messages. This habit has become even more widespread in text messages, where space is limited.

You may be familiar with the following acronyms:

BTW	by the way
FWIW	for what it's worth
FYI	for your information
IMHO	in my humble opinion
LOL	laugh out loud
TIA	thanks in advance
TTYL	talk to you later

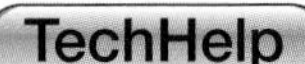

Electronic Language: Diacritics and Emoticons

Diacritics are not appropriate in many contexts. Here are some suggestions about using diacritics:

- Always be conscious of your audience when using acronyms. Email acronyms are never appropriate in professional email, such as a memo, a report, or an email to a professor. Include them only when the situation is appropriately informal.
- When writing to your friends, creativity is the rule, but take care not to overuse email diacritics or else the content of your message may become lost.
- If your email system doesn't allow underlining or italics, putting an asterisk before and after a word or phrase is the most common way to indicate emphasis or contrast:
  That exam was *way* too hard, if you ask me!
- Some people use UPPERCASE LETTERING for emphasis, but take care because this can seem like SHOUTING.
- Use emoticons only in extremely informal writing situations.

Emoticons are those combinations of standard keyboard characters that look like faces when turned sideways:

:) smile	;-) wink
:-o surprise or shock	: (frown

(Your email program may turn some of these emoticons—like the smile and the frown—into actual graphics automatically: ☺ ☹.)

Although these abbreviations are fine in informal messaging, they should never be used in formal communications of academic writing.

❻ Using file attachments

Most email systems allow you to attach files or documents to your messages. For sending your work to a classmate, using an attachment is more convenient

TechHelp

Dealing with Incompatible File Formats

Some word-processing programs save documents as file types that may not be recognized by other software. For example, *Microsoft Works*, the free program that comes loaded on many personal computers, automatically saves in a format that is not compatible with other Microsoft products (*.wps). Newer versions of *Microsoft Word* (e.g., 2007) may be incompatible with earlier formats. Here are some suggestions:

1. **Save your document as a plain text file (*.txt).** When you are saving your document, click on FILE > SAVE AS and then click on the arrow to open the SAVE AS TYPE dialogue box. Choose PLAIN TEXT for the most stripped-down text, which can be read by almost any other program.
2. **Save your document as a rich text file (*.rtf).** When you are saving your document, click on FILE > SAVE AS and then click on the arrow to open the SAVE AS TYPE dialogue box. Choose RICH TEXT FORMAT for a formatted text that can be read by most programs. Most of your formatting will be preserved in the rich text format.
3. **Save your document as HTML (*.htm or *.html).** Notice the other formats that are available to you, including saving as a Web page using HyperText Markup Language. By typing the correct file name, you can open HTML documents in any Web browser.

than cutting and pasting the work into your actual email, since it allows you to preserve the formatting. Instructors may ask that assignments be turned in as attachments so that they can see the formatting of your bibliography or subheadings, for example.

When you select the ATTACH feature, you will typically be prompted to browse for and select the file you wish to attach. Be sure that the file name shows up on the attachment line or that some other icon appears to indicate that you have successfully attached the file. The recipient of your message can then save the attachment and open it in a word-processing program for reading, comment, and response.

FOR COLLABORATION Using the ATTACHMENT feature of your email system, send a classmate a paper that you are currently working on. Specify the kind of advice you would find helpful. Discuss whether or not your classmate received and was able to save and open your attachment. Describe how using attachments might help you write and revise papers.

21c Use online networks effectively

Many Internet resources promote the building of online communities. These include electronic mailing lists, bulletin boards, and newsgroups, as well as real-time chat rooms, blogs, wikis, Web class tools, social networking sites, and other specialized Internet applications.

1 Electronic mailing lists

Guide to email discussion lists

Mailing lists, which are special-interest email lists, distribute messages simultaneously to their many participants or subscribers. Thousands—perhaps millions—of such lists exist to facilitate a myriad of activities: scholarly discussions, committee meetings, fan club talk, even class discussions and research projects. One subscriber hosts the list, providing the host server and the necessary software. (The most common software program is called **listserv**.)

Many lists allow anyone who wishes to join to do so; other lists are selective about their participants and limit the number who can join. In either case, you must **subscribe** to the list in order to participate or access its archives.

Mailing lists can help you become informed as you prepare for a research paper project. Joining a mailing list of science fiction enthusiasts, for example, might help you identify hot topics in science fiction. Take care, as with all online sources, that the list you join is a credible one, with knowledgeable participants. And take care not to request from subscribers information that is readily available elsewhere. If you use information from a mailing list in a research paper, the posting must be cited either in the text itself or in the list of works cited. Do not quote any mailing list posting without the permission of the author. Figure 21.1 is an example of a listserv posting, reprinted here by permission of Barrett M. Briggs.

See Chs. 12–14

See Fig. 21.1

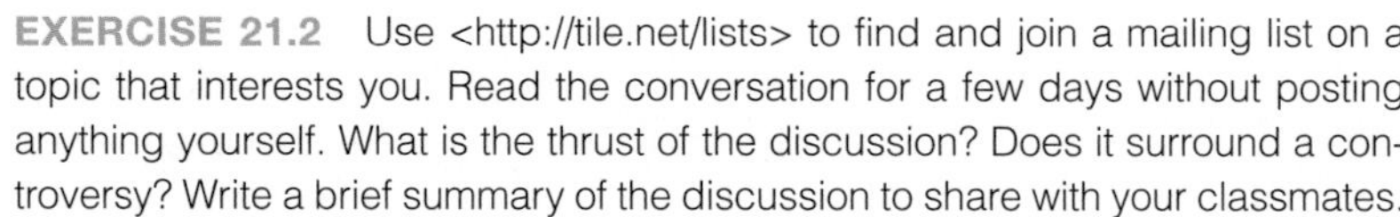

EXERCISE 21.2 Use <http://tile.net/lists> to find and join a mailing list on a topic that interests you. Read the conversation for a few days without posting anything yourself. What is the thrust of the discussion? Does it surround a controversy? Write a brief summary of the discussion to share with your classmates.

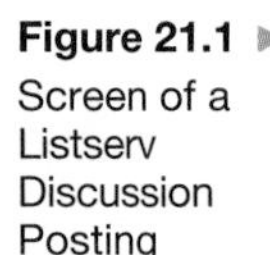

Figure 21.1 ▶ Screen of a Listserv Discussion Posting

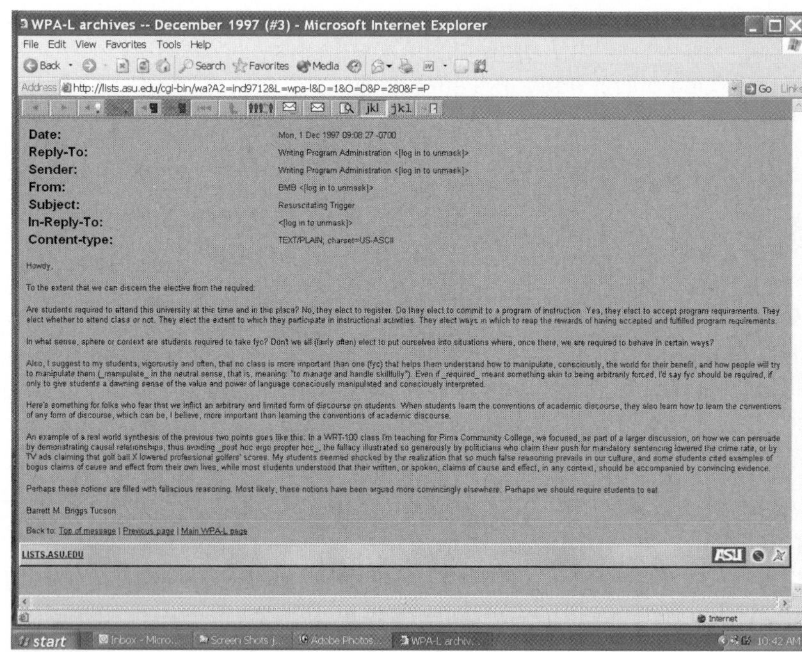

WPA-L archives -- December 1997 (#3) - Microsoft Internet Explorer

File Edit View Favorites Tools Help

Back Search Favorites Media

Address http://lists.asu.edu/cgi-bin/wa?A2=ind9712&L=wpa-l&D=1&O=D&P=280&F=P Go Links

Date: Mon, 1 Dec 1997 09:08:27 -0700

Reply-To: Writing Program Administration <[log in to unmask]>

Sender: Writing Program Administration <[log in to unmask]>

From: BMB <[log in to unmask]>

Subject: Resuscitating Trigger

In-Reply-To: <[log in to unmask]>

Content-type: TEXT/PLAIN; charset=US-ASCII

Howdy,

To the extent that we can discern the elective from the required:

Are students required to attend this university at this time and in this place? No, they elect to register. Do they elect to commit to a program of instruction Yes, they elect to accept program requirements. They elect whether to attend class or not. They elect the extent to which they participate in instructional activities. They elect ways in which to reap the rewards of having accepted and fulfilled program requirements.

In what sense, sphere or context are students required to take fyc? Don't we all (fairly often) elect to put ourselves into situations where, once there, we are required to behave in certain ways?

Also, I suggest to my students, vigorously and often, that no class is more important than one (fyc) that helps them understand how to manipulate, consciously, the world for their benefit, and how people will try to manipulate them (_manipulate_ in the neutral sense, that is, meaning: "to manage and handle skillfully"). Even if _required_ meant something akin to being arbitrarily forced, I'd say fyc should be required, if only to give students a dawning sense of the value and power of language consciously manipulated and consciously interpreted.

Here's something for folks who fear that we inflict an arbitrary and limited form of discourse on students. When students learn the conventions of academic discourse, they also learn how to learn the conventions of any form of discourse, which can be, I believe, more important than learning the conventions of academic discourse.

An example of a real world synthesis of the previous two points goes like this: In a WRT-100 class I'm teaching for Pima Community College, we focused, as part of a larger discussion, on how we can persuade by demonstrating causal relationships, thus avoiding _post hoc ergo propter hoc_, the fallacy illustrated so generously by politicians who claim their push for mandatory sentencing lowered the crime rate, or by TV ads claiming that golf ball X lowered professional golfers' scores. My students seemed shocked by the realization that so much false reasoning prevails in our culture, and some students cited examples of bogus claims of cause and effect from their own lives, while most students understood that their written, or spoken, claims of cause and effect, in any context, should be accompanied by convincing evidence.

Perhaps these notions are filled with fallacious reasoning. Most likely, these notions have been argued more convincingly elsewhere. Perhaps we should require students to eat.

Barrett M. Briggs Tucson

Back to: Top of message | Previous page | Main WPA-L page

LISTS.ASU.EDU

Internet

start Inbox - Micro... Screen Shots j... Adobe Photos... WPA-L archiv... 10:42 AM

❷ Bulletin boards, newsgroups, and Weblogs (blogs)

Newsgroups and blogs

Like mailing lists, **bulletin boards** provide a forum for discussion. Instead of sending email messages to subscribers, however, bulletin boards post messages electronically for anyone to access and read. There is no need to subscribe to read bulletin board messages.

A **newsgroup** is a type of bulletin board consisting of a collection of messages tied to a specific topic. *Usenet* has the most extensive array of public newsgroups. *Google Groups* has archived *Usenet* discussions going back for many years and has largely taken over the function of *Usenet.* See Figure 21.2 for a sample newsgroup screen.

See Fig. 21.2

The fastest growing use of the Internet is **Weblogs**, or **blogs**—personalized online journals. Blogs can be completely personal (an hourly recount of one individual's life) or organized around a topic like politics or sports. College courses sometimes have blogs for posting and sharing student work. Individual

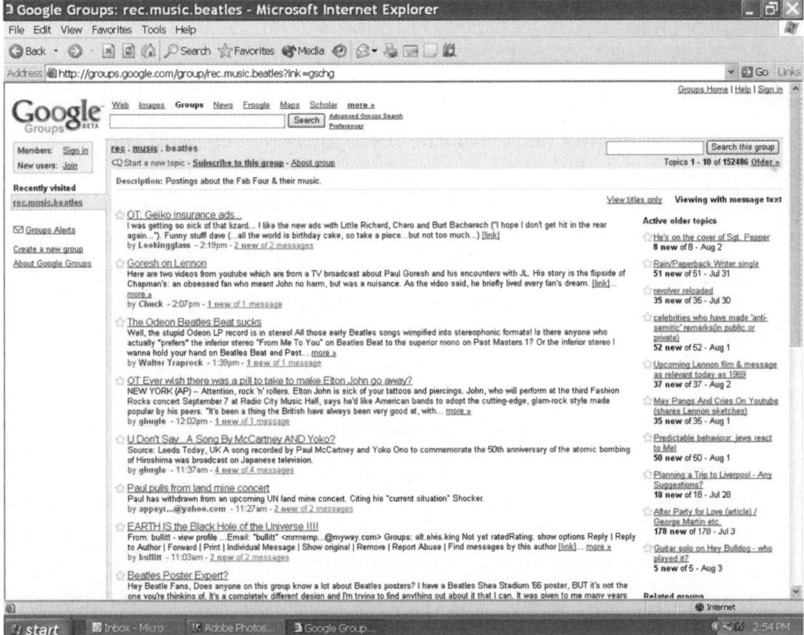

◄ **Figure 21.2**

Google Groups: <rec.music.beatles>

students may use blogs for a similar purpose—that is, as a collection site for notes, ideas, and work in progress.

EXERCISE 21.3 Choose a topic on *Google Groups* that interests you and read a few of the postings (<http://groups.google.com>). What is being discussed? Who are the participants in the newsgroup? Print out a few postings to discuss with your classmates, and then brainstorm about how you might use bulletin boards in a research project.

21d Use instant communication effectively

Email is called **asynchronous communication** because it does not take place in real time: users post and read messages at their convenience. Sometimes we prefer to communicate more rapidly, as if we were conversing face to face. A variety of tools are available for this kind of instant exchange, called **synchronous communication**. Instant-messaging and text-messaging are the most common forms of synchronous communication.

1 Instant-messaging

Instant-messaging allows you to create an online circle of friends, classmates, or colleagues. The instant-messaging service (such as *Yahoo!*, *Google Talk*, or *AmericaOnline*) then notifies you whenever someone in your group is online so that you can choose whether to chat. Depending on the service, you can include four or more people in your conversation, and the automatic typing indicator lets you know whenever someone is typing a response. See Figure 21.3 for a sample instant-messaging screen. For collaborative projects, your group might find it worthwhile to set up instant-messaging accounts on the same service.

See Fig. 21.3

The rhetoric of instant-messaging

As with other electronic communications, you need to pay attention to the rhetoric of instant-messaging. Most often it is used to communicate with friends and family. If you use an instant-messaging chat to discuss a collaborative project with classmates, you may find that you have to remind yourselves to stay focused on the work at hand. It is easy to stray into informal personal chatting in this medium.

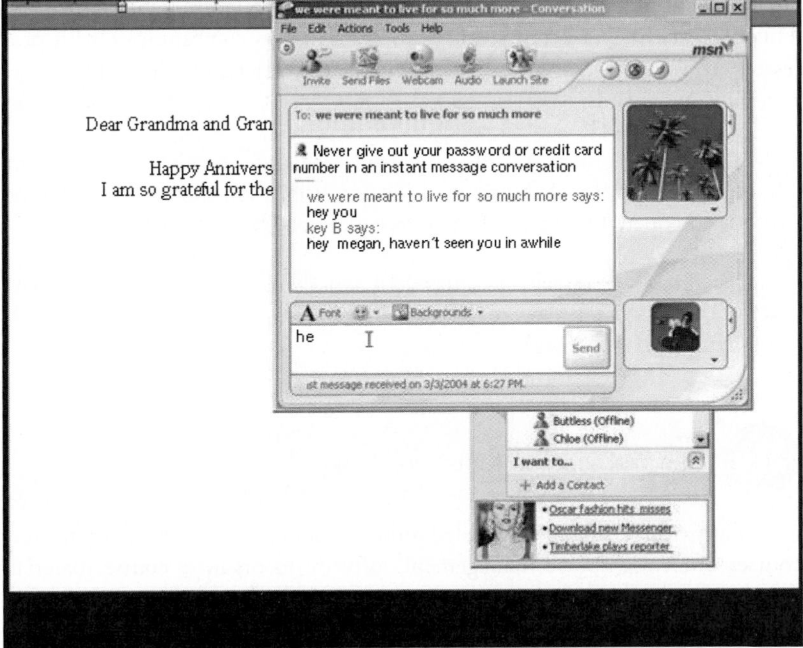

◄ **Figure 21.3**
Instant-Messaging Chat

Getting used to the timing of an instant-messaging discussion takes some patience, as there may be some lag time between when you post something and when someone else replies. This lag time is another reason it may be hard to keep focused when discussing via instant-messaging.

❷ Text-messaging

Most cell phones now permit users to exchange **text messages** as well as voice messages. Although text messages can move back and forth in real time at the rate of conversation, they can also be saved, accessed, and responded to later, as time permits.

The rhetoric of text-messaging

With text-messaging between cell phones, the rhetoric is difficult to control. Because of the constraints of the electronic medium itself, text messages are often full of shorthand, abbreviations, and truncated sentence structures. Thus, text messaging is rarely an appropriate way to communicate with professors. You should reserve text messaging for very brief and informal messages to family and friends.

EXERCISE 21.4 Sign up for an Instant Message account at *Yahoo.com.* Arrange an instant-messaging chat session with a few friends. How did the discussion go? What did you like or dislike about this electronic medium?

FOR COLLABORATION Discuss your experience using instant-messaging with your classmates. How might this medium be used to enhance class discussions or peer reviews?

21e Use Web course tools effectively

Many courses are now provided online, and professors in more traditional courses often use course management software to organize course material, assignments, and grades. **Course management software** (e.g., *Blackboard, MyCompLab* and others) allows instructors to post a syllabus, assignments, a schedule, and other class information on a Web site and to interact with students electronically. It also allows students to interact with one another electronically. If you are not currently participating in an electronically managed course environment, you probably will before your college career is over.

1 Getting started

Logging into the class

To begin using a Web classroom, you will first need to know the URL at which your class's Web site can be found. For example, the URL for Web classes at Utah State University is <http://blackboard.usu.edu>. On the opening page for your class's Web site, you will typically be asked to type in a user name and password that has been assigned to you by your teacher. Keep careful track of your user name and password, since they are your key to entering the Web classroom. One of the biggest problems that students have is finding themselves "locked out" of the classroom because they forgot their passwords!

Checklist

Web Course Questions

Following are some of the questions you might want to ask your instructor as you begin a course using a Web classroom:

- ✓ How often will the information on the class Web site be updated?
- ✓ How will I know when there is new information posted?
- ✓ Where do I go to find the course assignments?
- ✓ Where do I go to see how my assignments have been graded?
- ✓ Will there be quizzes, and how will they be administered and graded?
- ✓ What tools will we use to collaborate with our peers?
- ✓ What tools will we use to peer review each other's papers?
- ✓ Is there a discussion forum that we are required to participate in?
- ✓ What about a chat room? Are we expected to chat with our peers?
- ✓ Will your office hours be held in a chat room at a particular time?

Becoming familiar with the online classroom

When you are actually admitted to the online classroom, there will probably be an opening screen with a menu of options. There may be a "getting started" or introductory screen that will help you to become oriented to the tools available to you. There may also be course information provided by your instructor that helps you to understand the course policies and expectations. Take the time to become familiar with the classroom and its tools.

See Fig. 21.4

❷ Course information

Web classrooms may include a course calendar; a bulletin board for important messages from the instructor; a syllabus with a course outline; and course information such as meeting times, instructor's office hours, and descriptions of assignments. Read all of this information carefully. When instructors make use of online classrooms, they generally do not also provide you with printed hard copies of course information but rather rely on you to garner the relevant information directly from the Internet.

See Fig. 21.5

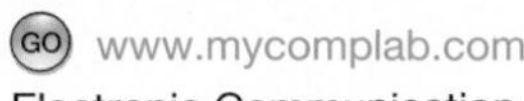

Figure 21.4 ▶ *WebCT* Welcome Screen

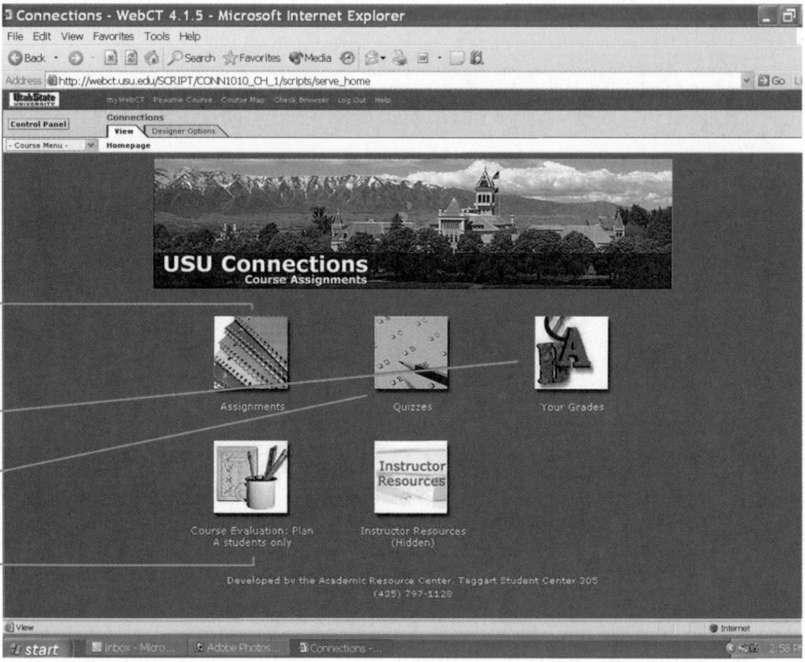

Descriptions of course assignments

Grades

Quizzes

Course evaluations

❸ Course communication tools

Your Web classroom will provide a number of tools that you will use to communicate with your teacher and others in your class. These may include class email or listservs, chat rooms, discussion forums, homework managers, and file-sharing spaces. Again, take the time to become familiar with the communication tools that your class will be using. We discussed the use of email and online networks in 21b and 21c. The comparable course tools in your Web classroom will function similarly (see Figure 21.6 for an illustration of a post on a discussion forum). The only difference will be that the tools will be gathered into one location on the Web, that of your particular Web classroom.

See 21b and 21c

See Fig. 21.6

Other course tools not previously described may include a homework manager and a file-sharing space. Both of these tools allow you to share your written work, either with the instructor alone (in the case of the homework manager) or with everyone in the class (with the file-sharing space).

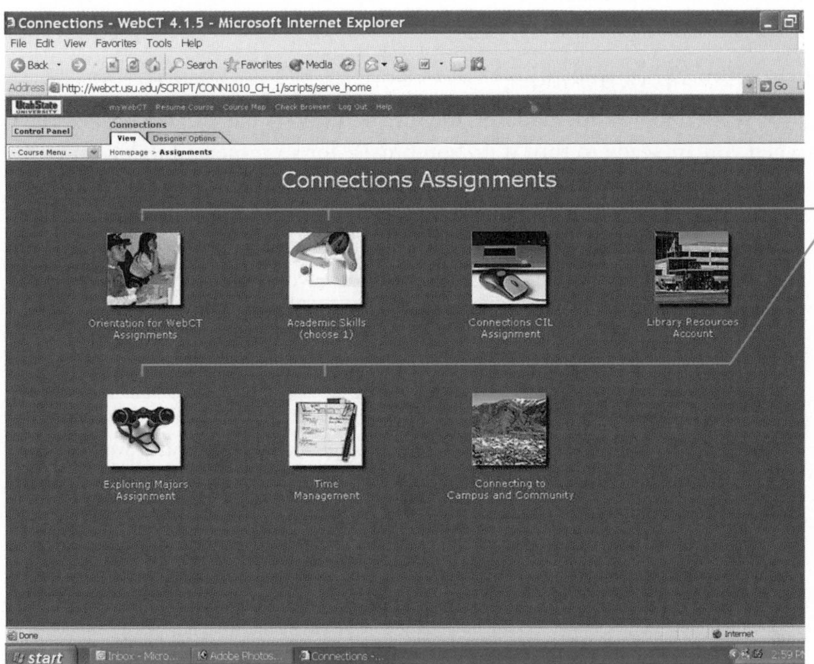

◄ **Figure 21.5**
WebCT Assignments Screen

◄ **Figure 21.6**
New Century Handbook WebCT Discussion Post

Reply Quote Save

[Prev Thread][Next Thread][Prev in Thread][Next in Thread]

Article No. 1: posted by **Christine Hult** on Wed, Oct. 25, 2006, 15:02

Subject: Portfolio review

```
Dear Class,

I've finished your first portfolio reviews and I'm very
happy with your work so far.  Please remember that your
argument first draft is due on the Homework Manager on
October 31.

Dr. Hult
```

[Prev Thread][Next Thread][Prev in Thread][Next in Thread]

Homework manager

With a homework manager, the instructor posts the assignment and then, when you are ready to turn it in, you browse for your file and upload it to the Web server. Your instructor in turn downloads your work, corrects it or comments on it electronically, and then uploads it once again to the class Web site. In this fashion, work can easily be submitted, graded, and returned without ever being printed out in a hard copy. Homework managers can also keep track of your grades and let you know how you are doing in the class.

File-sharing space

See Fig. 21.7

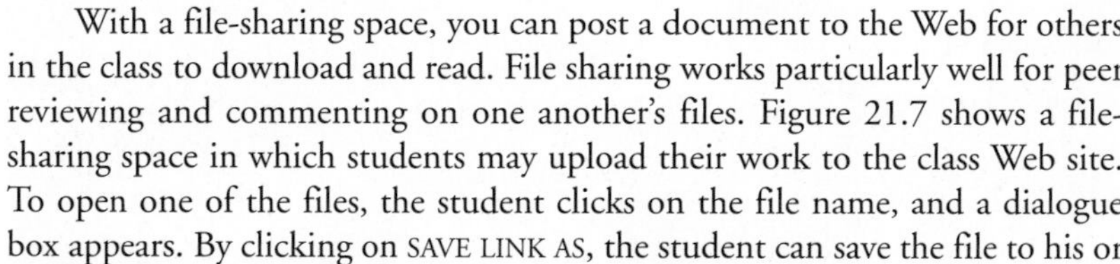

With a file-sharing space, you can post a document to the Web for others in the class to download and read. File sharing works particularly well for peer reviewing and commenting on one another's files. Figure 21.7 shows a file-sharing space in which students may upload their work to the class Web site. To open one of the files, the student clicks on the file name, and a dialogue box appears. By clicking on SAVE LINK AS, the student can save the file to his or

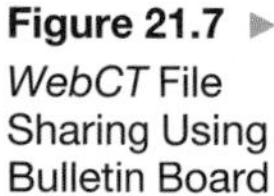

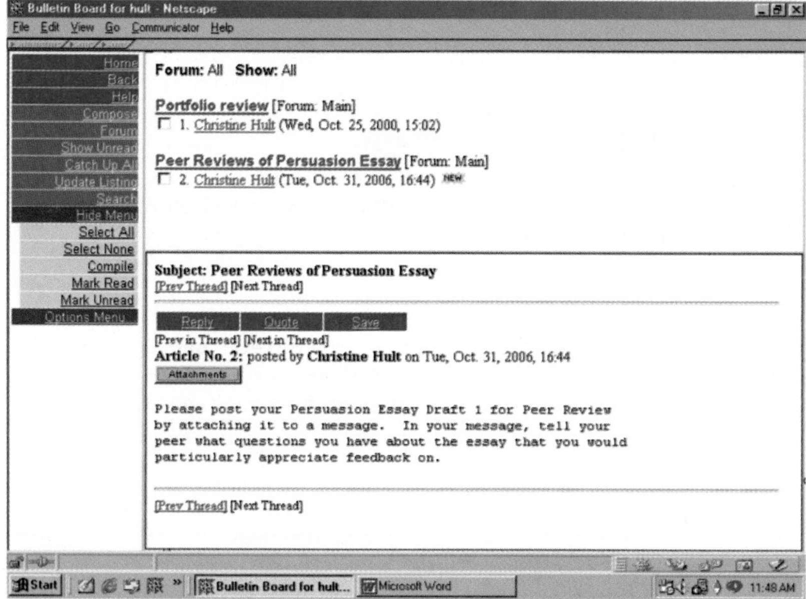

Figure 21.7 ▶ *WebCT* File Sharing Using Bulletin Board

her own data disk and then subsequently open it in a word-processing program for commenting. Using the DOCUMENT COMMENT feature of the word-processing program, the student can insert document comments as part of a peer review session. Once the document has been commented on, it is then uploaded once again to the file-sharing space so that the original author can read the comments. You will need to check with your instructor to learn exactly how the file-sharing system works for your particular Web classroom.

GO
See TechHelp 5e-3

FOR COLLABORATION If a course Web site is available to you, try revising a paper together with a friend by using an online discussion forum, chat room, or file-sharing tool. Discuss the experience with your classmates.

22 Business Correspondence and Reports

FAQs

- How do I write a good business letter? (22a)
- How do I prepare an electronic résumé? (22c-3)
- What's the difference between a memo and a report? (22e)

Writing at work differs significantly from writing in school:

SCHOOL WRITING	WORKPLACE WRITING
• Typically analyzes or reflects on some intellectual topic	• Typically addresses a practical problem and proposes a solution
• Is usually written for a single reader	• Is usually written for multiple readers
• Gets a thorough, careful reading	• May be only read in parts, or skimmed
• Is usually done alone	• Is often done in collaboration with others

Because workplace writing is so different from school writing in these and other ways, it puts a premium on clarity, conciseness, and conventional document structure.

22a Write concise and professional business letters

People write business letters for a variety of purposes: to make an inquiry or a request, to complain, to apply for a job, to issue an announcement, to sell something, to respond to a previous letter. Letters are typically addressed to a specific person, but they may be circulated to other readers as well. Thus, you should anticipate the possibility that people other than the addressee (an assistant, for example) might read it. Be clear and concise and try to strike a friendly, courteous, and professional tone.

See Ch. 38 and 43c

Rhetorical considerations

The best way to structure a letter depends on how you think the reader will react to its message. If your reader is likely to respond favorably or neutrally, take the *direct approach* by getting to the point quickly and providing necessary explanations and details later. On the other hand, if your reader is likely to respond to your message unfavorably or skeptically, take a more *indirect approach*, in which you begin with background information or some other form of "bad news buffer" before getting to the main point.

Try to give your letter as positive a tone as possible. Emphasize good news by putting it in positions of prominence (such as at the beginning and end of paragraphs). Try to word your sentences in ways that accentuate the positive. If possible, avoid words with negative connotations such as *regretfully, unfortunately, refuse, will not,* or *failure.* Of course, this should not be overdone; in business writing, clarity is more important than comfort.

Format

Guide to business letters

See Ch. 21

Today, the most common form of written correspondence in the business world, as in many other environments, is email. Because email is so easy and convenient to use, many writers do not give it the care and attention they should. But readers of business email are no different from readers of letters, reports, résumés, and memos, working under time pressure to solve practical problems. When you write business email, apply the same rhetorical considerations to it that you would to other forms of business correspondence: a clear purpose, sufficient background information, correct grammar and spelling, a friendly yet professional tone. Since email readers are likely to scroll quickly through a long message and may miss key items if they are buried in the text, email letters should focus on a single topic and be short enough, if possible, to fit on one screen. Always remember to observe proper netiquette and to consider your audience's reaction to the message.

The traditional hard-copy business letter is becoming increasingly outmoded. Still, there may be occasions when you will want to use it. In such cases, use a format such as in Figure 22.1.

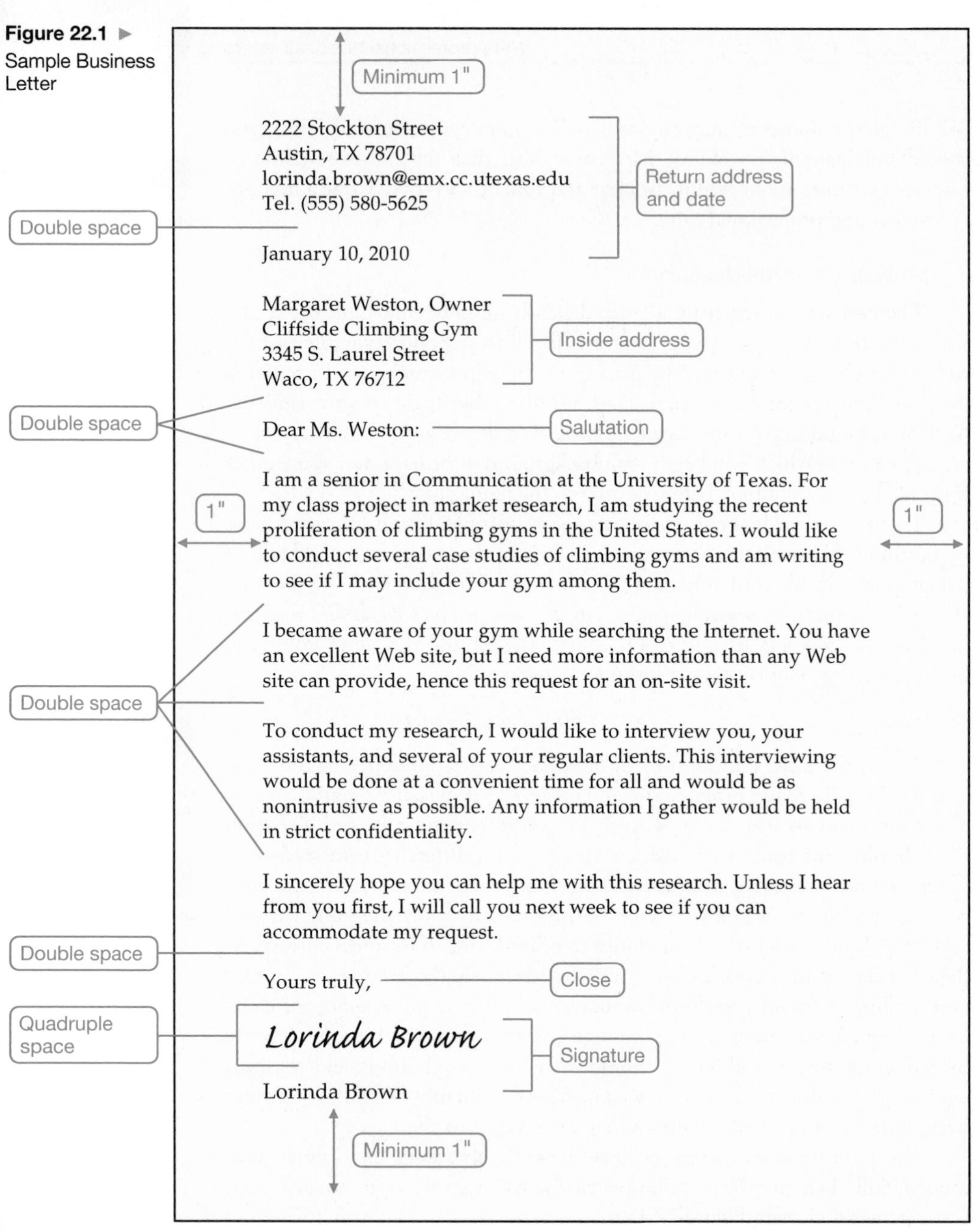

2222 Stockton Street
Austin, TX 78701
lorinda.brown@emx.cc.utexas.edu
Tel. (555) 580-5625

January 10, 2010

Margaret Weston, Owner
Cliffside Climbing Gym
3345 S. Laurel Street
Waco, TX 76712

Dear Ms. Weston:

I am a senior in Communication at the University of Texas. For my class project in market research, I am studying the recent proliferation of climbing gyms in the United States. I would like to conduct several case studies of climbing gyms and am writing to see if I may include your gym among them.

I became aware of your gym while searching the Internet. You have an excellent Web site, but I need more information than any Web site can provide, hence this request for an on-site visit.

To conduct my research, I would like to interview you, your assistants, and several of your regular clients. This interviewing would be done at a convenient time for all and would be as nonintrusive as possible. Any information I gather would be held in strict confidentiality.

I sincerely hope you can help me with this research. Unless I hear from you first, I will call you next week to see if you can accommodate my request.

Yours truly,

Lorinda Brown

Lorinda Brown

Figure 22.1 ▶ Sample Business Letter

Guidelines

Writing Email Letters

- Use the subject line to orient the reader.
- Provide any necessary background information in the first sentence or two; if appropriate, reference previous correspondence.
- Quickly establish your purpose.
- Focus on the main point.
- Use simple sentences and short paragraphs.
- Use personal pronouns and active verbs.
- Keep it short.
- Consider letting your letter sit for a while before sending it because once sent, it can't be retrieved.
- Remember that no email message is strictly confidential.

22b Write specifically tailored letters of application

Principles of business correspondence

Knowing how to write a good application letter is crucial to the job-seeking process. An application letter is a kind of sales pitch, where the product you are selling is yourself. It is usually the first thing a prospective employer sees from you, and, of course, you want to make a good first impression. There is no room for error in a letter of application—no room for beating around the bush, shyness, misrepresentations, or misspellings.

Writing Letters of Application

- **Keep it brief.** A one-page letter is the general rule.
- **Clearly state the position you are applying for** in the first paragraph.
- **Describe your primary credentials** for the position in the next paragraph or two.
- **Request an interview** and give the reader information about your availability in the closing paragraph.
- **Address the envelope** carefully and correctly, using standard abbreviations.

Usually, a letter of application is accompanied by a résumé and includes some of the same information. But unlike the résumé, the letter should be tailored to one specific job or program. Whereas a résumé contains a full summary of your past accomplishments, the letter includes only those accomplishments that are relevant to the job or program you are applying for. The tone of the letter should be polite, confident, and enthusiastic, but not pushy. Where possible, it should emphasize how your skills would benefit this particular organization. A sample letter of application is shown in Figure 22.2.

GO See Fig. 22.2

22c Write densely but appropriately packed résumés

A **résumé** is a concise summary of an individual's accomplishments, skills, experience, and personal interests. It is more complete and inclusive than a letter of application; the same résumé can be sent to more than one potential employer, whereas each letter of application should be different.

ESL NOTE In some countries, a résumé may include an individual's age, marital status, religious affiliation, and other highly personal information. In the United States, such information cannot legally be considered in hiring and so should not be included.

A résumé should be densely packed with appropriate information—never padded with irrelevant information or information that is not true.

Most résumés use five standard categories of information:

1. Position Desired or Objective
2. Education
3. Experience or Employment
4. Related Activities
5. References

If you think your experience or employment history is more impressive than your educational achievements, you may want to reverse the positions of those two categories. The entries within any one category are normally listed in reverse chronological order (that is, the most recent achievement is listed first). For most students and other workers just starting out, a résumé will be no longer than a single full page.

Figure 22.2
Sample Letter of Application

2222 Stockton Street
Austin, TX 78701
lorinda.brown@emx.cc.utexas.edu
Tel. (555) 580-5625

January 10, 2010

Mr. Jeffrey Lee
Director of Marketing Training
Future Consumer, Inc.
444 North Sycamore Avenue
Los Angeles, CA 90009-4444

Dear Mr. Lee:

I am writing to apply for acceptance into your marketing training program. I am especially impressed with the program's emphasis on market research, product planning, and catalog sales. As a marketing major at the University of Texas, I believe I am ready to undertake this challenge and would welcome the opportunity to prove myself.

Marketing has been a major focus of my college and work experience. My studies have provided a strong foundation in communication and business. I have also had experience in product testing and merchandising through my jobs in market research and retailing and have been on the "receiving end" of customer indecision and anxiety. My ability to handle difficult customers earned me a promotion from direct sales to sales management.

My résumé is attached. I will be graduating in early June and would be available for training immediately thereafter. I look forward to hearing from you.

Sincerely yours,

Lorinda Brown

Lorinda Brown

enclosure

An alternative to the standard résumé just described is the **functional résumé**, in which certain skills are emphasized through categories such as Computer Skills, Management Skills, and Language Skills or Ability to Solve Problems, Ability to Motivate Others, and Ability to Maintain Diverse Interests. If you do not have a long employment history but have been doing volunteer work or internships or want to emphasize your coursework, the functional résumé may be a better format for you to use. Keep in mind, though, that the functional résumé is somewhat unconventional; some employers may not care for it.

Today, résumés may be submitted and inspected in a variety of ways.

- A traditional hard-copy résumé, sent by post or fax or delivered by hand, may be reviewed personally by one or more people at the receiving company.
- A hard-copy résumé, sent by post or fax or delivered by hand, may be scanned into the receiving company's computer for review onscreen.
- An electronic résumé, sent by email, may be reviewed as is by one or more people at the receiving company.
- An electronic résumé, sent by email, may be converted by the receiving company into its own database format for review on screen.
- An electronic résumé, posted to a Web site, may be available for prospective employers to locate through a keyword search.

Also, it is becoming increasingly common for companies to have job applicants log on to their Web site and fill out electronic application forms, or **e-forms**, the information from which is then added to the company's résumé databank.

Given all this variety, you may want to prepare several versions of your résumé. In the next few pages, we will show you how. Many Internet sites can help you, too.

❶ Formatting a traditional résumé

A traditional hard-copy résumé should be designed to please the eye. It should be centered on the page and approximately fill the page. A skimpy résumé suggests that you have not accomplished much, while an overcrowded one puts too much pressure on the reader to absorb all the information provided. Use suitable margins (about 1 inch all around), and use white space to set off the major categories and groupings. Use boldface type for your name and for major headings and subheadings. Use verb phrases instead of full sentences to describe your various activities and achievements; consistent use of such phrases will produce an elegant parallelism. Using active-voice verbs will give you a dynamic image. Always use white or light-colored paper. Avoid printing in color, as it will not reproduce well on black-and-white copiers. A sample traditional résumé is shown in Figure 22.3. Note that the applicant added a category for Awards.

See Ch. 19

See Ch. 38, See 28g

TechHelp

Formatting a Scannable Résumé

- **Use nouns and noun phrases rather than verbs** as much as possible. Computer scanning of hard-copy résumés is based mainly on keyword searches, and keywords are usually nouns.

Instead of	Write
Performed maintenance	Maintenance mechanic
Designed a Web site	Web site designer
Tested products	Product tester
Worked in a laboratory	Laboratory technician
Developed software	Software developer
Wrote grant proposals	Grant proposal writer

- **Don't shy away from technical jargon.** Many computer programs use technical jargon to find appropriate candidates.
- **Put your keyword self-description at the beginning.** Some computer programs process only the first 50 to 75 words, so you may want to include a separate section at the beginning of your résumé that lists all your keyword self-descriptors.
- **Use white or light-colored paper,** standard size.
- **Always send an original,** not a photocopy.
- **Use a standard typeface** (Times, Palatino, Arial, Garamond, or Helvetica, for example) in 10- to 14-point font sizes. Don't use italics, underlining, or fancy or unusual type styles.
- **Don't use lines, graphics, boxes, or color.**
- **Use left justification,** not left/right justification, to keep normal spacing between letters and words.
- **Start every line at the left margin.** Don't use columns or tabs.
- **Don't fold or staple your résumé.**

Figure 22.3 ▶
Sample Traditional Résumé

Lorinda Brown
2222 Stockton Street
Austin, TX 78701
lorinda.brown@emx.cc.utexas.edu
(555) 580-5625

OBJECTIVE
Marketing/management trainee in the retail industry.
Am willing to relocate if necessary.

EDUCATION
Bachelor of Science, University of Texas at Austin, June 2010 (present GPA: 3.4)

Major: Communication. Minor: Marketing. Completed 25 credit hours in marketing and management.

BUSINESS EXPERIENCE
Retail sales, Stevens Brown Sports, Austin, since September 2009. Started with floor sales; promoted to assistant manager of weekend operations. Designed the company's Web site, which features links to local bike trails, golf courses, and other sites of recreational interest. Drew up new marketing plan that increased sales by 15%.

Intern, Frito-Lay, Inc., Austin, June–August 2006. Completed 10-week marketing internship, which included product testing and merchandising. Handled accounts during 6 weeks' absence of local representative.

Server, Tony Roma's Restaurant, Austin, September 2008–May 2009. Responsible for five-table section. Used sales and public relations techniques in a high-volume environment.

OTHER EXPERIENCE
Vice-President, University of Texas Black Student Association, September 2009 to present. Represented the Association at the 2009 Southwest meeting.

Counselor-Tutor, Upward Bound, Austin, January–May 2008.

AWARDS
Employee of the Month, Stevens Brown, November 2009.

REFERENCES
Available on request from the University of Texas Placement and Career Information Center, 350 SSB, Austin, TX 78704.
Tel. (555) 581-6186.

❷ Formatting a scannable résumé

Many companies are now using computer technology to scan large numbers of hard-copy résumés quickly and insert the results into a databank. Later, a keyword search can be used to select only those applicants whose self-descriptors fit a certain profile. If you are applying to technologically oriented organizations, you should format your résumé to take advantage of this technology. Some significant differences exist between the traditional résumé and the scannable résumé.

Computer scanners are not entirely reliable when it comes to distinguishing letters and other marks on paper. So, in putting together a scannable résumé, do everything you can to make things easy for the scanner. A scannable version of Lorinda Brown's résumé is shown in Figure 22.4.

❸ Formatting an electronic résumé

Increasingly, companies solicit résumés via email or the Internet. In such cases, you should format your résumé so that it conforms to the company's specifications.

Email résumés

If you plan to send your résumé by email to several different companies, you should put it into as simple and universal a format as possible. This means (1) using a simplified layout with a prominent keywords section, like that of the scannable résumé, and (2) putting the résumé in ASCII, text only, or simple text format. Most companies prefer that you embed the résumé in the email message itself, after the cover letter, rather than attaching a file. If the look of the résumé is of great importance to you, however, you might try using RTF (rich text format) and sending your résumé as an attachment to your email message. In this case, you would be wise to first send a test copy to a friend who has a different system than you do.

See 21b-6

Homepage résumés

Although designing your own homepage résumé can be fun, it is generally not the most effective way to go about searching for a job. Most potential employers will not go to the trouble of logging on to your Web site. You would make better use of your time logging on to *their* Web sites and submitting your résumé according to *their* specifications.

Figure 22.4 ►
Sample Scannable Résumé

Lorinda Brown
2222 Stockton Street
Austin, TX 78701
(555) 580-5625

KEY WORDS: Marketing/management trainee, retail sales, Web site designer, communication major, management experience, marketing planner, recreation industry, product testing, merchandising.

OBJECTIVE: Marketing/management trainee in the retail industry. Willing to relocate.

EDUCATION: Bachelor of Science, University of Texas at Austin, June 2010 (present GPA: 3.4). Major: Communication.
Minor: Marketing. Completed 25 credit hours in marketing and management.

BUSINESS EXPERIENCE: Retail sales, Stevens Brown Sports, Austin, since September 2009. Assistant manager, Web site designer, marketing planner. Management of weekend operations after promotion from floor sales. Web site design features links to local bike trails, golf courses, and other sites of recreational interest. New marketing plan has increased sales by 15%.

Intern, Frito-Lay, Inc., Austin, June–August 2009. Marketing internship, 10 weeks, which included product testing and merchandising. Did accounting during 6 weeks' absence of local representative.

Server, Tony Roma's Restaurant, Austin, September 2008–May 2009. Responsible for five-table section. Used sales and public relations techniques in a high-volume environment.

OTHER EXPERIENCE: Vice-President, University of Texas Black Student Association, September 2009 to present.
Representative for the Association at the 2009 Southwest meeting.
Counselor-Tutor, Upward Bound, Austin, January–May 2008.

AWARDS: Employee of the Month, Stevens Brown, November 2009.

REFERENCES: Available on request from the University of Texas Placement and Career Information Center, 350 SSB, Austin, TX 78704. Tel. (555) 581-6186.

TechHelp

Finding Online Information about Writing and Posting a Résumé

- *eRésumés*
  http://www.eresumes.com
- *Proven Resumes.com Career Center*
  http://www.provenresumes.com
- *Monster.com*
  http://www.monster.com
- *JobStar Resume Guide*
  http://www.jobsmart.org/tools/resume/
- *Guaranteed Résumés Career Library*
  http://www.gresumes.com/library.htm

If, however, you are determined to have your own homepage résumé, we suggest that you follow these guidelines.

See Ch. 20

1. Make sure that you are familiar with the principles of good Web page design.
2. Put your keyword self-descriptors up front, as in a scannable résumé.
3. Use keywords in your page's title and URL. Companies' search engines will not recognize your name, but they will recognize certain keywords.
4. For personal safety, do not include your home address or phone number. Give only an email address.
5. Consider creating an additional page containing an ASCII version of your résumé, with all HTML tags removed, in case employers want to copy it into their database.
6. Surf the Web and look at some other homepage résumés. If you look at enough of them, you will get a sense of what works and what does not.

EXERCISE 22.1 On the Internet, on a campus bulletin board, or in your local newspaper, find an advertisement for a job that you would want, and write a letter of application for the job.

FOR COLLABORATION Prepare a scannable résumé and share it with your group. Exchange ideas on how to improve the formatting of your résumé, as well as what additional or alternative keywords you may want to include.

22d Write clearly organized reports

A report, as the name implies, is a document that describes the results of an activity. If you do experiments in a chemistry lab, you will be expected to write them up in a lab report. If you research a topic for your composition class in the library, you may be asked to write a library report. Company employees who go on a business trip are usually asked to submit a trip report. Scientists and engineers conducting research projects are expected to submit ongoing progress reports and then, at the end, a final report. There are many other kinds of reports as well, including feasibility reports, environmental impact statements, and activity reports. A report can be as short as one or two pages or as long as a thousand pages. Short reports (for example, lab reports and trip reports) usually have a small, local readership; longer reports are often circulated to a variety of readers both inside and outside the organization in which they are written.

1 Making decisions about content, layout, and design

Designing reports is generally easier than designing brochures or newsletters because most instructors and businesses have specific formats or conventions that they expect you to follow. For example, the report in 17c follows a format commonly used in engineering courses. It is important to find out what format your instructor or supervisor expects you to use for a report.

2 Dividing the report into four basic parts

There are four basic parts to a report: a header, an introduction, a body, and a conclusion. Reports may have additional components as well, such as a title page, an abstract, attachments, a table of contents, and a cover letter or memo. If you do not have a specified format to follow, many word processors provide document templates that can help get you started.

Header

The first part of a report is called the header. It provides basic information about the document, such as for whom it is intended, who wrote it, when it was written, and what it is about. If you are writing a report in memo form, the header should contain four standard lines: TO, FROM,

SUBJECT (or RE), and DATE. Fill in each of these lines with the appropriate information. In a more formal report, you may want to use a title page instead of a header.

See 22d-3

Headers can include other information, such as a distribution list (recipients other than the person named on the TO line may be listed under DIST or CC), a list of enclosures or attachments (indicated by ENCL or ATTACHMENT), and a reference to previous correspondence (indicated by REF).

See student example, 17c

Introduction

The introduction serves the vitally important purpose of orienting and informing busy readers. Like brochures and newsletters, reports are often distributed to a variety of readers both inside and outside the organization from which they originate. Many of these readers may be unfamiliar with the report's subject matter. Furthermore, unlike college instructors, who are obligated to read entire student papers, readers in the "real world" often skim reports. In your introduction, you should tell readers quickly (1) what problem you are addressing, (2) how you have addressed it, and (3) what your findings and recommendations are. Begin with a brief problem statement, usually only one paragraph long, and then follow it with a separate summary, also only one paragraph long. (The engineering students in 17c stated the problem and their recommended solutions in a two-paragraph executive summary that preceded the report itself.)

Body

The main part of the report should contain your claim(s), present your evidence, lay out your reasoning, acknowledge counterarguments, and cite references—in short, provide a good, solid argument. If the problem statement on the first page of your report needs elaboration, elaborate at the beginning of the body. Visual aids, including typographical distinctions, itemized lists, graphs, and tables should be used throughout to distinguish and clarify important information. If your report is two or more pages, divide the body into sections, using informative headings such as Introduction, Method, Results, and Discussion. (The engineering students in 17c used the following headings for the body of their report: Introduction and Problem Statement, Four Proposed Alternative Solutions, Research Methods, and Results and Discussion.)

See Ch. 6

See Ch. 19

Conclusion

Conclude the report with a summary of your main points, a recommendation, a proposal for action, and/or an expression of appreciation. You can repeat information from the summary section of the introduction for emphasis.

See 17c

3 Adding optional parts

Title page

Formal reports of more than five pages often have a title page instead of a header. The title page should include the name of the person or group to whom the report is addressed, the names of any other recipients, the names of the writers, the date, the subject (that is, the title), and references to any funding sources.

Abstract

An *abstract* is a concise synopsis (100–150 words) of the report that

1. introduces the topic
2. briefly describes the method of investigation
3. details the main findings
4. states the general conclusions and implications of these findings.

If your report is published, the abstract may be separated from the report and entered into a computerized database; therefore, it should be comprehensible on its own.

Attachments

Many reports are based on detailed information—lengthy calculations, drawings, published articles, and other secondary matter—that not every reader will need or want to see. Rather than including such materials in the report, append them either as a formal appendix or as attachments. If you have multiple attachments, include a separate table of contents prior to the attachments.

See 17c

Table of contents

A table of contents helps readers get a sense of the overall structure of the report and allows busy readers to skip directly to those parts that interest them. If your report is fairly long and complex, with a title page, abstract, and attachments, you should include a table of contents just after the abstract.

Cover letter or memo

A cover letter (also called a letter of transmittal) or a memo often accompanies a long report sent to specific readers. This letter gives the writer an opportunity to (1) introduce the report to readers who are not expecting it and (2) draw readers' attention to specific parts of the report. Writers often send different cover letters to different readers. (The engineering students in 17c included a memo to introduce their report to readers.)

4 Formatting for the selective reader

Some readers will want to read the entire report, while others will want to read only parts of it. Thus, it is important that reports—especially long reports—be formatted to accommodate selective reading behavior.

EXERCISE 22.2 Write a two-page report evaluating the engineering students' report in 17c for ease of skimming. Use the Guidelines in 22e.

22e Write focused memos

One of the most important types of documents in business and professional contexts is the memorandum, or memo. People write memos for a variety of purposes: to inform, to summarize, to recommend, to make a request. Memos are usually quite short, informal in tone, and focused on a single topic. Unlike reports, memos are typically written to only a local audience, such as supervisors, colleagues, or employees internal to a company or department.

See 22d

Structurally, a memo has the same four basic parts as a report: a header, an introduction, a body, and a conclusion. In addition, like a report, a memo may have attachments. But all of these components are typically much

See 17c
See 18c

Making It Easy for Readers to Skim a Report

- Use an informative *title*.
- Provide a short *abstract*.
- At the very beginning, define the *problem* the report is addressing.
- Provide an *executive summary* on the first page of the report.
- Provide good *visual aids* to accompany appropriate text.
- Divide the report into logical sections, with informative *section headings*.
- Provide informative *subheadings* as well.
- Begin each paragraph with a good *topic sentence*.
- Give *typographical prominence* to key points (without overdoing it).
- Relegate supporting information (such as calculations and reference materials) to *appendixes*, making sure to reference such information in the body of the report.
- For a long report, include a *table of contents*.

See Ch. 19

See 5a

See 22a

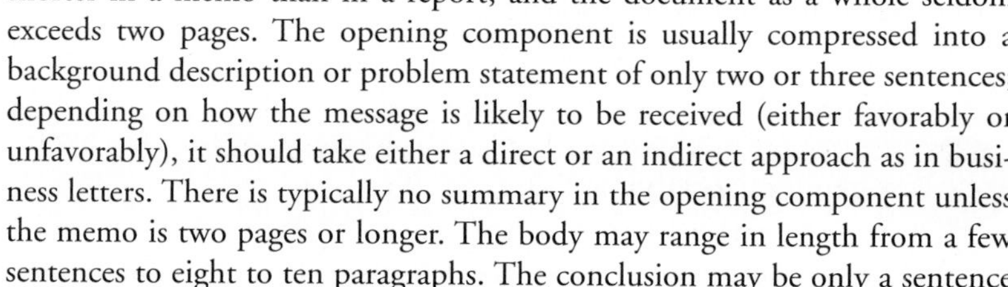

shorter in a memo than in a report, and the document as a whole seldom exceeds two pages. The opening component is usually compressed into a background description or problem statement of only two or three sentences; depending on how the message is likely to be received (either favorably or unfavorably), it should take either a direct or an indirect approach as in business letters. There is typically no summary in the opening component unless the memo is two pages or longer. The body may range in length from a few sentences to eight to ten paragraphs. The conclusion may be only a sentence or two.

With most word-processing programs, you can create a document template (a preset form). If your department or company has a standard format for memos, you can create a template that conforms to this standard.

The sample memo in Figure 22.5 was written by two students to their writing instructor. The instructor, Professor Gilbert, had asked all the students in the class to form two-person teams, call local nonprofit agencies to find a suitable service-learning project, and then submit to her a one-page memo describing their proposed project.

Figure 22.5
Sample Memo

To: Professor Gilbert

From: Mona Kitab and Fernando Marquez

Date: June 4, 2009

Subject: Proposal for a service-learning project

After telephoning five agencies, we have decided that the project we would most like to work on is an information brochure for the city's homeless shelter. Although about 150 homeless people use the shelter on a regular basis, the shelter is badly underfunded and needs more volunteers to help out. Miriam Hatcher, the shelter director, told us she thought that more university students would volunteer to help if they only knew more about it. She said that a well-written brochure answering students' questions about the shelter might be the answer, because it could be easily distributed all around campus.

We plan to create a six-panel, folded brochure that will answer the following questions:

- What is the homeless shelter?
- How many people does it serve, and in what way?
- Why does it need volunteer help? Why doesn't the government pay for it?
- If I volunteered, what would I be doing? How much time would it take?
- How do I sign up?

According to Ms. Hatcher, these are the questions that students are most likely to ask. The brochure will be well written, nicely illustrated, and elegantly formatted.

We are enthusiastic about this project, as it seems to address an important need in our community, and we hope that it meets your approval. We look forward to getting your feedback on this.

Header containing basic information

Introduction, describing the problem and proposed solution

Body of memo giving details

Conclusion, summarizing the main point of the memo

TechHelp

Using a Memo Template

1. On the FILE menu, select NEW.
2. When a screen pops up, select the desired option (for example, MEMO).
3. Select the desired style (for example, PROFESSIONAL MEMO).
4. Fill in the blanks or type over the text that is already there.
5. To customize the memo, follow the onscreen instructions.

FOR COLLABORATION With one or more members of your group, write a short memo to your instructor on a topic of your own choosing. For example, you might request special help on an upcoming writing project, pose some questions about English grammar, or describe a new Web site you recently discovered. If your computer has a document template program, use it to write your memo.

23 Oral Presentations Using *PowerPoint* and Other Tools

FAQs

- How can I organize my oral presentation? (23a)
- What kinds of visual aids are best for an oral presentation? (23b)
- What makes a good *PowerPoint* slide? (23c)
- How can I get over my nervousness? (23d and e)

In many occupations, the ability to communicate orally is just as important as the ability to write well. Simple conversations, interviews, phone calls, meetings—these are all staple forms of communication in the workplace. And so are oral presentations. This chapter offers advice on how to give good presentations.

23a Prepare thoroughly

The basic principle to keep in mind in preparing any kind of oral presentation is this: *All listeners have a limited attention span.* Their attention will probably wander from time to time, even if your presentation is only 10 minutes long. So, if you want to make sure your listeners will come away from your talk with your main points clear in their minds, you must organize your presentation in such a way that these main points stand out. Here is how to do it.

Analyze your audience and limit your topic accordingly. What do your listeners already know about the topic? What do they need or want to know about it? If you tell them what they already know, they'll be bored. If you give them too much new information too fast, they may not be able to keep up.

Determine your primary purpose. Is there some main point or idea you want to get across? If so, use it as the cornerstone on which to build your presentation.

Select effective supporting information. What kind of evidence will best support your main point? What kind of information will appeal to your listeners? These things will constitute the heart of your presentation, so put some thought into your selection.

Choose an appropriate pattern of organization. Do your subject matter and purpose lend themselves to a certain pattern of organization such as problem and solution, narrative, or classification? If so, building your presentation around such a pattern will help you organize and present the talk and make it easier for your listeners to follow.

Prepare an outline. Keep it brief: main points and main supporting points only. Arrange these points according to the pattern of development you chose earlier.

Select appropriate visual aids.

Prepare a suitable introduction. You must convince your listeners that what you have to say is important. Are you addressing some problem? Make sure you define it so that your listeners know exactly what it is and can appreciate your proposed solution. Are you taking sides on an issue and arguing for your point of view? If so, make sure your listeners know exactly what the issue is.

Prepare a closing summary. Listeners are typically very attentive at the beginning of a presentation, less attentive as it wears on, and then suddenly more attentive again as it comes to an end. You can take advantage of this fact by reemphasizing your main points at the end.

EXERCISE 23.1 Prepare a brief (5–10 minute) oral presentation using the guidelines in 23a.

23b Select visual aids carefully

Visual aids serve as "cue cards," reminding you of all your important points and allowing you to stay on track without reading from a manuscript or from notes. Visual aids also have tremendous power as attention-getters. Studies have shown that people remember the visual parts of speeches far better than they do the verbal parts. Finally, visual aids can help clarify your message.

▼ **Table 23.1** Types of Visual Aids Evaluated for Use with Oral Presentation

	POWERPOINT	OVER-HEADS	WHITE BOARD	FLIPCHARTS OR POSTERS	HAND-OUTS	3-D OBJECTS
Ease of preparation	Excellent	Good	Excellent	Fair	Good	Good
Ease of alteration	Fair	Good	Excellent	Fair	Poor	Poor
Audience control	Excellent	Excellent	Excellent	Excellent	Poor	Varies
Speed	Excellent	Good	Poor	Good	Excellent	Excellent
Amount of information	Good	Good	Fair	Good	Excellent	Fair
Audience size	Excellent	Excellent	Fair	Fair	Excellent	Fair
Reliability	Fair	Good	Excellent	Excellent	Excellent	Excellent
Future reference	Good	Poor	Poor	Poor	Excellent	Poor
Cueing	Excellent	Excellent	Poor	Excellent	Excellent	Good

Pick your visual aids carefully. Your basic options include *PowerPoint* projection, overhead transparencies, whiteboard, flip charts or posters, handouts, and three-dimensional objects. Each of these technologies has its own strengths and weaknesses. The following questions will help you pick the aid best suited to your needs and goals.

See Table 23.1

- Is it easy to prepare?
- Can it be altered easily during the presentation?
- Will it allow you to control the audience's attention—or will it distract attention from what you're saying?
- Will it let you present at an appropriate speed?

- How much information can it convey?
- How large an audience can you use it with?
- How reliable is it—does it depend on electronic equipment?
- Can the audience keep it for future reference?
- How well does it work as a "cue card"?

PowerPoint is probably the best overall visual aid for an oral presentation. It has more strengths and fewer weaknesses than any of the others presented in Table 23.1. But each of the others has its own good uses for particular situations and should not be overlooked.

EXERCISE 23.2 Decide what kinds of visual aids would be most appropriate for the oral presentation you prepared in Exercise 23.1. Be prepared to justify your choices.

Principles of business correspondence

23c Use *PowerPoint* effectively

Use of presentation software such as *PowerPoint* is becoming more common because this medium offers a number of special features. *PowerPoint* projects colors; it can include animation, video, and sound; it is easily managed with a laptop computer and projector; and the slides can be put on a Web site for later reference. The software comes with a wizard and templates that make it easy and fun to create slides and put together a presentation. Although the standard *PowerPoint* templates are business oriented, some of them can be adapted to academic presentations as well.

PowerPoint slides should be neatly formatted, easily readable, and uncluttered. For presentation in a darkened room, the slides should have a light background; for a well-lit room, they should have a darker background. Wherever possible, the slides should have some visual imagery, not just words; these images should be relevant to the theme of the slide or presentation, not used just for decoration.

Figures 23.1 and 23.2 illustrate before and after versions of a *PowerPoint* slide.

If you choose to use overhead transparencies, follow the same design principles suggested above.

Before

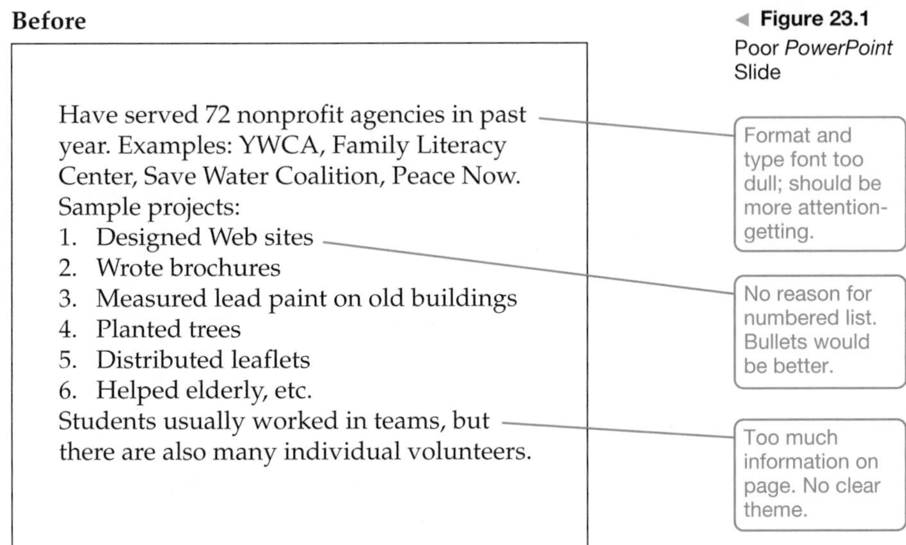

Have served 72 nonprofit agencies in past year. Examples: YWCA, Family Literacy Center, Save Water Coalition, Peace Now.
Sample projects:
1. Designed Web sites
2. Wrote brochures
3. Measured lead paint on old buildings
4. Planted trees
5. Distributed leaflets
6. Helped elderly, etc.
Students usually worked in teams, but there are also many individual volunteers.
Format and type font too dull; should be more attention-getting.
No reason for numbered list. Bullets would be better.
Too much information on page. No clear theme.

◀ **Figure 23.1**
Poor *PowerPoint* Slide

After

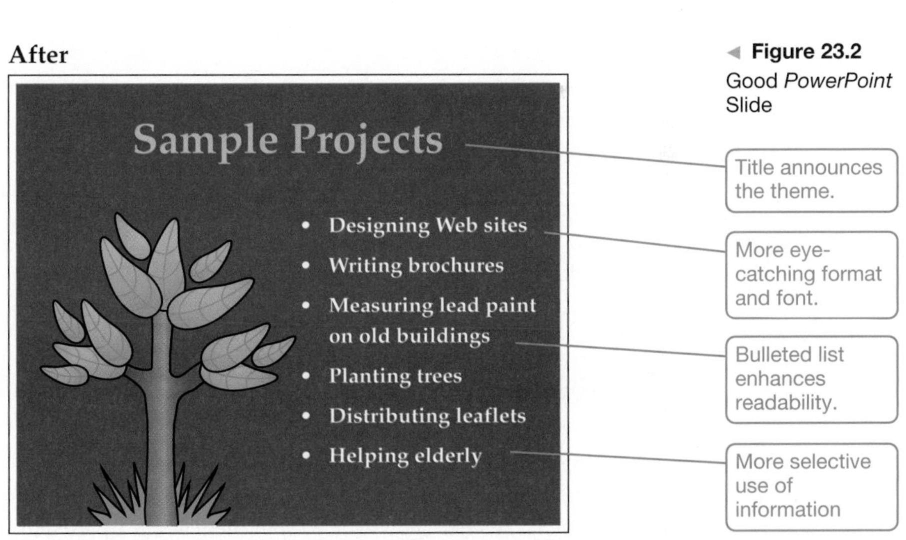

Sample Projects
• Designing Web sites
• Writing brochures
• Measuring lead paint on old buildings
• Planting trees
• Distributing leaflets
• Helping elderly
Title announces the theme.
More eye-catching format and font.
Bulleted list enhances readability.
More selective use of information

◀ **Figure 23.2**
Good *PowerPoint* Slide

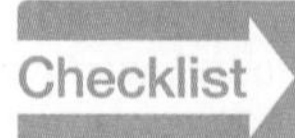

Using *PowerPoint*

PowerPoint presentations have obvious attractions, but they also have several potential pitfalls that you should be aware of. Be careful of the following.

✓ **Don't let the slides do your talking for you.** Your audience is there to hear what you have to say; slides should be support for that message. Prepare your talk first, and add slides later.

✓ **Don't make your presentation distractingly fancy.** *PowerPoint* technology offers a wide array of special effects, but they are easily overdone and can be distracting or even annoying.

✓ **Don't simply transfer note cards to the screen.** Look for opportunities to make your presentation visual, with appropriate images and graphics, not just written notes.

✓ **Keep in mind that *PowerPoint* is a one-way form of communication.** Don't let your audience become passive observers of a fast-moving slide show. Slow your pace, and try to provide opportunities for your audience to ask questions or raise comments.

EXERCISE 23.3 Using the presentation you prepared for Exercise 23.1, decide what points could be usefully illustrated with *PowerPoint* slides. Then find a computer with a *PowerPoint* program and create those slides.

FOR COLLABORATION Following the Guidelines on Using *PowerPoint*, deliver the presentation you designed for Exercise 23.3 to a small group of friends or fellow students. Afterward, ask them for feedback.

23d Practice, practice, practice

Nothing is more helpful to the success of an oral presentation than practice. Not even the best of speakers can give a totally effective presentation without first practicing it. Practice allows you to spot the flaws in a presentation and correct them. It enables you to work on making smooth transitions instead of awkward stops and starts. And practice gives you an idea of how long your presentation will take, allowing you to make adjustments so that you can deliver it at a comfortable tempo. All these benefits promote greater self-confidence, which will give you a more emphatic, convincing, and effective style of delivery.

The best way to practice a talk is by rounding up a few friends and trying it out on them. Ask them to hear you all the way through, taking notes but not interrupting you. Then ask them for an honest critique. In the absence of friends, you can use a video recorder or audiotape recorder and then critique yourself during playback. Here are some specific things to work on while practicing an oral presentation.

Devise ways of reiterating your important points without being too repetitive. Since your important points should all contribute to a single cumulative effect, it's a good idea to reiterate these points occasionally as you go along—especially in summary form at the end of your talk. However, exact repetition of a point can become annoyingly monotonous the third or fourth time around, so try to vary your wording.

Familiarize yourself with the equipment you'll be using. It's embarrassing—and annoying to the audience—to waste precious time fumbling with a computer, slide projector, or other equipment. Check out any equipment beforehand and become familiar with it, and have a backup plan in case something goes wrong.

Prepare yourself for questions. Listeners may raise questions at any point in your presentation, and it is vitally important that you answer them satisfactorily. If you don't, your most precious asset as a speaker—your credibility—may be jeopardized. So be sure you know your topic *well.* One way to prepare yourself is to have some friends listen to you and deliberately throw tough questions at you; if they succeed in stumping you, do some more research.

Develop your own speaking style. Practice presenting as if you were telling friends a story. Be natural and expressive. Use animated gestures and vary your intonation and rate of speech. In short, let your enthusiasm show! At the same time, try to get rid of any distracting habits you might have, such as leaning against something, pacing back and forth, or fiddling with a pencil.

If you will read from a manuscript, work on a lively, expressive intonation. There is a strong tendency when reading aloud to adopt a monotonous style of delivery that is boring for an audience. As you read aloud, practice varying your intonation as you would if you were talking spontaneously. Mark up the manuscript, underlining words that warrant special intonation and places where you may want to pause. Give special emphasis to contrasting terms.

EXERCISE 23.4 For practice, find a text of about 200 words that you could imagine reading aloud to someone. Print it out double-spaced. Read it aloud, trying to be as natural and expressive as you can. Go back and mark up the text, noting places where you want to use special intonation. Then read it aloud again.

23e Speak with enthusiasm and focus

As the time draws near for delivering your oral presentation, you will experience what all speakers do—nervousness. One key to an effective delivery is to convert your nervousness into the kind of energy that injects liveliness, enthusiasm, and animation into your speech.

How can you control your nervousness? First of all, make sure you're properly prepared for your talk. This means getting your visual aids and notes organized and making sure you're properly dressed and groomed. Your personal appearance is one of the most powerful "visual aids" you have. Looking your best will boost your confidence.

Second, as you are about to start your presentation, look for an opportunity to say something off-the-cuff. For example, you could acknowledge the occasion or share a spontaneous bit of humor. Don't feel you have to tell a prepared joke or story.

Finally, as you are actually giving your presentation, *concentrate your full attention on what you want to say.* Stick to your outline, and make sure you cover all your main supporting points. Persuade your listeners that the topic is important, and be enthusiastic about it. Show each of your visual aids long enough for the audience to understand and appreciate it, and then move on to the next one. Keep up the pace—don't dally.

Encourage questions from the audience, but don't let questions disrupt your presentation. Above all, do not show any antagonism toward a questioner. It will make your entire audience feel uncomfortable, and they may hold it against you even if the questioner is unfair or unpleasant.

FOR COLLABORATION With several friends or classmates as your audience, deliver the oral presentation that you prepared in Exercises 23.1–23.2. Afterward, ask your audience for constructive criticism.

24 Essay Exams

FAQs

- What can I do to prepare for an exam? (24a)
- How can I tell what exam questions are really asking? (24a-3)
- What steps should I follow in writing a response to an exam question? (24b)
- How can I avoid mistakes in my written exam? (24b-4)

24a Prepare for an essay exam

You can use a number of strategies to prepare for on-demand writing in general and essay exams in particular. These strategies include keeping up on your reading and notetaking, studying and reviewing your notes, and analyzing the exam question.

1 Keeping up with your reading and notetaking

Many instructors judge your success in a course by how well you are able to analyze and apply course material in a timed essay exam. In order to do a good job on such exams, you must be well prepared. Few essay exams are open-book, so you must learn the material well enough to be able to remember and write about it without access to your notes or textbooks.

You can prepare by keeping up with course assignments and discussions on a daily basis throughout the term. Attend every class and read your textbooks carefully, looking for key ideas and arguments. Pay close attention to chapter summaries, subheadings, and key terminology. Write the key ideas and terms down in a notebook for later review. When your instructor lectures, do not write down everything he or she says; rather, listen for and record main points and ideas that show relationships.

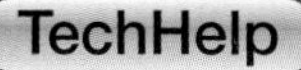

Using Keywords to Search Lecture Notes

If you keep your lecture notes in an electronic notebook, you can search for key information by doing the following:

1. Use your word-processing program's WORD COUNT feature to find out how many times a particular keyword appears in your notes.
2. Use your word-processing program's SEARCH function to search for each occurrence of the keyword.
3. Highlight the word by using italics or a contrasting color.
4. For review purposes, make a hard copy of pages that contain the keywords.

❷ Studying and reviewing your notes

As the exam date approaches, you will want to study more systematically. Ask the instructor if he or she is willing to provide models of previous exam questions or some general guidelines about the kinds of questions that might be included on the exam. Organize a study group to discuss and review the course materials. If possible, the study group should meet regularly during the term, either in person or through an email discussion group. Practice responding to course readings by taking a stance opposite that of the authors or by questioning the authors' position. Review your class notes, paying particular attention to your lists of key ideas and terms. For each key idea, develop a practice thesis statement that you could explore and support in an essay.

See 21c-1

Avoid the last-minute cram session. Cramming for several hours prior to the exam will not give you enough depth of knowledge to succeed on an essay exam. If you stay up all night before an exam studying, you will be in no condition to take it the next day. Instead, pace your studying over several days and try to get a good night's sleep so that you will be fresh for the exam itself.

TechHelp

Writing an Essay Exam in a Computer Lab

If your instructor allows you to write your timed response to an essay exam in a computer classroom or lab, do the following:

1. Briefly attend to the stages of the writing process, as described in 24b.
2. Budget your time carefully. Check your watch or the clock periodically.
3. Save your work frequently—to your disk or hard drive—so that you do not inadvertently lose your essay because of a computer glitch or power failure.
4. Run the spell checker before turning in your exam.

❸ Analyzing the exam question

Tips on writing essay exams

The first step in succeeding on an exam question is to analyze it carefully. The question itself will guide the organization of your response. An essay question will ask you to focus on a specific issue; address that issue rather than cataloging everything you learned from the course. Try to minimize your anxiety by taking a deep breath and focusing your thinking on the structure of your response. If the exam contains more than one question, determine how much time you have to devote to each question so that you do not run out of time before you complete your writing. Table 24.1 shows appropriate responses to some of the organizational cue words that typically appear in essay questions.

See Table 24.1

EXERCISE 24.1 Reread Chapter 2 of this handbook, and follow the suggestions outlined in 2b-2 and 2b-3 on taking and reviewing notes. Formulate a set of essay exam questions based on what you take to be the key ideas in Chapter 2.

FOR COLLABORATION Bring the essay exam questions that you generated in Exercise 24.1 to class. Discuss your exam questions with a group of your peers. How effective are the questions? What makes them effective or not effective?

Table 24.1 Cue Words in Essay Exam Questions

QUESTION	CUE WORD	HOW TO ORGANIZE YOUR RESPONSE
Analyze Shakespeare's use of dreams in Macbeth.	ANALYZE: Divide something into parts and discuss the parts in relationship to the whole.	1. State your thesis. 2. Discuss the play's major themes. 3. Identify places where dreams occur, and explain each instance in relation to the play's major themes. 4. State your conclusion.
Argue either for or against caps on political spending in presidential campaigns.	ARGUE: Take a position or stand and support it with reasoned arguments and evidence	1. Choose a side—either for or against such caps—and state that position in a thesis sentence. 2. List each point that supports your side, with evidence. 3. Conclude by restating your side.
Classify street people into types based on their sociological characteristics.	CLASSIFY: Divide some large whole into groups on the basis of shared traits.	1. State your thesis, pointing out the number of types of street people. 2. Identify one type and describe its characteristics. 3. Continue identifying types and describing their characteristics. 4. State your conclusion.
Describe the mechanism of the transmission of the disease typhus.	DESCRIBE: Systematically explain something's features, sometimes visually or sequentially.	1. State your thesis—that typhus is transmitted by parasites. 2. Describe the disease carrier—lice. 3. Explain how lice spread typhus. 4. State your conclusion.
Discuss the structure of US society in terms of its economic relationships.	DISCUSS: Consider as many important elements related to an issue as you can.	1. State your thesis, outlining what you take to be the important relationships. 2. Consider as many key elements of US society and economics as you can, such as monetary policy, agricultural policy, and political policy. 3. Conclude by restating your thesis.

(continued)

Table 24.1 *(continued)*

QUESTION	CUE WORD	HOW TO ORGANIZE YOUR RESPONSE
Evaluate the effectiveness of the performance of Handel's Water Music *by the San Francisco Symphony.*	EVALUATE: Give your opinion about something's value and provide the reasons on which your judgment is based.	1. State your opinion about the effectiveness of the performance in the form of a thesis. 2. Briefly summarize the performance. 3. List the reasons on which your opinion is based, with supporting evidence from the performance itself. 4. Conclude by restating your opinion.
Explain why an object thrown up into the air falls to the ground.	EXPLAIN: Tell about something that is complex in a way that makes it clear.	1. State the physical principle in the form of a thesis. 2. Tell about the nature of gravity that causes the object to fall. 3. Tell about the physical principles that determine how objects are affected by gravity, including the scientific formula for gravitational pull. 4. State your conclusion.
Illustrate the importance of color in Duchamp's Nude Descending a Staircase.	ILLUSTRATE: Provide examples and detail about something.	1. State in your thesis why color is important in the painting. 2. Provide an example relating to color. 3. Provide additional examples relating to color. 4. State your conclusion.
Summarize the major advantages of mainstreaming handicapped children in school.	SUMMARIZE: Repeat the main points in abbreviated form.	1. State your thesis. 2. List the advantages, one after another, along with reasons that support each point. 3. State your conclusion.

24b Attend to the writing process

See 3a

When you write an essay exam, you should briefly attend to each stage of the writing process.

❶ Preparing an outline

See 3e-5

When taking an essay exam, take a few minutes to jot down in an informal outline some of the key concepts you want to cover in your answer. Begin your response with a thesis statement and a short introductory paragraph that captures the main thrust of your response. Then, in subsequent paragraphs, elaborate with examples and details until you run out of time. As you outline, try to cover the most important points first, leaving the less important ones for last. If you have less than an hour to respond to the question, do not spend more than about five minutes planning and outlining your response.

❷ Drafting your response

Try to remain focused as you draft your response. Your instructor will have many essays to read and will not want to plow through a lot of extraneous information. If you know a great deal about the question, resist the temptation to write down everything. Rather, stick to your thesis, and plan your writing so that your response is coherent and organized. The easier it is for the instructor to follow your line of argument, the better.

❸ Analyzing and evaluating your response

As you draft your response, allow time to ensure that you have satisfied the demands of the assignment. When you read over your essay, you may find that you have overlooked the second part of a two-part question, for example, or that you have concentrated on defining terms when the question asked you to analyze information. Do not panic. If possible, write a new final paragraph that addresses the issues you missed. If you do not have time for that, write your instructor a brief message explaining where you went wrong and outlining how you would correct your essay if you had the time. Many instructors will give at least partial credit for such a response.

Also, look carefully at your thesis statement. Does it accurately reflect the direction of your essay? If not, then revise it. Check your organization. Does your essay read smoothly and flow logically? If not, then perhaps you can insert

Writing Successful Essay Exam Responses

- ✓ Have I shown my understanding of the question by including a thesis statement at the beginning of my response?
- ✓ Have I organized my response so as to present my ideas in a logical progression that supports my thesis?
- ✓ Have I used the specific details, facts, or analyses called for in the question?
- ✓ Have I shown my own independent thoughts and insights in my response?
- ✓ Have I concluded with a brief sentence that sums up the gist of my response?
- ✓ Have I evaluated and edited my response as time allowed?

transitional words or phrases that will help your instructor follow your argument. Have you included enough examples to support your thesis? If you need more, write a new paragraph and use an arrow to indicate where it should be inserted. Finally, does your conclusion provide a clear understanding of the main point of your essay? If not, add a sentence or two to sum up your argument.

4 Proofreading and editing your response

Your instructor will not expect your writing to be grammatically and structurally perfect in a timed writing situation. However, he or she will expect your exam response to be readable and clear. If possible, write your response in pencil so that you can easily erase and correct errors. Take a few minutes to proofread and also to check your penmanship. If your response is unreadable, your instructor cannot evaluate it fairly.

24c Review sample student responses to an essay exam question

To help you write better essay exam responses, we include here two student responses to the following exam question, which appeared on the midterm for a course in twentieth-century British literature.

TechHelp

Using Technology During Exams

The easy availability of technology has made it necessary for many professors to institute rules and regulations about using technology during exams. To avoid getting into trouble, be certain to find out from your professor what the rules are.

1. **Cell phones** are generally banned from exams because of the possibility of cheating by text-messaging.
2. **Personal digital assistants** (e.g., Palm Pilot or Blackberry) are generally banned because of email or text-messaging capability.
3. **Laptops or electronic notebooks** are often permissible for an open-book exam. Be sure to check with your professor before bringing a laptop to an exam, however. You may be required to load software that prevents you from accessing your own hard drive files.

Below you will find a quotation from a novel we read this term. Spend 15 minutes writing a short essay that performs a close reading of the passage. Pick out specific details from the quotation that illustrate some of the central themes or ideas of the novel. Your response should demonstrate both an ability to read closely and a general understanding of the novel.

From Henry James's *The Turn of the Screw:* "I remember feeling with Miles in especial as if he had had, as it were, nothing to call even an infinitesimal history. We expect of a small child scant enough 'antecedents', but there was in this beautiful little boy something extraordinarily sensitive, yet extraordinarily happy, that, more than in any creature of his age I have seen, struck me as beginning anew each day. . . . I could reconstitute nothing at all, and he was therefore an angel."

See Figs. 24.1 and 24.2

Figures 24.1 and 24.2 represent good and poor responses to the question.

The instructor wanted the exam responses to demonstrate both an ability to read closely and a general understanding of the novel. In the first response, the student shows a clear understanding of the major themes of the novel, using specific details from the quotation to illustrate that understanding and connect the passage to the larger themes of innocence and history. In contrast,

◀ **Figure 24.1**
A Good Student Exam Response

This quotation expresses the governess's naivete regarding the innocence of the children she is looking after. She assumes that just because they are children, they have had little experience and are, thus, pure "angels." Her perception of this, however, is erroneous and detrimental to Miles. Assuming that he is pure, she takes all measures to protect him from any horrors that may have happened in the past, not realizing that the past is part of Miles's history. His past takes the form of ghosts which haunt the governess, although they do not seem to frighten the children. In fact, the children are drawn to the ghosts and want the governess to go away. Her lack of experience and her innocence are actually greater than the children's, who no longer have parents and have experienced the death of two servants. Her inability to see this truth ends up killing Miles. Caught between the image of the governess and Peter Quint, Miles finally has to make evident to her what is so obvious to everyone else—Peter Quint exists, the past is a part of his present. Not willing to let Miles exist outside of her perceptions, the governess ironically reassures him, "I caught you." She strips him of his history, his identity, and he dies a young boy "dispossessed."

Figure 24.2 ▶
A Poor Student Response

> The governess here is expressing how she feels about the child Miles vs. the Miles she knew once upon a time. The use of the run-on sentence is a radical change from the accepted format of the past. The form represents thought put on paper and not interpreted through writing. The effect that the child had on her doesn't seem realistic. It seems more mystic and of fantasy.

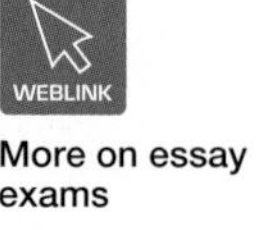

More on essay exams

the second response does not draw any specific connections between the quotation and the major issues or themes of the novel. It appears from the second response that this student did not really understand the novel. Furthermore, the second response does not answer the question posed. As reading these responses makes clear, you must understand both the subject and the question in order to answer well.

EXERCISE 24.2 Using the Checklist for Writing Successful Essay Exam Responses in 24b-4, analyze the two student essay exam responses. In each of the responses, which of the guidelines were observed? Which were not? How could each response have been improved?

25 Writing Portfolios

FAQs

- What is a portfolio, and why do I need one? (25a)
- How do I develop a writing portfolio? (25b)
- How do I prepare the final portfolio? (25c)
- What does a reflective cover letter look like? (25d)

Many courses, majors, and even entire college programs are now requiring students to submit portfolios as a part of their college work. Teachers report that students frequently misunderstand the purposes and audiences for these portfolios, so this chapter provides an overview of portfolios and the expectations that frequently lie behind this assignment.

25a Learn about types of portfolios

The three common types of portfolios you may encounter in your college career vary in rhetorical stance. You will need to work with your instructor to determine the type of portfolio you are going to compile, along with its purpose and audience. Similarly, you will need to consider carefully your own persona—that is, how you want to present yourself through the content and organization of your portfolio.

See 3b-2

❶ Types of portfolios

Course portfolio

Perhaps the most common type of portfolio is the individual course portfolio, which reflects your work for a particular term in a specific course. Many disciplines use portfolios for assessment purposes, as a way for students to display the work they have accomplished that term. Disciplines that typically use portfolios include written composition, art, photography, and education. As you can imagine, the items included in portfolios for different disciplines vary widely. In art and photography, for example, portfolios include primarily visual materials. In composition and education, portfolios consist largely of written documents in a variety of formats. An education portfolio, for example, typically includes lesson plans, whereas a composition portfolio typically includes essays and research papers.

See Fig. 25.1

Program assessment portfolio

The program assessment portfolio is used by a program to assess the progress of students. It is usually administered on a large scale—perhaps to all sophomores as a measure of their writing competency following the completion of the general education requirements. Be sure to find out exactly what is expected in the program assessment portfolio. Typically, a program will draw up

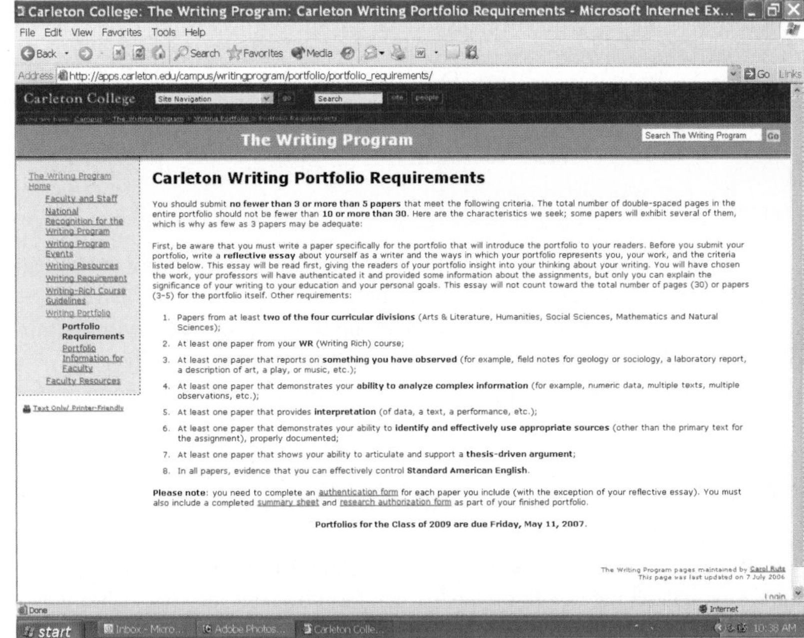

Carleton Writing Portfolio Requirements

You should submit **no fewer than 3 or more than 5 papers** that meet the following criteria. The total number of double-spaced pages in the entire portfolio should not be fewer than **10 or more than 30**. Here are the characteristics we seek; some papers will exhibit several of them, which is why as few as 3 papers may be adequate:

First, be aware that you must write a paper specifically for the portfolio that will introduce the portfolio to your readers. Before you submit your portfolio, write a **reflective essay** about yourself as a writer and the ways in which your portfolio represents you, your work, and the criteria listed below. This essay will be read first, giving the readers of your portfolio insight into your thinking about your writing. You will have chosen the work, your professors will have authenticated it and provided some information about the assignments, but only you can explain the significance of your writing to your education and your personal goals. This essay will not count toward the total number of pages (30) or papers (3-5) for the portfolio itself. Other requirements:

1. Papers from at least **two of the four curricular divisions** (Arts & Literature, Humanities, Social Sciences, Mathematics and Natural Sciences);
2. At least one paper from your **WR** (Writing Rich) course;
3. At least one paper that reports on **something you have observed** (for example, field notes for geology or sociology, a laboratory report, a description of art, a play, or music, etc.);
4. At least one paper that demonstrates your **ability to analyze complex information** (for example, numeric data, multiple texts, multiple observations, etc.);
5. At least one paper that provides **interpretation** (of data, a text, a performance, etc.);
6. At least one paper that demonstrates your ability to **identify and effectively use appropriate sources** (other than the primary text for the assignment), properly documented;
7. At least one paper that shows your ability to articulate and support a **thesis-driven argument**;
8. In all papers, evidence that you can effectively control **Standard American English**.

Please note: you need to complete an authentication form for each paper you include (with the exception of your reflective essay). You must also include a completed summary sheet and research authorization form as part of your finished portfolio.

Portfolios for the Class of 2009 are due Friday, May 11, 2007.

The Writing Program pages maintained by Carol Rutz
This page was last updated on 7 July 2006

Figure 25.1 ▶ Guidelines for Portfolios at Carleton College specific guidelines as to content and purpose. You would be well advised to follow such guidelines explicitly.

Student career portfolio

GO
See Fig. 25.2

The student career portfolio is used to track your progress through a major course of study. The main purpose of a career portfolio is to highlight the personal growth you have experienced over the length of your education. For example, an English major specializing in professional communication might compile such a portfolio as evidence of his or her job skills and potential as an employee. Students often find career portfolios useful when they go into the job market after graduation.

❷ Goals or purposes of portfolios

To many students the primary goal of a portfolio is to get a good grade in a course. However, as you work to reach that specific goal, you'll find that you have achieved other goals as well. For example, an important goal for any portfolio is

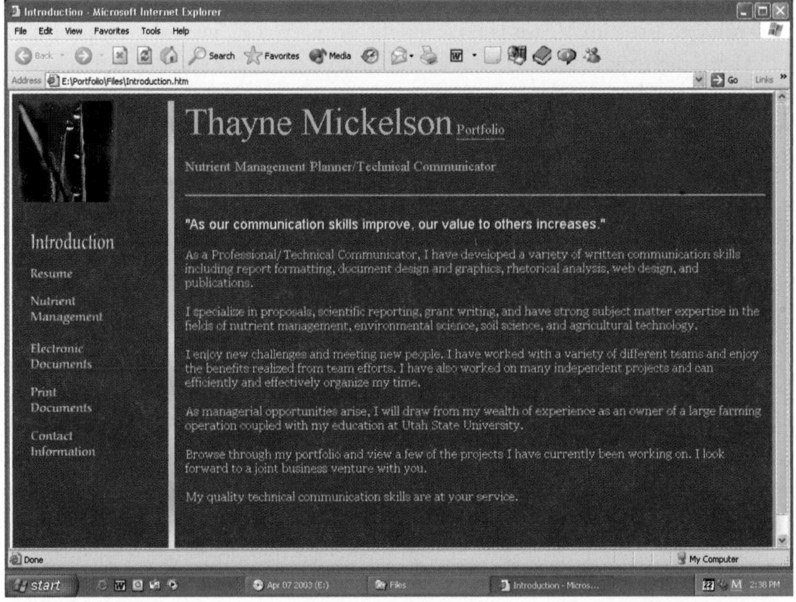

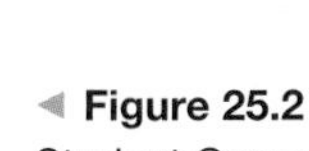
◄ **Figure 25.2**
Student Career Portfolio

to reflect the knowledge you have gained from a course or program of study. In content courses such as the humanities and social sciences—for example, music, history, or sociology—your portfolio needs to accurately reflect your understanding of the major concepts covered. If the portfolio is being used to assess a program, it needs to show that you have mastered the core concepts and skills of the program.

See 25b-3

Portfolios should also reflect an improvement in your writing skills and an effective presentation format and style. For composition and other writing-intensive courses such as those in the social sciences, your portfolio should show your growth as a writer. Including early drafts of pieces is one way of reflecting growth. Including a reflective cover letter is another. Your portfolio will need to show that you have mastered the conventions of Standard Edited English—that is, your writing should be correct and error-free. Similarly, portfolio readers will expect you to present your work effectively—that is, the portfolio should be organized, neat, and complete. How you present the portfolio will also send a message to your readers about your professionalism.

3 Audiences for portfolios

Your course's instructor is typically the primary audience for your portfolio. However, there may be other equally important secondary audiences. For example, other faculty evaluators and administrators may read the portfolio if it is used for program assessment. Peers may review your portfolio and provide advice, particularly if your instructor uses peer review as a feature of the course. Future employers may also read your portfolio. Many fields use portfolios as a measure of someone's work. A portfolio that results from work in a major capstone course can be particularly valuable when you are looking for employment.

4 Your persona

Because you are the primary author of the portfolio, you are ultimately responsible for its success. How you put together your portfolio will communicate your persona to your readers, whether you want it to or not. They will judge you as a "slacker" or a hard worker depending on how you present yourself through your portfolio. If you are diligent about meeting deadlines, revising and editing, visiting the writing center, and asking questions of your instructor when you are confused, you have every reason to believe your portfolio will be successful.

EXERCISE 25.1 Review the guidelines for portfolio assessment of writing from Carleton College shown in Figure 25.1. What is the purpose of the assessment? What do the students actually have to do to fulfill the requirement? Are these tasks suitable to the purpose?

FOR COLLABORATION Discuss the Carleton guidelines with a small group of your peers. What does your group think the purpose is for this assessment? Do you find the guidelines explicit enough for students to be successful?

25b Develop a writing portfolio

The type of writing portfolio you are developing, in addition to your audience, purpose, and persona, will help determine the materials to be included.

1 Using good writing habits

A portfolio should begin taking shape the minute you receive your first assignment for a course. Don't think of the portfolio as a "final exam" and put it off until the end. Rather, see the portfolio as a term-long project that will reflect the entire range of your work. The guidelines provided by this handbook can

Guidelines

Potential Writing Samples to Include in a Writing Portfolio

- Academic essay
- Business writing (résumé, business or application letter, memo)
- Creative writing (creative nonfiction, poem, short story)
- Essay exam
- Group or team collaborative writing project
- Lab report
- Long researched report
- Newsletter or brochure
- Personal essay
- Position paper
- *PowerPoint* presentation
- Proposal
- Report of primary research
- Researched argument with sources
- Short informal report
- Web hypertext or Web site

Creating a Writing Portfolio

Make sure that you understand the assignment completely before preparing your final portfolio. Ask yourself:

- ✓ Do I have options about the number and types of assignments I should include in my portfolio?
- ✓ Should I include rough drafts as well as polished pieces?
- ✓ Are other documents required in addition to my writing, such as a cover letter?
- ✓ If a reflective cover letter is required, what should be included in it?
- ✓ What should the portfolio convey about my overall learning?

If you can't answer these questions yourself, check with your instructor.

See Parts 6-12

help you in your writing and research for individual pieces in your portfolio. The latter parts of the handbook can help you with revising and editing your writing.

❷ Selecting materials to include

Many times portfolios fail not because the individual pieces within them are poor but rather because the wrong pieces have been selected or the portfolio itself is incomplete and disorganized. Find out from your instructor whether or not prewriting, research notes, rough drafts, outlines, and so on should be included. If the instructor allows choice and wants you to include process writing, don't take that as a blanket invitation to include everything. Be selective so as not to overwhelm your readers. Select finished writing that is clear, coherent, and appropriate for its audience; that has a strong thesis; and that is organized, thoughtfully developed, and correct.

❸ Reflecting on the process

A common feature of many portfolio assignments is the reflective statement or cover letter. Students are frequently confused about what to include in such a statement. Because you are the writer, editor, and compiler of the portfolio, the reflective statement should be written in your own unique voice and should reflect your personality. This is your opportunity to explain why you chose each piece and what, from your perspective, makes it stand out.

Your reflective statement should

- Focus on how you developed as a writer and/or how your knowledge and skills have improved.
- Give specific examples from your writing to illustrate each point—such as specific revisions that were done on individual pieces and overall features of your writing that have improved.
- Comment generally about the experience of the course and the entire portfolio process.
- Answer these questions: How has your writing improved? How have your critical thinking and analytical skills improved?

4 Organizing the final portfolio

Before you compile the final portfolio, look once again at the assignment sheet. Is there a required format? Some portfolios need to be submitted in folders with dividers, for example. Is there a specific order of contents? Find out if the reflective statement should come first as a cover letter and/or if a brief reflective statement needs to be included before each piece in the portfolio. Check to see how each piece should be labeled, and find out if you need a table of contents. Ask to see successful model portfolios that you can emulate. Following your instructor's guidelines explicitly will surely help you succeed.

25c Prepare the final portfolio

Now you have come to the final stages of your portfolio project. You have selected and organized the pieces to be included; you have written your reflective statement(s) and decided how to best order the contents; you have rechecked your instructor's guidelines and consulted models. Your portfolio will most likely be submitted in one of two ways: physically or electronically.

1 Physical submission

Your instructor or program may require you to submit an actual portfolio folder. In some cases, it will be supplied to you; in others, you will be expected to supply your own appropriate folder (a manila folder, a large envelope, a paper folder with pockets, or a hardbound or spiral folder). Do not substitute one folder for another; follow the guidelines *explicitly*. Your instructor has reasons for requiring the physical presentation a certain way. Check again to see in which order the materials should be placed—for example, table of contents followed by reflective cover letter. Use dividers, introductory statements, clear titles, and so on to help your readers navigate through your portfolio. Be consistent in the use of fonts and colors. Do not become overly elaborate and ornate—that will only distract your reader from the content. Remember, appearance and neatness count.

Sample online portfolios

2 Electronic submission

Many courses and programs use the latest technologies for submitting and storing portfolios electronically. Electronic portfolios provide a number of advantages: they allow for multimedia presentations, multiple paths for readers to navigate, and relatively unlimited storage and retrieval capabilities. Once again, it will be important for you to find out the exact specifications for electronic submission of your portfolio: on a disk, via email attachment, on a CD, or on a Web site. Electronic portfolios sometimes do not include rough drafts since these may not have been stored along the way. You should discover early on whether or not you need to save copies of early drafts to include in your electronic portfolio. Of course, an electronic portfolio has the added benefit of demonstrating your knowledge and expertise in electronic media. A word of caution: Be sure to back up your work electronically by saving it on a disk or a network prior to submission. Allow yourself extra time for those inevitable last-minute electronic glitches.

25d Review a sample reflective cover letter

See Fig. 25.3

The reflective cover letter shown in Figure 25.3 was written by a student in a first-year composition course. The student discusses the changes made to each paper in the portfolio and reflects on the concepts learned in the course.

◀ **Figure 25.3**
Student Reflective Cover Letter

Reflective Statement

Throughout the course of my first year in college, I think my writing has improved substantially. I have always enjoyed writing, and I usually use proper grammar, mechanics, punctuation, etc. However, this year I have learned to write more effectively using sophisticated sentences and active voice, yet also being concise in my thoughts and ideas. I have also learned many argumentative strategies that are useful for trying to persuade audiences. I noticed an improvement in each of my writings as the semester passed, learning to write more professionally and still appeal to the reader.

My first paper, a reflective argument about LBL, had very few mechanical errors. Only a small number of structural changes were required, so I had to revise it once more and make the necessary adjustments. Mainly, I needed to tighten some of my ideas and state my point in a more succinct manner. For example, I used prepositional phrases and some other words that were superfluous and had to be condensed. I also got rid of a nominalization by changing the noun formation back into a verb.

My second paper was a research report in which I stated and analyzed the results of a survey I conducted.

Figure 25.3 ▶ Student Reflective Cover Letter (*continued*)

2

Like my first paper, this one didn't have many grammatical errors, but it did have a few organizational problems. To correct these, I moved a couple of sentences around so that each sentence of every paragraph was related to the topic sentence of that paragraph. As always, there were some words that I changed and omitted in order to make sentences sound better and more suitable.

My last paper, a rhetorical analysis detailing the effects of alcohol in inner cities, had some minor errors that needed to be corrected. I had to clarify a few points and rearrange a sentence so that I could be understood better. Mainly, I changed several "be" verbs to action verbs and eliminated as many passive sentences as possible. This helped to make the paper more interesting and concise.

I have noticed several improvements in my writings as I progressed throughout the semester. I have tried to write using as many active verbs as possible and do away with needless words and phrases. To make my writings sound more professional, I have also tried to cut down on short, choppy sentences and write more elaborate, sophisticated sentences. However, I still attempt to organize my ideas so that they are condensed and logical to the reader. I learned to use the three

3

persuasive strategies: logos, ethos, and pathos. These are very important when trying to convince and influence others, and I will always try to use them when they are needed. I now know that writing can be a very effective means of communication, and when done correctly, it can be even better than speaking. If I continue to work on these areas of my writing, especially sentence structure and organization, I think I can become a good, maybe even great, writer as I continue on in college and the rest of my life.

Figure 25.3 Student Reflective Cover Letter (*continued*)

EXERCISE 25.2 Analyze the reflective cover letter shown in Figure 25.3. What did this student learn in the composition course? Are these important lessons? Did the student learn anything about global revision or just about details of grammar?

FOR COLLABORATION Discuss your analysis of the reflective cover letter in Figure 25.3 with a small group of your peers. Do you agree as to its effectiveness?

part 6

Sentence Grammar

26 Sentence Structure

FAQs

- What is an adverb? (26a-5)
- What is the difference between a participle and a gerund? (26a-10)
- What is a sentence subject? (26b-1)
- What is a predicate? (26b-2)

There is a fundamental difference between formal, academic writing and the kind of informal writing you do with your friends. When you're communicating with a friend, either orally or in writing, you don't need to spell out everything you mean. You and your friend share enough personal and contextual knowledge that you can take all sorts of shortcuts. You can use abbreviations, slang expressions, simple sentences or even parts of sentences, confident that your friend can fill in what's missing. In contrast, when you do formal, academic writing, you're trying to communicate with someone (your instructor) with whom you likely do *not* share such personal, contextual knowledge. In this case you cannot expect your reader to "figure out" what you mean; you need to make your meaning *explicit*. How do you do that? By crafting full sentences with proper grammatical structure and by choosing words that precisely capture your intended meaning.

This chapter and the ones that follow it in the next three parts of the book focus on grammatical structure. Because grammar checkers have many shortcomings, you cannot rely on them to fix grammatical errors in your writing. Instead, you need to know the basic elements of sentence structure and do much editing on your own.

26a Learn to identify parts of speech

In writing a sentence, you put words together in certain combinations. These combinations depend, in part, on the different kinds of words, or **parts of speech**, you use: nouns, pronouns, adjectives, verbs, adverbs, prepositions, conjunctions, articles, and interjections.

1 Nouns

A **noun** (n) is the name of a person, place, thing, quality, idea, or action. Some examples of nouns are

Picasso	Mexico	printer
honesty	democracy	juice

Common nouns refer to general persons, places, things, concepts, or qualities.

man city mouse philosophy generosity

Proper nouns, which are almost always capitalized, name particular persons, places, institutions, organizations, months, and days.

Lindsay Lohan	Salt Lake City	the World Court
Duke University	Buddhism	Monday

Concrete nouns specifically refer to things that can be sensed through sight, hearing, touch, taste, and smell.

bookshelf fork billboard hamburger

Abstract nouns refer to ideas, emotions, qualities, or other intangible concepts.

beauty sadness truth love

Count nouns name things that can be counted and thus can have a plural form.

lake(s) violin(s) baseball(s) goose (geese)

Noncount nouns, or **mass nouns**, name things that typically are not counted in English and thus cannot be made plural.

water snow hatred health news

Some nouns can serve as either count or noncount nouns, depending on their meaning. For example, *experience* can be used as a count noun (*I've had many interesting experiences*) or as a noncount noun (*Experience is the best teacher*).

See 56a

Collective nouns name groups; they are usually singular in both sense and form.

committee team class crowd

❷ Pronouns

A **pronoun** (pron), such as *she, they,* or *it,* is a word that substitutes for a noun and usually refers to a noun, which is called the **antecedent** of the pronoun. The noun antecedent usually precedes the pronoun in a sentence:

▸ *Lucinda* said *she* was not feeling well.

Sometimes the noun antecedent follows the pronoun:

See Ch. 27 for a discussion of pronoun case and Ch. 33 for a discussion of pronoun-antecedent agreement.

▸ Saying *she* was not feeling well, *Lucinda* left the room.

Pronouns can be singular or plural, and their case can vary depending on how they are used in a sentence. The change from *he* to *him* or *his* reflects pronoun use according to case—subjective, objective, or possessive.

❸ Adjectives

An **adjective** (adj) is a word that modifies a noun or pronoun by qualifying or describing it. In English, the adjective usually precedes the noun it modifies (an *old* tree, the *other* day), but in literary usage an adjective occasionally follows the noun (a woman *scorned*). In sentences such as "The program was *challenging,*" the adjective falls on the other side of a verb linking it to the noun it modifies. An adjective used in this way is called a **predicate adjective**.

See Ch. 30

Many adjectives have comparative and superlative forms created by the addition of *-er* and *-est* (*small, smaller, smallest*). Many other adjectives have the same form as the present or past participle of a verb (a *roaring* lion, a *deserted* island).

Types of Pronouns and Their Roles

Type	Role
Personal pronouns ***Singular:*** *I, you, he, she, it; me, you, him, her, it; mine, yours, his, hers, its* ***Plural:*** *we, you, they; us, you, them; ours, yours, theirs*	Refer to specific persons or things and serve to distinguish the speaker or writer (first person), the person or thing spoken to (second person), and the person or thing spoken about (third person): "Michael gave me his book and I gave him mine."
Demonstrative pronouns *this, that, these, those*	Point to their antecedent nouns: "That was an interesting idea!"
Indefinite pronouns *all, any, anybody, anyone, anything, both, everybody, everyone, everything, few, many, one, no one, nothing, somebody, someone, something, several, some*	Refer to nonspecific persons or things and do not require an antecedent: "Nothing could be done."
Relative pronouns *that, what, which, who, whom, whose, whoever, whichever, whatever*	Introduce dependent clauses: "She is the teacher who runs marathons."
Interrogative pronouns *who, whom, which, what, whose*	Introduce questions: "Whose bike is this?"
Reflexive and intensive pronouns (consist of a personal pronoun plus -self or -selves) ***Singular:*** *myself, yourself, himself, herself, itself* ***Plural:*** *ourselves, yourselves, themselves*	A reflexive pronoun refers back to the subject to show that the subject itself is the object of an action: "She saw herself in the mirror." An intensive pronoun is used for emphasis: "They did it themselves."
Reciprocal pronouns *one another, each other*	Refer to the separate parts of a plural antecedent: "They gave presents to each other."
Expletive pronouns *there, it*	Serve as introductory, "empty" words occupying the position of grammatical subject: "There are many kinds of hummingbirds."

Some of the pronouns discussed in 26a-2 can also function as **possessive adjectives** (*our* school), **demonstrative adjectives** (*this* page), **interrogative adjectives** (*Which* button do I push?), and **indefinite adjectives** (*some* money). These, along with **articles** (*the, a, an*), comprise the category of **determiners**. Determiners serve to introduce nouns and noun phrases:

the kitchen

my DVD player

some interesting news

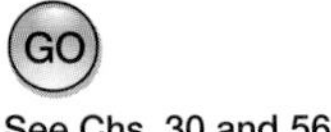

See Chs. 30 and 56

Unlike most adjectives, however, they do not occur as predicate adjectives, do not have comparative or superlative forms, and do not occur in combination.

4 Verbs

A **verb** (v) is a key word that expresses an action (*swim, read*) or a state of being (*is, seemed*). Main verbs are often accompanied by **auxiliary verbs** (also called **helping verbs**), which include forms of the verbs *be, have,* and *do,* and/or by **modal verbs**, such as *may, might, can, could, will, would, shall, should,* and *must.* Auxiliary and modal verbs are special verb forms that express questions, future tenses, past tenses, and various degrees of doubt about or qualification of the main verb's action.

See Ch. 28 for more on verbs

See 26b-2, 26b-3

Transitive verbs (VT) transfer action from an agent (usually the subject of the sentence) to an object or recipient (usually the direct object of the sentence): "Michael *fumbled* the ball." Some common transitive verbs are *carry, reject, show, build,* and *destroy*. **Intransitive verbs** (VI) may express action, but they do not transfer it to an object or recipient: "The bridge *collapsed*." Some common intransitive verbs are *sleep, fall, die, erupt,* and *disappear.* Many verbs can be used either intransitively or transitively: "Frank *eats* often, but he does not *eat* red meat." **Linking verbs** (LV) such as *be, seem,* and *appear* connect the subject of a sentence to a subject complement (typically an adjective), as in "Mary *is* Irish" or "Your friend *seems* bored." Some linking verbs express the result of an action: "The apples *turned* sour," "Her predictions *came* true."

The five major forms a verb takes are usually referred to as its **principal parts**. They are the **base form** (or **infinitive form**), **present tense** (third-person singular), **past tense**, **past participle**, and **present participle**.

Base form	Present tense	Past tense	Past participle	Present participle
(to) erase	erases	erased	(have) erased	(am) erasing
(to) run	runs	ran	(have) run	(am) running

These different forms of a verb serve different functions. For **regular verbs**, the past tense and the past participle are formed by adding *-d* or *-ed* to the base form (*erased*). For **irregular verbs**, the past tense and past participle are formed differently (*ran*/*run*).

See 28b for more on irregular verb forms.

Verbs also have an **active form**, called the **active voice** ("He *committed* the crime"), as well as a **passive form**, called the **passive voice**, consisting of a form of the verb *be* and a past participle ("The crime *was committed* by him"). In addition, verbs may take on alternative forms to reflect different **moods**. Normally they are in the **indicative mood**, used to make assertions, state opinions, and ask questions. But they can take past-tense forms to express unreal conditions or wishes, in the **subjunctive mood**: "I wish I *were* in Hawaii." They can appear in the base form, usually with no apparent subject, to issue a command, in the **imperative mood**: "Don't *do* that again!" or, occasionally, "Don't you *do* that again!" Finally, verb forms become verbals when they change their function and are used as nouns, adverbs, or adjectives.

See 26a-9,
See Chs. 28 and 57 for a more complete discussion of verbs.

❺ Adverbs

An **adverb** (adv) modifies a verb, an adjective, another adverb, or an entire clause or sentence. Adverbs usually answer one of the following questions: when? where? how? how often? to what extent?

- The mayor lives *alone* in a downtown apartment. [*Alone* modifies the verb *lives.*]
- She has a *very* busy schedule. [*Very* modifies the adjective *busy.*]
- She *almost* never takes a vacation. [*Almost* modifies the adverb *never.*]
- *Apparently,* she doesn't need one. [*Apparently* modifies the entire sentence.]

Many adverbs (*quickly, hopefully*) are formed by adding *-ly* to an adjective, but many others (*very, not, always, tomorrow, inside, therefore*) are not.

ESL NOTE Adverbs must be positioned properly within a sentence.

See 58d

See Ch. 37,
See Ch. 30 for a more detailed discussion of adverbs.

Conjunctive adverbs, such as *however, thus,* and *consequently,* modify an entire sentence or clause while linking it to the preceding sentence or clause.

► Today's weather will be beautiful. *However,* we expect rain tomorrow.

6 Prepositions

A **preposition** (prep) is a word such as *in, on, of, for,* or *by* that usually comes before a noun or pronoun and its modifiers to form a **prepositional phrase**. Some examples of prepositional phrases are *in the water, off the deep end,* and *toward them.* The noun or pronoun in such phrases (*water, end, them*) is called the **object of the preposition**. Here are some of the most common prepositions used in English:

about	beneath	into	through
above	beside	like	to
across	between	near	toward
after	by	of	under
along	despite	off	underneath
among	down	on	unlike
around	during	onto	until
at	except	out	up
before	for	outside	upon
behind	from	over	with
below	in	past	without

Prepositions also occur in multiword combinations: *according to, along with, because of, in case of, in spite of, on account of,* and *with respect to.*

Prepositions can be linked to certain verbs to form **phrasal verbs**, such as *do without, put up with,* and *look over.* In phrasal verbs, the preposition is called a **particle**. Compare the following sentences:

► She *came across* a dead animal. [*Came across* is a phrasal verb meaning "discovered."]

► She *came* across the bridge. [*Came* is a simple verb; *across* is part of the adverbial phrase *across the bridge.*]

See Chs. 57 and 59

ESL NOTE Phrasal verbs are common in idiomatic English.

7 Conjunctions

A **conjunction** (conj) joins two sentences, clauses, phrases, or words. The relationship between the two parts may be an equal, or coordinate, one; or it may be an unequal, or subordinate, one.

Coordinating conjunctions (*and, but, or, nor, yet, so, for*) connect sentences, clauses, phrases, or words that are parallel in meaning and grammatical structure. **Correlative conjunctions** (*both/and, neither/nor, either/or, not/but, whether/or, not only/but also*) are pairs of conjunctions that give extra emphasis to the two parts of a coordinated construction. **Subordinating conjunctions** introduce dependent clauses and connect them to main clauses. Some common subordinating conjunctions are *although, because, if, since, unless,* and *while.*

See 38c,
See Ch. 37 for further discussion of conjunctions.

8 Articles

An **article** is any one of three small words (*a, an, the*) used to signal the presence of a noun.

- *The* apartment next door has *a* new tenant.

9 Interjections

An **interjection** is a short utterance such as *Wow!, Ouch!, well,* or *oh* that usually expresses an emotional response. Interjections often stand alone and are often punctuated with an exclamation mark.

- *Wow!* What a show!
- *Oh*, I thought it was just so-so.

10 Verbals

In addition to the traditional parts of speech, there are also **verbals.** A verbal is a verb form that functions in a sentence as a noun, an adverb, or an adjective. There are three types of verbals: participles, gerunds, and infinitives.

Participles are words such as *sweeping* and *swept,* the present and past participles of a verb (*sweep*) that function as adjectives and can modify nouns or pronouns.

- Beware of *sweeping* generalizations.
- *Swept* floors make a house seem more livable.

Gerunds are verb forms that end in *-ing* and function as nouns.

▸ *Sweeping* the floors is something I do not enjoy.

An **infinitive** is the base form of a verb preceded by *to* (*to read, to fly, to ponder*). Infinitives can function as nouns, adjectives, or adverbs.

NOUN	*To quit* would be a mistake.
ADJECTIVE	Her desire *to quit* is understandable.
ADVERB	He is eager *to quit.*

26b Learn to identify basic sentence patterns

See Ch. 31 for more on fragments.

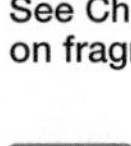

Parts of speech

Sentences are the basic units for expressing assertions, questions, commands, wishes, and exclamations. All grammatically complete sentences have a subject and a predicate. In a sentence fragment, one of these elements may be missing.

1 Sentence subjects

The **subject** (sub) of a sentence is a noun, a pronoun, or a noun phrase (a noun plus its modifiers) that identifies what the sentence is about. Usually it directly precedes the main verb.

▸ *You* probably have a pointing device (or PD) connected to your computer.

▸ *Some PDs* have a ball that rolls against wheels.

▸ *The rubber ball found inside some PDs* oxidizes over time and begins to slip.

▸ *The preference settings for double-click speed and for the ratio of hand or finger travel to pointer travel* are set in the OPTIONS menu.

The **simple subject** is always a noun or pronoun. In the example sentences, the simple subjects are *you, PDs, ball,* and *settings.* The **complete subject** is the simple subject plus all its modifiers; the complete subjects are italicized in the example sentences. Some sentences have a **compound subject** including two or more simple subjects.

▸ *Tips and techniques* can be found in the HELP menu.

In imperative sentences, which express a command or a request, the subject is understood to be *you,* even though it is not usually stated.

▶ [*You*] Use macros to automate repetitive tasks.

The subject of a sentence always agrees in number and person with the main verb. For example, a third-person singular subject such as *he* needs a third-person singular verb such as *runs.*

Subject-verb agreement is discussed further in Ch. 29.

EXERCISE 26.1 Put brackets around the complete subject in each of the following sentences. The first one has been done for you.

1. After its Industrial Revolution, [England] led the world as the most advanced nation in mechanization and mass production.
2. The Arts and Crafts Movement in Victorian England started as a mild rebellion by a group of artists, designers, and architects.
3. These artisans were concerned about the poor standard of design in English building and furnishings.
4. One of the most influential leaders of the Arts and Crafts Movement was William Morris (1834–1896).
5. Unable to find the fabrics he wanted for his home, Morris set up his own textile design firm in London in 1861.
6. Each year, the students at MIT compete to execute ever more creative pranks.
7. One year, they managed to park a car on top of a building.
8. In the winter, people need to be alert for signs that their heating systems are malfunctioning and emitting carbon monoxide gas.
9. The light breeze was welcome on that hot summer afternoon.
10. Most of us look forward to the hamburgers and potato salad served at summer cookouts.

❷ Predicates

The **predicate** is the part of a sentence that contains the verb and makes a statement about the subject. The **simple predicate** is the verb plus any auxiliary (helping) verbs.

▶ The World Wide Web *offers* information, graphics, music, movies, and much more.

▶ With a Web browser, you *can locate* information efficiently.

The **complete predicate** consists of the simple predicate plus any objects, complements, or adverbial modifiers.

▶ The World Wide Web *offers information, graphics, music, movies, and much more.*

A **compound predicate** has two or more verbs that have the same subject.

▶ A Web page *informs and entertains.*

See 26a-4

A **direct object** (DO) is a noun, a pronoun, or a noun phrase that completes the action of a transitive verb—one that is capable of transmitting action. In this sentence, *information* is the direct object of the verb *locate:*

Sub V DO

▶ You can locate *information.*

An **indirect object** (IO) is a noun, a pronoun, or a noun phrase that is affected indirectly by the action of a verb. It usually refers to the recipient or beneficiary of the action described by the verb and the direct object. The verbs *give, buy, bring, teach, tell,* and *offer* commonly take indirect objects.

Sub V IO DO

▶ The teacher told *us* a story.

Most indirect objects can be presented instead as the object of the preposition *to* or *for.*

▶ The teacher told *us* a story.

OR

▶ The teacher told a story *to us.*

▶ I bought *my mother* a plant.

OR

▶ I bought a plant *for my mother.*

An **object complement** (OC) is a noun, a noun phrase, an adjective, or an adjective phrase (an adjective plus its modifiers) that elaborates on or describes the direct object.

Sub V DO OC

▶ The news made us *depressed.*

Sub V DO OC

▶ They appointed Laurie *head of the task force.*

A **subject complement** (SC) is a noun, a noun phrase, an adjective, or an adjective phrase that follows a linking verb (such as *is, was,* or *seems*) and elaborates on the subject.

Sub LV SC

▶ She was *happy.*

Sub LV SC

▶ Laurie is *the new head of the task force.*

❸ Basic sentence patterns

The complete predicate is usually structured according to one of six basic sentence patterns:

Pattern 1: A sentence may have an intransitive verb and no object.

Pred

Sub V

▶ Time flies.

Pattern 2: A sentence may have a transitive verb with a direct object.

Pred

Sub VT DO

▶ Time heals all wounds.

Pattern 3: A sentence may have a transitive verb with a direct object and an indirect object.

Pred

Sub VT IO DO

▶ Free time gave us an opportunity.

Pattern 4: A sentence may have a transitive verb with a direct object and an object complement.

Pred

Sub VT DO OC

▶ Time pressures made us tense.

Pattern 5: A sentence may use a **linking verb**, which connects the subject to a subject complement, indicating a condition, quality, or state of being.

Pred
Sub LV SC
▶ Time is precious.

Pattern 6: A sentence may start with an auxiliary verb such as *is, do,* or *can* to form a question or exclamation.

Aux Sub V
▶ Does time fly?

EXERCISE 26.2 Insert a slash (/) between the subject and the predicate in each sentence.

1. I enrolled at Albany State in 1988.
2. My major interests were music and biology.
3. I was a soloist with the choir.
4. We sang three types of music.
5. The choir specialized in spirituals.
6. They had major injections of European musical harmony and composition.
7. Gospel music comprised a major part of black church music at the time.
8. Black choral singing was full, powerful, and richly ornate.
9. The hymns were offset by upbeat call-and-response songs.
10. People in church sang and prayed until they shouted.

26c Learn to expand sentences

The six basic sentence patterns can be expanded with **modifiers**, which are words, phrases, or clauses used to modify the subject or predicate.

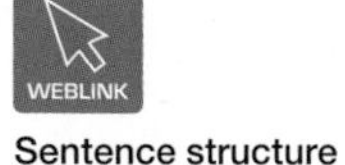

Sentence structure

1 Modifying with single words

Any simple sentence part can be modified, qualified, or described by appropriate single words. Verbs, adverbs, and adjectives can be modified by adverbs, and nouns can be modified by adjectives.

Sub V Adv

- Time flies *quickly.*

Adj Sub V Adv Adv

- *Spare* time flies *very quickly.*

Adjectives usually are placed before the noun or pronoun they modify (*terrible* burden). Adverbs are placed near the verb, adjective, or other adverb they modify. Adverbs that modify an entire sentence can be placed at the beginning, the middle, or the end of a sentence.

See Chs. 30 and 58 for more on placing adjectives and adverbs.

- *Frantically,* Martha crammed for the exam.
- Martha *frantically* crammed for the exam.
- Martha crammed for the exam *frantically.*

❷ Modifying with phrases

Sentence parts can also be modified by phrases. A **phrase** is a group of words consisting of (1) a noun and its related words or (2) a verbal and its related words. Phrases add detail to any of the subjects, verbs, objects, or complements used in the six basic sentence patterns.

Adding Prepositional Phrases

A preposition and its object (a noun or a pronoun) form a **prepositional phrase**: *in the dark, on time, outside Dallas.* Prepositional phrases can be used to modify nouns, verbs, or adjectives.

Sub Prep phr V Prep phr

- The TV *in the corner* does not work *without an antenna.*

Sub V Adj Prep phr

- Juan was jealous *beyond reason.*

Adding Verbal Phrases

A **verbal** is a verb form that functions as a noun, an adverb, or an adjective. The three kinds of verbals—infinitives, gerunds, and participles—can be combined with other words to form infinitive phrases, gerund phrases, and participial phrases.

See 26a-10

An **infinitive phrase** consists of the *to* form of a verb plus modifiers, objects, and/or complements. Such a phrase can function as a noun, an adjective, or an adverb.

- He wanted *to plant the garden.* [The infinitive phrase functions as a noun and is the object of *wanted.*]
- Free time gave us an opportunity *to reflect.* [The infinitive phrase functions as an adjective modifying *opportunity.*]
- The company was eager *to expand its operations.* [The infinitive phrase functions as an adverb modifying *eager.*]

A **gerund phrase** consists of the *-ing* form of a verb plus modifiers, objects, and/or complements. Gerund phrases function as nouns and thus can be used as sentence subjects, objects, or complements.

- *Lifting boxes all day* (Sub) made Stan tired.
- Rebecca hates *cooking.* (DO)
- Her favorite activity is *watching old movies.* (SC)

ESL NOTE Some English verbs can take only one kind of verbal as a complement—an infinitive ("I want *to go*") or a gerund ("I enjoy *biking*"); other verbs can take either ("Rebecca hates *cooking*" or "Rebecca hates *to cook*").

See Ch. 57

A **participial phrase** consists of a present participle (the *-ing* form of a verb) or a past participle (the *-ed* or *-en* form of a verb) plus modifiers, objects, and/or complements. Participial phrases function as adjectives, modifying subjects and objects of sentences.

- *Having decided to quit his job,* Roberto began looking for another one. [The participial phrase modifies the sentence subject, *Roberto.*]
- I caught someone *trying to break into my car.* [The participial phrase modifies the object *someone.*]

As these examples illustrate, participial phrases should be placed next to the words they modify. Failure to do so may produce dangling modifiers or other modification problems.

See Ch. 34

Adding Appositive Phrases

An **appositive phrase** is a noun phrase that describes or defines another noun. Appositive phrases directly follow or precede the nouns they modify and are usually set off by commas.

- ► *One of the world's most famous celebrities,* Muhammad Ali draws crowds wherever he goes.
- ► The Ford Mustang, *a car originally designed by Lee Iacocca,* has been an enduring icon of the US automotive industry.

Adding Absolute Phrases

An **absolute phrase** consists of a subject and an adjective phrase (most commonly a participial phrase). Unlike other kinds of phrases, which modify single words, absolute phrases are used to modify entire clauses or sentences.

Abs phr

Sub | Part phr

- ► *His curiosity satisfied,* Marco decided to move on to other topics.

Abs phr

Sub | Adj phr

- ► *Her face white as a sheet,* Sue put down the phone and slowly stood up.
- ► Maria could not wait to start writing another book,

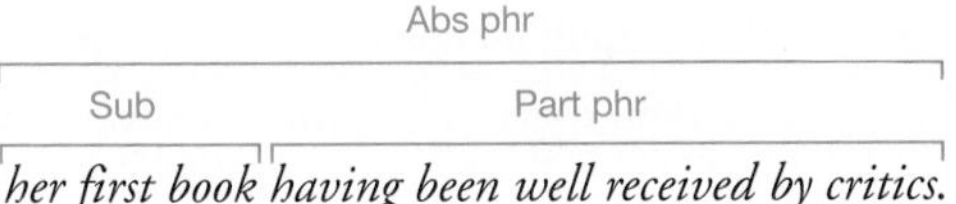

her first book having been well received by critics.

EXERCISE 26.3 Download several paragraphs from an Internet site or photocopy a newspaper or magazine article. In the text, find (1) three prepositional phrases, (2) two gerund phrases, (3) two participial phrases, and (4) an appositive phrase or an absolute phrase.

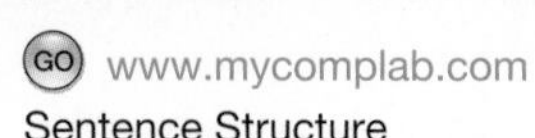

FOR COLLABORATION In your group, share the phrases you have identified and explain how you came to your conclusions.

❸ Modifying with clauses

A **clause** is a group of words that has a subject and a predicate. If a clause can stand alone as a sentence, it is an **independent clause** (or **main clause**); if it cannot, it is a **dependent clause** (or **subordinate clause**). There are three major types of dependent clauses: adjective, adverb, and noun.

Adjective clauses (also called **relative clauses**) modify nouns and pronouns. An adjective clause usually begins with a relative pronoun (*which, that, who, whose, whom*) or a subordinating conjunction (*where, when, why*) and immediately follows the noun or pronoun it modifies.

- ▶ The student *who is best prepared* is most likely to succeed.
- ▶ The place *where I work best* is in my basement.

If the relative pronoun is the direct or indirect object in the adjective clause, it can be omitted.

- ▶ The person [*whom*] *I gave the money to* has disappeared.

Ch. 33 discusses the correct use of relative pronouns; Ch. 37 describes how to use adjective clauses to subordinate ideas.

Adverb clauses modify verbs, adjectives, clauses, or other adverbs, answering questions such as the following: when? where? why? how? An adverb clause begins with a subordinating conjunction (*if, although, because, whenever, while*).

- ▶ *If you cannot find the topic you want,* double-click on the HELP button.
- ▶ *Although I have been late for work three times in the past two weeks,* my boss has not said anything to me. [The adverb clause modifies the entire main clause.]

See 27c

Noun clauses function in a sentence the way simple nouns do—as subjects, objects, complements, or appositives. Noun clauses typically begin with a *wh-* element such as *whoever, which,* or *whether;* with *that;* with *to* or *for;* or with a gerund (marked by *-ing*).

- ▶ *Whoever leaked the news* [Sub] should be punished.
- ▶ We told her *that she was wrong.* [DO]
- ▶ The plan is *to march on City Hall.* [SC]
- ▶ His one hobby, *collecting old bottles,* [App] takes up much of his time.

EXERCISE 26.4 Combine each of the following pairs of sentences to form a single sentence. In so doing, turn one of the sentences into a dependent clause attached to the main clause.

1. Some people live in a cold climate. They should anticipate car battery problems.
2. Your car will not start. You reach for some jumper cables.
3. You attach the cables to your battery. You should consider the possibility of explosion or injury.
4. Hydrogen gas in the battery case combines with air. It becomes a very explosive material.
5. There is a risk that an explosion will hurt your eyes. You should carry a pair of safety goggles with your cables.
6. Some drivers do not know how to use battery cables. They should not try to do it on their own.
7. You want to attempt a jump start. It is a good idea to read the owner's manual.
8. Car computers can lose memory when batteries fail. You will have to reset some things.
9. Prevent battery drain. Be certain to shut the car doors tightly.
10. It is easy to forget your headlights are on when you leave your car. Be sure to double-check.

TechALERT!

Electronic Language: "Filler Phrases"

People who do a lot of instant-messaging or informal emailing tend to overuse conversational noun clauses starting with *what: What I want to do is argue for a new health policy.* In academic writing, it is advisable to avoid or edit out such "filler" phrases so as to be more concise: *I want to argue for a new health policy.*

26d Learn how to classify sentences

Good writers vary the types of sentences they use in order to make their writing more interesting. The two main categories of sentence types are functional and structural.

1 Functional classifications

Sentences can be categorized functionally, or rhetorically, according to their role. A **declarative sentence**, for example, makes a direct assertion about something.

- Our political system is heavily influenced by corporate interests.

An **interrogative sentence** asks a question and ends with a question mark.

- Have you ever traveled overseas?

An **imperative sentence** makes a request, gives a command, or offers advice. Although it is always addressed to *you,* the pronoun is usually omitted.

- Use the TOOLBAR buttons to align or indent text.
- Please send me a short reply.

An **exclamatory sentence** expresses strong emotion and ends with an exclamation point. Sometimes an exclamatory sentence is written in a form that is not a complete sentence.

- We're finally connected!
- What a show [it was]! [Although not part of the sentence, *it was* is understood.]

❷ Structural classifications

Sentences can also be categorized structurally according to their overall grammatical construction. A **simple sentence** has a single independent clause and no dependent clauses. Though a simple sentence has only one clause, it may have many phrases and thus be quite long.

► I walk.

► The high plateau of western Bolivia, called the *altiplano,* is one of the world's highest elevation populated regions, with several towns at over 12,000 feet above sea level.

A **compound sentence** has two or more independent clauses and no dependent clauses. A compound sentence is created when two or more independent clauses are connected with a comma and a coordinating conjunction (*and, or, but, nor, for, so, yet*), with a semicolon and a conjunctive adverb (*therefore, however, otherwise, indeed*), with a semicolon alone, or with a correlative conjunction (*either/or, neither/nor, both/and, not only/but also*).

Ind cl — Ind cl

► An eagle once flew past our house, *but* I got only a brief glimpse of it.

Ind cl

► Personal computers are becoming more user-friendly*; therefore,*

Ind cl

more people are buying them.

Ind cl — Ind cl

► Feinstein voted for the bill*;* Boxer voted against it.

Ind cl — Ind cl

► *Either* we go to the movie *or* we stay home.

A **complex sentence** contains one independent clause and one or more dependent clauses.

Dep cl — Ind cl

► Although we stood in line for four hours, we didn't get tickets.

A **compound-complex sentence**, as the name implies, consists of two or more independent clauses and one or more dependent clauses.

Dep cl

► Millions upon millions of years before civilization had risen upon earth,

Ind cl

the central areas of this tremendous ocean were empty*; and*

Dep cl — Ind cl

where famous islands now exist, nothing rose above the rolling waves.

—James Michener, *Hawaii*

EXERCISE 26.5 Mark each sentence as declarative (D), imperative (Im), interrogative (In), or exclamatory (E) *and* as simple (S), compound (Cd), complex (Cx), or compound-complex (CC). The first one has been done for you.

1. Modern American Indian women are deeply engaged in the struggle to redefine themselves. (D, S)
2. They must reconcile traditional tribal definitions of women's roles with industrial society's definitions of these roles.
3. How does society define the role a woman should play?
4. If women are told they are powerless, they will believe it!
5. In the West, few images of women form part of the cultural mythos, and those that do are usually sexually charged.
6. The Native American tribes see women variously, but they do not question the power of femininity, which has always been a strong force.
7. Go cook the food.
8. Would you be friends with someone you couldn't trust?
9. The Indian women I have known have shown a wide range of personal styles and demeanors.
10. We must celebrate cultural differences!

EXERCISE 26.6 Log on to an Internet site of your choice, and download into a file a block of text of at least five sentences. (Alternatively, photocopy a block of text from a book or magazine.) Then classify each of the sentences according to the functional and structural classifications in this section.

FOR COLLABORATION Share your classifications, and the reasons for your decisions, with your group.

27 Pronoun Case

FAQs

- Is it correct to say "This is her"? (27a)
- How do I know when to use *who* or *whom*? (27d)
- What is wrong with "Mark likes school more than me"? (27f)

The kind of informal writing people do with friends (texting, IM'ing, email, etc.) typically uses a lot of *I's* and *you's* (or *u's*). More formal writing, by contrast, uses the full spectrum of pronouns: *I, you, he, she, it, we, they, our,* etc. It is important that you use the correct form (or **case**) of these pronouns.

Case refers to the form a pronoun takes to indicate its function in a sentence. For example, the difference between *he, him,* and *his* is a matter of case: *he* is the **subjective case**, indicating its use as a grammatical subject, whereas *him* is the **objective case**, indicating its use as a grammatical object, and *his* is the **possessive case**, indicating its use as a grammatical possessive.

	Subjective	Objective	Possessive
First-person singular	I	me	my, mine
Second-person singular	you	you	your, yours
Third-person singular	he, she, it	him, her, it	his, her, hers, its
First-person plural	we	us	our, ours
Second-person plural	you	you	your, yours
Third-person plural	they	them	their, theirs
Relative and interrogative	who, whoever	whom, whomever	whose

Writers and speakers familiar with English seldom have a problem using the correct case when a single pronoun occupies the position of subject, object, or possessive in a sentence.

SUBJECT	*She* hoped that *they* would do well. [Subjects in both clauses.]
OBJECT	The crew helped *her.* [Direct object] Sarah gave *him* timely help. [Indirect object]
OBJECT OF A PREPOSITION	Help came for *them* immediately, thanks to *her.*
POSSESSIVE	Two of *my* friends have recently quit *their* jobs.

In some special situations, however, choosing the correct pronoun form can be confusing.

27a Use *I, he, she, we, they,* or *who* for sentence or clause subjects and subject complements

The subjective case (*I, you, he, she, it, we, they, who, whoever*) is required for all pronouns used as subjects, including a pronoun paired with a noun to form a compound subject:

- ~~Her~~ *She* and Octavio are good friends. [Compound sentence subject]

- It seems that only Harrison and ~~me~~ *I* were not invited. [Compound clause subject]

See 28b-2

The subjective case is also required for subject complements where a pronoun renames the subject:

- Hello, is Carol there? Yes, this is ~~her~~ *she*. [Subject complement]

- Will the lead actor be ~~him~~ *he* or ~~me~~ *I*? [Subject complements]

In casual English, many people would say, "Yes, this is *her*" and ". . . *him* or *me*." But the antecedents of these pronouns are sentence subjects (*this, lead actor*), so in standard English the pronouns should be in the subjective case: *she, he,* and *I.*

27b Use *me, him, her, us, them,* or *whom* for sentence or clause objects

The objective case (*me, you, him, her, it, us, them, whom, whomever*) is required for all pronouns used as direct objects, indirect objects, and objects of a preposition. This can be tricky in situations involving compound objects where the pronoun is paired with a noun:

- ▶ The boss invited Janice and ~~he~~ him to lunch. [Pronoun as direct object]
- ▶ He gave Jose and ~~she~~ her a word of encouragement. [Pronoun as indirect object]
- ▶ Just between *you* and ~~I~~ me, don't you think Marty's been a little out of line lately? [Pronoun as object of a preposition]

In this last example, many people would say, "Just between you and *I*." But *between* is a preposition and the two pronouns are its objects, so the pronouns should be in the objective case: *you* and *me.*

27c Test for pronouns in compound constructions by using the pronoun alone

Pronoun usage

Most problems with pronoun case arise in compound constructions in which a pronoun is paired with a noun:

- ▶ The instructor gave *Natasha and ~~I~~* me an extra project to do.

The correct pronoun here is *me,* not *I,* because the pronoun is an object in this sentence. You can see this by trying the same sentence with just the pronoun:

The instructor gave *me* an extra project to do.

What about this sentence?

- ▶ *Natasha and ~~me~~* I like to work with music on.

Here the correct form is *I,* because the pronoun is part of the sentence subject. Again, you can test this by trying the sentence with just the pronoun:

I like to work with music on.

A special type of compound construction, called an **appositive**, occurs when a pronoun is conjoined with a noun.

- ▶ We ~~*Us*~~ *Americans* tend to be patriotic.
- ▶ Sometimes people from other countries complain about us ~~*we*~~ *Americans.*
- ▶ The sorority members chose to send *one person*— me ~~*I*~~—to the national convention.

Again, if you are unsure about which case to use in such situations, just omit the noun and see which pronoun form is correct.

We tend to be patriotic.

Sometimes people from other countries complain about *us.*

The sorority members chose to send *me* to the national convention.

EXERCISE 27.1 Circle the correct pronoun in each of the following sentences.

1. Are you going to invite her and [I, me] to your party?
2. It is unfair to make Paul and [I, me] do all the extra work by ourselves.
3. The coach asked Chris and [I, me] to design a new team logo.
4. Neither Paco nor [she, her] wants to go to Europe to study.
5. It is unfair to stereotype [we, us] Asians as people who do nothing but study all the time.
6. She is not willing to give up her ticket, and neither are Luis and [he, him].
7. [We, us] New Yorkers love the city life.
8. The neighborhood council has asked [we, us] club members to keep the sidewalk clean.
9. Tokashi and [I, me] do not always see eye to eye, but we are generally good friends.
10. She read the manuscript to Eiko and [I, me].

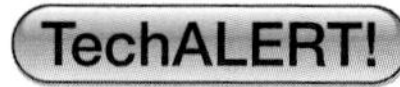

Grammar Checkers: Pronouns

Do not count on your grammar checker to identify pronoun case errors. When we ran our checker on the incorrect sentences in this chapter, it did not detect any errors at all!

Pronoun Case

Overusing *I*

INCORRECT The recruiter wants to see both you and *I.*

CORRECT The recruiter wants to see both you and *me.*

Many people use the pronoun *I* in places where *me* is the correct form. They may think that *I* is somehow more "correct." But it all depends on grammatical functions. In the example above, *both you and me* is the direct object of the verb *see*, so the pronoun should be in the objective case—*me*.

Misusing *me*

INCORRECT It seems that only Harrison and *me* were not invited.

CORRECT It seems that only Harrison and *I* were not invited.

Here too the choice of pronoun case depends on the pronoun's grammatical function in the sentence. *Harrison and I* is the subject of the subordinate clause, *Harrison and I were not invited.* That's why the subjective case (*I*) is correct.

Confusing *whoever* and *whomever*

INCORRECT You can invite *whomever* wants to come.

CORRECT You can invite *whoever* wants to come.

As always, the choice of pronoun case depends on how that pronoun functions in its immediate clause. In this example, *whoever* is the subject of the subordinate clause, *(somebody) wants to come.* That's why the subjective case (*whoever*) is correct.

27d Choose *who* or *whom* based on how it functions in its clause

See 26c-3

The *wh-* pronouns *who, whom, whoever, whomever,* and *whose* are used in questions and relative clauses. In questions, they are called **interrogative pronouns**; in clauses, they are called **relative pronouns**.

- *Who* reserved this book? [Interrogative pronoun]
- I'd like to find the person *who* reserved this book. [Relative pronoun]

Many people are uncertain about when to use *who* and *whom.* Just remember this: *Who* is used for sentence or clause *subjects*, and *whom* is used for *objects.*

- ~~*Who*~~ Whom are you going to invite to the wedding?

All about pronouns

In this sentence (which is also a clause), *whom* is the direct object of *invite.* You can see this by asking yourself this question: Would you say "You are going to invite *he* to the wedding" or "You are going to invite *him* to the wedding"? The correct answer, of course, is *him.* Since *him* is in the objective case, you should choose the objective-case *whom.*

Now consider this sentence:

- Marlowe, ~~*who*~~ whom Shakespeare greatly admired, died at age 29.

The relative clause *whom Shakespeare greatly admired* modifies *Marlowe.* It says, "Shakespeare greatly admired him"; *him* is the object of *admired.* In the relative clause version, *whom* substitutes for *him*; that's why it's in the objective case.

Similar reasoning can be used to distinguish between *whoever* (subjective case) and *whomever* (objective case).

- The place is open to ~~*whomever*~~ whoever wants to go there.

Here the *wh-* pronoun occurs in the relative clause ____ *wants to go there.* If it were an independent clause, it would require a subjective form in the slot before *wants*: *He* wants to go there, *She* wants to go there, etc. So the subjective form (*whoever*) is needed in the relative clause, not the objective form (*whomever*).

EXERCISE 27.2 Select the correct form of the pronoun in each sentence.

1. How can someone [who, whom] makes the minimum wage invest in the stock market?
2. My family doctor, [who, whom] everyone in the community knew, recently moved to New York.
3. [Who, Whom] does she wish to contact at the law firm?
4. She made it perfectly clear that [whoever, whomever] wants to come is welcome.
5. Judge Reynolds is a man in [who, whom] the community has placed great trust.
6. Barbara Ehrenreich is someone [who, whom] I have long admired.
7. He addressed his remarks to [whoever, whomever] would listen.
8. Fortune sometimes comes to those [who, whom] seek it.
9. Richard, [who, whom] updated his writing portfolio last week, now only has to write his final paper.
10. We will support [whoever, whomever] the people elect.

27e Distinguish between possessive adjectives and possessive pronouns

Possessive adjectives (*my, your, her, his, its, our, their*) precede and modify a noun:

This is *my* car.

Possessive pronouns (*mine, yours, hers, his, its, ours, theirs*) replace a noun and stand alone:

This car is *mine.*

Mine is the one in back.

Note that the possessive forms ending in *-s* (*yours, hers, ours, its, theirs*) do not take an apostrophe.

Gerunds require a possessive adjective, not a possessive pronoun:

See 50a-1, See 26a-9, See 26a-3

His

~~Him~~ wanting to do extra work was what impressed me.

In this sentence, *wanting to do extra work* is a gerund phrase. Since gerunds act as nouns, the possessive modifier in this case should be the adjective *his,* not the pronoun *him.*

Pronoun case problems

27f Use pronouns in comparisons (with *than* or *as)* based on how they would function in a full sentence

How do you know when to use . . . *more than me* or . . . *more than I*? When you are using a pronoun in a comparison, test for case by imagining how it would be in a full sentence. Consider this sentence:

▸ Mark likes school more than *me*.

You are saying, "Mark likes school more than *he likes me*." But now consider this sentence:

▸ Mark likes school more than *I*.

Here, you are saying, "Mark likes school more than *I like school*." In both instances, the case of the pronoun reflects how it would function in a full sentence.

The same holds true for *as* . . . *as* sentences.

▸ President Obama's wife is as much a Democrat as ~~*him*~~ *he*.

The correct pronoun is *he* (not *him*), as you see from the complete sentence:

President Obama's wife is as much a Democrat as *he is (a Democrat)*.

EXERCISE 27.3 Circle the correct pronoun in each sentence.

1. My brother is as conservative as [me, I].
2. The recruiter rated Susan higher than [me, I].
3. Trang claims that she enjoys the opera as much as [him, he].
4. Mark went to Paris this summer and liked it as much as [we, us].
5. Without even realizing it, Pia hurt Kelly's feelings today as much as she hurt [my, mine] last week.
6. Ronaldo does not play volleyball as well as [her, she].
7. I think it was Martin who said that Stacy is taller than [him, he].
8. Are you going to talk to [he, him] about the controversy created by the proposal?
9. He is as much to blame for the tension in the office as [her, she].
10. Ahmad felt that Jerry was better suited for the position than [me, I].

FOR COLLABORATION Discuss your conclusions for the above exercise, and the reasons for your decisions, with your group.

28 Verbs

FAQs

- What is wrong with the sentence "He believed that his thesis is credible"? (28e-2)
- How can I decide when to use *sit* or *set*? (28f)
- When I make an "if" statement, where should I put the *would*? (28h-1)

Informal writing among friends (texting, IM'ing, etc.) typically consists of simple thoughts about the recent past, the present, or the immediate future. It therefore uses short, simple sentences or even just parts of sentences (fragments). Verbs are restricted to the simple past, present, or future tense. Academic writing, on the other hand, is meant to convey complex ideas, and do so in a way that sometimes shuttles back and forth between the distant past and the distant future. It therefore tends to use complex sentence structure and a variety of verb forms.

Using verbs correctly can help make writing lively and precise. This chapter explains some of the major aspects of verb usage: form, tense, voice, and mood.

Another aspect, number, is discussed in 29a.

28a Learn the regular verb forms

All verbs in English, except *be,* have five basic forms or **principal parts**.

Most English verbs are **regular verbs**. That is, starting with the base form, their forms follow the pattern of the examples in the box: adding *-s* (or *-es*) to the base form to make the third-person singular present tense, adding *-d* (or *-ed*) to make the past tense and past participle, and adding *-ing* to the base form (and sometimes dropping the final *e*) to make the present participle.

Base form	Present tense (third-person singular)	Past tense	Past participle	Present participle
jump	jumps	jumped	jumped	jumping
erase	erases	erased	erased	erasing
add	adds	added	added	adding
veto	vetoes	vetoed	vetoed	vetoing

The **base form**, or **simple form**, of a verb—the form listed in a dictionary—is normally used with subjects that are plural nouns or the pronouns *I, you, we,* or *they* to make statements in the present tense.

- Hummingbirds *migrate* south in winter.
- I *walk* two miles every day.

When the subject of a sentence is a singular noun or a third-person singular pronoun (*he, she* or *it*), the **present tense** of the verb has an *-s* added to it.

- She *visits* New York every month.
- My neighbor *walks* laps around our block.

Sometimes a slight change is required in the spelling of the base form (*fly/flies, veto/vetoes*).

The **past tense** of a verb is used to describe action that occurred in the past. For a regular verb, add *-d* or *-ed* to the base form to get the past tense:

- ABC *televised* Super Bowl XL.
- We *wanted* to see the game.

The **past participle** of a regular verb is similar in form to the past tense. The past participle can be used (1) with *has* or *have* in the present perfect tense, (2) with *had* in the past perfect tense, (3) with some form of *be* to create a passive-voice construction, and (4) by itself, as an adjective, to modify a noun.

- We *have petitioned* the school board for a new crosswalk. [Present perfect]
- Before last night's meeting, we *had talked* about going directly to the mayor. [Past perfect]

- Last year, two students *were injured* trying to cross this street. [Passive voice]
- The parents of the *injured* students are supporting our cause. [Adjective]

The **present participle** is created by adding *-ing* to the base form of a verb. It is used (1) with some form of *be* to indicate ongoing action (the progressive tense), (2) as a gerund, and (3) as an adjective.

Verbs

Misusing irregular verbs

INCORRECT	The budget has *shrinked.*
INCORRECT	The budget has *shrank.*
CORRECT	The budget has *shrunk.*

Many verbs in English have irregular forms for the past or perfect tenses. You need to learn them one by one.

See 28b

Confusing *sit* and *set, lie* and *lay, rise* and *raise*

INCORRECT	She tried to *raise up* from the chair but couldn't.
CORRECT	She tried to *rise up* from the chair but couldn't.

Verbs like *set, lay,* and *raise* are transitive: They transfer an action from the subject to an object. Verbs like *sit, lie,* and *rise* are intransitive: They don't transfer an action to an object.

See 28f

Misusing *would* in conditional sentences

INCORRECT	If the coach *would* have been there, he would have done something.
CORRECT	If the coach *had* been there, he would have done something.

In most sentences beginning with *if,* the verb in the *if* clause should be in the subjunctive form.

See 28h

- Joaquin *is working* on a new project. [Progressive tense]
- He enjoys *working.* [Gerund]
- This is a *working* draft of my paper. [Adjective]

EXERCISE 28.1 What are the principal parts of the following regular verbs?

1. print
2. drown
3. compile
4. drag

28b Learn common irregular verb forms

An **irregular verb** is one whose past tense and past participle are not created by adding *-d* or *-ed* to the base form. Instead, these forms often have different internal vowels than in the base form (base form: *find;* past tense: *found;* past participle: *found*). Alternatively, the past tense and past participle may be the same as the base form (*set/set/set*) or may be radically different (*go/went/gone*). (Note: *Be* and *have* also have irregular present-tense forms.)

ESL NOTE English has so many irregular verbs because it was derived from different source languages (e.g., Latin and German) that create their verb forms in different ways.

Base form	*Past tense*	*Past participle*
beat	beat	beaten
become	became	become
begin	began	begun
bite	bit	bit, bitten
blow	blew	blown
break	broke	broken
bring	brought	brought
build	built	built
burn	burned, burnt	burned, burnt
buy	bought	bought

Base form	*Past tense*	*Past participle*
catch	caught	caught
choose	chose	chosen
come	came	come
cost	cost	cost
cut	cut	cut
dig	dug	dug
dive	dove, dived	dived
do	did	done
draw	drew	drawn
drink	drank	drunk
drive	drove	driven
eat	ate	eaten
fall	fell	fallen
feel	felt	felt
fight	fought	fought
find	found	found
fly	flew	flown
forget	forgot	forgotten, forgot
freeze	froze	frozen
get	got	gotten, got
give	gave	given
go	went	gone
grow	grew	grown
hang	hung	hung
have	had	had
hear	heard	heard
hide	hid	hidden
hit	hit	hit
keep	kept	kept
know	knew	known
lay	laid	laid
lead	led	led
leave	left	left
lend	lent	lent
lie	lay	lain
lose	lost	lost

Base form	*Past tense*	*Past participle*
make	made	made
mean	meant	meant
pay	paid	paid
prove	proved	proved, proven
read	read	read
ride	rode	ridden
run	ran	run
say	said	said
see	saw	seen
send	sent	sent
set	set	set
shake	shook	shaken
shoot	shot	shot
show	showed	shown, showed
shrink	shrank	shrunk
sing	sang	sung
sink	sank	sunk
sit	sat	sat
sleep	slept	slept
speak	spoke	spoken
steal	stole	stolen
stick	stuck	stuck
strike	struck	struck, stricken
swear	swore	sworn
swim	swam	swum
swing	swung	swung
take	took	taken
teach	taught	taught
tear	tore	torn
think	thought	thought
throw	threw	thrown
wake	woke, waked	woken, waked
wear	wore	worn
win	won	won
write	wrote	written

Electronic Language: Technology Verbs (*to google*, *to text*)

New tech-oriented verbs such as *google, flame, blog,* and *IM* are not acceptable (yet) in academic or formal writing. Over time, this may change, as language gradually adjusts to the needs of its users. For example, it wasn't so long ago that *email* entered the English language as a new verb. At first it was considered slang and was not acceptable in formal usage. But today it can be found in all standard dictionaries as both a noun and a verb. New verbs like those listed above may undergo the same evolution. For now, however, it is best to avoid them in academic or formal writing.

As you can see, many of the most common verbs in the English language are irregular. Therefore, it is important that you learn their forms.

The two most common verbs in English, *be* and *have,* are also two of the most irregular. The third-person singular present tense of *have* is not *haves* but *has.* See the Forms of *be* chart on this page for a complete outline of the forms of this irregular verb.

Forms of *be*

Present Tense

	Singular	*Plural*
First person	I *am*	we *are*
Second person	you *are*	you *are*
Third person	he/she/it *is*	they *are*
	Michael *is*	people *are*

Past Tense

	Singular	*Plural*
First person	I *was*	we *were*
Second person	you *were*	you *were*
Third person	he/she/it *was*	they *were*
	Michael *was*	people *were*

EXERCISE 28.2 What are the principal parts of each of the following irregular verbs? (To figure out the past tense form, use the verb in a sentence with *yesterday*. To figure out the participle, use the verb in a sentence with *have*.)

1. arise
2. dream
3. ring
4. stand
5. sweep

28c Know how to use auxiliary verbs

See 28d,
See 28h,
See 28g

An **auxiliary verb** (or **helping verb**) is used with a main verb to indicate tense, mood or voice. The most common auxiliary verbs are *be, have,* and *do.* Some form of one of these helping verbs is frequently used with a base form, present participle, or past participle of a main verb to create a more complex **verb phrase**.

- She *is finishing* her paper. [Progressive tense, indicating ongoing action]
- The college *has adopted* a new honor code. [Present perfect tense, indicating past action with ongoing effects]
- We *do need* to get going. [Emphasis]
- My roommate *has been asked* to run for the student senate. [Passive voice, present perfect tense]
- *Does* he *know* what's involved? [Question]

Other important helping verbs are the **modal auxiliary verbs** (*may/might, can/could, will/would, shall/should, must, ought to,* and *have to*). These verbs communicate degrees of probability, necessity, or obligation. A modal auxiliary verb is used only with the base form of another verb:

- The concert *might be* sold out.
- We *should get* tickets before it is too late.

Most of the modal auxiliaries do not have a third-person present *-s* form or a participle form; *have to* is the only exception.

- ▶ Sandra *has to* write a paper.
- ▶ Yesterday she *had to* spend all afternoon in science lab.
- ▶ Earlier she *had had to* prepare for a math test.

Modal auxiliaries can be used with forms of *be, have,* or *do,* but not with other modal auxiliaries. For example, "We might could do that" is ungrammatical in standard English. You can often create a standard English version of such a double-modal expression by substituting a synonymous verb phrase for one of the modal auxiliaries:

NONSTANDARD	We might *could* do that.
REVISED	We might *be able to* do that.

In some cases, you can simply eliminate one of the modal auxiliaries:

NONSTANDARD	Sally *should ought to* cancel her appointment.
REVISED	Sally *should* cancel her appointment.
OR	
	Sally *ought to* cancel her appointment.

EXERCISE 28.3 In the following sentences, underline the verb phrases, circle the modal auxiliary verbs, and correct any double modals.

1. Joey is working on his chemistry assignment tonight.
2. Li-Ping wanted Michael to have lunch with her, but he told her that he might ought to work.
3. Angelica must should go with us to see the soccer match.
4. I heard that the company has adopted a new policy with regard to employee absences.
5. Does she know that he might not come to the play with us?
6. Fernando is staying home tonight.
7. He must not leave the house while he is recovering from knee surgery.
8. School uniforms should ought to be the standard in the public schools.
9. Ikuto may be walking over to our house right now.
10. My neighbor has been accused of stealing company office supplies.

28d Learn the verb tenses

Verb tense expresses the time of the action or the state of being indicated by a verb. English has three basic tenses: past, present, and future. Each tense can also take on a **verbal aspect**, indicating duration or completion of the verb's action or state of being. The three verbal aspects in English are progressive, perfect, and perfect progressive. With all possible combinations of tenses and aspects, English has twelve verb tenses.

SIMPLE PRESENT TENSE	we wonder
PRESENT PROGRESSIVE TENSE	we are wondering
PRESENT PERFECT TENSE	we have wondered
PRESENT PERFECT PROGRESSIVE TENSE	we have been wondering
SIMPLE PAST TENSE	we wondered
PAST PROGRESSIVE TENSE	we were wondering
PAST PERFECT TENSE	we had wondered
PAST PERFECT PROGRESSIVE TENSE	we had been wondering
FUTURE TENSE	we will wonder
FUTURE PROGRESSIVE TENSE	we will be wondering
FUTURE PERFECT TENSE	we will have wondered
FUTURE PERFECT PROGRESSIVE TENSE	we will have been wondering

1 Present tenses

The **simple present tense** is used to express a general truth, to make an observation, or to describe a habitual activity.

- ▶ A rolling stone *gathers* no moss.
- ▶ Oates's stories *depress* me.
- ▶ My father *mows* the lawn every week.

With an appropriate time expression, the simple present can be used to refer to a scheduled future event.

- ▶ The show *begins* in five minutes.

The simple present is used in stage directions and in critical discussions of literary works.

- ▶ Max suddenly *appears* at the door.
- ▶ In *The Tempest,* all the action *occurs* in one place during one day.

The simple present also is used to express a scientific fact or law.

- ▶ Water *boils* at 100° Celsius.
- ▶ Gravity *causes* objects to fall.

The **present progressive tense** is formed with the auxiliary verb *am, are,* or *is* and the present participle (*-ing* form) of a main verb. The present progressive is used to indicate action occurring at the present time.

- ▶ Jennifer *is preparing* for the MCAT exam.

With an appropriate time expression, the present progressive can be used to announce future events.

- ▶ A new supermarket *is opening* next week.

ESL NOTE Certain verbs, called **stative verbs**, do not have any progressive tenses. These verbs include *know, believe, need, consist,* and *exist.* Thus, it is incorrect to say "I am needing a new computer".

See 57f

The **present perfect tense** is formed with the auxiliary verb *have* or *has* and the past participle of a main verb. The present perfect is used to indicate action that began in the past and either is continuing or has continuing effects in the present.

- ▶ Many people *have expressed* alarm about environmental degradation.

ESL NOTE The present perfect tense and the simple past tense cannot be used interchangeably. The present perfect implies *duration* of past action; the simple past tense expresses *completed* past action. The sentence "She was at the university since 2004" is incorrect, because the *since* phrase refers to a continuous time period. The grammatically correct version of this sentence is "She *has been* at the university since 2004".

The **present perfect progressive tense** is formed by combining *have been* or *has been* with the present participle of a main verb. The present perfect progressive is used similarly to the present perfect but emphasizes the ongoing nature of the activity.

▶ Eric *has been studying* German for two years.

This sentence means that Eric is still studying German, whereas the sentence "Eric *has studied* German for two years" could mean that he is not currently studying it (although he might again study it someday).

❷ Past tenses

The **simple past tense** is used to describe actions or conditions that occurred or applied entirely in the past.

▶ Jonas Salk *invented* the polio vaccine.

▶ In 1950, the United States *consisted* of only forty-eight states.

The **past progressive tense** is formed by combining the auxiliary verb *was* or *were* with the present participle of a main verb. The past progressive describes action continuing over a period of time in the past. It is often used to set the stage for another action of shorter duration.

▶ He *was cleaning* the living room when the phone rang.

The **past perfect tense** is created by combining the auxiliary verb *had* with the past participle of a main verb. The past perfect is used to describe a past action that preceded another past action.

▶ Amanda *had thought* of volunteering for the job, but then she got sick.

The **past perfect progressive tense** functions like the past perfect tense but puts more emphasis on the continuing or repetitive nature of the past action. The past perfect progressive is formed by combining *had been* with the present participle of a main verb.

▶ Amanda *had been thinking* of volunteering for the job, but then she got sick.

EXERCISE 28.4 Correct the verb tense errors in the following sentences.

1. Eli Whitney has invented the cotton gin in 1793.
2. She divulged the secret, even though she promised not to.
3. It was five years since I last saw Aihua.
4. Three years ago, I had visited China.
5. The United States first was consisting of thirteen colonies.

6. Joseph Conrad was writing *The Heart of Darkness* in English, his third language.
7. She waited for the phone to ring when her brother came into the bedroom.
8. Miguel did well in the course until last week, when he unexpectedly received a D on an important quiz.
9. Tim has learned the results of his preliminary examinations two weeks after he took them.
10. He was my best friend, even though he had been two years older.

❸ Future tenses

The **simple future tense**, as its name implies, expresses actions or conditions that will occur in the future. The simple future consists of the modal auxiliary verb *will* and the base form of a main verb.

GO For *shall*, see the Glossary of Usage

▶ Ames *will be* a half hour late.

ESL NOTE In casual English, future conditions are often expressed using the modal auxiliary *is going to* instead of *will*, as in "Ames *is going to* be a half hour late." It is best to avoid this usage in formal English.

The **future progressive tense** is formed by combining *will be* with the present participle of a main verb. The future progressive expresses action that will be continuing or repeated in the future.

▶ Right now my son is working, but next year he *will be going* to college.

The **future perfect tense** consists of *will have* and the past participle of a main verb. The future perfect is used to describe an action that will occur in the future but before some specified time.

▶ By the end of this year, gun-related violence *will have taken* the lives of more than 2000 American teenagers.

The **future perfect progressive tense** is similar to the future perfect but emphasizes the continuous or repetitive nature of the action. The future perfect progressive consists of *will have been* plus the present participle of a main verb.

▶ By tomorrow morning, I *will have been working* on this paper for eighteen hours.

Verb tense sequencing

28e Observe sequence of tenses

Good writing presents a coherent framework of time. Since time is indicated in part by verb tense, it is important to select verb tenses carefully and logically. The relationship between two or more verbs in the same sentence or in adjacent sentences is called the **sequence of tenses**.

❶ Sequence of verb tenses in compound or adjacent sentences

Two or more independent clauses about closely related events or situations may be connected by a coordinating conjunction (*and, or, but*) to form a compound sentence. Alternatively, two related independent clauses may be presented as consecutive sentences. Typically, the main verbs in each clause or sentence have the same tense.

- Joe *wants* to go to the game, but Lori *does* not.
- He *likes* baseball. She *dislikes* the game.

Sometimes, however, one event or action may logically precede or follow the other, requiring different verb tenses to indicate which of the two came first.

- Joe *could* not *go* to the game, because he *had* not *done* his homework.

❷ Sequence of verb tenses in complex sentences

See 26d-2

A complex sentence has one independent clause and one or more dependent clauses. Each clause has its own main verb. The appropriate tense for each main verb depends on the context and the intended meaning. If the actions expressed by these verbs occur at approximately the same time, the verbs should be in the same tense.

- When the conductor *gives* the signal, the musicians *start* playing.
- Before you *sit* down, *adjust* the height of your chair.

When you need to make it clear that one past action or event preceded another, use the past perfect or past perfect progressive tense in one clause and the simple past tense in the other clause.

- Although Amanda *had thought* of volunteering for the job, she *was* now no longer interested.

When you need to show that a past action or event preceded a present or future one, use the present perfect or present perfect progressive tense to express the past action or event.

▸ Since the Pope *has been* to Poland already, he probably *will* not *go* again.

③ Sequence of verb tenses with infinitives

There are two kinds of infinitives: the **present infinitive** (*to* plus the base form of a verb) and the **perfect infinitive** (*to have* plus the past participle of a verb). Use the present infinitive for an action that occurs at the same time as or later than the action expressed by the main verb.

GO
See 26a-9

▸ Samantha *wants* me *to pick up* the car.

Use the perfect infinitive for an action that occurs prior to the action expressed by the main verb.

▸ Samantha *wants* me *to have picked up* the car.

④ Sequence of verb tenses with participles

The **present participle** (the *-ing* form of a verb) can be used to represent an action that occurs at the same time as that expressed by the main verb.

▸ *Walking* into the house, Jim sensed that something was wrong.

Choosing the Correct Tense Sequence

1. Consider the two adjacent clauses: Does the action in clause A occur at approximately the same time as the action in clause B? If so, use the same verb tense in both clauses.
2. If the action in clause A *precedes* the action in clause B, follow these guidelines:
   a. If clause B is in the *present* tense, put clause A in the *past* or *present perfect.*
   b. If clause B is in the *past* tense, put clause A in the *past perfect.*
   c. If clause B is in the *future* tense, put clause A in the *present* or *present perfect.*

The **past participle** is used to indicate that an action occurs before or during the action expressed by the main verb.

- *Stung* by criticism of his latest film, Costner is working hard on a new one.

The **present perfect participle** (*having* plus the past participle) expresses an action occurring prior to the action of the main verb.

- *Having signed* a contract, Deanna was afraid she had to go through with the deal.

EXERCISE 28.5 Correct any sequence-of-tense errors in the following sentences.

1. As soon as she entered the room, several people rush over to say hello.
2. He was disappointed when some of his sources are found to be fraudulent.
3. He believed that his thesis is credible.
4. We insisted on using pesticides, even though this is not proven to be the best solution to an insect problem.
5. Her eyesight has begun to fail, and she turned to the radio for information.
6. Who expected that old car to lasted all these years?
7. His roommate has expected him to have done the laundry by Friday.
8. Entering the workplace, they have understood the safety concerns of the employees.
9. Having fired the employees who reported the safety problem, the manager had faced a lawsuit.
10. Concerned that the number of beds in the emergency shelter would be inadequate, the city council votes to open another shelter during the winter.

28f Use transitive and intransitive verbs correctly: *sit/set*, *lie/lay*, *rise/raise*

See 26a-4

A **transitive verb** is a verb that takes a direct object. In other words, a transitive verb transfers an action from a subject to an object. The sentence "A virus damaged my hard drive" has a transitive verb (*damaged*) that transfers the action to the direct object (*hard drive*). Some typical transitive verbs are *see, hear, consult, kick, recognize,* and *mix*. Transitive verbs are usually marked in dictionaries with the abbreviation *vt* or *tr*.

An **intransitive verb** is one that does not take a direct object. Some typical intransitive verbs are *sleep, relax, die, go, fall, come,* and *walk*.

Intransitive verbs are usually identified in dictionaries by the abbreviation *vi* or *intr.*

Many English verbs can be used either transitively or intransitively. For example, the verb *jump* is transitive in the sentence "Mike jumped the fence" but intransitive in the sentence "Mike jumped for joy." Some other common "two-way" verbs are *run, dream, write, eat, grow,* and *develop.*

Many speakers of English confuse *sit* and *set, lie* and *lay,* and *rise* and *raise.* The two verbs in each of these pairs sound somewhat alike and have related meanings, but they differ as to whether they can take an object. The first member of each pair is intransitive and cannot take an object; the second member is transitive and does take an object.

See 26b-3

INTRANSITIVE Jorge *will sit* over there. [The verb has no object.]

TRANSITIVE Jorge *will set* the *flowers* over there. [The verb has an object, *flowers.*]

INTRANSITIVE I think I *will lie* down. [The verb has no object.]

TRANSITIVE We *will lay* the *groundwork* for the project. [The verb has an object, *groundwork.*]

INTRANSITIVE The sun *rises* in the east. [The verb has no object.]

TRANSITIVE The senator always *raises* a lot of *money* for his reelection campaigns. [The verb has an object, *money.*]

EXERCISE 28.6 Select the correct verb in each of the following sentences.

You may want to consult the list of irregular verbs in 28b.

1. We should all (sit, set) our watches for daylight saving time.
2. The winner usually (raises, rises) the trophy over his head.
3. Russ was so tired he (lay, laid) down for a quick nap.
4. If the dictator tries to stay in power, the people may (raise up, rise up) and overthrow him.
5. Please (set, sit) down and make yourself comfortable.
6. The young mother wanted to (lay, lie) her baby on the counter to change its diaper.
7. A member of the audience (rose, raised) from his seat.
8. The jury (sat, set) still for more than three hours.
9. The parents (laid, lay) a wreath on their son's grave.
10. Congress is talking about (rising, raising) the minimum wage.

28g Favor active over passive voice

See 26b, See 28f

Voice is the characteristic of a verb that indicates whether the subject of a sentence is acting or being acted upon. In the **active voice**, the subject of the sentence performs an action on a direct object. In the **passive voice**, the subject of the sentence is acted upon. Only transitive verbs can be cast in active and passive voice.

ACTIVE ▶ My friend Julie *handcrafted* this pin. [The subject acts upon an object.] (Subject/Actor: My friend Julie; DO: this pin)

PASSIVE ▶ This pin *was handcrafted* by my friend Julie. [The subject is acted upon by the object following the verb.] (Subject: This pin; Actor: my friend Julie)

See 28a

The passive voice consists of an appropriate form of the auxiliary verb *be* and the past participle of a main verb. A passive-voice sentence may refer to the performer of the action in a *by* phrase following the verb. In practice, though, such a *by* phrase is often omitted, which has the effect of concealing or de-emphasizing the performer of the action.

PASSIVE This pin *was handcrafted.* [The phrase *by my friend Julie* is omitted.]

See 36d

In general, good writers favor the active voice over the passive voice. The active voice is more concise and more direct—and thus more vigorous—than the passive. In some cases, however, the passive voice works better than the active voice. For example, when identifying the performer of an action is unimportant or difficult, using the passive voice allows you to write a grammatical sentence without mentioning the actor.

▶ Bacterial infections are usually treated with antibiotics.

EXERCISE 28.7 Some of the following sentences are in the passive voice; others are in the active voice. For practice, change all passive-voice sentences to active-voice sentences (which may require inventing an actor) and

Grammar Checkers: Passive Voice

Your grammar checker may flag some of your passive sentences and miss others. In any case, you need to use your own judgment: If the performer of the action is obvious or unimportant, you may want to keep the passive and omit mention of the actor. (In 28g, we used nine passive sentences. Our grammar checker flagged eight of them, all of which we decided to keep.)

all actives to passives (which may involve omitting the actor). (Note: Some sentences have intransitive verbs, which cannot be changed.)

1. We can recycle most ordinary materials.
2. Twelve protesters were arrested by the police.
3. Cartilage serves as padding material in joints.
4. It keeps bones from grinding on bones.
5. You can use toolbar buttons instead of menu or keyboard commands.
6. A group of marine scientists and conservationists in 2000 voted Palau, Micronesia's coral reef, one of the seven underwater wonders of the world.
7. *A Tale of Two Cities* by Charles Dickens should be reread by everyone who thinks reading it in high school was enough.
8. In the summer of 1996, scientific evidence pointing to the possible existence of life beyond Earth was announced by NASA.
9. The purported evidence was found in a 4.5-pound meteorite that landed in Antarctica 13,000 years ago.
10. Did someone switch off the copier?

28h Make sure verbs are in the proper mood

The **mood** of a verb indicates the type of statement being made by the sentence—an assertion, a question, a command, a wish, or a hypothetical condition. English verbs have three moods: indicative, imperative, and subjunctive.

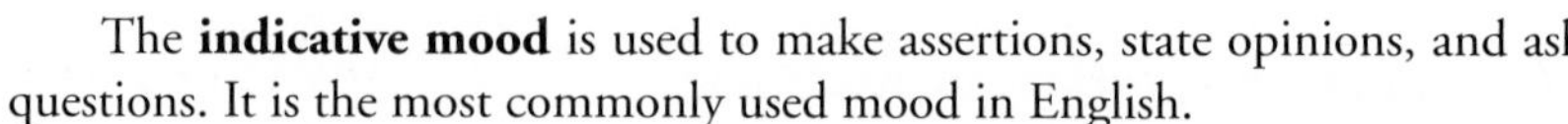

See 26a-4

The **indicative mood** is used to make assertions, state opinions, and ask questions. It is the most commonly used mood in English.

- Washington *was* the first president of the United States. [Assertion]
- Citizens *should take* more interest in local government. [Opinion]
- *Do* you *want* to vote? [Question]

See 26b-1

The **imperative mood** is used to express commands and give instructions. Commands are always addressed to a second person, although the explicit *you* is normally omitted. Instructions are often cast in the imperative mood.

- *Insert* Setup Disk 1 in the CD drive. Then *run* the program.

The **subjunctive mood** is used for hypothetical conditions, polite requests, wishes, and other uncertain statements. A verb in the subjunctive mood often appears in dependent clauses beginning with *if* or *that.* The present subjunctive is the same as the base form of the verb. The past subjunctive is identical to the past tense of the verb. The only exception is *were,* which is used for all subjunctive uses of *be* except after verbs of requesting, requiring, or recommending, where *be* is used.

- I wish I *were* an A student!
- The defense attorney requested that her client *be* given probation.

The past perfect subjunctive has the same form as the ordinary past perfect.

Verb resources

1 Hypothetical *if* constructions

When an *if* clause expresses a contrary-to-fact or unreal condition, the verb of the clause should be in the past subjunctive or past perfect subjunctive mood. The main clause verb should include the modal auxiliary *would, could,* or *might.*

- If I *were* you, I *would* make up my Incompletes as soon as possible. [Expresses a hypothetical future condition.]
- If John *had been* there, he *might* have been able to help. [Expresses a hypothetical past condition.]

Do not use *would, could,* or *might* in a hypothetical *if* clause. In contrary-to-fact sentences, modal auxiliaries such as *would* and *could* belong in the main clause, not in the conditional (subordinate) clause. Use the subjunctive in the conditional clause.

SUBJUNCTIVE FORM REVISED

▶ If we ~~would live~~ *lived* closer to San Francisco, we would go there more often.

❷ Dependent clauses expressing a wish

In a dependent clause following the verb *wish,* use the past subjunctive for present contrary-to-fact conditions and the past perfect subjunctive for past contrary-to-fact conditions.

▶ I wish [that] he *were* here.

▶ I wish [that] he *had stayed.*

❸ Dependent clauses expressing a request, suggestion, or demand

Verbs such as *require, demand, suggest,* and *insist* are usually followed by a dependent clause beginning with *that.* The verb in the *that* clause should be in the subjunctive mood. (Note: Sometimes *that* is omitted.)

▶ The police require that all pets *be* kept on a leash.

▶ They suggested that he *go* to the emergency room.

EXERCISE 28.8 Correct any errors in mood in the following sentences.

1. If I was rich, I would go on a world tour.
2. If Denju would get a job, he could move out of his parents' house.
3. If she would have been more careful, the accident might never have occurred.
4. I might believe you if you would have been more honest with me in the past.
5. Rahim knew that if he was to eat less, he would lose weight.
6. I wish that Shu-Chuan was still my roommate.
7. Nedra might be able to leave town for the weekend if she would finish her history research paper before Friday night.
8. Was he to actually consider Joanne's stock-option offer, he might take more interest in the future of the company.

9. If Josh was any better a dancer, he could probably be in an MTV video.
10. If he could have gone to the store, I am sure he would have remembered to buy the strawberries.

FOR COLLABORATION Select one exercise in this chapter to share with your group. (You may want to discuss an exercise that was particularly difficult for you.)

29 Subject-Verb Agreement

FAQs

- Is it correct to write "Meg's circle of friends give her a lot of support"? (29b)
- What's wrong with "Neither my parents nor my sister are coming"? (29d)
- Which is correct: "Athletics *are* . . ." or "Athletics *is* . . ."? (29g)

In every English sentence, the subject and its verb must agree in **number:** If the subject is singular, the verb must be singular, too; if the subject is plural, the verb must be plural as well. Subject and verb should also agree in **person:** "He *go* to work at nine o'clock" is ungrammatical because the subject *he* is third-person singular while the verb *go* is not; the third-person singular form of *go* is *goes.*

See 35a

29a Use plural verbs with plural subjects and singular verbs with singular subjects

A **subject** is a noun, pronoun, or noun phrase that identifies what the sentence is about. Plural subjects usually have a distinctive *-s* or *-es* ending (*friends, trees, boxes*), while singular subjects do not (*friend, tree, box*). Verbs, on the other hand, are alike for both plural and singular—with the exception of the third-person singular present-tense verb, which typically ends with an *-s* or *-es.*

See 26b-1

The verb *be* is also exceptional; see the box on page 611.

FIRST-PERSON SINGULAR	I *go* to work.
SECOND-PERSON SINGULAR	You *go* to work.
THIRD-PERSON SINGULAR	He or she *goes* to work.

TechALERT!

Grammar Checkers: Subject-Verb Agreement

Your grammar checker may identify some errors in subject-verb number agreement, but will likely miss many. When we tested our grammar checker on the preceding paragraph after deliberately making all the subjects and verbs *disagree,* our grammar checker detected only three of the six errors.

FIRST-PERSON PLURAL	We *go* to work.
SECOND-PERSON PLURAL	You *go* to work.
THIRD-PERSON PLURAL	They *go* to work.

With a subject that is third-person singular, be sure to use a third-person singular verb form.

▶ Megan ~~ride~~ *rides* the bus every day.

Be sure *not* to use a third-person singular verb form with a subject that is *not* third-person singular.

▶ We ~~rides~~ *ride* the bus every day.

29b With a modified subject, make the verb agree with the simple subject

See 26b-1

A **simple subject** is a single noun or pronoun. In cases where the subject has modifiers, the verb should agree with the simple subject.

▶ Meg's circle of friends gives her a lot of support. [*Circle* is the simple subject of the phrase *Meg's circle of friends.*]

When a singular subject is followed by a phrase beginning with *as well as, along with, in addition to,* or *together with,* the verb should be in the singular.

▶ Meg, as well as her friends, usually votes for the more liberal candidate.

If this seems awkward to you, you can restructure the sentence to create a compound subject (which takes a plural verb):

- Meg and her friends usually vote for the more liberal candidate.

29c Use plural verbs with most compound subjects

WEBLINK

Guide to subject-verb agreement

Compound subjects refer to two or more people, places, or things and are formed with the conjunction *and.* In most cases, compound subjects have a plural sense and thus require plural verbs.

- Geography and history are my favorite subjects.

In some cases, a compound subject has a singular sense and requires a singular verb.

- Law and order is a desirable feature for all modern societies.
- Rock and roll has remained popular for decades.

29d With subjects joined by *or* or *nor*, make the verb agree in number and person with the second part of the subject

- Either my sister or my parents are coming.
- Neither my parents nor my sister is coming.

If the singular verb, as in the second example above, sounds awkward to you, you can switch the two parts of the subject and use the plural form of the verb:

- Neither my sister nor my parents are coming.

29e Use singular verbs with most indefinite pronouns

Indefinite pronouns include *anybody, everyone, nothing, each,* and *much.* Unlike regular pronouns, they do not necessarily refer to any particular person or thing. Most indefinite pronouns are grammatically singular. Therefore, when used as subjects, they should have singular verbs.

Subject-Verb Agreement

Subjects separated from verbs

The most common agreement errors occur when the subject contains both singular and plural nouns. In such cases, the main verb should agree with the *simple* subject.

INCORRECT The purpose of these exercises are to help you write better.

CORRECT The purpose of these exercises is to help you write better.

The simple subject in this sentence is *purpose,* which is singular, so the main verb should be singular, too.

The pronoun *each*

Especially problematic for many writers and speakers is the pronoun *each.*

INCORRECT Each of my friends are having problems.

CORRECT Each of my friends is having problems.

Here the simple subject is *each,* which is singular. Therefore, the main verb should be singular as well.

See 29b

- No one is here.
- Something needs to be done about this.
- Each of the candidates is giving a short speech.

A few indefinite pronouns, including *both* and *others,* are plural and therefore require plural verbs. Other indefinite pronouns, such as *some, all, any, more,* and *none,* can take either singular or plural verb forms, depending on what they refer to.

- All of the committee members were at the meeting.
- All of their attention was directed at the speaker.

In the first example, *all* is plural because it refers to the plural noun *members; all of the committee members* could be replaced by the plural pronoun *they.* In the second example, *all* is singular because it refers to the singular noun *attention; all of their attention* could be replaced by the singular pronoun *it.*

29f Use singular verbs with most collective nouns

Collective nouns such as *team, faculty, jury,* and *committee* refer to groups. They can have either a singular or a plural sense depending on whether they refer to the group or to the individuals within the group. These nouns usually take singular verbs.

GO See 26a-1

- The team is doing better than expected.
- The band seems to be road-weary.

When the noun refers to individuals within the group, use a plural verb:

- The faculty are divided in their opinion of the new president.

To emphasize the plural sense of collective nouns, simply insert an appropriate plural noun.

- The band members seem to be road-weary.

OR

- The members of the band seem to be road-weary.

29g Use singular verbs with nouns that are plural in form but singular in sense

Words such as *mathematics, athletics, politics, economics, physics,* and *news* look like plural nouns because of the *-s* ending. However, these nouns are usually singular in meaning and thus require singular verbs.

- Economics is my favorite subject.
- The news from Lake Wobegon always interests me.

Likewise, titles of creative works and names of companies that look plural in form but actually refer to a singular entity take a singular verb.

- *The Brothers Karamazov* was probably Dostoevsky's best novel.
- Allyn & Bacon publishes college textbooks.

In some cases, however, a word may take either a singular or a plural verb depending on whether it refers to an entire field (singular) or to a set of activities or properties (plural).

- At our school, physics is required for all college-bound seniors. [Here, *physics* refers to a field of study.]
- The physics of fiber-optic technology are pretty complicated. [Here, *physics* refers to properties.]

29h Make a linking verb agree with its subject

See 26b-3

Sometimes you may be faced with a sentence of the form "*X* is *Y*," in which the subject *X* is singular and the subject complement *Y* is plural, or vice versa. In such cases, the linking verb should agree in number with the subject, not with the subject complement.

- Her main interest is boys.
- Boys are her main interest.

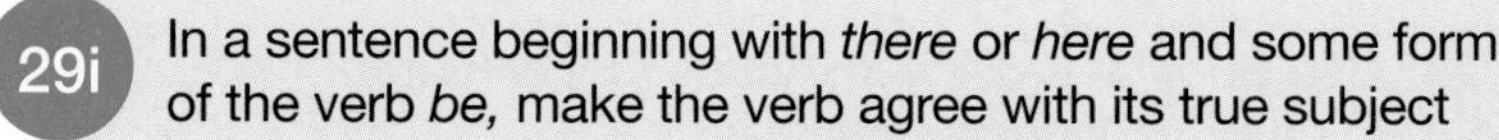

29i In a sentence beginning with *there* or *here* and some form of the verb *be,* make the verb agree with its true subject

The true (grammatical) subject of such a sentence is usually the noun that immediately follows the *be* verb form.

- There are some people at the door.
- Here is the address you were looking for.

ESL NOTE Many languages besides English have similar constructions (for example, *hay* in Spanish, *il y a* in French, *es gibt* in German), but number agreement between the verb and the noun following the verb generally is not required.

EXERCISE 29.1 In each of the following sentences, circle the correct verb form and underline the simple subject. The first one has been done for you.

1. The clocks in this building [run, runs] slow.
2. Basketball and football [is, are] Lucy's favorite sports.
3. Either my brother or my cousins [is, are] coming to babysit the children.
4. Neither my sisters nor Todd [is, are] interested in going to college.
5. Each of the Spanish club members [is, are] going to bring an authentic Hispanic dish to share.
6. All of the Norwegians studying in the United States [celebrates, celebrate] Norwegian Independence Day on May 17.
7. All of her love [was, were] manifest in the poem she wrote him.
8. The faculty of the English department [decides, decide] how many fellowships are granted each year.
9. Many Americans believe that White House politics [is, are] corrupt.
10. There [is, are] several different dresses you can try on that are in your size.

30 Adjectives and Adverbs

FAQs

- What is the difference between an adjective and an adverb? (30a, 30c)
- Should I say "I feel bad" or "I feel badly"? (30d)
- What is wrong with saying "most unique"? (30e)

Informal writing and texting among friends typically does not use a lot of adjectives and adverbs. But formal, academic writing often uses many of them. Adjectives and adverbs, used correctly, allow writers to add details to their work, making it more precise and colorful.

30a Use adjectives to modify nouns

See 26a-3

An **adjective** is a word that modifies a noun. Typically, adjectives answer one of the following questions: which? what kind? how many? Sometimes an adjective is placed next to the noun it modifies, either directly before the noun (an *ancient* building, the *first* page) or directly after (a dream *forsaken,* his curiosity *satisfied*). Other times an adjective is separated from the noun it modifies, as in the sentence "The movie was *exciting.*" In these cases, a linking verb (such as *is, was,* or *seemed*) connects the noun and its modifier.

Some adjectives have "pure" forms; others are derived from nouns or verbs by adding a suffix. Examples of pure adjectives include *small, hot, blue, quick, correct, ambiguous, ornery,* and *sharp.* Examples of derived adjectives are *harmful, interesting, desirable, biological, worthwhile, foolproof,* and *sweaty.*

Base form	*Suffix*	*Adjective*
harm	-ful	harmful
interest	-ing	interesting
desire	-able	desirable
biology	-ical	biological
worth	-while	worthwhile
fool	-proof	foolproof
sweat	-y	sweaty

Many adjectives have the same form as the present and past participles of verbs (a *roaring* lion, a *deserted* island). There also are many pronoun-like adjectives: **possessive adjectives** (*her* guitar), **demonstrative adjectives** (*that* tree), **interrogative adjectives** (*Which* way do I go?), and **indefinite adjectives** (*some* ideas).

30b Avoid overuse of nouns as modifiers

Adjective basics

A noun can modify another noun and thus function as an adjective. Some examples are *park* bench, *soda* pop, *letter* opener, *telephone* book, *fender* bender, *tape* player, and *movie* theater. Indeed, this **noun compounding** is so common in English that some noun-noun combinations eventually become single words (*windshield, placekicker, flowerpot, dishrag, sideshow, screwdriver*). And it is not uncommon to find three nouns in a row, with the first two serving as adjectival modifiers of the third (*soda pop dispenser, brass letter opener, tape player cabinet, movie theater lobby*). In principle, a limitless number of nouns can be stacked up as adjectives before another noun. (Here is an example from a cookbook: *rose-hip jam dessert ideas.* Can you figure out what it means?)

Noun compounding can help you save a few words—*windshield* is more concise than *shield against the wind*—but it can be confusing for readers, especially if you use more than three nouns in a row. To avoid long noun strings such as *the picnic table cross brace,* use a prepositional phrase: *the cross brace under the picnic table.* Such phrasing may take a few more words, but the meaning will be clearer.

TechALERT!

Grammar Checkers: Noun Strings

Grammar checkers typically flag any string of four or more nouns. But they often have trouble distinguishing nouns from other parts of speech. For example, our grammar checker flagged *picnic table leg brace* but missed *picnic table cross brace;* apparently, it thought *cross* was a verb!

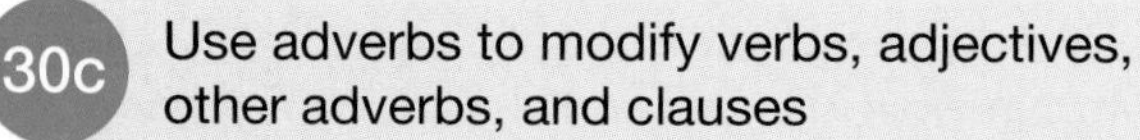

30c Use adverbs to modify verbs, adjectives, other adverbs, and clauses

See 26a-5

An **adverb** is a word that modifies a verb, an adjective, another adverb, or a clause. Adverbs modify verbs by answering one of the following questions: when? how? how often? where?

- Bob *quickly* raised his hand.
- Linda *often* goes to the gym to work out.

In the following examples, the adverb modifies a clause, an adjective, or another adverb.

- *Luckily,* I was able to find a backup disk. [Modifies the entire clause]
- They made a *very* bad mistake. [Modifies the adjective *bad*]
- The car was turned *almost* upside down. [Modifies the adverb *upside down*]

ESL NOTE Do not put an adverb between a verb and its object. Nonnative speakers sometimes make the mistake of positioning an adverb between the verb and its object or objects.

FAULTY Javier writes *often* letters to his family.

REVISED Javier *often* writes letters to his family.

Adverb basics

30d Don't confuse *good* and *well* or *bad* and *badly*

The pairs of words *good/well* and *bad/badly* are misused by many writers who fail to recognize that *good* and *bad* are usually adjectives, while *well* and

TechALERT!

Electronic Language: Amplifying Adverbs

If you do much instant-messaging or informal emailing, you may use lots of amplifying adverbs such as *very, totally,* and *absolutely.* You may also tend to separate your adjectives from the nouns they modify: *We took a route home that was totally foolproof* instead of *We took a foolproof route home.* Be aware that such stylistic habits should be avoided in academic writing.

badly are adverbs. The sentence "Shaq runs *good* for a man his size" is ungrammatical. The correct version is

► Shaq runs *well* for a man his size. [The adverb *well* modifies the verb *runs.*]

The adjective *good* is appropriate when the word being modified is a noun.

► He has a *good,* long stride. [The adjective *good* modifies the noun *stride.*]

When the main verb expresses a feeling or a perception (such verbs include *look, appear, feel, seem, taste,* and *smell*), the correct modifier is an adjective complement such as *bad, good,* or *wonderful.*

► I feel *bad* about what I did. [Not *badly; bad* modifies *I*]

► This gazpacho tastes *good.* [Not *well; good* modifies *gazpacho*]

► You look *wonderful.* [Not *wonderfully; wonderful* modifies *You*]

NOTE Though normally an adverb, well is an adjective when used in the sense of "not sick."

► She's not feeling ~~good~~ *well* today.

Though normally an adjective, *good* can be used as a noun to mean "something good."

► He says he wants to do *good.*

EXERCISE 30.1 Circle the correct adjective or adverb in each sentence.

1. Although David played [good, well] for the audition, he did not get the job.
2. Many students study long hours, sleep [bad, badly], and have trouble concentrating in class.
3. Mariko looked [good, well] in her new school uniform.

4. The senator felt [bad, badly] about his involvement in the scandal.
5. It seems like a [good, well] idea to refrigerate the leftovers.
6. Whenever I do too much heavy lifting, I ache [bad, badly] the next day.
7. After the sultry heat of the afternoon sun, it feels [good, well] to sleep in the shade.
8. After Tom eats garlic, his breath smells [bad, badly].
9. The athlete swam [good, well] in spite of her injured knee.
10. Teresa got off to a [bad, badly] start in the fourth race.

Differences between adjectives and adverbs

30e Use comparative and superlative forms of adjectives and adverbs correctly

Most adjectives and many adverbs can be used to make comparisons.

- Ted works *hard.* He is *determined* to get ahead.
- Ted works *harder* than I do. He is *more determined* than I am. [Comparative forms]
- Ted works the *hardest* of anybody I know. He is the *most determined* person I have ever met. [Superlative forms]

Adjectives of one or two syllables usually add *-er* and *-est* in their comparative and superlative forms. For adjectives with more than two syllables, the comparative and superlative forms typically consist of the positive base form with *more* and *most.*

Positive	*Comparative*	*Superlative*
smart	smarter	smartest
tasty	tastier	tastiest
beautiful	more beautiful	most beautiful
interesting	more interesting	most interesting

A few common adjectives have irregular comparative and superlative forms:

good	better	best
bad	worse	worst
far	farther/further	farthest/furthest

Many adverbs have regular comparative and superlative forms, including the following:

Positive	*Comparative*	*Superlative*
early	earlier	earliest
fast	faster	fastest
hard	harder	hardest
late	later	latest
long	longer	longest
near	nearer	nearest
quickly	more quickly	most quickly
carefully	more carefully	most carefully
elegantly	more elegantly	most elegantly

Several other adverbs have irregular forms:

badly	worse	worst
far	farther/further	farthest/furthest
little	less	least
much	more	most
well	better	best

❶ Avoid redundancy of comparative or superlative forms

Using both *more* (or *less*) and a comparative form of an adjective or adverb (with the *-er* ending) is incorrect:

▶ Ted works ~~more~~ harder than I do.

Likewise, using both *most* (or *least*) and a superlative form of an adjective or adverb (with the *-est* ending) is incorrect:

▶ Ted is the ~~most~~ hardest working person I know.

❷ When making comparisons, be accurate, complete, and logical

When comparing two items, use the comparative form. When comparing three or more items, use the superlative form.

▶ Of the two candidates, I like Johnson *better.*

▶ Of the three candidates, I like Johnson *best.*

Adjectives and Adverbs

Confusing *good* (adj) and *well* (adv)

- Thanks to her new study habits, Sharon is doing ~~good~~ well in her courses.
- She also has a *good* tutor.

Confusing *bad* (adj) and *badly* (adv)

- The fish tasted ~~badly~~ bad.
- It had been seasoned *badly*.

Confusing *less* and *fewer*

- There were ~~less~~ fewer people at the meeting than I expected.
- We had *less* disagreement among the members.

3 Use *fewer* and *less* correctly

Use *few, fewer,* or *fewest* with count nouns (such as *books, calories, flowers,* and *dollars*). Use *little, less,* or *least* with noncount nouns (such as *water, understanding,* and *progress*).

- The team has *fewer* fans that it used to have.
- The new package contains *less* rice.

More on adverbs

4 Make sure the terms of a comparison are complete

Do not write a sentence such as "This headache remedy works better." Many readers will wonder, "Better than what?" Including a *than* phrase as part of the comparison makes it clear:

- This headache remedy works better *than any other.*

Occasionally, the context allows you to omit the *than* phrase. For example, if you have been discussing the movies *Star Wars* and *The Empire Strikes Back,* you could say, "I think *Star Wars* is better."

Grammar Checkers: Comparative/Superlative Forms

Your grammar checker will probably flag redundant comparative and superlative forms such as *more better* and *most hardest,* as well as illogical colloquialisms such as *most unique.* It should also catch misuses of *fewer, fewest, less,* and *least.* However, it will probably not detect a more subtle error such as *Of the two candidates, I like Johnson best.*

5 Do not qualify inherently absolute terms

Certain adjectives, by definition, express an absolute condition or quality and thus logically cannot have different degrees. Words such as *unique, dead, pregnant, final,* and *incomparable* belong in this category. It makes no sense to say that something or someone is *more unique* or *less dead.*

▶ Kobe Bryant is the most ~~unique~~ talented basketball player in the world.

EXERCISE 30.2 Correct the errors of comparative or superlative form in the following sentences.

1. Chris is the most smartest friend I have.
2. I went to the grocery checkout line marked "Twelve Items or Less."
3. The morning paper will give us a more newer update on the situation in the Middle East.
4. The most far that AAA recommends driving in a single day is 200 miles.
5. My grandmother's chocolate cheesecake is my most favorite dessert.
6. The store manager told the cashiers that they had to dress less casual for work.
7. A 1990 study by the Federal Reserve Board showed that African Americans and Latinos were 60 percent more likelier than European Americans to be rejected for home mortgages.
8. There are experts who believe that in some more early societies women and men may have been social equals.

9. These societies had lesser gender discrimination than does the contemporary world.
10. Forced to choose among several appealing options on the menu, I opted for the one that intrigued me more.

FOR COLLABORATION Discuss the results of the exercise above in your group. Share with your group which kinds of errors are most difficult for you to identify.

part 7 Correct Sentences

31 Sentence Fragments

FAQs

- What is a "sentence fragment"?
- How can I identify fragments in my writing? (31a)
- How can I fix a fragment? (31b, 31c)

A **fragment** is a grammatically incomplete sentence. Here are some examples:

The one in the corner.

Runs like the wind.

Because we had no choice.

Whichever film you prefer.

See 26c-3

In informal writing and ordinary conversation, people say things like the above. But these are not complete sentences, and formal English requires complete sentences. Complete sentences (1) have a grammatical subject, (2) have a complete predicate, and (3) do not begin with a subordinating conjunction or relative pronoun unless they are connected to a main clause. In the four examples of fragments, the first has no predicate, the second has no subject, the third begins with an unattached subordinating conjunction (*Because*), and the fourth begins with an unattached relative pronoun (*Whichever*).

31a Make sentences grammatically complete

1 Does the sentence have a subject?

See 26b

In standard English, all sentences (except commands) must have a grammatical subject.

Grammar Checkers: Sentence Fragments

Your grammar checker should identify most of the sentence fragments in your writing. But it will not be able to tell you how to fix them. When we ran a grammar check on this chapter, our word processor flagged only three of the fragments listed at the beginning. For the first two, it said only "This does not seem to be a complete sentence"; for the third, it said, "This sentence does not seem to contain a main clause." So, even with a good grammar checker, you will need to solve these problems on your own.

Sometimes, a fragment can be corrected by simply inserting an appropriate subject and making other related changes:

▸ Most of today's sitcoms are not about families in suburbia. ~~*But*~~ Rather, they are ~~*rather*~~ *about young adults in the big city.*

Sometimes, simply changing the punctuation and making the fragment part of the previous sentence will correct the error:

▸ Most of today's sitcoms are not about families in suburbia, but ~~*But*~~ *rather about young adults in the big city.*

By removing the period after *suburbia*, you allow *most of today's sitcoms* to serve as the subject for the rest of the sentence, thereby eliminating the fragment.

❷ Does the sentence have a complete predicate?

In standard formal English, all sentences must have a complete predicate—that is, a main verb plus any necessary helping verbs and complements. The main verb must be a *finite* (full) verb, not an infinitive (*to* form) or a participle (*-ing* form).

The second part of the following example has been incorrectly set off as a separate sentence; it does not have a finite verb and so cannot be a full sentence:

Seven is a very symbolic number in Judeo-Christian culture. *Appearing often in the Bible and other sacred texts.*

TechALERT!

Grammar Checkers: Sentences Beginning with *And* or *But*

Your grammar checker will probably flag any sentence beginning with *and*, *but*, or another coordinating conjunction and suggest that you replace the word with a conjunctive adverb such as *in addition* or *however*. There is no ironclad rule, however. If what follows the *and* or *but* is a grammatically complete sentence, and if you want to set it off for emphasis, using *and* or *but* at the beginning is acceptable, even to most expert writers.

Simply replacing the period with a comma will correct the problem:

- Seven is a very symbolic number in Judeo-Christian culture, *appearing often in the Bible and other sacred texts.*

❸ Are the subordinating phrases or clauses connected to a main clause?

Check to be sure that word clusters beginning with a subordinating conjunction (such as *because, although,* or *if*) or a relative pronoun (such as *which, who,* or *that*) are connected or subordinated to a main subject and predicate.

GO See 31b

FRAGMENT	We did what the landlord asked us to. *Because we had no choice.*
REVISED	We did what the landlord asked us to, *because we had no choice.*

Some Common Subordinating Conjunctions

after	before	though	whenever
although	even if	unless	wherever
as	if	until	whether
because	since	when	while

31b Connect dependent clauses

Dependent clauses have a subject and a predicate but are linked to a main clause with a subordinating conjunction (such as *because, although,* or *if*) or a relative pronoun (such as *which, who,* or *that*). Because dependent clauses depend on their connection to a main clause for their meaning, they cannot stand alone. Therefore, if you begin a clause with a subordinating conjunction or relative pronoun and then end it with a period or semicolon before connecting it to a main clause, you have produced a fragment, not a sentence. In the following case, changing the period to a comma allows the *Before* clause to serve as a dependent clause:

FRAGMENT *Before you delve into critically analyzing the characters.* You should first discuss the opening sequence.

REVISED *Before you delve into critically analyzing the characters,* you should first discuss the opening sequence.

Below, the solution is simply to eliminate the period, joining the two fragments:

▶ What seems annoying to me~~. May~~ *may* not bother you at all.

31c Connect phrases

See 26c-2

Phrases are similar to clauses except that they lack full verbs. Phrases can be used as modifiers, subjects, objects, or complements—but never as sentences. Make sure that all of your phrases are connected to main clauses.

Sentence fragments, with exercises

FRAGMENT *To prevent powerful foreign corporations from gaining too much influence.* Some African governments insisted on owning 51 percent of key national industries.

REVISED *To prevent powerful foreign corporations from gaining too much influence,* some African governments insisted on owning 51 percent of key national industries. [Putting a comma after *influence* connects the modifying phrase (*To . . . influence*) to the main clause.]

FRAGMENT Many nations began to process their own food, minerals, and other raw materials. *Using foreign aid and investments to back their efforts.*

REVISED Many nations began to process their own food, minerals, and other raw materials, *using foreign aid and investments to back their efforts.*

Checklist

Fixing Fragments

✓ Can I connect the fragment to an independent clause by changing the punctuation?

FRAGMENT Some African nations emphasized the growing of export crops. *Which provided badly needed capital for development.*

REVISED Some African nations emphasized the growing of export crops, *which provided badly needed capital for development.* [Inserting a comma after *crops* connects the relative clause (*which . . . development*) to the main clause.]

FRAGMENT Agricultural development was hampered by natural disasters. *Such as locust plagues and cattle diseases.*

REVISED Agricultural development was hampered by natural disasters *such as locust plagues and cattle diseases.* [The phrase beginning with *such* has been attached to the main clause.]

✓ Can I turn the fragment into a separate sentence?

FRAGMENT Some of the problems facing African nations can be traced to colonialism. *Some European nations doing little to prepare their colonies for independence.*

REVISED Some of the problems facing African nations can be traced to colonialism. *Some European nations did little to prepare their colonies for independence.* [Changing the participle in the fragment into a full verb turns the fragment into an independent sentence.]

EXERCISE 31.1 Correct the fragments in the following sentences.

1. John Lennon was killed in 1980. By a deranged young man.
2. Were it not for the dynamics of racism in US society. Chuck Berry probably would have been crowned king of rock and roll.
3. It was the phenomenal success of "Rapper's Delight." That first alerted the mainstream media to the existence of hip hop.
4. Barry Bonds hit seventy-three home runs in one year. Setting a new record.
5. Mauritania is an Islamic country. Which is located in northwest Africa.
6. Lamarck thought that acquired traits could be passed on to one's offspring. His ideas being challenged much later by Charles Darwin.
7. Having thought about our situation. I have decided I should take a second job.
8. This is a good economic arrangement. For working and taking care of the children.
9. Two years after his disastrous invasion of Russia in 1812. Napoleon was exiled to the island of Elba.
10. He regained power the following year. But was defeated at Waterloo.

31d Use sentence fragments only for special effect

More on fragments, with exercises

Occasionally sentence fragments can be used for special effect, to add emphasis or to make writing sound conversational. Here is an example from the writing of Molly Ivins:

> Shrub's proposal to cut property taxes, on which our public schools depend, by $1 billion merely shifts the tax burden even more dramatically to the folks with the least money. *Nice work, Shrub.*
>
> —Molly Ivins, "Truly Happy News"

In this editorial column, Ivins is criticizing a state politician. After giving her interpretation of the politician's proposal in the first sentence, she uses a common conversational expression in the form of a fragment—"Nice work"—to make a sarcastic comment.

Be cautious about using fragments in any kind of formal writing you do. Since they are rarely found in such writing, readers might see them only as grammatical mistakes, not as "special effects."

EXERCISE 31.2 Fragments are commonly seen in advertisements. Find a magazine ad or Internet ad containing at least three sentence fragments.

1. Underline all the fragments in the ad.
2. Rewrite the ad, turning the fragments into complete sentences.

FOR COLLABORATION In your group, explain why you think the writers of the ad chose to include the fragments.

32 Comma Splices and Run-on Sentences

FAQs

- What is a "comma splice"?
- How do I know when I have written a run-on sentence?
- How do I correct a comma splice or a run-on sentence? (32a–32d)

Joining two independent clauses with a comma creates a **comma splice:**

> The best keyboard for one-handed users is the Dvorak keyboard, it has a more convenient layout than the standard Qwerty keyboard.

Or this, from an instant-messaging conversation:

> i don't think you would want what i am going through right now, i would actually like to go back to school

Comma splices like these are commonplace and perfectly acceptable in casual English, where speed matters more than formal correctness or the careful editing it requires. In formal American English, however, comma splices are considered to be grammatical errors (except with short, idiomatic expressions such as *Sometimes you win, sometimes you lose*).

Comma splices, with exercises

ESL NOTE The comma splice is unique to American English. In British English, Australian English, and other Englishes around the world, comma splices are fully acceptable.

Putting two independent clauses together without a conjunction or any punctuation creates a **run-on sentence** (or *fused sentence*):

> Dvorak keyboards put the most frequently typed characters within easy reach they are often used in speed-typing competitions.

TechALERT!

Grammar Checkers: Comma Splices

Grammar checkers do not reliably identify comma splices and run-on sentences. When we ran a grammar check on the ten flawed sentences in Exercise 32.1, it spotted and corrected only two errors (both comma splices).

Run-on sentences are incorrect in standard English and are often confusing to readers. There are four main ways to correct comma splices and run-on sentences:

- Turn one clause into a subordinate clause.
- Add a comma and a coordinating conjunction.
- Separate the clauses with a semicolon.
- Separate the clauses with a period.

32a Turn one clause into a subordinate clause

Often the best way to correct a comma splice or run-on sentence is to convert one of the two clauses into a subordinate clause. This can be done by using either a subordinating conjunction (such as *while, although, because,* or *if*) or a relative pronoun (such as *which, that,* or *who*).

▶ The best keyboard for one-handed users is the Dvorak keyboard, ~~it~~ *which* has a more convenient layout than the standard Qwerty keyboard.

▶ *Because* Dvorak keyboards put the most frequently typed characters within easy reach, they are often used in speed-typing competitions.

Sometimes this technique may require switching the two clauses around:

▶ *Because* it has a more convenient layout than the standard Qwerty keyboard, the best keyboard for one-handed users is the Dvorak keyboard.

32b Separate clauses with a comma and a coordinating conjunction

If the two parts of a comma splice or run-on sentence are of equal importance, you can put a comma and a coordinating conjunction (such as *and, or, but, nor,* or *yet*) between them:

- An eagle once flew past our house [, but] I got only a brief glimpse of it.
- My uncle introduced me to stamps when I was ten years old [, and] I've been a stamp collector ever since.

Simply inserting a comma in a run-on sentence is not enough, for that produces another error (a comma splice); you must also insert a conjunction.

32c Separate independent clauses with a semicolon

If the two parts of a comma splice or run-on sentence are of equal importance, you can insert a semicolon between them:

- Desktop computers usually have bigger screens than laptops do [;] laptops are easier to carry around.

If you use a conjunctive adverb such as *however, therefore,* or *for example,* place the semicolon before it:

- Laptops are coming down in price [;] *therefore,* more people are buying them.

32d Separate independent clauses with a period

Checklist of common errors

Often the easiest way to correct a comma splice or run-on sentence is by inserting a period between the two independent clauses:

- Amelia Earhart was a famous aviator~~, in~~ [. In] 1932 she became the first woman to fly across the Atlantic alone.

► The railroads grew out of commercial rivalry among Eastern cities, Baltimore led the way.

Although adding a period is the easiest way to correct these errors, it is not usually the best way. Inserting a period between the two clauses turns them into two separate sentences, thereby making it more difficult for the reader to see the relationship between them. As a general rule, try to use one of the other three methods before settling on this one.

EXERCISE 32.1 Correct the following comma splices and run-on sentences.

1. Ritchie Valens was the first Chicano rock-and-roll star, he recorded a string of hits before his fatal plane crash in February 1959.
2. In order to access the Internet via modem you must install the Dial-Up Networking option click here to start.
3. I started reading Russian literature when I was young, though I did not know that it was Russian, in fact I was not even aware that I lived in a country with any distinct existence of its own.
4. We always ate dinner at eight o'clock we spent the whole day anticipating the time we could talk and eat together as a family.
5. Mine is a Spanish-speaking household we use Spanish exclusively.
6. The side pockets of her jacket were always bulging they were filled with rocks, candy, chewing gum, and other trinkets only a child could appreciate.
7. Some people seem to be able to eat everything they want they do not gain weight.
8. The VCR was not a popular piece of equipment with movie moguls, the studios quickly adapted.
9. Some magazines survive without advertising, they are supported by readers who pay for subscriptions.
10. A multimillion-dollar diet industry has developed, they sell liquid diets, freeze-dried foods, artificial sweeteners, and diet books by the hundreds.

33 Pronoun Reference and Agreement

FAQs

- Can my computer help me spot pronoun problems? (33a-3)
- Is there anything wrong with beginning a sentence with *this*? (33b)
- When should I use *that* and when should I use *which*? (33d)
- Should I say "The jury took *its* time" or "The jury took *their* time"? (33e)

Using pronouns in place of nouns often makes writing more concise and readable. Social writing (such as texting, instant-messaging, or emailing a friend) is very interactive and personal, so it makes heavy use of first- and second-person pronouns: *I, me, you* (or *u*), *we, us.* Academic writing, on the other hand, is about other people and other things, and so it makes far more use of third-person pronouns (*he, she, it, they*). If these latter pronouns are not used carefully, they can cause the reader considerable confusion.

33a Refer to a specific noun antecedent

Pronouns (such as *she, it,* and *that*) work best when they refer back to a particular noun, called the **antecedent.**

- The conductor announced to the orchestra members that *she* was resigning.
- Only one of the new hockey players knew what *his* position would be.

1 Avoiding use of generalized *they* or *you*

In casual speech, people often use pronouns in vague ways, without explicit antecedents ("*They* say that television is dulling our brains"). In formal writing, however, such vagueness can sabotage meaning and must be avoided.

VAGUE *THEY* REVISED

Some people
~~They~~ say that television is dulling our brains.

Similarly, avoid using the pronoun *you* unless you are addressing the reader directly.

VAGUE *YOU* REVISED

One never knows
~~You never know~~ when calamity will strike.

2 Avoiding use of implied antecedents

Pronouns should refer back to specific antecedents, not implied ones.

IMPLIED REFERENCE REVISED

the notes
Notetaking is very helpful in doing research, especially if ~~they~~ are well organized.

3 Clarifying references with more than one possible antecedent

Writers sometimes get into trouble by using a pronoun that could refer to more than one noun.

VAGUE REFERENCE

Hannibal's troops used elephants to carry equipment across the Alps, but many of *them* died in the harsh winter weather.

In this sentence, the pronoun *them* could refer to either Hannibal's troops or their elephants, since both are plural. In such cases, you should either replace the pronoun with its specific antecedent or reword the sentence to eliminate the vagueness.

Identifying Pronoun Reference Problems

1. Open the SEARCH feature of your word-processing program.
2. Enter *it* in the SEARCH field.
3. Run the search.
4. Whenever the program highlights an *it,* use the guidelines in this chapter to determine whether you have used the word correctly.
5. Do a similar search for *this, that,* and *which.*

VAGUE REFERENCE REVISED

Hannibal's troops used elephants to carry equipment across the Alps, but many of ~~them~~ the elephants died in the harsh winter weather. [Specifies the antecedent]

OR

Hannibal's ~~troops~~ army used elephants to carry equipment across the Alps, but many of them died in the harsh winter weather. [Replaces one of the plural antecedents with a singular one, eliminating the vagueness]

33b Avoid vague use of *this, that, which,* and *it*

The pronouns *this, that, which,* and *it* may be used with care to refer broadly to an entire statement:

▶ According to the linguistic school currently on top, human beings are all born with a genetic endowment for recognizing and formulating language. *This* must mean that we possess genes for all kinds of information, with strands of special, peculiarly human DNA for the discernment of meaning in syntax.

—Lewis Thomas, *Lives of a Cell*

CommonErrors

Pronoun Reference

Using *they* or *you* in making a general statement (33a)

VAGUE *They* say that Kennedy was shot by more than one person. [Who does *they* refer to?]

CLEAR *Some people* believe that Kennedy was shot by more than one person.

Using *which, this, it,* or *that* to refer vaguely to some referent (33b)

VAGUE Many observers have commented on the increased use of entertainment as a substitute for dealing directly with our problems—*which* is not a constructive form of action. [What does *which* refer to?]

CLEAR Many observers have commented on the increased use of entertainment as a substitute for dealing directly with our problems. *This refusal to face reality* is not a constructive form of action.

Using *his, he, him, she,* or *her* to refer to both males and females (33f)

SEXIST A good *teacher* always treats *her* students with respect. [Are all teachers female?]

FAIR AND ACCURATE Good *teachers* always treat *their* students with respect.

In this excerpt, the word *this* leading off the second sentence refers clearly to the main clause of the first sentence ("human beings . . . language").

This and *that* are frequently used in instant messaging and similar kinds of informal writing because the subject matter is simple and writer and reader are closely attuned to each other. In academic writing, however, the subject matter is more complex and the reader may have little knowledge of the writer. In such cases, using pronouns like *this* and *that* (or *it*) for broad reference may confuse the reader. What does *it* refer to in the following paragraph?

Watching *Monday Night Football* has become a ritual for countless American sports lovers. *It* is symbolic of contemporary American life.

It could refer to (1) *Monday Night Football*, (2) watching *Monday Night Football*, or (3) watching *Monday Night Football* has become a ritual for countless American sports lovers. One way to resolve this ambiguity is to replace the pronoun with a full noun phrase:

VAGUE REFERENCE REVISED

Watching *Monday Night Football* has become a ritual for countless American sports lovers. ~~*It*~~ *Monday Night Football* is symbolic of contemporary American life.

33c Avoid mixed uses of *it*

See 33b

The word *it* can function either as a pronoun or as an expletive. Do not use the word both ways in the same sentence:

▸ ~~In the manual *it*~~ The manual says that *it* is important to turn off all other applications before installing a new program.

33d Be consistent with use of *that, which,* and *who*

Pronoun references

The relative pronoun *that* is used only with essential (restrictive) relative clauses—clauses that are necessary to identify the nouns they modify:

ESSENTIAL CLAUSE

First prize went to the long-haired collie *that came all the way from Hartford.* [There were other long-haired collies in the competition.]

Although many people prefer using the relative pronoun *which* only with nonessential relative clauses—clauses that merely add extra information—*which* can also be used with essential relative clauses.

See 47e, 47j

NONESSENTIAL CLAUSE

First prize went to the long-haired collie, *which came all the way from Hartford.* [It was the only long-haired collie in the competition.]

ESSENTIAL CLAUSE

First prize went to the long-haired collie *which came all the way from Hartford.* [There were other long-haired collies in the competition.]

It is conventional to use the personal relative pronouns *who, whose,* and *whom,* rather than *which* or *that,* when referring to people.

PERSONAL REFERENCE REVISED

This is the ambulance driver ~~which~~ *who* rescued me.

NOTE In references to objects and nonspecific or unnamed animals, it is conventional to use *that, which,* and *whose,* not *who.*

EXERCISE 33.1 Correct the pronoun errors in the following sentences.

1. *Sesame Street* is a valuable children's program. Not only is one able to learn from a show like this, one also is able to fall in love with your favorite character who has the ability to become your friend and teacher.
2. Then there is the Disney book club, that provides short-story versions of the animated films.
3. The most popular sitcoms today are set in big cities and do not have anything to do with family, which is a change from the sitcoms of old.
4. We do not tear your clothing with machinery. We do it carefully by hand.
5. Every student must bring their books to class tomorrow and be prepared to discuss Chapter 6. It is important for you to do this.

TechALERT!

Grammar Checkers: *That* and *Which*

Your grammar checker may suggest that you use *that* with essential clauses, but this usage is not required. Many expert writers use either *that* or *which* in essential clauses, depending on how formal they want their writing to sound. (*Which* is slightly more formal than *that.*)

6. Only one of the members of the House of Representatives decided that they would vote against the proposed bill.
7. They say that drinking and driving kills more people each year than cancer. They should not drink and drive.
8. Filling out college applications and worrying about SAT scores are annual rituals for many high school seniors. It is a part of the admissions process.
9. In the annual report it says it has been a disappointing year for the company.
10. The dog which chases my cat lives in the house across the street.

33e Make pronouns and antecedents agree in number and gender

Singular pronouns should have singular antecedents; plural pronouns should have plural antecedents.

Antecedent — Pronoun

▶ *Bad luck* can happen to anyone, and *it* can happen at any time.

In this sentence, *bad luck* and *it* are both singular; therefore, they agree in **number.** They also agree in **gender** because *bad luck* is neuter (neither masculine nor feminine) and *it* can serve as a pronoun for neuter antecedents.

Be especially careful about agreement when the pronoun is far away from its antecedent:

▶ *Each* of the graduating football players was asked to say a few words about what ~~*they*~~ *he* thought was the highlight of the season.

Following are some rules on pronoun-antecedent agreement.

1 A compound antecedent usually is plural and thus requires a plural pronoun

A **compound antecedent** is a noun phrase containing two or more terms joined by *and.*

▶ *Mr. and Mrs. Kwan* are here for *their* appointment.

Some compound antecedents, such as company names, are used in a singular sense and thus require a singular pronoun.

- *Brown and Root*, a major construction firm, had *its* headquarters in Texas.

Pronoun agreement, with exercises

❷ With disjunctive antecedents, the pronoun should agree in number with the nearest part

A **disjunctive antecedent** is a noun phrase consisting of two or more terms joined by *or* or *nor*. When a disjunctive antecedent contains both a singular and a plural part, making the pronoun agree with the nearest part works well if the singular noun precedes the plural one.

- Either Tamara Wilson or *the Changs* will bring *their* barbeque set to the next picnic.
- Neither the President nor *the Democrats* will give *their* support to this bill.

If the plural noun precedes the singular one, however, following the rule usually leads to an awkward-sounding sentence:

Neither the Democrats nor *the President* will give *his* support to this bill.

In such cases, it is better to either put the singular noun before the plural one and use the plural pronoun *their* (as above) or reword the sentence to eliminate the pronoun:

- Neither the Democrats nor the President will support this bill.

❸ A collective noun can be either singular or plural, depending on its sense

Both of these sentences are correct:

- *The jury* took only two hours to reach *its* verdict.
- *The jury* took only two hours to reach *their* verdict.

The first sentence emphasizes the singularity of the jury as a body, while the second puts more emphasis on the jury as a group of individuals.

4 Pronouns must agree with antecedents that are indefinite pronouns

Most indefinite pronouns (such as *everything, anything,* and *each*) are singular. When such a pronoun serves as the antecedent for another pronoun, that pronoun should also be singular.

- *Everything* was in *its* place.
- *Each* of the women had *her* reasons for opposing the plan.

Some indefinite pronouns (*some, all, more*) can have either a singular or a plural sense. When one of these indefinite pronouns is used as the antecedent for another pronoun, the other pronoun can be either singular or plural, depending on the sense of the sentence.

- *Some* of the *news* was as bad as we thought *it* would be.
- *Some* of the team's *players* have lost *their* motivation.

Still other indefinite pronouns (*everyone, everybody, nobody*) have a plural, collective sense, which is often reflected in plural pronouns referring back to them.

- *Everyone* hoped *they* would get a raise.
- *Everybody* applauded me, and I was glad *they* did.

Note, however, that such pronouns are treated as grammatically singular when it comes to subject-verb agreement.

- *Everyone hopes* they will get a raise.
- *Nobody wants* other people to think badly of them.

33f Avoid sexist use of pronouns

Agreement issues

In the past, a sentence such as the following would have been acceptable:

A doctor should listen carefully to his patients.

Today that is no longer the case. Because doctors can be male or female, using only the male pronoun (*his*) to refer to all doctors is inaccurate and sexist.

The three most effective techniques for avoiding sexist pronoun usage are (1) making the pronoun and its antecedent plural, (2) rewording the sentence, and (3) using an occasional disjunctive pronoun such as *he or she.*

- *Doctors* should listen carefully to *their* patients. [Plural]
- An important part of medical practice is listening carefully to patients. [Rewording]
- *A doctor* should listen carefully to *his or her* patients. [Disjunctive pronoun]

See 42c

These three revisions of the unacceptable sentence have subtle differences in tone and meaning. One version might work best in a certain context; another might be best in a different context. Good writers do not rely exclusively on any single technique for avoiding sexism but instead use whichever they deem most appropriate in the given situation.

In conversation, many people use the third-person plural pronoun (*they*) to refer back to a singular antecedent, as in this sentence:

If *a doctor* is conscientious, *they* will listen carefully to *their* patients.

In formal writing, such usage is incorrect. You can correct the error by making all the referents plural, as shown below:

- If *doctors* are conscientious, *they* will listen carefully to *their* patients.

EXERCISE 33.2 Select the correct pronoun in each of the following sentences, and draw an arrow to its antecedent.

1. Earthquakes most often occur near a fault line, and [it, they] are usually impossible to predict.
2. Tony and Michiyo are here to pick up [his, their] final research projects.
3. Some of the coaches have lost [its, their] faith in the team.
4. Drinking and driving can cause fatal automobile accidents, but [it, they] can easily be prevented.
5. Everything in the office was in [its, their] proper place.
6. The members of the committee took three hours to make [its, their] decision.
7. Choong was required to take physics during his undergraduate course of study, and he was sure that [it, they] would be a very difficult subject.
8. The NBA imposes fines on [its, their] athletes if they break the rules.
9. Neither the former owners nor the current owner could find [his, their] signature on any of the documents.
10. A lawyer should always treat [his or her, their] clients with respect.

34 Misplaced and Dangling Modifiers

FAQs

- What is a modifier?
- How can I tell when I have misused a modifier? (34b–34d)
- What is a "split infinitive"? (34d-2)
- What is a "dangling modifier"? (34e)

Modifiers are words, phrases, or clauses that qualify other words, phrases, or clauses. Used properly, modifiers can make writing richer and more precise. Informal writing, because it often deals with simple subjects, usually contains few modifiers. Academic writing, by contrast, which typically deals with complex subjects, uses many modifiers.

34a Position modifiers close to the words they modify

For maximum clarity, modifiers should be placed as close as possible to (ideally, right next to) the words they modify.

Unlike George,
- Kramer does not need the approval of anyone~~, unlike George.~~

frequently
- Businesses publish the URLs for their Web sites ~~frequently~~ in advertisements.

Take special care with modifiers such as *only, just, even, not,* and *almost,* which are often used imprecisely in ordinary speech. In formal writing,

TechALERT!

See 34d-2

Grammar Checkers: Misplaced Modifiers

With the exception of disruptive modifiers that create split infinitives, grammar checkers typically cannot identify misplaced or dangling modifiers.

they should generally be positioned directly before the word or phrase they modify.

- The yucca plant ~~only~~ grows well ^only in full sunlight.
- England ~~did not win~~ won the battle ^not because of superior firepower but because of better tactics.

Misplaced modifiers

34b Avoid ambiguity

A modifier that is not carefully positioned may lead the reader to make the wrong interpretation. Consider this newspaper headline:

> MARYLAND STUDENT EXPELLED FOR ATTACK ON TEACHER CLAIMING BIAS

It sounds as if the teacher is the one who is claiming bias, when actually it's the student. The following version, with the modifier (*claiming bias*) repositioned next to the word it modifies (*student*), makes the intended meaning clearer:

- MARYLAND STUDENT, CLAIMING BIAS, EXPELLED FOR ATTACK ON TEACHER

Adverbs such as *happily, quickly,* and *easily* are often ambiguous if they are positioned between two verb phrases.

> Most people who responded to the ad *quickly* decided not to look at the car.

In this sentence, does *quickly* modify *responded* or *decided?* The ambiguity can be resolved by repositioning the modifier:

- Most people who *quickly* responded to the ad decided not to look at the car.

OR

- Most people who responded to the ad decided *quickly* not to look at the car.

Shifting the position of certain limiting adverbs can alter the meaning or emphasis in a sentence. The following sentences differ in meaning because of the different locations of *only*:

See 34a

- *Only* Martha crammed for the exam. [Other students did not cram.]
- Martha *only* crammed for the exam. [She did not prepare in any other way.]
- Martha crammed for the exam *only*. [She did not cram for quizzes and other assignments.]

34c Try to put lengthy modifiers at the beginning or end of a sentence

When a lengthy modifier is placed in the middle of a sentence, it tends to disrupt the basic structure (subject–verb–complement) of the sentence. By moving such modifiers to the beginning or end of the sentence, you preserve the basic structure and make the sentence more readable.

MODIFIER IN THE MIDDLE OF THE SENTENCE

A television network usually, after it airs a documentary, makes the film available to groups for a nominal rental fee.

REVISED

After it airs a documentary, a television network usually makes the film available to groups for a nominal rental fee.

34d Avoid disruptive modifiers

English sentences are made up of subgroupings of words, such as the verb and its object or the word *to* and the rest of the infinitive construction. When modifiers are inserted into these subgroupings, there is a risk of interrupting and obscuring the vital connections between key words.

1 Modifiers between the verb and its object

Sentences are easiest to read when the main predicate goes from verb to object without interruption. For this reason, it is best to avoid inserting any interrupting modifiers between the verb and its object.

quickly
▸ The magician shuffled ~~quickly~~ the cards.

See 34c

Sometimes, in following this advice, you may also be heeding the guideline that recommends moving a lengthy modifier to the beginning or end of the sentence.

After reading the news report, several
▸ ~~Several~~ customers decided~~, after reading the news report~~, to boycott the store.

2 Split infinitives

A **split infinitive** occurs when the two parts of a *to* infinitive construction (*to escape*) are separated, as in "He hoped *to* easily *escape.*" Traditionalists claim that split infinitives are ungrammatical, but this belief is based on an eighteenth-century confusion between Latin and English grammar. In any case, most readers have no trouble with such sentences; indeed, *Star Trek* fans have long enjoyed the split infinitive in their motto, "Star Trekkers hope *to boldly, loyally, and optimistically go* where none have gone before."

See 40d

As a general guideline, though, it is best to avoid any long or complex "splits" in a *to* infinitive. "He hoped to easily escape" would be acceptable to most readers, but "He hoped to without detection escape" would not.

34e Avoid dangling modifiers

Using modifiers correctly

A mistake that plagues many writers is the use of the **dangling modifier,** a verbal phrase that does not have a clear referent.

Having studied until late at night, it was time to get some sleep.

Who did the studying? Without any mention of a specific agent, readers don't know. The following version is clearer:

▸ Having studied until late at night, I decided it was time to get some sleep.

Simply mentioning the missing referent somewhere in the main clause is not enough; the referent must be in the subject position so that it is next to the modifying phrase:

Running down the hall, an elderly patient collided with Nurse Summers.

Was it the elderly patient who was running down the hall? That's what this sentence says. If it was Nurse Summers who was running down the hall, the sentence should be rewritten with the modifying phrase next to *Nurse Summers.*

▸ Running down the hall, Nurse Summers collided with an elderly patient.

EXERCISE 34.1 Correct the modifier errors in the following sentences.

1. Politicians who run for office frequently need to raise a lot of money.
2. Three homes were reported vandalized by the Springdale police.
3. To get the job, his résumé had to be completely revised.
4. Please take a moment to view the photos that are on display with your family.
5. Before installing a new program, all other applications should be turned off.
6. Having missed class four times in three weeks, Professor Kateb decided that Melissa should be penalized.
7. Angelina Jolie will talk about her pet dog that was killed by an intruder in an interview with Oprah.
8. The patient was seen by a dentist with an abscessed tooth.
9. A church leader was found guilty of public lewdness in a Virginia court.
10. In 2001 he put the family home up for sale, along with his mother.

FOR COLLABORATION Find some examples of dangling modifiers on the Internet, and share them with your group.

35 Faulty Shifts

FAQs

- What does it mean to say that writing is "inconsistent"? (35a–35c)
- What is a "mixed construction," and how can I avoid it? (35d)

Readers expect writers to use a consistent tone, time frame, and point of view. Writers should try to satisfy this expectation by avoiding unnecessary shifts.

Inappropriate tense shifts

35a Avoid unnecessary shifts in person and number

Person, which indicates to whom a discourse refers, is denoted mainly by pronouns. The first-person pronouns *I, me, we,* and *us* refer to the writer or speaker. The second-person pronoun *you* refers to the reader or listener. The third-person pronouns *he, him, she, her, they,* and *them* refer to people being written or spoken about. Use care when making shifts in person.

- You should start writing a paper well before the deadline; otherwise, ~~one~~ *you* may end up doing it at the last minute, with no chance to revise it.
- We were hoping to get tickets to the Phish concert. But the line was so long ~~you~~ *we* had no chance.

See Ch. 29

Number refers to whether a noun, pronoun, or verb is singular or plural. If you use two or more words to refer to the same thing, make sure that they are consistently singular or consistently plural.

- Anyone who weaves in and out of traffic is endangering ~~their~~ *his or her* fellow drivers.

OR

- ~~Anyone~~ *People* who weave~~s~~ in and out of traffic ~~is~~ *are* endangering their fellow drivers.

35b Avoid unnecessary shifts in verb tense, mood, subject, and voice

See 28e

Verb tense indicates the time frame of an action. Readers will be confused by arbitrary shifts in time frame. Unless you are describing a situation where there is a natural or logical difference in time frames, it is best to use the same verb tense throughout.

- In 1995, the median pay for full-time female workers in the United States was $22,497, while the median pay for males was $31,496. In other words, women ~~make~~ made seventy-one cents to a man's dollar.

Accounts of literary narratives are usually written consistently in the present tense:

- Huxley's *Brave New World* depicts a nightmare utopia in which there ~~was~~ is no passion, no frustration, and no deviation from normalcy.

See 28h

There are three **moods** in English: indicative, imperative, and subjunctive. The **indicative mood** is used for facts and assertions, the **imperative mood** for commands, and the **subjunctive mood** for conditions that are contrary to fact. If you mix moods in the same sentence, you may confuse your readers:

INCONSISTENT MOOD

If China were a democracy, it will have elections at periodic intervals.

Is China a democracy? Does it have regular elections? Or is the writer just posing a hypothetical idea? The mixing of subjunctive mood (in the first clause) and indicative mood (in the second clause) makes it impossible to know. Either of the following revisions would clarify the meaning:

REVISED

- If China *becomes* a democracy, it *will have* elections at periodic intervals. [Both verbs are in the indicative, suggesting a factual assertion.]
- If China *were* a democracy, it *would have* elections at periodic intervals. [Both verbs are in the subjunctive, indicating a contrary-to-fact condition.]

TechALERT!

Grammar Checkers: Faulty Shifts

Grammar checkers are not programmed to identify faulty shifts. You will have to find them on your own.

See 26b-1

The grammatical **subject** of a sentence serves as a focal point for the reader. It usually indicates what the sentence is about or who is performing the verb's action. By repeating the same subject from one sentence to the next, the writer helps readers maintain focus on it. Conversely, by shifting from one subject to another in sentence after sentence, the writer may disorient readers.

INCONSISTENT SUBJECT

> When people try to move an accident victim, they should use proper lifting techniques. The legs should be used, not the back. The body should be bent at the knees and hips, and all twisting should be avoided.

Notice how the grammatical subjects change from one clause to another:

> people
> they
> the legs
> the body
> all twisting

A better version would retain the focus on *people* by keeping it in the subject position:

REVISED

> When *people* try to move an accident victim, *they* should use proper lifting techniques. *They* should use their legs, not their backs. *They* should bend their bodies at the knees and hips and avoid all twisting.

Maintaining a consistent subject usually helps maintain a consistent **voice** as well. Voice is a feature of the verb that indicates whether the subject of a sentence is acting or being acted upon. In the Inconsistent Subject example above, the first sentence is in active voice and the next two are in passive voice. The Revised version consistently uses the active voice throughout.

See 28g

35c Avoid shifts in tone

See 41c

Tone refers to the writer's attitude toward the subject matter or the audience. It can be formal or informal, ironic or direct, friendly or hostile, and so on. Since readers need to get a clear sense of what the writer's attitude is, a writer should strive to maintain a consistent authorial tone.

INCONSISTENT TONE

> The world of folklore and fairy tales is one that attracts adults and children alike. As adults, we look back fondly on childhood cartoons and still get a kick out of 'em.

Because most of this passage is written in a fairly formal tone, the colloquial "still get a kick out of 'em" is jarring. The following revision has a more consistent tone:

REVISED

> The world of folklore and fairy tales is one that attracts adults and children alike. As adults, we look back fondly on childhood cartoons and find them as enjoyable as ever.

EXERCISE 35.1 Correct the shifts in the following sentences.

1. One should do some type of physical activity at least three times a week for thirty minutes. Regular exercise is good for your heart and lungs.
2. We wanted to go to the U2 concert. However, the tickets sold out before I even got there, and there was no chance that you could buy them from scalpers for less than $200.
3. Someone who does not love themselves can never hope to love anyone else.
4. We hike up in the mountains every Saturday morning. We love the feeling of sheer exhilaration. We were happy to be tired.

5. Elizabeth Bishop's *A First Death in Nova Scotia* discusses death from the point of view of a child. It painted a picture of a young girl's emotional reaction to the death of her cousin.
6. If she were rich, she will buy all her clothes at Nordstrom and Lord & Taylor.
7. If you want to learn to speed-read, you have to first learn to concentrate. We need to focus on the words on the page. It is important not to let the attention wander. The eyes should always catch the center of each page.
8. If our goal is educational and economic equity and parity, then we need affirmative action to catch up. We are behind as a result of discrimination and denial of opportunity, and that is totally not fair.
9. Married couples make a deep commitment to one another and to society; in exchange, society extends certain benefits to them, which really helps them out with money and other stuff.
10. There can be no excuse for what you did. The act is shameful, and one should not be forgiven for it.

Consistency, with quiz

35d Avoid mixed constructions

Mixed constructions are those that result when a writer starts a sentence in a certain way but then changes track and finishes it differently. The two parts of the sentence end up being incompatible—and confusing to the reader.

MIXED In the world created by movies and television makes fiction seem like reality.

Where is the grammatical subject in this sentence? The writer began with a prepositional phrase but then apparently got sidetracked and failed to create a complete main clause. One way of revising this sentence would be to turn the prepositional phrase into a noun phrase, which could then serve as the grammatical subject.

REVISED The world created by movies and television makes fiction seem like reality.

Another option would be to set off the prepositional phrase with a comma and then reconstruct the rest of the sentence to form a main clause.

REVISED In the world created by movies and television, fiction seems like reality.

Subordinating adverbs such as *although, since, because,* and *if* are used only in subordinate clauses. Thus, if you start a sentence with such an adverb, you must finish the subordinate clause and then construct a main clause.

MIXED Since the campus parking situation makes you want to take the bus.

REVISED Since the campus parking situation is bad, you will want to take the bus.

Alternatively, you can omit the subordinating adverb and reconstruct the entire sentence.

REVISED The campus parking situation makes you want to take the bus.

35e Create consistency between subjects and predicates

Subjects and predicates should always harmonize, both logically and grammatically. When they do not, the result is **faulty predication.**

FAULTY Writer's block is when you cannot get started writing.

In this sentence, a noun (*writer's block*) is connected to an adverb of time (*when*). This is ungrammatical and illogical. In a sentence of the form *A is B*, the *A* and *B* terms must be of the same grammatical type.

See 26b

REVISED *Writer's block* [N] is *a condition* [N] in which you cannot get started writing.

Make sure the predicate fits logically with the subject.

FAULTY Shaw's *Pygmalion* wins out over the snobbish aristocrat, Henry Higgins.

Pygmalion is the name of a play, so it cannot "win out" over one of its characters.

REVISED In Shaw's *Pygmalion*, the lowborn Eliza Doolittle wins out over the snobbish aristocrat, Henry Higgins.

35f Avoid unmarked shifts between direct and indirect discourse

Direct discourse is language that is taken word for word from another source and thus is enclosed in quotation marks. **Indirect discourse** is language that is paraphrased and therefore is *not* enclosed in quotation marks. If you shift from one mode to the other, you may have to alter not only punctuation but also pronouns and verb tenses so as not to confuse your readers.

CONFUSING Agassiz, the legendary Swiss scientist and teacher, once said I cannot afford to waste my time making money. [Without quotation marks, this statement seems to refer to two different people: Agassiz and the writer.]

REVISED Agassiz, the legendary Swiss scientist and teacher, once said, "I cannot afford to waste my time making money." [By signaling direct discourse, the quotation marks make it clear that Agassiz is talking about himself.]

REVISED Agassiz, the legendary Swiss scientist and teacher, once said that he could not afford to waste his time making money. [Without quotation marks but with the pronoun *he* and consistent past-tense verbs, the statement clearly refers only to Agassiz. This is an example of indirect discourse.]

EXERCISE 35.2 Correct the mixed constructions and faulty predications in the following sentences.

1. By using the terms *alligator* and *crocodile* to refer to the same reptile misleads many people.
2. A foot is when you can measure 12 inches.
3. The job of all UPS drivers delivered packages from its city of origin to their final destinations.
4. She asked did you like the concert?
5. One reason the Slavic Festival was so popular was because they had a band play polka music.
6. To creative writers, such as Lita, romanticized her adventures.

7. The reason why strawberries are picked while slightly green is because if left to ripen they rot before they are picked.
8. When the homecoming parade included William Smith and Ted Jackson became school heroes.
9. In processing caramel at high heat softens their centers.
10. The Great Salt Lake is a lake that is easy to swim in where there is a high salt content to make the water more buoyant.

part

8

Effective Sentences

36 Clarity and Conciseness

FAQs

- What is a passive sentence? (36d)
- How can I tighten up my writing so that it's not so wordy? (36e)
- How can I be sure that readers will understand my meaning? (36g–36j)

Unlike the quick give-and-take of informal, conversational writing, the kind of writing you are expected to do in college is designed for readers who may not know you or have the same background knowledge as you. This more formal kind of writing should convey its message as clearly and completely as possible without being unnecessarily wordy.

The errors discussed in this chapter afflict academic writing much more than they do the sort of informal writing you might do with friends.

36a Avoid excessively long sentences

Sentences that are more than about twenty-five words long can sometimes be difficult for a reader, especially if the sentences are complicated.

> Despite their significance in contemporary society, social movements seldom solve social problems, because in order to mobilize resources a movement must appeal to a broad constituency, which means that the group must focus on large-scale issues which are deeply embedded in society.

This sentence is forty-two words long. The following three shorter sentences say the same thing and are much easier for the reader to understand:

- Despite their significance in contemporary society, social movements seldom solve social problems. To mobilize resources, a movement must appeal to a broad constituency. This means that the group must focus on large-scale issues which are deeply embedded in society.

36b Avoid unnecessary repetition and redundancy

A certain amount of repetition is necessary, both for emphasis and to maintain focus. Repetition is especially useful for linking one sentence to another. However, unnecessary repetition will only clutter your writing and irritate readers.

See 5c

▶ Life offers many lessons ~~about life~~.

▶ People seem to learn things best when they ~~learn~~ *experience* them firsthand.

If you repeat nouns too often, you will end up with a dull, heavy writing style. The best way to avoid repetition of nouns is to use pronouns. Pronouns can establish and maintain coherence in paragraphs just as repeated nouns do, but with a lighter touch.

See 26a-2

Redundancy is the use of words that could be left out without changing the meaning of the sentence. Saying that something is *blue in color* is redundant, because readers already know that blue *is* a color. Some other redundant phrases are *repeat again, combine together, end result, true fact,* and *basic essentials.* Such phrases should always be pruned.

▶ I was caught ~~unexpectedly~~ off guard by the boss's telling me I had ~~successfully~~ made the grade in my new job.

36c Use expletives only where appropriate

An **expletive** is an "empty" word, such as *there* or *it,* that occupies the subject position in a sentence but is not its grammatical subject. Expletives have useful functions: for example, *there is* (*are, was, were*) typically introduces a new topic for discussion, whereas *it is* (*was*) typically creates special emphasis. Because expletives can be overused, however, look for opportunities to convert expletive constructions into more direct expressions.

▶ ~~There are many new features that can be found in my computer.~~ *My computer has many new features.*

▶ ~~It is recommended that~~ *A*~~a~~ll candidates *should* be on time for their interviews.

36d Use passive voice only where appropriate

See 28g

In passive-voice constructions, the subject position is occupied not by the agent of the verb's action but by the recipient. Since passive-voice constructions tend to be wordier and less direct than active-voice constructions, try to write most of your sentences in the active voice.

PASSIVE Flexible songs, containing a variety of motifs arranged to its liking, are sung by the robin.

ACTIVE The robin sings flexible songs, containing a variety of motifs arranged to its liking.

The passive version of this sentence is wordy and confusing, whereas the active version is direct and clear.

Passive sentences are appropriate when the recipient of the verb action is the topic of discussion or when the agent can be omitted without loss of clarity.

- Over the past ten years, more than three million white-collar jobs have been eliminated in the United States.

Using the active voice would force the writer to mention the agent of this job elimination (presumably management), taking the focus of the sentence off the loss of jobs.

Over the past ten years, management has eliminated more than three million white-collar jobs in the United States.

36e Eliminate wordy phrases

Concise writing

Many commonly used phrases are unnecessarily long. If you can replace them with no loss of meaning, you should do so.

- ~~In a very real sense~~, ~~t~~T trickle-down economics ~~exhibits a tendency~~ tends to make money trickle up, benefiting mainly the wealthy.

TechALERT!

Grammar Checkers: Wordy Phrases

Although a typical grammar checker will identify many wordy phrases, it will also miss quite a few. Therefore, you need to be vigilant and double-check your writing. For example, our grammar checker flagged *as a matter of fact* and *due to the fact that* but not *in the final analysis* or *in the event that.*

Wordy phrases	*Concise phrases*
as a matter of fact	in fact
at the present time	today, presently
at this point in time	now
due to the fact that	because
in spite of the fact that	although, even though
in the event that	if
in the final analysis	finally, ultimately
until such time as	until

EXERCISE 36.1 Revise the following sentences to make them as clear and concise as possible.

1. Millions of people witnessed the first lunar landing on the moon.
2. She did the daily paperwork every day.
3. I experienced a frightening experience when my teenage daughter took me out for a drive.
4. The quarterback who had been injured early in the season and had undergone extensive knee surgery to repair the damage had been conscientious about his rehabilitation exercises and was therefore feeling ready to play again only four months after the surgery.
5. The lack of a warm pair of mittens and a hat on that very cold morning led to the trumpeter's inability to play well during the halftime show at the Thanksgiving game.
6. Several unusual songs were sung by the Girl Scouts during their annual awards ceremony.
7. The Boy Scout Eagle rank was achieved by a boy who works with my son during the summer.
8. Hundreds of items were marked down by the store management for the annual August clearance sale.

9. There are many people in this society who do not have enough leisure time.
10. It is often that students find their work piling up at finals time.

Writing clear, concise sentences

36f Avoid a noun-heavy style

A noun-heavy writing style is characterized by many more nouns than verbs. It tends to involve excessive use of the verb *be* (*am, are, is, was, were*) and strings of prepositional phrases. A noun-heavy style results partly from the use of **nominalizations**—that is, nouns derived from verbs. For example, *determination* is a nominalization derived from the verb *determine.* Other examples include *remove/removal, insist/insistence, develop/development,* and *jog/jogging.* Although nominalizations can be useful for certain purposes, using too many of them will make your style ponderous and dull. Turning some of your nominalizations into verbs will make your writing more active and concise.

NOUN-HEAVY	The preference of most writers is for an understanding of their composing as a species of fine frenzy.
MORE VERBAL	Most writers prefer having it understood that they compose in a fine frenzy.
NOUN-HEAVY	Thomas Jefferson was not a believer in the divinity of Jesus Christ and indeed was the author of a version of the Four Gospels that included the removal of all references to "miraculous" events.
MORE VERBAL	Thomas Jefferson did not believe in the divinity of Jesus Christ and indeed wrote a version of the Four Gospels from which he removed all references to "miraculous" events.

Noun-heavy writing also is created through the use of phrasal expressions such as *perform an examination* instead of simple verbs such as *examine.*

- Before ~~making the purchase of~~ purchasing a used car, one should always ~~perform an examination on~~ examine it.

EXERCISE 36.2 The following phrasal expressions are characteristic of a wordy, noun-heavy style. Convert them into simpler verb forms. (The first one has already been done.)

1. create an improvement in ___*improve*___
2. give a summary of ______________
3. put emphasis on ______________
4. perform an operation on ______________
5. do an analysis of ______________
6. make an estimate of ______________
7. come to the realization that ______________
8. provide an explanation for ______________
9. have a lot of sympathy for ______________
10. conduct an inspection of ______________

EXERCISE 36.3 Revise the following sentences to make them less noun-heavy.

1. The scientist came to the conclusion that she had made an important discovery.
2. The United Nations wanted to conduct an inspection of the country's weapons storage facilities.
3. The committee reached a decision to hire the man it had interviewed.
4. The stance of the institution in regard to the question of affirmative action was unclear.
5. The group held the belief that disaster was coming at the close of the century.
6. The opinion of my mechanic is that there is nothing wrong with the transmission of my car.
7. Their press release gave an explanation for the behavior of the demonstrators.
8. The education reform law passed by the legislature demands that schools make improvements in their ways of teaching.
9. The composition of a piece of music is a requirement of the music theory course.
10. The man was justifiably proud of the achievement of his goal.

TechALERT!

Grammar Checkers: Noun-Heavy Writing

Although most grammar checkers are supposed to flag a noun-heavy style, especially long strings of prepositional phrases, they seldom do. For example, when we ran a grammar check on the three noun-heavy sentences given above, it failed to detect anything wrong.

A somewhat more reliable indicator of a noun-heavy style can be found in readability statistics (see TOOLS > OPTIONS > SPELLING & GRAMMAR). For example, the three noun-heavy sentences given above were rated at the twelfth-grade reading level, while the revised versions of these same sentences were rated two grades easier. Of course, readability statistics are only a superficial indicator; to make specific improvements in your style, apply the advice found in this chapter.

36g Choose words that express your meaning precisely

Good writing conveys its meaning efficiently, with precision. Such precision is achieved largely through the careful selection of words. Minimize your use of vague nouns such as *area, aspect, factor, kind, nature, situation, sort, thing,* and *type,* as well as your use of vague adjectives such as *bad, good, interesting, nice,* and *weird* and vague adverbs such as *basically, completely, definitely, really,* and *very.*

Word use is discussed in more detail in Part 9.

▶ ~~A democratic type of government basically~~ Democracy requires ~~a pretty~~ an informed citizenry.

36h Use *that* to clarify sentence structure

Clear sentence structure helps the reader see how the pieces of a sentence fit together. In sentences with a main clause followed by a *that* clause, it usually helps to include the *that.*

Clarity and Conciseness

Using redundant expressions

- It's a ~~true~~ fact that Yao Ming is very tall ~~in height~~.
  [By definition, facts are true, and *tall* is a measure of height.]

Using wordy expressions

- emphasize
  In this paper I want to ~~put emphasis on~~ the role of the media in globalization.
- Europeans
  ~~People from Europe~~ first learned about smoking tobacco from the
  American Indians.
  ~~original natives of America~~.

Using vague words

- is the study of plant life.
  Botany ~~has to do with living things like plants~~.
- is very introspective and idealistic.
  Hamlet ~~basically likes to think a lot and has some good ideals~~.

- that
  It is important ^ we understand the instructions before we proceed.

Sometimes, failure to include *that* can cause the reader to misinterpret the sentence initially.

> Some people are claiming their rights have been violated by the government.

By beginning with a string of words that looks like a sentence in itself ("Some people are claiming their rights . . ."), the writer of this sentence risks misleading the reader. Inserting *that* after *claiming* helps to clarify the sentence structure.

- Some people are claiming *that* their rights have been violated by the government.

TechALERT!

Grammar Checkers: Comparative Constructions

Although grammar checkers may spot certain kinds of problematic comparative constructions (such as the ambiguous "We need more thorough employees"), they miss many others. For example, our grammar checker did not flag either the Incomplete sentence or the Ambiguous sentence below.

36i Make comparisons complete and clear

Comparative constructions inherently involve two terms: "*A* is ________ er than *B*." In casual conversation, speakers sometimes omit the *B* term on the assumption that listeners can easily figure out what it is. In writing, however, you should make both terms of the comparison explicit.

INCOMPLETE Talk radio has become a popular form of entertainment because it gets people more involved. [More involved than what?]

COMPLETE Talk radio has become a popular form of entertainment because it gets people more involved than most other media do.

Comparative constructions are sometimes open to two possible interpretations. In such cases, add a few words to help the reader know which interpretation is meant.

AMBIGUOUS Abstract expressionism was more influenced by cubism than surrealism.

CLEAR Abstract expressionism was more influenced by cubism than surrealism *was.*

CLEAR Abstract expressionism was more influenced by cubism than *by* surrealism.

See 30e on comparative and superlative forms.

36j Avoid multiple negation

A single negative word, such as *no, not, never, nobody, unhappy,* or *unpleasant,* can change the entire meaning of a sentence. If you put two or more negative words in the same sentence, you may change the meaning in multiple ways and confuse the reader.

CONFUSING Not many of the assignments were left unfinished, but none of the students did all of them.

By rewriting the first part of the sentence in positive rather than negative terms, you can make its meaning much clearer:

CLEAR Most of the assignments were finished, but none of the students did all of them.

ESL NOTE In many languages, multiple negation is correct and clear. In Spanish, for example, "don't say anything to anybody" is rendered as *no le digas nada a nadie* (literally, "don't say nothing to nobody").

FOR COLLABORATION Make the following sentences as concise as you can without changing the meaning. Then compare your answers with those of two other students and see whose version uses the fewest number of words.

1. I think that people learn the most from personal experience and hard work, not from memorizing dates or facts, and that hard times or failure is a success if you learn something from it and improve.
2. In our natural childbirth class, I planned a calm and relaxing natural childbirth plan for my own pregnancy.
3. This book contains a significant amount of information on art in history because without a knowledge of art history, one may find it difficult to discern the principles of art which are clearly crucial to an understanding of the aspects of art today.
4. I have come to conclude that to serve the purpose of conveying the overall benefit of chemical weapons incineration, the report should maintain an argumentative tone while clarifying the success of chemical weapons incineration and the safety standards followed by those who carry it out, and through this, to contradict any negative views.

5. Although she was in a family way, she continued in the fulfillment of her familial and employment responsibilities.
6. In recent months, research has come to light that bright red, green, yellow, and other colored fruits and vegetables may be instrumental in preventing lung cancer.
7. The weather, which was hostile, and the native inhabitants, the Indians, led to the death of most of the expedition members, who died.
8. The grassy area, which contains grass and trees, will be turned into a parking lot, so that students can park their cars there.
9. During that time period, many people who were car buyers preferred cars that were large in size and bright in color but not of a cheap quality.
10. Truly, for all intents and purposes, the industrial productivity in America generally depends on various and certain factors which are really usually more psychological in kind than of any true given technological aspect.

37 Coordination and Subordination

FAQs

- What is the best way to avoid "choppy" writing? (37a)
- How can I emphasize some ideas and de-emphasize others? (37c)

Texting, instant messaging, and other kinds of informal writing seldom have sentences longer than a few words. Academic or formal writing is very different. Here long sentences are quite common, including sentences with two or more clauses. In such cases, it is important to either coordinate the two clauses or subordinate one to the other. Remember, *form should reflect content.* If the ideas in the two clauses are equally important, *coordinate* them by giving them equal grammatical status. If they are not equally important, put the less important idea in a grammatically *subordinate* form.

37a Look for a way to combine closely related sentences

Combining sentences

Writing that contains one short sentence after another not only is unpleasantly choppy but also fails to emphasize some sentences more than others.

TOO CHOPPY

> I was born and raised in a small midwestern town. It was easy to make friends. I got to know a lot of people. I was able to achieve almost all of my goals. I could do almost anything I wanted to. School and sports were a challenge. But I could always make my way to where I wanted to be.

This paragraph is so choppy that it is hard to get a sense of what the writer's main point is. The writer could solve this problem by noticing that several pairs of sentences are closely related and combining these sentences.

REVISED VERSION

> I was born and raised in a small midwestern town. It was easy to make friends, *and so* I got to know a lot of people. *Since* I could do almost anything I wanted to, I was able to achieve almost all of my goals. School and sports were a challenge, *but* I could always make my way to where I wanted to be.

Instead of seven sentences, there are now four sentences, each conveying a single idea. This reorganization helps readers get a sense of the writer's main point—that growing up in a small town made it easy for him to be popular and successful.

The revised paragraph has three instances of sentence combining. In two of these cases, the sentences seemed to be of equal value and so *coordination* was used.

- ▸ It was easy to make friends, *and so* I got to know a lot of people.
- ▸ School and sports were a challenge, *but* I could always make my way to where I wanted to be.

In the third case, one sentence seemed to be more important than the other, so *subordination* was used.

- ▸ *Since* I could do almost anything I wanted to, I was able to achieve almost all of my goals.

Whenever you have written two closely related sentences, you should consider combining them into one with a conjunction, an adverb, or punctuation.

TechALERT!

Grammar Checkers: Choppy Style

Your grammar checker will not be able to tell you how to combine closely related sentences or even when to do so. But it can alert you to an unpleasantly choppy style. When we ran our grammar checker on the Too Choppy paragraph above, it was judged to be at an elementary (fifth-grade) level. The style of the revised version, in contrast, was found to be at the seventh-grade level—more appropriate for a mature audience.

37b Coordinate related sentences of equal value

Coordination is the pairing of sentences or sentence elements by putting them in the same grammatical form and linking them via a coordinating conjunction, conjunctive adverb, or semicolon. The coordinating conjunctions are *and, but, or, nor, for, so,* and *yet.*

See 26a-7

Some Common Conjunctive Adverbs

also	hence	likewise	otherwise
consequently	however	meanwhile	similarly
finally	indeed	moreover	therefore
furthermore	instead	nevertheless	thus

USE OF A COORDINATING CONJUNCTION

A high-fiber diet appears to lower the risk of certain cancers, *so* the National Cancer Institute recommends consuming 25–35 grams of fiber a day.

Conjunctive adverbs provide another way of giving equal emphasis to two conjoined sentences. The conjunctive adverbs include *however, consequently, therefore,* and *otherwise.* A conjunctive adverb is often preceded by a semicolon.

See 26a-5

USE OF A CONJUNCTIVE ADVERB

The 1928 Pact of Paris offended nobody, since it included no compulsory machinery of enforcement; *hence,* the European nations rushed to sign it.

A coordinate relationship also can be created between two sentences simply by using a semicolon.

USE OF A SEMICOLON

People are affected by social forces sometimes far removed from their immediate perceptions; they perceive only a relatively small portion of the influences that play upon them.

See Chapter 48 for further discussion of semicolon use.

37c Subordinate less important ideas

See 26c-3

To combine two closely related but unequal ideas, use **subordination;** put the more important idea in a main clause and the lesser one in a subordinate clause. Subordinate clauses are typically set off by subordinating conjunctions (such as *although, because, if, since, though, unless, until,* and *while*) or by relative pronouns (such as *that, which, who, whom,* and *whose*).

Consider these two sentences:

We know that advertisers are "out to get us."

We do not make much of an attempt to refute advertising messages.

These two statements are closely related, so they could be combined. Since the author's point is that people allow themselves to be seduced by advertising, the second statement is more important (that is, more topic-oriented) than the first. Therefore, the second statement should become the main clause and the first statement should become the subordinate clause.

USE OF A SUBORDINATING CONJUNCTION

Even though we know that advertisers are "out to get us," we do not make much of an attempt to refute their messages.

Here is another example of how a subordinating conjunction can be used to set off a subordinate clause:

Using hands-on experience is one of the best ways of learning. It helps the student learn on a more interactive level.

USE OF A SUBORDINATING CONJUNCTION

Using hands-on experience is one of the best ways of learning, *as* it helps the student learn on a more interactive level.

When one sentence adds information to the entire preceding sentence, it is often possible to convert the second sentence to a relative clause.

The Great Lakes cool the hot winds of summer and warm the cold winds of winter. This gives the state of Michigan a milder climate than some of the other north central states.

USE OF A RELATIVE CLAUSE

The Great Lakes cool the hot winds of summer and warm the cold winds of winter, *which gives* the state of Michigan a milder climate than some of the other north central states.

Relative clauses can sometimes be shortened by getting rid of the relative pronoun.

The Great Lakes cool the hot winds of summer and warm the cold winds of winter, *giving* the state of Michigan a milder climate than some of the other north central states.

When two sentences modify the same noun, you can sometimes embed one into the other as an appositive.

See 26c-2

Julia Cameron was a British photographer. She is considered one of the most important portraitists of the nineteenth century.

USE OF AN APPOSITIVE

Julia Cameron, *a British photographer*, is considered one of the most important portraitists of the nineteenth century.

EXERCISE 37.1 Each of the following items contains two or more sentences that can be combined into one. Use coordination or subordination, as appropriate, to do the combining. (You may rearrange the order of the information any way you like.)

1. In a Molière comedy, the central character is a type, only slightly individualized.
   Tartuffe, for example, is a great artistic creation.
   He is not a living human being.
2. In his youth, Watergate burglar G. Gordon Liddy listened to Hitler's speeches in German on the radio.
   Liddy knew only a few German phrases.
   Liddy often found these speeches very persuasive.
3. In 1848, the Treaty of Guadalupe Hidalgo was signed.
   This treaty ended the Mexican War.
   About half the territory of Mexico was incorporated into the United States.

4. With the land came its inhabitants.
   Many of these inhabitants were Mexican citizens of Spanish or Spanish-Indian descent.
   The majority were Indians.
5. Under the terms of the treaty, former Mexican citizens were granted US citizenship.
   The Indians were treated in the traditional American fashion.
   The subsequent history of Mexican Americans has been one of dispossession and discrimination.
6. There are many ways to form opinions about current events.
   First, you have to gather information.
   You can gather information from a variety of sources, such as newspapers, magazines, and television.
7. When you write a paper, the statements should be your own.
   You should never claim a statement as your own if it is not.
   That is called plagiarism.
8. You can help shape your audience.
   You can send your writing to a particular person or persons.
   You can also send your writing to a publication chosen for its readership.
9. Spoken conversation is different from written conversation.
   In spoken conversation, you have limited control over whom you will talk with.
   In written conversation, you have many more options and wider-ranging possibilities in determining the conversation's participants.
10. Margaret Mead was an anthropologist.
    She communicated with many different groups of people, from Samoan tribe people to international political leaders.
    Her writing reflects her unique sense of audience.

FOR COLLABORATION Bring a sample piece of writing to your group; exchange your writing samples, and identify any areas of choppy writing that could be improved.

38 Parallelism

FAQs

- What does it mean to make sentences "parallel"?
- If I want to make two or more sentences parallel, how can I ensure that they match each other? (38a)
- How do parallel sentence elements work to make comparisons? (38d)
- Why is a set of parallel elements sometimes considered "incomplete"? (38e)

When two or more sentence elements represent comparable ideas, putting them in the same grammatical form helps the reader to see the relationship between them. This stylistic device is called **parallelism.** When Benjamin Franklin wrote "A penny saved is a penny earned," he was using parallelism. The adjective *saved* parallels in content and form the adjective *earned.* If he had written "A penny saved is a penny that someone has earned," his sentence would have been out of balance (and would not have been so memorable!).

38a Put parallel content in parallel form

Parallelism

Words and phrases that are linked by the coordinating conjunction *and, but, or,* or *nor* often are parallel in content. When that is the case, they also should be parallel in form.

cease and *desist* [Both verbs]

hook, line, and *sinker* [All nouns]

of the people, by the people, [and] *for the people* [All prepositional phrases]

Sometimes parallel structures are complicated, as in this famous sentence from Abraham Lincoln's Gettysburg Address, contrasting politicians' speeches with soldiers' bravery:

The world will	little note,	*nor*		
	long remember,		what we say here,	*but*
it can	never forget		what they did here.	

To make sure that you use parallelism appropriately, follow this three-step procedure:

1. Whenever you write a sentence that has words or phrases joined by *and, but, or,* or *nor,* ask yourself whether there is comparable content somewhere on each side of the conjunction. If so, identify exactly what that comparable content is. In the sentence from the Gettysburg Address, for example, "what we say here" is compared with "what they did here."
2. Check to see whether the comparable parts are in the same grammatical form. The two parts cited from the Gettysburg Address are both relative clauses, beginning with the same relative pronoun (*what*), followed by a personal pronoun (*we/they*), a verb (*say/did*), and the same adverb (*here*).
3. If the comparable parts are not in the same grammatical form—but should be—use the elements in one part of the sentence as a model and put the elements in the other parts in the same grammatical form.

▶ The world will little note *nor* ~~remember forever~~ long remember . . .

All of this may seem complicated, but it is worth learning because parallelism is one of the most powerful tools a writer has for presenting ideas clearly and memorably.

In the following sentence, the conjunction *and* alerts the reader to the possibility that there is comparable content in the two parts of the sentence. The writer seems to be saying that creativity has two identifying characteristics of a similar kind, and the sentence seems to have this kind of structure: Creativity = $X + Y$.

FAULTY Creativity is being able to identify a situation or problem and the knowledge of how to solve it.

Are *X* and *Y* in the same grammatical form? No: "being able to identify a situation or problem" is a gerund (*-ing*) phrase, whereas "the knowledge of how to solve it" is a noun phrase.

To fix this problem, use the first part of the sentence as a model for the second part. The first part is a gerund phrase, so you can create parallelism by turning the second part into a gerund phrase as well: "knowing how to solve it."

REVISED Creativity is *being* able to identify a situation or problem and *knowing* how to solve it.

Consider these additional examples of similar sentence elements that can be confusing if they are not made parallel:

FAULTY An expert is someone who knows more and more about increasingly little.

REVISED An expert is someone who knows *more and more* about *less and less*.

FAULTY The young talk about what they are doing; old people reminisce about the past; fools only tell what their plans are.

REVISED The young talk about what they are doing; the old about what they have done; the foolish about what they plan to do. [Old French proverb]

TechHelp

Finding Places to Use Parallelism

1. Open the SEARCH (or FIND) feature of your word-processing program.
2. Enter the word *and* in the search field, and run the program.
3. Whenever the program highlights an *and*, examine the words or phrases linked by it to see whether they represent comparable or equivalent content. If they do, they should be in parallel form.
4. Follow the same procedure with *but, or*, and *nor*.

EXERCISE 38.1 Correct the faulty parallelism in the following sentences.

1. Her interests include skiing, running, and bike rides.
2. We must either turn left on Martin Luther King Drive or take a right turn on Main Street.
3. Nothing in the world can take the place of persistence: talent will not, genius will not, being educated won't.
4. My present occupation is repairing appliances, VCRs, and refinishing floors.
5. Mark Twain claimed that a friend is one who will side with you when you are wrong, since when you are right anyone is willing to be on your side.
6. Prejudice is the real robber, and vice murders us.
7. What we call the beginning is often the end, and what we referred to as an ending was a place to begin.
8. Destiny is not a matter of chance. It is a matter to be chosen. It is not a thing to be waited for. It is a thing you should try to be achieving.
9. Ask not what your country can do for you; ask what can be done by you for your country.
10. The television commercial is not at all about the character of the products to be consumed. It is about the product consumers' character.

EXERCISE 38.2 Select a sample of your own writing. Following the instructions in the preceding TechHelp box, identify all words and phrases that should be parallel. Where necessary, make appropriate corrections.

Make all items in a list or series parallel

Whenever you present any kind of listing in formal or academic writing, whether it is a formatted list such as an outline or just a series of items in a sentence, all of the items should be in the same grammatical form. They are, in effect, being lined up for comparison on an "apples with apples" basis, and readers expect each item to be in similar form. For example, the headings in this chapter constitute a formatted list, with each item set off with a number and letter. Notice how each heading is in the form of an imperative verb phrase ("Put parallel content in . . .," "Make all items in . . .," "Use parallelism with . . ."). This parallel structure helps the reader approach each guideline for writing in a similar way; phrasing that goes off in different directions is likely to distract the reader.

CommonErrors

Parallelism

Not putting all items in a list in parallel form

FAULTY The building is 72 feet wide, 130 feet in length, and has a height of five stories.

PARALLEL The building is 72 feet wide, 130 feet long, and five stories high.

Not using enough parallelism to make the meaning clear

UNCLEAR Human language is different from other animals' communication systems, just as the elephant's trunk doesn't look like the nostrils of non-elephants.

CLEAR Human language is as different from other animals' communication systems, as the elephant's trunk is different from other animals' noses.

- The last decades of the nineteenth century through the early decades of the twentieth century marked a period when Americans confronted rapid industrialization, a communications revolution, and ~~big business was growing~~ *the growth of big business.* [A third noun phrase is put into the series to replace the distracting clause.]
- All addictions are characterized by compulsion, loss of control, ~~there are~~ negative consequences, and ~~people deny they're addicted~~ *denial.* [Turning the last two items into noun phrases makes it clear that the sentence contains a series of four items.]

38c Use parallelism with correlative conjunctions

Whenever you use correlative conjunctions such as *both/and, either/or, neither/nor,* and *not only/but,* you are lining up two sentence elements for comparison. Thus, those elements require parallel grammatical form.

See 26a-7

- Either *we go full speed ahead* or *we stop right here.*

In lining up the sentence elements, make sure you place the two conjunctions exactly where they belong, so that the elements after each conjunction are grammatically parallel to each other.

INCORRECT Solar energy is both used to heat homes and to run small appliances.

REVISED Solar energy is used *both* to heat homes *and* to run small appliances.

INCORRECT These three books by Morrison have not only received critical acclaim but also have been widely read.

REVISED These three books by Morrison *not only* have received critical acclaim *but also* have been widely read.

38d Use parallelism for comparisons or contrasts

A comparison or contrast involves two statements or terms that are seen as somehow equivalent; indeed, this equivalence allows them to be compared. These two statements or terms therefore should be parallel. Abraham Lincoln's use of parallelism in the Gettysburg Address excerpt is a good example. Another good example of contrasting parallelism can be found in Neil Armstrong's famous utterance upon first stepping on the moon: "That's one small step for man, one giant leap for mankind."

More on parallelism, with exercises

Make parallel constructions complete and clear

In addition to similar grammatical form, parallelism generally involves one or more words that appear in both parts of the construction. In the Gettysburg Address example, the words *what* and *here* are found in both parts of the sentence; *world* is referred to again with the pronoun *it.* Usually only a few matching words are needed. As writers create parallel sentences, they sometimes forget to pull all the grammatical elements together to make the comparison complete. Sometimes an extra word or two is all that is needed to complete the parallelism and clarify the connection for the reader.

▶ It seems apparent to even the casual observer that all people crave some form of recognition, *that* no one lives in total isolation, and *that* any healthy society will find some way to meet this human imperative. [Inserting *that* makes it clearer that there are three things that "seem apparent."]

In other cases, a rearrangement of words or phrases is called for.

UNCLEAR Speculation leads to learning, in the same way that science is supported by theory.

In this sentence, the conceptual analogy between the first part of the sentence and the second part is not clear. Rearranging the words of the mixed comparison and repeating the words *leads to* solves the problem.

CLEARER Speculation leads to learning, just as theory leads to science. [The revision puts the second part of the sentence into the active voice, matching the first part and enabling the reader to line up *speculation* and *theory* on the one hand and *learning* and *science* on the other.]

38f Use parallelism to enhance coherence

See 5e

As mentioned in Chapter 5, parallelism promotes coherence within paragraphs. If two related sentences are equivalent in function and content, show their relatedness by putting both in the same grammatical form. In the following example from a psychology text, two similar *if* constructions are used to create parallel explanations.

▶ The distinction between formative and summative assessment is based on how the results are used. The same assessment procedure can be used for either purpose. If the goal is to obtain information about student learning for planning purposes, the assessment is formative. If the purpose is to determine final achievement (and help determine a course grade), the assessment is summative.

—Anita E. Woolfolk, *Educational Psychology*

Checklist

Parallelism with Grouped Elements

✓ Find sentences that have words or phrases joined by *and*, *but*, *or*, or *nor*. (You can use the SEARCH, or FIND, feature to identify them. See the box in 38b.) *Example:* "She liked apples, but pears were what she always preferred."

✓ Check to see whether these sentences have equivalent content linked by the conjunctions—elements that might be compared or contrasted. If they do, identify exactly what those equivalent elements are. *Example:* ". . . liked apples" and "pears . . . preferred."

✓ Check to see whether these comparable sentence elements are in the same grammatical form. If not, use the elements in one part of the sentence as a model, and arrange the other parts in the same grammatical form, so that all parts are consistent. *Example:* "She liked apples but always preferred pears."

EXERCISE 38.3 Correct the faulty parallelism in the following sentences.

1. We live in a time when people seem afraid to be themselves, when a hard, shiny exterior is preferred to the genuineness of deeply felt emotion.
2. Most people prefer to watch others exercise rather than participate because exercise is so difficult and it is so easy to lie on a couch.
3. The responsibilities of a stagehand include keeping track of props, changing scenery, and they sometimes help out with special effects.
4. Two complaints being investigated by the task force were lack of promotions for women and writing company memos that were not gender inclusive.
5. Just a generation ago, people would not have dreamed of eating strawberries in September, nor would corn have been available in May.
6. Objectivity is assumed to be fundamental to news reporting, but public relations and advertising personnel are not assumed to be objective.
7. The history of television is a history of technology and policy, economics and sociology, and entertainment and news are part of it, too.
8. Watching an animal in its natural habitat is the most authentic form of animal-viewing experience, followed by a circus or zoo, showing one televised in its natural habitat, and seeing one featured on a late-night talk show.

9. Good therapists will assess a client's general problem fairly early, and provisional goals will be set for the client.
10. Minor hassles—losing your keys, the grocery bag rips on the way to the door, you slipped and fell in front of everyone in a new class, finding that you went through the whole afternoon with a big chunk of spinach stuck in your front teeth—may seem unimportant, but the cumulative effect of these minor hassles may be stressful enough to be harmful.

FOR COLLABORATION Proverbs often use parallelism. Working together with a friend or classmate, complete each of the following proverbs by putting the words in parentheses into a form that parallels the first part of the sentence. The first one is already done for you.

1. A wise man knows his own ignorance; (fool, thinks, knows, everything).
   Answer: A wise man knows his own ignorance; a fool thinks he knows everything.
2. Love is a furnace, but (not cook, the stew).
3. If a man steals gold, he is put in prison; (if, land, made, king).
4. You can hardly make a friend in a year, but (easily offend, an hour).
5. Perspective continues to be our greatest shortage, just as (our ironies, most abundant product).
6. We promise according to our hopes, and (perform, fears).
7. She who leaves nothing to chance will do few things ill, but (she, very few things).
8. Fear less, hope more (eat, chew; whine, breathe; talk, say; hate, love); and all good things are yours.
9. The harder the conflict, (glorious, triumph). What we obtain too cheap, (esteem, lightly).
10. Live your own life, for (you, die, death).

39 Emphasis

FAQs

- How can I make my main ideas stand out more? (39a–39d)
- Why should I avoid using underlined words or fancy typography to create emphasis? (39d)

With any writing, some ideas are more important than others, and it helps your readers if you make those ideas stand out. This is where emphasis comes in. With all the formatting options available on your computer, you can create emphasis through punctuation, typeface, and other formatting options. You can use underlining, **boldface,** *italics,* ALL CAPS, or a special font to draw attention to certain words and phrases. You can also use exclamation points and dashes. (Note that quotation marks are *not* used for emphasis!) You can use white space, bulleted lists, or boxes. In casual email, you can even use emoticons, such as :-o to represent shock.) However, these stylistic tricks should be used sparingly, if at all, in formal or academic writing. Learn to rely instead on the techniques described in this chapter.

See 46g, 52e-f, 19b, 21b–e

39a Create emphasis through end-weight

The most emphatic part of a sentence is its ending. This explains the power of Franklin Roosevelt's famous line "The only thing we have to fear is fear itself." If you read that sentence aloud, you can hear your voice rising naturally at the end before abruptly falling. This natural intonation pattern underlies **end-weight.** Using end-weight means putting a key word or phrase where intonation naturally gives it emphasis—at the end of the sentence. If FDR had said "Fear itself is the only thing we have to fear," he would have missed out on a good opportunity to apply this principle.

As you edit your writing, look for opportunities to give end-weight to key concepts. Note how the writer of the following example made the phrase *better and wiser* more prominent by shifting it toward the end of the second sentence:

FIRST DRAFT We all muddle through life, falling along the way. But we will become better and wiser people if we pick ourselves up and keep moving on.

REVISION We all muddle through life, falling along the way. But if we pick ourselves up and keep moving on, we will become better and wiser for it.

EXERCISE 39.1 The following are email tag lines, rewritten in a form less elegant than their original form. Using the end-weight principle, try to restore them to their original form. (Suggestion: First identify a key concept; then try to move the phrase related to that concept to the end of the sentence.) The first has been done for you.

1. Television is very educational: I go to my room and read a book the minute someone turns it on. Answer: Television is very educational: The minute someone turns it on, I go to my room and read a book.
2. Recycled electrons were used to print this message.
3. The tree of liberty grows only when the blood of tyrants waters it.
4. Where ignorance is bliss, to be wise is folly.
5. The heart has its reasons which are not known by reason.
6. You risk even more if you do not risk anything is the trouble.
7. Life is nothing if it is not a daring adventure.
8. Time is the stuff life is made of. Do not squander time if you love life.
9. To gain your heart's desire and to lose it are the two tragedies in life.
10. Courage is the mastery of fear. It is not the absence of it.

39b Create emphasis through selective repetition

Another powerful way of emphasizing important ideas is through repetition—especially when combined with some form of grammatical parallelism. Notice how Studs Terkel uses the repetition of the simple pronoun *my* to emphasize the personal significance of his work:

▶ A further personal note. I find some delight in *my* job as a radio broadcaster. I'm able to set *my* own pace, *my* own standards, and determine for

> *my*self the substance of each program. Some days are more sunny than others, some hours less astonishing than I'd hoped for; *my* occasional slovenliness infuriates me . . . but it is, for better or worse, in *my* hands.
>
> —Studs Terkel, *Working*

See 36b

Repetition is effective only if used judiciously. Overdoing repetition will make your writing boring and wordy.

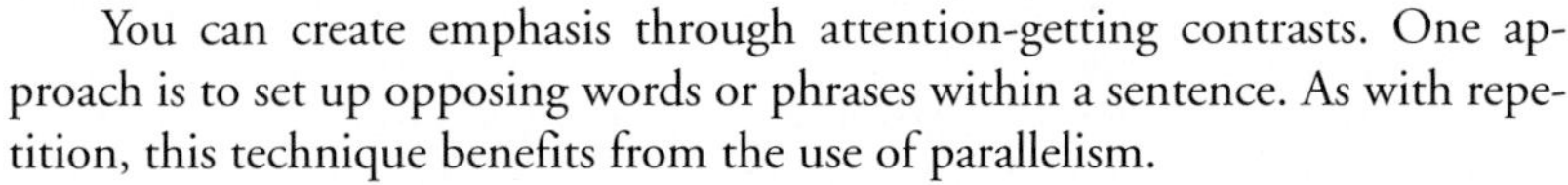

39c Create emphasis through contrast

See 38d

You can create emphasis through attention-getting contrasts. One approach is to set up opposing words or phrases within a sentence. As with repetition, this technique benefits from the use of parallelism.

> ▸ The democratic faith is based not as much upon the assumption of leadership by the few as upon the wisdom and conscience of the many.
>
> —Norman Cousins, *Human Options*

In this sentence, the author uses the contrast between *few* and *many* to emphasize the broad-based nature of democratic governance. Note the parallelism between *leadership by the few* and *wisdom and conscience of the many.* If the author had written "The democratic faith is based mainly upon the wisdom and conscience of many people," the statement would have been less emphatic.

See 5c-1

Another way of creating emphasis through contrast is by using transitional expressions such as *however, though, while, yet,* or *but* to "trump" one idea with another. In this example from a discussion of investigative journalism, the writer uses *though* and *while* to emphasize her main point:

> ▸ *While* most newspapers carry on a continuous series of investigations of local and often national or international issues, these investigations are limited in their scope. In particular, local journalistic investigations tend to be focused on the illegal, unethical, or personally extravagant activities of public officials or the harmful actions of private individuals or business firms acting against the public interest. *Though* there is often great value to these investigations in keeping both public officials and private interests from plundering the commonweal, they too infrequently address questions like the efficacy or wisdom of the public proposals and plans.
>
> —Phyllis Kaniss, *Making Local News*

 39d Create emphasis through careful word choice

Adding emphasis

GO
See Ch. 41, Ch. 6

You can often produce emphatic writing simply by using vivid, powerful words. Even a single carefully chosen word can have a powerful effect. Note the effect Angela Napper achieves by using the words *rages* and *take a stand* in the opening paragraph of her essay on cybercensorship:

▶ With more and more regulations being formed about what citizens are allowed to view on the Internet, concerns as to the constitutional rights of these citizens are being raised. At public libraries, at colleges and universities, and at businesses the debate *rages* as to how much privacy users should have, and whether censorship of certain materials is needed to protect the public welfare. More and more it is becoming clear that citizens need to *take a stand* to protect their right to privacy and freedom of speech . . . [italics added]

Angela could have chosen milder expressions such as *there is a debate* and *act,* but these would not have the power of *the debate rages* and *take a stand.* The more emphatic expressions draw the reader's attention and encourage him or her to take action.

Even simple adverbs can make a difference in how emphatic a statement is. Which of the following sentences seems more emphatic to you?

▶ Robert's GPA is 3.79.
▶ Robert's GPA is *just under* 3.8.
▶ Robert's GPA is *nearly* 3.8.

All three sentences say essentially the same thing, but the second and especially the third subtly imply that Robert's GPA is very high.

See 6f-2, Ch. 44

In using emphatic vocabulary, be sure to be accurate. If you use powerful words just for shock effect without regard for accuracy, you will be accused of *hyperbole* (exaggeration for effect) and will lose your credibility. To find appropriate powerful replacements for dull expressions, consult your online thesaurus and dictionary.

FOR COLLABORATION Pair off with another student and exchange compositions that you have written. Try to find at least three sentences in your partner's composition that lack emphasis. Following the guidelines in this chapter, revise these sentences.

EXERCISE 39.2 Restructure (and slightly reword, if necessary) the following sentences so that emphasis is created not by punctuation and typography but by sentence structure. The first one is done for you.

1. Gravity is the law (and it is also a good idea). Answer: Not only is gravity a good idea—it's also the law.
2. Truth can set you free, and it is the only thing that can. (Hint: "The only thing that . . .")
3. Keep moving, by all means, if you can't fly, run, walk, or crawl." (Hint: "If you can't fly, run; if you can't run, . . .")
4. It was Polish that was Joseph Conrad's first language, not English, and most people do not realize that. (Hint: "Most people do not . . .")
5. It would be a LIE if I said that I did not want to see you again. (Hint: "If I said . . .")
6. Falling out of love is simply awful, even though it's awfully simple to fall in love. (Hint: "To fall in love is awfully simple, but . . .")
7. Telling the truth becomes a revolutionary act during times of universal deceit. (Hint: "During times of . . .")
8. It was **Emily** Brontë who wrote *Wuthering Heights,* not her sister Charlotte. (Hint: "It was not Charlotte . . .")
9. The family cannot be replaced when it comes to keeping children away from drugs. Schools, religious institutions, the police—they can all help. (Hint: "When it comes to keeping . . .")
10. All truth goes through three stages: Before it is accepted as self-evident, it is violently opposed, and before that, ridiculed. (Hint: "All truth goes through three stages: First, it is ridiculed; second, it . . .") [source: http://sayings.wordpress.com/tag/sayings/]

40 Variety

FAQs

- How can I jazz up my writing style? (40a–40c)
- How much variety should I aim for in my writing? Are there some situations that call for more variety than others? (40d)

Good writers always try to make their writing interesting, not only in content but also in style. This is where variety comes in. By varying your sentence and word patterns, you change the rhythm of your writing and make it more interesting for your readers. Conversely, if you use the same words and the same types of sentences over and over, you'll bore your readers to death.

40a Vary sentence length

One of the easiest and most effective ways to alter the rhythm of your writing is to vary the length of your sentences. Readers usually process one sentence at a time. If sentences are all of similar length, the result will be a monotonous tempo that will bore readers. A mixture of long, short, and medium-length sentences is much more interesting. You do not have to change length with every sentence, but you should do so from time to time. Note how Barbara Kingsolver varies sentence length in the opening paragraph of *The Bean Trees:*

> I have been afraid of putting air in a tire ever since I saw a tractor tire blow up and throw Newt Hardbine's father over the top of the Standard Oil sign. I'm not lying. He got stuck up there. About nineteen people congregated during the time it took for Norman Strick to walk up to the Courthouse and blow the whistle for the volunteer fire department.

> They eventually did come with the ladder and haul him down, and he wasn't dead but lost his hearing and in many other ways was never the same afterward. They said he overfilled the tire.
>
> —Barbara Kingsolver, *The Bean Trees*

The six sentences in this paragraph vary in number of words as follows: 32-3-5-27-29-6. Not only is this kind of variety pleasing for variety's sake; it also allows the author to emphasize the three short sentences and spin out details in the three long sentences.

Of course, creative writers like Kingsolver are supposed to do whatever they can to make their writing interesting. But does this principle apply to the kind of ordinary, everyday writing the rest of us do? Yes, it does. Varying the length of your sentences will make your writing more interesting—more readable—no matter what kind of writing it is. Even textbooks can benefit from varied sentence length:

> ▶ The world around us contains a staggering number of living organisms with very different appearances and lifestyles. Despite the diversity of sizes and habits, all living things perform the same basic functions. They respond to changes in their immediate environment. You move your hand away from a hot stove, dogs bark at approaching strangers, fish are scared by loud noises, and tiny amoebas glide toward potential prey. Living things also show adaptability, and their internal operations and responses to stimulation can vary from moment to moment.
>
> —Frederic Martini, *Fundamentals of Anatomy and Physiology*

The sentences in this passage vary in length as follows: 17-15-8-27-19. There is not as much sentence-length variation as in the Kingsolver excerpt, but the variation here does improve readability. Notice in particular how the short third sentence makes the main point, while the long fourth sentence provides supporting details. As well as creating a pleasingly diverse tempo, varying sentence length helps the reader distinguish between main points and details.

EXERCISE 40.1 Examine a sample of your own writing. Do your sentences vary in length? (Use the WORD COUNT feature of your word processor to check.) If not, try to revise them so that they do.

40b Vary sentence structure

Creating variety

See 26c-3, 26d-2

Another way to alter the rhythm and cadence of your writing is by varying the structure of your sentences. Based on clause structure, sentences can be divided into four basic types:

> A **simple sentence** contains one independent clause and no other clauses.
>
> A **compound sentence** contains two independent clauses.
>
> A **complex sentence** contains one independent clause and one or more subordinate clauses.
>
> A **compound-complex sentence** contains two independent clauses and at least one subordinate clause.

All four sentence types are found in the following paragraph.

	One of the great paradoxes in history is that the truest
Complex	expression of Christianity is to be found not in the West but
	in the East. In India countless millions of people are living
Complex	out the ideas of Christ, though they do not call themselves
	Christians and are unfamiliar with Christian theology. They
Simple	are the poor, the meek, the merciful, and the pure in heart.
Compound	They regard life as sacred and they will not harm it in any of
Simple	its forms. They practice renunciation. They believe in non-
	violence and they worship the memory of a human being
Compound-	who perhaps has come closer to enacting Christianity than
Complex	anyone in modern history. Interestingly enough, Gandhi's
Simple	struggle was directed against a Western Christian nation.

—Norman Cousins, *Human Options*

Notice how pleasing this paragraph is to the ear. By using a variety of sentence structures, Cousins changes the tempo of the writing, avoiding monotony. Notice, too, how the changes in tempo lead to sentences of different length, ranging from three to twenty-six words. Thus, the two strategies—varying sentence length and varying sentence structure—work together.

TechALERT!

Grammar Checkers: Variety

Your grammar checker is not programmed to check for variety in sentence structure. You will have to check for this yourself.

40c Avoid excessive repetition

See Ch. 38, 39b

Repetition always draws attention. If you use it deliberately to create parallelism or emphasis, that is fine. But if you use it for no particular reason, you will only draw attention to your repetitiveness—not a good way to liven up your style! Excessive repetition can arise in a number of ways. Following are some typical sources of excessive repetition:

1. Continual use of sentences of the same length.
2. Continual use of the same sentence type.
3. Overuse of a special grammatical form (for example, passive voice, *there is,* or *it is*).
4. Continual use of the same grammatical subject.
5. Frequent use of the same kind of sentence opener (for example, a subordinate clause, transitional phrase, or adverbial phrase).
6. Frequent use of the same word.

Here is how to avoid these problems: After you have written a draft or two and are ready to edit for style, read the text aloud. Listen especially for rhythm and cadence—the tempo of the writing. Do you notice a consistent tempo from one sentence to the next, creating a sing-song rhythm? If so, revise your writing, following one or more of the Guidelines for Increasing Sentence Variety in 40c.

Let's see how revision for variety can improve the following short essay.

ORIGINAL

Out of all the experiences I've had throughout my life, I've learned the most through real-life experiences. Working with people, how a hospital system works, and the value of health are a few of the skills I've gained through volunteer work at Rosewood Hospital.

First, working with people has been one of the greatest joys I've had the opportunity to learn. For example, in the hospital there are many patients who need special attention. I am often asked to get them supplies, help them with reading, or just be there for someone to talk to. Through volunteering to help with patients, I've learned how to work easily with others.

Next, gaining knowledge about how the hospital system works is something else I've learned. Watching nurses care for patients and running errands for them to other areas of the hospital has given me this knowledge. Observing the hospital system has also helped me realize that I want to study for a health career in the future.

Finally, the principle of the value of health is the skill I hold most valuable. Taking care of sick patients has made me realize how valuable health is. For instance, ...

If you read this essay aloud, you will notice that it suffers from a monotonous rhythm, which almost lulls you to sleep. This is because the sentences are similar in length, type, and structure. Except for the second one, the sentences vary in length from only thirteen to twenty-one words. Most are complex sentences, and many start with a gerund phrase (*First, working with people; Next, gaining knowledge about*). It seems that the writer is trying overly hard to categorize the different things she has done and learned.

The following revision incorporates many changes that contribute to sentence variety.

REVISED

Of all the learning experiences I've had throughout my life, real-life ones have taught me the most. By doing volunteer work at Rosewood Hospital, for example, I've learned how to work with people, how a hospital system operates, and how important health is.

Learning how to work with people has been a particular joy. Many patients need special attention, and I am often asked to get them supplies, help them with reading, or just be there for someone to talk to. In this way, I've learned how to interact easily with others.

> Something else I've learned is how the hospital system works. By watching nurses care for patients and running errands for them to other areas of the hospital, I've learned enough about the hospital system to know that I want to begin studying for a future career in healthcare.
>
> Finally, and most importantly, taking care of sick patients has made me realize how valuable health is. For instance, ...

What changes have been made? First, deleting unnecessary verbiage has reduced the total number of words by about 17 percent (from 196 to 162). Second, sentence combining has created eight sentences from the original eleven. The result is sentences of varying length—some as short as ten words, others as long as thirty-eight. Third, the types of sentences vary more; now only half the sentences are complex. Furthermore, putting the writer (*I*) more frequently into the grammatical subject position has broken up the heavy pattern of starting sentences or clauses with a gerund phrase.

See Ch. 34, 36a

CAUTION In making stylistic changes, be careful not to violate any of the guidelines discussed in Chapters 31 through 39. For example, do not create an excessively long sentence; if you decide to move a modifier, do not misplace it.

Guidelines

See Ch. 36

Increasing Sentence Variety

- ✓ Revise for clarity and conciseness.
- ✓ If sentences sound short and choppy, try forming an occasional long sentence by combining two shorter ones.
- ✓ If sentences are so long that you have to take a deep breath after each one, create some shorter sentences by dividing a few of the long ones.
- ✓ Move some transitional expressions; they do not always have to be at the beginning of the sentence.
- ✓ Move some modifiers; they often can either precede or follow what they are modifying.
- ✓ Restructure some sentences.
- ✓ Eliminate excessive repetition of words and phrases.

EXERCISE 40.2 Test a sample of your own writing for sentence variety. Read it aloud, then revise it as necessary, following the Guidelines for Increasing Sentence Variety.

FOR COLLABORATION Exchange samples with a friend or member of your group. Offer suggestions for revision by increasing sentence variety.

40d Respect different standards and purposes

Spicing up your writing

In seeking to make your writing more varied and interesting, be sensitive to the kind of writing you are doing and to your audience. In technical and business writing, for example, stylistic variety is not valued as highly as it is in, say, literary or magazine writing. Your biology or accounting instructor will probably be less concerned about variety than will your English or history instructor. Different academic fields value different writing styles. The guidelines offered in this chapter will be especially useful in those classes where the instructor puts a premium on stylistic variety.

See Ch. 22, Ch. 16

In nonacademic situations, such as when writing emails to friends, you will probably want to use sentence variety for the same reason—to spice up your writing and make it more interesting. But in this case, you can do it in different ways—with sentence fragments, quick shifts of topic, jokes, or digressions. In this type of writing, you can punctuate your sentences any way you like—even with emoticons.

See Ch. 21

Another issue of concern is correctness, especially when you are writing in formal (Standard Edited) English. Dictionaries, grammar books, and handbooks have long included guidelines about what constitutes correct usage and what does not. In general, it is best to observe such guidelines, especially when they are based on the actual practices of our best writers. On the other hand, there are certain other "rules" that are passed along by folklore yet have no linguistic or communicative logic to them, such as "Never split an infinitive," "Do not end a sentence with a preposition," and "Do not use *hopefully* to mean *I hope*." Expert writers routinely disregard such "rules," and so should you.

See 34d-2

part

9

Effective Words

41 Choosing the Right Words

FAQs

- How can I improve my choice of words?
- Is there anything I can do to make my writing more colorful? Should I try using figures of speech? (41f-1, 41f-2)
- What are "clichés"? What is wrong with using them? (41f-3)

Since meaning is conveyed through words, a writer's choice of words, or **diction**, is crucial. Choose your words carefully, and you will make your writing clearer and more interesting; choose your words carelessly, and you may leave your readers frustrated.

Commonly confused words

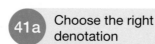

41a Choose the right denotation

The **denotation** of a word is its basic dictionary meaning. Your first obligation in choosing words is to select ones that accurately denote what you are trying to convey. For example, the word *growl* denotes a low-pitched menacing sound; the word *shriek* denotes a high-pitched frantic cry. If you are writing about the sound a monkey makes when fleeing from a predator, you should use *shriek*, not *growl*.

By choosing among the various words denoting an event, activity, idea, or object, you can make your focus general or specific, abstract or concrete.

1 General statements versus specific details

All good writing involves a mixture of general statements and specific details. General statements establish main points, while specific details make these points precise, vivid, and memorable. Good writers thus continually make choices among words whose denotations range from general to specific. For example, consider this sentence:

> Immediately after the accident, Julie *went* to the nearest house.

The phrase "went to the nearest house" serves as a general description of what Julie did after the accident. But consider these alternatives:

> Immediately after the accident, Julie *ran* to the nearest house.
>
> Immediately after the accident, Julie *walked* to the nearest house.
>
> Immediately after the accident, Julie *crawled* to the nearest house.

The specificity of each of these alternative versions adds vividness to the description and tells us something about the seriousness of the accident and about Julie's state of mind.

Always look for ways to add specific details to your generalizations. As you do, take care to choose the words that most accurately depict those details.

EXERCISE 41.1 Rearrange the words in each of the following sets in order of increasing specificity. The first one has been done for you.

1. vegetation, tree, small tree, small fir tree, small subalpine fir tree
2. pollution, smog, air pollution, dense urban smog, urban smog
3. decoration, plants, ferns, potted plants, interior decoration
4. log cabin, dwelling, old log cabin, building, cabin
5. animal, cow, organism, grazing animal, Guernsey cow
6. wood, building material, hardwood, oak, material
7. casserole, food, shrimp creole, main dish, rice casserole
8. sport, tennis, recreational activity, racquet sport, mixed-doubles tennis
9. garment, men's suit, clothing, tuxedo, suit
10. ceremony, baptism, religious ceremony, baptism by immersion, ritual

❷ Abstract versus concrete nouns

Abstract nouns, such as *power, romance*, and *democracy*, have broad, often vague denotations; they refer to concepts rather than to tangible objects. **Concrete nouns** refer to things that are available to the senses—things that we can see, touch, hear, smell, or taste. For example, *raccoon, Statue of Liberty*, and *radishes* all bring to mind tangible, concrete objects. As with general statements and specific details, you should aim for a mixture of the abstract and the concrete. Abstractions state ideas, while concrete expressions make those ideas more vivid and real.

In the following example, Norman Cousins defines and describes an abstract concept (despair) by means of a series of vivid concrete images: *calling out to one another, frozen faces, clouds racing across the sky.* He even talks about the "breaking up" of words!

> ▶ Human despair or default can reach a point where even the most stirring visions lose their regenerating and radiating powers. It will be reached only when human beings are no longer capable of calling out to one another, when words in their poetry break up before their eyes, when their faces become frozen toward their young, and when they fail to make pictures out of clouds racing across the sky.
>
> —Norman Cousins, *Human Options*

❸ Commonly confused word pairs

Certain words are commonly confused with certain other words. For example, *imply* is often misused for *infer*, and vice versa. *Imply* means "suggest without stating outright," while *infer* means "derive a conclusion from what is not explicitly stated." *Imply* is something that writers and speakers do; *infer* is something that readers and listeners do:

▶ When he spoke to the employees, Mr. Adams ~~inferred~~ *implied* that they would get a raise.

▶ Some employees ~~implied~~ *inferred* from his comments that it would be a big raise.

TechALERT!

See 45b

Grammar Checkers: Commonly Confused Words

Grammar checkers flag only those words that are in their list of "commonly confused words"—typically a restricted list. For example, *Microsoft Word 2000* has eighty-six entries in its list, most of which are confused only in spelling, not pronunciation, such as *yolk/yoke, urn/earn,* and *no/know*. It does not include any of the words mentioned above, which are often confused in both spelling *and* pronunciation. Thus, do not rely on your grammar checker to identify commonly confused words for you. You'll have to distinguish such words yourself.

In other words, *imply* and *infer* have different denotations, and as a careful user of English you should observe this difference.

Other word pairs that are often confused include *install/instill, emigrate/immigrate, adapt/adopt, specially/especially, respectfully/respectively, raise/rise, lay/lie,* and *sit/set.* If you are uncertain about any of these, consult the Usage Glossary at the end of this book.

41b Choose the right connotation

WEBLINK

Denotation, connotation, and clichés

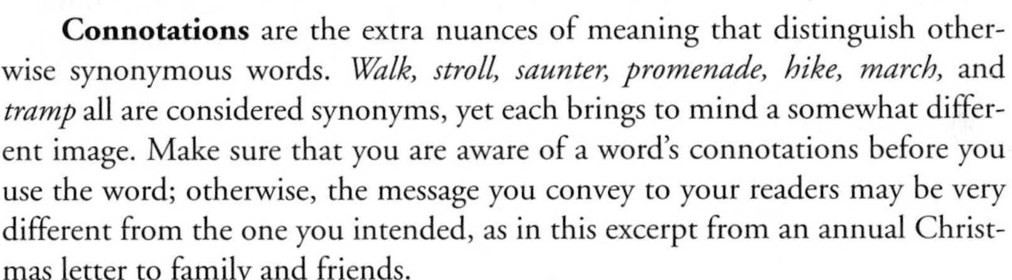

Connotations are the extra nuances of meaning that distinguish otherwise synonymous words. *Walk, stroll, saunter, promenade, hike, march,* and *tramp* all are considered synonyms, yet each brings to mind a somewhat different image. Make sure that you are aware of a word's connotations before you use the word; otherwise, the message you convey to your readers may be very different from the one you intended, as in this excerpt from an annual Christmas letter to family and friends.

MISLEADING It was another interesting year on the social scene. People say we have the most *contrived* parties in town.

The writer meant to say that their parties reflect ingenuity and cleverness. But *contrived* connotes an artificiality that the author did not mean to convey.

EXERCISE 41.2 The synonyms in each of the following sets can be used to describe people. But some of the terms have more favorable connotations than others. Rearrange each set to order the terms from most favorable to least favorable. If you are unsure of the synonyms' connotations, choose the most common term in the group and look it up in a dictionary. You may find usage notes there to help you.

1. apt, intelligent, clever, bright, smart, shrewd
2. gaunt, skinny, slender, thin, slim, lanky
3. aggressive, domineering, dynamic, assertive, pushy, forceful
4. funny, silly, humorous, comical, amusing, ridiculous
5. poor, insolvent, destitute, broke, penniless, indigent
6. clique, circle, clan, faction, gang
7. solitary, independent, self-reliant, separate, autonomous

8. immature, childlike, innocent, green, callow
9. animalistic, bestial, wild, untamed, unbroken
10. unkempt, sloppy, disheveled, messy, untidy

41c Find the right level of formality

Sometime in the course of growing up, children learn that they should speak more formally, or "correctly," to adults than to their peers. In other words, they learn to shift **registers**, or levels of formality. People continue to adjust registers naturally, if imperfectly, throughout their lives, in part through their selection of words. Words vary in their level of formality, from very formal to colloquial. Always listen to what you are writing, to make sure that you consistently use words in the appropriate register.

1 Formal, academic vocabulary

Virtually all writing you do for school and college assignments (except for special cases such as creative writing or personal narratives) should be in a fairly formal register, as is this handbook. Formal, academic vocabulary consists largely of words derived from Latin and Greek—words like *inevitable, hypothesis, perception, theory,* and *superfluous*—which is why you are tested on such words when you take the SAT or ACT exam. A fairly formal register excludes colloquialisms (such as *uptight* and *get movin'*); an even more formal register excludes contractions (such as *can't, they'll,* and *you're*).

See Ch. 43

Try to learn as many Greco-Latinate words as you can. And once you have learned them well, feel free to use them wherever they seem appropriate. *Appropriate* is the key word here; simply using as many "big words" as possible will not impress anyone. If you overdo it, you will likely misuse some of the words; in any case, your writing will sound stuffy and pretentious.

2 Informal vocabulary

Informal words are those you might use in ordinary, everyday contexts such as talking or texting with friends. The informal register consists mainly of words derived from the Germanic roots of English—words such as *keep, laugh, throw, sleep,* and *ground.* Such words tend to be shorter than their Latinate equivalents, but they are often used with prepositions to form longer **idiomatic**

expressions. For example, the formal Latinate words *inspect* and *examine* have as their equivalent the informal idiomatic phrase *take a close look at.* The informal register also contains many **contractions**, such as *can't, she's*, and *they'll.*

ESL NOTE The difficulties of idiomatic phrases for non–English speakers are discussed in Chapter 59.

See 59c

Although informal vocabulary is sometimes acceptable in formal writing, you should generally try to use the more formal equivalents where possible.

Informal	*Formal*	*Informal*	*Formal*
friendly	amicable	do again	repeat
worn out	exhausted	go faster	accelerate
hard-working	industrious	take apart	dismantle
funny	amusing	get hold of	seize

EXERCISE 41.3 Give a formal equivalent for each of the following informal terms.

1. cheap
2. put up with
3. take into account
4. under the weather
5. a lot of clapping
6. kind of like
7. put down
8. get something straight
9. take grief from
10. a bunch of

TechALERT!

Grammar Checkers: Colloquialisms

Your grammar checker will probably identify some common colloquialisms, such as *real, totally, kind of*, and *plenty*, but it will generally not draw your attention to informal expressions such as those listed above. You will need to monitor your own word usage.

EXERCISE 41.4 Translate each of the following sentences into a more formal register.

1. If you turn up any glitches in the program, let me know.
2. Ahab was so hung up on tracking down the white whale, he went out of his mind.
3. When the savings and loans started going belly up in the 1980s, many small investors found themselves up a creek without a paddle.
4. Right now, good jobs are hard to come by.
5. Too often the blame for all the ills of welfare is put on the backs of social workers.
6. The guy next door got taken by a con artist selling vinyl siding.
7. My kid brother fixes cars at the garage downtown.
8. The food at the new restaurant is cheap but good.
9. Customers shouldn't have to put up with crappy service.
10. Government waste makes me sick.

41d Avoid jargon, slang, and dialect

There are many versions of English, only one of which—Standard Edited English—is represented in this book. Standard Edited English is the version most widely used in academic and professional contexts and most widely understood around the world. Other versions, including jargon, slang, and dialect, are valuable in their own right. However, they are less widely understood, and thus you should refrain from using them except with audiences composed of "insiders" or members of special interest groups.

Jargon is any technical language used by professionals, sports enthusiasts, hobbyists, or other special interest groups. By naming objects and concepts that are unique to a group's special interests, jargon facilitates communication among members of the group. (Imagine computer engineers trying to get by without terms like *buffer, cache, serial port, CPU,* and *configuration.*) But it has the opposite effect when used with outsiders. Unless you are addressing an audience of fellow insiders, avoid using jargon.

Used by teenagers and other subcultures, **slang** is a deliberately colorful form of speech whose appeal depends on novelty and freshness. For this reason, slang terms tend to be short-lived, quickly giving way to newer, fresher

TechALERT!

Electronic Language: Abbreviations

Abbreviations like UR ("you're"), OMG ("oh my god"), and LOL ("laugh out loud") are appropriate for texting, social network posts, and other forms of casual communication with friends. They are *not* appropriate, however, in formal writing or in written correspondence with your instructor.

replacements. At the time this book was written, student slang included terms such as *sick, diss, phat, chill,* and *stoked,* and hacker slang included *barfulous, fritterware, geekasm, frob,* and *cruft* (all of which are now probably outdated). Like jargon, slang is understood and appreciated only by insiders. If you are trying to reach a broad audience, avoid using it.

A **dialect** is the type of speech used by a specific social, ethnic, or regional group. Dialects typically have a distinctive accent, many unique words and expressions, and even some grammatical patterns that differ from those of Standard Edited English. For example, in some dialects you might hear a sentence like "She be working hard" or "They might could of done it." While perfectly logical and correct within the dialect, such sentences are likely to confuse outsiders—that is, people who do not speak that dialect. Thus, if you are addressing a broad audience, avoid using dialect in your writing.

EXERCISE 41.5 Log on to a chat room, newsgroup, or other Internet site where slang, jargon, or dialect is being used. Print out several sentences, and translate them into Standard Edited English.

FOR COLLABORATION Share both the initial sentences and your "translated" versions with your group.

41e Avoid pretentiousness

College students are continually exposed to the discourse of academics—professors, scholars, textbook writers—who have spent most of their adult lives developing a large vocabulary and an embellished style of writing. If you find yourself tempted to imitate this style of discourse, do so with great caution. You are at risk of sounding pretentious.

PRETENTIOUS By virtue of their immersion in a heterogeneity of subcultures, the majority of individuals have internalized an extensive repository of collective aphorisms about a multitude of quotidian concerns.

The following rewritten version says essentially the same thing but in clearer, simpler language:

BETTER Because of their participation in a variety of subcultures, most people know a large number of common sayings about many everyday issues.

Pretentiousness has two common causes:

1. *Using literary language in nonliterary writing.* When you are reading a great work of literature such as *Moby Dick*, you may become enthralled with words such as *doleful, naught,* and *convivial.* But such words have very restricted conditions of usage; indeed, that is one reason why poets and other creative writers like to use them. Unless you know exactly how these words should be used, do not use them—you will only sound foolish.

2. *Using big words just because they are big.* Academic vocabulary has many long, Latinate words such as *recalcitrant, egalitarian,* and *indissoluble.* Be sure you know exactly what these words mean and how to use them, however, or you will likely misuse them.

EXERCISE 41.6 Common sayings and proverbs usually use simple words so that children can easily learn them. Notice how silly they sound when reworded below with pretentious vocabulary. Restore these sentences to their normal form.

1. In locales displaying visible fumes, one can expect to find combustion.
2. A dyad of uppermost anatomical extremities outperforms a single such entity.
3. Genetically similar members of the avian realm manifest a pronounced desire to congregate.
4. The greater the number of alterations in whatever is perceived to have a separate existence, the greater the amount of equivalency in those entities.

5. The fruit of any of the various trees of the genus *Quercus*, after moving under the influence of gravity, does not come to rest at any considerable distance from the parent plant.
6. Irrespective of the direction in which one moves, one finds oneself in that particular place.
7. Your harsh, abrupt canine utterance is directed upward at the incorrect tall, woody plant.
8. A single complete movement of a threaded needle when accomplished within a certain amount of passing time prevents nine such movements.
9. Human beings who inhabit dwellings fashioned from brittle transparent material ought not to hurl projectiles consisting of mineral matter.
10. It is futile to make inarticulate sobbing sounds after whitish liquid falls out of its container.

41f Use figurative language thoughtfully

Figurative language uses words in nonliteral, creative ways to enhance the reader's understanding. Such nonliteral uses of words are called **figures of speech**. Two of the most common figures of speech are simile and metaphor, both of which attempt to explain the unfamiliar by comparing it to the familiar.

1 Similes

A **simile** is the explicit use of one thing (called the *vehicle*) to describe another (the *tenor*). In the following example, scientist Carl Sagan uses similes to explain how the two hemispheres of the brain work:

> ▶ The left hemisphere processes information sequentially; the right hemisphere simultaneously, accessing several inputs at once. The left hemisphere works in series; the right in parallel. *The left hemisphere is something like a digital computer; the right like an analog computer.*
>
> —Carl Sagan, *The Dragons of Eden*

Assuming that readers are more familiar with computer technology than with neuroscience, Sagan uses the former to explain the latter.

When crafting a simile, be sure that it does not undermine or belittle your point:

INEPT She had a deep, throaty, genuine laugh, like the sound a dog makes just before it throws up.

See 41b

Unless you mean to ridicule the woman's laugh, comparing it to the sound of a sick dog evokes the wrong imagery.

Similes are created in the space of a single sentence, normally using the word *like* or *as* to make a simple, straightforward comparison. When a simile extends beyond one sentence, it is called an **analogy**.

❷ Metaphors

A **metaphor** is an implicit simile. It draws the reader's attention to a surprising similarity between otherwise dissimilar things, but it does so without using *like, as*, or other explicit markers. Metaphors are much more common than similes. In fact, some scholars claim that most of our everyday language is metaphorical in nature. When you say "Her ideas *cast some light* on the subject" or "I *fell* into a deep depression," you are speaking metaphorically. Feel free to use metaphors in your writing, as Gretel Ehrlich does in this passage describing springtime in the Wyoming plains:

> ▸ Spring weather is capricious and mean. It snows, then blisters with heat. There have been tornadoes. They lay their elephant trunks out in the sage until they find houses, then slurp everything up and leave. I've noticed that melting snowbanks hiss and rot, viperous, then drip into calm pools where ducklings hatch and livestock, being trailed to summer range, drink. With the ice cover gone, rivers churn a milkshake brown, taking culverts and small bridges with them.
>
> —Gretel Ehrlich, *The Solace of Open Spaces*

Ehrlich's use of metaphor gives us a vivid picture of Wyoming spring weather. She describes tornadoes in terms of elephants, melting snowbanks in terms of snakes (*viperous*), and rivers in terms of milkshakes. In using words such as *capricious* and *mean*, she gives the weather a distinct human personality. This is an example of the use of **personification**, in which inanimate objects or abstractions are described as having human traits.

You can use different metaphors in a single piece of writing, as Ehrlich does, so long as they don't conflict. Otherwise, you will have what is called a **mixed metaphor**.

MIXED METAPHOR His thoughts tumbled in his head, making and breaking alliances like underpants in a dryer without fabric softener.

This sentence describes thoughts in two incompatible metaphorical ways: as things that can make alliances and as underpants that stick together in the dryer.

Choosing Words

Relying excessively on abstract, general words or on specific, concrete words

- ▶ If you have a ~~conduit that is emitting aqueous fluid,~~ *leaky pipe,* ~~solicit the aid of a plumbing repair specialist.~~ *call a plumber.*

Using words that have an unwanted connotation

- ▶ *The Diary of Anne Frank* is a ~~tear-jerking~~ *heartbreaking* story.
  [*Tear-jerking* demeans the seriousness of this tragic tale.]

Using informal words in formal writing

- ▶ Plato was 28 years old when his teacher, Socrates, ~~kicked the bucket.~~ *died.*

Using similes that do not support the point you are trying to make

- ▶ He was deeply in love. When she spoke, he thought he heard bells, as if she were a garbage truck backing up.

Using clichés

- ▶ Without a good education, it's very difficult to ~~climb the ladder of success.~~ *have a successful career.*

3300 clichés

③ Clichés

When they are fresh, metaphors add sparkle to writing. But over time, if they are used heavily, they become worn out and lose their charm. An overused metaphor is called a **cliché**. Clichés are especially common in political discourse, because when a catchy phrase scores well with the public, politicians like to use it over and over. In a 1996 television appearance, presidential candidate Ross Perot used the term "a giant sucking sound" to describe the thousands of American jobs being transferred to Mexico via the North American Free Trade Agreement. It went over so well with the viewing audience that other politicians and media figures began using it. Soon, however, it had lost its freshness and was just another hackneyed expression.

See 41c-2, 59c

How do clichés differ from ordinary idiomatic expressions such as *take a close look at, taken for a ride*, and *learn the nuts and bolts* (of something), which are also used frequently? Clichés are simply more noticeable, either because they evoke extremely vivid images (*white as a ghost, climbing the ladder of success*) or because they are repeated so frequently in ads or elsewhere (*It's the real thing, Get over it*). They draw attention, which makes them more effective at first but also causes them to wear out quickly.

Clichés are generally less irritating in conversation than they are in writing because, like idiomatic expressions, they help speakers cope with the moment-to-moment pressure of putting ideas into words. When you have time to *plan* your thoughts—as you do when writing—you should make an effort to be original or at least use fewer hackneyed expressions.

Advertisers and headline writers sometimes use clichés and other idiomatic expressions in creative ways. For example, an ad for a dual-processor computer was headlined "Two brains are better than one," a catchy twist on the cliché "Two heads are better than one." Such playfulness is less common in academic writing.

TechALERT!

Grammar Checkers: Clichés

Most grammar checkers are programmed to identify certain clichés and overused expressions. But this means that they do *not* identify *other* clichés and overused expressions. Thus, you'll have to be vigilant yourself and try to develop an ear for detecting such expressions.

EXERCISE 41.7 Think of five clichés and write them down. Where have you heard them? What does this tell you about your customary sources of information? Just for fun, imagine that you are a subversive graffiti artist. How would you alter these clichés to make them interesting or truthful? (For example, instead of the advertising slogan "Come to where the flavor is," you might write "Come to where the *cancer* is.")

EXERCISE 41.8 Revise the following sentences (from *The Word Wild Web* <http://therussler.tripod.com>) to get rid of the clichés and mixed metaphors:

1. She's been burning the midnight oil on both ends.
2. He's really low dog on the totem pole.
3. I could beat him with my eyes tied behind my back.
4. It looks like the cows have come home to roost.
5. It's as American as killing two birds with one apple pie.
6. Now that the ball is in our court, let's go for the touchdown.
7. Sometimes I feel like I'm swimming uphill against the grain.
8. Take time to stop and smell the tunnel at the end of the rainbow.
9. The ship of state has a difficult road ahead.
10. You can lead a gift horse to water but you can't look him in the mouth.

42 Language and Power

FAQs

- Is there just one correct form of English? (42a)
- What is *bias*, and how is it expressed? (42b)
- What is sexist about a sentence such as "Everyone should pay attention to his spelling"? (42c-2)
- How can I avoid stereotyping? (42c-3, 42f)

Language is arguably the single most powerful tool we humans have. It is what sets us apart from all other species. It helps us think through problems. It allows us to explore and understand highly nuanced, abstract ideas. It lets us record complex information for future use. And every day, it routinely lets us communicate with other people near and far.

For all these things to happen, our use of language must satisfy two conditions. First, it must *conform to certain conventions or norms.* If you're stopped at an intersection and your friend says, "The light's green," you make sense of her utterance by knowing that "light" probably refers to the traffic light, that "green" refers to its color, that "*'s*" is a contraction of "is," and that the utterance as a whole constitutes a statement about the color of the traffic signal. These understandings are all based on conventions of word meaning and word order in English. Indeed, knowing English means knowing such *conventions of language.* Furthermore, you need to know certain *conventions of culture,* in this case the fact that a green traffic light in the United States authorizes drivers to proceed ahead. Finally, you need to know certain *conventions of situated meaning,* whereby in a case such as this you interpret your friend's remark not simply as a description of the traffic signal but as a suggestion to drive ahead.

Second, our use of language must be *flexible and creative* enough to accommodate changing circumstances and communicative needs. Each situation we encounter is different, with its own demands. Sometimes, the best way to deal with such situations is to be creative and "bend the rules" of language. This kind of creative adaptation is commonplace in society. When new technologies, ideas, events, and so on occur, we often invent new names for them: *spyware, blog, Weaponsgate.* If we move to a new geographic area, we may have to adapt our language to regional differences: a *cooler* in one part of the country might be called an *ice chest* in another. Even in the course of a day, as we move from one context to another, we may alter our use of language in subtle, unconscious ways. "The light's green," for example, could have a different meaning in a different context. If your friend knows you have a romantic interest in a new acquaintance, and she discovers he's unattached, she might say "The light's green" to give you encouragement.

These two qualities—conventionality and flexibility—are in opposition to each other, creating a productive tension. We need to observe conventional norms so as to communicate with each other—this is a basic requirement. But by "bending the rules" at times, we can also adapt to new situations and needs. Furthermore, by being flexible we can inject creativity and playfulness into our interactions with other people, adding spice to these interactions and enhancing our social identities.

42a "Correctness"

Many students begin a writing course thinking that there is only one "correct" type of English, that all others are "incorrect." It's true that in US colleges and universities, Standard Edited English is considered the norm. Standard Edited English is the English used not only in academia but in virtually every profession and occupation that requires higher education. It is used by broadcasters and newspapers across the nation, giving it widespread influence and prestige in our media-saturated society. Therefore, to help prepare you both for college writing assignments and for your future career, your writing instructor will no doubt insist that you adhere to Standard Edited English. In other words, you should use Standard Edited English in the context of a college-level composition class, and the guidelines laid down in Parts 6–12 of this book are designed accordingly.

See 41d

Bear in mind, though, that correctness of language use is always relative to a context and purpose. In an informal setting, such as chatting with other students or texting a friend, you may prefer to use an informal style sprinkled with slang or accentuated with dialect. In the workplace or on the playing field, you may find it most comfortable to use lots of technical or sports jargon. In situations such as these, you are interacting with a small group of "insiders" who share a common purpose or background. Using slang, jargon, or dialect may be more appropriate than using Standard Edited English in these contexts because it enables you to convey ideas more efficiently and it reinforces the cultural bond you have with your audience. Indeed, the power of language is maximized to the extent that you have *mastery* of different styles (or norms) and can *shift* from one style to another as the situation requires.

42b Language and identity

See 3b-2

Language not only conveys information about some topic but also information about you and your audience. That is, your use of language in a particular situation reveals much about your social identity, or *persona*, how you view the world, and how you perceive the relationship between you and the person(s) you are speaking or writing to. If you want to promote personal rapport between you and your audience, one way to do so is by adopting a style of language that you and your audience are comfortable with, a style that indicates shared experiences and shared beliefs.

The power of language can also be used negatively, however. One of the main ways in which language can cause harm is through **bias**, the one-sided (usually negative) characterization of an entire group. Bias can be either direct ("All Catholics are ______________") or indirect ("Jody's a southerner, so she tends to ______________"). It can arise from a single discriminatory term, an ill-conceived sentence, or a poorly chosen example or illustration. Bias is so endemic to all human societies that people often are not even conscious of it. That, however, does not make it acceptable. Writers should try at all times to avoid bias in their writing, in ways that the following sections suggest.

Gender bias

42c Avoid biased gender references

In the past, men and women had distinctly different roles in society. The tasks performed primarily by men were considered high-status jobs. The work done mostly by women was considered of lower status. Language developed accordingly. The head of a committee was called a chair*man*, the work done collectively by the labor force was known as *man*power, and humanity itself was referred to as *man*kind or just *man.* A doctor was presumed to be male; in the relatively few cases where a woman happened to be a doctor, she was referred to as a *woman doctor.* A nurse, on the other hand, was presumed to be female; gender was indicated only in those relatively few cases involving a *male nurse.* And the default pronoun for secretaries, elementary school teachers, or flight attendants was *she.*

Today, women are pursuing career paths long dominated by men, participating in what were once considered male sports, and challenging the myth of male superiority in other ways. Also, men are following career paths once thought to be for women only. To acknowledge and encourage this trend, we all need to rethink our use of gender references. Since language is our primary means of communicating, we need to be more conscious of how we use it.

1 Gender-specific nouns

Many nouns in the English language implicitly discriminate against women because they emphasize one gender over another. If you use a word like *chairmen* to refer to a group of men and women, you are discriminating against the women in the group; a better choice would be *chairpersons* or just *chairs.* Likewise, female-marked terms such as *poetess* and *hostess* unnecessarily highlight the gender of the person involved; unless you think the person prefers such a term, use *poet* and *host* instead. In general, do not use gender-marked terms in situations where a person's gender should not be of any relevance. Fortunately, it is relatively easy to find nonsexist equivalents for such words. Your grammar checker should be helpful.

Sexist	*Gender-neutral*
businessmen	businesspersons
chairmen	chairs, chairpersons

congressmen	representatives
foremen	supervisors
mankind	humanity, humankind
manpower	personnel, staff
policemen	police officers
salesmen	salesclerks, salespersons
stewardesses	flight attendants
workmen	workers

❷ Generic pronouns

Pronouns are more of a challenge, because the English language lacks a gender-neutral pronoun in the third-person singular. Traditionally, *he, him,* and *his* were used as **generic pronouns** to refer to all members of a group, regardless of sex. A sentence such as "Everyone should pay attention to his spelling" would (in theory) apply to both males and females. But studies have shown that when people are asked to visualize the meaning of such a sentence, they usually think of a male. Thus, the so-called generic pronoun is actually discriminatory in its psychological effects.

There is no simple way around this problem. The Guidelines for How to Avoid the Generic Pronoun Problem list four techniques, all of which are employed by expert writers.

❸ Stereotyping in examples

Stereotyping can arise unwittingly through the careless use of examples and illustrations. If you use examples that consistently portray women as homemakers and men as breadwinners, you will be reinforcing a longstanding stereotype. Try to vary the roles of men and women in your examples, thereby broadening the spectrum of possibilities for both sexes.

TechALERT!

Grammar Checkers: Generic Pronouns

Most grammar checkers will flag gender-specific nouns such as those listed above. However, they will not flag generic pronouns. Thus, you will have to deal with this problem yourself.

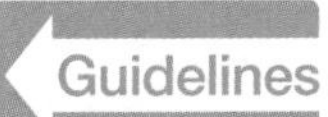

Avoiding the Generic Pronoun Problem

1. *Pluralize the antecedent and use* they/their: "All writers should pay attention to their spelling."
2. *Restructure the entire sentence to get rid of the pronoun:* "Spelling deserves careful attention." This often works, but it lacks the vividness of the personal pronoun.
3. *Keep the singular antecedent and use* he or she (*or* his or her, *or* him or her): "Everyone should pay attention to his or her spelling." This is a cumbersome solution and should be used sparingly.
4. *Use the passive voice to get rid of an antecedent subject:* "Spelling should be paid close attention to." This solution produces an indirect statement that is less forceful than an active-voice statement; it too should be used sparingly.

42d Avoid biased language about race and ethnicity

Just as offensive as gender stereotyping is language that either intentionally or unintentionally discriminates against people because of their race or ethnicity. Obviously this type of language includes slurs, which are clearly a form of deliberate verbal aggression. But it also includes the sort of disparaging stereotyping evident in ethnic jokes and in statements like "__________ would do better if they just worked harder."

Terms such as *inner-city residents* and *illegal immigrants* also can be discriminatory if they are consistently linked to a specific ethnic or racial group. Although such terms do have legitimate uses, they are often used as indirect labels, or "code words," to refer only to certain kinds of inner-city residents or illegal immigrants. Do not let yourself be drawn into this kind of stereotyping.

Like sexism, ethnic and racial stereotypes can be reinforced by poorly chosen examples and illustrations. If you are writing about welfare recipients, for instance, and you use a single, teenaged African American mother as your main example, you will be perpetuating a longstanding, discriminatory myth. (Most welfare recipients in the United States are, in fact, white.)

Understandably, people are sensitive about the names used to describe their ethnic or racial identity because of the connotations that invariably attach to them. Since ethnic and racial labels often change over time, the issue can be confusing: should you use *American Indian* or *Native American? Hispanic* or *Latino? African American* or *black?* The best rule of thumb is to call people by whatever term they prefer, just as you should pronounce their personal name however they want it pronounced. If you are unsure of what name to use to describe a certain group of people, just ask members of that group.

42e Avoid biased language about age

In our youth-oriented culture, it is not uncommon to hear demeaning references to age. Indeed, the adjective *old* often is used as a way of denigrating others, as in "When the first President Bush lost reelection, people said that was the end of the line for old George." (This is the same man who, five years later, took up skydiving!) Some of the changes people undergo as they age are undesirable, but others are for the better. Avoid focusing on the negative aspects of aging and assuming that anyone beyond a certain age is unworthy of respect. Do not use expressions like *old fogey, one foot in the grave*, and *over the hill*, and avoid age-related stereotypes in examples and jokes.

42f Avoid biased language about other differences

Occupational, religious, political, regional, socioeconomic, sexual-orientation, and disability-related groups are among the many other groupings in our society that are subject to stereotyping. As with ethnic groups, it is generally best to refer to such groups in ways that they themselves prefer. For example, most people with physical disabilities prefer to be called *physically disabled* rather than *handicapped,* and most people who clean buildings prefer the title of *custodian* rather than that of *janitor.* Political *conservatives* usually do not like being called *right-wingers,* nor do *Pentecostals* appreciate the label *holy rollers.* Sometimes people invent new labels just to exalt themselves, as in the case of one airline's flight attendants who decided to call themselves *personal service managers.* Most of the time, however, relabeling is driven by a desire to cast off undesirable connotations. This is a legitimate desire, worthy of respect.

EXERCISE 42.1 Remove the biased language from the following sentences, and replace it with more acceptable terminology.

1. The newly revised cookbook would be a welcome addition to any woman's library.
2. Orientals are good at math.
3. A professional nurse has a responsibility to keep up with developments in her field.
4. The old man must be pretty senile to believe that!
5. The church held a food drive to make sure that no little black children went hungry.
6. We await the day when man discovers a cure for the common cold.
7. Old people are not able to look after themselves.
8. The physical education teacher told the two boys not to speak Puerto Rican in her class.
9. We must pay attention to the needs of the deaf and dumb.
10. The shrewd Jewish businessman made a handsome profit.

EXERCISE 42.2 Revise the following passage to make it bias-free.

The clear superiority of the Anglo-American culture placed great pressure on the wretched immigrants to blend into this better way of life. Poor immigrant urchins learned more quickly than the old people to drop their backward ways and language for the more progressive customs of English-speaking Americans. In fact, just a few short years after their forefathers had arrived poverty-stricken, illiterate, and disease-ridden from the slums of Europe, the grandsons of immigrants had embraced a new American identity and way of life.

FOR COLLABORATION Share your revised versions of the passage with your group.

43 Building a Powerful Vocabulary

FAQs

- How can I best improve my vocabulary?
- Word definitions are always referring to meanings from ancient languages like Latin and Greek. Why should I pay attention to those meanings? (43a)

The best way to learn the sort of vocabulary needed for academic and professional writing is through reading. Reading exposes you to a greater variety of words than does television, radio, conversation, or any other form of communication. As you come across new words in your reading, you can accelerate your learning of them by employing some basic strategies.

Learn roots, prefixes, and suffixes

Sometimes when you encounter an unfamiliar word, you can make an educated guess at its meaning by looking closely at its parts—its root and whatever prefixes or suffixes it may have. The **root** (or **stem**) of a word is its core, the part to which prefixes and suffixes are attached. A **prefix** is a word part that precedes the root; a **suffix** is one that follows it. Thus, in the word *renewal, -new-* is the root, *re-* is the prefix, and *-al* is the suffix. By recognizing that *re-* sometimes means "again," *-new-* means "new," and *-al* marks a noun form, you can guess that *renewal* is a noun meaning something like "making new again."

This kind of educated guesswork can be very productive in enlarging your vocabulary, especially that needed for academic and professional writing. Most of the specialized terms found in academic and professional discourse were created from Latin and Greek roots, prefixes, and suffixes. *Introvert, counter intuitive, antibiotic*, and *hypothesis* are typical of words formed from Latin and Greek parts. By recognizing the parts and then noting the context in which a word is found, you can narrow down the possible meanings. With multiple exposures to a word—and perhaps some help from a dictionary—you can gradually learn the exact meaning of the word and how it should be used.

Some Common Roots

Build a better vocabulary

Root	*Meaning*	*Examples of words*
-audi- (L)	to hear	audible, audience, auditorium
-bene- (L)	good, well	benefit, benevolent, benefactor
-bio- (G)	life	biology, biography, biosphere
-chrono- (G)	time	chronological, chronometer, synchronic
-cogni- (L)	know	cognition, recognize, incognito
-dict- (L)	say, speak	diction, dictaphone, predictable
-duc- (L)	lead, make	ductile, production, reduce
-fac- (L)	make, do	factory, facsimile, manufacture
-gen- (L)	kind, class	gene, generalization, genesis
-graph- (G)	write	graphic, photography, geography
-jur-, -jus- (L)	law	jury, perjure, justice
-log- (G)	reason, speech	logic, sociology, dialog
-luc- (L)	light	lucid, elucidate, translucent
-manu- (L)	hand	manuscript, manual, manufacture
-mis-, -mit- (L)	send	mission, transmit, emit
-path- (G)	feel, suffer	pathetic, pathology, sympathy
-phon- (G)	voice, sound	phonetics, phonograph, telephone
-port- (L)	carry	port, portable, transport
-prim- (L)	first	prime, primary, primitive
-scient- (L)	know	scientific, science, omniscient
-scrib-, -script- (L)	write	scribble, prescribe, description
-sens-, -sent- (L)	feel	sense, sensation, sentiment
-spect- (L)	see	spectacle, inspect, circumspect
-terr- (L)	earth	terrain, territory, inter
-therm- (G)	heat	thermal, thermometer, thermodynamics

(continued)

Root	Meaning	Examples of words
-vert- (L)	turn	convert, diversion, versatile
-vid-, -vis- (L)	see	video, visible, envision
-voca- (L)	call	vocal, vocation, provoke

Some Common Prefixes

Prefix	Meaning	Examples of words
anti-	against, opposite	antibiotic, anticommunist, antithesis
co-, con-	together, with	cooperate, collaborate, conspire
dis-	opposite, apart	disagree, disable, disappear
e-, ex-	out of	emit, evoke, export
hyper-	excessive(ly)	hypercorrect, hypersensitive, hyperbole
il-, im-, in-	not	illegal, immoral, inactive
im-, in-	in	immigrate, inaugurate, invade
inter-	between	intermission, intercept, international
intra-	within	intramural, intravenous, intracellular
intro-	inside	introduce, introverted, introspection
mono-	one	monologue, mononucleosis, monotony
neo-	new	neo-Nazi, neocolonialism, neoconservative
omni-	all	omnipresent, omniscient, omnivorous
out-	to surpass	outshine, outperform, outclass
over-	excessive	overworked, overexcited, overenthusiastic
re-	again	redesign, renew, reload
syn-	same	synonym, synchronize, syndrome
trans-	across	transmit, translate, transcontinental
uni-	one	uniform, unicycle, unisex

Some Common Suffixes

Suffix used to create a noun	***Meaning***	***Examples of words***
-al	act of	portrayal, dismissal
-ance	process of	acceptance, maintenance
-ism	practice of, belief	Taoism, activism
-ment	process of	government, atonement
-ness	state of being	kindness, dampness
-ship	condition	hardship, fellowship
-tion	action of	pollution, abstraction
Suffix used to create a verb	***Meaning***	***Examples of words***
-ate	cause to become	activate, irritate
-en	cause to become	strengthen, lessen
-ize	cause to become	memorialize, minimize
Suffix used to create an adjective	***Meaning***	***Examples of words***
-able, -ible	capable of being	desirable, edible
-al	relating to	national, political
-ful	having or promoting	powerful, useful
-ous, -ious	characterized by	monstrous, fictitious
Suffix used to create an adverb	***Meaning***	***Examples of words***
-ly	in this manner	quickly, suddenly

EXERCISE 43.1 Using the roots, prefixes, and suffixes listed in this section (and others that you know), try to determine what the following words mean. Keep in mind that the task is not simply a matter of decoding, as word meanings often change over time.

1. transcribe
2. synchronize
3. convocation
4. omnipotent
5. hyperconscientiousness

6. inducement
7. introvert
8. audiologist
9. omniscient
10. dismiss

EXERCISE 43.2 Identify the common root in each of the following sets of words, and try to determine its meaning. Also try to determine the meanings of any of the words you do not already know.

1. paternal, paternalism, patriot
2. congregate, gregarious, egregious
3. fluid, effluent, confluence
4. emerge, immersion, merger
5. distend, tensile, extensive
6. agitate, agenda, action
7. astronaut, astrology, disaster
8. unicorn, cornea, cornet
9. pedal, pedestal, pedigree
10. sedentary, reside, session

43b Learn denotations and connotations

See 41a

See 41b

As you develop your vocabulary, try to learn both the exact dictionary meanings of words and the associations attached to them. The **denotation** of a word is its standard dictionary meaning—that is, what it means to anyone who knows the word. Many words have more than one denotation. For example, *sanitize* means "to make sanitary" or "to make more acceptable by removing undesired features (as in a document)." The **connotations** of a word are the additional, often emotive, meanings it has for some people due to its association with certain contexts. For example, the word *lawyer* denotes a person whose profession involves advising clients on legal rights and obligations and representing them in a court of law. However, for some, *lawyer* may connote someone who files inappropriate lawsuits or otherwise abuses the legal system. Such negative connotations have led many legal practitioners to call themselves *attorneys.*

Using words accurately is a vital part of writing. The best way to learn how to use words correctly is through extensive reading, which allows you to encounter words in their natural contexts. Frequently two words with similar basic meanings, such as *heinous* and *infamous*, differ somewhat in nuance and usage. If you encounter such words often enough, you will figure out how they should be used, primarily by using other nearby words and phrases as *context clues* to the meaning and usage of the target word. Common context clues include informal definitions, synonyms, contrasts, and examples. The following passage illustrates three of these:

> Allergic rhinitis, commonly called hay fever, is similar to asthma except in one respect. In asthma, an airborne substance causes an allergic, or hypersensitive, reaction in your lungs and chest. In allergic rhinitis, the reaction occurs in your eyes, nose, and throat.
>
> —*American Medical Association Family Medical Guide*

This passage twice uses synonyms to clarify the meaning of less common terms (*hay fever* for *allergic rhinitis* and *hypersensitive* for *allergic*), it contrasts allergic rhinitis to asthma, and it contains an informal definition: "Allergic rhinitis [is a disease in which] an airborne substance causes an allergic . . . reaction . . . in your eyes, nose, and throat."

Be aware, however, that context clues are not always reliable. If you are not certain about the meaning or usage of a word, consult a good dictionary.

See Ch. 44

43c Learn related words

Learn new words

Although a word can be seen in isolation, as a thing unto itself, readers normally experience words in relation to other words, as part of a word system. All words are related to certain other words. Knowing these relationships helps you as a writer, because it allows you to choose just the right word to express your meaning. There are three important ways in which words are related: in collocations, as synonyms, and as antonyms.

1 Collocations

Words often occur in combination with certain other words. These word relationships are called **collocations**. Some collocations, such as *bread and butter,* *cease and desist,* and *reinvent the wheel,* are so common as to be formulaic. Just hearing the first part of such a collocation allows you to fill in the rest: *beat around the* _____, *make a mountain out of a* _____, *leave someone holding the* _____. Other collocations are less predictable. The word *rumor,* for example, is commonly used with at least five different verbs: *spread, circulate, deny, confirm,* and *hear.* The phrase "I heard a rumor" sounds like normal everyday English; "I absorbed a rumor" does not. So, the words *hear* and *rumor* commonly go together, or collocate, whereas *absorb* and *rumor* do not. To learn to speak and write well, you should familiarize yourself with as many collocations as possible. Such knowledge will make it easier for you to construct idiomatic, or natural-sounding, sentences. It also will serve you well on those occasions when you want to create a humorous or stylish twist on a timeworn expression.

See 41f-3

Be careful, though, not to overuse collocations. If you depend exclusively on common word combinations, your writing will lack originality and may be laden with clichés.

See 59b

ESL NOTE Collocations are especially troublesome for non–English speakers.

EXERCISE 43.3 Each of the following sentences contains a word that does not quite fit. Replace it with a suitable collocating word.

1. My family is probably one of the closest families anyone could come around.
2. The best way to learn is by doing mistakes and learning from them.
3. Education is important to me because it is my only hope to gain my goals.
4. To be creative in the food industry you need to have an open mind and a feeling of adventure.
5. Children aren't born knowing how to decipher right from wrong, so they must be taught by their parents.
6. Traffic was stalled because of a mishap involving several cars.
7. Contrary to myth, the Pilgrims did not solemnize Thanksgiving.
8. Many latent supporters are watching the gubernatorial candidate as she campaigns.
9. The referee called far fewer transgressions in last night's game than he has called in previous games.
10. The pirate distinguished the spot where the treasure was buried.

Using Word Games to Build Vocabulary

A fun way to build your vocabulary is by playing word games. There are some excellent free Websites that offer crossword puzzles, word morphs, anagrams, word-in-a-word, cryptoquotes, and other word games. Such sites include <http://www.wordplays.com>, <http://www.eastoftheweb.com>, and <http://wordsmith.org>.

❷ Synonyms

Synonyms are words that mean essentially the same thing: *dreary/gloomy, fury/rage,* and *injure/damage* are all synonymous pairs. You can often use synonymous words to avoid the sort of heavy repetition that makes for an irritatingly dull style. Bear in mind, though, that there are almost no perfect synonyms in English (or in any other language). That is, rarely can two words be freely substituted for each other with exactly the same meaning in all contexts. Consider the words *injure* and *damage.* Although they have similar meanings, *injure* is used only with reference to humans and animals while *damage* can refer to inanimate objects. It would sound odd to say "I injured my computer." An important part of building your vocabulary is learning these subtle differences among synonyms. Consulting a thesaurus, or book of synonyms, can be a big help in this respect. Remember, however, to choose carefully among the synonyms listed; each one has its own particular uses and nuances. Better dictionaries often contain cross-references and usage notes that explain the differences among common synonyms.

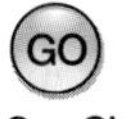

See Ch. 44

❸ Antonyms

Antonyms are words that have opposite meanings: *wrong/right, tall/short,* and *hate/love* are examples. Antonyms are useful in creating humor, irony, sarcasm, and other special effects. For example, a well-chosen antonym can be used effectively in tongue-in-cheek fashion to ridicule someone you do not want to accuse directly: "Senator ____________ is the most *undefiled* [read *corrupt*] public servant we are privileged to know." Antonyms also can help you learn new words. By knowing the opposite of a word, you can get a better sense of what the word itself means.

EXERCISE 43.4 Each of the following sentences contains an italicized word or phrase that is not quite right for the context. Consult your thesaurus, and then substitute an appropriate synonym.

1. Efforts to *fulfill* economic growth in Latin America have been hindered by overpopulation.
2. Political *confusion* in Latin America, as elsewhere, has often led to violations of human rights.
3. The United States strongly opposed the *diffusion* of communism in the Western Hemisphere.
4. For several decades, Brazil *fantasized* about entering the twenty-first century as one of the world's industrial giants.
5. Relations between the United States and Latin America have been *branded* both by friendship and by tension.
6. He *infracted* the city's ordinance that bans the feeding of birds on public property.
7. She *conveyed* her application in plenty of time to meet the deadline.
8. The rotten meat *issued* a sickening odor, which could be smelled throughout the house.
9. I made a list of ten *intentions* on New Year's Day.
10. The body of the *inanimate* president lay in state for three days.

FOR COLLABORATION Bring some examples of unusual words, and their definitions, to your group. Discuss some ideas for continuing to build a more powerful vocabulary.

44 Using a Thesaurus and a Dictionary

FAQs

- Do I really need a thesaurus? (44a)
- How can I get help if I am thinking of a certain concept but cannot remember the word for it? (44a-1)
- If a dictionary gives several different meanings for a word, how do I know which one to use? (44-b)

A writer needs tools, and two of the best are a good thesaurus and a good dictionary. A thesaurus such as *Roget's International Thesaurus*, 6th ed. (New York: HarperCollins, 2002), *Bartlett's Roget's Thesaurus* (Boston: Little Brown, 2003), or *Random House Webster's College Thesaurus*, revised ed. (New York: Random House, 2005) can be of great use in selecting appropriate words. A dictionary such as *The American Heritage College Dictionary*, 4th ed. (Boston: Houghton Mifflin, 2002), *The Random House Webster's College Dictionary* (New York: Random House, 2005), *Merriam-Webster's Collegiate Dictionary*, 11th ed. (Springfield: Merriam-Webster, 2003), or *Webster's New World College Dictionary*, 4th ed. (New York: Macmillan, 2004) can provide indispensable information about spelling, pronunciation, meaning, usage, word division, and etymology (word origin). These reference works are especially useful in describing Standard Edited English, the kind of English you are expected to use in college and in most professional careers.

Online tools

See 40d

ESL NOTE If you are a non–English speaker, consider getting one of the specialized dictionaries that contain information about count and noncount nouns, phrasal verbs, verb complements, and collocations and also offer many sample sentences. (See Chapter 59 for specific references.)

See 56a, 57a, 57b, 59b

 44a Use a thesaurus to find the exact word

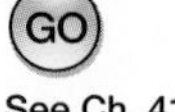
See Ch. 41

See 40c

Part of being a good writer is choosing words that accurately express your thoughts. Do you ever find yourself thinking of a concept and knowing that there is a word to describe it, yet not being able to come up with the word? Do you find yourself wanting to vary your word choices to avoid excessive repetition, yet not knowing exactly which substitute words to use? In these situations, a thesaurus is of great help. A **thesaurus** is a book of synonyms and antonyms that allows you to zero in on the exact word you are looking for.

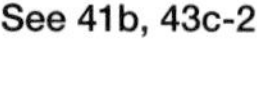
See 41b, 43c-2

A word of advice: Do not use a thesaurus just to find ornamental words with which to dress up your writing. As synonyms often have special conditions of use and are not freely interchangeable, substituting fancy synonyms for more common words just to impress your readers is likely to have the opposite effect.

Online thesaurus

1 Electronic thesaurus

Today, most word-processing programs have a built-in thesaurus, which you can use as you write. (It is usually on the same menu as the spell checker.) You can also find thesauruses on the Internet. Use *thesaurus* as your search term, and bookmark whatever good sites you find. One such site can be found at <http://thesaurus.reference.com>. Alternatively, you can buy a thesaurus on a CD-ROM, either by itself or as a supplement to a dictionary.

An **electronic thesaurus** is a great writing tool that is quick and easy to use. If you notice that a word you have written is not quite the word you want to use, all you have to do is select the word and then click on THESAURUS. You will get a listing of synonyms and, in some cases, antonyms and related words.

Sometimes, you quickly find the word you need; other times, the exact word does not pop up immediately. In these cases, you will have to be a little more inventive.

For example, when Jennie Lee was writing an essay called "Ride the Bus!" she used the thesaurus a number of times. At one point, she wanted to criticize students who think they have to own a car to get around. She wrote this sentence:

> Many people have been tricked into believing that owning a vehicle is the best means of meeting personal transportation needs.

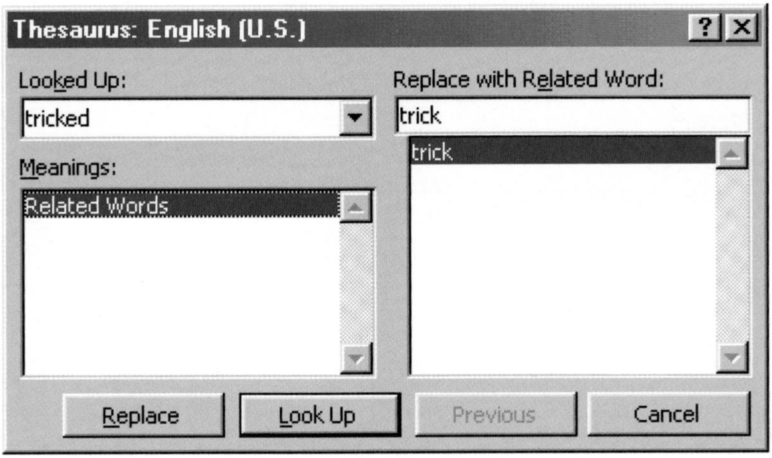

Figure 44.1 Thesaurus Screen for *tricked*

At first this sentence seemed okay, but when Jennie was revising her draft she felt the word *tricked* was a little too strong. So she selected it with her mouse and clicked on THESAURUS. Figure 44.1 shows the computer screen that came up. Clicking on RELATED WORDS gave her the screen shown in Figure 44.2. The only verb form listed here was *deceive*, which was not

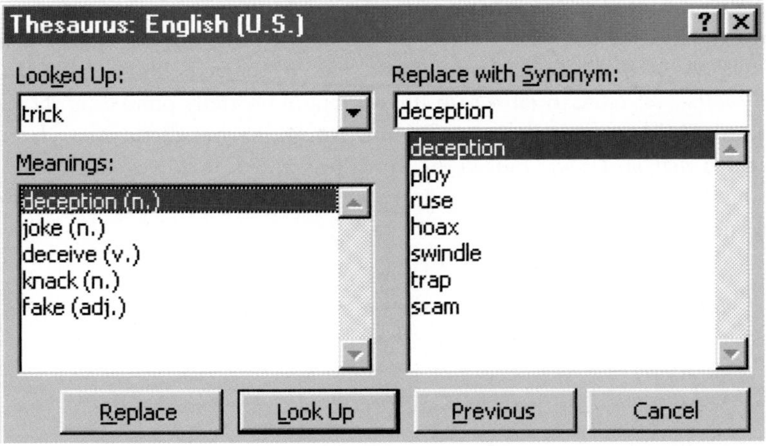

Figure 44.2 Thesaurus Screen Showing Related Words for *tricked*

Figure 44.3 ▶
Thesaurus Screen for *deceive*

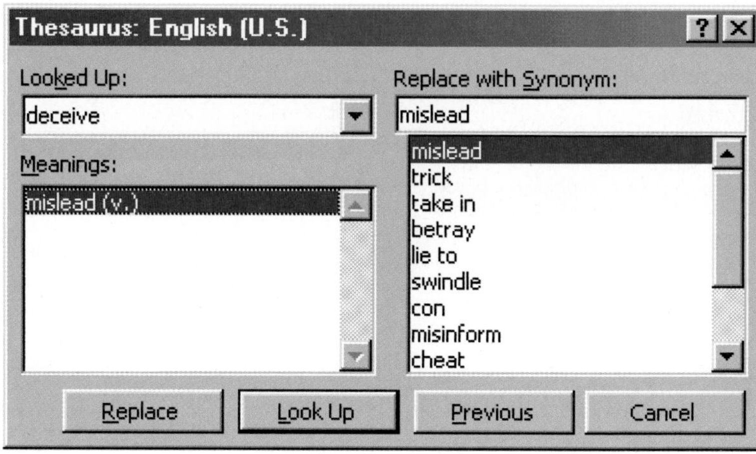

quite the word she was looking for, either. But she decided to click on it anyway, to see what it would bring up. She got the list of synonyms shown in Figure 44.3.

Aha! *Mislead.* Yes, thought Jennie, *that* was the word she was looking for! "Many people have been *misled* into believing that owning a vehicle is the best means of meeting personal transportation needs." Just to make sure, she examined all the synonyms listed and decided that although all of them conveyed a sense of deception, most, like *trick*, were too strong. Only *misinform* was close to *mislead* in its connotation. Briefly pondering the difference between these two words—and consulting her dictionary—Jennie decided that *misled* was indeed the word she wanted. It conveyed the idea of being deceived, but in a vague sense, without implying a specific agent of deception.

What is the moral of this story?

- *Take advantage of your electronic thesaurus.* It will let you quickly search for the word you want. (This entire search took Jennie less than a minute.)
- *Be persistent.* If at first you don't succeed, do some exploring.

❷ Traditional thesaurus

You should also feel comfortable using a thesaurus in traditional book form. The pocket-size versions are handy for carrying around; larger, desk-size thesauruses are found in all libraries and many offices. In many pocket-size thesauruses, the words are arranged alphabetically, as in a dictionary. With most desk-size thesauruses, you first look up the word in an index at the back of the book and then turn to the most relevant sections indicated.

Whereas multiple clicks and extended searching are often required to find the word you are looking for in an electronic thesaurus, traditional thesauruses typically present a number of words in one place, allowing you to get a comprehensive look at the full set of synonyms for a word. For example, when we used our electronic thesaurus to look up the word *succinct,* we were presented with a screen containing nine synonyms. But when we checked in a modest traditional thesaurus, we were given seventeen: *concise, terse, short, brief, curt, laconic, pithy, trenchant, pointed, crisp, neat, compact, summary, condensed, shortened, abbreviated,* and *compressed.* Furthermore, unlike the electronic thesaurus, the traditional thesaurus gave us five antonyms: *verbose, prolix, loquacious, long-winded,* and *garrulous.* In short, the traditional thesaurus offered a more comprehensive sense of what the word *succinct* means.

EXERCISE 44.1 Each of the following sentences contains an italicized word that does not quite fit with the rest of the sentence. Use a thesaurus to find a synonym that sounds better.

1. When I am bored, I like to go *observe* a movie.
2. A true New Englander enjoys a *segment* of pie for breakfast.
3. The Brothers Grimm were collectors of German fairy *narratives.*
4. The man playing third base is a very promising *neophyte.*
5. The couple went to the market to buy *comestibles.*
6. Most of us love to *vocalize* along with the radio.
7. Before starting the job, the teacher signed an employee *pact.*
8. We will need to measure the *girth* of the piano to see if it will fit through the door.
9. Ron and Sylvia have a *rendezvous* on Friday.
10. The board should *summon* a special meeting of the leadership to review the current situation.

TechHelp

Using Special Electronic Thesaurus Features

Some Websites offer electronic thesauruses with special search features:

- *A reverse dictionary.* If you have a certain concept in mind but cannot think of the exact word for it, you can enter descriptive terms or concepts in the search field and have the program use these to find the exact word.
- *A wildcard pattern.* Let's say you are thinking of a word that begins with *clar* but can not remember the rest. You enter "clar*" and the program will search its database for candidate words. (This feature is particularly handy for doing crossword puzzles or finding words that rhyme!)

A good place to start at is <http://www.onelook.com>.

Online dictionary

44b Use a dictionary to learn about words

Do you sometimes come across a new word in your reading and wonder what it means? Have you ever argued with a classmate about how a word should be pronounced? Have you ever had an instructor circle a word in one of your papers and write *usage* in the margin? Are you curious about where a word like *maverick* comes from? When using your thesaurus, do you find yourself trying to decide how the various words listed as synonyms differ? A good dictionary will help you out in all of these situations and more.

1 Kinds of dictionaries

Traditional, hardbound dictionaries come in two types: pocket size and desk size. The pocket size is handy, but the desk size contains more complete information. Electronic dictionaries usually have as much information as desk-size types.

There are two kinds of electronic dictionaries: those on CD-ROM and those on the Internet. Although the preferred method of using the CD-ROM type is to download it to your hard drive, you can play it directly from your CD-ROM drive. To use the Internet type of electronic dictionary, you log on to a Web site such as *Merriam-Webster Online* at <http://www.m-w.com/

dictionary.htm>, the *Oxford English Dictionary* at <http://www.oed.com>, or *OneLook Dictionaries* at <http://www.onelook.com>. In some cases, you may have to pay a subscription fee.

A typical entry from a comprehensive dictionary, whether hardbound or electronic, will look something like the one in Figure 44.4, from *The American Heritage College Dictionary,* 4th ed.

Pronunciation | Part of speech | Word endings

Spelling and word division

Word senses (definitions)

ha•rass (hăr′əs, hə-răs′) *tr.v.* **ha•rassed, ha•rass•ing, ha•rass•es. 1.** To irritate or torment persistently. **2.** To wear out; exhaust. **3.** To impede and exhaust (an enemy) by repeated attacks or raids. [French *harasser,* possibly from Old French *harer,* to set a dog on, from *hare,* interjection used to set a dog on, of Germanic origin.] **—ha•rass′er** *n.* **—ha•rass′ment** *n.*

Etymology

Related words

Words having similar meanings, with examples

SYNONYMS: *harass, harry, hound, badger, pester, plague, bait.* These verbs are compared as they mean to trouble persistently or incessantly. *Harass* and *harry* imply systematic persecution by besieging with repeated annoyances, threats, demands, or misfortunes: *The landlord harassed tenants who were behind in their rent. "Of all the griefs that harass the distress'd"* (Samuel Johnson). *A gang of delinquents harried the storekeeper. Hound* suggests unrelenting pursuit to gain a desired end: *Reporters hounded the celebrity for an interview.* To *badger* is to nag or tease persistently: *The child badgered his parents to buy him a new bicycle.* To *pester* is to inflict a succession of petty annoyances: *"How she would have pursued and pestered me with questions and surmises"* (Charlotte Brontë). *Plague* refers to the infliction of tribulations, such as worry or vexation, likened to an epidemic disease: *"As I have no estate, I am plagued with no tenants or stewards"*(Henry Fielding). To *bait* is to torment by or as if by taunting, insulting, or ridiculing: *Hecklers baited the speaker mercilessly.*

USAGE NOTE: Educated usage appears to be evenly divided on the pronunciation of *harass.* In a recent survey 50 percent of the Usage Panel preferred a pronunciation with stress on the first syllable, while 50 percent preferred stress on the second syllable. Curiously, the Panelists' comments appear to indicate that each side regards itself as an embattled minority.

Authoritative opinions about correct usage

▲ **Figure 44.4** Entry from *The American Heritage College Dictionary*

TechHelp

Using an Electronic Dictionary

Some online dictionaries—for example, <http://m-w.com.downloads.htm> and <http://encarta.msn.com>—allow you to put a dictionary icon on your toolbar or right-click on any word on a Web page and get a definition for it.

❷ Spelling, word division, and pronunciation

See 55e

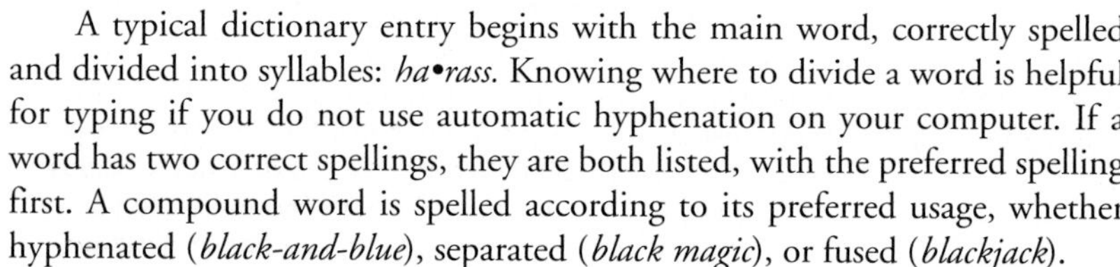

A typical dictionary entry begins with the main word, correctly spelled and divided into syllables: *ha•rass.* Knowing where to divide a word is helpful for typing if you do not use automatic hyphenation on your computer. If a word has two correct spellings, they are both listed, with the preferred spelling first. A compound word is spelled according to its preferred usage, whether hyphenated (*black-and-blue*), separated (*black magic*), or fused (*blackjack*).

The word's pronunciation is indicated next, in parentheses: (hăr′əs, hə-răs′). Most modern dictionaries have a pronunciation key at the bottom of the page to help you decipher the pronunciation. For words of more than one syllable, a heavy accent mark (**′**) indicates which syllable should receive primary stress; some words have a secondary accent (′) as well. Some electronic dictionaries allow you to click on a button and get a voice recording of the correct pronunciation of the word.

❸ Parts of speech and word endings

See Ch. 26 for an introduction to the parts of speech.

After the pronunciation guide come symbols describing some aspect of the word—for example, what part of speech it is (such as a noun, verb, or adjective) or whether it is singular or plural. The most common abbreviations follow:

adj.	adjective	*intr.*	intransitive	*pron.*	pronoun
adv.	adverb	*n.*	noun	*sing.*	singular
aux.	auxiliary	*pl.*	plural	*suff.*	suffix
conj.	conjunction	*pref.*	prefix	*tr.*	transitive
interj.	interjection	*prep.*	preposition	*v.*	verb

Often an entry will include variants of the main word, showing different word endings. For verbs, for example, a comprehensive dictionary will give the principal tenses. In the example shown in Figure 44.4, *The American Heritage College Dictionary* gives the past tense (*harassed*), the present participle (*harassing*), and the simple present tense (*harasses*). For other word types, you can expect to find other kinds of word endings. Adjectives, for example, will usually have their comparative and superlative forms listed. Nouns with irregular plural forms will have those listed.

See 28d

4 Word senses

Many words have more than one meaning, or **sense**. Each sense is given separately in an entry, generally preceded by a boldfaced number. In some dictionaries, these senses are arranged historically, according to when they entered the language; in other dictionaries, senses are listed according to current popularity, with the most commonly used sense appearing first. (It is a good idea to consult the front of your dictionary to see which system it uses.) Sometimes the main senses are further divided into subsenses, generally indicated by a boldface lowercase letter.

5 Etymology and related words and expressions

Information about a word's origin, or **etymology**, is given in square brackets. This information can help you to learn the word and use it accurately. Sometimes, **related words**—words derived from the same root—are given as well. These might include related expressions such as phrasal verbs and idioms.

See 57a, 59c

6 Synonyms and usage notes

Some dictionaries list synonyms for certain words, along with explanations of the differences among them and examples. Also, some dictionaries provide **usage notes**, which typically represent the judgments of a panel of authorities about "correct" usage. In many dictionaries, particular senses of a word may be given **usage labels** such as *informal, colloquial, nonstandard, slang, vulgar, obscene, offensive, archaic*, or *obsolete*. You may want to check the front of your dictionary to see how the different kinds of usage are defined.

See 40d

7 Field labels

If a word sense applies to a certain field of study or activity, many dictionaries will label it accordingly. For example, a *genoa* is a type of sail on a sailboat, so this definition may be labeled *Naut.* (for nautical). Some other common field labels are *Anat.* (for anatomy), *Biochem.* (for biochemistry), *Comp. Sci.* (for computer science), *Gk. Myth.* (for Greek mythology), *Mus.* (for music), and *Phys.* (for physics). A full listing of field labels can usually be found in the dictionary's front matter.

EXERCISE 44.2 Select two interesting new words from your course readings. Go to a library or bookstore and look them up in three of the newest dictionaries. Take note of the differences among the three definitions. Write a two-page report describing these differences and recommending one dictionary over the other two.

FOR COLLABORATION Share your conclusions with your group; is there a consensus on which dictionaries were preferred?

45 Spelling

FAQs

- My spell checker is too slow. Can I make it go faster? (45a)
- Are there certain times when I should not depend on a spell checker for help? (45b)
- What are some helpful spelling rules? (45d)

Modern English is a product of many other languages, including German, French, Latin, Greek, Scandinavian, and Spanish. One unfortunate result of this hybridization is an irregular system of spelling that causes problems for many users of the language. If you are one of those people, be assured that you are not alone. However, it is important that you work on your spelling and keep trying to improve it. Many readers, including employers and customers in the workplace, have little tolerance for bad spelling. In fact, studies have shown that even a few misspellings on a résumé can cause a job applicant to be eliminated from consideration.

45a Use a spell checker

Advice for spell checker use

A computerized **spell checker** makes it easy to review your work for spelling errors. If you are not already doing so, you should routinely run a final spell check on any important document you write. Some word processors allow you to set the spell checker so that it will identify possible misspellings either while you are typing or after you have finished. Although spell checking can be frustratingly slow, there are things you can do to speed it up.

See TechHelp box in 45a

TechHelp

Speeding Up Spell Checking

You can spell check faster by taking these steps:

1. Uncheck the CHECK GRAMMAR box.
2. Each time your spell checker flags a specialized term or name, click on IGNORE ALL or ADD TO DICTIONARY. This way, it won't flag that item again.

Spell checkers are far from perfect. Sometimes they flag words that are spelled correctly (especially names), and sometimes they fail to flag words that are spelled incorrectly. The first problem is particularly annoying, but it can be resolved. For example, suppose you are writing a paper on Hemingway and your spell checker keeps flagging the name *Hemingway.* Instead of clicking IGNORE every time, you can customize the spell checker so that it will recognize the name. With most spell checkers, you can customize as you write.

Identifying misspellings that the spell checker missed is a more difficult problem. A spell checker will accept any word that happens to match a word form in its dictionary, even if the word is misused. For example, if you write *golf coarse,* the spell checker will not recognize the misspelling of *course* because the word *coarse* is in its dictionary. Thus, even with a spell checker, you must have the knowledge to prevent or correct misspellings. The most effective ways to gain such knowledge are by (1) mastering troublesome homophones, (2) guarding against common spelling errors, and (3) learning some general spelling rules and patterns. The remainder of this chapter is devoted to these topics.

EXERCISE 45.1 Create a document called "Personal Spelling Demons" on your word processor, and enter any words that you have trouble spelling.

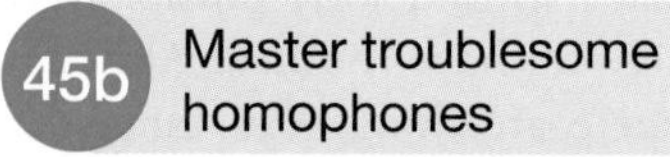

45b Master troublesome homophones

Homophones are words that sound alike but are spelled differently and have different meanings. They are one of the most common causes of misspelling

TechALERT!

Grammar Checkers: Homophones

Although homophones slip past a spell checker, some of them are flagged by a grammar checker. But most homophones are overlooked, even by the best grammar checkers. For example, the grammar checker in *MS Word 2002* identifies only about one-fourth of the homophones listed here.

in English and cannot be detected by a spell checker. For this reason, you should study them and learn their differences, especially those listed below.

affect	verb: "to have an influence on"
effect	verb: "to bring about"; noun: "result"
its	possessive pronoun
it's	contraction of *it is*
loose	adjective: "free, not tightly secured"
lose	verb: "to fail to keep"
their	possessive form of *they*
there	adverb: "in that place"
they're	contraction of *they are*
to	preposition
too	adverb: "also"
two	adjective and noun: "2"
who's	contraction of *who is*
whose	possessive form of *who*
your	possessive form of *you*
you're	contraction of *you are*

Some other frequently confused homophones and near homophones include the following:

advice	recommendation
advise	to recommend
all ready	fully prepared
already	by now
all together	everyone or everything in one place
altogether	completely

allude elude	to refer to to avoid or escape
allusion illusion	reference to misleading appearance
brake break	to stop to reduce to pieces, destroy
breath breathe	air inhaled and exhaled to inhale and exhale air
choose chose	to select past tense of *choose*
cite sight site	to quote as an authority vision place, location
clothes cloths	garments pieces of fabric
coarse course	rough path, track; academic class
conscience conscious	sense of right and wrong aware
dairy diary	place where milk is produced personal daily journal
desert dessert	dry, barren area sweet food at the end of a meal
device devise	apparatus, tool to plan or invent
dominant dominate	controlling, ruling to control, govern
elicit illicit	to call forth, evoke illegal
eminent immanent imminent	distinguished existing within, inherent about to happen

envelop	to surround
envelope	flat paper container
fair	equitable, permissible, acceptable
fare	transportation charge
formally	in a formal manner
formerly	previously
forth	forward or onward
fourth	in position 4 in a countable series
gorilla	ape
guerrilla	irregular soldier
heard	past tense of *hear*
herd	group of animals
hole	opening
whole	entire, complete
human	referring to people
humane	compassionate
lead	to guide or direct
led	past tense of *lead*
may be	might be
maybe	perhaps
miner	someone who works in a mine
minor	underage person
patience	perseverance, endurance
patients	doctor's clients
peace	absence of war
piece	fragment, part
personal	individual, private
personnel	employees
plain	ordinary, simple, clear
plane	flat surface; airplane
presence	being in attendance
presents	gifts

principal principle	leading person; a capital sum; most important rule or guideline
quiet quite	silent completely; somewhat
rain reign rein	water drops falling to earth period of rule strap to control a horse
respectfully respectively	with respect in that order
right rite write	correct; opposite of left ceremony to put words on paper
sense since	reason, feeling because, subsequently
stationary stationery	standing still writing paper
than then	in comparison with at that time
threw through thorough	past tense of *throw* in one side and out another complete
waist waste	midsection of body useless byproduct; to use needlessly
weak week	opposite of strong seven days
weather whether	atmospheric conditions if it is the case that
were where	past tense of *are* at or in what place

EXERCISE 45.2 In the following sentences, choose the correct spelling from each pair of words in brackets. Add any words you get wrong to your Personal Spelling Demons document. (See Exercise 45.1.)

1. The doctor [who's, whose] license was revoked by the medical [bored, board] is no longer allowed to treat [patients, patience].
2. The television [diary, dairy] is one of the [devices, devises] used by A. C. Nielsen to research the programs people choose.
3. The [peace, piece] of [advice, advise] Ann Landers gave was simple, practical, and [fare, fair].
4. The poster [sighted, cited] Jesse Jackson, who said, "Your children need your [presents, presence] more than your [presents, presence]."
5. Because he is an excellent magician, he always allows the audience a [through, thorough] inspection of his props before he creates his wonderful [allusions, illusions].
6. More than once last [weak, week], the tardy student managed to [allude, elude] the [principal, principle] as she entered the building.
7. At a gorgeous [site, sight] atop a hill, the women gathered for a bonding [right, rite], calling forth the [immanent, eminent] wisdom from each person present.
8. The [personal, personnel] department's intense search for a [principle, principal] engineer to [led, lead] the department [led, lead] to the promotion of a woman [who's, whose] talent had [formally, formerly] gone unrecognized.
9. When the camouflaged [gorilla, guerrilla] [herd, heard] something moving in the underbrush, he tried to determine [weather, whether] it was an enemy soldier.
10. The small craft carrying [elicit, illicit] drugs encountered bad [whether, weather] that night and traveled far from [it's, its] intended [coarse, course].

45c Guard against common spelling errors

Although a spell checker can flag many spelling errors for you, it is still worth learning the correct spelling of the most commonly misspelled words. Some of these words follow.

Commonly Misspelled Words

accidentally	achieved	apparent
accommodate	address	appropriate

argument
basically
beneficial
calendar
committee
definitely
dependent
develops
environment
exaggerate
exceed

February
government
heroes
lose
maintenance
manageable
misspell
necessary
noticeable
occasionally
occurred

parallel
quantity
receive
recommend
seize
separate
success
therefore
truly
until
without

If you find your spell checker flagging the same misspelled words over and over, add them to your Personal Spelling Demons document and study them from time to time. Most spell checkers will allow you to enter such words into a file with just a single mouse click.

Many words include letters or syllables that are not pronounced in casual speech (or even, in some cases, in careful speech). Here are examples of such words; try to "see" the silent letters or syllables as you visualize these words.

address
candidate
different
dumb
environment
February
foreign

government
interest
library
parallel
pneumonia
privilege
probably

quantity
recognize
restaurant
surprise
therefore
tomatoes
Wednesday

If you are unsure about a certain letter in a word, try to think of a related word; it may provide a clue. For example, suppose you are wondering whether *grammar* or *grammer* is correct. If you think of *grammatical*, you will spell *grammar* correctly. Here are some other examples:

	Think of
competition or compitition?	compete
democracy or democricy?	democrat
mystery or mystry?	mysterious
relative or relitive?	relate

TechALERT!

Electronic Language: Slang Spellings

Slang spellings used for instant-messaging and text-messaging, such as *pls, u/ur, b4, wut,* and *2nite,* are not appropriate in formal or academic writing.

EXERCISE 45.3 In the following paragraph, choose the correct spelling from each pair of words in brackets. Add any words you get wrong to your Personal Spelling Demons document.

On the second [Wensday, Wednesday] in [Febuary, February], those running for various positions in town [government, goverment] gathered for a [Candidates', Canidates'] Night. At the event, the two [canidates, candidates] for school [comittee, committee] expressed [diffrent, different] opinions about how to [accomodate, accommodate] the new state education standards without having to [excede, exceed] the available amount of money. Mr. Smith believes that the state legislature is right to make [forein, foreign] language a required course. He also pointed out that an up-to-date school [libary, library] is [neccessary, necessary] for student [sucess, success]. Ms. Jones, on the other hand, [basically, basicly] believes that, although beneficial, both [forein, foreign] language courses and school [libaries, libraries] are less important than other things, such as regular school building [maintainance, maintenance]. The [canidates, candidates] then had an [arguement, argument] about building [maintainance, maintenance], Ms. Jones [reccomending, recommending] that the town [seize, sieze] the opportunity to repair current buildings and Mr. Smith stating that the [maintainance, maintenance] budget is [exagerated, exaggerated] and proposing that the town defer some of the repairs in order to spend more on educational programming. Because the debate highlighted [noticeable, noticable] [diffrences, differences] between the [canidates, candidates], the voters who attended the event were well served.

45d Learn general spelling rules and patterns

Spelling rules

Although English is not the simplest language in the world when it comes to spelling, it does have a number of general rules and patterns that can be helpful.

See 43a

See 55a

❶ Prefixes

Prefixes are small word parts, like *re-, anti-*, and *pre-*, placed at the beginnings of words. Prefixes do not change the spelling of the root word: *anti-* added to *-freeze* becomes *antifreeze.* In some cases, though, a hyphen is required: *anti-* plus *-intellectual* is spelled *anti-intellectual.*

mis + spell = misspell
un + necessary = unnecessary
re + entry = reentry
dis + service = disservice

❷ Suffixes

See 43a

Suffixes are small word parts, like *-age, -ence, -ing*, and *-tion*, placed at the ends of words. By adding suffixes to a root word such as *sense-*, you can create different meanings: *sensitive, sensual, sensory, senseless.* In doing so, however, you must observe the following spelling rules.

1. If the word ends in a silent *e* and the suffix starts with a vowel, drop the *e.*

imagine + ation = imagination
debate + able = debatable
pure + ist = purist
perspire + ing = perspiring

There are some exceptions. Some words need to retain the final *e* in order to be distinguished from similar words (*dyeing/dying*), to prevent mispronunciation (*mileage, being*), or to keep a soft *c* or *g* sound (*noticeable, courageous*).

2. If the word ends in a silent *e* and the suffix starts with a consonant, do not drop the *e.*

require + ment = requirement
spine + less = spineless
hate + ful = hateful
definite + ly = definitely

Some exceptions are *argument, awful, ninth, truly*, and *wholly.*

EXERCISE 45.4 Combine the following words and suffixes, keeping or dropping the silent *e* as necessary. Add any words that you spell incorrectly to your Personal Spelling Demons document.

1. complete + ly
2. grace + ious
3. grieve + ance
4. wholesome + ness
5. exercise + ing
6. trace + able
7. continue + ous
8. sole + ly
9. argue + ment
10. sedate + ive

3. When adding a suffix to a word that ends in *y*, change the *y* to *i* if the letter preceding the *y* is a consonant.

study + ous = studious
joy + ous = joyous
comply + ance = compliance
pay + ment = payment

Exceptions are words with the suffix *-ing*, which keep the *y* in all cases: *studying, carrying, drying, paying.*

4. In creating adverbs from adjectives, add *-ly* to the adjective unless the adjective ends in *-ic,* in which case use *-ally.*

silent + ly = silently
hopeful + ly = hopefully
vile + ly = vilely
wild + ly = wildly
terrific + ally = terrifically
basic + ally = basically

An exception is *publicly.*

5. In choosing between *-able* and *-ible*, use *-able* if the root word can stand alone; otherwise, use *-ible.*

understand + able = understandable
change + able = changeable
agree + able = agreeable
vis + ible = visible
ed + ible = edible
aud + ible = audible

Some exceptions are *resistible, probable*, and *culpable.*

6. Double the final consonant of the root word if (a) the root word ends with a single accented vowel and a single consonant and (b) the suffix begins with a vowel.

drop + ed = dropped
slim + er = slimmer
occur + ence = occurrence
begin + ing = beginning
laugh + ed = laughed [Root word does not end with a single consonant.]
sleep + ing = sleeping [Root word has two vowels.]
commit + ment = commitment [Suffix does not start with a vowel.]
happen + ing = happening [Root word does not end with an accented vowel.]

EXERCISES 45.5 In each case, combine the root word and the suffix so as to form a single, correctly spelled word. Add any words you get wrong to your Personal Spelling Demons document.

1. room + mate =
2. hesitant + ly =
3. shop + ing =
4. control + (able or ible?) =
5. plaus + (able or ible?) =
6. cool + er =
7. drastic + (ly or ally?) =
8. quiet + est =
9. thin + ness =
10. public + (ly or ally?) =

FOR COLLABORATION In your group, share your lists of Personal Spelling Demons. How many words appear on more than one person's list?

3 Plurals

English has several different ways of forming plurals from singular nouns. Following are some rules for forming plurals.

1. For most words, add *-s.*

tool, tools
window, windows
minute, minutes

2. For words ending with *s, sh, ch, x,* or *z,* add *-es.*

bus, buses
crash, crashes
quiz, quizzes [Note the doubled final consonant.]
sandwich, sandwiches
fox, foxes

3. For words ending with a consonant followed by *y*, change the *y* to *i* and add *-es.*

enemy, enemies	strawberry, strawberries
mystery, mysteries	theory, theories

4. For some words ending with *f* or *fe*, change the *f* or *fe* to *v* and add *-es.*

calf, calves	life, lives
half, halves	thief, thieves
knife, knives	yourself, yourselves

Some exceptions are *belief, beliefs; chief, chiefs; proof, proofs*; and *motif, motifs.*

5. For compound nouns written as single words, add the plural ending as you would to an ordinary noun.

laptop, laptops	database, databases
workstation, workstations	

6. For compound nouns written as two or more words or hyphenated, add the plural ending to the noun being modified.

video game, video games [The noun being modified is *game.*]
word processor, word processors [The noun being modified is *processor.*]
sister-in-law, sisters-in-law [The noun being modified is *sister.*]

Irregular plurals must be learned individually. Sometimes, an internal vowel must be changed to make a noun plural:

woman, women	mouse, mice
tooth, teeth	

With some nouns derived from Latin or Greek, a final *us, um*, or *on* must be changed to *i* or *a*:

syllabus, syllabi	curriculum, curricula
alumnus, alumni	medium, media
stimulus, stimuli	criterion, criteria

Some nouns have the same form for both singular and plural:

deer, deer	species, species
sheep, sheep	

EXERCISE 45.6 Make the following words plural. If necessary, check your dictionary.

1. device
2. memorandum
3. church
4. goose
5. moose
6. kiss
7. sky
8. syllabus
9. mailbox
10. mouse

❹ The "*i* before *e*" rule

The rule you had to memorize in elementary school is worth keeping in mind: "*i* before *e* except after *c* or when sounded like *ay*, as in *neighbor* or *weigh*."

I BEFORE *E*

achieve	field
believe	friend
brief	piece

EXCEPT AFTER *C*

ceiling	deceive
conceive	receive

OR WHEN SOUNDED LIKE *AY*

eight	vein
neighbor	weigh

Some exceptions are *ancient, caffeine, conscience, counterfeit, either, foreign, height, leisure, neither, seize, science,* and *weird.*

EXERCISE 45.7 Insert the correct form (*ei* or *ie*) in the following words:

1. exper______nce
2. perc______ve
3. h______ght
4. ch______f
5. v______n
6. dec______t
7. for______gn
8. th______f
9. b______ge
10. anc______nt

part

10

Punctuation

46 End Punctuation

FAQs

- Which is correct, *FBI* or *F.B.I.*? (46d)
- Should a question mark go inside or outside quotation marks? (46e-1)
- What is an "indirect question," and how do I punctuate it? (46f)

It is important to end sentences with proper punctuation so that readers know what types of statements are being made and what kinds of silent intonation to give each one. There are three ways to punctuate a sentence: with a period, a question mark, or an exclamation point.

All about end punctuation

THE PERIOD

The period is used for several purposes: to indicate the end of a statement, to punctuate initials and abbreviations, and to mark basic divisions in units and computer names.

46a Use a period to mark the end of a statement

See Ch. 31

See 51e

Sometimes called a "full stop," the period is most commonly used to mark the end of a sentence. Just make sure before you place the period that the words form a *complete grammatical sentence*, or else you will be creating a sentence fragment.

If the sentence ends with a quotation mark, place the period *inside* the quotation mark:

- One commentator said that "rainforest destruction, overpopulation, and the global arms trade are problems for the entire world**.** "

If the sentence ends with a parenthesis, place the period *outside* the parenthesis unless the entire sentence is a parenthetical comment:

See 52a to 52c

▸ Mexicans voted Sunday in elections that could weaken the power of the world's longest ruling political party, the Institutional Revolutionary Party (PRI).

46b Use periods to punctuate initials and many abbreviations

Initials that stand for middle names or first names take periods:

Mary W. Shelley   O. J. Simpson   F. Scott Fitzgerald

Leave one space after each period when punctuating initials in names.

Most abbreviations ending in lowercase letters take periods:

Ms.	a.m.	St.	Jan.
Mrs.	p.m.	Ave.	i.e.
Mr.	etc.	Rd.	Jr.
Dr.	e.g.	apt.	Inc.

See also Ch. 54

46c Use periods to mark basic divisions in units and computer names

Basic divisions in money, measurements, email addresses, and file names are indicated by periods:

$99.50	3.2 meters	13.5 gallons
English.paper.doc	michael.okiwara@u.c.utah.edu	

46d Avoid common misuses of periods

1. *Do not use a period to mark just any pause.* If you insert a period whenever you want readers to pause, you risk creating sentence fragments. Consider this example:

Attempts to challenge reactionary political views are often branded as "politically correct" by those same reactionaries. Who support only their own versions of "free speech."

See Ch. 31, Ch. 47

The second statement is a fragment; the writer has incorrectly set it off as a separate sentence. The correct way to signal a pause is to insert a comma, thus turning the fragment into a relative clause:

▸ Attempts to challenge reactionary political views are often branded as "politically correct" by those same reactionaries**,** who support only their own versions of "free speech."

2. *Do not use periods with acronyms and other all uppercase abbreviations.* The recent trend is not to use periods with common abbreviations for states, countries, organizations, computer programs, famous people, and other entities:

CA	NJ	USA	UN	FBI
NOW	NAACP	MS-DOS	CD-ROM	HTML
MIT	NBA	JFK	FDR	AAA

3. *Do not use periods at the end of stand-alone titles or headings.* The title of this chapter and its numbered headings are examples of stand-alone titles and headings, respectively.

4. *Do not use periods at the end of sentences within sentences.* Here is an example of a sentence within a sentence:

▸ The famous statement "I think, therefore I am" originated in an essay by the French philosopher Descartes.

5. *Do not use periods after items in a formatted list (except for full sentences).* The table of contents for this handbook is an example of a formatted list. Only when the items in the list are full sentences is it acceptable to end them with periods.

Question marks

THE QUESTION MARK

See 47j (number 6)

Question marks are placed after direct questions, whereas periods follow indirect questions. Do not use a comma or a period after a question mark unless the question mark is part of a title.

46e Use a question mark after a direct request

REQUESTING INFORMATION	Who wrote *Jesus Christ, Superstar*?
ASKING FOR CONFIRMATION	It's a complicated situation, isn't it?
MAKING A POLITE REQUEST	Could you please be a little quieter?

❶ Using question marks with quotation marks

If the quotation is a question and it is at the end of the sentence, put the question mark inside the quotation marks.

▸ The police officer asked me, "Do you live here?"

If the quotation is a statement embedded within a question and it comes at the end of the sentence, put the question mark outside the quotation marks.

See Ch. 51 for more on quotation marks.

▸ Who said, "Those who forget history are condemned to repeat it"?

❷ Using question marks in a series

It is acceptable to put a question mark after each independent item, even if it is not a full sentence.

▸ Will our homeless population continue to grow? Stay about the same? Get smaller?

If the question is an either/or type, put a question mark only at the end.

▸ Are you coming with us or staying here?

46f Do not use a question mark after an indirect question

An indirect question is the writer's rewording of a question posed by someone else.

▸ A tourist asked me where the Lincoln Memorial was.

THE EXCLAMATION POINT

Exclamation points are used to show strong emotion, including amazement and sarcasm. Do not use a comma or a period after an exclamation point. (The one exception is when the exclamation point is part of a title; see 47j.)

46g Use an exclamation point to signal a strong statement

The statement marked with an exclamation point does not have to be a full sentence.

AN OUTCRY OR COMMAND	Oh**!** Watch out**!**
STRONG EMPHASIS	People before profits**!**
ASTONISHMENT	Imagine reading this news report and not getting upset**!**
SARCASM	And the cigarette companies claim that smoking is not addictive**!**

❶ Using exclamation points with quotation marks

If the quotation itself is an exclamation, put the exclamation point inside the quotation marks.

▶ It is not a good idea to go into a crowded movie theater and shout "Fire**!"**

Otherwise, the exclamation point should be placed outside the quotation marks.

▶ I can't believe he said, "Alice doesn't live here**"!**

❷ Avoiding overuse of exclamation points

Exclamation points are rarely used in college papers, essays, and other kinds of formal writing. Try not to use them except in highly unusual circumstances. Any kind of writing—even informal writing—that has too many exclamations sounds juvenile. There are better ways to express your enthusiasm.

See Ch. 39

EXERCISE 46.1 The following email message contains a number of errors in end punctuation. Make the appropriate corrections.

Guess what

I just found the Web site for NoF.X. Which I have been meaning to search out. It's NoF.X.@www.nofxofficialwebsite.com.

I just got their new C.D. it was a real deal At WEJones Music downtown—$12 99 I'm listening to it now—it rules.

That's it for now I have to write a paper (yuck) due Tues It's on F.D.R. and W.W.II Got to go

Later :)

EXERCISE 46.2 The end punctuation marks have been deleted from the following paragraphs. Supply the appropriate punctuation marks.

1. How long have human beings been concerned about population growth If you believe the warnings, we have long been on the verge of overpopulating the earth In a warning written around AD 200, a Roman writer named Tertullian lamented that "we are burdensome to the world and the resources are scarcely adequate to us" The population at the time is believed to have been 200 million, barely 3 percent of today's 5.8 billion He thought *he* had reason for concern
2. Can a program ever be believed once it stages an incident Sometimes it can NBC's *Dateline* was not the first network to fake a car crash when it used igniters in its dramatization of the hazards of GM trucks; all three networks had done the same Unfortunately, the public was not told that program personnel "helped" ignite the fire Why did the network do it They did it because of competition for viewers The line between entertainment and news was badly blurred What was the reason for the media error *Dateline* anchor Jane Pauley replied, "Because on one side of the line is an Emmy; the other, the abyss"

47 The Comma

FAQs

- Should I use a comma before *and* or *but*? (47b)
- How should I punctuate a series of items? (47c)
- In addresses, is there a comma between the state and the zip code? (47g-2)
- Should I put a comma after *such as*? (47j)

See Ch. 28

The comma is the most common and most useful punctuation mark in academic writing—and also the most difficult to master. Commas are used mainly to indicate sentence structure and thereby clarify meaning. This chapter provides some guidelines (not absolute rules) for the use of commas.

Main uses of commas

See 28b-1

47a Use a comma to set off an introductory phrase or clause

When readers start to read a sentence, one of the first things they do (unconsciously) is try to locate the grammatical subject. Help them do this by setting off with a comma any potentially distracting words that *precede* the subject. In the following excerpt, note how the commas allow the reader to identify easily the sentence subjects that follow them: *cultural relativism, most US citizens*, and *bullfighting*.

- *Because we tend to use our own culture to judge others*, cultural relativism presents a challenge to ordinary thinking.
- *For example*, most US citizens appear to have strong feelings against raising bulls for the sole purpose of stabbing them to death in front of crowds shouting "Olé!"

- ▶ *According to cultural relativism, however,* bullfighting must be viewed strictly within the context of the culture in which it takes place—its history, its folklore, its ideas of bravery, and its ideas of sex roles.

The writer has put a comma after an introductory subordinate clause (*Because we tend to use our own culture to judge others*), a transitional phrase (*For example*), and a prepositional phrase and conjunctive adverb (*According to cultural relativism, however*). In each sentence, the comma marks off everything preceding the subject, allowing the reader to locate the subject easily.

Using a comma after an introductory element is sometimes necessary to prevent possible confusion.

CONFUSING Soon after starting the car began making funny noises.

CLEAR Soon after starting, the car began making funny noises.

Exception: If the introductory element is short and unemphatic, you do not need to insert a comma.

- ▶ *Today* I have class from 9:00 a.m. to 1:00 p.m.
- ▶ *On most days* the mail does not get here until late afternoon.

47b Use a comma before a coordinating conjunction to separate independent clauses

The combination of a comma and a coordinating conjunction (*and, but, or, nor, for, so, yet*) is one of the most common ways of connecting independent clauses.

See 28c-3

- ▶ Members of a mainstream culture often feel threatened by a counterculture, *and* they sometimes move against it in the attempt to affirm their own values.
- ▶ Conflict theorists acknowledge that social institutions were originally designed to meet basic survival needs, *but* they do not see social institutions as working harmoniously for the common good.

Using a comma before a coordinating conjunction to separate independent clauses, as in these examples, clarifies for the reader that each clause is making a separate statement.

When the two clauses are closely linked, however, you may want to omit the comma, as in this example.

► It was very hot and the men had marched a long way. They slumped under the weight of their packs and the curiously black faces were glistening with sweat.

—George Orwell, "Marrakech"

When you are using a coordinating conjunction to link phrases rather than clauses, you generally do not insert a comma.

INCORRECT Acupuncture has proved effective for treating chronic pain, and for blocking acute pain briefly.

CORRECT Acupuncture has proved effective for treating chronic pain and for blocking acute pain briefly.

However, writers sometimes insert a comma to create more separation between the two parts.

See 26d, 31b, and Ch. 32 for more on using phrases and clauses in sentences.

► Acupressure is similar to acupuncture, but does not use needles.

Here the writer has put a comma between the two verb phrases in order to emphasize the contrast in meaning between them.

EXERCISE 47.1 Correct the comma errors in the following sentences:

1. In comparison with ordinary soap the production of detergents exerts a more intense environmental impact.
2. Three out of four Americans claim to believe in God and four out of ten go to church regularly.
3. If a typical book contains 500 pages the information content of a single chromosome corresponds to some 4,000 volumes.
4. There are numerous private daycare centers in the United States but the employees are often underpaid and weary from looking after too many children.
5. In many countries people cannot conceive of themselves apart from the family or group they belong to. In the United States on the other hand self-reliance is the fundamental virtue.
6. The English language surrounds us like a sea and like the waters of the deep it is full of mysteries.

7. Of all the world's languages (which now number some 2,700) English is arguably the richest in vocabulary.
8. For most people body temperature drops at night, and then rises in the morning.
9. Enjoyment and appreciation are related terms but they are not synonymous.
10. Although one can enjoy music without understanding it appreciation of music requires some knowledge.

47c Use commas between items in a series

A series of three or more items generally has commas after all but the last item.

- My super-patriotic neighbor says *red, white, and blue* are his favorite colors.
- Each day, cigarettes contribute to over 1,000 deaths from *cancer, heart disease, and respiratory diseases.*

Some writers, however, drop the final comma (or **serial comma**), especially in fields such as journalism, advertising, and business.

- My uncle used to work for *Pierce, Fenner and Smith.*

Using the serial comma is never wrong, however; and sometimes it helps clarify the meaning of a sentence.

UNCLEAR The three balls were colored red, blue and white and green.

CLEAR The three balls were colored red, blue and white, and green.

OR

CLEAR The three balls were colored red, blue, and white and green.

47d Use commas to separate coordinate adjectives

When the adjectives in a series could be arranged in any order or could be (but are not) strung together with the use of *and,* they are termed **coordinate adjectives.** To show their loose relationship and to avoid confusion with adjectives

GO
See 47j

that cumulate in a particular order to modify each other, separate coordinate adjectives with commas.

- A *rusty,* *dented,* *broken-down* car was left behind.

In this example, each adjective modifies the word *car*, and the string of adjectives could be rearranged:

- A *broken-down, dented, rusty* car was left behind.

 47e Use commas to set off nonessential elements

See 47j, 52e, 52a

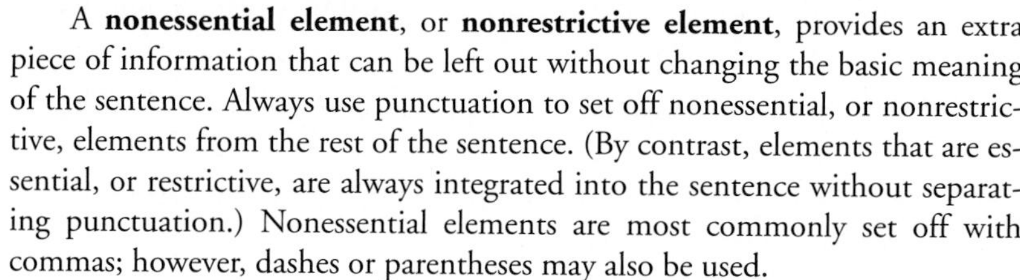

A **nonessential element**, or **nonrestrictive element**, provides an extra piece of information that can be left out without changing the basic meaning of the sentence. Always use punctuation to set off nonessential, or nonrestrictive, elements from the rest of the sentence. (By contrast, elements that are essential, or restrictive, are always integrated into the sentence without separating punctuation.) Nonessential elements are most commonly set off with commas; however, dashes or parentheses may also be used.

- Lung cancer, *the leading cause of cancer deaths in the United States,* kills more than 153,000 Americans each year. [A nonessential appositive is set off with commas.]
- Many other illnesses, *like the common cold and even back strain,* are self-limiting and will improve in time. [A nonessential phrase is set off with commas.]
- Universal health care, *which guarantees every citizen at least basic medical benefits,* is found in every industrialized country in the world except the United States and South Africa. [A nonessential clause is set off with commas.]

In each of these sentences, the writer could have omitted the italicized elements without affecting the basic meaning:

> Lung cancer . . . kills more than 153,000 Americans each year.
>
> Many other illnesses . . . are self-limiting and will improve in time.
>
> Universal health care . . . is found in every industrialized country in the world except the United States and South Africa.

Instead, she chose to insert extra information to help the reader.

Unless the nonessential element ends the sentence, be sure to use *two* commas to set it off, not just one.

INCORRECT Alzheimer's disease, *a progressive impairment of the brain* strikes over 4 million older Americans every year.

CORRECT Alzheimer's disease, *a progressive impairment of the brain,* strikes over 4 million older Americans every year.

When should you use commas instead of dashes or parentheses to set off nonrestrictive elements? Commas represent less of a break in the flow of thought, so the elements they enclose are a bit more closely attached to the main part of the sentence. Dashes give more emphasis to the nonrestrictive element, while parentheses can make the nonrestrictive element seem almost like an afterthought.

See 52e, 52a

EXERCISE 47.2 Correct the comma errors in the following sentences.

1. The antitax group collected 65,202 signatures, on a petition, in support of an immediate tax cut.
2. Although this is more than the required 64,928 signatures it still may not be enough.
3. Because of duplications, illegible signatures and people improperly signing for other family members a minimum margin of at least 2,000 is usually needed, to withstand challenges experts say.
4. At one time many states often barred the sale of contraceptives to minors prohibited the display of contraceptives or, even, banned their sale altogether.
5. Today condoms are sold in the grocery store and some television stations, even air ads for them.
6. The capital campaign which was off to a great start, hoped to net $1.2 million.

Grammar Checkers: Comma Errors

TechALERT!

Do not expect your grammar checker to catch comma errors. Exercise 47.2 contains twenty such errors, and our grammar checker failed to detect any of them.

7. When we shop we want to get the most for our money.
8. Herbalists practice herbal medicine which is based on the medicinal qualities of plants or herbs.
9. Economically and culturally overshadowed by the United States Canada has nonetheless managed to carve out a feisty independent identity since World War II.
10. The participants who had been carefully chosen by Akron's political and community establishment expressed a range of views.

47f Use commas to set off conjunctive adverbs

See 37b

Conjunctive adverbs include such words and phrases as *however, therefore, consequently, thus, furthermore, on the other hand, in general,* and *in other words.* They serve as useful transitional devices, helping the reader to follow the flow of the writer's thinking. By setting off conjunctive adverbs with commas, you give them more prominence, clearly marking a shift in thinking.

- Over eighty million people in the United States suffer from chronic health conditions. Their access to health care**,** *however***,** is largely determined by whether or not they have health insurance.
- Resistance training exercises cause microscopic damage to muscle fibers, which take twenty-four to forty-eight hours to heal; *therefore***,** resistance training programs require at least one day of rest between workouts.

47g Use commas with dates, place names and addresses, titles and degrees, and numbers

1 Using commas with dates

When writing a date in the traditional American format—month, day, and year—set off the year by placing a comma after the day.

- John F. Kennedy died on November 22**,** 1963**,** in Dallas, Texas.

Do not use a comma if only the month and year are given.

- John F. Kennedy died in November 1963 in Dallas, Texas.

Do not use a comma when writing the date in inverse order (day, month, year).

- John F. Kennedy died on 22 November 1963 in Dallas, Texas.

❷ Using commas in place names and addresses

Use commas after all major elements in a place name or address. However, do not put a comma before a zip code.

- Aretha Franklin was born in Memphis, Tennessee, on March 25, 1942.
- Alfredo's new address is 112 Ivy Lane, Englewood, NJ 07631.

❸ Using commas with titles and degrees

See 54a

Use commas to set off a title or degree following a person's name.

- Stella Martinez, MD, was the attending physician.
- Ken Griffey, Jr., will never break Barry Bonds's home run record.

❹ Using commas in numbers

Use a comma in numbers having five digits or more, to form three-digit groups. In a number with four digits, the comma is optional.

2,400 or 2400

56,397

1,000,000

Exceptions: Do not use commas in street numbers, zip codes, telephone numbers, account numbers, model numbers, or years.

47h Use commas with speaker tags

If you are quoting someone and using a speaker tag (such as *he said, according to Freud,* or *notes Laurel Stuart*), put a comma between the tag and the quotation.

- *Thomas Edison said,* "Genius is 1 percent inspiration and 99 percent perspiration."

▸ "The only thing about the fishing industry that has not changed much," *she writes,* "is the fishermen themselves."

See 51e

Note that if a quotation ends in a comma, the comma goes *inside* the quotation marks.

A comma is not used if the quotation ends in another punctuation mark.

▸ "What a marvelous performance!" exclaimed the Queen.

A comma is not used if the quotation is introduced with *that.*

▸ Rush Limbaugh claims that "the poorest people in America are better off than the mainstream families in Europe."

47i Use commas with markers of direct address

Put commas around words that indicate that you are talking directly to the reader: words such as *yes* or *no,* the reader's name (*Bob*), a question tag (*don't you agree?*), or a mild initiator (*Well* or *Oh*).

▸ *Yes,* the stock market is likely to turn around.

▸ Do you really think, *Grace,* that Professor Wilson will postpone the test?

▸ Intelligence is impossible to measure with just one type of test, *don't you think?*

▸ Some people say we should all have guns to protect ourselves. *Well,* I do not agree.

EXERCISE 47.3 Correct the comma errors in the following sentences.

1. One fictitious address used by advertisers is John and Mary Jones 100 Main Street Anytown USA 12345.
2. We are a nation of shoppers aren't we?
3. Easy access to birth control however, was not always the case.
4. "It would be good to have this question on the ballot" the governor said.
5. Dr. Martin Luther King Jr. often quoted lines from the Bible.
6. For example, he would sometimes say "Let justice roll down like the waters."
7. A Renoir exhibition organized and first shown by the National Gallery of Canada in Ottawa Ontario opened at the Art Institute of Chicago, on October 21 1997 and ran through January 4th, of the next year.

8. Much to the irritation of its neighbor, for instance Canada keeps friendly ties with Fidel Castro's Cuba.
9. Lee surrendered to Grant at Appomattox Court House Virginia on April 9 1865.
10. According to the police there were more than 10000 protestors at the rally.

 47j Avoid misuse of commas

Illustrated guide to commas

1. *Never use a single comma between the subject and predicate.* When a complex subject begins a sentence, writers sometimes feel inclined to add an inappropriate comma that splits the subject and predicate.

INCORRECT Numerous psychological and social factors, have a strong influence on how people age.

CORRECT Numerous psychological and social factors have a strong influence on how people age.

This mistake arises only if you insert a *single* comma between subject and predicate. A nonrestrictive element between the subject and the predicate may be set off by two commas.

- Police discretion, the decision as to whether to arrest someone or even to ignore a matter, is a routine part of police work.

2. *Never put commas around essential elements.* **Essential** (or **restrictive**) **elements** are phrases or clauses that help define some other element in the sentence. Unlike nonessential elements, they should not be set off with commas.

See 47e

INCORRECT Consumers, who are considering using a hospital or clinic, should scrutinize the facility's accreditation.

CORRECT Consumers who are considering using a hospital or clinic should scrutinize the facility's accreditation. [Omitting the commas makes it clear that the writer is referring only to those consumers who are considering using a hospital or clinic.]

INCORRECT Be sure to use a filtration system, which will destroy all harmful bacteria in the water.

CORRECT Be sure to use a filtration system which will destroy all harmful bacteria in the water. [Omitting the comma before the modifying phrase makes it clear that the writer is referring only to a certain type of filtration system, not just any filtration system.]

Essential elements include names that come immediately after a common noun and define what the noun refers to:

- The film *Citizen Kane* is an all-time classic. [The name *Citizen Kane* serves as a restrictive appositive, identifying a specific film.]
- The Chilean novelist Isabel Allende is an acclaimed defender of human rights. [The name Isabel Allende is a restrictive appositive, identifying a particular Chilean novelist.]

3. *Avoid using commas with cumulative adjectives.* Adjectives that accumulate before a noun, each one modifying those that follow, are called **cumulative adjectives**. Their modifying relationships, which depend on their order, are likely to be confused by the separating commas that are common with adjectives in a coordinate series.

INCORRECT The suspect was seen driving a *small, new, Italian, luxury* car.

CORRECT The suspect was seen driving a *small new Italian luxury* car.

Cumulative adjectives follow a certain order. Therefore, one way of identifying such adjectives is to see whether they can be reordered. If the result sounds awkward (*a luxury Italian new small car*), the original ordering is cumulative.

See 47d

Coordinate adjectives are different. Instead of modifying the following adjectives, they each modify the noun directly. Therefore, it is appropriate to separate them with commas.

4. *Avoid putting a comma before* than. Resist the urge to heighten a comparison or contrast by using commas to separate the *than* phrase from the rest of the sentence.

INCORRECT Beating our arch rival was more important, than getting to the state playoffs.

CORRECT Beating our arch rival was more important than getting to the state playoffs.

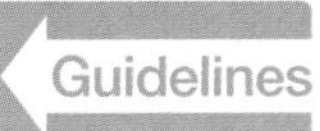

Using Commas

Use commas to separate or set off

- Introductory phrases or clauses, especially if they tend to obscure the subject (47a)
- Independent clauses connected with a coordinating conjunction (47b)
- Three or more items in a series (47c)
- A string of adjectives that could be rearranged or linked by *and* (47d)
- Nonessential phrases or clauses that add to but do not restrict the sentence's basic meaning (47e)
- Conjunctive adverbs used as transitional devices (47f)
- Speaker tags (47h)
- Markers of direct address (47i)

Do not use commas to separate or set off

- A subject and a predicate that would be split with a single comma
- Restrictive phrases or clauses that are essential to a sentence's basic meaning
- Adjectives that depend on their order to show modification in meaning
- Items in a series of only two items
- Phrases beginning with *than*
- Subordinating conjunctions
- Independent clauses that are not connected with a coordinating conjunction (32c, 47b)

5. *Avoid using a comma after a subordinating conjunction.* A comma should not be used to separate a subordinating conjunction from its own clause.

INCORRECT Although**,** the car is fifteen years old, it seems to be in good shape.

CORRECT Although the car is fifteen years old, it seems to be in good shape.

6. *Do not use a comma before parentheses or after a question mark or exclamation point.* A comma is superfluous with an opening parenthesis, a question mark, or an exclamation point, unless the punctuation mark is part of a title.

INCORRECT Muhammad was born in Mecca**,** (now in Saudi Arabia) and founded the religion of Islam around AD 610.

CORRECT	Muhammad was born in Mecca (now in Saudi Arabia) and founded the religion of Islam around AD 610.
INCORRECT	"Where are you going**?,**" he asked.
CORRECT	"Where are you going**?"** he asked.
BUT	According to the book *Culture Shock*!**,** 57% of Americans are Protestants.

For exceptions, see 49a.

7. *Do not insert a comma before a list.* Resist the urge to punctuate before a listed series.

INCORRECT	Some countries, such as**,** Holland, Sweden, and Denmark, have very compassionate welfare systems.
CORRECT	Some countries, such as Holland, Sweden, and Denmark, have very compassionate welfare systems.
INCORRECT	My toughest subjects are**,** math, biology, and physics.
CORRECT	My toughest subjects are math, biology, and physics.

8. *Do not use a comma in a two-item series.* While commas are needed to separate three or more items in a series, separating two items with a comma is unnecessary and distracting.

INCORRECT	Her outfit used strong contrasts between red**,** and blue.
CORRECT	Her outfit used strong contrasts between red and blue.

EXERCISE 47.4 Remove commas where necessary from the following sentences.

1. Tiger Woods has more competition, than he did five years ago.
2. My favorite sports are team sports such as, basketball and football.
3. Anyone, who appreciates classic art, would enjoy a visit to the Prado museum in Madrid.
4. The cues of daylight and darkness, help to keep plants and animals synchronized with the environment.
5. Someday, when we begin to assemble a kind of time map of the body's various rhythms, everyone will be surprised and perhaps delighted to recognize rhythms already observed in themselves.
6. Although, they often find Americans welcoming, and friendly, this is not altogether an easy country for foreigners to travel in.

7. Rodney gave his girlfriend a necklace with a beautiful, large, black, gemstone in it.
8. I normally use the Internet portal, *Yahoo*!, but my mother prefers *Excite*.
9. The objective of the US school system, is to bestow a broad education on every youngster.
10. Unless, they frequently trade in their car for a new one, people normally search for a car, that will last many years.

EXERCISE 47.5 Insert or remove commas where appropriate in the following sentences.

1. Length area and volume, are properties that can be measured.
2. Many plants are poisonous and others can be toxic if used in high doses.
3. We spend more on health care than does any other nation yet, unlike the rest of the industrialized world we do not provide access to health care for our entire population.
4. Stereotypes concerning inevitable intellectual decline among the elderly, have largely been refuted.
5. Classified advertisements are lists of ads set in small, type sizes, that advertise jobs items for sale and garage sales.
6. Long detailed explanations, can put a listener to sleep.
7. People, who are good shoppers, spend many hours planning their purchases.
8. They check sale circulars, from the newspaper and use the telephone to compare prices.
9. When they, finally, find an item at the best possible price they make their purchase.
10. Celebrations, marking the year 2000, were held in cities and towns across the continent.

EXERCISE 47.6 The following passage contains a number of comma errors (not in the original). Make the appropriate corrections.

To survive on the Earth human beings require the stable continuing existence of a suitable environment. Yet the evidence is overwhelming, that the way, in which we now live on the Earth is driving its thin life-supporting skin, and ourselves with it to destruction. To understand this calamity we need to begin with a close look, at the nature of the environment itself. Most of us find this a difficult thing to do for there is a kind of ambiguity, in our relation to the environment. Biologically human beings *participate* in the environmental system as subsidiary parts of the whole. Yet, human society is designed to *exploit* the environment as a whole to produce wealth. The paradoxical role we play in the natural environment—at once participant, and exploiter—distorts our perception of it.

Among primitive people a person is seen as a dependent part of nature, a frail reed in a harsh world governed by natural laws, that must be obeyed if he is to survive. Pressed by this need primitive peoples can achieve a remarkable knowledge of their environment. The African Bushman lives in one of the most stringent habitats on earth; food and water are scarce and the weather is extreme. The Bushman survives, because he has an incredibly intimate understanding of this environment. A Bushman can, for example return after many months, and miles of travel to find a single underground tuber noted in his previous wanderings when he needs it, for his water supply in the dry season.

—Barry Commoner, *The Closing Circle*

FOR COLLABORATION Share your corrected paragraphs with a friend or member of your group. Notice which revisions do the most to improve the paragraphs.

48 The Semicolon

FAQs

- When should I use a semicolon? (48a–48c)
- Do semicolons go inside or outside quotation marks? (48d)

Semicolons have three main functions: (1) linking closely related independent clauses without an intervening *and, but, or, nor, for, so,* or *yet*; (2) linking closely related independent clauses with an intervening *however, therefore,* or other conjunctive adverb; and (3) punctuating a complex list of items.

48a Use a semicolon to link independent clauses without a coordinating conjunction

Guide to semicolons

There are three ways to show a close relationship between independent clauses: with a *comma* and coordinating conjunction, with a *colon*, or with a *semicolon.* A semicolon is used when the two clauses have a coordinate relationship—that is, when they convey equally important ideas—but do not have a coordinating conjunction (*and, but, or, nor, for, so, yet*) between them.

See 47b, 49b, 37b

- The first panacea for a mismanaged nation is inflation of the currency**;** the second is war. Both bring a temporary prosperity**;** both bring a permanent ruin.

—Ernest Hemingway, *Notes on the Next War*

48b Use a semicolon to connect independent clauses separated by a conjunctive adverb

If you separate two independent clauses with a conjunctive adverb like *however, therefore,* or *nevertheless,* you must use a semicolon.

See list in 32c

- More than 185 countries belong to the United Nations**;** *however,* only five of them have veto power.
- Japan and Germany are now among the five most powerful nations in the world**;** *therefore*, they would like to have veto power, too.

48c Use semicolons in a series with internal punctuation

GO See 47c

A **complex series** is one that has internal punctuation. Normally, commas are used to separate items in a series; however, if the individual items themselves contain commas, it can be difficult for readers to determine what the items are. In these cases, semicolons are used to separate the items.

- I have lived in Boulder, Colorado**;** Corpus Christi, Texas**;** and Vero Beach, Florida.

48d Place semicolons outside quotation marks

Semicolons are always positioned outside quotation marks.

- Those who feel abortion is not a woman's prerogative say they are "prolife"**;** those who feel it is say they are "pro-choice."

48e Avoid common semicolon errors

See Ch. 47, Ch. 49

Most errors with semicolons occur as a result of confusing semicolons with commas or with colons.

1. *Do not use a semicolon between an independent clause and a dependent clause or phrase.* Dependent clauses or phrases are linked to independent clauses most often by commas, not semicolons.

INCORRECT	When we say that a country is "underdeveloped"**;** we imply that it is backward in some way.
CORRECT	When we say that a country is "underdeveloped**,"** we imply that it is backward in some way.

TechALERT!

Grammar Checkers: Semicolon Errors

A grammar checker is unlikely to identify semicolon errors with any reliability. You'll do better to learn the principles laid out in this chapter and apply them on your own.

More on semicolons

INCORRECT In *MS Word*, you can remove several items from a document and then insert them as a group into another document by using the Spike**;** a scrapbook-like feature.

CORRECT In *MS Word*, you can remove several items from a document and then insert them as a group into another document by using the Spike**,** a scrapbook-like feature.

2. *Do not use a semicolon to introduce a list.* Use a colon instead of a semicolon to introduce a list.

GO See 49a

INCORRECT Utah has five national parks**;** Arches, Bryce, Canyonlands, Capitol Reef, and Zion.

CORRECT Utah has five national parks**:** Arches, Bryce, Canyonlands, Capitol Reef, and Zion.

EXERCISE 48.1 Correct the punctuation errors in the following sentences.

1. Socrates disliked being called a "teacher," he preferred to think of himself as an intellectual midwife.
2. Tests will be given on the following dates; Monday, November 2, Friday, November 20, and Monday, December 7.
3. The scientific naming and classification of all organisms is known as *taxonomy*, both living and extinct organisms are taxonomically classified.
4. A single category of a species is called a *taxon*, multiple categories are *taxa*.
5. Since laughter seems to help the body heal; many doctors and hospitals are prescribing humor for their patients.
6. Beethoven was deaf when he wrote his final symphonies, nevertheless, they are considered musical masterpieces.
7. Some people think that watching a video at home is more fun than going to a movie, movie theaters are often crowded and noisy.

8. The lifeguards closed the beach when a shark was spotted, a few hours later some fishermen reported seeing the shark leave; so the beach was reopened.
9. The feeling of balance is controlled by the ears, inside each ear are three small tubes filled with fluid.
10. Since its opening in 1955; Disneyland has been an important part of American culture, it has the ability to reflect and reinforce American beliefs, values, and ideals.

49 The Colon

FAQs

- How does the colon differ from the semicolon? (49b)
- What punctuation mark should I use to introduce a quotation? (49c)

In formal writing, the colon is used mainly at the end of a general statement to announce details related in some way to the statement. These details may be given in a list of items, an appositive, an explanatory statement, or a quotation.

49a Use a colon to introduce a list or an appositive

Using the colon

- In creating a macro, you can assign it to any one of three places**:** the toolbar, the keyboard, or a menu.
- One principle should govern your choice**:** which one is most convenient?

In using a colon to introduce a list or an appositive, be sure that the introductory part of the sentence is a grammatically complete independent clause.

FAULTY COLON USE

The four main parts of a memo are**:** header, introduction, summary, and details.

FAULTY COLON USE REVISED

A memo has four main parts**:** header, introduction, summary, and details.

OR

There are four main parts to a memo**:** header, introduction, summary, and details.

Electronic Language: Punctuation-Based Emoticons

Emoticons using colons, semicolons, and other punctuation marks, such as :-o, :-/, and ;-), are not appropriate in formal or academic writing, including email to an instructor or on the job.

In academic writing, the phrase *as follows* is often used. It directly precedes the colon.

- There are four main parts to a memo, as follows**:** header, introduction, summary, and details.

49b Use a colon to set off a second independent clause that explains the first

- Rock climbing is like vertical chess**:** in making each move up the wall, you should have a broad strategy in mind.
- Eighteenth century French philosophers were the godfathers of American democracy**:** Their writings, which influenced many of the Founders, advocated religious tolerance, individual liberty, majority rule, and checks and balances in government.

NOTE You may begin the clause after the colon with either an uppercase letter or a lowercase letter.

49c Use a colon to introduce a quotation

See 49a

When a colon is used to introduce a quotation, the part of the sentence that precedes the colon should be grammatically independent.

- In *Against Empire,* Michael Parenti states his concern about American foreign policy**:** "We should pay less attention to what US policymakers profess as their motives—for anyone can avouch dedication to noble causes—and give more attention to what they actually do."

If the part introducing the quotation is not an independent clause, use a comma instead of a colon.

▸ In *Against Empire*, Michael Parenti states, "We should pay less attention. . . ."

NOTE If the quotation serves only as an example and is set off from the sentence that introduces it, a colon is not required. For instance, the sentence about *Against Empire* is set apart, by indentation and extra spacing, as an example. That is why there is no colon following the preceding sentence, which introduces it.

49d Use colons in titles

Colons are often used in the titles of academic papers and reports. The part of the title that follows the colon is called the *subtitle*. It usually provides a more explicit description of the topic than does the title.

▸ Nature and the Poetic Imagination**:** Death and Rebirth in "Ode to the West Wind"

49e Use colons in business letters and memos

In business letters and memos, colons are used with salutations (*Dear Ms. Townsend***:**), to separate the writer's initials from the typist's initials (*TH***:***ab*), and in memo headings (*To***:**, *From***:**, *Date***:**, *Subject***:**, *Dist***:**).

See Ch. 24 for more on business writing.

49f Use colons in numbers and addresses

More on colon use

Colons are used in Biblical citations to distinguish chapter from verse (*Matthew 4***:***11, Genesis 3***:***9*), in clock times to separate hours from minutes and minutes from seconds (*5***:***44 p.m.*), in ratios (*3***:***1*), and in Web site addresses (*http://www.fray.com*).

EXERCISE 49.1 Correct the punctuation errors in the following sentences.

1. There are several steps involved in writing an effective summary; read the original carefully, choose the material for your summary rewrite the material in a concise manner, identify the source of the original text.
2. We need to buy several ingredients in order to bake the cookies, brown sugar, chocolate chips eggs, and milk.
3. In *Becoming a Critical Thinker*, Ruggiero states, "Truth is not something we create to fit our desires. Rather, it is a reality to be discovered."
4. There are three important characteristics that all critical thinkers possess; the ability to be honest with themselves, the ability to resist manipulation, and the ability to ask questions.
5. Experts say swimming is one of the best forms of exercise, it burns as many calories as running but is low-impact.
6. The hacker apparently logged on to <http//www.au.org> at 9.03 a.m.
7. There are four qualities of a diamond that a prospective buyer should be aware of, color, clarity, cut, and carat weight.
8. In *The Language Instinct*, Steven Pinker discusses the inherent nature of language, "We are all born with the instinct to learn, speak, and understand language."
9. There are six major speech organs which are used to articulate sounds; the larynx, soft palate, tongue body, tongue tip, tongue root, and lips.
10. Denise titled her paper "Howls of Delight; Reintroduction of the Wolf into Yellowstone National Park."

50 The Apostrophe

FAQs

- What is the difference between *its* and *it's*? (50a-1)
- How do I show possession with two names, like *Maria and Roberto*? (50a-2)
- Should I write *1990's* or *1990s*? (50c-2)

The apostrophe is used to indicate possession, to signal contractions and omitted letters, and to form certain plurals.

50a Use apostrophes with nouns to indicate possession

America's apostrophe catastrophe

In its grammatical sense, *possession* refers to ownership or some other special relationship between two nouns, such as that between an amount and the noun it quantifies. With singular nouns, possession is usually indicated by attaching *'s* to the end of the noun.

Sue Ellen's jacket	everyone's dream
my mother's photo	yesterday's bad weather
the club's treasurer	Gandhi's place in history
Ahmad's smile	a week's worth of work
Mr. Linder's class	

There are two exceptions to this rule:

1. If the rule would lead to awkward pronunciation, the extra *s* may be omitted: *Euripides' plays, Moses' laws, Mister Rogers' Neighborhood.*
2. In names of places, companies, and institutions, the apostrophe is often omitted: *Robbers Roost, Kings County, Starbucks, Peoples Republic.*

For plural nouns ending in *s*, form the possessive by just adding an apostrophe at the end:

the Browns' car the Yankees' star pitcher my parents' friends

For plural nouns not ending in *s*, form the possessive by adding *'s:*

women's rights children's section sheep's wool

1 Avoiding apostrophes with possessive pronouns

See 27e

Pronouns never take apostrophes to indicate possession. They have their own possessive forms: *its, his, her/hers, your/yours, their/theirs, our/ours, my/mine.*

Be careful not to confuse *its* and *it's.* The former is possessive; the latter is a contraction for *it is.*

POSSESSIVE The university has revised its policy on hate speech.

CONTRACTION If you fall way behind in your studies, it's hard to catch up.

2 Showing possession with multiple nouns

With multiple nouns, use apostrophes according to your intended meaning. If you want to indicate joint possession, add an apostrophe only to the last of the nouns:

Bill and Hillary's wedding

Siskel and Ebert's recommendations

If you want to show *separate* possession, put an apostrophe after each of the nouns:

Julie's and Kathy's weddings

Omar's, Gretchen's, and Mike's birthdays

50b Use apostrophes to indicate contractions and omitted letters

In casual speech, syllables are sometimes omitted from common word combinations. For example, *cannot* becomes *can't.* In formal writing, such contractions are generally inappropriate. In much informal writing, however,

Grammar Checkers: Apostrophe Errors

Your grammar checker should flag most of the apostrophe errors described in this chapter, including all three of the common errors listed in the box. However, it may not tell you exactly how to fix the problem. For example, in the sentence "TV news reporting *seem's* like yet another form of entertainment," our grammar checker identified *seem's* as problematic but offered five different alternatives, only one of which was correct. You will have to exercise your own judgment in such cases. The guidelines in this chapter should help you.

such as email messages and personal letters, contractions are quite common. Just be sure to punctuate them correctly with an apostrophe.

will not → won't	should not → shouldn't	it is → it's
I am→ I'm	you have → you've	they are → they're

The apostrophe also can be used for less common contractions, especially if you are trying to create a colloquial, slangy tone.

the 1990s → the '90s	magazine → 'zine
underneath → 'neath	neighborhood → 'hood

50c Use apostrophes to mark certain plural forms

When a letter or symbol is used as a noun, the usual way of pluralizing nouns (adding an *-s* or *-es*) does not work well: "There are four *ss* in *sassafras*." In such cases, an apostrophe can help out: "There are four *s*'s in *sassafras*."

1 Forming the plurals of letters, symbols, and words referred to as words

Adding *'s* instead of *s* clarifies the plural forms of unusual nouns.

How can she have two @'s in her email address?

My instructor said I have too many *there*'s in my paper.

❷ Forming the plurals of numbers and abbreviations

Both the Modern Language Association and the American Psychological Association recommend omitting the apostrophe in forming plurals like the following:

the 1990s several IOUs
a pair of 6s a shipment of PCs

More on apostrophes

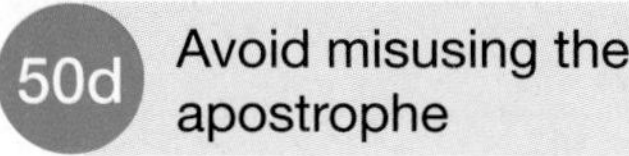

50d Avoid misusing the apostrophe

Be careful not to use apostrophes where they do not belong. The box below lists some of the most common apostrophe errors.

EXERCISE 50.1 Each of the following sentences contains at least one error involving the use of apostrophes. Make the appropriate correction(s).

1. Its unfortunate that Bobs' birthday falls on February 29.
2. I wanted to go to Maria's and Roberto's party, but I wasnt able to.
3. The snake sheds it's skin many times during its life.

Apostrophes

Using an apostrophe for the possessive form of *it*

NO Her dog lost *it's* collar.

YES Her dog lost *its* collar.

Using an apostrophe with a nonpossessive noun

NO This report discusses four major *features'* of modern mass media.

NO This report discusses four major *feature's* of modern mass media.

YES This report discusses four major *features* of modern mass media.

Using an apostrophe with a present-tense verb

NO TV news reporting *seem's* like yet another form of entertainment.

YES TV news reporting *seems* like yet another form of entertainment.

4. Does the mens' group meet here?
5. No, its a womens' group that meets in this room on Thursdays.
6. I can't wait til my vacation comes!
7. Im taking my lawyers advice on such matter's.
8. All of the orchestra member's instruments seemed to be out of tune.
9. The driver and passenger's airbags both deployed after the accident.
10. Kevin's and Lauren's older sister is in high school now.

FOR COLLABORATION Take note of apostrophe errors that you see on campus or in your neighborhood; share your examples with your group.

51 Quotation Marks

FAQs

- Should I use quotation marks if I am only paraphrasing someone's words? (51a-1)
- Should a comma go inside or outside the quotation mark? (51e)
- How do I introduce a quotation? (51e)

The primary use of quotation marks is to acknowledge other people's words and statements. Using quotation marks is especially important in academic writing, which puts a premium on the ownership of ideas.

Quotation marks

51a Use quotation marks for exact direct quotations

Quotation marks should be placed around any words, phrases, or sentences that you have borrowed from someone else (unless the quotations are so lengthy that you prefer to set them off as an indented block).

- In *The End of Work,* Jeremy Rifkin said, "In the years ahead, more than 90 million jobs in a labor force of 124 million are potentially vulnerable to replacement by machines."
- One reviewer called it "a very readable and timely book."
- Some years ago, a group of artists designed a "space bridge" between Los Angeles and New York.

1 Paraphrasing or quoting indirectly

A summarization, restatement, or paraphrase of a statement made by someone else is a form of **indirect discourse,** and quotation marks are not used. Putting quotation marks around words that were not those of the speaker or writer would be extremely misleading.

▶ Rifkin argues that in the future more than two-thirds of the American workforce could be displaced by automation.

❷ Setting off long quotations in block form

A long quotation (more than four lines) should be set off as an indented block without quotation marks.

▶ Rifkin sees this reduction of the workforce as having profound social effects:

> The wholesale substitution of machines for workers is going to force every nation to rethink the role of human beings in the social process. Redefining opportunities and responsibilities for millions of people in a society absent of mass formal employment is likely to be the single most pressing social issue of the coming century. (Rifkin xv)

For a student example, see 16c-2.

51b Use quotation marks to suggest skepticism about a term

Sometimes you may find yourself writing about a concept that you think does not deserve the respect other people are giving it. In such cases, you can convey your skepticism by putting the concept name in quotation marks.

▶ Some politicians who claim to support **"**family values**"** have been found to be unfaithful to their spouses and abusive of their children.

In this example, the quotation marks around *family values* suggest that the writer has a skeptical view of the term.

This application of quotation marks (sometimes referred to as "scare quotes") should be reserved for cases where you believe that a term is being misused by others. Only on rare occasions should you use quotation marks simply to make ironic or sarcastic comments.

INCORRECT Action films are very **"**intellectual,**"** aren't they?

CORRECT Action films are not very intellectual, are they?

51c Use quotation marks to indicate shifts of register

Quotation marks can be used occasionally to set off a colloquial term from the more formal discourse surrounding it.

- One should always try to avoid an inflexible, "cookie-cutter" approach to rhetorical criticism.

NOTE Colloquialisms should be used sparingly in formal writing, even when punctuated with quotation marks.

51d Use quotation marks when citing titles of short works

When referring by title to short stories, book chapters, poems, essays, songs, and other brief works, enclose the titles in quotation marks.

- I will never forget the first time I read Shirley Jackson's short story "The Lottery."
- "Smells Like Teen Spirit" is a musical classic.
- Chapter 20, "Design Principles and Graphics," talks about the functionality and aesthetics of formatting.

See 53e

Titles of longer or more encompassing works are italicized or underlined.

51e Follow standard practice in using other punctuation with quotations

Quoted material is commonly combined and mixed with a writer's original material. Here are common guidelines for using other punctuation with quotations.

1. *Put commas and periods inside the end quotation mark.* Standard American editorial practice calls for commas and periods to be placed as shown in the following passage:

► “The definition of community implicit in the market model**,”** argues Patricia Hill Collins, “sees community as arbitrary and fragile, structured fundamentally by competition and domination**.”**

NOTE Readers of British publications may see exceptions to this rule, as the British style is to place commas and periods outside quotation marks. When quoting from British sources, you should standardize punctuation for consistency with modern American usage, placing periods and commas inside quotation marks.

2. *Put colons and semicolons outside the end quotation mark.*

► One critic called 1990 “the year in which rock and roll was reborn**”:** the fusing of metal and rap by groups like Living Colour and Faith No More broke down racial barriers in a way reminiscent of early rock and roll.

► One of the things that distinguished Snoop Doggy Dogg from other rappers was his style, which was described in the *New York Times* as “gentle**”;** “where many rappers scream,” said *Times* reporter Touré, “he speaks softly.”

3. *Put other punctuation marks inside the end quotation mark if they are part of the quotation; otherwise, put them outside the end quotation mark.* Question marks, exclamation points, dashes, parentheses, and other punctuation marks should be positioned according to meaning.

PART OF QUOTED TITLE

Whitney Houston’s “How Will I Know**?”** entered the pop charts at number one.

PART OF SENTENCE

What do you think of controversial songs like “Deep Cover” and “Cop Killer**”?**

4. *Use single quotation marks (‘ ’) for quotation marks within quotation marks.*

► Garofalo notes that “on cuts like **‘**JC**’** and **‘**Swimsuit Issue,**’** Sonic Youth combined an overt sexuality with uncompromisingly feminist lyrics about women’s issues.”

► The last line of the stanza reads, “Quoth the raven, **‘**Nevermore.**’**”

CommonErrors

Quotation Marks

Using quotation marks just to call attention to something

NO Pete Sampras won the Wimbledon championship "seven" times.

YES Pete Sampras won the Wimbledon championship seven times.

See 35f

Using quotation marks for indirect discourse

NO President Bush said "he was a compassionate conservative."

YES President Bush said he was a compassionate conservative.

See 18a for an example.

Putting quotation marks around the title of your paper on a title page or at the head of the paper

If your title contains within it the title of *another* short work, however, that work's title should be enclosed in quotation marks.

▸ Death and Rebirth in "Ode to the West Wind"

5. *Introduce quotations with the punctuation standard grammar calls for.* If the introduction to a quotation is not a full clause, do not use any punctuation.

▸ The conservative Parents Music Resource Center said that heavy metal was "the most disturbing element in contemporary music."

If the introduction to a quotation *is* a full clause, use a colon.

▸ The conservative Parents Music Resource Center said that heavy metal was harmful to society**:** "It's the most disturbing element in contemporary music."

See 49h

Exception: If the introduction to a quotation is a speaker tag such as *she said* or *he notes*, use a comma.

TechHelp

Using Smart Quotation Marks

To use the more elegant smart (curly) quotation marks, instead of straight ones, click on TOOLS > AUTOCORRECT > AUTOFORMAT and then check "replace straight quotes with smart quotes."

▶ *Rolling Stone* noted, "Beneath the 'save the children' rhetoric is an attempt by a politically powerful minority to impose its morality on the rest of us."

EXERCISE 51.1 Correct the punctuation errors in the following sentences.

1. The question is not "why some rappers are so offensive, but rather, why do so many fans find offensive rappers appealing"?
2. "When you hear your record company has been sold for 20 or 30 times its earnings", said Tim Collins, Aerosmith's manager, "you think, "I want a piece of that"."
3. According to one critic, the 2006 Lollapalooza summer tour was, "way too male and way too guitar-oriented."
4. The biggest lottery prize in history, shared by eight workers in a Nebraska meatpacking plant, was worth "$365 million."
5. PMRC's Pam Howar expressed the concern that Madonna was teaching young girls: "how to be porn queens in heat".
6. In announcing that US superskier Picabo Street would miss the World Cup races because of a knee injury, her coach told the press", When the mind is ready but the body is not [. . .] there is danger of another injury".
7. The citation for the 2004 Nobel Peace Prize given to Kenyan activist Wangari Maathai reads, in part: She represents an example and a source of inspiration for everyone in Africa fighting for sustainable development, democracy and peace.
8. There are people who really enjoy line dances like "YMCA" and "The Electric Slide", although there are others who think those dances are silly.
9. Older people are often labeled "old and sick", "old and helpless", old and useless, or old and dependent:" in fact, the general image of old age is negative.
10. The Celtic tune "Greensleeves" is the melody used for the carol "What Child Is This"?

52 Other Punctuation Marks

FAQs

- When should I use dashes instead of parentheses? (52e–52f)
- How should I use brackets and ellipses in quotations? (52h–52j, 52k, 52m)

See 21b for a discussion of punctuating with email diacritics.

Parentheses, dashes, brackets, ellipses, or slashes can be used, in moderation and in the proper contexts, to clarify meaning and add interest to writing.

Dashes and parentheses

PARENTHESES ( )

52a Use parentheses to insert extra information

Parenthetical comments—clarifications, asides, examples, or other extra pieces of information—are often embedded within sentences. They can be as short as a single word or as long as an entire sentence.

- Many components of biological diversity (biodiversity) are dwindling.
- You can get a free annual credit report from any of the nation's three largest agencies (visit *annualcreditreport.com*).
- For most right-handed people, the left hemisphere of the brain controls manual skill and language. (The opposite is true for most left-handed people.)
- Manual skill (that is, the skill associated with making and using tools) is usually localized in the same hemisphere as speech.

Another common use of parentheses is in documentation. The scientific reference style calls for inserting reference citations in parentheses within sentences. This parenthetical style is the preferred method of the MLA and APA.

See 12a and 13a

- We need to think about the implications of our future liberation (Eastman and Hayford).
- In antiquity and through the Middle Ages, memory was a valued skill (Hacking, 1995).

52b Do not overuse parentheses

Parentheses are so handy that you may be tempted to overuse them. Resist the temptation. Too many parentheses can make it difficult for readers to follow the main train of thought. If you find yourself developing a parenthesis habit, look for ways to rewrite some of the parenthetical comments as modifiers or as subordinate clauses.

See 26c, 37c

52c Use parentheses around letters or numbers to set off embedded lists

Listed phrases or clauses embedded in a longer sentence may be itemized with numbers or letters placed within parentheses.

- Socialism has three essential components: (1) the public ownership of the means of production, (2) central planning, and (3) distribution of goods without a profit motive.

52d Use parentheses to acknowledge editorial emphasis within a quotation

When you quote a passage, you may want to emphasize a certain part of it that is not emphasized in the original. You can do so by underlining or italicizing that part and then, at the end of the passage, acknowledging the change by writing *emphasis added* or *italics mine* between parentheses.

- Scheuer states, "Our popular and political cultures are dominated by money and profit, imagery and spin, hype and personality—and there can be no doubt that *the chief culprit* is commercial television." (emphasis added)

EXERCISE 52.1 The following passage has too many parentheses. Rewrite it, using the suggestions given in 26c and 37c.

Abatement of water pollution in the United States (like that of air pollution) has been largely a success story. It also is one of the longest running (its legislative origins go back to the turn of the century). Until the 1970s, most legislation addressed public health issues and included provisions for helping communities build treatment plants (specifically, for water and sewage). With passage of the Water Pollution Control Act in 1972 (later called the Clean Water Act), the federal government turned its attention to cleaning up the nation's waterways (they had become badly polluted from industrial effluents and inadequately treated sewage).

FOR COLLABORATION If you feel that you have a parenthesis habit, give a sample piece of writing to a friend or member of your group, and ask him or her for suggestions for revision.

DASHES —

Although dashes are a slightly less formal kind of punctuation than parentheses, they have several good uses. You can create a dash by typing two consecutive hyphens, which most word processors will then convert into a solid dash. If you first type a space before the hyphens, you'll get a short *en dash*; if you don't type such a space, you'll get a longer *em dash.* (The former is preferred for narrow-column writing such as in newspapers, the latter for full-page columns such as in college papers.)

52e Use dashes to highlight extra informational comments

Dashes set off internal, informational comments in a more emphatic way than parentheses do.

- The first great American myth—the myth of the Chosen People—emerged among the Puritans in the colonial period.

- The modern industrial food chain has been unrivaled for its productivity—on average, a single US farmer today grows enough food each year to feed 100 people.
- Public decision makers have a tendency to focus mostly on the more obvious and immediate environmental problems—usually described as "pollution"—rather than on the deterioration of natural ecosystems upon whose continued functioning global civilization depends.

Dashes are particularly useful for setting off an internal list of items.

- Particularly resistant to increased pollution controls have been small businesses in California—paint dealers, gas stations, and dry-cleaning establishments—which the state began regulating in 1990.

52f Use dashes to set off important or surprising points

If not overused, dashes can be a dramatic way to set off an inserted comment.

- While the Marshall Islanders continue to wrestle with the consequences of nuclear testing, a new proposal is on the table that will make the islands a dumping ground for American garbage—literally.
- A US waste disposal company, Admiralty Pacific, proposes to ship household waste from the west coast of the United States to the Pacific islands—an estimated 34 billion pounds of waste in the first five years of the program alone.

52g Confine yourself to one pair of dashes per sentence

Dashes, like parentheses, can be overused. If you need to add more than one informational comment to a sentence, use commas or parentheses around the other comments. Too many dashes in a paragraph are a sign of poorly integrated ideas.

See 47e

EXERCISE 52.2 Insert appropriate punctuation if needed (parentheses, dashes, or commas) in the places marked in the following sentences.

1. In 1987, officials in the Guatemalan government and the US Drug Enforcement Agency___DEA___entered into an agreement to defoliate vast areas of Guatemala's north and northwest___a region that contains a wildlife refuge and the largest area of unplundered rainforest remaining in Central America.
2. On the Internet are thousands of Usenet newsgroups, made up of people who communicate about almost any conceivable topic___from donkey racing and bird watching to sociology and quantum physics___.
3. People look forward to communicating almost daily with others in their newsgroup, with whom they share personal, sometimes intimate, matters about themselves___even though they have "met" only electronically___.
4. There is no theory that would have led anyone to expect that after World War II, Japan___with a religion that stressed fatalism, with two major cities destroyed by atomic bombs, and stripped of its colonies___would become an economic powerhouse able to turn the Western world on its head.
5. Although the distinction between race and ethnicity is clear___one is biological, the other cultural___people often confuse the two.
6. The United Nations defines seven basic types of families, including single-parent families, communal families___unrelated people living together for ideological, economic, or other reasons___, extended families, and others.
7. By the late 1980s, the proportion of adult Americans who were single by choice or by chance___often after failed marriages___had increased to slightly over 25 percent of adult men and over 20 percent of adult women.
8. If you were to go on a survival trip, which would you take with you___food or water___?
9. The key to a successful exercise program is to begin at a very low intensity, progress slowly___and stay with it___!
10. The three branches of the US government___the executive, the legislative, and the judicial___are roughly equal in power and authority.

Using punctuation marks, common and rare

BRACKETS [ ]

Use brackets to insert editorial comments or clarifications into quotations

Quotations represent someone's exact words. If you choose to alter those words (because of a misspelling in the original quotation or to add explanatory information, for example), you must indicate that you have done so by putting brackets around the alterations.

► "One of the things that will produce a stalemate in Rio [the site of the 1992 UN conference on the environment] is the failure of the chief negotiators, from both the north and the south, to recognize the contradictions between the free market and environmental protection."

The reference to Rio in this quotation might not be understood out of context, so the author has inserted a brief clarification between brackets.

Whenever you insert a quotation from your reading into your writing, be aware that you may need to give the reader important information that was located in the sentences immediately preceding or following it in the original. Any necessary clarification may be added either outside the actual quotation or within it, in which case it should be in brackets. Say, for example, that you have come across this passage in your reading and want to quote the final sentence:

> Sea snails are the source of highly refined painkilling chemicals now being tested for human use. One scientist describes these as "little chemical factories" that are in essence doing what drug companies are trying to do. They have created thousands of chemical compounds and refined them to be exquisitely sensitive and potent.

If you just quoted the final sentence word for word, readers would not know what *They* referred to. Therefore, you should write the sentence in one of the following two ways:

► Sea snails "have created thousands of chemical compounds and refined them to be exquisitely sensitive and potent."

OR

► "[Sea snails] have created thousands of chemical compounds and refined them to be exquisitely sensitive and potent."

52i Use brackets with the word *sic*

The Latin word *sic* (meaning "so" or "thus") indicates a mechanical error—for example, an error of grammar, usage, or spelling—in a quotation. You may want to use it to show both that you recognize an error in a quote and that you did not introduce the error when transposing the quote into your writing. Place it in brackets in the quotation, immediately following the error.

- "Any government that wants to more and more restrict freedoms will do it by financial means, by creating financial vacums [*sic*]."

If you frequently quote Internet messages like this one, you may have many opportunities to use *sic*. Overusing it, though, may make your writing sound snobbish.

52j Use brackets for parenthetical comments within parentheses

If one parenthetical comment is nested within another, the inner one should be punctuated with brackets to distinguish it from the outer one.

- The spectacular palace that King Louis XIV built at Versailles (which is located 19 kilometers [12 miles] west of Paris) required 35,000 workers and 27 years to construct.

ELLIPSES . . .

An **ellipsis** (plural: *ellipses*) is a series of three periods, used to indicate a deletion from a quotation or a pause in a sentence. An ellipsis consists of three *spaced* periods (. . .), not three bunched ones (...).

52k Use an ellipsis to indicate a deletion from a quotation

The sentence with an ellipsis should not be significantly different in meaning from the original sentence, nor should it be ungrammatical.

- "Practically any region on earth will harbor some insect
  . . .
  species—~~native or exotic~~—that are functioning near the limits of their temperature or moisture tolerance."

If you end a sentence with an ellipsis, use a fourth period to indicate the end of the sentence.

▶ "The notion of literature as a secular scripture extends roughly from Matthew Arnold to Northrop Frye. . . ."

52l Use an ellipsis to indicate a pause in a sentence

To mark a pause for dramatic emphasis in your own writing, use an ellipsis.

▶ I was ready to trash the whole thing . . . but then I thought better of it.

Beware, however, of overusing ellipses to indicate pauses.

EXERCISE 52.3 Reduce the following passage to a two-sentence quotation, using at least one set of brackets and one ellipsis.

Preserving the planet's remaining natural areas is one of our most urgent responsibilities. Such places are fundamental to every economy in the world, no matter how divorced from "nature" it might appear to be, and no conceivable development will lessen that dependence. There is no substitute for a stable hydrological cycle, healthy pollinator populations, or the general ecological stability that only natural areas can confer. We need these places in ways that are direct enough to satisfy even the most hard-nosed economist, but we also need them for reasons that are harder to quantify.

52m Use brackets around ellipses in quotations to differentiate them from the author's ellipses

See 12a

MLA style recommends that you place brackets around your ellipsis marks if necessary to differentiate them from ellipsis marks the original author used. One space should be inserted before the opening bracket and one space after the closing bracket, unless it is followed by another punctuation mark. There should be no space between a bracket and the ellipsis mark itself. Thus, someone quoting the example sentence in 52l above might insert additional ellipsis marks as follows:

▶ "The writer states: 'I was ready to trash the whole thing . . . but [. . .] thought better of it.' "

Note that this bracketing applies only to quotations. It is *not* done with statements of your own.

SLASHES /

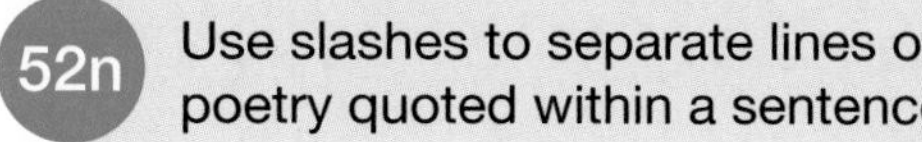

52n Use slashes to separate lines of poetry quoted within a sentence

If you are quoting lines of poetry without setting them off in separate lines as they appear in the poem, put a slash (surrounded by spaces) between the lines.

- Gerard Manley Hopkins's poetry features what he called "sprung rhythms," as can be heard in these lines from "The Windhover": "No wonder of it: sheer plod makes plow down sillion / Shine, and blue-bleak embers, ah my dear, / Fall, gall themselves, and gash gold-vermilion."

52o Use a slash to show alternatives

Slashes (with no surrounding spaces) are used in expressions such as *either/or, pass/fail, on/off, win/win* and *writer/editor.* Readers may object, though, if you overuse them. The expressions *he/she, his/her*, and *s/he* are admirable attempts at gender neutrality, but many people dislike their phonetic clumsiness. We suggest you use *he or she* and *his or her* or find other ways of avoiding sexist pronouns.

See 42c

52p Use a slash to indicate a fraction

Fractions that would be set in formal mathematics on separate lines also can be shown on one line, with a slash dividing the numerator from the denominator:

1/3 3/8 2 2/5

Your word-processing program may automatically convert fractions into more elegant versions like $\frac{1}{2}$ and $\frac{1}{4}$, but first you have to type them with slashes. (Check under AUTOFORMAT to see whether your program will format fractions for you.)

52q Use slashes in Internet addresses

Slashes are indispensable components of URLs (Web site addresses), such as <http://mediachannel.org/views/>. Include the last slash if it brackets a directory, but not if it brackets an HTML file. (Tip: If your browser automatically adds a final slash to the address, that tells you the final term names a directory, not a file.)

52r Use slashes in writing dates informally

Instead of writing out a date like June 16, 2006, you can write the date informally: 6/16/06. (Note: In many other countries, this date would be written 16/06/06.)

part

11

Mechanics

53 Capital Letters and Italics

FAQs

- Should I capitalize the first word of a sentence in parentheses? (53a)
- Should I capitalize directions like *east* and *northwest*? (53b)
- Do I need to capitalize email addresses? (53d)
- If I cite a URL, should I put it in italics? (53f)
- Should all foreign words be italicized? (53h)

Capitalization

CAPITAL LETTERS

Capital (uppercase) letters are used to indicate the start of a new sentence. They are also used for proper names, proper adjectives, and some abbreviations.

53a Capitalize the first word of all free standing sentences

Sentences like the one you are reading should always start with a capital letter. Sentences that are embedded in other sentences, however, may or may not start with a capital letter, depending on the situation.

If a sentence follows a colon or dash, capitalization is optional:

- Some employees have strong objections to mandatory drug testing in the workplace**: T**hey believe that their civil liberties are being violated.

  OR

- Some employees have strong objections to mandatory drug testing in the workplace**: t**hey believe that their civil liberties are being violated.

TechALERT!

Electronic Language: Using Capital Letters

Many people like to write emails and text messages without capital letters. This very informal style is fine for writing to friends. Bear in mind, however, that all-lowercase writing is harder to read and is not acceptable in academic papers or projects, more formal emails, or other formal, academic writing.

You should be sure to pick one capitalization style for this situation, however, and use it consistently throughout your writing.

If a sentence occurs in parentheses within another sentence, the first word of the parenthetical sentence should not be capitalized:

- ▶ Major league baseball no longer seems to enjoy the civic loyalty it used to (~~For~~ *for* example, several teams have threatened to leave their cities if new facilities are not built).

If, however, the parenthesized sentence is set off as a separate sentence, the first word should be capitalized:

- ▶ Major league baseball no longer seems to enjoy the civic loyalty it used to. (For example, several teams have threatened to leave their cities if new facilities are not built.)

If a sentence occurs as a quotation within another sentence and is set off by a colon, comma, or dash, the first word should be capitalized:

- ▶ Rush Limbaugh once said, "~~vegetarians~~ *Vegetarians* are a bunch of weaklings who wouldn't be able to bench press 50 pounds after one of their meals."

However, if the quotation is not set off by a colon, comma, or dash, the first word should be lowercase:

- ▶ Rush Limbaugh once said that "~~Vegetarians~~ *vegetarians* are a bunch of weaklings who wouldn't be able to bench press 50 pounds after one of their meals."

Question fragments can also be capitalized.

- ▶ Will the stock market keep booming? Level off? Take a dive?

If you are quoting a poem, capitalize the first letter of each line (if the original did so).

▸ Long as the heart beats life within her breast
  Thy child will bless thee, guardian mother mild,
And far away thy memory will be blest
  By children of the children of thy child.

—Alfred, Lord Tennyson, 1864

More on capitalization

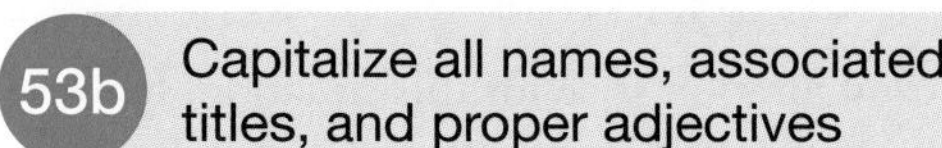

53b Capitalize all names, associated titles, and proper adjectives

Capitalize the first letter of any name, title, or proper adjective referring to a particular person, place, or thing.

1. *Capitalize names and associated titles of people.*

Ralph Nader	Aunt May
Ruth Bader Ginsburg	Dr. Harris
Professor Mixco	Ken Griffey, Jr.

NOTE Professional titles and family relationships are *not* capitalized if they are not used as part of the person's name:

▸ My aunt is a doctor specializing in internal medicine.

2. *Capitalize place names.*

San Diego, California	the Rockies
Lake Michigan	Maple Street
the Great Northwest	Apartment 34
Long Island	Yellowstone National Park
the Mississippi River	Africa

NOTE Compass points (*north, southwest*) are capitalized only when they are incorporated into a name (*North Carolina*) or when they function as nouns denoting a particular region (*the Southwest*).

3. *Capitalize the names of historic events.*

World War II	the Boston Tea Party
Reconstruction	the Sand Creek Massacre
the Middle Ages	the Cold War

4. *Capitalize the names of days, months, holidays, and eras.*

Monday
April
the Gilded Age
the Reagan Era
Thanksgiving
Veteran's Day

NOTE Seasons of the year usually are not capitalized:

last fall winter sports spring semester

5. *Capitalize the names of organizations, companies, and institutions.*

Common Cause
the National Rifle Association
Time-Warner, Inc.
the United Nations
the Central Intelligence Agency
Intel Corporation
New York University
Alameda Community College

6. *Capitalize the names of certain objects and products.* In most cases, only the first letter of each word in an object or product name is capitalized:

the Power Mac
the Plymouth Voyager
the Hope Diamond
the *Titanic*
the North Star
the Boeing 767

Some manufacturers, however, especially in the computer industry, use intercaps:

WordPerfect
HotJava
QuarkXPress
GlobalFax

Many objects and products have abbreviated names in all uppercase letters: *HDTV, AOL, RISC.*

See 54d

7. *Capitalize religious, national, and ethnic names.*

Catholicism
the Koran
Buddha
the Bible
Korean
Chicana
Passover
the Prophet
Holy Communion
the Ten Commandments
African American
Polynesian

8. *Capitalize adjectives based on proper nouns.*

American football
French history
Newtonian physics
Jewish literature
Southern hospitality
Islamic tradition

53c Capitalize all significant words in titles

In titles of books, poems, articles, plays, films, and other cultural works, every word except articles (*a, an, the*), conjunctions, and short prepositions should be capitalized. The first word of the title and of the subtitle should be capitalized, even if it is an article, conjunction, or short preposition.

For Whom the Bell Tolls
The Joy Luck Club
Death of a Salesman
Pulp Fiction
"Ode to the West Wind"
"Learning in Context: A Qualitative Study"

See 13a

NOTE The APA reference style calls for capitalizing only the first word of the title and of the subtitle and any proper nouns.

53d Follow the owner's preferences in capitalizing email addresses and URLs

Although most of the Internet is not case-sensitive, there are two important reasons for writing email and Internet addresses exactly as the owners do. First, some parts of these addresses, such as the pathnames that follow the first single slash in URLs, *are* case-sensitive. Second, some people use uppercase and lowercase letters to make important distinctions in their addresses. For example, Holli Burgon uses uppercase and lowercase letters to help users make sense of her email name. As the middle child in her family, she came up with *HbMidKid,* which is easier to decipher than *hbmidkid.*

EXERCISE 53.1 Correct the capitalization errors in the following sentences.

1. On july 17, 1996, a Trans World airlines passenger plane crashed into the atlantic ocean, killing all 230 people aboard.
2. Bound for paris, france, the boeing 747 disappeared from Radar screens at 8:48 p.m.
3. The plane was about fifty miles East of the Airport when it plunged into the Ocean about ten miles South of East Moriches, long island.
4. The US coast guard conducted a futile rescue effort, and the national transportation safety board carried out a long investigation.

Grammar Checkers: Capitalization

Your grammar checker will probably flag—and in some cases automatically correct—errors of capitalization involving names of people, days, months, countries, major cities, religions, and so on. But it will miss many other proper names, especially names that resemble common nouns. For example, when we wrote *boston tea party,* our grammar checker flagged *boston* but let *tea* and *party* go. So you should not count on your computer to identify all errors of capitalization.

5. Meanwhile, rumors circulated on the internet and a well-known Politician claimed, "the plane was shot down by a US navy missile."
6. I logged on to <HTTP://WWW.cbpp.org/pa-1.htm> and found a report called "Pulling apart: a State-by-state analysis of income Trends."
7. The report, published by the center on Budget and policy priorities, says that "in 48 States, the gap between the incomes of the richest 20 percent of families with children and the incomes of the poorest 20 percent of families with children is significantly wider than it was two Decades ago." (only Alaska and north Dakota bucked the trend.)
8. Individual states could counteract this National trend (Few, however, have done so).
9. My Nephew, Julius Evans, jr., is a Junior at San Francisco state university.
10. So, we'll sit no more a'writing
        so late into the night,
    though our minds be still a burning,
        and our thoughts be still as bright.
    [The first stanza of a poem by Doug Downs]

ITALICS

Using italics

In published documents, *italic* type is used for a number of purposes, which will be described in the sections that follow. Although most word processors permit the selection of an italic font, many instructors prefer that students use underlining instead of italics in their papers, as underlined letters and words stand out more than italicized ones. If you are a student and wish to use italics rather than underlining, check with your instructor first.

53e Italicize titles of independent creative works

See Ch. 12

Titles of books, magazines, digital magazines (e-zines), newspapers, and other creative products that are independently packaged and distributed to a public audience should be written with italics. Here are some examples:

BOOKS	*The Scarlet Letter*
MAGAZINES	*National Geographic*
E-ZINES	*Salon*
NEWSPAPERS	*Los Angeles Times*
LONG POEMS	*Paradise Lost*
MOVIES	*Ocean's Eleven*
PLAYS	*The Iceman Cometh*
TV PROGRAMS	*The O.C.*
PAINTINGS	*Nude Descending a Staircase*
SCULPTURES	Rodin's *The Kiss*
CDS	*Back to Bedlam*
MUSIC VIDEOS	*Closure*
COMPUTER GAMES	*Mortal Kombat*
ONLINE WORKS	*Encarta*

NOTE The names of personal or commercial homepages should not be underlined or italicized.

53f Italicize URLs and email addresses

When writing an Internet or email address in the body of a text, use underlining or italics, unless the address is enclosed in angle brackets.

▶ Helpful information about current Congressional legislation can be found at *http://thomas.loc.gov/.* The email address is *thomas@loc.gov.*

53g Italicize names of vehicles

Names of particular vehicles, not types of vehicles, should be italicized. These include the names of spacecraft, airplanes, ships, and trains.

Voyager 2

Spirit of St. Louis

Titanic

Wabash Cannonball

53h Italicize foreign words and phrases

In general, it is best to avoid using foreign words and phrases when writing in English. However, if you need to use a foreign expression (for example, because there is no good English equivalent), write it with underlining or italics and, if possible, provide a brief English explanation.

▶ One of the nice things about Brazilian culture is the custom of giving a *jeitinho,* or helping someone work things out.

▶ My Dutch friends say they like being in a *gezellig* environment, one that has a lot of human warmth.

Latin names for plants, animals, and diseases should be underlined or italicized.

▶ The sandwich tern (*Sterna sandvicensis*) is slightly larger than the common tern.

If foreign words and phrases have been so thoroughly assimilated, or Anglicized, that they are commonly recognized, however, they do not need underlining. Here are some examples:

machete (Spanish)	judo (Japanese)
sauerkraut (German)	coffee (Arabic)

pasta (Italian) data (Latin)
cologne (French) criteria (Greek)

The richness of the English language comes from borrowings like these, and they can all be found in a standard English dictionary. The best rule of thumb is to underline or italicize only truly foreign expressions. If the expression can be found in a standard English dictionary, do not underline or italicize it.

53i Italicize words, letters, and numbers referred to as such

When you write a word, letter, or number so as to talk about it as a word, letter, or number, use underlining or italics.

- Many people misspell the word *misspell;* they write it with only one *s*.
- The witness said the license plate had two *5*s in it.

Underlining or italics is also appropriate for a word you are about to define. (Alternatively, boldface type can be used.)

- Before starting up a cliff, rock climbers sometimes like to get *beta*—advice from someone who has already done the climb.

53j Italicize words for emphasis

You can use underlining or italics to emphasize a certain word or phrase.

- Unfortunately, those who cannot remember the past tend to repeat it, which explains why U.S. officials continue to repeat the propaganda strategies of the 1950s. Rather than changing the way we actually *relate* to the people of the Middle East, they still dream of fixing their image through some new marketing campaign cooked up in Hollywood or on Madison Avenue.

—Sheldon Rampton and John Stauber, *Weapons of Mass Deception*

Be sure that you do not overuse this kind of emphasis, however, as you may irritate your readers. It is better to rely on word choice and syntactic structuring to create emphasis.

See Ch. 39

TechALERT!

Electronic Language: Symbols for Emphasis

Ways of creating emphasis in email, instant messages, and text messages—such as placing an asterisk or an underscore on each side of a word or using all caps—are inappropriate for formal academic writing.

EXERCISE 53.2 In each of the following sentences, add italics to those words and phrases that need it.

1. My favorite poem in Robert Creeley's book For Love is "A Wicker Basket."
2. Juan says the new drama teacher is very simpático.
3. Of the fifty people interviewed, twenty-two said that 13 is an unlucky number.
4. You can keep track of the spaceship NEAR's progress at http://spacelink.nasa.gov/.
5. Smoking also contributes to platelet adhesiveness, or the sticking together of red blood cells that is associated with blood clots.
6. She's an easy teacher—she gives all A's and B's.
7. For me, the best track on Fleetwood Mac's Greatest Hits is "Rhiannon."
8. The flower that does best under these conditions is the prairie zinnia (Zinnia grandiflora).
9. For further information, email us at johnsonco@waterworks.com.
10. The term dementia implies deficits in memory, spatial orientation, language, or personality. This definition sets it apart from delirium, which usually involves changing levels of consciousness, restlessness, confusion, and hallucinations.

54 Abbreviations and Numbers

FAQs

- Is it okay to use acronyms in formal writing? (54d)
- When should I spell out numbers? (54f–54j)

ABBREVIATIONS

Abbreviations include shortened versions of words (*Mr., Rev., fig.*), initialisms formed from the first letters of a series of words (*FBI, NBC, IBM*), and acronyms, or initialisms that are pronounced as words (*OPEC, NASA, RAM*). In formal writing, abbreviations should be used sparingly. If you are not sure that readers will know what a certain abbreviation stands for, spell out the word the first time it is used and put the abbreviation in parentheses right after it:

- The Internet uses a domain name system (DNS) for all its servers worldwide.

Using abbreviations

54a Abbreviate titles, ranks, and degrees only before or after full names

Title before full name	*Degree or rank after full name*
Ms. Yuko Shinoda	Jan Stankowski, DDS
Mr. Steven D. Gold	Derek Rudick, CPA
Dr. Teresa Rivera	Teresa Rivera, MD
Prof. Jamie Smith-Weber	Young-Sook Kim, PhD
Rev. Martin Luther King, Jr.	James Norton, PFC
Rep. Nancy Pelosi	Chris L. Miller, DSW

When titles or ranks are followed by only a surname, they should be spelled out:

General Clark　　Senator Lott　　Professor Davis

54b Use abbreviations after numerical dates and times

The following abbreviations are commonly used in writing dates and times:

124 BC ("before Christ") OR 124 BCE ("before the common era")

AD 567 (*anno Domini,* or "year of our Lord") OR 567 CE ("common era")

9:40 a.m. (*ante meridiem*) OR 0940 hrs (military or international 24-hour time)

4:23 p.m. (*post meridiem*) OR 1623 hrs

Avoid using *a.m.* or *p.m.* unless it is adjoined to a specific number:

▸ The package arrived late in the ~~a.m.~~ morning.

Avoid abbreviating the names of months, days, and holidays in formal writing:

▸ This year ~~Xmas~~ Christmas fell on a ~~Thurs.~~ Thursday.

54c Use Latin abbreviations sparingly

The following abbreviations, derived from Latin, are appropriate in academic writing. Be careful, however, not to overuse them.

Abbreviation	*Latin term*	*English meaning*
cf.	*confer*	compare
e.g.	*exempli gratia*	for example
et al.	*et alii*	and others
etc.	*et cetera*	and so forth
i.e.	*id est*	that is
N.B.	*nota bene*	note well

54d Use acronyms and initialisms only if their meaning is clear

An **initialism** is an abbreviation formed from the first letters of a name—for example, *FBI* (for *Federal Bureau of Investigation*). Usually the letters are all capitalized. An **acronym** is an initialism that is pronounced as a word—for example, *ASCII, PAC, AIDS.* Some abbreviations, such as *JPEG, MS-DOS,* and *DRAM,* are **semiacronyms:** part of the term is pronounced as one or more letters, the rest as a word (for example, "jay-peg"). Some initialisms and acronyms have morphed into a verb, gerund, or participle. In such cases, use uppercase letters only for the abbreviated part: *ID'd, MUDding, IMing.*

Because they are convenient and quickly written, initialisms and acronyms tend to be overused. But in many cases, especially in the computer world, they are virtually indispensable. As long as your audience knows what they mean and as long as you do not overdo it, it is okay to use such abbreviations where appropriate.

The Abbreviation and Acronym Server

54e Avoid most other abbreviations in formal writing

Place names, including the names of states, countries, provinces, continents, and other localities, should not be abbreviated except in addresses and occasionally when used as adjectives (for example, in *US government*). Organization and company names should not be abbreviated unless they are extremely familiar: *IBM, CBS, UPS, UCLA, NYU.* Many official company names, however, include one or more abbreviations, which should be kept as is: *Canon, Inc.; Braun AG; Mac Pro.* Fields of study should not be abbreviated. Write *political science* (not *poli sci*) and *psychology* (not *psych*).

In formal, nontechnical writing, most units of measure should be spelled out: *inches, yards, meters, square feet, gallons.* In technical and scientific writing, the use of abbreviations is standard: *m, kg, bps, dpi, mips, GB, rpm.* Symbols such as @, #, &, +, and = should not be used in the body of a paper. They can be used, though, in graphs, tables, and email addresses and for other similar purposes.

TechALERT!

See 21b-4

Electronic Language: TM and IM Shorthand

Abbreviations commonly used in text-messaging, instant-messaging, and emailing—such as *pls, tx, u, msg, gr8, w/, b/c, lol, BTW, TIA, FYI,* and *ASAP*—should be avoided in formal writing.

EXERCISE 54.1 In the following sentences, correct any abbreviations that are not in the proper form and write out any expressions that are not appropriately abbreviated in academic writing.

1. Dr. Ernesto Garcia, M.D, is a specialist in the treatment of A.I.D.S.
2. There has always been a friendly rivalry between people who live in N.H. and those who live in Mass.
3. The Girl Scouts of Tr. 76 visited Representative Harriet Stanley at the Mass. State House.
4. Among the questions the girls asked Rep. Stanley were several about a proposal to extend the school year into July and Aug.
5. The G.O.P. and the Dems have very different positions on that bill.
6. Many colleges have a phys. ed. requirement.
7. When I drive to work in the a.m., my usual radio station is 1030 a.m.
8. The unit of blood one gives at a blood drive measures 450 ml.
9. It was a dramatic advance in science when DNA was 1st used to clone a sheep.
10. HTML is the fundamental language of the WWW.

NUMBERS

Using numbers

54f Use figures with abbreviations and conventionally numerical references

Time

7:00 a.m.	0700 hrs	seven o'clock in the morning
2:45 p.m.	1445 hrs	two forty-five in the afternoon

Dates

65 BC (or BCE)	AD 126 (or 126 CE)	the 1890s	May 15, 1996
from 1996 to 1998	1996–1998	1996–98	

Money

$23.4 billion $12,566 $7.99 45¢ forty-five cents one dollar

Rates of speed

55 mph	33.6 bps
200 MHz	3000 rpm

Decimals and percentages

.05 (or 0.05)   5 percent (or 5%)

Telephone numbers

617-555-1284 [US]   +1 (617) 555 1284 [International]

Addresses

233 East 19th Street   PO Box 45   Route 66
New York, NY 10011

Divisions of books and plays

volume 2, chapter 11, pages 346–55
King Lear, act II, scene i, lines 5–7 OR *King Lear* II.i.5–7
The Alchemist, act 2, scene 1, lines 5–7 OR *The Alchemist* 2.1.5–7

54g Write out other numbers that can be expressed in one or two words

One to ninety-nine

fifteen   twenty-two   eighty-four

Fractions

two-thirds   one-fourth   five-sixteenths

Large round numbers

thirteen hundred   four thousand   thirty million

Decades and centuries

the eighties (or the '80s)
the twenty-first century (or the 21st century)

54h Write out numbers that begin sentences

FAULTY 18% of Americans believe that career preparation should begin in elementary school.

REVISED Eighteen percent of Americans believe that career preparation should begin in elementary school.

When a number is too large to write out (more than two words), keep the numerical form but rearrange the sentence so as to avoid beginning with a number.

FAULTY 240,183 people could be fed for one year with the food we Americans waste in one day.

REVISED We Americans waste enough food in one day to feed 240,183 people for one year.

54i When one number modifies another, write one as a figure and the other as a word

- We bought fourteen $25 tickets.
- There were 75 twelfth-graders at the dance.

54j Write related numbers alike

When comparing two or more numbers in the same sentence or paragraph, make the comparison easy to see by putting the numbers in the same form, as either words or figures.

- It takes ~~nine hundred~~ 900 hours of training to become a licensed hair braider in New York but only 117 hours to become an emergency medical technician.

EXERCISE 54.2 Correct the use of numbers in the following sentences.

1. 200 prayers are sent to the Wailing Wall each day by email.
2. 1998 is the year in which Hong Kong was turned back to the Chinese government.
3. Some workers now work two eight-hour jobs back to back.
4. In 1582, Pope Gregory the 13th instituted the calendar we still use today.
5. At one time, mathematicians were able to work with only the 3 dimensions they could visualize, but now they have analytic methods that allow them to deal with 4, 5, or more dimensions.

6. Much has changed over the years, but the price of Boardwalk remains $200 in Monopoly.
7. The long passage of 16th notes in that piece makes it a difficult one for a beginner to play.
8. Abraham, patriarch of Christianity, Judaism, and Islam, was probably alive in about 1800 B.C.E.
9. The university hopes to increase its endowment by 50% over the next 5 years.
10. In the early 80s, home mortgage interest rates were as high as 16 or 17%.

55 The Hyphen

FAQs

- Should I hyphenate a term like *third grader*? (55b)
- What are the rules for hyphenating a word at the end of a line? (55e)

The hyphen (-) is typed as a single keystroke, with no space before or after. It differs from a dash, which can be typed as two consecutive hyphens (--) and then converted by the computer into what looks like a long hyphen (—).

55a Hyphenate certain compound terms

Using hyphens

A **compound** is a term made up of two or more words. Sometimes these words are connected by a hyphen (*screen-test*), sometimes they are separated by a space (*screen pass*), and sometimes they are fused (*screensaver*). There are no firm rules for determining how to write a particular compound, so it is best to check your dictionary. *Wired Style* says, "When in doubt, close it up," giving examples such as *email, homepage,* and *offline.*

Grammar Checkers: Hyphenated Compounds

A grammar checker will consult the computer's dictionary for you, to determine whether a compound should be hyphenated. But most computerized dictionaries lack full coverage of compounds; therefore, grammar checkers are limited in what they can do. For example, after we deliberately mishyphenated the compounds in the previous paragraph, our grammar checker failed to detect all but two of the erroneous compounds.

Complex compounds are compounds made up of three or more words, such as *cut-and-paste* and *up-to-date.* When you hyphenate a complex compound, be sure to hyphenate all its parts—put hyphens between all the terms.

- I do a lot of *cut-and-paste* revising.
- My boyfriend needs a more *up-to-date* computer.

In cases where two or more hyphenated compounds occur before a single noun, the recurring part can usually be omitted from all but the last compounds, though the hyphen should be kept, as in this example:

- Martha teaches *seventh-* and *eighth-grade* English. [The hyphen after *seventh* helps the reader understand that the writer is referring to *seventh-grade.*]

55b Hyphenate compounds acting as adjectives before nouns

When a compound is placed in front of a noun to act as a modifier, the compound is usually hyphenated.

- I teach *seventh-grade* algebra.

Notice that the same compound, when *not* placed before a noun, is *not* hyphenated.

- I teach algebra to the *seventh grade.*

Hyphenate only compounds that *precede* nouns, not those that follow.

- She goes to a *little-known* college. The college is *little known.*

Exceptions to this rule include everyday compounds such as *science fiction, long distance,* and *zip code,* which can be used as modifiers without hyphens.

- Do you have a *zip code directory?*
- There's something wrong with my *phone mail system.*

55c Hyphenate spelled-out fractions and numbers from twenty-one through ninety-nine

one-half	three-eighths	forty-four
two-fifths	twenty-six	seventy-nine

55d Hyphenate to avoid ambiguity and awkward spellings

Some words, especially those with the prefix *re-*, *pre-*, or *anti-*, require hyphens to prevent misreadings, mispronunciations, and awkward-looking spellings:

- Now that Professor Muller has complicated the problem, we will have to re-solve ~~resolve~~ it. [Without the hyphen, *re-solve*, "to solve again," would be read as *resolve*, "to deal with successfully."]
- Pre-emergent ~~Preemergent~~ weedkillers are best used in springtime. [Without the hyphen, some readers might see *preem* as a single, unrecognizable syllable.]

55e Use hyphens for end-of-line word division

In general, it is best to avoid dividing a word at the end of a line. But there are situations where word division is desirable. For example, if you are trying to arrange text in columns (in a brochure or résumé, for instance), end-of-line hyphenation may provide valuable extra space. (Note: You should be able to turn the automatic hyphenation feature on or off.) General principles for end-of-line word division follow.

1 Dividing words only between syllables

If you are using a computer, you can have the word processor divide words for you. Otherwise, consult a dictionary to find out where the syllable breaks are. (In most dictionaries, a dot indicates a syllable break.) For example,

TechHelp

See 19b-4

Using Automatic Hyphenation

1. Can the document have a ragged right margin?
   a. If so, you can disable your word-processing program's automatic end-of-line hyphenation without running the risk of having large gaps, or *rivers,* in the middle of lines. Rivers reduce readability.
   b. If the document is a brochure or newsletter, for example, and requires block-justified text, activate the automatic hyphenation feature so as to avoid internal rivers.
2. Does the justified text have too many hyphenated lines? If so, further steps are needed, as excessive hyphenation can interfere with readability.
   a. You may want to adjust some of the hyphenated lines manually.
   b. You might consider changing the width of your columns.

the entry **den•si•ty** means that the word can be hyphenated as either *den-sity* or *densi-ty.*

❷ Avoiding a second hyphen in a hyphenated word

Words with prefixes like *self-*, *ex-*, and *all-* and complex compounds should not be hyphenated anywhere else.

► Jimmy Carter has set a new standard for civic activism by ex-~~presi-~~ presidents. ~~dents~~.

❸ Leaving at least two letters on a line

Do not divide a word so that a single letter is left hanging either on the first line or on the second line.

► Stress management requires an examination of one's ~~e-~~ emo- tional ~~motional~~ responses to others.

If you have to divide a name that includes two or more initials, keep the initials together.

▶ In the movement for racial equality, few stand taller than ~~W. E.~~ W. E. B. ~~B.~~ Dubois.

④ Avoiding consecutive lines ending in hyphens

Ending three or more lines in a row with hyphens looks ungainly and detracts from readability.

> Admitting to your feelings and allowing them to be ex-
> pressed through either communication or action is a stress-
> management technique that can help you through many diffi-
> cult situations.

You can prevent such situations by clicking on LIMIT CONSECUTIVE HYPHENS in your word-processing program and setting the maximum number of hyphens in a row at two. Alternatively, you can widen the hyphenation zone (which determines the range in the width of a line).

EXERCISE 55.1 Correct the hyphenation errors in the following paragraphs.

1. Stress-management calls for the development of positive self esteem, which can help you cope with stressful situations. Self esteem skills are instilled through learned habits. Stress management also requires that you learn to see stressors not as adversaries but as exercises in life. These skills, along wi-th other stress management techniques, can help you get through many difficult situations.
2. Smoke-less tobacco is used by approximately 12-million Americans, one fourth of whom are under the age of twenty one. Most users are teen-age and young adult males, who are often emulating a professional sports-figure or a family-member.
3. In a consumer oriented environment, many hospitals are making efforts to improve patient care. Many are now designated as trauma-centers. They have helicopters to transport victims, they have in house specialty physicians available around-the clock, and they have specialized-diagnostic equipment. Though very expensive to run, trauma-centers have dramatically reduced mortality-rates for trauma-patients.

4. Hispanics made up the fastest growing segment of the US-population during the 1990s. However, Hispanics constitute diverse groups, having come from a variety of Spanish speaking countries at different times in the nation's history- Because the United States at one time seized large amounts of land from Mexico- the largest group of Hispanics are of Mexican-descent. Newspapers serving these descendants are called the Chicano-press and are printed in Spanish, English, or sometimes both languages.
5. Felice Schwartz (1989) suggested that corporations offer women a choice of two parallel career paths. The "fast-track" consists of high powered, demanding positions that require sixty-or-seventy hours of work per week, regular responsibilities, emergencies, out of town meetings, and a briefcase jammed with work on week-ends. The second track, the "mommy-track," would stress both career and family. Less would be expected of a woman on the mommy-track, for her commitment to the firm would be lower and her commitment to her family higher.

FOR COLLABORATION Exchange your corrected paragraphs with another member of your group for checking. See what types of hyphenation errors are particularly troublesome for you.

part

12

ESL Issues

56 Tips on Nouns and Articles

FAQs

- Why is it necessary to use articles?
- How do I know whether to use *a* or *the*? (56b–56d)
- When is it okay to use no article at all? (56e)

Articles (*a, an, the*) are important in the English language because they clarify what nouns refer to. There is a significant difference in meaning between "I found *a* new Web site" and "I found *the* new Web site." The first sentence introduces new information, while the second sentence implies that the new Web site is something the reader or listener already knew about. Articles can be used to mark other subtleties as well. Because many other languages do not use articles in this way, though, many nonnative speakers of English have trouble with articles.

Count and noncount nouns

See 56f

56a Use the plural only with count nouns

To use articles correctly, you first need a clear understanding of the difference between count nouns and noncount nouns. **Count nouns** refer to things that have a distinct physical or mental form and thus can be counted, such as *book, apple, diskette, scientist,* and *idea.* Count nouns can be enumerated and pluralized—for example, *eight books, three apples, several diskettes, two scientists,* and *many ideas.*

Noncount (or **mass**) **nouns** are words such as *air, rice, electricity, excitement,* and *coverage* that do not have a distinct form as a whole. (Though each grain of rice may have a distinct form, rice as a mass quantity is variable in form.) Noncount nouns are neither enumerated nor pluralized. No one would

Common Examples of Two-Way Nouns

As a count noun	*As a noncount noun*
a *wine* (a type of wine)	*wine* (the fermented juice of grapes)
a *cloth* (a piece of cloth)	*cloth* (fabric made by weaving or knitting)
a *thought* (an idea)	*thought* (mental activity, cogitation)
a *beauty* (a lovely person or thing)	*beauty* (loveliness)
a *hair* (a single strand of hair)	*hair* (filamentous mass growing out of the skin)

say *eight airs, three rices, several electricities, two excitements,* or *many coverages.* Noncount nouns can be quantified with expressions like *a lot of, much, some,* and *a cup of*—for example, *some air, a cup of rice, much excitement,* and *a lot of coverage.*

Some nouns can be used as either count or noncount nouns. In such cases, the countable sense is more specific than the uncountable sense. For example, *reading* as a noncount noun refers to the general activity ("I enjoy *reading*"), while *reading* as a count noun refers to a particular type of reading—for example, a text ("We were assigned a collection of *readings*"), an interpretation ("I made several *readings* of the data"), or a performance ("We were invited to a public *reading*"). See the box on Common Examples of Two-Way Nouns.

See also 26a-1 for more on count and noncount nouns.

EXERCISE 56.1 Decide whether each of the nouns listed below is countable, noncountable, or both (depending on context). If the noun is countable, write its plural counterpart next to it. If the noun can be either countable or noncountable, explain in what context it would be appropriate to pluralize the noun.

1. idea
2. money
3. math problem
4. government
5. party
6. memorization
7. computer program
8. silence
9. tobacco
10. movie

More on count and noncount nouns

Using articles correctly

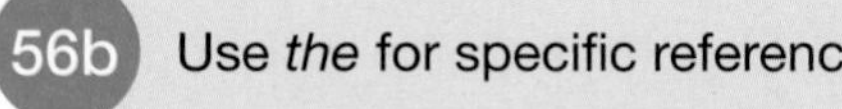

56b Use *the* for specific references

In deciding whether to use *the, a, an,* or no article at all, keep in mind the concept of specificity. Does the noun refer to some particular thing or set of things, or does it refer to something general? As mentioned in the introduction to this chapter, "*the* Web site" refers to a specific, unique Web site, whereas "*a* Web site" refers to any Web site.

There are many types of situations in which nouns refer to specific things and must be preceded by *the*. In all these cases, the writer assumes that the reader knows *which* thing or set of things is being referred to. If you are using a noun that names something unique and specific, use the definite article *the* with the noun, whether or not the noun is countable. (Note: This guideline applies to common nouns only, not to most proper nouns.)

1 Using *the* with superlative adjectives

Adjectives like *best, worst,* and *most interesting* single out one particular thing among many.

- Roger Federer was *the best tennis player* in the world.

2 Using *the* with unique things

The past, the present, the sun, and *the solar system* all have unique identities. There is only one past, only one present, only one sun (in our solar system anyway).

- Thirty minutes after we boarded, the plane was still on *the ground.*

3 Using *the* with nouns followed by a modifier

Many nouns are followed by a phrase or clause that restricts the noun's identity.

- *The theory of relativity* was developed by Einstein.
- *The girl in the corner* is in my physics class.

❹ Using *the* to refer to a previous mention

Once something has been mentioned, it becomes part of the reader's knowledge. If you refer to it again, use *the* so that the reader knows that you are talking about the same thing.

► I went shopping today and bought beans, rice, and *chicken*. We can cook *the chicken* for dinner.

NOTE For clarity or emphasis, the demonstrative adjective *this, that, those,* or *these* may be used instead of *the* if the second mention occurs closely after the first.

❺ Using *the* to draw on shared knowledge

If you and your reader can draw on shared experience to identify something in particular, use *the* to mark it.

► Please shut down *the computer* when you are done with it.

❻ Using *the* for contextual specificity

Sometimes the context of a situation allows you and your reader to identify something as unique. Consider, for example, the word *printer*. There are many printers in the world, but if you are writing about a computer and you want to mention the printer attached to it, use *the* to indicate that it is the only printer in this particular context.

► I was using my friend's computer and could not get *the printer* to work.

❼ Using *the* to denote an entire class of things

The can be used with a singular count noun to denote an entire class or genre of things.

► *The earthworm* is one of nature's most valuable creatures.

► *The personal computer* has revolutionized modern life.

NOTE This generic use of *the* to refer to an entire class of things applies only to singular count nouns, not to plural count nouns or noncount nouns.

EXERCISE 56.2 Study the following paragraph and insert *the* where appropriate.

Do animals have morals? Many people do not think so. Those who would put ______ humans on a pedestal above all other creatures feel threatened by ______ possibility of morality in ______ animals, since it seems to threaten ______ special and unique status of ______ humans. This idea that ______ humans are ______ most virtuous creatures usually comes from ______ religion, so to say ______ animals can be moral is sometimes perceived as a threat against some deeply held religious beliefs. But it's not. The only thing that is threatened by ______ proposition that ______ animals are ______ moral beings is ______ belief that ______ morality alone defines our "human nature." [M. Bekoff, *The Emotional Lives of Animals,* p. 90]

Help with nouns and articles

56c Use *the* with most proper nouns derived from common nouns

Proper nouns are names of things such as persons, places, holidays, religions, companies, and organizations. Most proper nouns, even though they uniquely identify somebody or something, do not take the definite article:

Muhammad Ali	Mother Theresa	New York	China
Christmas	Ramadan	Catholicism	Microsoft
September	Greenpeace	*Hamlet*	

Many proper nouns, though, do take the definite article:

the Rolling Stones	the United States
the Panama Canal	the International Red Cross
the Vietnam War	the Golden Gate Bridge
the Himalayan Mountains	the University of Chicago
the Fourth of July	the *Encyclopedia Britannica*

Do you see a general pattern that distinguishes these two kinds of proper nouns? Those that take the definite article have a head noun derived from a common English noun: *stones, states, canal, cross, war, bridge, mountains, university, fourth,* and *encyclopedia.*

There are many exceptions, however, to this pattern. Many common-noun names do not take the definite article: *Elm Street, Salt Lake City, Lookout Mountain, Pine Creek, Capitol Hill, Burger King.* And a few names not derived from a common noun nonetheless do take the definite article: *the Vatican, the Amazon, the Congo, the Hague.* In general, major landmarks tend to take the definite article, while lesser ones do not: *the Pacific Ocean* vs. *Pine Creek, the United Kingdom* vs. *Burger King.* This is not an absolute rule, however: Michigan State University and the University of Michigan are of comparable size, yet only one is referred to with the definite article. We suggest that you pay close attention to each proper name you encounter and note whether it is used with *the.*

NOTE English uses the definite article with titles, place names, and other proper nouns less consistently than Spanish does. For example, *El señor Lopez está enfermo* in English is simply *Mr. Lopez is sick,* without an article. *La Suecia* is simply *Sweden. El catolicismo* is simply *Catholicism.*

56d Use *a* or *an* in nonspecific references to singular count nouns

Nonspecific nouns refer to *types* of things rather than to specific things. With nonspecific singular count nouns, such as *shirt, jacket, belt,* and *hat,* you must use an indefinite article (either *a* or, if the next sound is a vowel sound, *an*) or some other determiner (for example, *my, your, this,* or *each*).

- I bought a shirt and an overcoat.

56e Use no article in nonspecific references to plural count nouns or noncount nouns

With nonspecific plural count nouns, such as *shirts, jackets, belts,* and *hats,* no article is used. You may, however, use determiners such as *our, some, these,* and *no.*

- There were *socks* and *shorts* on sale, but *no belts.*

Nonspecific noncount nouns, such as *clothing, apparel,* and *merchandise,* do not take articles either. They can, however, take determiners such as *some, much, enough, your, their, this,* and *no.*

- *People* were buying *lots of clothing,* but I did not have *enough money* to get everything I needed.

EXERCISE 56.3 Study the following sentences, and insert *a, an,* or *the* where appropriate.

1. Sarah used to play ______ soccer for her high school team, and she was ______ star player.
2. He gave me ______ good advice.
3. ______ anecdote is ______ type of illustration.
4. You should give credit to _____ people who did _____ work.
5. ______ professor surprised ______ students with ______ quiz.
6. All of ______ dogs in ______ neighborhood started to bark when ______ power went out.
7. Vera bought ______ new pink dress for graduation, but, unfortunately, ______ dress was too big.

EXERCISE 56.4 Study the following paragraphs, and insert *a, an,* or *the* where appropriate.

1. In ______ different societies, ______ gift giving is usually ritualized. ______ ritual is ______ set of multiple, symbolic behaviors that occurs in ______ fixed sequence. Gift-giving rituals in our society usually involve the choosing of ______ proper gift by ______ giver, ______ removing of ______ price tag, wrapping of ______ gift, timing ______ gift giving, and waiting for ______ reaction (either positive or negative) from ______ recipient.
2. In ______ latter part of ______ nineteenth century, ______ capitalism was characterized by ______ growth of ______ giant corporations. Control of most of ______ important industries became more and more concentrated. Accompanying this concentration of industry was ______ equally striking concentration of ______ income in ______ hands of a small percentage of ______ population.

Self-study quizzes

56f Use other determiners correctly

Articles belong to the class of **determiners.** A determiner is a word or phrase that begins a noun phrase. Other determiners include quantifiers (such as *many, some, no*), demonstratives (*this, these, that, those*), and possessive adjectives (such as *my, your, their*). Do not use more than one determiner with any one noun phrase.

1. Quantifiers indicate some amount of a noun. Some quantifiers are used only with count nouns, such as *many, several, few, a few, a couple of, every,* and *each.* Other quantifiers are used only with noncount nouns, such as *much, not much, little,* and *a little.* Still others are used with either count or noncount nouns, such as *some, no, enough, any,* and *a lot of.* (Note: *Few* and *little* have negative connotations, while *a few* and *a little* have positive connotations.)

▶ Loners have ~~*a few*~~ few friends.

▶ A poor person has ~~*a little*~~ little money.

2. Demonstratives specify the person or thing referred to. *This* and *these* indicate something nearby or just mentioned; *that* and *those* indicate something more distant.

▶ *This* book should help you with your English.

▶ *That* computer you bought five years ago might be outdated now.

This and *that* are used with noncount nouns and singular count nouns. *These* and *those* are used with plural count nouns.

3. Possessive adjectives indicate ownership. They resemble possessive pronouns (*mine, yours, theirs,* and so on) but differ in function and location. Possessive adjectives occur in the determiner position, initiating a noun phrase. Possessive pronouns substitute for noun phrases; they do not initiate noun phrases.

POSSESSIVE ADJECTIVE *Your* book is on the chair.

POSSESSIVE PRONOUN This book is *yours.*

Note that *yours,* like other possessive pronouns, is spelled without an apostrophe.

See 50a-1

57 Tips on Verbs

FAQs

- I have a lot of trouble with verbs like *look out for* and *look over.* Do I need to learn them? (57a)
- If it is okay to say "I like to read," what's wrong with "I dislike to read"? (57b–57c)
- What is wrong with "The program is consisting of four parts"? (57f)
- What are the correct verb tenses for sentences with *if* clauses? (57i–57k)

The main features of the English verb system are discussed in Chapter 28; subject-verb agreement in Chapter 29; and tense, mood, and voice in 35b. This chapter addresses aspects of the verb system that may present special difficulties: phrasal verbs, verb complements, verbs of state, modal auxiliary verbs, and conditional sentences.

Phrasal verbs

PHRASAL VERBS

Phrasal verbs are made up of a verb and one or two particles (prepositions or adverbs)—for example, *pick over, look into, get away with.* For this reason, they are sometimes called **two-word verbs** or **three-word verbs.** Phrasal verbs are common in English, especially in informal speech. Some phrasal verbs mean something quite different from their associated simple verbs. For example, if a friend of yours says, "I just *ran into* Nguyen in the library," the incident probably had nothing to do with running. *To run into* means "to encounter unintentionally." Other phrasal verbs are used merely to intensify the meaning of the simple verb. For example, *fill up* is a more emphatic version of *fill.*

Some phrasal verbs are **transitive** (that is, they have direct objects), while others are **intransitive**. For example, *dig up* (meaning "find") is transitive ("I *dug up* some information for my paper"), but *speak up* (meaning "speak louder") is intransitive ("Please *speak up*"). Some phrasal verbs have both transitive and intransitive meanings. For example, *show up* can mean either "expose or embarrass (someone)" or "appear," depending on whether it is used transitively or intransitively: "He tried to *show up* the teacher" (transitive) versus "He never *shows up* on time" (intransitive).

See 26a-4 and 28f for more on transitive and intransitive verbs.

Some transitive phrasal verbs are **separable**, meaning that the particle may be placed after the object of the verb: "I quickly *looked over* my paper" or "I quickly *looked* my paper *over.*" Other transitive phrasal verbs are **inseparable**, meaning that the verb and the particle must be kept together: "I quickly *went over* my paper," not "I quickly *went* my paper *over.*"

57a Note phrasal verbs as you listen and read

Quizzes on phrasal verbs

To master idiomatic English, you must learn hundreds of phrasal verbs. The best way to do so is by listening to and reading as much informal English as you can and noting the phrasal verbs. Also consult a good pocket dictionary of phrasal verbs, such as the *Handbook of Commonly Used American Idioms,* 4th ed., by A. Makkai, M. Boatner, and J. Gates (New York: Barron's, 2004). A good Web site to visit is Dave Sperling's *Phrasal Verb Page* at <http://www.eslcafe.com/pv/>.

VERB COMPLEMENTS

Verb complements include gerunds (*swimming*), and infinitives (*to swim*). English verbs differ in the kinds of verb complements they can take.

I *dislike* [V] *swimming.* [Comp] [Not "I dislike to swim" or "I dislike swim"]

I *want* [V] *to swim.* [Comp] [Not "I want swimming" or "I want swim"]

I *like* [V] *swimming.* [Comp] OR I *like* [V] *to swim.* [Comp] [Not "I like swim"]

WEBLINK
Verb complements

57b Learn which verbs take *-ing* verb complements

The following verbs take gerunds (verbals ending in *-ing*), but not infinitives, as complements, as in "Maria *acknowledged skipping* class."

acknowledge	deny	give up	put off
admit	depend on	have trouble	quit
advise	detest	imagine	recommend
anticipate	discuss	insist on	regret
appreciate	dislike	keep	resist
avoid	dream about	miss	result in
cannot (can't) help	enjoy	object to	risk
consider	escape	plan on	succeed in
consist of	evade	postpone	suggest
delay	finish	practice	talk about

57c Learn which verbs take *to* verb complements

The following verbs take infinitives (verbals consisting of *to* followed by a verb's base form) but not gerunds, as complements, as in "Kim cannot *afford to buy* a car."

afford	decide	intend	offer	seem
agree	demand	learn	plan	struggle
ask	expect	like	prepare	tend
attempt	fail	manage	pretend	threaten
claim	hesitate	mean	promise	wait
consent	hope	need	refuse	want

57d Learn which verbs take either *-ing* or *to* verb complements

The following verbs can take either a gerund or an infinitive as a complement: "He *began learning* English as a small child" or "He *began to learn* English as a small child."

begin	dread	like	stop*
cannot (can't) stand	forget*	love	try
continue	hate	remember*	

For those verbs marked with an asterisk, the meaning depends on the type of complement: "He *forgot to go* to the store" means that he didn't go to the store, while "He *forgot going* to the store" means that he did go to the store but didn't remember going there.

57e Learn the special properties of *have*, *help*, *let*, and *make*

There are four verbs that, when followed by a noun or pronoun, take an infinitive without *to*, as in "She *let him pay* for dinner." These verbs are

have help let make

(Note that *help* can also take an infinitive with *to* as a complement.)

EXERCISE 57.1 In the following sentences, fill each blank with the correct form of the verb in parentheses.

1. Professor Adams refused (change) ___________ the student's grade.
2. The student believed that (change) ___________ the grade was the only fair course of action.
3. The student also insisted on (discuss) ___________ the matter with the dean of the college.
4. The student hoped (convince) ___________ the dean that the professor was being unjust in her refusal to change the grade.
5. The dean, however, decided (side) ___________ with the professor, so the student's grade was never changed from a B to an A.
6. The famous scientist offered (speak) ___________ at the university graduation ceremony.
7. Most students dislike (study) ___________ for final examinations.

VERBS OF STATE

Many English verbs depict states or conditions rather than events or actions. These verbs are called **verbs of state**.

57f Do not use verbs of state such as *understand* and *exist* in the *-ing* form

GO See 28d

Verbs of state generally cannot occur in the progressive tense, which indicates continuous action rather than a static condition. For example, *consist of* is a verb of state and therefore cannot occur in the progressive tense, which is composed of some form of the verb *be* and the *-ing* form of the main verb.

▶ The program ~~*is consisting*~~ consists of four parts.

The following verbs do not occur in the progressive tense:

appear	contain	know	result in
believe	correspond	mean	seem
belong	differ from	need	suppose
consist of	exist	possess	understand
constitute	involve	represent	want

MODAL AUXILIARY VERBS

See 26a-4, 28c

The **modal auxiliary verbs** include *can, could, may, might, must, will, would,* and *should.* They are used to express a variety of conditions, including possibility, necessity, ability, permission, and obligation. Each modal auxiliary has at least two principal meanings, one relating to social interaction and the other to logical probability. For example, the word *may* in a sentence like "*May* I sit down?" requests permission, an aspect of social interaction, while the word *may* in a sentence like "It *may* rain today" denotes logical possibility. Within these two general categories, the modal auxiliaries carry different degrees of strength, as shown in the box on the next page. Modal auxiliary verbs have certain distinct grammatical features that can cause problems for nonnative speakers.

57g Use only a verb's base form immediately after a modal auxiliary

Any verb immediately following a modal auxiliary must be in the base, or simple, form (for example, *teach, have, go, run*), not in the infinitive or gerund form.

NO History *can to teach* us many good lessons.

YES History *can teach* us many good lessons.

NO The UN *should done* more to help stop the Rwandan civil war.

YES The UN *should have done* more to help stop the Rwandan civil war.

Modal Auxiliaries Ranked by Strength

Modal verb	***Social interaction meaning***	***Logical probability meaning***	***Strength***
will	intention	certainty	Strong
must	obligation	logical necessity	↑
would	conditionality	conditional certainty	
should	advisability	probability	
may	permission, possibility	possibility	
can	permission	possibility	↓
might/could	very polite permission, possibility	low possibility	Weak

57h Do not use more than one modal at a time

NO If I study hard, I *might could* get an A.

YES If I study hard, I *might* get an A.

YES If I study hard, I *could* get an A.

If you want to combine a modal auxiliary verb with some other modal meaning, use a modal phrase such as *be able to, be allowed to,* or *have to.*

YES If I study hard, I *might be able to* get an A.

EXERCISE 57.2 The following sentences have verb errors. Make the appropriate corrections.

1. A formal academic essay usually is containing an introduction, the main discussion, and a conclusion.
2. My parents must will send me some money.

3. A thesis statement should to present the main idea of the essay.
4. Right now, Marinela studies in the library for a test in her one o'clock class.
5. Yuka could not imagining to miss even a day of her ESL conversation class.
6. Many students enjoy to study in small groups.
7. Many students are not understanding that the organization of an essay is as important as its content.

CONDITIONAL SENTENCES

Conditional sentences have two parts: a subordinate clause beginning with *if* (or *when* or *unless*) that sets a condition and a main clause that expresses a result. The tense and mood of the verb in the subordinate clause depend on the tense and mood of the verb in the main clause. There are three main types of conditional sentences: factual, predictive, and hypothetical.

57i In factual conditionals, use the same verb tense in both parts

Factual conditional sentences depict factual relationships. The conditional clause begins with *if, when, whenever,* or some other condition-setting expression; the conditional clause verb is cast in the same tense as the result clause verb.

- If you don't *get* enough rest, you *get* tired.
- When we *had* a day off, we *went* hiking in the mountains.

57j In predictive conditionals, use a present-tense verb in the *if* clause and an appropriate modal in the result clause

Predictive conditional sentences express future possible conditions and results. The conditional clause starts with *if* or *unless* and has a present-tense verb; the result clause verb is formed with a modal (*will, can, should, may,* or *might*) and the base form of the verb.

- If we *leave* now, we *can be* there by five o'clock.
- She *will lose* her place in class unless she *registers* today.

57k In hypothetical conditionals, use a past-tense verb in the *if* clause and *would, could,* or *might* in the result clause

See 28h

Hypothetical conditional sentences depict situations that are unlikely to happen or are contrary to fact. For hypothetical past situations, the verb in the conditional clause should be in the past perfect tense and the verb in the main clause should be formed from *would have, could have,* or *might have* and the past participle.

► If we *had invested* our money in stocks instead of bonds, we *would have gained* a lot more.

For hypothetical present or future situations, the verb in the conditional clause should be in the past tense and the verb in the main clause should be formed from *would, could,* or *might* and the base form.

► If we *invested* our money in stocks instead of bonds, we *would gain* a lot more.

EXERCISE 57.3 Choose the correct verb in the following sentences.

1. If Frank studied harder, he (*got, would get, will get*) better grades.
2. Whenever Suzy turns on her computer, she (*gets, would get, will get*) an error message.
3. If we plan ahead, we (*finish, should finish, would finish*) the project on schedule.
4. You will disappoint your parents unless you (*call, may call, should call*) them soon.
5. If the rain (*stopped, has stopped, had stopped*) sooner, there would not have been so much flooding.
6. If Serena Williams retires, tennis (*loses, should lose, will lose*) one of its most exciting players.
7. Just when you think things can't get worse, they sometimes (*do, might, would*).
8. Unless the price of oil comes down, world financial markets (*are, will be, would be*) in trouble.
9. If you like good art, you (*go, will go, should go*) to the Guggenheim Museum in New York.
10. If Mozart had lived a full life, he (*composed, had composed, might have composed*) much more music.

58 Tips on Vocabulary

FAQs

- How can I best learn common phrases and expressions? (58b)
- Can I use idiomatic expressions in academic writing? (58c)

Many nonnative speakers of English feel that they just do not know enough words to express their thoughts as fully as they would like. Knowing enough words, and knowing them well, is a challenge for almost all nonnative speakers of English; indeed, it is a challenge for many native speakers, too. This chapter covers some of the most common vocabulary problems for non-native speakers—those related to cognates, collocations, and idioms.

58a Look for cognates, but watch out for "false friends"

Cognates are words that have a formal relation to similar words in another language. They are usually quite recognizable. For example, the English *telephone* and Spanish *teléfono* are cognates, and it is easy for speakers of either language to recognize this word when learning the other language. Cognates are either derived from a common ancestor language or borrowed by one language from another. Sometimes the borrowing process involves minor alterations, as in *telephone/teléfono;* sometimes it involves more significant changes, as in the English *northwest* and Spanish *noroeste.*

If your native language is closely related to English, cognate recognition is a good strategy for learning new words. In most cases, you can trust a cognate to carry more or less the same meaning in your second language as it has in your first language. Of course, there are often subtle differences that you should pay attention to. For example, although the word *collar* is used in both

Some Spanish/English False Cognates

Spanish	*Meaning*	*English*	*Meaning*
bonanza	fair weather	*bonanza*	a treasure
coraje	anger, rage	*courage*	bravery, valor
desgracia	misfortune	*disgrace*	dishonor
eventual	possible	*eventual*	final, ultimate
falacia	deceit, fraud	*fallacy*	false reasoning
informal	unreliable	*informal*	casual
lunático	temperamental	*lunatic*	insane
particular	private, personal	*particular*	specific
sensible	sensitive	*sensible*	reasonable
voluble	moody, fickle	*voluble*	talkative

English and Spanish to refer to the band around the neck of an animal, in Spanish it is also used to mean "necklace" whereas in English it more often refers to the top of a shirt.

Sometimes, however, words that look similar in two different languages have entirely different meanings. These words are called **false cognates.** An example of a false cognate is the English *jubilation* and Spanish *jubilación.* The English word means "great happiness," while the Spanish one means "retirement, pension (money)." You should always be on the alert for false cognates. Never assume that two words mean the same thing just because they look similar.

EXERCISE 58.1 If your native language is related to English, create a special document on your word processor called "False Cognates." Set up a table like the one above, and enter as many false cognates as you can think of. Use this document as an ongoing resource for vocabulary building.

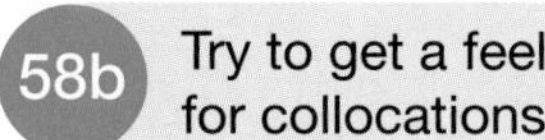

58b Try to get a feel for collocations

WEBLINK Quiz on collocations

Collocations are words that commonly occur together (see 45c-1). For example, the word *advice* commonly occurs with the verbs *give, get,* and *receive* and with the adjectives *good, bad,* and *sound.* This is why the sentence "She gave me some good advice" sounds like normal American English, while the sentence "She presented me some nice advice" does not.

- ▸ An intermission allows theatergoers to ~~extend~~ stretch their legs.
- ▸ A steep ~~upshoot~~ rise in grain prices could topple many governments in the Third World.
- ▸ On Christmas Day, the children were bubbling ~~up~~ over with excitement.
- ▸ Lazy thinkers tend to make ~~wide~~ broad generalizations about things.

The best way to develop your knowledge of collocations is to pay attention to them in the English you see and hear around you. In this way, you will develop a feel for which words go with which. Another good strategy is to consult collocational dictionaries such as the *Advanced Learner's English Dictionary*, 4th ed. (London: Collins COBUILD, 2004), which is based on a 500-million-word corpus of actual written and spoken English.

You can also get help with collocations through a specialized English learner's dictionary that provides plenty of example sentences. Good choices include the *Longman Dictionary of Contemporary English*, 4th ed. (London: Longman, 2003), the *Longman Dictionary of American English*, 3rd ed. (New York: Pearson, 2004), and the *Oxford Advanced Learner's Dictionary*, 7th ed. (New York: Oxford University Press, 2005). On the Internet, try *OneLook Dictionaries* at <http://www.onelook.com>.

EXERCISE 58.2 In each of the following sentences, replace the underlined word to form a collocation. You may want to consult an appropriate dictionary for help. The first sentence has already been done.

1. Kenya has one of the ~~tallest~~ highest standards of living in sub-Saharan Africa.
2. Gone are the days when a doctor would make house visits.
3. Let's all give the winner a volley of applause.
4. The students were on their promise not to cheat.
5. She was the first woman to achieve the finish line at the Boston Marathon.
6. The young actor had to learn his lines to heart.
7. I just got an A on my English paper, and things are seeing up.
8. He told the waiter that he would eat the specialty of the house.

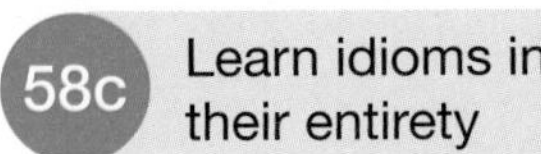

58c Learn idioms in their entirety

Learning idioms

A special type of collocation, an **idiomatic expression,** or **idiom,** is a fixed phrase whose meaning cannot be deduced from the meanings of its parts. For example, even if you know the words *kick* and *bucket,* you may not know what the idiom *kick the bucket* means (it means "die"). Because of their unpredictability, you have to learn idioms in their entirety, one at a time. And you have to use them in exactly the right form. If you said *kick a bucket* or *kick the pail,* many listeners would not know what you meant.

The best way to learn a language's idioms is by listening to native speakers. Some good Web sites can also help: Dave Sperling's *ESL Idiom Page* at <http://www.pacificnet.net/~sperling/idioms.cgi>, *ESL Idioms and Slang* at <http://iteslj.org/links/ESL/Idioms_and_Slang>, and *Vocabulary on the Internet* at <http://ec.hku.hk/vec/vocab/vocint.htm>.

See 41c

Self-study for ESL students

The same holds true for other idioms like *beat around the bush, have a screw loose,* or *lip service.* Because most idioms are colloquial, you should generally avoid them in formal written English. They are most often used for casual communication, as in ordinary conversation, email correspondence, or chat groups. Some idioms, though, such as *by and large, out of the question,* and *on the other hand,* are quite acceptable in more formal uses.

Glossary of Grammatical and Rhetorical Terms

absolute phrase A subject and an adjective phrase (often a participial phrase) used to modify an entire clause—for example, "*Her curiosity satisfied,* she left the meeting." (26c-2)

abstract noun A word that names an idea, emotion, quality, or other intangible concept—for example, *beauty, passion, despair.* (26a-1, 41a-2)

acronym A pronounceable word formed from the first letters of a multiword name and usually written in uppercase letters—for example, *UNESCO, ASCII, RAM.* (54d)

active form *See* active voice.

active voice The form a transitive verb takes to indicate that the subject is performing the action on the direct object. Also called the *active form.* (26a-4, 28g)

adjective A word that modifies a noun by qualifying or describing it—for example, *new, interesting.* (26a-3, Chapter 30). *See also specific types of adjectives.*

adjective clause A dependent clause, usually introduced by a relative pronoun, that modifies a noun or pronoun. Also called a *relative clause.* (26c-3)

adverb A word that modifies a verb, adjective, clause, sentence, or other adverb—for example, *quickly, well.* (26a-5, Chapter 30). *See also specific types of adverbs.*

adverb clause A dependent clause that begins with a subordinating conjunction and answers a question such as the following: when? where? how? why? (26c-3)

agreement The grammatical requirement that a verb and its subject have the same number (either plural or singular) and that a pronoun and its antecedent have the same number and gender. (Chapter 29)

analogy The noting of a similarity between otherwise dissimilar things; a less explicit version of a simile. (41f-1)

analytical writing Writing that examines the whole of a work in relationship to its component parts. (16a-3)

annotating Making summary notes in the margin, as well as underlining or highlighting important words and passages. (2b-3)

antecedent The noun that precedes and is replaced by a pronoun. For example, in the sentence "David is proud of himself," *David* is the antecedent of *himself.* A pronoun should agree in number and gender with its antecedent. (26a-2, 33a)

antonyms Two words having opposite meanings—for example, *love* and *hate.* (43c-3)

appositive A special type of pronoun-noun pairing in which a pronoun is conjoined with a noun—for example, *we students.* Also, a noun that is placed next to the subject to give it extra characterization (27c). *See also* appositive phrase.

appositive phrase A noun phrase, placed next to another noun, that describes or defines the other noun and is usually set off by commas—for example, "Sammy Sosa, *my favorite baseball player,* may someday break the home run record." Also called an *appositive.* (26c-2)

argument A course of reasoning that puts forth a claim and supports it with evidence. (Chapter 4)

article A word that precedes a noun and indicates definiteness or indefiniteness. Standard Edited English has three articles: *a, an, the.* (26a-3, Chapter 56)

aspect *See* verbal aspect.

auxiliary verb A verb, such as *has, be,* or *do,* that combines with a main verb to form a simple predicate—for example, "The guests *have* left." Also called a *helping verb.* (26a-4, 28c)

base form The main form of a verb, given as the headword in the dictionary—for example, *run, ask, consider.* Also called *simple form.* (26a-4, 28a)

bibliography Any listing of books and articles on a particular subject. (7d)

Boolean operators Specific words (AND, NOT, OR) that are combined with other words or phrases to focus search terms during a database search. (8c-1)

brainstorming Generating random ideas or fragments of thought about a topic. (3c-1)

case The form a pronoun takes to indicate its grammatical relation to other words in the sentence. (Chapter 27). *See also* objective case, possessive case, subjective case.

clause A group of words that has a subject and a predicate. (26c-3). *See also specific types of clauses.*

cliché An overused expression—for example, *sick and tired, climbing the ladder of success.* (41g-3)

clustering A prewriting technique that helps a writer see relationships among ideas. (3c-4)

cognates Two words from different languages that are similar in form and meaning—for example, the English *disaster* and the Spanish *desastre.* (58a)

coherence The characteristic of writing that makes it "stick together" from sentence to sentence and paragraph to paragraph. (5a-2)

collective noun A singular word that names a group—for example, *team, band, trio.* (26a-1)

collocation The relationship between two or more words that frequently occur together—for example, *write* and *check.* (43c-1, 58b)

comma splice Two independent clauses joined only by a comma. Comma splices are not acceptable in formal English. (Chapter 32)

common noun A word that names one or more persons, places, things, concepts, or qualities as a general category—for example, *flowers, telephone, determination.* Common nouns are lowercased. (26a-1)

complement *See* object complement, subject complement, verb complement.

complete predicate The simple predicate plus any objects, complements, or adverbial modifiers. (26b-2)

complete subject The simple subject of a sentence, plus all modifiers. (26b-1)

complex compound A word made up of three or more words. (55b)

complex sentence A sentence that has a single independent clause and one or more dependent clauses. (26d-2, 40b)

complex series A series in which individual items contain internal commas, necessitating the use of semicolons to separate the items. (48c)

compound A word made up of two smaller words. (55a)

compound antecedent A noun phrase consisting of two or more terms joined by *and*—for example, *Kim and her brother.* It is usually considered plural; therefore, if it is referred to later by a pronoun, the pronoun should be plural. (29b)

compound-complex sentence A sentence that has two or more independent clauses and one or more dependent clauses. (26d-2, 40b)

compound predicate A predicate containing two or more verbs with the same subject. (26b-1)

compound sentence A sentence that has two or more independent clauses and no dependent clauses. (26d-2, 40b)

compound subject A sentence subject consisting of two or more simple subjects. (26b-1)

concrete noun A word that names something that can be touched, seen, heard, smelled, or tasted—for example, *automobile, music, cloud.* (26a-1, 41a-2)

conditional sentence A sentence composed of a subordinate clause (usually beginning with *if*) and a main clause—for example, "If I'm late, please start the meeting without me." (57i–k)

conjunction A word that joins two sentences, clauses, phrases, or words—for example, *and, or, but.* (26a-7). *See also specific types of conjunctions.*

conjunctive adverb An adverb that modifies an entire sentence or clause while linking it to the preceding sentence or clause—for example, *however, therefore.* (26a-5, 47f)

connotation Extra meaning that a word has, beyond its basic meaning. (41b, 43b)

contraction A reduced form of a word or pair of words—for example, *can't* for *cannot, I'll* for *I will.* (41c-2)

coordinate adjectives A series of adjectives, separated by commas, that can be arranged in any order—for example, a *rusty, dented, broken-down* car. (47d)

coordinating conjunction A conjunction used to connect sentences, clauses, phrases, or words that are parallel in meaning and grammatical structure—for example, *and, but, or, nor.* (26a-7)

coordination The pairing of equivalent sentences or sentence elements by putting them in the same grammatical form and linking them via a coordinating conjunction, conjunctive adverb, or semicolon. (37b)

correlative conjunctions Conjunctions that are used in pairs—for example, *both/and, either/or, neither/nor.* The two elements connected by such conjunctions should be in parallel grammatical form. (26a-7)

count noun A word that names something that can be counted and pluralized—for example, a *book*, some *friends*, three *dollars.* (26a-1, 56a)

cumulative adjectives A series of adjectives, each one modifying those following it—for example, *a small new Italian luxury* car. These adjectives must follow a certain order, and commas are not used to separate them. (47j)

dangling modifier An introductory verbal phrase that does not refer to the subject of the sentence. Dangling modifiers are unacceptable in formal English. (34e)

debating A prewriting technique that helps writers to examine arguments for and against a controversial issue. (3c-5)

declarative sentence A sentence that makes a statement about something. In most writing, declarative sentences predominate. (26d-1)

deductive reasoning Argumentation that starts with some general rule or assumption and then applies it to a specific fact to arrive at a logical conclusion. (4a-2)

demonstrative adjective An adjective that singles out a specific noun—for example, *this* book, *those* promises. (26a-3, 30a)

demonstrative pronoun A pronoun that points to its antecedent noun—for example, *this, those.* (26a-2)

demonstratives Short for demonstrative pronouns and/or demonstrative adjectives.

denotation The dictionary meaning of a word. Compare with *connotation.* (41a, 43b)

dependent clause A clause that cannot stand alone as a sentence but must be attached to a main clause. A dependent clause typically begins with a subordinating conjunction or relative pronoun. The three types of dependent clauses are adjective, adverb, and noun clauses. Also called a *subordinate clause.* (26c-3, 31b)

descriptors *See* keywords.

determiner A word such as *the, this,* or *her* that initiates a noun phrase. (26a-3, 56f)

development The depth of coverage given to key ideas in a piece of writing. (5a-2)

dialect Speech that is identified with a particular social, ethnic, or regional group. (41d)

diction A writer's choice of words. (Chapter 41)

direct discourse Language that is taken word for word from another source and is enclosed in quotation marks. (35f)

direct object A noun, pronoun, or noun phrase that completes the action of the verb in an active sentence—for example, "Our neighbor plays *the piano.*" (26b-2)

disciplinary discourse The language conventions and genres typically used by a particular academic discipline, (such as political science or physics). (15b)

disjunctive antecedent A noun phrase consisting of two or more terms joined by *or* or *nor*—for example, *the wife or the husband.* If the disjunctive antecedent is referred to later by a pronoun, the pronoun should agree in number with the last term in the phrase. (29b)

disjunctive subject A sentence subject consisting of two nouns or pronouns joined by *or* or *nor.* (29a-4)

ellipsis Three spaced periods marking the omission of a word or phrase. (10b-2, 52j)

end-weight The emphasis that falls naturally on the words located at the end of a clause or sentence. (39a)

enthymeme A syllogism with one of the premises unstated. (6a-2)

etymology Information about a word's historical development. (44b-5)

exclamatory sentence A sentence that expresses strong emotion and is punctuated with an exclamation point. (26d-1)

exemplification The use of examples to make difficult concepts understandable. (5b-8)

expletive An introductory word (*it, there*) that opens a sentence but carries little meaning. Expletives are sometimes overused. (36c)

fallacy A false statement or line of reasoning. (4g)

false cognates Two words from different languages that resemble each other but have different meanings—for example, the Spanish *compromiso* and the English *compromise.* Also called *false friends.* (59a)

false friends *See* false cognates.

faulty predication An ungrammatical sentence in which the subject and the predicate are not consistent with each other. (35e)

figure of speech A figurative, or nonliteral, use of language such as a metaphor or simile. (41g)

final bibliography The final listing of sources actually used in writing a research paper, formatted according to a particular documentation style. (7d)

focus The extent to which a piece of writing adheres to its topic and purpose. (5a-2)

format (*n*) The way a piece of writing delineates its subtopics and parts through headings, typeface, typestyle, and so forth. (*v*) To set up a piece of writing's visual style. (6a-2)

fragment *See* sentence fragment.

freewriting Writing down thoughts in connected sentences as they come to mind. (3c-2)

functional résumé A résumé in which certain skills are emphasized through the use of categories such as "Computer Skills" and "Language Skills." (21c)

fused sentence *See* run-on sentence.

future perfect progressive tense A verb tense formed by combining *will have been* and the *-ing* form of the main verb. It emphasizes the continuous or repetitive nature of the action—for example, "Next month, my father *will have been teaching* for 30 years." (28d-3)

future perfect tense A verb tense formed by combining *will have* and the past participle of the main verb. It describes an action that will occur in the future but before some specified time—for example, "Soon I *will have completed* all the requirements." (28d-3)

future progressive tense A verb tense formed by combining *will be* and the *-ing* form of the main verb. It expresses action that will be continuing or repeated in the future—for example, "My daughter is on vacation now, but she *will be going* back to school in the fall." (28d-3)

future tense A verb tense formed by combining the modal auxiliary *will* and the base form of the main verb. It expresses actions or conditions that will occur in the future—for example, "The final exam *will be* hard."Also called *simple future tense.* (28d-3)

gender Classification of a noun or pronoun as masculine, feminine, or neuter. (29b)

generic pronoun A pronoun used to refer to people in general, regardless of gender. (42a-2)

genre The kind of writing form used, such as an essay, poem, song lyric, or report. (3b-3). *See also* literary genre.

gerund A verb form that ends in *ing* and functions as a noun—for example, "We went *skiing* last week." (26a-9)

gerund phrase A phrase consisting of a gerund and any modifiers, objects, and/or complements—for example, *"Running a business* can be difficult." (26c-2)

helping verb *See* auxiliary verb.

homophones Words that sound alike but are spelled differently and have different meanings—for example, *brake* and *break.* (45b)

Identifiers *See* keywords.

idiom *See* idiomatic expression.

idiomatic expression A phrase whose meaning differs from that of its individual words—for example, *kick the bucket.* Also called an *idiom.* (41c-2, 58c)

imperative mood A grammatical form of a verb used to express a command or a strong request and give instructions. Imperative sentences are always addressed to an understood subject, *you,* which is usually omitted. (26a-4, 28h, 35b)

imperative sentence A sentence that expresses a command, a request, or a suggestion, usually with the understood subject *you*—for example, "Don't fret!" "Try using the toolbar buttons." (26d-1)

indefinite adjective A nonspecific adjective—for example, *some* people. (26a-3, 30a)

indefinite pronoun A pronoun that refers to one or more nonspecific persons, places, or things and does not require an antecedent—for example, *anybody, anything.* (26a-2)

independent clause A group of words that includes a subject and predicate and can stand alone as a sentence. Also called a *main clause.* (26c-3)

indicative mood A grammatical form of a verb used to make assertions, state opinions, and ask questions. (26a-4, 28h, 35b)

indirect discourse A summarization, restatement, or paraphrase of a statement made by someone else. (35f, 51a-1)

indirect object A noun, pronoun, or noun phrase that is indirectly affected by the action of the verb—for example, "My boyfriend gave *me* a present." (26b-2)

inductive reasoning A pattern in which the writer states the main claim for an argument late in the work, in order to first present a skeptical audience with supporting evidence. (4a-2)

infinitive The base form of a verb preceded by *to.* It can function as a noun, adjective, or adverb. (26a-4, 26a-9). *See also* perfect infinitive, present infinitive.

infinitive phrase A phrase consisting of an infinitive and any modifiers, objects, and/or complements—for example, "Kevin said he wanted *to make his own way.*" (26c-2)

initialism An abbreviation formed from the first letters of a multiword name and usually written in uppercase letters—for example, *FBI, CPU.* (54d)

inseparable verb A transitive phrasal verb whose particle must be kept together with the verb—for example, "I quickly *went over* my paper." Compare with *separable verb.* (Chapter 57)

intensive pronoun A pronoun that consists of a personal pronoun plus *-self* or *-selves* and is used for emphasis—for example, "They did it *themselves.*" (26a-2)

interjection A word or short phrase that expresses an emotional outcry and is punctuated with an exclamation point. (26a-8)

interpretive writing Writing that discusses another person's intended meaning or the impact of a work on an audience. (16a-2)

interrogative adjective An adjective that raises a question about a noun—for example, "*Which* way do I go?" "*Whose* hat is this?" (26a-3, 30a)

interrogative pronoun A pronoun that introduces a question—for example, *who, what, whose.* (26a-2, 27d)

interrogative sentence A sentence that raises a question and is punctuated with a question mark. (26d-1)

intransitive verb A verb that does not take a direct object—for example, "My driver's license *has expired.*" (26a-4, 28f, Chapter 57)

invisible writing A computer freewriting technique designed to release writers from inhibitions created by seeing their own words on screen. (3c-3)

irregular verb A verb whose past tense and past participle are not formed through the standard pattern of adding *-d* or *-ed* to the base form—for example, *run* (*ran, run*); *know (knew, known).* (26a-4, 28b)

jargon Specialized, technical language used by a professional or special interest group. (41d)

keywords Words that are used to identify the subjects found in electronic databases. Also called *descriptors* or *identifiers.* (7e-2)

linking verb A verb that joins a sentence subject to a subject complement, indicating a condition, quality, or state of being—for example, "They *will be* late." (26a-4, 26b-3)

literary genre Type of literature, such as poetry, fiction, or drama. (16a-1)

main clause *See* independent clause.

mass noun *See* noncount noun.

metaphor A figure of speech in which the writer describes something in a way normally reserved for something else, thus presenting the thing being described in a new light. (41g-2)

mixed construction An ungrammatical sentence that starts out one way but finishes in another. (35d)

mixed metaphors Two different metaphors put close together in a piece of writing—for example, "Milwaukee is the golden egg that the rest of the state wants to milk." Mixed metaphors should be avoided. (41g-2)

modal auxiliary verb A special type of verb that indicates necessity, probability, or permission—for example, *may, might, should, can.* Also called a *modal verb.* (26a-4, 28c, 57f). *See also* auxiliary verb.

modal verb *See* modal auxiliary verb.

modifier A word, phrase, or clause that adds detail to another word, phrase, or clause. (26c, Chapter 34). *See also* dangling modifier, split infinitive.

mood Classification of a verb according to the type of statement made—indicative, imperative, or subjunctive. (26a-4, 28h, 35b)

narrative A type of writing that tells a story in a time-ordered sequence. (5b-7)

nominalization A noun derived from a verb—for example, *removal* (derived from *remove*), *fascination* (derived from *fascinate*). The frequent use of nominalizations results in a noun-heavy style. (36f)

noncount noun A word that names something that typically is not counted or pluralized—for example, *milk, generosity, rain.* Also called a *mass noun.* (26a-1, 57a)

nonessential element *See* nonrestrictive element.

nonrestrictive element A phrase or clause that provides extra information in a sentence. A nonrestrictive element can be omitted without changing the basic meaning of the sentence; it is set off with commas, dashes, or parentheses. Also called a *nonessential element.* (47e)

noun A word that names a person, place, thing, quality, idea, or action. (26a-1). *See also specific types of nouns.*

noun clause A dependent clause that begins with a relative pronoun and functions as a sentence subject, object, complement, or appositive. (26c-3)

noun compound A sequence of two or more nouns, with the right-most noun being the head noun and the other noun(s) serving to modify it—for example, *income tax form.* (30b)

number Classification of a noun, pronoun, or verb as singular or plural. (29b, 35a)

object *See* direct object, indirect object, object of a preposition.

object complement A noun, noun phrase, adjective, or adjective phrase that elaborates on or describes the direct object of a sentence—for example, "The film made me *angry.*" (26b-2)

object of a preposition A noun or pronoun in a prepositional phrase—for example, "He was on the *boat.*" (26a-6)

objective case The form a pronoun takes when it is used as a grammatical object. (Chapter 27)

organization The plan that a piece of writing follows, typically based on the thesis and opening paragraphs. (5a-2)

paragraph A sentence or group of sentences, presented in a text as a unit, that develops a main idea. (Chapter 5)

parallel form *See* parallelism.

parallel structure *See* parallelism.

parallelism The use of similar grammatical form for words or phrases that have a coordinate relationship. Also called *parallel structure* or *parallel form.* (5e, Chapter 38)

participial phrase A phrase consisting of a present or past participle plus any objects, modifiers, and/or complements—for example, "I saw someone *running down the street.*" (26c-2)

participle A verb form that can serve as an adjective—for example, *earned* income or *earning* power. (26a-9). *See also* past participle, present participle, pres-ent perfect participle.

particle A preposition or adverb that, when attached to a verb, creates a phrasal verb—for example, look *into*, see *through*, knock *out.* (26a-6)

parts of speech The different categories in which words can be classified according to their grammatical function: nouns, verbs, adjectives, adverbs, pronouns, prepositions, conjunctions, verbals, and expletives. (26a)

passive form *See* passive voice.

passive voice The form a transitive verb takes to indicate that the subject is being acted upon. Also called the *passive form.* (26a-4, 28g)

past participle A verb form that can be used by itself as an adjective or can be combined with some form of the auxiliary *have* to form perfect tenses or with some form of the verb *be* to create passive-voice sentences. For regular verbs, it is similar in form to the past tense—for example, *picked, opened.* (26a-4, 26a-9, 28a, 28e-4)

past perfect progressive tense A verb tense formed by combining *had been* and the present participle of the main verb. It puts emphasis on the continuing or repetitive nature of a past action—for example, "By the time he crossed the bridge, Roy *had been running* for two hours." (28d-2)

past perfect tense A verb tense created by combining *had* and the past participle of the main verb. It is used to describe a past action that preceded another past activity—for example, "Before she injured her knee, Beth *had hoped* to become a top ski racer." (28d-2)

past progressive tense A verb tense formed by combining the auxiliary verb *was* or *were* and the present participle of the main verb—for example, "I *was* just *starting* to cook when our guest arrived." (28d-2)

past tense A verb tense that indicates past action—for example, "World War I *started* in 1914." For a regular verb, the past tense is formed by adding *-d* or *-ed* to the base form. Also called *simple past tense.* (26a-4, 28a, 28a-2)

perfect infinitive A verb form consisting of *to have* plus the past participle of the verb—for example, *to have changed, to have stopped.* It is used for an action that occurs prior to the action expressed by the main verb. (28e-3)

person Classification of a pronoun based on whether it refers to the speaker (first person: *I, me, us*), the person spoken to (second person: *you*), or someone or something spoken about (third person: *she, him, it, they*). (35a)

persona A writer's presentation of him- or herself through a piece of writing. (3b-2)

personal pronoun A pronoun that refers to one or more specific persons, places, or things—for example, *she, it, they.* (26a-2)

personification A type of metaphor in which an inanimate object or abstraction is described as having human traits. (41g-2)

phrasal verb A verb consisting of a verb and one or two particles—for example, *pick over, look into, get away with.* Also called a *two-word verb* or *three-word verb.* (26a-6, 57a)

phrase A group of related words that does not have both a subject and a complete predicate (compare with *clause*). Phrases can function as nouns, verbs, or modifiers. (26c-2). *See also specific types of phrases.*

plagiarism Unauthorized or misleading use of the language or thoughts of another author. (10a-3)

possessive adjective An adjective that indicates possession—for example, *my* coat, *their* country. (26a-3, 27e, 30a, 56f)

possessive case The form a pronoun takes when it is used as a grammatical possessive. (Chapter 27)

possessive pronoun A pronoun such as *mine, yours,* or *hers* that stands by itself—for example, "This seat is *mine.*" (27e)

predicate The part of a sentence that contains the verb and makes a statement about the subject. (26b-2)

predicate adjective An adjective that follows a linking verb and refers back to the noun subject. (26a-3)

prefix A word part, such as *anti-, re-,* or *dis-,* that is attached to the beginning of a word—for example, *anti*freeze, *re*new, *dis*cover. (43a, 45d-1)

preposition A word that indicates a relationship between a noun or pronoun and some other part of the sentence—for example, *to, in, at, from, on.* Also called a *particle* when part of a phrasal verb. (26a-6)

prepositional phrase A group of words consisting of a preposition plus a noun or pronoun and its modifiers. (26a-6, 26c-2)

present infinitive A verb form consisting of *to* plus the base form of the verb—for example, *to go, to hesitate.* It is used for an action that occurs at the same time as or later than the action expressed by the main verb. (28e-3)

present participle A verb form created by adding *-ing* to the base form—for example, *sewing, writing.* It can be used by itself as an adjective or noun or can be combined with some form of the verb *be* to form the progressive tenses. (26a-4, 26a-8, 28a, 28e-4)

present perfect participle A verb form consisting of *having* plus the past participle of the verb. It is used to express an action occurring prior to the action of the main verb—for example, "*Having changed* my PIN number, I cannot remember it." (28e-4)

present perfect progressive tense A verb tense formed by combining *have been* or *has been* and the present participle of the main verb. It typically emphasizes the ongoing nature of the activity—for example, "People *have been complaining* about the working conditions for years." (28d-1)

present perfect tense A verb tense formed by combining the auxiliary verb *have* or *has* and the past participle of the main verb. It is used to indicate action that began in the past and either is continuing or has continuing effects in the present—for example, "The United Nations *has served* many purposes." (28d-1)

present progressive tense A verb tense formed by combining the auxiliary verb *am, is,* or *are* and the *-ing* form of a main verb. It is typically used to indicate present action—for example, "Mike *is taking* a heavy load of classes this term." (28d-1)

present tense The verb tense used to express a general statement, make an observation, or describe a habitual activity—for example, "Geese *fly* south in autumn." Also called *simple present tense.* (26a-4, 28a, 28d-1)

primary research Generating information or data through processes such as interviewing, administering questionnaires, and observing. (7a-1, 7f-6)

principal parts The major forms of a verb: base form, present tense, past tense, past participle, and present participle. (26a-4, 28a)

process description A type of writing that depicts a step-by-step procedure. (5b-7)

pronoun A word that substitutes for a noun and always refers to a noun. (26a-2, 29b). *See also specific types of pronouns.*

proper noun A word that names a particular person, place, institution, organization, month, or day—for example, *Anne, New York City, Monday.* Proper nouns are almost always capitalized. (26a-1)

quantifier An adjective such as *many, little,* or *every* that indicates some amount of a noun. (56f)

reciprocal pronoun A pronoun that refers to the separate parts of a plural antecedent—for example, "They made promises to *one another.*" (26a-2)

redundancy The use of words that could be left out without changing the meaning of a sentence. (36b)

reflexive pronoun A pronoun that consists of a personal pronoun plus *-self* or *-selves.* It refers back to the subject to show that the subject is the object of an action—for example, "Katy cut *herself.*" (26a-2)

register The overall degree of formality of a piece of writing, including its identification with a particular field or community of users. (41c)

regular verb A verb that forms the third-person singular present tense by adding *-s* or *-es* to the base form, forms the present participle by adding *-ing* to the base form, and forms the past tense and past participle by adding *-d* or *-ed* to the base form. (26a-4, 28a)

related words Words derived from the same root. (44b-5)

relative clause *See* adjective clause.

relative pronoun A pronoun that introduces a dependent clause—for example, *that, which, whom.* (26a-2, 27d)

restrictive element Information essential to the precise meaning of a sentence and thus not set off with commas. Compare with *nonrestrictive element.* (47j)

résumé A concise summary of an individual's accomplishments, skills, experience, and personal interests. (22c). *See also* functional résumé.

rhetorical stance A writer's approach to his or her topic, encompassing purpose, persona, and audience. (3b-2)

root The main part of a word, to which prefixes and suffixes can be attached—for example, the root of *telephonic* is *phon.* Also called a *stem.* (43a)

run-on sentence Two independent clauses fused together without any intervening conjunction or punctuation. Run-on sentences are not acceptable in formal English. Also called a *fused sentence.* (Chapter 32)

secondary research Finding information in secondary, or previously published, sources. (7a-1, 7f-1 to 7f-5)

semiacronym An abbreviation in which part of the term is pronounced as a word and the rest as one or more letters—for example, *jpeg,* pronounced "jay-peg." (54d)

sense The meaning of a word. (44b-4)

sentence The basic unit of written language for expressing a thought. All sentences except commands have a stated grammatical subject and a predicate. (26b). *See also specific types of sentences.*

sentence fragment A grammatically incomplete sentence. (Chapter 31)

sentence subject *See* subject.

separable verb A transitive phrasal verb whose particle may be placed after the object of the verb—for example, "I quickly *looked* my paper *over.*" Compare with *inseparable verb.* (Chapter 57)

sequence of tenses The time relationship among verbs in a block of text, expressed by verb tenses. (28e)

serial comma In a series of items, the comma that separates the items. (47c)

signal phrase The introductory phrase that signals a quotation to follow. (10b-2)

simile A figure of speech in which the writer uses one thing to describe another. Similes typically employ the word *like* or *as*—for example, "The brain is somewhat *like* a computer." (41g-1)

simple form *See* base form.

simple future tense *See* future tense.

simple past tense *See* past tense.

simple predicate A main verb plus any auxiliary verbs. Also called a *verb phrase.* (26b-2). *See also* predicate.

simple present tense *See* present tense.

simple sentence A sentence that has a single independent clause and no dependent clauses. (26d-2, 40b)

simple subject The noun or pronoun that constitutes the heart of a sentence subject. (26b-1)

slang Nonstandard language characterized by short-lived, colorful expressions. It is most commonly used by teenagers and tight-knit subcultures. (41d)

split infinitive An infinitive with one or more words between *to* and the verb—for example, *to quickly retreat.* (34d-2)

stative verb *See* verb of state.

stem *See* root.

subject A noun, pronoun, or noun phrase that indicates what a sentence is about and typically precedes the main verb of the sentence. (26b-1, 29a-1, 35b). *See also specific types of subjects.*

subject complement A noun, noun phrase, adjective, or adjective phrase that elaborates on the subject of a sentence and usually follows a linking verb—for example, "Joanne was elected *student body president.*" (26b-2)

subjective case The form a pronoun takes when it is used as a grammatical subject. (Chapter 27)

subjunctive mood A grammatical form of a verb used to express hypothetical conditions, wishes, and other uncertain statements. Verbs in subjunctive mood often appear in dependent clauses beginning with *if* or *that.* (26a-4, 28h, 35b)

subordinate clause *See* dependent clause.

subordinating conjunction A conjunction that is used to introduce a dependent clause and connect it to an independent clause—for example, *although, because, if, since.* (26a-7)

subordination In a sentence containing two ideas that are not equal in importance, making the lesser idea into a subordinate, or dependent, clause. (37c)

suffix A word part, such as *-ful, -ship,* or *-ness,* that is attached to the end of a word—for example, boast*ful,* fellow*ship,* kind*ness.* (43a, 45d-2)

syllogism A form of deductive logic consisting of a major premise, a minor premise, and a conclusion. (4a-2)

synonyms Words that are similar in meaning—for example, *desire* and *want.* (43c-2)

tense *See* verb tense.

theoretical writing Writing that examines individual works or events to determine how they exemplify broader trends. (16a-3)

thesaurus A collection of synonyms and antonyms. (44a)

thesis statement A sentence or two that concisely identifies the topic and main point of a piece of writing. (3e-2)

three-word verb *See* phrasal verb.

tone The tone of a piece of writing, including the attitude a writer conveys toward the subject through language choices. (5a-2, 35c)

topic sentence A sentence, usually at the beginning of a paragraph, that gives readers an overview of the paragraph. (5a-1)

transitive verb A verb that acts on an object—for example, *carry, show.* In the active voice, a transitive verb acts on the direct object of the sentence. In the passive voice, it acts on the subject. (26a-4, 28f, Chapter 57)

two-word verb *See* phrasal verb.

unified paragraph A paragraph that focuses on and develops a single main idea. (5a)

usage label In dictionaries, a notation indicating a particular sense of a word—for example, *Informal, Archaic.* (44b-6)

usage note In dictionaries, an expert judgment about the correct use of a word. (44b-6)

verb A word that expresses action, occurrence, or existence. (26a-4, Chapter 28). *See also specific types of verbs.*

verb complement A participial or infinitive phrase attached to a verb—for example, in the sentence "I like to swim," *to swim* is the complement of the verb *like.* (57b)

verb of state A verb that expresses a condition or state, rather than an action or event—for example, *involve, need, consist of.* Verbs of state do not have progressive tense forms. Also called a *stative verb.* (28d-1, 57f)

verb phrase A main verb plus any auxiliary verbs. Also called a *simple predicate.* (28c)

verb tense The form a verb takes to indicate the time of the action or the state of being. (28d, 35b)

verbal A verb form that functions in a sentence as a noun, adverb, or adjective. There are three types of verbals: participles, gerunds, and infinitives. (26a-9, 26c-2)

verbal aspect The particular form a verb takes, within its tense, to indicate duration or completion of the verb's action or state of being. Standard Edited English has three verbal aspects: perfect, progressive, and perfect progressive. Also called *aspect.* (28d)

voice The form a transitive verb takes to indicate whether the subject is acting (*active voice*) or being acted upon (*passive voice*). (28g, 35b). Sometimes used to refer to the tone of a piece of writing. (11a-3.)

warrant An assumption in the form of a general statement or rule (often unstated) that logically connects the evidence or data a writer is using to the point he or she is making. (4e-2)

working bibliography A listing of all the sources encountered while researching a topic. The entries may not be in final citation format. (7d)

Glossary of Usage

a, an Use *a* before words beginning with a consonant sound: *a program, a uniform.* Use *an* before words beginning with a vowel sound: *an open book, an uncle.*

accept, except *Accept* is a verb meaning "to receive gladly." *Except* is usually a preposition meaning "with the exclusion of."

adapt, adopt *Adapt* means "to adjust" or "to make suitable." *Adopt* means "to take as one's own." *If you adopt a child, you will have to adapt to it.*

adverse, averse *Adverse* means "unfavorable." *Averse* means "opposed to." *I am averse to anything that has adverse consequences.*

advice, advise *Advice* is a noun meaning "guidance." *Advise* is a verb meaning "to guide." *I advised her to take my advice.*

affect, effect *Affect* is usually a verb meaning "to influence." *Bad weather seems to affect my mood. Effect* is usually a noun meaning "result." As a verb, *effect* means "to bring about." *The new policy will effect important changes.*

aggravate "To make worse." *Donna's asthma was aggravated by the polluted air.* Also commonly used to mean "to irritate," though some experts consider this incorrect.

ain't Nonstandard. *Am not, is not, are not,* or *have not* are preferred in standard English.

all ready, already *All ready* is an adjective phrase meaning "all prepared." *They were all ready to go. Already* is an adverb meaning "by this time." *They have already left.*

all right Should be spelled as two words. An adjective phrase meaning "satisfactory."

all together, altogether *All together* means "in unison, as a group." *Altogether* means "completely." *The witnesses spoke out all together. They were altogether happy to get the chance.*

allusion, illusion *Allusion* means "indirect reference." *Illusion* means "false perception of reality."

a lot Spelled as two words, not *alot* or *allot.* Informal. In formal writing, use *much* or *many* instead.

among, between See *between, among.*

amongst British equivalent of *among.*

amoral, immoral *Amoral* means "neither moral nor immoral"; to some, it connotes "not caring about right and wrong." *Immoral* means "not moral."

amount, number *Amount* is used with noncount nouns; *number* is used with count nouns. *A number of people said that they had a large amount of money to give.*

an, a See *a, an.*

and etc. Redundant. Use *etc.* or *and so on.*

ante-, anti- *Ante-* is a prefix meaning "before." *The broker asked us to antedate the check. Anti-* is a prefix meaning "against." *Our planes encountered anti-aircraft fire.*

anxious, eager *Anxious* means "uneasy, worried." *We were anxious about the weather. Eager* means "having a strong desire." *We were eager to see the show.*

anymore Should be used only in negative sentences. *She doesn't live here anymore.* In positive sentences, use *nowadays. I have many friends nowadays.*

anyplace Informal for *anywhere.*

anyways, anywheres Nonstandard for *anyway* and *anywhere.*

as Be careful when using *as* as a substitute for *because* or *since. As I fell asleep, I lost track of the time.* Does *as* in this case mean "because" or "while"?

as, like See *like, as.*

assure, ensure, insure These words have the same basic meaning of "to make certain." However, *assure* has the more personal orientation of "to set someone's mind at ease." *Ensure* and *insure* both mean, roughly, "to guarantee"; the latter carries a financial connotation.

at Redundant when used with *where.* The colloquial *Where is he at?* should be shortened in formal writing to *Where is he?*

at this point in time Wordy. Use *now, at present,* or *currently.*

averse, adverse See *adverse, averse.*

awesome "Inspiring awe." *The Himalayas are awesome.* Should not be used in formal writing to mean simply "excellent" or "outstanding."

awful, awfully Avoid using these to mean "very," except in informal communication.

bad, badly *Bad* is an adjective and *badly* is an adverb; avoid confusing these functions, as in *I feel badly* or *He plays bad.*

because of, due to Use *because of* when referring to a clause. *She had a headache because of stress.* Use *due to* when referring to a noun. *Her headache was due to stress.*

being as, being that These phrases are colloquial when used in such sentences as *Being as the roads are icy, we should drive carefully.* In formal writing, replace them with *because* or *since.*

better, had better *Had better* is an idiomatic expression meaning "should." *You had better leave.* It is acceptable in formal writing. *You better leave* is too colloquial.

between, among Use *between* when referring to distinct individuals, especially two of them. *Let's divide it up between you and me.* Use *among* when referring to a mass or collectivity. *Let's divide it up among our friends.*

bring, take *Bring* suggests motion toward the writer or speaker; *take* suggests motion away from the writer or speaker. You *bring* something here, but you *take* something there.

but May be used to begin a sentence. Be aware, however, that some traditionalists may disagree with such usage.

calculate, figure, reckon Colloquial expressions for "to guess" or "to suppose," as in *I calculate we'll have a losing season again.* In formal writing, use *suppose, surmise,* or *imagine.*

can, may *Can* is preferred when expressing ability; *may* is preferred when requesting permission. *May I have another piece? Can she walk without crutches?*

can't hardly, can't scarcely Nonstandard. In formal writing, use *can hardly* or *can scarcely. Even accountants can hardly make sense of the tax code.*

censor, censure *Censor* means "to remove objectionable ideas from." Censure means "to condemn." *Church authorities censored the film and censured the film's producers.*

center around In formal writing, *center on* is preferred. *My paper will center on hate speech.*

cite, site *Cite* is a verb meaning "to quote." *Site* is a noun meaning "place."

climactic, climatic *Climactic* is the adjective form of *climax. King Lear's death is the climactic event of the play. Climatic* is the adjective form of climate. *Global warming could be a climatic disaster.*

complement, compliment A *complement* is something that completes a whole. *The flowers beautifully complemented the table setting.* A *compliment* is an expression of praise. *She complimented me on my dancing.*

compose, comprise *Compose* means "to make up or constitute." *Comprise* means "to consist of." *Seven days compose one week; one week comprises seven days.*

conscience, conscious *Conscience* is a noun meaning "a sense of right and wrong." *Conscious* is an adjective meaning "aware" or "intentional." *Todd made a conscious decision to clear his guilty conscience.*

continual, continuous *Continual* means "repeated at intervals." *Continuous* means "without interruption." The flow of time is *continuous,* but a heartbeat is *continual.*

could of Nonstandard for *could have. He could have tried harder.*

council, counsel A *council* is an assembly of people who advise or regulate. *Counsel* means "advice or guidance." *A council can give counsel.*

criterion, criteria *Criterion* is singular, meaning "standard of judgment." *Criteria* is the plural form.

data Traditionally, *data* was used only as the plural form of *datum.* However, it is now also commonly used as a singular form meaning "numerical information."

device, devise *Device* is a noun meaning "small machine" or "scheme." *Devise* is a verb meaning "to plan or invent."

different from, different than In formal writing, use *different from* when the comparison is between two persons or things. *My opinion is different from hers.* Use *different than* when the object of comparison is a full clause. *The party turned out different than I wanted it to be.*

discreet, discrete *Discreet* means "tactful" or "modest." *Discrete* means "distinct" or "separate."

disinterested, uninterested *Disinterested* means "neutral, unbiased." *Unintere- sted* means "unconcerned, indifferent to." *Although good judges are always disinterested in the case before them, they are not likely to be uninterested in it.*

due to, because of See *because of, due to.*

eager, anxious See *anxious, eager.*

effect, affect See *affect, effect.*

elicit, illicit *Elicit* is a verb meaning "to call forth." *Illicit* is an adjective meaning "illegal."

emigrate, immigrate, migrate *Emigrate* means "to move permanently away from." *Immigrate* means "to move permanently to." *Migrate* means "to move temporarily from one place to another."

eminent, immanent, imminent *Eminent* means "distinguished." *She is an eminent scholar. Immanent* means "inherent." *God's spirit is immanent in nature. Imminent* means "about to occur." *A stock market crash is imminent.*

ensure See *assure, ensure, insure.*

enthused As an adjective, *enthused* is nonstandard. In formal writing, use *enthusiastic.*

especially, specially *Especially* means "deserving of special emphasis" or "particularly." *I am especially happy about my math grade. Specially* is the adverb form of special; it means "exceptionally" or "for a particular reason." *Today is a specially designated holiday.*

-ess A noun suffix used to denote a female, as in *lioness* or *hostess.* In cases where gender is irrelevant, use of this suffix has sexist connotations. Instead of terms such as *poetess* and *sculptress,* use *poet* and *sculptor.*

et al. Abbreviation for Latin *et alia* ("and others"). Should be used only to avoid repeated reference to three or more authors of a single work. *Johnson et al. make the same argument.*

etc. Abbreviation for Latin *et cetera* ("and the rest"). Should not refer to people and should not be used in formal writing. Instead of *She likes Cezanne, Matisse, etc.,* write *She likes artists such as Cezanne and Matisse* or *She likes Cezanne, Matisse, and other such artists.*

everyone, every one *Everyone* is an indefinite pronoun. *Everyone is here.* In *every one, one* is a pronoun and *every* is a quantifier. *Every one of the guests has been seated.*

except, accept See *accept, except.*

expect Verb meaning "to anticipate." In formal writing, should not be used to mean "to presume" or "to suppose."

farther, further *Farther* refers to physical distance. *She hit the ball farther than anyone else. Further* refers to time or degree. *Should we go further with our research?*

fewer, less Use *fewer* with items that can be counted. Use *less* with general amounts. *He had fewer problems and less anxiety than I did.*

figure See *calculate, figure, reckon.*

firstly, secondly, thirdly Common in British English, but considered pretentious in American English. Use *first, second, third.*

get Informal in most uses, especially idiomatic expressions such as *get cracking* or *get around to.* A thesaurus will suggest more formal alternatives for many of these expressions.

good, well *Good* is an adjective; *well* is an adverb. *I feel good. I write well.*

gorilla, guerrilla A *gorilla* is a large ape. A *guerrilla* is a member of a rebel army.

had better, better See *better, had better.*

hanged, hung Use *hanged* for executions, *hung* for all other past-tense meanings. *The prisoner was hanged at dawn. The flag was hung from the railing.*

hardly, scarcely These adverbs have a negative meaning ("almost not at all"); using them with *not* creates a double negative, which is nonstandard in English. *It hardly matters* (not *It doesn't hardly matter*).

he, him, his Using this singular masculine pronoun generically (that is, to refer to a mixed-gender group of people) is considered sexist by many. For ways around this problem, see 42c-2.

he/she, him/her, his/her These forms can be used to avoid the sexism of generic *he, him,* or *his.* Use them sparingly, however. (See 42c.)

heard, herd *Heard* is the past form of hear. *Herd* may be used as a noun to refer to a group of animals or as a verb, as in *to herd* cattle.

hisself Nonstandard for *himself. He shot himself in the foot.*

hole, whole *Hole* is a noun meaning "gap" or "cavity." *Whole* is an adjective meaning "complete" or "entire."

hopefully Used widely as a sentence adverb, as in *Hopefully, the war will soon be over.* Although this usage is grammatically correct, some readers object to it because there is no subject to be full of hope.

hung, hang See *hang, hung.*

if, whether Although both of these conjunctions can be used to express an alternative, *whether* is clearer. *She doesn't know whether she can go.*

illicit, elicit See *elicit, illicit.*

illusion, allusion See *allusion, illusion.*

immanent See *eminent, immanent, imminent.*

immigrate See *emigrate, immigrate, migrate.*

immoral, amoral See *amoral, immoral.*

imply, infer *Imply* means "to suggest indirectly." *Infer* means "to draw a conclusion from what someone else has said." *The owner implied that I didn't have enough experience. I inferred that she would not offer me the job.*

incredible, incredulous *Incredible* means "unbelievable." *His performance was incredible. Incredulous* means "disbelieving." *He was incredulous when he heard the news.*

individual, person *Individual* is overused as a substitute for *person. Individual* should be reserved for situations emphasizing a person's distinctiveness. *Elizabeth Cady Stanton was a* *remarkable individual. Person* can be used in all other cases. *The person who stole my laptop will be caught sooner or later.*

infer, imply See *imply, infer.*

ingenious, ingenuous *Ingenious* means "inventive, clever." *Ingenuous* means "unsophisticated, candid."

in regards to Nonstandard. Use *in regard to, regarding,* or *as regards.*

instill, install *Instill* means "to implant." *A good parent instills good character in a child. Install* means "to set in position for use." *I should install new brakes in my car.*

insure See *assure, ensure, insure.*

irregardless Nonstandard for *regardless.*

its, it's *Its* is the possessive form of *it. It's* is the contracted form of *it is. It's important that a company give its employees a sense of security.*

kind of, sort of, type of Be careful to observe number agreement with these modifiers. Use *this kind of book* (all singular) or *these kinds of books* (all plural), not *these kind of books, these kinds of book,* or *this kind of books.*

lay, lie *Lay* takes a direct object. *They want to lay a wreath at his grave. Lie* does not take a direct object. *I think I'll lie down for a while.*

lead, led *Lead* is a noun referring to a certain type of metal. *Led* is the past form of the verb lead. *Our efforts have led to nothing.*

leave, let *Leave* means "to go away." *She plans to leave tomorrow. Let* means "to allow." *Let me pay for this.*

lend, loan These verbs both mean "to give something temporarily." But *loan* is used only for monetary transactions, while *lend* can be used for more figurative meanings, such as *lend someone a hand.*

less, fewer See *fewer, less.*

lie, lay See *lay, lie.*

like, as In formal writing, use *like* as a preposition before a noun phrase and *as* as a conjunction before a clause: *She looked like her mother* versus *She looked as I thought she would.*

loan, lend See *lend, loan.*

lose, loose *Lose* is a verb meaning "to fail to keep." *Loose* is an adjective meaning "not fastened."

lots Informal. Use *many* or *much.*

man, mankind Avoid these terms in situations where gender-inclusive terms such as *people, humanity, humans, humankind,* or *men and women* can be used instead.

may, can See *can, may.*

might of Nonstandard for *might have. They might have left.*

migrate See *emigrate, immigrate, migrate.*

moral, morale A *moral* is a lesson taught in a story. *Morale* is a state of mind regarding confidence and cheerfulness.

must of Nonstandard for *must have. They must have lost their way.*

number, amount See *amount, number.*

okay, OK, O.K. Informal. In formal writing, use more precise terms such as *enjoyable, acceptable,* or *pleasing.*

person, individual See *individual, person.*

personal, personnel *Personal* is an adjective meaning "private" or "individual." *Personnel* is a noun meaning "the people employed by an organization." *The personnel office keeps personal files on all the company's employees.*

phenomenon, phenomena A *phenomenon* is a perceivable occurrence or fact. *Phenomena* is the plural form.

plus Colloquial when used in place of *moreover. We had gone past the deadline; moreover* (not *plus*), *we were over budget.*

precede, proceed *Precede* means "to come before." *Proceed* means "to go ahead."

pretty In formal writing, avoid using *pretty* as an adverb. *JFK was a very* (not *pretty*) *good writer.*

principal, principle *Principal* is an adjective meaning "foremost." *Principle* is a noun meaning "rule" or "standard." *Our principal concern is to maintain our high principles.*

raise, rise *Raise* is a transitive verb meaning "to lift" or "to build." *He raised his hand. Rise* is an intransitive verb meaning "to stand up" or "to ascend." *She rose from her chair.*

real, really *Real* is an adjective; *really* is an adverb. In most cases, both of these terms should be avoided in formal writing. *The economy is doing very* (not *real* or *really*) well.

reason . . . is because Colloquial. Use *reason . . . is that* in formal writing. *The reason the Yankees won is that they had better pitching.*

reckon See *calculate, figure, reckon.*

respectfully, respectively *Respectfully* means "with respect." *Respectively* means "in the order given." *The teacher called on Bart and Juana, respectively.*

rise, raise See *raise, rise.*

set, sit *Set* is used most often as a transitive verb meaning "to place" or "to arrange." *Set the table. Sit* is an intransitive verb meaning "to take a seat." *Sit down over here.*

shall, will In American English, *shall* is used only for polite questions in the first person (*Shall we sit down?*) and in legalistic writing. Otherwise, *will* is the standard modal verb for future tenses.

should of Nonstandard for *should have.*

site, cite See *cite, site.*

somewheres Nonstandard for *somewhere.*

sort of See *kind of, sort of, type of.*

specially, especially See *especially, specially.*

stationary, stationery *Stationary* is an adjective meaning "not moving." *Stationery* is a noun meaning "writing materials."

take, bring See *bring, take.*

than, then *Than* is a conjunction used to introduce the second part of a comparison: *Donna is taller than Jo. Then* is an adverb meaning "at that time."

that, which As a relative pronoun, *that* is used only in essential clauses. *The storm that* (or *which*) *everyone talks about occurred ten years ago. Which* can be used with either essential or nonessential clauses. *The storm of 1989, which I'll never forget, destroyed part of our roof.*

their, there, they're *Their* is the possessive form of *they. They retrieved their car. There* is an adverb of place; it is also used in expletive constructions. *There is someone at the door.* (See 29i, 36c.) *They're* is a contraction of *they are. They're too young to drive.*

theirselves Nonstandard. Use *themselves.*

threw, through/thru *Threw* is the past form of the verb *throw. Through* is a preposition, as in *walk through the house.* Do not use *thru* in formal writing.

till, until, 'til *Till* and *until* are both acceptable in formal writing. '*Til* is informal.

totally "Entirely" or "completely." *The building was totally demolished.* Should not be used in formal writing to mean "very."

type of See *kind of, sort of, type of.*

uninterested, disinterested See *disinterested, uninterested.*

unique "The only one of its kind." In formal English, *unique* should be used without any degree modification. *Tiger Woods is a unique* (not *very unique*) *athlete.*

until See *till, until, 'til.*

use, utilize In most cases, *use* is the better choice. *Utilize* means "to make practical use of" and should be used only with this meaning.

way Should not be used in formal writing as an adjective. Instead of *The test was way hard,* write *The test was very hard*

weak, week *Weak* is the opposite of strong. *Week* is a period of seven days.

weather, whether Use *weather* as a noun meaning "atmospheric conditions." Use *whether* as a conjunction meaning "if" or "either."

well, good See *good, well.*

whether, if See *if, whether.*

will, shall See *shall, will.*

which, that See *that, which.*

whole, hole See *hole, whole.*

who, whom *Who* and *whom* are used as interrogative or relative pronouns. *Who* stands for a grammatical subject; *whom* stands for a grammatical object. (See 26a-2.)

who's, whose *Who's* is a contraction for *who is. Whose* is the possessive form of *who.*
would have Should not be used in the *if* part of a conditional sentence. *If I had* (not *would have*) *started sooner, I would have finished the paper on time.* (See 57k.)
would of Nonstandard for *would have.*
your, you're *Your* is the possessive form of *you. You're* is a contraction of *you are. You're loyal to your friends.*

Credits

Adbusters Reprints, "Joe Chemo" advertisement. Reprinted by permission.
American Heritage College Dictionary, The. Copyright © 2006 by Houghton Mifflin Harcourt Publishing Company. Reproduced by permission from *The American Heritage College Dictionary, Fourth Edition*.
B.C. (cartoon). By permission of John L. Hart FLP, and Creators Syndicate, Inc.
Beebe, Steven A., and Susan J. Beebe, *Public Speaking: An Audience-Centered Approach*. 5th ed. Boston: Allyn, 2003.
Beers, Burton F. *World History*. Englewood Cliffs, NJ: Prentice, 1990. 719.
Billitteri, T. J. (2008, December 5). Reducing Your Carbon Footprint. *CQ Researcher*, 18, 985–1008. Copyright © 2008 by CQ Press, a division of SAGE Publications. Reprinted by permission.
Bishop, Elizabeth. "One Art" from THE COMPLETE POEMS: 1927–1979. Copyright © 1979, 1983 by Alice Helen Methfessel. Reprinted by permission of Farrar, Straus and Giroux, LLC.
Briggs, Barrett M. "Resuscitating Trigger." Online posting. Writing Program Administrator Listserv. 1 Dec. 1997.
Brody, Jane E. "Personal Health: Cigar Smoking," *The New York Times*, May 29, 1996. Copyright © 1996 by The New York Times Co. Reproduced with permission.
Chaika, Elaine. *Language: The Social Mirror*. Cambridge, MA: Newbury House, 1989. 90.
Children's Defense Fund and Citizens for Tax Justice, "Effects of the Bush Tax Cut, 2004-2010," http://www.ctj.org./html/gwb0602.htm>.
Claywell, Gina. *The Allyn & Bacon Guide to Writing Portfolios*. Boston: Allyn, 2001. 77–78.
Cole, K.C. *The Scientific Aesthetic*. New York: Discover, 1983. Reprinted by permission of the author.
Cousins, Norman. *Human Options*. New York: Berkley, 1981. 41–42, 63, 90.
Dominguez, Joe, and Vicki Robin. *Your Money or Your Life*. New York: Viking, 1992. 13.
Donatelle, Rebecca J. *Access to Health*. 8th ed. Benjamin Cummings, 2004.
EBSCOHost Academic Search Elite search results page, advanced searching page, screen-shot of an online journal article with annotations, and full-text article results page. Copyright © EBSCO Publishing, Inc. All rights reserved.
Ehrlich, Gretel. *The Solace of Open Spaces*. New York: Viking, 1985. 7.
Farb, Peter. *Living Earth*. New York: Harper, 1959.
Fund and Citizens for Tax Justice. "Effects of the Bush Tax Cut, 2004–2010," Children's Defense Fund and Citizens for Tax Justice, http://www.ctj.org./html/gwb0602.htm>.
Hardgrave, Robert L., Jr., *American Government*. Orlando: Harcourt, 1986. 477.

Henslin, James M. *Sociology: A Down-to-Earth Approach.* 6th ed. Boston: Allyn, 2003. Copyright © 2003 by Allyn & Bacon. Reprinted by permission.

Hopper, Vincent F., and Bernard D. N. Grebanier. *Essentials of European Literature.* Vol. 2. Great Neck, NY: Barron's, 1952.

Hult, C. HETI Final Report. 2 Sept. 1997. 7 Oct. 1997. http://english.usu.edu.

Kaniss, Phyllis. *Making Local News.* Chicago: U of Chicago P, 1991. 88–89.

Kingsolver, Barbara. *The Bean Trees.* New York: Harper, 1988. 1.

Martini, Frederic. *Fundamentals of Anatomy and Physiology.* Englewood Cliffs, NJ: Prentice, 1989. 3.

Melville Society home page reprinted by permission of The Melville Society.

Microsoft product screen shot reprinted with permission from Microsoft Corporation.

Miller, Kenneth R., and Joseph Levine. *Biology.* Englewood Cliffs, NJ: Prentice, 1991. 76.

New Book of Knowledge, The. New York: Grolier, 1998.

Niethammer, Carolyn. *Daughters of the Sky.* New York: Macmillan, 1997. 96.

Ogden Standard Examiner (front page), May 1, 2006 and March 23, 2009. Reprinted by permission of the *Ogden Standard.*

Okelberry, Christopher. Screen captures from the SyllaBase website are courtesy, Christopher Okelberry and the Department of English at Utah State University. Reprinted with permission.

Pew Center on Global Climate Change, 2006. Homepage: http://www.pewclimate.org. Reprinted by permission.

Pew Center on Global Climate Change, 2006. Race To The Top: The Expanding Role of U.S. State Renewable Portfolio Standards Report page. http://www.pewclimate.org/global-warming-indepth/all-reports/rac_to_the_top/index.cfm. Reprinted by permission.

Rifkin, Jeremy. *The End of Work.* New York: Putnam, 1995.

Rosenthal, Angela. From "Raising Hair," in *Eighteenth Century Studies* 38.1 (2004). Copyright © 2004 by Angela Rosenthal. Reprinted by permission of the author.

Rutz, Carol. Director, Writing Program, Carleton College. Used by permission.

Sacks, Glenn. "Title IX Lawsuits Are Endangering Men's College Sports." Reprinted by permission.

Saturn VUE advertisement. General Motors Corp. Used with permission, GM Media Archives.

Schwartz, John. Technology: "With Cable TV at M.I.T., Who Needs Napster?" *The New York Times,* October 27, 2003. Copyright © 2003 by The New York Times Co. Reproduced with permission.

Science & Technology Review, Jul./Aug. 2003, Lawrence Livermore National Laboratory.

Sen, Amartya. *Inequality Reexamined.* Cambridge, MA: Harvard UP, 1992. 21

SparkNotes.com screen capture. http://sparknotes.com, Courtesy, SparkNotes, LLC.

Sternberg, Robert J. *Pathways to Psychology.* 2nd ed. For Worth: Harcourt, 2000. 14.

Terkel, Studs. *Working.* New York: Avon, 1972. xix.

Twitter page of the CDC. Reprinted by permission of Twitter, Inc.

Utah State University Libraries, http://library.usu.edu/main/inabs/index.php, courtesy Utah State University—Merril Cazier Library.

Wall Street Journal (Front page with annotations). Reprinted with permission of *The Wall Street Journal*, Copyright © 2004 Dow Jones & Company, Inc. All rights reserved worldwide.

Woolfolk, Anita E. *Educational Psychology.* 9th ed. Boston: Allyn, 2004. 122. Copyright © 2004 by Allyn & Bacon. Reprinted by permission.

WWF Climate Change website screen capture. http://www.panda.org/about_wwf/what_we_do/climate_change/our_solutions/index.cfm.

Yahoo! [Online]. Text and artwork copyright © 1998 by Yahoo! Inc. All rights reserved. YAHOO! And the YAHOO! Logo are trademarks of Yahoo! Inc.

Index

A

C

E

G

J

K

L

P

T

U

Revision Symbols

Boldface Letters and Numbers refer to chapters in the handbook.

Symbol	Meaning	Chapter
ab	abbreviation	**54a–c**
ad	form of adjective/adverb	**30**
agr	agreement	**29**
awk	awkward diction or construction	**34, 41**
ca	case form	**27**
cap	capitalization	**53a–d**
coh	coherence	**5b–c**
coord	coordination	**37b**
cs	comma splice	**32**
d	diction, word choice	**41, 43, 44**
dev	development needed	**3, 5f**
dm	dangling modifier	**34e**
doc	check documentation	**12, 13, 14**
emph	emphasis needed	**39**
frag	sentence fragment	**31**
fs	fused sentence	**32**
hyph	hyphen	**55**
inc	incomplete construction	**26b, 35**
ital	italics	**53e–j**
lc	lowercase letter	**53a–d**
log	logic	**4h**
mm	misplaced modifier	**34a–d**
ms	manuscript form	**11f**
mix	mixed construction	**35d**
no ¶	no paragraph needed	**5**
num	number	**54f-j**
¶	paragraph	**5**
¶ dev	paragraph development needed	**5**

Symbol	Meaning	Chapter
ref	unclear pronoun reference	**33**
rep	unnecessary repetition	**36**
search	check research or citation	**9, 10, 12, 13, 14**
sp	spelling error	**45**
shift	inconsistent, shifted construction	**35a–c**
subord	sentence subordination	**37c**
t	verb tense error	**28d–e**
trans	transition needed	**5g**
var	sentence variety	**40**
vb	verb form error	**28**
w	wordy	**36e**
ww/wc	wrong word; word choice	**41, 43**
//	faulty parallelism	**38**
.?!	end punctuation	**46**
:	colon	**49**
ˇ’	apostrophe	**50**
—	dash	**52e–g**
( )	parentheses	**52a–d**
[ ]	brackets	**52h–j**
. . .	ellipses	**52k–m**
/	slash	**52n–r**
;	semicolon	**48**
“ ”	quotation marks	**51**
^,	comma	**47**
⁀	close up	
^	insert a missing element	
ℓ	delete	
∿	transpose order	

TECH HELP

Creating a Double-Column Notebook (2b)
Exploring Topics on the Internet (3b)
Using Computer Journals to Invent and Prewrite (3c)
Brainstorming On-Screen (3c)
Writing Invisibly on the Computer (3c)
Organizing Your Files (3d)
Outlining with Word Processing (3e)
Combining documents (3f)
Saving Document Drafts (3f)
Collaborating via Computer (3g)
Keeping Track of an Argument (4i)
Designing an Argument for a Web Site (4j)
Revising your Document (6a)
Rewriting your Document (6b)
Comparing Document Drafts (6b)
Using the SEARCH Function to Revise (6b)
Using the Grammar Checker Appropriately (6b)
Checking Sentence Structure on the Computer (6c)
Checking Word Choice on the Computer (6c)
Proofreading On-Screen and in Print (6d)
Using Document COMMENT Function (6e)
Exploring Topics on the Internet (7a)
Web Searches: Using *Google* and *Google Scholar* Effectively (7a)
Printing Internet Sources (7c)
Downloading Internet Sources (7c)
Using a Computer Bibliography Program (7d)
Using the FAVORITES or BOOKMARK Feature (8b)
Using the HISTORY Feature of Your Web Browser (8b)
Using Social Bookmarking Sites (8c)
Finding a Site's Homepage (9a)
Web Searches: Using the Internet to Assess Author Credibility (9a)
Web Searches: Using Domains and URLs to Assess Internet Sources (9a)
Web Searches: Identifying Sites as Personal Homepages (9a)
Web Searches: Assessing the Appropriateness of Web Sources (9a)
Web Searches: Using *Wikipedia* Appropriately (9a)
Using INSERT to Number Pages (11d)
Using a Computer FOOTNOTE Program (11e)
Using PAGE SETUP and FORMAT (11e)
Italicizing, Not Underlining (12a)
Numbering Pages (19b)
Creating an Itemized List (19b)
Editing Photographs Digitally (19c)
Aligning Graphics with Text (19c)
Using Document Templates (20a)
Publishing Your Web Pages (20d)
Creating and Previewing Your Web Page with *Word* (20e)
Determining Which Etool to Use (21a)
Electronic Language: Diacritics and Emoticons (21b)
Dealing with Incompatible File Formats (21b)
Formatting a Scannable Résumé (22c)
Finding Online Information about Writing and Posting a Résumé (22c)
Using a Memo Template (22e)
Using Keywords to Search Lecture Notes (24a)
Writing an Essay Exam in a Computer Lab (24a)
Using Technology During Exams (24c)
Identifying Pronoun Reference Problems (33a)
Finding Places to Use Parallelism (38a)
Using Word Games to Build Vocabulary (43c)
Using Special Electronic Thesaurus Features (44a)
Using an Electronic Dictionary (44b)
Speeding Up Spell Checking (45a)
Using Smart Quotation Marks (51e)
Using Automatic Hyphenation (55e)

TECH ALERT! **Electronic Language**

"Filler" Phrases (26c)
Technology Verbs (*to google, to text*) (28b)
Amplifying Adverbs (30d)
Abbreviations (41d)
Slang Spellings (45c)
Punctuation-Based Emoticons (49a)
Using Capital Letters (53a)
Symbols for Emphasis (53j)
TM and IM Shorthand (54e)

TECH ALERT! **Grammar Checkers**

Pronouns (27c)
Passive Voice (28g)
Subject-Verb Agreement (29a)
Noun Strings (30b)
Comparative/Superlative Forms (30e)
Sentence Fragments (31a)
Sentences Beginning with *And* or *But* (31a)
Comma Splices (32a)
That and *Which* (33d)
Misplaced Modifiers (34a)
Faulty Shifts (35b)
Wordy Phrases (36e)
Noun-Heavy Writing (36f)
Comparative Constructions (36h)
Choppy Style (37a)

← See preceding page for a list of Revision Symbols.